Human–Computer Interaction Series

Editors-in-Chief

Desney Tan
Microsoft Research, Redmond, WA, USA

Jean Vanderdonckt
Louvain School of Management, Université catholique de Louvain,
Louvain-La-Neuve, Belgium

The Human–Computer Interaction Series, launched in 2004, publishes books that advance the science and technology of developing systems which are effective and satisfying for people in a wide variety of contexts. Titles focus on theoretical perspectives (such as formal approaches drawn from a variety of behavioural sciences), practical approaches (such as techniques for effectively integrating user needs in system development), and social issues (such as the determinants of utility, usability and acceptability).

HCI is a multidisciplinary field and focuses on the human aspects in the development of computer technology. As technology becomes increasingly more pervasive the need to take a human-centred approach in the design and development of computer-based systems becomes ever more important.

Titles published within the Human–Computer Interaction Series are included in Thomson Reuters' Book Citation Index, The DBLP Computer Science Bibliography and The HCI Bibliography.

More information about this series at http://www.springer.com/series/6033

Boris Galitsky

Artificial Intelligence for Customer Relationship Management

Solving Customer Problems

 Springer

Boris Galitsky
Oracle Labs
Redwood Shores, CA, USA

ISSN 1571-5035   ISSN 2524-4477 (electronic)
Human–Computer Interaction Series
ISBN 978-3-030-61643-4   ISBN 978-3-030-61641-0 (eBook)
https://doi.org/10.1007/978-3-030-61641-0

This Springer imprint is published by the registered company Springer Nature Switzerland AG
The registered company address is: Gewerbestrasse 11, 6330 Cham, Switzerland

Preface to Volume 2

The second volume of the book on Artificial Intelligence for Customer Relationship Management presents a broad spectrum of application domains with a focus on solving customer problems. We design a chatbot to specifically address issues customer experiences, as well as a system that tries to understand the customer complaint, his mood, and what can be done to resolve an issue with the product or service.

In the first volume of the book, we addressed the key issues of modern CRM systems, which frequently cannot handle the high volume of calls and chats. The main limitations of CRM today is a lack of machine understanding of what a customer is trying to say, what are the issues he is trying to communicate or attempts to conceal. To attack these limitations, we proposed a number of Natural Language Understanding (NLU) techniques with the focus on deep language analysis and reasoning.

Nothing repels customers as much as irrelevant, annoying, intrusive answers and low-quality content. The inability to find information users need is a major reason they are unsatisfied with a producer of a provider. In the first volume, we shared the evaluations of question-answering components, verified their explainability features and observed a satisfactory lab performance for major CRM tasks. We concluded that keeping the customers informed is key to their acquisition and retention. For example, in Fig. 1, fast access to information on who owns the bird is critical for a smooth transaction.

In this second volume, we make the next step to the heart of the customer retention issue: solving a customer problem. Now just understanding what the customer is saying is not enough anymore: we need to involve a formalized knowledge about a product and reason about it. To solve a customer problem efficiently and effectively, we focus on dialogue management. A dialogue with the customer is maintained in such a way so that the problem can be clarified and multiple ways to fix it can be sought.

If the CRM is not intelligent enough, it is not very usable. In particular, CRMs are used by people who sell, and as such, they are often traveling to customer sites, away from their desk, in front of clients, and are paid to generates sales, so communication with a CRM is often an afterthought. Salespeople are not hired for their computer or data entry skills but instead for their ability to sell. If they close a significant deal and

Fig. 1 Communicating
specific features of products
with a buyer

Catcher In The Sky

PET STORE | DETROIT, MI, USA | RIGHT | DECEMBER 28, 2009

Customer: "How much is this bird?"

Me: "Sir, how did you get the bird out of the cage? The cage was locked."

Customer: "Oh, I got this one from the birds you have outside by the door."

Me: "Those aren't our birds."

Customer: "What?"

Me: "Sir, you picked up a wild bird. But congratulations, because I can't imagine it was a simple task."

boredpanda.com

Fig. 2 Charles Fillmore's
example for joint sentence
discourse

• **Please use the toilet NOT the pool**

• **Pool for members only**

never entered it into the CRM, something may be said after the congratulations on the sale, but no one would complain about not using the CRM. The general consensus among sales representatives is simple: no one likes dumb CRM. They are frequently overly-complex, clunky systems without a conversational interface that do not help them sell and even obstruct the sales process. So the personnel may use unintelligent CRM as little as possible. More than a third of businesses face low adoption rates of CRM systems.

Our dialogue management is based on discourse analysis, a systematic linguistic way to handle the thought process of an author. Discourse analysis is a method for studying the natural language in relation to its social context. Discourse analysis tracks how language is used in real-life situations. A well-known American linguist Charles Fillmore demonstrates that two sentences taken together as a single discourse can have meanings different from each one taken separately (Fig. 2).

The objects of discourse analysis (texts, conversations, communicative events) are defined in terms of coherent sequences of sentences, propositions and speech acts. Sometimes discourse analysis even helps to get a consumer out of trouble by making a conversation convincing (Fig. 3). A dialogue structure can take a peculiar form for a conversation between two apple maggots (Fig. 4).

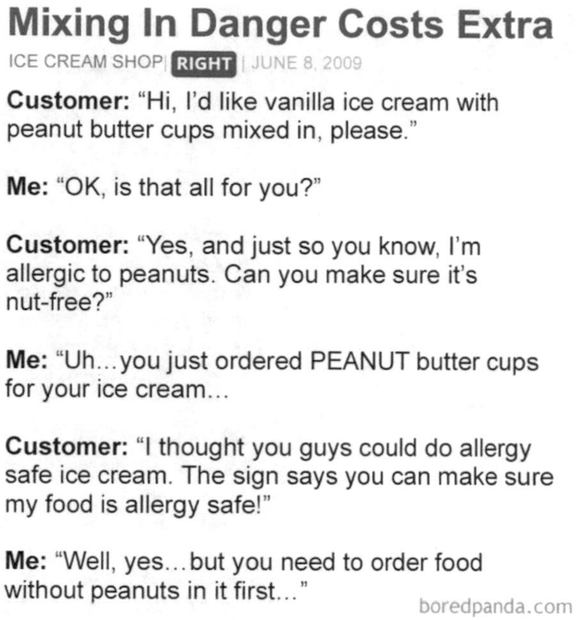

Fig. 3 Finding a contradiction in customer's request and communicating it

Mixing In Danger Costs Extra

ICE CREAM SHOP | **RIGHT** | JUNE 8, 2009

Customer: "Hi, I'd like vanilla ice cream with peanut butter cups mixed in, please."

Me: "OK, is that all for you?"

Customer: "Yes, and just so you know, I'm allergic to peanuts. Can you make sure it's nut-free?"

Me: "Uh…you just ordered PEANUT butter cups for your ice cream…

Customer: "I thought you guys could do allergy safe ice cream. The sign says you can make sure my food is allergy safe!"

Me: "Well, yes…but you need to order food without peanuts in it first…"

boredpanda.com

Fig. 4 A conversational structure of two apple maggots

We demonstrate how a dialogue structure can be built from an initial utterance. We also introduce real and imaginary discourse trees as a means to represent an explicit and implicit discourse of text. A problem of involving background knowledge on-demand, answering questions is addressed as well. We outline the *Doc2Dialogue* algorithm for converting a paragraph of text into a hypothetical dialogue based on an analysis of a discourse tree for this paragraph. This technique allows for a substantial extension of chatbot training datasets in an arbitrary domain.

Fig. 5 An example of
hypocrisy

How About A Side Of Hypocrisy

FAST FOOD, RESTAURANT | **RIGHT** | JULY 13, 2009

Me: *preparing a gyro wrap for a customer*
"Would you like cheese on it?"

Customer: "Oh my God, no! I'm a VEGAN! Don't
you know what they do to cows in those horrible
farms? They force them to get pregnant all the
time, and then they take away their babies and kill
them so we humans can steal their milk! Dairy
products are cruelty! "

Me: "Okay, okay. No cheese. Moving along. What
sauces would you like on that?"

Customer: "Tzatziki sauce, please."

*(Note: the particular brand of tzatziki we
purchased included both yogurt and sour cream.)*

Me: "Ah, I'm afraid that's a dairy prod–"

Customer: "I DON'T CARE! PUT IT ON!"

boredpanda.com

We compute user sentiments and personal traits to tailor dialogue management and content to individual customers. We also design several dialogue scenarios for CRM with replies following certain patterns and propose virtual and social dialogues for various modalities of communication with a customer.

To detect fake content, deception and hypocrisy (Fig. 5), we need to analyze associated discourse patterns, which turned out to differ from the ones for genuine, honest writing. With discourse analysis, we can zoom in further and characterize customer complaints with respect to the best way to resolve them. We simulate the mental states, attitudes and emotions of a complainant and try to predict his behavior. Having suggested graph-based formal representations of complaint scenarios, we machine-learn them to identify the best action the customer support organization can choose to retain the complainant as a customer.

Customer complaints are classified as valid (requiring some kind of compensation) or invalid (requiring reassuring and calming down) the customer. Scenarios are represented by directed graphs with labeled vertices (for communicative actions) and arcs (for temporal and causal relationships between these actions and their parameters). The classification of a scenario is computed by comparing a partial matching of its graph with graphs of positive and negative examples. We illustrate machine learning of graph structures using the Nearest

Neighbor approach as well as concept learning, which minimizes the number of false negatives and takes advantage of a more accurate way of matching sequences of communicative actions.

Redwood Shores, CA, USA   Boris Galitsky

Acknowledgements

The author is grateful to Dmitri Ilvovsky, Tatyana Machalova, Saveli Goldberg, Sergey O. Kuznetsov, Dina Pisarevskaya and other co-authors for fruitful discussions on the topics of this book.

The author appreciates the help of his colleagues from the Digital Assistant team at Oracle Corp. Gautam Singaraju, Vishal Vishnoi, Anfernee Xu, Stephen McRitchie, Saba Teserra, Jay Taylor, Sri Gadde, Sundararaman Shenbagam and Sanga Viswanathan.

The author acknowledges substantial contribution of the legal team at Oracle to make this book more readable, thorough and comprehensive. Kim Kanzaki, Stephen Due, Mark Mathison and Cindy Rickett worked on the patents described in this book and stimulated a lot of ideas which found implementation in this book.

Dmitry Ilvovsky contributed to the book Chap. 1 Volume 2 within the framework of the National Research University Higher School of Economics Basic Research Program and funded by the Russian Academic Excellence Project '5–100'.

Contents

Chapter 1
Chatbots for CRM and Dialogue Management

Abstract In this chapter, we learn how to manage a dialogue relying on the discourse of its utterances. We show how a dialogue structure can be built from an initial utterance. After that, we introduce an imaginary discourse tree to address the problem of involving background knowledge on demand, answering questions. An approach to dialogue management based on a lattice walk is described. We also propose *Doc2Dialogue* algorithm of converting a paragraph of text into a hypothetical dialogue based on an analysis of a discourse tree for this paragraph. This technique allows for a substantial extension of chatbot training datasets in an arbitrary domain. We evaluate constructed dialogues and conclude that deploying the proposed algorithm is a key in successful chatbot development in a broad range of domains where manual coding for dialogue management and providing relevant content is not practical.

1.1 Introduction: Maintaining Cohesive Session Flow

The growing popularity of smart devices, personal assistants, and CRM systems has stimulated the research community to develop various new methodologies for chatbots. Two general types of systems have become dominant: retrieval-based (IR), and generative, data-driven. While the former produces clear and smooth output, the latter brings flexibility and the ability to generate new unseen answers (Serban et al. 2016; Csaky 2019). We attempt to combine the best of these two worlds and to implement a dialogue manager based on hand-crafted rules and automated learning from the discourse structure of questions, requests and answers (LeThanh et al. 2004; Galitsky and Ilovsky 2017a).

In this chapter, we explore how a chatbot dialog can be managed to rely on the logic of conversation, employing the discourse analysis (Galitsky 2019a). Why is pragmatic/discourse analysis thought to be the most promising way to control dialogues compared with syntactic, semantic analyses or just learning from dialogue examples?

(1) Discourse analysis is the most formalized level of text analysis so that the logical representation, along with the availability of tagged corpus, allows for a most systematic treatment of dialogue structure, combining reasoning and learning.
(2) Discourse analysis (as well as syntactic one) is domain-independent, and once discourse machinery of dialogues is built, it can be applied to any knowledge domain.
(3) Discourse analysis is supposed to be language independent. Although discourse parsers of languages other than English are limited, discourse structure itself is designed in a language-independent manner and is supposed to support dialogues in any language.

If a dialogue is not constructed by pragmatic means, it can either be hard-coded or random. Hard-coded dialogue scenarios can take a user through a sequence of interactions such as a financial operation or an order of a service, but it is hard to demonstrate an advantage over a traditional interface such as a web form. Hard-coded dialogue management neither impresses a user with a human-like understanding nor tailors a dialogue to specific user needs (Galitsky et al. 2019).

On the other hand, attempts to imitate human-like dialogue without a full understanding of communicative discourse, learning from a high volume of dialogue scripts, lead to a random sequence of utterances. Trying to simulate human-like conversation, these kinds of chatbots can possibly keep user attention but would hardly perform a useful task. With random, irresponsible dialogue management, it is hard to accomplish a user task, provide a recommendation to a user or enable her with some knowledge.

Recent advances in deep learning, language modeling and language generation have introduced new ideas to the chatbot field. Deep neural models such as sequence-to-sequence, Memory Networks, and the Transformer have attempted to become key components of experimental chatbots in academia. While those models are able to generate meaningful responses even in an unseen situation, they need a lot of training data to build a reliable model. Thus, most real-world chatbots still follow traditional IR-based approaches and even hand-crafted rules, due to their robustness and effectiveness, especially for vertical-domain conversations in CRM.

Another option is that a poorly designed search engine is advertised as a chatbot or a virtual assistant but does not really have dialogue management (Fig. 1.1). For a query "*Restricted stock unit distribution*" it gives a definition of the entity "Restricted stock unit" but does not tell about its "distribution".

The most useful applications of chatbots such as digital personas are currently goal-oriented and transactional (Kostelník et al. 2019): the system needs to understand a user request and complete a related task with a clear goal within a limited number of dialog turns. The workhorse of traditional dialog systems is slot-filling (Wang and Lemon 2013), which predefines the structure of a dialog state as a set of slots to be filled during the dialog. For a home service reservation system such as carpenter or plumber, such slots can be the location, price range or type of project. Slot filling is a reliable way of dialogue management, but it is hard to scale it to new

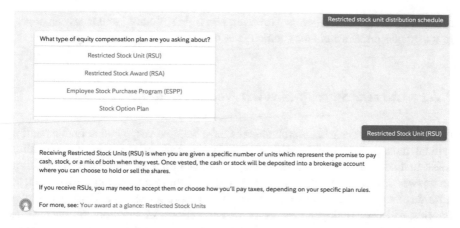

Fig. 1.1 An attempt with a limited success at building a virtual assistant for customer service (as of March 2020) due, in particular, to a lack of dialogue management and also a lack of ontology support for the entities involved

domains. It sounds implausible to manually encode all features and slots that users might refer to in a conversation, ordering a certain type of service.

Nowadays, chatbots are becoming future directions of a unified interface for the whole web and entering people's minds as the main communication media of the future. Over the last two decades, conversational agents captured imaginations and were fascinating to play with (Wilks 1999), but their application areas were unclear. The modern users of text-based AI would want to avoid typing keywords into a major search engine, browsing through lists of search result snippets, and feeling their dependence on search engine optimization and marketing to deliver the best content. Demand for high-quality content with efficient access is expected to be satisfied by chatbots that possess data from adequate sources, can navigate it efficiently and personalize to the needs of a user (such as domain expertise, an intent to acquire knowledge or to request a transaction, Galitsky 2016).

Over the last ten years, Siri for iPhone and Cortana for Windows Phone have been designed to serve as digital assistants. Excluding voice recognition, they analyze input question sentences and return suitable answers for users' queries (Kerly et al. 2007). However, they assume patterned word sequences as input commands. This requires users' memory of the commands, and therefore is not necessarily a user-friendly user interface. Moreover, there are previous studies that combine NLP with ontology technology to implement a computer system for intellectual conversation. For example, Agostaro et al. (2005) proposed the method based on the idea of Latent Semantic Analysis that utilized cosine similarity of morpheme appearance in user queries and in knowledge base sentences. Augello et al. (2017) proposed the tree structure that includes sentence structures in expected queries. There are chatbot systems like ALICE3 (2018), which utilizes an ontology like Cyc. Most of these methods expected the correct formulation of a question, certain domain knowledge and a rigid grammatical structure in user query sentences, and assumed patterns of query sentences to find answers. However, less rigid structured sentences can appear in a user utterance in a chatbot, which is in the style of spoken language.

1.1.1   *Current State-of-the-Art: Not Good for CRM*

Over the last two decades, search engines have become very good at understanding typical, most popular user intents, recognizing the topic of a question and providing relevant links. However, these search engines are not necessarily capable of providing an answer that would match the style, personal circumstances, knowledge state, an attitude of a user who formulated a query. This is particularly true for long, complex queries, and for a dialogue-based type of interactions. In a chatbot, a flow such as *query—clarification request—clarification response—candidate answer* should be cohesive; it should not just maintain a topic of a conversation.

Moreover, modern search engines and modern chatbots are unable to leverage immediate, explicit user feedback on what is most interesting and relevant to this user. For a given query, a search engine learns what are most popular search results, selected by a broad audience, and associate them with this query for future searches. It can only be done by major search engines with high search volume and for popular queries. Answering tail questions still needs to be done via keyword relevance and linguistic means.

Developing a robust chatbot traditionally requires a substantial amount of hand-crafted rules combined with various statistical components. However, selecting answers and replies based on user choice for previous search sessions sounds like a promising approach for many chatbot designers. Recently, a nontrivial dialogue management problem for task-oriented chatbots has been formulated as *a reinforcement learning* that can be automatically optimized through human interaction (Young et al. 2013). In this approach, the system learns by a trial and error process driven by a potentially delayed learning objective, a reward function that determines dialogue success. However, it is hard to define this reward function to cover a broad variety of conversational modes required in a real-life dialogue.

Users rely on Amazon's Alexa, Apple's Siri, Google Now, Api.ai and Microsoft's QnA Maker to receive answers to entertaining or factoid questions. Modern chatbots are embedded within common platforms like Slack, Skype, and Facebook Messenger. For this family of bots, the content is manually curated and is of high quality, but with limited coverage. On the other hand, deep learning-based chatbots learn from conversational logs and, therefore, can answer a broad spectrum of questions, but approximately and non-systematically. This family of bots is designed to imitate human intellectual activity, maintaining a dialogue; they try to build a plausible sequence of words to serve as an automated response to a user query, and most plausible sequences of words do not necessarily mean the best answers or clarification requests. End-to-end neural-based dialogue systems can potentially generate tailored and coherent responses for user inputs. However, most of the existing systems produce universal and non-informative responses, and they have not gone beyond chit-chat yet. To tackle these problems, Dialog System Technology Challenges were developed to focus on building a dialogue system that produces informational responses that are grounded on external knowledge (Tanaka et al. 2020).

Supervised learning has also been used in dialogue research where a dialogue management policy is trained to produce an example response when a certain dialogue state is given. One family of supervised learning approaches relies on collecting domain-specific training corpora (Kelley 1984). Over the last few years, an extensive body of research has attempted to train a neural network-based dialogue model (Bordes and Weston 2016). The dialogue management systems were directly trained on past dialogues without detailed specification of the internal dialogue state.

There are multiple issues in relying on learning from previous dialogues:

(1) The effects of selecting an action on the future course of the dialogue are not considered;
(2) There may be a very large number of dialogue states for which an appropriate response must be generated. Therefore in most cases, a training set may lack sufficient coverage.
(3) There is no reason to suppose a human wizard is acting optimally, especially at high noise levels;

These issues become more visible in larger domains where multi-step planning is needed. Thus, learning to mimic a human wizard does not necessarily lead to optimal behavior.

Task-oriented CRM chatbots tend to be highly specialized: they perform well as long as users do not deviate too far from their expected domain. Outside of CRM fields, chit-chat chatbots are designed to better handle a wide variety of conversational topics. The open-domain dialog research community investigates a complementary approach attempting to develop a chatbot that is not specialized but can still chat about anything a user wants. Such a chatbot could lead to many interesting applications, such as further humanizing computer interactions, improving foreign language practice, and making relatable, interactive movie and videogame characters.

However, current open-domain chatbots have a critical flaw: their utterances are not meaningful in most cases. They sometimes say things that are inconsistent with what has been said so far, or lack common sense and basic knowledge about the world. Moreover, chatbots often give responses that are not specific to the current context. For example, "I don't know," is a sensible response to any question, but it's not specific. Current chatbots do this much more often than people because it covers many possible user inputs.

Adiwardana et al. (2020) built Meena, a 2.6 billion parameter end-to-end trained neural conversational model. The authors attempted to form conversations that are more sensible and specific than existing state-of-the-art chatbots. A new human evaluation metric was proposed for open-domain chatbots, called Sensibleness and Specificity Average (SSA), which tried to reflect basic, but important attributes of human conversation. This metric strongly correlates with perplexity, an automatic metric that is readily available to any neural conversational model. Meena conversations may look cohesive but they lack a goal and still look meaningless

Fig. 1.2 Cleverbot answers questions *"Who/what/which technology was used in creating you"*

Who created you.

Human.

When.

About 24 years ago.

Which technology was used.

Alien. *share!*

say to cleverbot...   ≡ ◓

think about it   think for me   thoughts so far

with regards to its purpose and hardly applicable to CRM. Once Meena encounters a customer with a problem, it would "propose a solution" averaged through 341 GB of text, filtered from public domain social media conversations. It is easy to imagine how this common solution would upset a customer with his particular issue needing resolution.

Existing human evaluation metrics for chatbot quality tend to be complex and do not yield a consistent agreement between reviewers. To improve the meaningfulness of chatbot conversations, Adiwardana et al. (2020) crowd-sourced free-form conversation with the well-known open-domain chatbots, including Mitsuku, Cleverbot, XiaoIce, and DialoGPT, which are in turn conduct a hardly meaningful and useful conversation. Some of these chatbots have an online demo so that the user can objectively assess the quality of conversation that is neither cohesive nor meaningful (Fig. 1.2).

In order to ensure consistency between evaluations, each conversation starts with the same greeting, "Hi!". For each utterance, Amazon Mechanical Turk workers answer two questions, *"is it meaningful & specific?"*. The worker is asked to use common sense to judge if a response is completely reasonable in context. Once an utterance is off: confusing, illogical, out of context, then it is tagged as meaningless. The chatbot designers even attempted to tag factually wrong answers, hoping that Meena would learn all true facts in the world!

If the response makes sense, the utterance is then assessed to determine if it is specific to the given context. For example, if a user says *"I love cats"* and the chatbot responds, *"That's nice"* then the utterance should be marked as non-specific. That reply could be used in dozens of different contexts. However, if the chatbot responds instead, *"Me too, I buy special food for my pet"* then it is marked as specific since it is topically relevant to what is being discussed. Developers of data-driven chatbots optimize perplexity that measures the uncertainty of a language model. The lower the perplexity, the more confident the model is in generating the next token (character, subword, or word). Conceptually, perplexity represents the number of choices the model is trying to choose from when producing the next token. Experiments showed that the lower the perplexity, the better the SSA score is for the model. The measure for human SSA performance is 86%, for Meena is 79%, and for Cleverbot (that can be tested to fail on the second utterance) is 56%. Since there is no online demo for Meena, one can conclude that SSA is hardly correlated with dialogue meaningfulness...

1.2 Chatbot Architectures and Dialogue Manager

Chatbots are often represented, designed, and developed as a process flow between several communicating components (Fig. 1.3). In most charts across this book, boxes represent key processing stages and arrows link one stage to another—arrow text highlights the form of data being sent between processes.

Natural language understanding (NLU) component produces a semantic representation of user utterances (Jurafsky and Martin 2000) such as an intent class or a logic form, extracting the "meaning" of an utterance.

Following the NLU in the chatbot process is the dialogue manager (DM), a critical module that orchestrates the flow of the dialogue and communicates with other subsystems and components. DM also facilitates interactions between the chatbot and the user.

In addition to NLU and DM, a search engine or question answering (Chap. 3 Volume 1) are other major mission-critical components of the chatbot. Frequently, when a business employs the chatbot, it already has its own functioning search engine. The transition from the search engine to the chatbot interface includes improving search relevance and building the DM that fits the existing search domain and adds transactional capabilities to the user interface (Rizk et al. 2020).

In order to support the interaction between the chatbot and the user, DM must receive user input from the NLU and produce the system responses at a concept

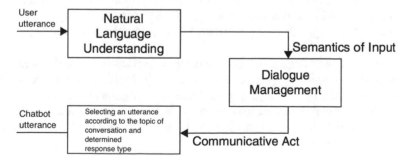

Fig. 1.3 Basic architecture of a chatbot with dialogue management

level to the natural language generator (NLG) or select answers from candidate search results. Which response DM chooses will depend on the strategy that has been chosen. Strategies are related to maintaining a conversational state and the ability to model the dialogue structure beyond that of a single utterance (Jurafsky and Martin 2000).

In order for chatbots to achieve flexible dialogues with users, DM needs to model a formalized dialogue structure, to perform a contextual interpretation (compute disambiguation and identify phrases connected by various kinds of references), to implement the domain knowledge management (the skill to reason about the domain and access information sources) and to select the chatbot action.

Contextual interpretation usually requires keeping some form of dialogue context, which can be used to resolve anaphora. A context may have a number of constituents: dialogue history, task records, and other models (e.g., user models), which all can be used as knowledge sources and together may be collectively referred to as a dialogue model (Zhao et al. 2020). DM is expected to be capable of reasoning about the domain in which it is placed; part of that involves the representation it keeps about the conversation domain.

The way in which a DM chooses its actions also has an effect on who has initiative through the conversation. In chatbots, initiative refers to the participant who has control of the dialogue at any given time. Peers should be able to choose how much to say and what to talk about. At one extreme, there exists a system-initiative chatbot that leads the user through the conversation, prompting her at every stage. At the other end, there are user-driven DMs that allow the user to have complete control over the flow of conversations (Galitsky et al. 2017). Some task-oriented systems are fairly robust in how the user drives a dialogue. There also exist mixed-initiative chatbots, in the middle of this range, which has an overall end-goal that must be achieved. Driven for the DM, these chatbots will allow the user a higher degree of freedom in how they proceed through a conversation. A number of methodologies to select actions have been proposed in the literature; they include methodologies from the finite-state machines, used in early chatbots, to ML techniques adopted in recent systems.

The key capabilities of a DM are as follows (Morbini et al. 2012):

(1) Supports a mixed-initiative system by fielding spontaneous input from either participant and routing it to the appropriate components;
(2) Tackles non-linguistic dialogue events by accepting them and routing them to the Context Tracker;
(3) Supports meta-dialogues between the chatbot itself and either peer. An example might be a question of a dialogue participant about the status of the chatbot;
(4) Acts as a central point for rectifying dialogue management errors;
(5) DM builds reliable associations between the user utterances and the system's actions (which themselves may be utterances), and keeps track of the information that it leverages to reach that goal.

The key expected outcome of the DM is a semantic representation of communicative action (Galitsky and Shpitsberg 2015). For example, DM interprets an intention: 'I need to *ask* the *user* for their *name*' as *ask(user, name)*.

NLG (natural language generator), an important component of a DM, receives a communicative act from the DM and generates a matching textual representation. There are two functions that the NLG must perform: content planning and language generation. Content planning involves deciding the semantic and pragmatic content, communicative action and its subject, what the system intends to convey to the user. Language generation, in contrast, is the interpretation of the meaning by choosing the syntactic structures and words needed to express the meaning:

(1) The DM in a travel assistance chatbot (Ivanov et al. 2020) decides that during the next turn, it must give the user traveler an update of their location in a city relative to the points of interest.
(2) The DM sends the conceptual representation (Galitsky and Kovalerchuk 2014) of communicative action that it intends to use to fulfill its goal of informing the user.
(3) The NLG, having received the communicative action, expands it into language by forming a semantic representation: '*Your position is at ... and you are near town ...*' Here, it is the responsibility of the NLG to decide what information is included in the response, and how it should be presented in language.

In the above example, the DM has decided the end state it intends to achieve through communication (provide an update on the user's situation), but it is the NLG that decides how to get there by developing the language and content that will be used.

We will focus on NLG in Chap. 5 Volume 2, developing an algorithm for building a detailed, conclusive answer. In the remainder of this chapter, we will focus on deterministic and statistical and discourse level learning-based DMs. We then proceed to more advanced, discourse-level-based DM in Chap. 4 Volume 2 (see also Galitsky and Ilvovsky 2017a, b).

1.3 Building Dialogue Structure from a Discourse Tree of an Initial Question

In this section, we propose a DT reasoning-based approach to dialogue management for a customer support chatbot. To build a dialogue scenario, we analyze the discourse tree (DT) of an initial query of a customer support dialogue that is frequently complex and multi-sentence. We then enforce a rhetorical agreement between DT of the initial query and that of the answers, requests and responses (Galitsky 2019b). The chatbot finds answers, which are not only relevant by topic but are also suitable for a given step of a conversation and match the question by style, argumentation patterns, communication means, experience level and other domain-independent attributes. We evaluate the performance of the proposed algorithm in the car repair domain and observe a

5–10% improvement for single and three-step dialogues, respectively, in comparison with baseline keyword approaches to dialogue management.

Answering questions, a chatbot needs to reason to properly select answers from candidates. In industrial applications of search, the reasoning is often substituted by learning from conversational logs or user choices. It helps to make the search more relevant as long as a similar question has been asked many times. If there is no data on a previous similar question, which is frequently the case, a chatbot needs to apply some form of reasoning to select from candidate answers (Wilks 1999; Galitsky et al. 2013).

The most frequent type of reasoning is associated with topical relevance; it requires a thesaurus and is domain-specific. Difficulties in building domain thesauri are well known, and in this chapter, we are taking a different reasoning-based approach. Once a set of candidate answers or replies are available, how to select the most suitable ones? The suitability criteria are two-dimensional: (1) topical relevance and (2) appropriateness not associated with the topic but instead connected with communicative discourse. Whereas topical relevance has been thoroughly investigated, chatbot's capability to maintain the cohesive flow, style and merits of conversation is an underexplored area.

The main foundation of our dialogue construction algorithm is Rhetoric structure theory (RST, Mann and Thompson 1988), since this discourse theory represents how a text author organizes her thoughts. RST structure outlines which entities are primary and being introduced first and which other entities and their attributes would follow. If an author has a hypothetical proponent or opponent who expresses confirmation or doubts about what is being claimed about these entities by the text author, the desired dialogue occurs. The structure of such dialogue is described by the same discourse representation as the original text. Hence we will rely on the RST representation of text for selecting text fragments.

Rhetorical relations (RR) for text can be represented by a discourse tree (DT), that is a labeled tree in which the leaves of the tree correspond to contiguous units for clauses (elementary discourse units, EDUs). Adjacent EDUs, as well as higher-level (larger) discourse units, are organized in a hierarchy by rhetorical relation (e.g., *Background, Attribution*). An anti-symmetric relation involves a pair of EDUs: nuclei, which are core parts of the relation, and satellites, which are the supportive parts of the rhetorical relation.

When a question is detailed and includes multiple sentences, there are certain expectations concerning the style of an answer. Although an issue of a topical agreement between questions and answers has been extensively addressed, a correspondence in style and suitability for the given step of a dialogue between questions and answers has not been thoroughly explored. In this chapter, we focus on the assessment of the cohesiveness of the Q/A flow, which is important for a chatbots supporting longer conversation (Galitsky 2019c). When an answer is in a style disagreement with a question, a user can find this answer inappropriate even when a topical relevance is high. Matching rhetorical structures of questions and answers is a systematic way to implement high-level reasoning for dialogue management, to be explored in this work.

A problem in communicative discourse occurs mostly for complex questions (Chali et al. 2009; Galitsky 2017a), arising in miscommunication, a lack of under-standing, and requiring clarification, argumentation and other means to bring the answer's author point across. Rhetorical disagreement is associated with a broken dialogue and is usually evident via the means an answer is communicated, explained or backed up.

1.3.1 Setting a Dialogue Style and Structure by a Query

Once we have a detailed initial question, we frequently can determine which direction we can take a given dialogue. If an answer is formulated in a straightforward way, then a definitional or factual answer is to follow. Otherwise, if a question includes a doubt, a request to dig deeper into a topic, or to address controversy, the dialogue should be handled with replies, including attribution, communicating a contrast, explicit handling of what was expected and what actually happened. Hence from the identified rhetorical relations (RRs) in the initial query, the chatbot can select one set of answers over the other not only to cover the main topic, but also to address the associated issues raised by the user. It can be done even if the initial query is short and its DT is trivial.

A good example of how it is possible to form a dialogue structure from the initial utterance comes from the medical field. Doctors only spend 11 s on average listening to patients before interrupting them, according to a new study (Singh Ospina et al. 2018). In primary care visits, only about half of patients were able to explain their agendas, while in specialty visits, only a fifth part of patients was allowed to explain their reason for visiting. For specialty care visits, eight out of 10 patients were interrupted, even if they were allowed to share their agenda. Since medical doctors are capable of building a conversation in the domain with such high responsibility as medical, chatbots are expected to be able to manage a dialogue from the first utterance in less critical domains as well.

In the following example, we consider two options for Q:

(1) Define an entity;
(2) Define an entity and explain what it is if there is an inconsistency between the naming of this entity and its actual role;

This can be expressed, for example, by two respective templates;

- *Does E do certain things?* (a null DT);
- *E is supposed to do certain things, but does it really do it?* (DT with a single rhetorical relation *Contrast* between *E—supposed to do* and *E really does*).

Notice that Q_1 and Q_2 are about the same entity, so a traditional search engineering technique is supposed to deliver the same answer for Q_1 and Q_2, which is a significant flaw. Instead, the discourse analysis is expected to help us to determine whether we want A_1 with a default DT (one without *Contrast* relation) or A_2 with a DT with *Contrast*.

Q_1: *Does law enforcement fight corruption in Russia?*
Q_2: *Does law enforcement **really** fight corruption in Russia?*
A_1: *The Russian government is sending out two very different messages in its declared war on corruption. On the one hand it is trying to curtail the efforts of civil society organizations as they go about their business, including Transparency International Russia, with a series of inspections that are hampering their operations. But at the same time, the government is taking measures to stop officials from hiding illicit wealth as part of its program to curb corruption.*
A_2: *Corruption significantly impedes businesses operating or planning to invest in Russia. High-level and petty corruption are common, especially in the judicial system and public procurement. The Russian Federal Anti-Corruption Law requires companies to actively implement anti-corruption compliance programs. However, compliance with these provisions in practice is lagging behind. Russian law criminalizes active and passive bribery, facilitation payments, gifts and other benefits. However, effective enforcement of anti-corruption legislation is hindered by a politicized and corrupt judicial system.*

To differentiate between default and controversial answer, one needs to look at the relation of *Contrast*, which is expected for a Q with an indication that an A addressing this controversy is expected (Fig. 1.4). Such RRs as *Background* and *Enablement* can occur in both DTs and do not determine how controversial the answer is.

Now imagine that for each of the answers, we obtain multiple candidates with distinct entities. How would the chatbot know which entity in an answer would be of a higher interest to a user? The chatbot needs to include a clarification procedure, asking, for example: *Are you interested in* (1) *private, individual corruption* (2) *corporate corruption.*

For a single Q/A pair, we refer to their coordination as a rhetorical agreement (Chap. 4 Volume 2). For the dialogue management problem, where a sequence of answers A_i needs to be in agreement with an initial question Q, we refer the proposed solution as *maintaining communicative discourse in a dialogue*. It includes three components:

(1) Finding a sequence of answers A_i to be in agreement with an initial question Q;
(2) Maintaining clarification procedure where for each i we have multiple candidate answers and need to rely on a user to select which one to deliver;
(3) We also allow the chatbot user to specify additional constraints and formulate more specific questions as answers A_i are being delivered.

1.3.2   Building a Dialogue Structure in Customer Support Dialogues

Let us start with an example of a customer support dialogue, where a customer support agent tries to figure out a root cause of a problem (Fig. 1.6). Customer support scenarios form a special class of dialogues where customers attempt to resolve certain problems, get their questions answered and get to their desired outcomes unreachable using default business procedures. Customer support dialogues frequently start

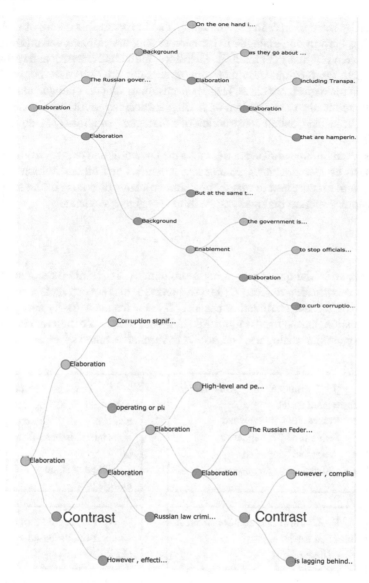

On the one hand i...

Background
as they go about ...

The Russian gover...
Elaboration
Including Transpa.

Elaboration
Elaboration

Elaboration
that are hamperin.

Elaboration

But at the same t...

Background
the government is...

Enablement
to stop officials...

Elaboration

to curb corruptio...

Corruption signif...

Elaboration

High-level and pe...

operating or pl₂
Elaboration
The Russian Feder...

Elaboration
Elaboration
However , complia

Elaboration

Contrast
Russian law crimi...
Contrast

However , effecti...
Is lagging behind..

Fig. 1.4 DTs for a default (on the top) and a controversial (on the bottom) answer, given respective Qs

with an initial question, a multi-sentence statement of problems Q, from which an experienced customer support personnel frequently plan a resolution strategy.

The personnel comes up with a sequence of recommendations and explanations for them addressing customer concerns expressed in Q. Also, the personnel comes up with some questions to the customer to adjust their recommendations to the needs expressed by the customer in Q. Frequently, due to the diverse nature of most businesses, it is hard to find dialogue in a customer support problem that addresses this exact problem (Galitsky et al. 2009). Therefore, individual answers and recommendations from the previous customer support sessions are used, not the whole such sessions, in the majority of cases. Hence the customer support dialogue management cannot be reduced to the problem of finding sufficiently similar dialogue and just following it: instead, actual construction of a dialogue to address Q is required most of the times.

The system finds candidate answers with the keywords and phrases from the initial query, such as *Google Earth, cannot see, attention* and others. Which candidate answers would be the best to match the communicative discourse of the query?

A customer support dialogue can be represented as a sequence

$$Q, A_1, C_1, A_2, C_2, \ldots,$$

where Q is an initial query describing a problem, A_1 is an initial recommendation and also a clarification request, C_1 is a response to this request, A_2 is a consecutive recommendation and clarification request, C_2 is a response to A_2 and possibly a further question, and so forth. Figure 1.5 shows our model structure for certain kinds of customer support dialogues. Our goal is to simulate a broad spectrum of dialogue

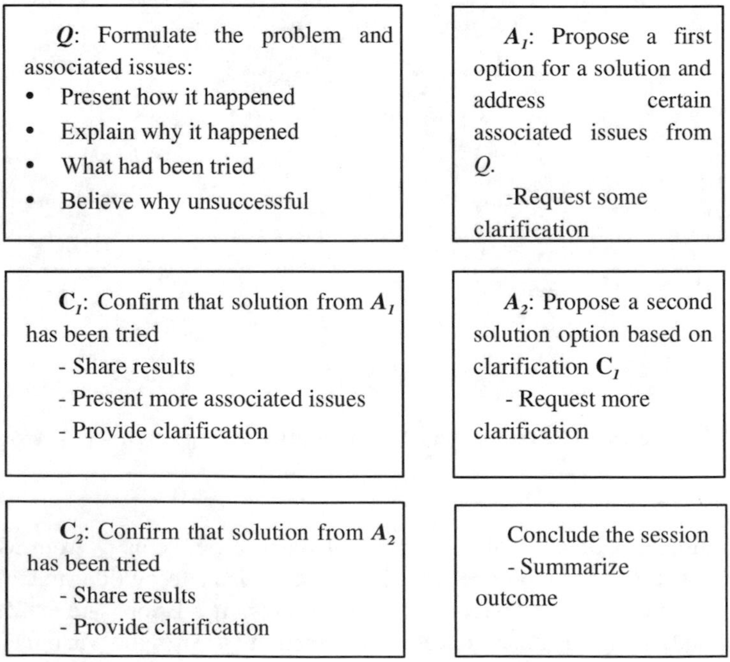

Q: Formulate the problem and associated issues: • Present how it happened • Explain why it happened • What had been tried • Believe why unsuccessful	A_1: Propose a first option for a solution and address certain associated issues from Q. -Request some clarification
C_1: Confirm that solution from A_1 has been tried - Share results - Present more associated issues - Provide clarification	A_2: Propose a second solution option based on clarification C_1 - Request more clarification
C_2: Confirm that solution from A_2 has been tried - Share results - Provide clarification	Conclude the session - Summarize outcome

Fig. 1.5 A high-level view of some types of customer support dialogue

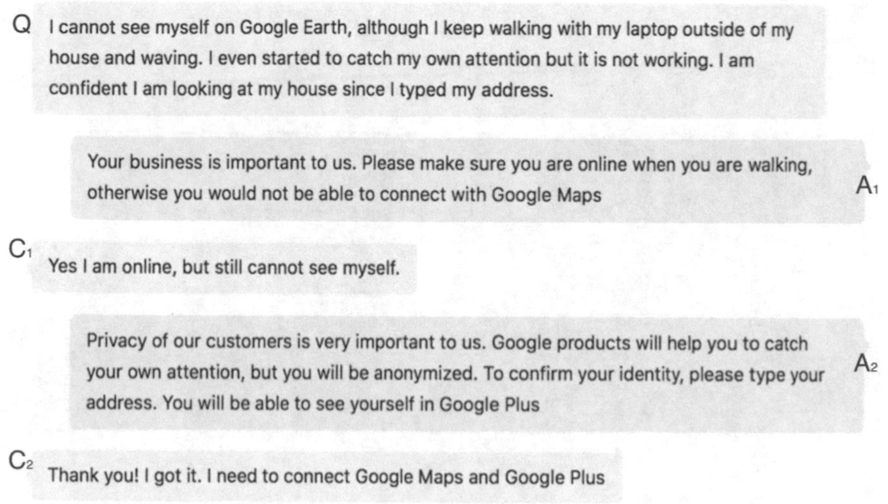

Q   I cannot see myself on Google Earth, although I keep walking with my laptop outside of my
house and waving. I even started to catch my own attention but it is not working. I am
confident I am looking at my house since I typed my address.

     Your business is important to us. Please make sure you are online when you are walking,
otherwise you would not be able to connect with Google Maps A_1

C₁
    Yes I am online, but still cannot see myself.

     Privacy of our customers is very important to us. Google products will help you to catch
your own attention, but you will be anonymized. To confirm your identity, please type your A_2
address. You will be able to see yourself in Google Plus

C₂
    Thank you! I got it. I need to connect Google Maps and Google Plus

Fig. 1.6 An example of a customer support dialogue

structures via correspondence of discourse trees of utterances. This way, once Q is
given, the chatbot can maintain the sequence of answers A_i for Q (Fig. 1.6).

1.3.3   Finding a Sequence of Answers to be in Agreement with a Question

The DT for the Q, and the DT for the sequence of two answers A1 and A2 are shown
in Fig. 1.7. We now demonstrate that a *chain* of nodes in DT-Q is determining a
corresponding chain of nodes in DT-A. This chain is defined as a path in a DT. The
chain of rhetorical relations with entities are *Elaboration [see myself Google Earth]-*
Contrast [walk laptop house]-Temporal [waiving] on the top of DT-Q is addressed
by the chain *Elaboration [online]-Same_Unit [walking]-Contract [Otherwise, not*
able connect] in the first answer A_1. We use the label

$$RR[abbreviated\ phrase]$$

for each node of a chain in DT. Notice that not only *RRs* are supposed to be
coordinated, but the entities in *phrases* as well.

     The second answer A_2 attempts to address in a complete way the issues raised
in the second part of Q. The first mapping is between the chain RR *Elaboration*
[catch my attention]—Contrast [not working] in Q and the chain *Elaboration [catch*
my attention]—Contrast [anonymized]. The second mapping is between the chain
Same-unit [confident]—Attribution [looking at my house] and the chain *Elaboration*

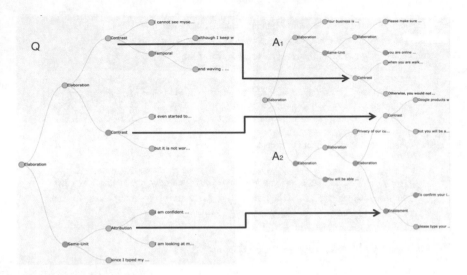

Fig. 1.7 The discourse tree of a question Q (on the left) and a sequence (pair) of combined discourse trees (on the right) for answers A_i. Arrows show which chains of DT-Q determine which chains of DT-A_i

[privacy]-Elaboration [confirm identity]—Enablement [type address]. Hence we built a mapping $Q \rightarrow \{A_1, A_2\}$.

The main observation here is that the question itself gives us a hint on a possible sequence of answers or on order the issues in the question are raised. One can look at the DT-Q and form a dialogue scenario (*first do this, obtain confirmation, then do that ...*). Since the dialogue is built from available answer fragments (e.g., from conversational logs), we take the candidate answers, form the candidate DTs from them and see if they match DT-Q. Hence a single nontrivial *DT-Q* determines *both DT-A_1* and *DT-A_2*. We refer to this capability as *determining the structure of a dialogue* (the structure of a sequence of answers) by the initial Q. We intentionally selected this anecdotal, meaningless example of a customer support dialogue to demonstrate that a full "understanding" of a query is not required; instead, the logical structure of interrelations between the entities in this query is essential to find a sequence of answers.

Is it possible to come up with a rule for *DT-A_i* given *DT-Q*, to formalize the notion of "addressing" an issue in Q by an A? A simple rule would be for a chain of RST relations for an A to be a sub-chain of that of a Q, also maintaining respective entities. But this rule turns out to be too restrictive and even invalid in some cases. Our observation is that *DT-A* does not have to copy *DT-Q* or its parts but instead have some complementarity features. There are two types of considerations for *DT-A_i*:

(1) Each nontrivial RR in *DT-Q* needs to be addressed by a RR in *DT-A_i*.
(2) There should be a rhetorical agreement between Q and A_i (Chap. 4 Volume 2, Galitsky 2017b), defined for a search engine. Whereas rhetorical agreement introduces a pair-wise constraint that can be learned from examples of good and

bad Q/A pairs, in this section, we extend it to one-to-many relation between a single Q and a sequence of A_i.

For an RR in $DT\text{-}A_i$ to address an RR in Q, it does not necessarily need to be the same RR, but it should not be a default RR such as *Elaboration* or *Joint*. *Attribution* and *Enablement*, for example, can address *Contrast*. Also, for a $RR(a_{q1}, EDU_{q2})$ in Q to be covered by $RR(EDU_{ai1}, EDU_{ai2})$ in A_i, entities E should be shared between EDU_{q1} and $EDU_{ai1} : EDU_{q1} \cap EDU_{ai1} = E : E \neq \emptyset$.

1.3.4 Searching for Answers with Specified RR for Dialogue Construction

Once we established the rules for addressing RRs in Q, we can implement a search for a series of answers A_i given Q. Assuming we have a corpus of dialogues with utterances tagged as A or Q, it should be indexed offline in at least two following fields:

(1) keywords of A;
(2) RRs with their EDUs.

Then once we receive Q, build $DT\text{-}Q$, and split $DT\text{-}Q$ into subtrees, each of which contains at least a single non-default RR. Then for each *subtree-DT-Q*, we form a query against these fields:

(1) keywords from the *EDU-subtree-DT-Q*;
(2) non-default RR from *subtree-DT-Q*.

For each candidate answer satisfying the query, we still have to verify *rhetorical_agreement(subtree-DT-Q, A_i)*.

Once the answer A_i is selected and given to the user, the user responds with C_i that in a general case contains some clarification expressed in A_i and also an additional question part Q_i. The latter would then require an additional answer that should be added to A_i if it has been already computed.

The high-level view of the search algorithm that supports the dialogue is as follows:

---

1) Build $DT\text{-}Q$;
2) Split $DT\text{-}Q$ into parts $Q_1, Q_2,...$ to correspond to $A_1, A_2...$;
3) Form search query for A_i from Q_i in the form *RST-relation [phrase]* ;
4) Run the search against the set of dialogue utterances and obtain the list of candidate answers for the first step $A_{1candidate}$;
5) Build $DT\text{-}A_{1candidate}$ for each candidate and approve/reject each based on *rhetorical_agreement(DT–Q, DT-A$_{1candidate}$)*. Select the best candidate A_1;
6) Respond to the user with the selected A_1 and receive C_1;
7) Form search query for A_2 from $Q_i\&C_i$;
8) Repeat steps 4) and 5) for A_2, respond to the user with the selected A_2 and receive C_2;
9) Conclude the session or switch to a human agent

Hence the dialogue management problem can be formulated as a search with constraints on DTs and can be implemented via traditional search engineering means plus discourse parsing when an adequate set of chat logs is available. Discourse tree-based dialogue management does not cover all possibilities of assuring smooth dialogue flows but provides a plausible mechanism to select suitable utterances from the available set. It allows avoiding solving NL generation problem for dialogues that is a source of a substantial distortion of conversation flow and a noise in the meaning of utterances.

In this subsection, we suggested a mechanism to build a dialogue structure where the first utterance formulated a detailed question requiring some knowledge and explanation. If this Q is detailed enough, then the chatbot can attempt to find a sequence of answers to address all issues raised in Q, and anticipate consequent user questions as well.

Some goals related to dialogue management do not need to be achieved via DTs. For example, an implementation of a *clarification* feature can be hard-coded and does not require specific RRs. When a user asks a broad question, the chatbot forms the topics for this user to choose from. Once such a topic is selected, the full answer is provided (Fig. 1.6, A_2).

We have built an algorithm for mapping $Q \rightarrow A_i$. When multiple valid candidate answers for each i are obtained, a clarification procedure is needed to have the user-selected A_{ij} from the set A_i of answers or recommendations valid from both relevance and rhetorical agreement perspectives. We now update step 6) of the search algorithm, which requests a clarification when multiple suitable answers are available.

---

5) ...
6)   Respond to the user with the list of choices selected $\{A_{1s} \mid s=0..n\}$ and receive clarification result
     with possibly additional constraint request C_1 (which includes the choice A_{1j});
7)   ...

Further improvement of this algorithm can be based on the differentiation between answers sharing knowledge and the ones providing recommendations on how to fix a problem.

1.3.5   Datasets for Evaluation

We experiment with the TREC datasets of the Web 2009 and Web 2010 tracks that contain collectively 100 queries and their relevance assessments on the Clueweb09 category B dataset2 (50+ m web pages in English crawled between January and February 2009). We choose these datasets because they are used widely in the community, allowing comparisons with the state-of-the-art. We consider a subset of this collection, consisting of the top 1000 documents that have been retrieved in response to each query by the baseline retrieval model on tuned settings using the (Indri IR 2018) system.

We also form a dataset of Q/A pairs related to car repair recommendations. These pairs were extracted from dialogues as first and second utterance so that the question is 7–15 keywords, and the answer is three to six sentences. This resource was obtained to train a dialog support system, but it also proved to be useful to evaluate search. This dataset is scraped from CarPros (2017) and is available at Car Repair Dataset (2017).

Our other source is Yahoo! Answers (Webscope 2017), a set of question–answer pairs with broad topics. Out of the set of 140k user questions, we selected 3300 of those, which included three to five sentences. The answers for most questions are fairly detailed, so no filtering by sentence length was applied (Galitsky 2019a).

Our social media dataset includes the Request-Response pairs mainly from postings on Facebook. We also used a smaller portion of LinkedIn.com and vk.com conversations related to employment. The authors formed the training sets from their own accounts and also public Facebook accounts available via API over a number of years (at the time of writing Facebook API for getting messages is unavailable). In addition, we used 860 email threads from Enron dataset (Cohen 2018). Also, we collected the data of manual responses to postings of an agent that automatically generates posts on behalf of human users-hosts (Galitsky et al. 2014). We form 4000 pairs from various social network sources. We compiled a dataset of financial questions scraped from Fidelity (2018) as well.

1.3.6 Evaluation of the Dialogue Construction from the First Query

As we proceed to the evaluation, we share an example of dialogue from the evaluation domain of recommendations on a car repair. Important characteristics of this domain are the importance of accurate recommendation, adequate dialogue structure, lesser bios than in other domains such as political, and an availability of complete and accurate coverage of a broad spectrum of car problems. We provide an example of a sample dialogue:

Q_1: *I have checked the spark plugs, replaced the battery, also replaced ignition coils and the solenoid, but I still could not start my car.*
A_1: *Is the engine getting spark and fuel? Will it start for a couple seconds using starting fluid?*
Q_2: *It did at first but not anymore. What should I do?*
A_2: *Check fuel pressure. But if no pressure, check the fuel pump for possible fault. If you have fuel pressure, then using a noid light make sure you have injector pulse. The light should blink when cranking.*

If light is not blinking does the check engine light come on with key on and engine off? If no light then look for a bad main relay or no power to the engine control module.

In this example, since Q_1 includes rhetorical relation of *Contrast* (something is done correctly but still not working), a detailed answer should include *Contrast, Condition*, or other RR that would address *Contrast* in *Q*. A certain recommended action is performed either correctly or incorrectly, and both these cases need to be addressed (Fig. 1.8). Correlation between DT-Q_1 and DT-A_2 would be trivial if Q_1 does not include a contradiction but instead just formulates a question of the form '*X is not working—how to fix it?*'.

To automate the relevance assessment, we considered the dialogue built *correctly* if an *actual* dialogue from the dataset is formed, given the first Q as a seed. Otherwise,

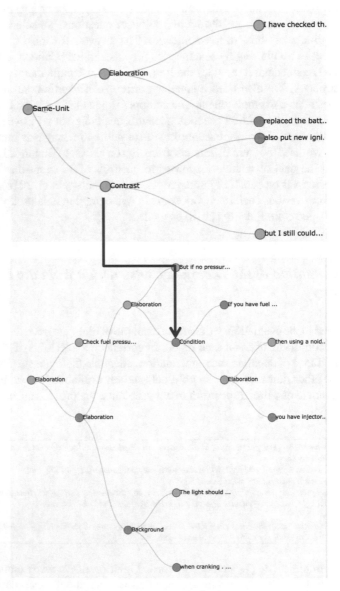

Fig. 1.8 On the top: DT for question Q_1 in Car Repair domain. On the bottom: DT for the detailed answer A_2 for Q_1

Table 1.1 Correctness of dialogue formation

Dialogue type	Q-A	Q-A1-C	Q-A1-C-A2	Q-A1-C1-A2-C2-A3
Baseline 1	62.3 ± 4.5	60.2 ± 5.6	58.2 ± 5.0	52.5 ± 5.7
Baseline 2	67.0 ± 4.8	63.8 ± 4.8	57.3 ± 5.3	55.6 ± 5.9
DT-Q dialogue formation	72.3 ± 5.6	70.3 ± 4.9	65.1 ± 5.5	65.9 ± 5.7

if the sequence of utterances does not occur in the dataset, we consider it to be *incorrect*. There are some deficiencies in this approach since some actual dialogs are illogical and some synthetic dialogues built from distinct ones can be plausible, but it allows avoiding manual tagging and construction of dialogues. The number of formed answers is limit to three: once initial Q is given, the system forms A_1, a set of A_{2i} and A_{3j}. A_1 is followed by the actual C_1 from the dialogue Q, so the proper A_2 needs to be selected. Analogously, once actual C_2 (if applicable) is provided, the proper A_3 needs to be selected.

As a first baseline approach (Baseline 1, the second row in Table 1.1), we select dialogue construction based on keyword similarity only, without taking into account a dialogue flow by considering a DT-Q. As a second baseline approach (Baseline 2, the third row in Table 1.1), we augment keyword similarity with linguistic relevance by computing maximal common sub- parse trees between the Q and A_i (Chap. 2 Volume 1).

For the selected dataset, the baseline approach is capable of building the correct scenarios in cases where similar keywords or similar linguistic phrases deliver the only dialogue scenario that is correct. On the contrary, *DT-Q* dialogue formation does not always succeed because some scenarios deviate from actual ones in the training set, although these scenarios are still plausible. Hence we see 10 and 5% improvement over the first and second baselines, respectively, for a basic, single-step scenario (Table 1.1).

As scenarios become more complex, the chance that the proper scenario is selected by topic relevance decreases. At the same time, the overall scenario formation complexity increases, and therefore an error rate for the *DT-Q* approach increases as well. For the most complex, 3-step dialogue scenarios, the *DT-Q* approach exceeds the baselines by 13 and 10%, respectively.

In this section we discovered that a dialogue structure could be built from the discourse tree of an initial question. This structure is built on top of the default conversational structure implementing such features as clarification, personalization or recommendation. If clarification scenario type is chosen, topics are automatically formed by the chatbot and are presented for a user to choose. For personalization, for a user query, the customer support chatbot system reduces the list of resolution scenarios based on what information is available for the given user. Chatbot's recommendation scenario proposes a solution to a problem by finding the one accepted by users similar to the current one (Galitsky 2016). Whereas a clarification, personalization and recommendation scenario covers only a small portion of plausible customer support scenarios, discourse analysis of dialogues supports dialogue management in a *universal* way for a *broad range* of available text fragments and previously accumulated responses.

1.4 Dialogue Management Based on Real and Imaginary Discourse Trees

In spite of the great success of search technologies, the problem of involving background knowledge is still on the agenda of search engineering, for both conventional and learning-based systems. Background knowledge ontologies are difficult and expensive to build, and knowledge graphs-based approaches usually have limited expressiveness and coverage (Galitsky 2013). In this section, we explore how a discourse analysis (which is domain-independent) can substitute certain features of ontology-based search.

Ontologies are in great demand for answering complex, multi-sentence questions in such domain as finance, legal, engineering and health. In the educational domain, this type of question is referred to as *convergent*: answers are usually within a very finite range of acceptable accuracy. These may be at several different levels of cognition, including comprehension, application, analysis, or ones where the answerer makes inferences or conjectures based on material read, presented or known. Answering convergent questions is an underexplored Q/A domain that can leverage discourse analysis (Kuyten et al. 2015).

Discourse trees (DT) became a standard for representing how thoughts are organized in text, in particular in a paragraph of text, such as an answer. Discourse-level analysis has been shown to assist in a number of NLP tasks where learning linguistic structures is essential (Louis et al. 2010; Lioma et al. 2012). DTs outline the relationship between entities being introduced by an author. Obviously, there are multiple ways the same entities and their attributes are introduced, and not all rhetorical relations that hold between these entities occur in a DT for a given paragraph.

In this section, we introduce a concept of an *imaginary discourse tree* to improve question-answering recall for complex, multi-sentence, convergent questions. Augmenting a discourse tree of an answer with tree fragments obtained from thesauri, we obtain a canonical discourse representation of this answer that is independent of a thought structure of an author of this answer. This mechanism is critical for finding answers which are not only relevant in terms of questions entities but are also suitable in terms of interrelations between these entities in these answers and their style. We evaluate the Q/A system enabled with imaginary discourse trees and observe a substantial increase of accuracy answering complex questions such as Yahoo! Answers and www.2carpros.com.

When DTs are used to coordinate questions and answers, we would want to obtain an "ideal" DT for an answer, where all rhetorical relations between involved entities occur (Galitsky 2014). To do that, we need to augment an actual (available) DT of the answer instance with certain rhetorical relations that are missing in the given answer instance but can be mined from text corpora or from the web. Hence to verify that an answer A is good for a given question Q, we first verify that their DTs (*DT-A* and *DT-Q*) agree, and after that, we usually need to augment the *DT-A* with fragments of other DTs to make sure all entities in Q are communicated (addressed) in augmented *DT-A*.

Hence instead of relying on an ontology, which would have definitions of entities missing in a candidate answer, we mine for rhetorical relations between these entities online. This procedure allows us to avoid an offline building of bulky and costly ontology (Chap. 6 Volume 1, Galitsky 2019d). At the same time, the proposed approach can be implemented on top of a conventional search engine.

1.4.1   Answering Questions via Entities and Discourse Trees

The baseline requirement for an A to be relevant to Q is that entities (*En*) of A cover the entities of Q: $E\text{-}Q \subseteq E\text{-}A$. Naturally, some $E\text{-}A$ is not explicitly mentioned in Q but is needed to provide a recipe-type A.

The next step is to follow the logical flow of Q by A. Since it is hard to establish relations between En, being domain-dependent, we try to approximate them by a logical flow of Q and A, expressible in domain-independent terms

$$EnDT\text{-}Q \sim EnDT\text{-}A.$$

However, a common case is that some entities E are not explicitly mentioned in Q but instead are assumed. Moreover, some entities in A used to answer Q do not occur in A but instead, more specific or general entities do. How would we know that these more specific entities are indeed addressing issues from Q? We need some external, additional source that we call *imaginary EnDT-A* to establish these relationships. This source contains the information on inter-relationships between *En*, which is omitted in Q and/or A but is assumed to be known by the peer. For an automated Q/A system, we want to obtain this knowledge at the discourse level:

$$EnDT\text{-}Q \sim EnDT\text{-}A + imaginary\ EnDT\text{-}A.$$

We start with a simple Example 1:
Q: *What is an advantage of electric car?*
A: *No need for gas.*
How can a search engine figure out that A is a good one for Q? We have an abstract general-sense entity *advantage* and a regular noun entity *car*. We need to link explicit entities in A {*need, gas*}. The fragments of a possible *imaginary EnDT-A* are shown: [*... No need...—Elaborate—Advantage*] ... [*gas—Enablement—engine*]...[*engine— Enablement—car*]. We do not need to know the details of how this *Enablement* occurs; we just need evidence that these rhetorical links exist. We could have used

semantic links between these entities but for that, we would need a domain-specific ontology.

We now present the second example to demonstrate how the Imaginary DT component would improve a web search (Fig. 1.9). Currently, search engines show certain keywords they do not identify in a given search result. However, it is possible to indicate how these keywords are relevant to this search result by finding documents where these unidentified keywords are rhetorically connected with the ones occurring in the query. This feature would naturally improve the answer relevance on the one hand and provide explainability for the user on how her keywords are addressed in the answer.

Now we proceed to another example. Let us explain how a match between a *Q* and an *A* is facilitated by DTs (Fig. 1.10).

Q: [When driving the cruise control][the engine will turn off][when I want to accelerate,][although the check engine light was off.] [I have turned on the ignition][and listen for the engine pump running][to see][if it is building up vacuum.] [Could there be a problem with the brake sensor under the dash ?] [Looks like there could be a little play in the plug.]

A: [A faulty brake switch can effect the cruise control.] [If it is,][there should be a code][stored in the engine control module.] [Since it is not an emissions fault,][the check engine light will not illuminate.] [First of all, watch the tachometer][to see][if engine speed increases 200 rpm][when this happens.] [If it does,][the torque converter is unlocking transmission.]

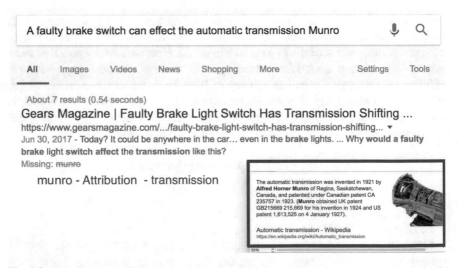

Fig. 1.9 How Imaginary DTs would enable Google search to explain missing keywords in the search results. In the default search, *munro* is missing. However, by trying to rhetorically connect *munro* with the entities in the question, the Imaginary DT system finds out that *Munro* is a person who is an inventor of automatic transmission. DT fragment is shown with rhetorical relation Attribution, as well as the Wikipedia source for Imaginary DT

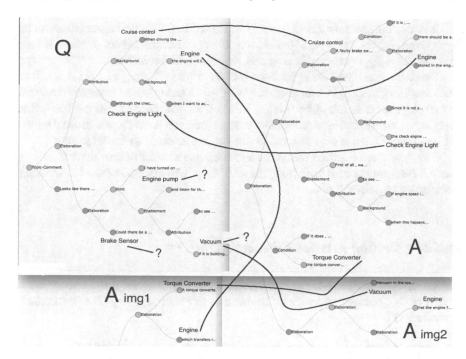

Fig. 1.10 DTs of Q, A and imaginary DT-A_{img1} and DT-A_{img2}

A explains a situation and also offers some interpretation, as well as recommends a certain course of action. A introduces extra entities which are not in Q, and needs to involve background knowledge to communicate how they are related to E-Q. We do it by setting a correspondence between E-Q and E-A, shown by the horizontal curly (red) arcs.

Notice that some entities E_0 in Q are *unaddressed*: they are not mentioned in A. E_0-Q includes {*Engine pump, Brake sensor* and *Vacuum*}. It means that either A is not fully relevant to Q omitting some of its entities E_0 or it uses some other entities instead. Are E_0-Q ignored in A? To verify the latter possibility, we need to apply some form of background knowledge finding entities E_{img} which are linked to both E_0-Q and E-A.

It is unclear how En-A = *Torque Convertor* is connected to Q. To verify this connection, we obtain a fragment of text from Wikipedia (or another source) about *Torque Convertor*, build DT-A_{img1} (shown on the left-bottom of Fig. 1.10) and observe that it is connected with *Engine* via rhetorical relation of *Elaboration*. Hence we confirm that En-A = *Torque Convertor* is indeed relevant for Q (*a vertical blue arc*). We obtained this confirmation without building an offline thesaurus linking entities and learning relations between then: instead, we rely on discourse–level context to confirm that A includes relevant entities.

It is also unclear how *En-Q pump* is addressed in *Q*. We find a document on the web about *Engine Pump* and *Vacuum* and attempt to connect them to *En-A*. It turns out that $DT\text{-}A_{img2}$ connects *Vacuum* and *Engine* via *Elaboration*.

Hence the combined *DT-A* includes real *DT-A* plus $DT\text{-}A_{img1}$ and $DT\text{-}A_{img2}$. Both real and imaginary DTs are necessary to demonstrate that an answer is relevant by employing background knowledge in a domain-independent manner: no offline ontology construction is required. Documents found on the web, which are the basis of imaginary DTs can also be used to support an answer in a chatbot setting.

Search relevance is then measured as the inverse number of unaddressed $En_0 - Q$ once *DT-A* is augmented with imaginary $DT\text{-}A_{img}$. This discourse-based relevance is then added to a default one.

1.4.2   Question Answer Filtering Algorithm

Given a *Q*, we outline an algorithm that finds the most relevant *A* such that it has as much of *En-Q* addressed by *En-A*, having a source for imaginary DTs (background knowledge) *B*.

---

1) Build *EnDT-Q*
2) Obtain *En-Q* and form a query for *En-A*
3) Obtain a set of candidate *As*
4) For each   candidate $Ac \in As$:
   a) Build *DT-Ac*
   b) Establish mapping $En\text{-}Q \rightarrow E\text{-}Ac$
   c) Identify $En_0\text{-}Q$
   d) Form queries from $En_0 - Q$ and $En_0 - Ac$ (entities which are not in $En_0 - Q$)
   e) Obtain search results from *B* for queries d) and build imaginary *DTs-Ac*
   f) Calculate the score $|En_0|$ remaining;
5) Select A with the best score.

Besides this algorithm, we outline a machine learning approach to classifying *<EnDT-Q, EnDT-A>* pair as correct or incorrect. The training set should include good Q/A pairs and bad Q/A pairs. Therefore a DT-kernel learning approach (SVM TK, Joty and Moschitti 2014; Galitsky 2017a, b) is selected, which applies SVM learning to a set of all sub-DTs of the DT for Q/A pair. Tree kernel family of approaches is not very sensitive to errors in parsing (syntactic and rhetoric) because erroneous sub-trees are mostly random and will unlikely be common among different elements of a training set.

An EnDT can be represented by a vector V of integer counts of each sub-tree type (without taking into account its ancestors): $V(T) = (\#\ of\ subtrees\ of\ type\ 1,$ …). Given two tree segments $EnDT_1$ and $EnDT_2$, the tree kernel function $K(EnDT_1, EnDT_2) = <V(EnDT_1), V(EnDT_2)> = \Sigma_{n1} \Sigma_{n2} \Sigma_i I_i(n_1) * I_i(n_2)$, where $n_1 \in N_1$, n_2

$\in N_2$ where N_1 and N_2 are the sets of all nodes in $EnDT_1$ and $EnDT_2$, respectively; $I_i(n)$ is the indicator function: $I_i(n) = \{1$ iff a subtree of type i occurs with root at node; 0 otherwise$\}$.

1.4.3 Experiments with Answering Convergent Questions

Traditional Q/A datasets for factoid and non-factoid questions, as well as SemEval and neural Q/A evaluations, are not suitable since the questions are shorter and not as complicated to observe a potential contribution of discourse-level analysis. For our evaluation, we formed two convergent Q/A sets (Sect. 1.3.5):

(1) Yahoo! Answer (Webscope 2017) set of question–answer pairs with broad topics;
(2) Car repair conversations, including 9300 Q/A pairs of car problem descriptions versus recommendation on how to rectify them.

For each of these sets, we form the positive one from actual Q/A pairs and the negative one from $Q/A_{similar-entities}$: $En-A_{similar-entities}$ has a strong overlap with E-A, although $A_{similar-entities}$ is not a really correct, comprehensive and exact answer. Hence Q/A is reduced to a classification task (Galitsky et al. 2015a; Galitsky and Makowski 2017) measured via precision and recall of relating a Q/A pair into a class of correct pairs.

Top two rows in Table 1.2 show the baseline performance of Q/A and demonstrate that in a complicated domain transition from keyword to matched entities delivers a performance boost of more than 13%. The bottom three rows show the Q/A accuracy when discourse analysis is applied. Assuring a rule-based correspondence between DT-A and DT-Q gives 13% increase over the baseline (real DTs), and using imaginary

Table 1.2 Evaluation of Q/A accuracy

Source	Yahoo! Answers			Car repair		
Search method	P	R	F1	P	R	F1
Baseline TF*IDF	41.8	42.9	42.3	42.5	37.4	39.8
IEn-Q ∩ En-AI	53.0	57.8	55.3	54.6	49.3	51.8
IEnDT-Q ∩ EnDT-AI	66.3	64.1	65.1	66.8	60.3	63.4
IEnDT-Q ∩ EnDT-A + EnDT-A$_{imgi}$ I	76.3	78.1	77.2 ± 3.4	72.1	72.0	72.0 ± 3.6
SVM TK for <EnDT-Q ∩ EnDT-A + EnDT-A$_{imgi}$>	83.5	82.1	82.8 ± 3.1	80.8	78.5	79.6 ± 4.1
Human assessment of SVM TK for <EnDT-Q ∩ EnDT-A + EnDT-A$_{imgi}$>	81.9	79.7	80.8 ± 7.1	80.3	81.0	80.7 ± 6.8

DTs—further 10%. Finally, proceeding from rule-based to machine-learned Q/A correspondence (SVM TK) gives a performance gain of about 7%. The difference between the best performing row *SVM TK for <EnDT-Q ∩ EnDT-A + EnDT-A$_{imgi}$>* row and the row above it is only the machine learning algorithm: representation is the same. A_{imgi} denotes *i*-th candidate answer associated with an imaginary DT.

The bottom row shows the human evaluation of Q/A on a reduced dataset of 200 questions for each domain. We used human evaluation to make sure the way we form the training dataset reflects the Q/A relevance as perceived by humans.

1.5   Dialogue Management Based on Lattice Walking

In this section, we focus on chatbot dialogues related to product recommendation (to be continued in Chap. 2 Volume 2). These are totally different chatbot interaction scenarios to the previous sections: they do not take into account the mental states of the user but instead navigate through the information states of product features. Hence the underlying algorithm is tailored to represent objects (items, products) and their features. It is fairly important to visualize those (Kovalerchuk and Kovalerchuk 2017) so that the user is aware of where he is driven to by the system and what are his current options.

The screen-shot of the interactive recommendation platform for advanced users is shown at the top of Fig. 1.11. The purpose of this view is to create a visual impression for the user of which features are advantageous or disadvantageous for a series of products of the same category. The data feed for this view is the result of extracting information from customer reviews. The initial lattice is drawn automatically, and the user may re-locate nodes of interest or add/remove labels when interests and focuses change. For every product and its disadvantageous features, the lattice allows the identification of products where these features are better. The user can continue the exploration of these recommended products and attempt to further express his needs to the system.

On the right, users choose their current products of interest. At any time, they can add new products by selecting the checkboxes for available products in order to obtain more comparative information. Similarly, users can remove products from the current view for more comprehensive visualization of remaining products. The lattice will be updated accordingly. When a given product is selected, one can see all nodes (highlighted) of the lattice that contains features of this product, and, conversely, for every positive or negative feature, one can see all products having these features. The concept of lattice is shown on the bottom of Fig. 1.11 in a higher resolution. It visualizes the generalization of products' features: the user can move upwards for a higher-level view of product features, considering a larger number of products. Conversely, moving down, the scope of products is reduced and the user can drill into for more specific product analysis. Navigating all the way down, the user arrives

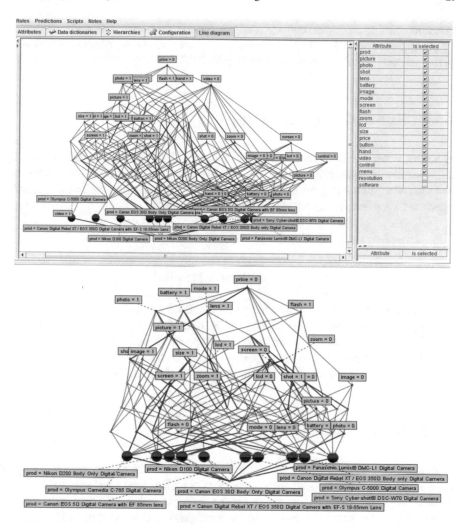

Fig. 1.11 Browsing of features for a series of comparable products (on the top). Visualization of a recommendation platform via the concept lattice of features of digital cameras

at individual products. Chatbot implementation does not necessarily need this visualization: the user is offered options to navigate the concept lattice up or down and the chatbot enumerates the corresponding sets of products and features.

Concept lattices have been employed by a wide variety of information retrieval techniques and systems (Kaytoue et al. 2015). Concept lattices can represent precisely a document and its query space that can be used as an index for automatic retrieval. In the last years, the Boolean information retrieval model has been considered as too limited for modern information retrieval requirements for search engines, chatbots, large datasets and complex document representations. Pattern structures have shown a great potential of the formal concept analysis-based information retrieval techniques by providing support for complex document representations, such as numerical and heterogeneous indexes (Codocedo and Napoli 2014).

1.5.1 Formal Concept Analysis

A formal context is a triple (G, M, I), where G and M are sets, called the set of objects and attributes, respectively. Let I be a relation $I \subseteq G \times M$ between objects and attributes, that is, $(g, m) \in I$ if the object g has the attribute m. The derivation operator $(\cdot)$ are defined for $A \subseteq G$ and $B \subseteq M$ as follows:

$$A' = \{m \in M | \forall g \in A : gIm\}$$

$$B' = \{g \in G | \forall m \in B : gIm\}$$

A' is the set of attributes common to all objects of A and B' is the set of objects sharing all attributes of B. The double application of $(\cdot)$ is a closure operator, that is, $(\cdot)''$ is extensive, idempotent and monotone. Sets $(A)''$ and $(B)''$ are referred to as closed. A formal concept is a pair (A, B), where $A \subseteq G$, $B \subseteq M$ and $A' = B$, $B' = A$. A and B are called the formal extent and the formal intent, respectively.

1.5.2 Lattice Walker Example

In this section, we simulate the interaction of a task-oriented chatbot for knowledge access for a user in the case where a query does not allow a search engine to identify a "small enough" set of responses. In other words, we propose an approach where a specified lattice-based description of the user query is computed in an interactive manner in order to provide a minimal set of responses with maximal variability of parameters that matter less to the user.

This chatbot might be used in e-commerce, for real-estate agency services or any other field where users face a big amount of objects that form an ontology and is described by well-defined (structured) parameters/characteristics.

Here we present a model of the interactive search where the chatbot clarifies the user needs in the course of navigation. During the interaction, the chatbot is sending the refined queries to a search engine. The received snippets, that is, short descriptions of the found items, are grouped in clusters of similar snippets wherein the shared description of a cluster (its centroid) represents a specified query. Under a specified query, we mean a description of this query with the information for drilling in. Among computed specified queries, the user chooses a relevant one, according to his current interest, that is used as a new refined query. The specification (updating the set of constraints) for the queries continues till the user does not find any more appropriate specification or a snippet that corresponds exactly to the information she searched for is found. The similarity of snippets is defined not only by its syntactic similarity but also by the relevance weights that are received from the web search engine.

Let us imagine we have a number of digital cameras (objects) {*Nikon, Kodak, Sony, Canon, Vivitar, KINGEAR, Olympus, The Imaging World, Yasolote, Vmotal, Polaroid, HeroFiber*}. Their features and their values (objects' features) are as follows: {*Avg. Customer Review: 5, 4, 3, 2, 1, Viewscreen Display Size: Under 2 in., 2 to 2.9 in., 3 to 3.9 in., 4 to 4.9 in., 5 to 6.9 in., Over 7 in., Price: Under 25,25 to 50,50 to 100,100 to 200,200 and Above, Camera Viewfinder Type: LCD, Optical, Both, Video Capture Resolution: 4 K UHD (2160p), FHD (1080p), HD (720p), SD (480p)*} (Table 1.3).

Now a user starts with a query '*Camera like Vivitar with 7 in. display*'. We now look for all cameras with features like *Vivitar* but having *7 in. display* instead of *6 in.* We find *Yasolote* camera with *7 in.*, or *Sony* camera but with the same *star number* and *Viewfinder = optical*. We then issue a clarification request to the user:

(1) *Yasolote camera with 7 in.? OR*
(2) *Sony with the same number of reviews and Viewfinder = optical OR*
(3) *Codak or Polaroid having FHD resolution.*

Therefore, each option has a certain combination of objects and properties induced by the original object and the desired feature. The initial query instead can mention a single object or a list of features.

Now imagine the user selects option 2. We now focus on *Sony* and cameras most similar to *Sony* with *star number 2* and *Viewfinder = optical*.

(1) *Sony*
(2) *Nicon*
(3) *Imaging World*

The user then either selects a particular item (object) or gives up on the current search session and starts over.

1.5.3 Lattice Navigation Algorithm

To arrive to an initial lattice node, the user is suggested to formulate a query. This query can contain object names, attribute names, and object descriptions. As a result of running the keyword query, we get the set of attributes and objects (O_q, A_q) where O_q is a set of objects satisfying this query, and A_q is a set of attributes satisfying this query. From this pair, we identify the initial lattice node (O_0, A_0), which is the closest pair to (O_q, A_q) in the sense of a minimal number of added/removed elements of the summed object and attributed to derive (O_0, A_0) from (O_q, A_q).

Table 1.3 Digital cameras (objects) and their grouped features

	Avg. customer review				Viewscreen display size						Price				Camera viewfinder type		Video capture resolution			
	5	4	3	2	2–3	3–4	4–5	5–6	6–7	7–8	25	50	100	200	LCD	Optical	UHD	FHD	HD	SD
Nikon		1						1				1				1			1	
Kodak			1				1						1		1			1		
Sony				1		1								1	1		1			
Canon		1						1							1					1
Vivitar				1				1					1			1		1		
Kingear	1					1								1		1	1			
Olympus			1				1					1			1		1			
Imaging World		1				1							1			1			1	
Yasolote				1					1			1				1				1
Vmotal	1						1								1		1			
Polaroid		1						1			1				1			1		
HeroFiber		1				1						1			1					1

Once (O_0, A_0) is identified, we fix the lattice node and the chatbot enumerates O_q, A_q to the user. Then at each iteration i the user is expected to request one of the following:

(1) update

- reduce the set of object of interest $O_i \Rightarrow O_{i+1}$. That can be requested via the utterance '*remove/I am not interested/avoid objects/products*'—ΔO_i.
  This is a jump up the lattice as we have fewer objects and more attributes.
- extend the set of object of interest $O_i \Rightarrow O_{i+1}$. That can be requested via the utterance 'add/I am interested/extend objects/products/items'—ΔO_i
  This is a jump down the lattice as we have more objects and fewer attributes.
- reduce the set of attributes of interest $A_i \Rightarrow A_{i+1}$. That can be requested via the utterance '*remove/I am not interested/avoid attributes/features/properties*'—ΔA_i
  This is a jump down the lattice as we have more objects and have fewer attributes.
- extend the set of object of interest $A_i \Rightarrow A_{i+1}$. That can be requested via the utterance '*add/I am interested/extend objects/products/items*'—ΔA_i
  This is a jump up the lattice as we have fewer objects and have more attributes.

(2) abrupt change of interest

- Proceed to new set O_{i+1}. That can be requested via the utterance "switch to O_{i+1}"
- Proceed to new set A_{i+1}. That can be requested via the utterance "switch to A_{i+1}"
- Run new query and go to (O_q, A_q)
  All of these three cases are a long-distance jump to a new area in the lattice.

(3) Focus on a selected attribute or product O_q, A_q The utterance is *tell me more about/lets focus on product* O_{qk} (*product x*) *or attribute/feature* O_{qy} (*feature y*). It is a long-distance jump up on the lattice to the second row from the top for the selected attribute and to the second row from the bottom for the selected object.

(4) Add/remove negation of attributes. The utterance is '*make it without/get rid of*' A_{qx}.

- These three cases is a short jump on the lattice analogous to 1).

(5) Finding a similar product to O_{ix}. The utterance is '*Find/show/give me/take me to similar products for* O_{ix}'.
  This operation retains the current set A_i but will now switch to new objects O_i* which does not include O_{ix};
  This is a horizontal shift operation on the lattice.

(6) Finding a similar product with the feature to A_{ix}. The utterance is '*Find/show/give me/take me to similar products with attribute* A_{ix}'.
  This operation find similar products to $O_i + A_i - A_{ix}$, which satisfy A_{ix} and returns the user multiple lattice nodes in the vicinity of the node (O_i, A_i).

1.6   Automated Building a Dialogue from an Arbitrary Document

In spite of the success of building dialogue systems, the bottleneck of training data remains. In most problem domains, designers of chatbots are unable to obtain training dialogue datasets of desired quality and quantity and therefore attempt to find alternative, lower quality datasets and techniques such as transfer learning. As a result, the relevance and dialogue cohesiveness are frequently unsatisfactory.

We discover a general mechanism of conversion of a paragraph of text of various styles and genres into a dialogue form. The paragraph is split into text fragments serving as a set of answers, and questions are automatically formed from some of these text fragments. The problem of building dialogue from text T is formulated as splitting it into a sequence of answers $A = [A_1...A_n]$ to form a dialogue

$$[A_1, < Q_1, A_2 >, \ldots, < Q_{n-1}, A_n >],$$

where A_i answers A_{i-1} and possibly previous question, and $\cup A_i = T$. Q_{i-1} needs to be derived from the whole or a part of A_i by linguistic means and generalization; also some inventiveness may be required to make these questions sound natural. To achieve it, we try to find a semantically similar phrase on the web and merge it with the candidate question. Dialogue generation is somewhat related to a general content (sentence) generation problem; however, questions should be less random than the ones potentially generated by methods such as sequence-to-sequence deep learning.

Question generation has gained increased interest (Du et al. 2017; Yuan et al. 2017; Heilman and Smith 2010), branching from the general Q/A problem. The task is to generate an NL question conditioned on an answer and the corresponding document. Among its many applications, question generation has been used to improve Q/A systems.

A dialogue is formed from the text by the following rule: once nucleus EDU is finished, and before satellite EDU starts, questions against this satellite EDU is inserted. In terms of a dialogue flow between a text author and a person asking a question, the latter "interrupts" the author to ask him this question such that the satellite EDU and possibly consecutive text would be an answer to this question. This question is supposed to be about the entity from the nucleus, but this nucleus does not contain an answer to this question. The person asking questions only interrupts the text author when his question sounds suitable; it does not have to be asked for all nucleus-satellite transitions.

Communicative discourse trees are designed to combine rhetorical information with arcs labeled with expressions for communicative actions. These expressions are logic predicates expressing the agents involved in the respective speech acts and their subjects.

The arguments of logical predicates are formed in accordance with respective semantic roles, as proposed by a framework such as VerbNet (Kipper et al. 2008). If a text already includes an a subject (underlined in our example) of communicative actions (bolded) in a satellite, it can be naturally converted into a question: '*A potential PG&E bankruptcy is **seen** as putting pressure on California lawmakers to provide a bailout and avoid more turmoil for the state's largest utility*' → {'*Why put pressure on California lawmakers?*', '*What should California lawmakers provide?*', ...}.

1.6.1 Forming a Dialogue from a Discourse Tree of a Text

Let us consider a paragraph from a controversial domain of Theranos investigation (Fig. 1.12):

> ...But Theranos has struggled behind the scenes to turn the excitement over its technology into reality. At the end of 2014, the lab instrument developed as the linchpin of its strategy handled just a small fraction of the tests then sold to consumers, according to four former employees.

To convert it into a dialogue, we need to build a DT for it and form a question for each satellite for each its relation:

- But Theranos has struggled...
- Struggled for what?
- ... behind the scenes to turn the excitement over its technology into reality. At the end of 2014, the lab instrument developed as ...
- What's the role of instrument development?
- ... the linchpin of its strategy handled just a small fraction of the tests then sold to consumers, ...
- Who said that?
- ... according to four former employees.

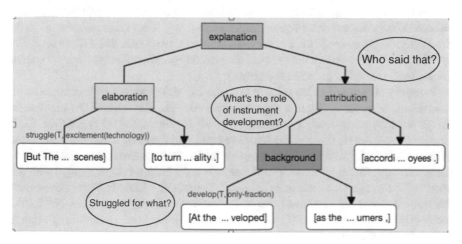

Fig. 1.12 A CDT for a text and questions attached to satellite nodes

Once we split a text into EDUs, we know which text fragments will serve as an answer to questions: satellites of all relations. *Elaboration* rhetorical relation is default and *What*-question to a verb phrase is formed. *Background* relation yields another *What*-question for the satellite '...*as <predicate>-<subject>*'. Finally, *Attribution* relation is a basis of "What/who is source" question.

A trivial approach to question generation would be to just convert satellite EDU into a question. But it would make it too specific and unnatural, such as '*the linchpin of its strategy handled just a small fraction of the tests then sold to whom?*'. Instead, a natural dialogue should be formed with more general questions like '*What does its strategy handle?*'.

Communicative actions help to formulate questions for satellite EDUs as well. For *struggle(T, excitement(technology))* attached to the relation of *Elaboration,* the question can be '*Was there an excitement about [Theranos] technology?*', and for *develop(T, small-fraction)* the possible question is '*Does Theranos only did a small fraction of tests?*'.

1.6.2 Question Formation and Diversification

When we obtain a candidate for a question, it is subject to reduction to avoid being too specific. For example, '*What is a British rock band that formed in London in 1970 and received Grammy Hall of Fame Award in 2004?*' would be too specific and should be reduced, for instance, to '*What is a British rock band that formed in London*'. To achieve a proper level of generalization for questions, we take an extended set of questions such as Stanford Q/A database (SQuAD), perform pairwise syntactic generalization (Galitsky et al. 2012) and retain the most frequent question templates. SQuAD corpus (Rajpurkar et al. 2016) is a machine comprehension dataset consisting of over 100k crowd-sourced question–answer pairs on five hundred Wikipedia articles. For example, generalizing '*What is the purpose of life on Earth*' and '*Tell me the purpose of complex numbers*' we obtain '*the-DT purpose-NN of-PRP *-NP*' where we retain the part-of-speech tags. We collect the most frequent generalization results (question templates).

We apply phrase-reduction rules at both the individual phrase and sentence level. As a result, we want to obtain a question from an original satellite EDU expression that is as close to a question template as possible. Hence for every satellite EDU expression, we iterate through the templates and find the most similar one. In terms of syntactic generalization, it is the template which delivers a maximal common sub-parse tree with this expression. For the sentence "[I built a bridge]$_{nucleus}$ [with the purpose of fast access to the forest]$_{satellite}$", the satellite EDU is better covered by the template from our previous paragraph than, for example, by "access-NN to-TO forest-NN" or 'access-NN to-TO NP' in terms of the number of common terms (parse tree nodes) of the generalization result.

To improve the meaningfulness, interestingness and diversity of a formed and generalized question, we rely on the wisdom of the web. We form a web search query from the formed question and attempt to find an expression from a web document as close to this question as possible and also from a reputable source. We iterate through web search results obtained by Bing API and score document titles, snippet sentences and other expressions in found documents to be semantically similar to the query. Semantic similarity is assessed via the syntactic generalization score between the candidate query and a search result. If such expression from the document is found, its entities need to be substituted by the ones from the original question. As a result, a candidate question will look more popular, mature and in more common terms.

To verify that the formed and modified question obtained from a satellite EDU text has this text as a good answer, we apply the open-domain Q/A technique (Galitsky 2017a). Given the whole original text and a formed question, we verify that the answer is the EDU; this question was formed from and did not correspond to another EDU. A wrong text fragment could appear as an answer if the question was substantially distorted by generalization or web mining. We use (DeepPavlov.ai 2020) deep learning Q/A system for this verification.

1.6.3 System Architecture

The architecture of the system for automated building of a dialogue from a document is shown in Fig. 1.13. A text is split into paragraphs and the CDT for each paragraph is built. Once we identify all satellite EDUs in all obtained CDTs, we try to insert a querying utterance before each of these satellite EDUs. To do that, we consider each such satellite EDU as an answer and attempt to formulate a question for it, generalizing it. We apply certain rules to achieve a proper generalization level: if the question is too broad or too specific, the fixed answer (the satellite EDU) would look unnatural. We also apply the rules to maintain proper question focus. As a candidate question is formed, it is sent as a query to the web to turn it into a question other people asked in some situations, assumed to be similar to the one described by the current paragraph. Once we form such the question, we insert it after the previous nucleus EDU and before the current satellite EDU.

To form a question from a nucleus EDU to get a set of questions, the following steps are applied (Fig. 1.14):

1) Build a parse tree
2) Select parse tree nodes for nouns, verbs and adjectives. Also add nodes linked by coreferences such as pronouns. More complex node selection rules can be applied (Finn 1975).
3) For every selected node, form a reduction of a parse tree by removing this node.
4) Build a question for this reduction by substitution a Wh word for this node
5) Select a proper Wh word following the rules: noun -> Who or What, verb ->'what ... do', adjective 'Which way', 'How is'.

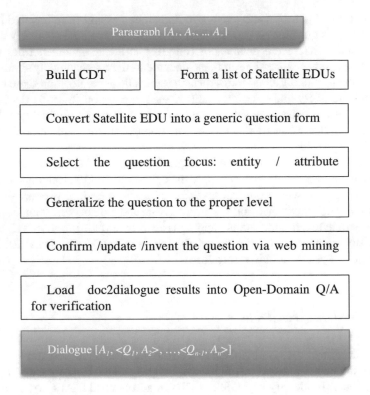

Fig. 1.13 System architecture

1.6.4 Evaluation of the Dialogue Builder

We measure the performance of our dialogue construction algorithm via a number of operations a human editor would need to apply to obtain a satisfactory dialogue. Table 1.4 contains the data for individual questions.

The second column contains the percentages of formed questions that need to be corrected. The third to fifth columns show contributions of three various methods of improving attempts for the formed questions. The last, sixth column estimates the percentages of problematic questions after these three methods are applied sequentially.

One way to evaluate the dialogue formation quality is to follow along the line of the dialogue generation assessment. The word-overlap metrics such as BLEU adopted from machine translation have become popular to compare a machine-generated response to a single target response (Papineni et al. 2002). In our case, it corresponds to the overlap between a formed question and a respective response from the original text. Since the response to the input context in dialogue could be very diverse and open, a single target response is not able to cover all acceptable question–answer (Q/A) pairs. Liu et al. (2016) demonstrated that word-overlap metrics do not agree

---

1) Build a parse tree

2) Select parse tree nodes for nouns, verbs and adjectives. Also add nodes linked by coreferences such as pronouns. More complex node selection rules can be applied (Finn 1975).

3) For every selected node, form a reduction of a parse tree by removing this node.

4) Build a question for this reduction by substitution a Wh word for this node

5) Select a proper Wh word following the rules: noun -> Who or What, verb ->'what ... do', adjective 'Which way', 'How is'.

Joe   packed his   tools   and materials neatly

Node deleted	
Tools and materials (NNS)	What did Joe pack neatly
Joe (NNP) , his (PRP$)	Who packed tools and materials neatly? Whose tools and materials were packed neatly
Neatly (RB)	How did Joe pack?

Fig. 1.14   Transforming a statement into a question

Table 1.4   Evaluation of dialogue construction

Construction/correction method	DT-satellite rephrasing into Q, necessary corrections (error rate) (%)	Using CA, decrease (%)	Using web mining, decrease (%)	Verifying by open-domain Q/A, decrease (%)	Hybrid improvement (combined decrease)
Correcting grammar	27	21	16	16	11
Removing too specific words	17	19	23	21	17
Adding words to make question more concrete	22	25	12	14	9
Reject Q as meaningless	9	9	5	7	3
Overall modification	39	32	34	30	19

well with the reply quality judgments from human annotators. The word embedding metric only accesses synonymy rather than general appropriateness of a question for an answer. Hence to assess the performance of the proposed algorithm, we use evaluation methods based on the editing of formed questions by human annotators.

One of the problems in formed questions is that they do not obey the proper grammar. Almost a third of formed questions have grammar errors, once we apply a generalization to it. As we apply web mining and Q/A verification, the error rate decreases by almost half.

Although questions are subject to generalization, in almost one out of five questions, further generalization is required. Fewer generalization steps are required when the satellite EDU includes communicative actions since their subjects are usually already close to how people formulate questions. Web mining sometimes breaks a proper level of generalization since a search result can be too specific. Q/A verification does not help to reach proper generalization either.

Conversely, some questions turn out to be too general so that the individual question, as well as the dialogue, looks unnatural. We observe that relying on CA does not make these questions more specific; however, web mining helps a lot with ideas on what to add to the questions. It might not necessarily fit the whole dialogue well but makes an individual question more natural and assists with question diversity. Getting expressions from the web by searching over-generalized questions reduces their number by a half.

About a tenth part of the questions is meaningless and should be rejected. CAs do not help but web mining helps a lot to filter them out. Also, Q/A verification helps with this task to some degree since meaningless questions cause different answers to the ones these questions were intended for.

Notice that all these errors in questions do not affect significantly the overall dialogue flow that is determined by the original text.

1.6.5   Rhetorical Map of a Dialogue

In our dialogue model, the dialog starts with the utterance introducing a topic. This utterance is followed by the second utterance, which is a question formed from the first satellite EDU of a text. What if we want to start a dialogue with a question? How can it be formed?

In our previous study (Galitsky and Ilvovsky 2019; Ilvovsky et al. 2020) we discovered that the most adequate questions for a portion of text as an answer are obtained from the nucleus of the DT for this text.

From the DT in Fig. 1.15, the following are the questions which can be answered by this text as a whole:

<What for/Why/When> did Theranos struggle? (Nucleus of the *Elaboration*).

<When/How/Why/What> was the lab instrument developed? (Nucleus for the *Background*).

In Fig. 1.15 we tag each EDU with respect to its role for forming questions: Nucleuses serve as '*global*' questions **Q** and can be initial questions to start a conversation. Conversely, satellites can serve as '*local*' questions **q** to form a dialogue but not to be asked, expecting the whole text as an answer.

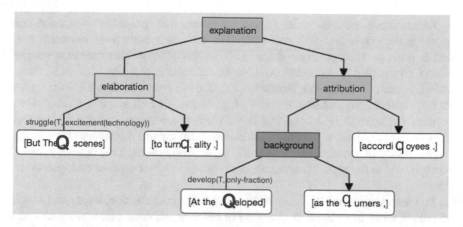

Fig. 1.15 Global questions Q to the whole text and local dialogue questions q for individual satellite EDUs

This split into global questions for the whole text and local questions for its individual parts via dialogue is reliable as long as the rhetorical parsing is correct. In the real life, some local questions would be good for the whole text, and some global questions would not be fully/adequately answered by this text; however, for the purpose of dialogue management, this split provides a reliable tool.

Hence within our developed framework, a dialogue in our training dataset starts with a global question, followed by local questions (Galitsky et al. 2015b). Now, what happens in real-time when a user starts asking questions? We outline a dialogue management algorithm based on a direct match of user utterances against the ones in the training set dialogues. We will compare this algorithm with a more popular learning-based approach.

An initial user question U_1 is matched with global questions $\{Q_g\}$, and a set of suitable dialogues S is formed, possibly with the most relevant representative $D^* \in S$. Each such dialogue D_1 has its Q_g containing the same entities as U_1.

A first answer A_1 from this representative is given. Once the user produces her second utterance U_2, it is matched with the Q_1 from the set of suitable dialogues. For A_1 it can be D, a different dialogue from D^* as long as its Q_j or A_j, is most relevant to U_2. Each consecutive U_i should be answered by $D \in S$ with the most relevant Q_j or A_j.

1.6.6 Evaluation of Chatbot Performance Improvement Building Datasets on Demand

In this section, we evaluate the boost in chatbot performance once we can automatically expand the training set on demand.

As a baseline, we select a fixed dataset of human dialogues obtained from the car repair recommendations resource. User questions are usually 5–15 keywords long and answers by their peers are three to six sentences long. This dataset is scraped from CarPros (2017) and split into dialogue utterances. It is available as a chatbot training dataset (Car Repair Dataset 2017). This dataset includes 9300 dialogues, so for a specific car problem, there is a high chance of a shortage of similar repair scenarios to learn from. Notice that it is a much more comprehensive dataset than the ones mostly used in chatbot evaluations, with coherent conversations, higher responsibility of answers and higher clarity of instructions. This dataset provides much more "to the point" answers than a typical customer support dialogue would do.

To generate queries which can be the start of the conversation, we extract a topic of conversation from the first utterance in our evaluation dataset and try to find a similar question in Yahoo! Answers dataset by searching via answers.search.yahoo. com and scraping the answers. This way, we obtain realistic questions that are foreign to our dataset. For some of them, there are answers in Car Repair Dataset (2017) and for some, there are none, so a mining of an additional source is required. Yahoo! Answers can serve not only as a source of questions but the source for comprehensive answers as well.

We experiment with acquiring an additional training dataset when the chatbot determines that a query includes an entity or a combination of entities that are not covered by the current dataset of dialogues. The chatbot then goes to the web and tries to find webpages relevant to the user queries. We used original scraped webpages, convert them into dialogues and also used conversion results where the generated queries are confirmed by searching the web with candidate question phrasings.

In this evaluation, we use popular dialogue construction measures BLEU and ROUGE (Lin 2004). Although these measures are weakly correlated with quality, topical and rhetorical relevance of answers, we use them to demonstrate the contribution of an extended training dataset.

We also use semantic assessment based on word2vec similarity. The embedding average constructs a vector for a piece of text by taking the average of the word embeddings of its constituent words. Then, the vectors for the chatbot response and for the gold human answer are compared using the cosine similarity. Also, greedy matching was introduced in the context of intelligent tutoring systems (Rus and Lintean 2012). It matches each word in the chatbot utterance to the most similar word in the gold human response, where the similarity is measured as the cosine between the corresponding word embeddings, multiplied by a weighting term:

$$greedy(u_1, u_2) = \frac{\sum_{v \in u_1} weight(v) * \max_{w \in u_2} \cos(v, w)}{\sum_{v \in u_1} weight(v)}$$

We present the results of chatbot functionality according to the word overlap model results in Table 1.5 and according to semantic similarity of produced and gold standard answers—in Table 1.6.

Table 1.5 Chatbot performance evaluation with keyword overlap

	BLEU 1	BLEU 2	BLEU 3	BLEU 4	ROUGE-L
Only relying on available dialogues	27.6	14.2	12.6	10.3	20.3
Identified webpages	32.4	17.1	15.9	13.2	23.7
Constructed dialogues without further web confirmation	35.1	21.5	18.5	14.6	28.1
Constructed dialogues with further web confirmation	36.5	20.8	19.0	14.0	28.0

Table 1.6 Chatbot performance evaluation with semantic similarity

	Embedding average	Greedy match	Manual (%)
Only relying on available dialogues	65.6	36.2	68.9
Identified webpages	70.3	37.1	74.5
Constructed dialogues without further web confirmation	72.1	39.0	78.2
Constructed dialogues with further web confirmation	71.7	37.9	76.8

One can observe that both BLEU and ROUGE-L measure of word overlap improves as we mine for the relevant content as the chatbot determines that it is lacking. In the baseline scenario, the chatbot gives answers which are available from the initial training set. In the baseline model, for the borderline questions, the chatbot gives less relevant answers, and refuses to answer questions distant from the initial training dataset. As we proceed to the scenario of acquiring content on demand, the chatbot starts getting the chunks of conversational data that cover new areas of user interest, and more relevant answers are delivered instead. These higher relevance answers are obtained on-demand in the cases when the chatbot is having low relevance for available answers.

If we obtain relevant webpages for foreign questions, we improve the keyword overlap measure by 3%. Once we build a dialogue from these webpages obtained on demand, we get a further 3% improvement since the chatbot now can handle multi-turn dialogue on the subjects not prepared by the baseline system. A web confirmation of the formed questions inserted into formed dialogue does not give a noticeable improvement for keyword overlap performance.

Relying on a semantic measure of chatbot performance and its human assessment, the performance boost of mined webpages is 1–5%, compared to the baseline. The dialogue generation provides further 2–4% improvement, and the web confirmation drops the performance by 1–2%. Hence whereas the web confirmation of formed questions helps with human perception of the quality of constructed dialogue, it has an inverse effect on the resultant chatbot functionality. At the same time, the extension of the training set on-demand turns out to be a fruitful feature assuring coverage of a Q/A domain.

1.7   Open Source Implementation

Although there is an abundance of chatbot development platforms, not too many open-source chatbot systems are available. To mention one, Augello et al. (2017) analyze open source technologies, focusing on their potential to implement a social chatbot.

In our open source implemented version, the application of parse thicket generalization for search occurs according to the following scenarios (Galitsky 2017a, b). For the question and candidate answer, we build a pair of parse thickets. Then we perform generalization of parse thickets, either without loss of information, finding a maximum common parse thicket subgraph, or with a loss of information, approximating the paths of resultant subgraph by generalizing thicket phrases. A search relevance score is computed accordingly as a total number of vertexes in a common maximum subgraph in the first case, and is calculated as the number of words in maximal common sub-phrases, taking into account the weight for parts of speech (Galitsky et al. 2012), in the second case. Alternatively, the tree kernel technology applied to parse thicket classifies an answer into the class of valid or invalid (Chap. 9 of Volume 1) .

The textual input is subject to a conventional text processing flow such as sentence splitting, tokenizing, stemming, part-of-speech assignment, building of parse trees and coreferences assignment for each sentence. This flow is implemented by either OpenNLP or Stanford NLP, and the parse thicket is built based on the algorithm presented in Galitsky et al. (2013). The coreferences and RST components rely on Stanford NLP's rule-based approach to finding correlated mentions, based on the multi-pass sieves.

The code for dialogue management is available at

https://github.com/bgalitsky/relevance-based-on-parse-trees/tree/master/src/main/java/opennlp/tools/chatbot.

1.8   Related Work

Typically, every part in most coherent text has some plausible reason for its presence, some function that it performs to the overall semantics of the text. Rhetorical relations such as *Contrast, Cause, Explanation* describe how the parts of a text are linked to each other. Rhetorical relations indicate the different ways in which the parts of a text are linked to each other to form a coherent whole.

Marir and Haouam (2004) introduced a thematic relationship between parts of text using RST based on cue phrases to determine the set of rhetorical relations. Once these structures are determined, they are put in an index, which can then be searched not only by keywords, as traditional information retrieval systems do, but also by rhetorical relations.

Lioma et al. (2012) studied if there is a correlation between certain rhetorical relations and retrieval performance. The authors also addressed a question on whether

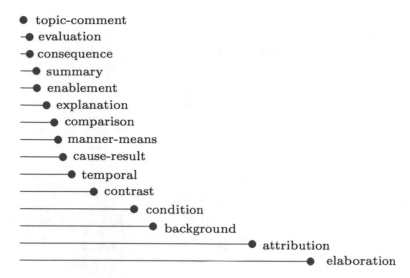

Fig. 1.16 Percentages of all RR as extracted by SPADE (Soricut and Marcu 2003)

knowledge about a document's rhetorical relations be useful to search re-ranking and presented a retrieval model that conditions the probability of relevance between a query and a document on the rhetorical relations occurring in that document.

The authors observed that different rhetorical relations perform differently across evaluation measures and query sets. The four rhetorical relations that improve performance over the baseline consistently for all evaluation measures and query sets are: *Background, Cause-Result, Condition* and *Topic-comment. Topic-comment* is one of the overall best-performing rhetorical relation that means that boosting the weight of the topical part of a document improves its estimation of relevance. These relations are not very frequent (Teufel and Moens 2002, Fig. 1.16).

Zidrasco et al. (2010) annotated conversational data taken from Wikipedia Talk page with 27 rhetorical relations (Table 1.7). Wikpedia Talk pages reflect short and long dialogues about ideas, requests and suggestions about page editing, to come to a common point about a topic or an item. To investigate the relationship between consensus building and appropriateness of structure, the authors counted frequencies of bigrams of rhetorical relations (Fig. 1.17). In dialogues with the focus on argumentation, the most frequent bi-grams and tri-grams are those including generalized RRs of *Agreement* and *Disagreement* (Table 1.8).

Discourse analysis and rhetorical structures have been studied in the context of several automatic text processing applications. This has been partly enabled by the availability of discourse parsers. Sun and Chai (2007) investigated the role of discourse processing and its implication on query expansion for a sequence of questions in scenario-based context Q/A. They considered a sequence of questions as a mini discourse. An empirical examination of three discourse theoretic models indicates that their discourse-based approach can significantly improve Q/A performance

Table 1.7 Frequent individual RRs

Level	Sublevel	Tag name
Requirement		Req_evidence
		Req_detail
		Req_yes/no
Response	Answer	Affirmation
		Negation
	Argumentation	Evidence
		Explanation_argumentative
		Example
		Background
	Consensus	Agreement
		Disagreement
Action request		Request_to_do
		Suggestion
Politeness		Gratitude
		Apology

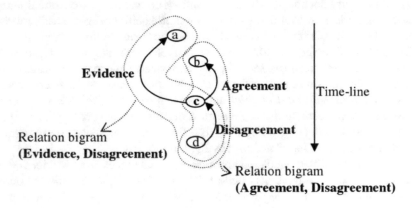

Fig. 1.17 Bi-grams and N-grams of RRs

over a baseline of plain reference resolution. In a different task, Wang et al. (2010) parsed Web user forum threads to determine the discourse dependencies between posts in order to improve information access over Web forum archives.

Heerschop et al. (2011) performed document sentiment analysis based on a document's discourse structure. The authors assessed the hypothesis that by splitting a text into important and less important text spans, and by subsequently making use of this information by weighting the sentiment conveyed by distinct text spans in accordance with their importance, they could improve the performance of a sentiment classifier. A document's discourse structure is obtained by applying rhetorical structure theory

Table 1.8 Bi-grams (on the tope) and tri-grams of RRs

Relation	Frequency	Percentage (%)
Explanation_argumentative	115	18
Agreement	108	17
Disagreement	94	15
Evidence	67	11
Suggestion	49	7.8
Justification	33	5.3
Req_evidence	26	4.2
Request_to_do	22	3.5
Req_detail	19	3.0
Affirmation	10	1.6
Other rhetorical relations	32	5.1
Total	627	100

Relation trigram			Frequency	Percentage (%)
r_1	r_2	r_3		
	Agreement	Agreement	4	1.7
	Evidence	Agreement	3	1.3
	Evidence	Agreement	3	1.3
	Explanation_Argumentative	Explanation_argumentative	3	1.3
	Disagreement	Evidence	3	1.3
	Suggestion	Req_detail	3	1.3
	Suggestion	Agreement	3	1.3

(continued)

Table 1.8 (continued)

Relation trigram			Frequency	Percentage (%)
r_1	r_2	r_3		
Disagreement	Evidence	Disagreement	3	1.3
Suggestion	Disagreement	Explanation_argumentative	3	1.3
Explanation_argumentative	Explanation_Argumentative	Agreement	3	1.3
Other rhetorical relations trigrams			199	83
Total			230	100

on a sentence level. The authors report a 4.5% improvement in sentiment classification accuracy when considering discourse, in comparison to a non-discourse based baseline. Similarly to this study, Somasundaran et al. (2009), Galitsky et al. (2009), Galitsky and McKenna (2017) achieve improvements to opinion polarity classification when using discourse and Morato et al. (2003) report a positive dependence between classification performance and certain discourse variables. Nagarajan and Chandrasekar (2014) address the expectation-related sentiment polarity.

In the area of text compression, Louis et al. (2010) study the usefulness of rhetorical relations between sentences for summarization. They find that most of the significant rhetorical relations are associated with non-discriminative sentences, that is, sentences that are not important for summarization. The authors observe that RRs that may be intuitively perceived as highly salient does not provide strong indicators of being informative; instead, the usefulness of RRs is in providing constraints for navigating through the text's structure. These findings are compatible with the study of Clarke and Lapata (2010) into constraining text compression on the basis of rhetorical relations. For a more in-depth look into the impact of individual rhetorical relations to summarization, the reader is recommended to consult (Teufel and Moens 2002).

Wang et al. (2006) extend an IR ranking model by adding a re-ranking strategy based on document discourse. Specifically, their re-ranking formula consists of the default retrieval status value, which is then multiplied by a function that linearly combines inverse document frequency and term distance for each query term within a discourse unit. They focus on one discourse type only (advantage disadvantage), which they identify manually in queries, and show that their approach improves retrieval performance for these queries. Also, Suwandaratna and Perera (2010) present a re-ranking approach for Web search that uses discourse structure. They report a heuristic algorithm for refining search results based on their rhetorical relations. Their implementation and evaluation are partly based on a series of ad-hoc choices, making it hard to compare with other approaches. They report a positive user-based evaluation of their system for ten test cases.

From the logical formalization of a search standpoint, anti-unification appears to be useful for various tasks in natural language processing: semantic classification of sentences based on their syntactic parse trees (Sidorov et al. 2012), grounded language learning, semantic text similarity, insight grammar learning, metaphor modeling. The major anti-unification technique in these applications is the original method for first-order terms over fixed-arity alphabets, introduced by Plotkin (1970). Amiridze and Kutsia (2018) provide an overview of existing linguistic applications of anti-unification, propose two flexible generalization computation algorithms, and discuss their potential use in NLP tasks.

Recently, rhetorical parsing became more reliable and efficient (Joty et al. 2013; Feng and Hirst 2014); however, the number of applications for resultant discourse trees (DTs) is mostly limited to content generation and summarization. Discourse features are valuable for passage re-ranking (Jansen et al. 2014). DTs have been found to assist in answer indexing to make search more relevant: query keywords should occur in the nucleus rather than a satellite of a rhetorical relation (Galitsky et al. 2015a, b).

The most popular approach in the last few years is to learn topical relevance and dialogue management together, using deep learning. This family of
approaches also fall into the answer category of data-driven (Serban et al. 2017);
they require huge dialogue datasets. Vorontsov and Potapenko (2015) combine probabilistic assumptions with linguistic and problem-specific requirements in a single
multi-objective topic model.

Zhao et al. (2012) present DAViewer, an interactive visualization system for
assisting computational linguistics researchers to explore, compare, evaluate and
annotate the results of discourse parsers. Relying on this system, a discourse linguistics scientist can move beyond a manual exploration and comparisons of discourse
structures to get intuitions for improving and deploying rhetorical parsing algorithms.
The DAViewer interface (Fig. 1.18) includes a detailed panel that shows the discourse
tree structures of the focused algorithms and documents as node-link or dendrograms,
as well as a status panel that provides the basic properties of the currently selected
items together with a legend for filtering operations. An annotation panel that allows
users to edit annotations is shown in the top-right. A text panel showing the content
of the current document is shown on the bottom right.

The problem of reducing the space of possible utterances under dialogue construction has been addressed in the extensive body of research. This reduction is based on

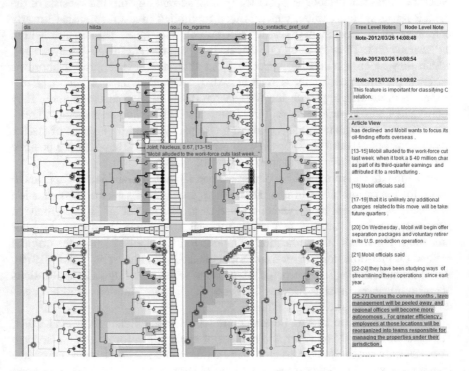

Fig. 1.18 DAViewer, an interactive visualization system for exploration, comparison, evaluation
and annotation of the results of discourse parsers (Zhao et al. 2012)

syntactic and possibly semantic features, but not discourse ones. A dialogue management system can narrow the number of plausible answer utterances to a small list, and an ML model would select the most appropriate responses from this list (Lowe et al. 2016). This next utterance classification task is derived from the IR-based metrics for information-retrieval-based approaches, which is easy to interpret and tune the complexity by changing the number of false responses.

Modern search engines and chatbots, from vertical to horizontal, do not implement reasoning via discourse-level analysis, to the best of our knowledge. This is due to its computational load and hard compatibility with big data technologies. Most search engineers consider discourse analysis too abstract and too distant from applications.

Since rhetorical parsers for English has become more available and accurate, their application in search engine indexing is becoming more feasible. As precision and recall of search systems ignoring discourse-level information deteriorates, users do not find products, services and information they need, therefore, leveraging the linguistic technologies, including discourse, become realistic and necessary for industrial systems.

Most chatbot vendors these days, such as www.botframework.com and www.dia logflow.com, provide NLP platforms so that the content providers feed them with Q/A pairs and expect satisfactory performance. It is hard to formally evaluate these systems, but anecdotal evidence is that their performance is rather limited. Another family of chatbots is focused on the simulation of the intelligent activity of humans instead of providing efficient content to information. This family is also frequently based on deep learning of a huge set of conversations. Being capable of supporting a conversation on an arbitrary topic, building plausible phrases, these systems are nevertheless hardly applicable for industrial applications such as customer support.

At any point in the discourse, some entities are considered more salient than others (occurring in nucleus parts of DTs), and consequently are expected to exhibit different properties. In Centering Theory (Grosz et al. 1995; Poesio et al. 2004), entity importance determines how they are realized in an utterance, including pronominalized relation between them. In other discourse theories, entity importance can be defined via topicality and cognitive accessibility (Gundel et al. 1993).

Barzilay and Lapata (2008) automatically abstracts a text into a set of entity transition sequences and records distributional, syntactic, and referential information about discourse entities. The authors formulated the coherence assessment as a learning task and show that their entity-based representation is well-suited for ranking-based generation and text classification tasks.

Nguyen and Joty (2017) present a local coherence model based on a convolutional neural network that operates over the distributed representation of entity transitions in the grid representation of a text. Their architecture can model sufficiently long entity transitions, and can incorporate entity-specific features without losing generalization power. Kuyten et al. (2015) developed a search engine that leverages the discourse structure in documents to overcome the limitations associated with the bag-of-words document representations in information retrieval. This system does not address the problem of rhetorical coordination between Q and A, but given a Q, this search engine can retrieve both the relevant *A* and individual statements from the *A* that describe some rhetorical relations to the query.

1.9 Conclusions

We built a dialogue management system for a chatbot with iterative content exploration that leads a user through a personalized knowledge acquisition session. The chatbot is designed as an automated customer support or product recommendation agent that assists a user in learning product features, product usability, suitability, troubleshooting and other related tasks.

Answering questions in the domain of this study is a significantly more complex task than a factoid Q/A such as Stanford Q/A database (Rajpurkar et al. 2016), where it is just necessary to involve one or two entities and their parameters. To answer a "how to solve a problem" question, one needs to maintain the logical flow connecting the entities in the questions. Since some entities from *Q* are inevitably omitted, these would need to be restored from some background knowledge text about these omitted entities and the ones presented in *Q*. Moreover, a logical flow needs to complement that of the *Q*.

Domain-specific thesauri, such as the ones related to mechanical problems with cars, are very hard and costly to build. In this chapter, we proposed a substitute via domain-independent discourse level analysis where we attempt to cover unaddressed parts of *DT-A* on the fly, finding text fragments in a background knowledge corpus such as Wikipedia. Hence we can do without an ontology that would have to maintain relations between involved entities (Galitsky et al. 2011).

The proposed imaginary DT feature of a Q/A system delivers a substantial increase of accuracy in answering complex convergent questions. Whereas using DTs for answer style matching improves Q/A accuracy by more than 10%, compared to the relevance-focused baseline, relying on imaginary DTs gives a further 10% improvement.

Since we explored the complementarity relation between DT-A and DT-Q and proposed a way to identify imaginary DT-A on demand, the learning feature space is substantially reduced and learning from an available dataset of a limited size becomes plausible. The interplay between a nucleus and a satellite in a discourse tree for managing a dialogue on the fly is fairly important (Fig. 1.19).

Although there has been a substantial advancement in document-level RST parsing, including the rich linguistic features-based of parsing models (Joty et al. 2013), a document level discourse analysis has not found a broad range of applications such as search. The most valuable information from DT includes global discourse features and long-range structural dependencies between DT constituents.

A number of studies including Surdeanu et al. (2015) showed that discourse information is beneficial for search. We believe this chapter is the first study explicitly showing how discourse trees help to navigate search. To be a valid answer for a question, its keywords need to occur in the adjacent EDU chain of this answer so

Fig. 1.19 An interaction between the nucleus and satellite nodes in a DT is important for dialogue management (on the left). To build a dialogue from a document, there is always a place to cut the document and insert a question (on the right). The proposed algorithm for building dialogues can produce as much data as needed (on the bottom, cartoonbank 2020)

that these EDUs are fully ordered and connected by Nucleus - Satellite relations. Note the difference between the proximity in the text as a sequence of words and proximity in a DT. An answer is expected to be invalid if the questions' keywords occur in the answer's satellite EDUs and not in their nucleus EDUs. The purpose of the rhetorical map of an answer is to prevent it from being fired by questions whose keywords occur in non-adjacent areas of this map.

Discourse trees and their extensions is a very promising subject of study for logical AI. Logical AI studies subjects such as logic forms and logic programs, which are very limited in quantity in the real world. But logical AI tries to make sense of them: discourse trees are fairly interpretable structures. Statistical/deep machine learning has big text data available at its disposal but not really making sense of it from the perspective of Logical AI. Communicative discourse trees can be obtained in large quantity on the one hand and they are an adequate Logical AI subject, on the other hand. That is why discourse trees and their extension is such an important subject of study for search engineering and chatbots.

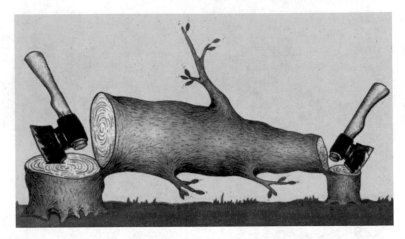

Fig. 1.20 Illustration of the method of bridging inference in discourse analysis (Cartoonbank 2020)

Hardalov et al. (2019) propose a CRM Q/A technique that adapts a deep neural architecture from the domain of machine reading comprehension to re-rank the suggested answers from different models using the question as context. The authors train their model using negative sampling based on Q/A pairs from the Twitter Customer Support Dataset. The evaluation shows that the proposed re-ranking framework improves the accuracy in terms of word overlap and semantic measures.

The idea of using imaginary discourse trees to bridge entities not explicitly associated is not novel (Fig. 1.20). Irmer (2010) explores the role bridging inferences play in discourse interpretation. Bridging inference in the form of the resolution of indirect anaphoric relationships between entities in a text or a discourse must be made by recipients in order to make sense of the linguistic input, which often does not fully specify the intended meaning of utterances. Contextual knowledge has to be taken into account for successfully determining the meaning of texts and discourses. The author examines the interpretation of discourses in general and bridging inferences in particular, from formal, computational, cognitive, and psychological points of view. He develops a formalization that can account for under-specification in cohesion and coherence of discourses and permits the integration of bridging inferences in the construction of a structured discourse representation.

1.9.1 Conclusions on Building a Dialogue

This is the first system, to the best of our knowledge, that builds dialogues from arbitrary texts. Hence the developed technology supports the transition from search engine-based information access that relied on indexed documents, to dialogue systems, in an arbitrary domain. Doc2Dialogue is a configurable system that can include web mining, forming queries based on communicative actions, and other question refinement means. The system of Novikova et al. (2017) of NL generation (NLG) evaluation produces ungrammatical output by word-by-word-based generation and learning from noisy data.

Reinforcement learning (Sutton and Barto 1998) allowed the authors to use policy gradient to directly optimize task-specific rewards such as BLEU, which are otherwise non-differentiable and hard to optimize (Kumar et al. 2018).

Word-based metrics rely on the assumption that human-generated references are a correct and complete gold standard, these assumptions are invalid for corpus-based NLG. This is especially true for crowdsourced dialogue datasets. Grammar-based metrics neither rely on human-generated references nor are affected by their quality.

Wang et al. (2017) proposed a generative machine comprehension model that machine leans to form questions and to answer them based on documents. The proposed model uses a sequence-to-sequence framework that encodes the document and generates a question (answer) given an answer (question). Significant improvement in model performance is observed empirically on the SQuAD corpus, confirming our hypothesis that the model benefits from jointly learning to perform both tasks.

It is well known that manually creating meaningful and relevant questions to texts is a time-consuming and challenging task. For example, while evaluating students on reading comprehension, it is tedious for a teacher to manually create questions, find answers to those questions, and thereafter evaluate answers. Traditional approaches have either used a linguistically motivated set of transformation rules for transforming a given sentence into a question or a set of manually created templates with slot fillers to generate questions. Recently, neural network-based techniques such as sequence-to-sequence learning have achieved remarkable success in various NLP tasks, including question generation. A recent deep learning approach to question generation by Serban et al. (2016) investigates a simpler task of generating questions only from a triplet of subject, relation and object. Du et al. (2017) propose a sequence-to-sequence model with attention for question generation from the text. Kumar et al. (2018) generate question–answer pairs from text using pointer networks.

Whereas a majority of neural network approaches (Nakamura et al. 2018) generate dialogues to support real-time conversation, mostly based on data of limited quality, the current study produces dialogues in a given domain to improve the overall performance of conversational systems requiring extensive dataset, such as neural-based. Hence this work complements popular approaches to dialogue generation rather than competes for the generation process itself. Instead of using a very peculiar, hardly generalizable and not very natural for an automated chatbot dataset such as Switchboard (Godfrey and Holliman 1997), we provide a tool to generate a high-volume of dialogues for a given domain on demand.

Dialogue generation approaches rely on a limited set of dialogues that are very different from what a user would expect from chatbots operating in the domains of interest, such as finance, legal, health. These datasets are rather peculiar in style and content; it is hard to extend their conversational logic to other domains. These datasets include:

(1) Movie Triples corpus (Banchs 2012) covers a wide range of topics with few spelling mistakes, but its small size of about a quarter of a million makes it difficult to train a dialogue model. We thought that this scenario would really benefit from the proposed adversarial generation.

(2) Ubuntu Dialogue Corpus has a limited scope of topics but contains almost 2 million conversations with an average of 5 utterances per conversation (Lowe et al. 2015).

(3) A new open dataset for Customer Support on Twitter (Kaggle 2019). It contains 3 M tweets and very short replies for twenty big companies such as Amazon, Apple, Uber, Delta, and Spotify, among others. As customer support topics from different organizations are generally unrelated to each other, we focus only on tweets related to Apple support, which represents the largest number of tweets in the corpus. The content coverage is very sparse so this dataset cannot be used to provide a piece of knowledge. Instead, this dataset can be used to capture a style of how users formulate their questions to customer support.

(4) The only available conversational dataset with adequate domain coverage. Car Repair dataset that we formed for evaluation of dialogue management algorithm (Galitsky et al. 2019) includes pairs extracted from dialogues as first and second utterance so that the question is 1–15 keywords and answer is three to six sentences. This resource was obtained to train a dialog support system, but it also proved to be useful to evaluate search. This dataset is scraped from Car Pros.com and is available at Car Repair Dataset (2017).

The technique presented in this chapter allows building dialogue matching content, style and cohesiveness of the target chatbot conversations. The content quality, factual accuracy, coherence and thoroughness of text is dramatically higher than the ones possibly obtained from a dialogue corpus compiled with the purpose different from a chatbot training.

Yuan et al. (2017) reframe the standard machine comprehension task: rather than answering questions about a document; the authors teach machines to ask questions. Our work has several motivations. First, we believe that posing appropriate questions is an important aspect of information acquisition in intelligent systems. Second, learning to ask questions may improve the ability to answer them. Singer and Donlan (1982) demonstrated that having students devise questions before reading can increase scores on subsequent comprehension tests. Third, answering the questions in most existing Q/A datasets is an extractive task—it requires selecting some span of text within the document—while question asking is comparatively abstractive—it requires the generation of text that may not appear in the document.

Although question-building task has attracted significant attention in the past decade, it is hard to find the research where attempts are made to form dialogue from the arbitrary text. The question generation task requires an alteration of a general Q/A problem formulation and a satisfactory solution can be provided by an end-to-end system once a sufficient training set is available. Conversely, the dialogue construction problem needs to rely on insights from discourse analysis; discourse tree topology plays an essential role here.

Our rule-based dialogue formation algorithm is designed to build training sets for data-hungry approaches such as statistical and deep learning. Notice that if deep learning composes a training set, it would not be the best one to feed another deep learning system for dialogue management since its shortcomings will be generalized and amplified.

Once generated dialogue data is available, chatbots can penetrate in the domains which are very distinctive by nature from the ones for which real human dialogues are currently available. Less formalized, user-generated and under-represented domains can be enabled with chatbots so that manual dialogue management efforts would not be required (Galitsky and Ilvovsky 2017b).

Acknowledgements I am grateful to my colleagues **Dmitry Ilvovsky** and **Tatyana Makhalova** for help in the preparation of this chapter.

References

Adiwardana DD, Luong M, So DR, Hall J, Fiedel N, Thoppilan R, Yang Z, Kulshreshtha A, Nemade G, Lu Y, Le QV (2020) Towards a human-like open-domain chatbot. arXiv:2001.09977

Agostaro F, Augello A, Pilato G, Vassallo G, Gaglio S (2005) A conversational agent based on a conceptual interpretation of a data driven semantic space. In: Proceedings of AI*IA, LNAI, vol 3673, pp 381–392

Amiridze N, Kutsia T (2018) Anti-unification and natural language processing. In: Fifth workshop on natural language and computer science, NLCS'18, EasyChair Preprint no. 203

Augello A, Gentile M, Dignum F (2017) An overview of open-source chatbots social skills. In: Diplaris S, Satsiou A, Følstad A, Vafopoulos M, Vilarinho T (eds) Internet science. Lecture notes in computer science, vol 10750, pp 236–248

Banchs RE (2012) Movie-DiC: a movie dialogue corpus for research and development. In: Proceedings of the 50th annual meeting of the association for computational linguistics, pp 203–207

Barzilay R, Lapata M (2008) Modeling local coherence: an entity-based approach. Comput Linguist 34(1):1–34

Bordes A, Weston J (2016) Learning end-to-end goal-oriented dialog. In: ICRL 2017

CarPros Car Repair Dataset (2017) https://github.com/bgalitsky/relevance-based-on-parse-trees/ blob/master/examples/CarRepairData_AnswerAnatomyDataset2.csv.zip. Obtained from https:// www.2carpros.com.

Cartoonbank (2020) https://cartoonbank.ru/?page_id=29&category=5&offset=80

Chali Y, Joty SR, Hasan SA (2009) Complex question answering: unsupervised learning approaches and experiments. J Artif Int Res 35

Clarke J, Lapata M (2010) Discourse constraints for document compression. Comput Linguist 36(3):411–441

Codocedo V, Napoli A (2014) A proposition for combining pattern structures and relational concept analysis. In: Glodeanu CV, Kaytoue M, Sacarea C (eds) ICFCA 2014. LNCS (LNAI), vol 8478. Springer, Heidelberg, pp 96–111

Cohen W (2018) Enron email dataset. https://www.cs.cmu.edu/~./enron/. Accessed 10 July 2018

Csaky R (2019) Deep learning based chatbot models. arXiv:1908.08835

DeepPavlov.ai (2020) DeepPavlov: an open source conversational AI framework. https://deeppavlo v.ai/

Du X, Shao J, Cardie C (2017) Learning to ask: neural question generation for reading comprehension. arXiv:1705.00106

Feng WV, Hirst G (2014) A linear-time bottom-up discourse parser with constraints and post-editing. In: Proceedings of the 52nd annual meeting of the association for computational linguistics (ACL 2014), Baltimore, USA, June 2014

Fidelity (2018) https://github.com/bgalitsky/relevance-based-on-parse-trees/blob/master/examples/Fidelity_FAQs_AnswerAnatomyDataset1.csv.zip

Galitsky B (2013) Transfer learning of syntactic structures for building taxonomies for search engines. Eng Appl Artif Intell 26(10):2504–2515

Galitsky B (2014) Learning parse structure of paragraphs and its applications in search. Eng Appl Artif Intell 32:160–184

Galitsky B (2016) Providing personalized recommendation for attending events based on individual interest profiles. AI Res 5(1) (Sciedu Press)

Galitsky, B, Chen H, Du S (2009) Inverting semantic structure of customer opinions expressed in forums and blogs. In: 17th international conference on conceptual structures, Suppl Proc

Galitsky B, Kovalerchuk B (2014) Improving web search relevance with learning structure of domain concepts. Clusters Orders Trees: Methods Appl 92:341–376

Galitsky B, Kuznetsov SO, Usikov D (2013) Parse thicket representation for multi-sentence search. In: International conference on conceptual structures, pp 153–172

Galitsky B, Dobrocsi G, de la Rosa JL (2012) Inferring the semantic properties of sentences by mining syntactic parse trees. Data Knowl Eng 81:21–45

Galitsky B, Ilvovsky D, Kuznetsov SO (2015a) Text classification into abstract classes based on discourse structure. In: Proceedings of recent advances in natural language processing, Hissar, Bulgaria, pp 200–207, 7–9 Sept 2015

Galitsky B, Ilvovsky D, Kuznetsov SO (2015b) Rhetoric map of an answer to compound queries. In: ACL-2, pp 681–686

Galitsky B (2017a) Matching parse thickets for open domain question answering. Data Knowl Eng 107:24–50

Galitsky B (2017b) Discovering rhetorical agreement between a request and response. Dialogue Discourse 8(2):167–205

Galitsky (2019a) Automated building of expanded datasets for training of autonomous agents. US Patent Application 16/426,878

Galitsky B (2019b) Rhetorical agreement: maintaining cohesive conversations. Developing enterprise chatbots. Springer, Cham, pp 327–363

Galitsky B (2019c) Semantic skeleton thesauri for question answering bots. Developing enterprise chatbots. Springer, Cham, pp 163–176

Galitsky B (2019d) Building chatbot thesaurus. In: Developing enterprise chatbots. Springer, Cham, pp 221–252

Galitsky B, Ilvovsky D (2017a) Chatbot with a discourse structure-driven dialogue management. In: EACL demo program

Galitsky B, Ilvovsky D (2017b) On a chat bot finding answers with optimal rhetoric representation. In: Proceedings of recent advances in natural language processing, Varna, Bulgaria, pp 253–259, 4–6 Sept 2017

Galitsky B, Makowski G (2017) Document classifier for a data loss prevention system based on learning rhetoric relations. In: CICLing 2017 Budapest, Hungary, 17–23 Apr 2017

Galitsky B, McKenna EW (2017) Sentiment extraction from consumer reviews for providing product recommendations. US Patent 9646078B2

Galitsky B, Ilvovsky D (2019) On a chatbot conducting virtual dialogues. In: Proceedings of the 28th ACM International Conference on Information and Knowledge Management, pp 2925–2928.

Galitsky B, Ilvovsky D, Makhalova T (2019) Discourse-level dialogue management. In: Developing enterprise chatbots. Springer, Cham, Switzerland

Galitsky B, Shpitsberg I (2015) Evaluating assistance to individuals with autism in reasoning about mental world. Artificial intelligence applied to assistive technologies and smart environments: papers from the 2015 AAAI workshop

Galitsky B, Ilvovsky D, Lebedeva N, Usikov D (2014) Improving trust in automation of social promotion. In: AAAI Spring symposium on the intersection of robust intelligence and trust in autonomous systems, Stanford, CA

Galitsky B, Parnis A, Usikov D (2017) Exploring discourse structure of user-generated content. In: CICLing 2017, Budapest, Hungary, 17–23 Apr 2017

Galitsky B, Dobrocsi G, de la Rosa JL, Sergei O Kuznetsov (2011) Using generalization of syntactic parse trees for taxonomy capture on the web. In: 19th international conference on conceptual structures, ICCS 2011, pp 104–117

Godfrey J, Holliman E (1997) Switchboard-1 release 2. Linguistic Data Consortium, Philadelphia

Grosz B, Joshi AK, Scott Weinstein S (1995) Centering: a framework for modeling the local coherence of discourse. Comput Linguist 21(2):203–225

Gundel JK, Hedberg N, Zacharski R (1993) Cognitive status and the form of referring expressions in discourse. Language 69(2):274–307

Hardalov M, Koychev I, Nakov P (2019) Machine reading comprehension for answer re-ranking in customer support chatbots. arXiv:1902.04574

Heerschop B, Goossen F, Hogenboom A, Frasincar F, Kaymak U, de Jong F (2011) Polarity analysis of texts using discourse structure. In: Proceedings of the 20th ACM international conference on information and knowledge management, CIKM '11. ACM, New York, NY, USA, pp 1061–1070

Heilman M, Smith NA (2010) Good question! statistical ranking for question generation. In: Human language technologies: the 2010 annual conference of the North American chapter of the Association for Computational Linguistics, pp 609–617

Ilvovsky D, Kirillovich A, Galitsky B (2020) Controlling chat bot multi-document navigation with the extended discourse trees. CLIB 63 71

Indri IR (2018) https://www.lemurproject.org/indri/. Accessed 11 Sept 2018

Irmer M (2010) Bridging inferences in discourse interpretation. PhD dissertation, University of Leipzig, Germany

Ivanov S, Webster C, Stoilova E, Slobodskoy D (2020) Biosecurity, automation technologies and economic resilience of travel, tourism and hospitality companies. osf.io

Jansen P, Surdeanu M, Clark P (2014) Discourse complements lexical semantics for nonfactoid answer reranking. ACL.

Joty SR, Moschitti A (2014) Discriminative reranking of discourse parses using tree kernels. In: Proceedings of the 2014 conference on empirical methods in natural language processing (EMNLP)

Joty SR, Carenini G, Ng RT, Mehdad Y (2013) Combining intra-and multi-sentential rhetorical parsing for document-level discourse analysis. In: ACL (1), pp 486–496

Jurafsky D, Martin JH (2000) Speech and language processing: an introduction to natural language processing, computational linguistics, and speech recognition. Prentice Hall, Upper Saddle River

Kaggle (2019) Customer support on Twitter. https://www.kaggle.com/thoughtvector/customer-support-on-twitter. Accessed 18 Feb 2019

Kaytoue M, Codocedo V, Buzmakov A, Baixeries J, Kuznetsov SO, Napoli A (2015) Pattern structures and concept lattices for data mining and knowledge processing. In: Joint European conference on machine learning and knowledge discovery in databases. Springer, Cham, pp 227–231

Kelley JF (1984) An iterative design methodology for user-friendly natural language office information applications. ACM Trans Inf Syst

Kerly A, Hall P, Bull S (2007) Bringing chatbots into education: towards natural language negotiation of open learner models. Knowl-Based Syst 20(2):177–185

Kipper K, Korhonen A, Ryant N, Palmer M (2008) A large-scale classification of English verbs. Lang Resour Eval J 42:21–40

Kostelník P, Pisařovic I, Muroň M, Dařena F, Procházka D (2019) Chatbots for enterprises: outlook. Acta Univ Agric Silvic Mendel Brun 67:1541–1550

Kovalerchuk B, Kovalerchuk M (2017) Toward virtual data scientist with visual means. In: IJCNN

Kumar V, Ramakrishnan G, Li Y (2018) A framework for automatic question generation from text using deep reinforcement learning. CoRR. arXiv:1808.04

Kuyten P, Bollegala D, Hollerit B, Prendinger H, Aizawa K (2015) A discourse search engine based on rhetorical structure theory. In: Hanbury A, Kazai G, Rauber A, Fuhr N (eds) Advances in information retrieval. ECIR 2015. Lecture notes in computer science, vol 9022. Springer, Cham

LeThanh H, Abeysinghe G, Huyck C (2004) Generating discourse structures for written texts. In: Proceedings of the 20th international conference on computational linguistics, COLING '04, Geneva, Switzerland. Association for Computational Linguistics.

Lin CY (2004) ROUGE: a package for automatic evaluation of summaries. In: Proceedings of the ACL workshop on text summarization branches out, Barcelona, Spain, pp 74–81, 25–26 July 2004

Lioma C, Larsen B, Lu W (2012) Rhetorical relations for information retrieval. In: SIGIR, Portland, Oregon, USA, 12–16 Aug 2012

Liu C-W, Lowe R, Serban I, Noseworthy M, Charlin L, Pineau J (2016) How not to evaluate your dialogue system: an empirical study of unsupervised evaluation metrics for dialogue response generation. In: EMNLP, pp 2122–2132

Louis A, Joshi AK, Nenkova A (2010) Discourse indicators for content selection in summarization. In: Fernandez R, Katagiri Y, Komatani K, Lemon O, Nakano M (eds) SIGDIAL conference. The Association for Computer Linguistics, pp 147–156

Lowe R, Pow N, Serban I, Pineau J (2015) The Ubuntu Dialogue Corpus: a large dataset for research in unstructured multi-turn dialogue systems. In: 16th annual meeting of the special interest group on discourse and dialogue, Prague, Czech Republic, pp 285–294, 2–4 Sept 2015

Lowe R, Serban IV, Noseworthy M, Charlin L, Pineau J (2016) On the evaluation of dialogue systems with next utterance classification. In: Special interest group on discourse and dialogue

Mann W, Thompson S (1988) Rhetorical structure theory: towards a functional theory of text organization. Text Interdiscip J Study Discourse 8(3):243–281

Marir F, Haouam K (2004) Rhetorical structure theory for content-based indexing and retrieval of web documents. In: ITRE 2004. 2nd international conference information technology: research and education, pp 160–164

Morato J, Llorens J, Genova G, Moreiro JA (2003) Experiments in discourse analysis impact on information classification and retrieval algorithms. Inf Process Manag 39:825–851

Morbini F, Forbell E, DeVault D, Sagae K Traum DR, Rizzo AA (2012) A mixed-initiative conversational dialogue system for healthcare. In: SIGDIAL '12: proceedings of the 13th annual meeting of the special interest group on discourse and dialogue, pp 137–139, July 2012

Nagarajan V, Chandrasekar P (2014) Pivotal Sentiment Tree Classifier. IJSTR 3, I(11)

Nakamura R, Sudoh K, Yoshino K, Nakamura S (2018) Another diversity-promoting objective function for neural dialogue generation. arXiv:1811.08100

Nguyen DT, Joty S (2017) A neural local coherence model. ACL 1:1320–1330

Novikova J, Dusek O, Curry AC, Rieser V (2017) Why we need new evaluation metrics for NLG. In: EMNLP

Papineni K, Roukos S, Ward T, Zhu WJ (2002) BLEU: a method for automatic evaluation of machine translation (PDF). In: ACL-2002: 40th annual meeting of the Association for Computational Linguistics, pp 311–318

Plotkin GD (1970) A note on inductive generalization. Mach Intell 5(1):153–163

Poesio M, Stevenson R, Di Eugenio B, Hitzeman J (2004) Centering: a parametric theory and its instantiations. Comput Linguist 30(3):309–363

Rajpurkar P, Zhang J, Lopyrev K, Liang P (2016) Squad: 100,000+ questions for machine comprehension of text. arXiv:1606.05250

Rizk Y, Bhandwalder A, Boag S, Chakraborti T, Isahagian V, Khazaeni Y, Pollock F, Unuvar M (2020) A unified conversational assistant framework for business process automation. arXiv: 2001.03543

Rus V, Lintean M (2012) A comparison of greedy and optimal assessment of natural language student input using word-to-word similarity metrics. In: Proceedings of the seventh workshop on building educational applications using NLP, Montreal, QC, Canada, pp 157–162

Serban IV, Lowe R, Henderson P, Charlin L, Pineau J (2017) A survey of available corpora for building data-driven dialogue systems. arXiv:1512.05742

Serban IV, García-Duran A, Gulcehre C, Ahn S, Chandar S, Courville A, Bengio Y (2016) Generating factoid questions with recurrent neural networks: the 30m factoid question-answer corpus. arXiv:1603.06807

Sidorov G, Velasquez F, Stamatatos E, Gelbukh A, Chanona-Hernández L (2012) Syntactic dependency-based N-grams as classification features. In: LNAI, vol 7630, pp 1–11

Singer H, Donlan D (1982) Active comprehension: Problem-solving schema with question generation for comprehension of complex short stories. Read Res Q 166–186

Singh Ospina N, Phillips KA, Rodriguez-Gutierrez R, Castaneda-Guarderas A, Gionfriddo MR, Branda ME, Montori VM (2018) Eliciting the patient's agenda—secondary analysis of recorded clinical encounters. J Gen Intern Med 1–5

Somasundaran S, Namata G, Wiebe J, Getoor L (2009) Supervised and unsupervised methods in employing discourse relations for improving opinion polarity classification. In: EMNLP. ACL, pp 170–179

Soricut R, Marcu D (2003) Sentence level discourse parsing using syntactic and lexical information. In: HLT-NAACL

Sun M, Chai JY (2007) Discourse processing for context question answering based on linguistic knowledge. Knowl-Based Syst 20:511–526

Surdeanu M, Hicks T, Valenzuela-Escarcega MA (2015) Two practical rhetorical structure theory parsers. In: Proceedings of the conference of the North American chapter of the Association for Computational Linguistics—human language technologies: software demonstrations (NAACL HLT)

Sutton RS, Barto AG (1998) Introduction to reinforcement learning, vol 135. MIT Press, Cambridge

Suwandaratna N, Perera U (2010) Discourse marker based topic identification and search results refining. In: 2010 5th international conference on information and automation for sustainability (ICIAFs), pp 119–125

Tanaka R, Ozeki A, Kato S, Lee A (2020) Context and knowledge aware conversational model and system combination for grounded response generation. Comput Speech Lang 62

Teufel S, Moens M (2002) Summarizing scientific articles: experiments with relevance and rhetorical status. Comput Linguist 28(4):409–445

Vorontsov K, Potapenko A (2015) Additive regularization of topic models. Mach Learn 101(1–3):303–323

Wang T, Yuan X, Trischler A (2017) A joint model for question answering and question generation. arXiv:1706.01450

Wang DY, Luk RWP, Wong K-F, Kwok KL (2006) An information retrieval approach based on discourse type. In: Kop C, Fliedl G, Mayr HC, Métais E (eds) NLDB. Lecture notes in computer science, vol 3999. Springer, pp 197–202

Wang W, Su J, Tan CL (2010) Kernel based discourse relation recognition with temporal ordering information. ACL

Wang Z, Lemon O (2013) A simple and generic belief tracking mechanism for the dialog state tracking challenge: on the believability of observed information. In: Proceedings of the SIGDIAL.

Webscope (2017). Yahoo! Answers dataset. https://webscope.sandbox.yahoo.com/catalog.php?dat atype=l

Wilks YA (ed) (1999) Machine conversations. Kluwer

Young S, Gasic M, Thomson B, Williams J (2013) POMDP-based statistical spoken dialogue systems: a review. Proc IEEE 99:1–20

Yuan X, Wang T, Gulcehre C, Sordoni A, Bachman P, Subramanian S, Zhang S and Trischler A (2017) Machine comprehension by text-to-text neural question generation. arXiv:1705.02012

Zhao J, Chevalier F, Collins C, Balakrishnan R (2012) Facilitating discourse analysis with interactive visualization. IEEE Trans Vis Comput Graph 18(12):2639–2648

Zhao X, Wu W, Tao C, Xu C, Zhao D, Yan R (2020) Low-resource knowledge-grounded dialogue generation. arXiv:2002.10348

Zidrasco T, Shiramatsu S, Takasaki J, Ozono T, Shintani T (2010) Building and analyzing corpus to investigate appropriateness of argumentative discourse structure for facilitating consensus. In: García-Pedrajas N, Herrera F, Fyfe C, Benítez JM, Ali M (eds) Trends in applied intelligent systems. IEA/AIE 2010. Lecture notes in computer science, vol 6097. Springer, Berlin, Heidelberg

Chapter 2
Recommendation by Joining a Human Conversation

Abstract We propose a novel way of the conversational recommendation where instead of asking user questions to acquire her preferences, the recommender tracks her conversations with other people, including customer support agents (CSA) and joins the conversation only when there is something important to recommend and the time is correct to do so. Building a recommender that joins a human conversation (RJC), we propose information extraction, discourse and argumentation analyses, as well as dialogue management techniques to compute a recommendation for a product and service that is badly needed by the customer, as inferred from the conversation. A special case of such conversations is considered where the customer raises his problem with a CSA in an attempt to resolve it, along with receiving a recommendation for a product with features addressing this problem. The performance of RJC is evaluated in a number of human–human and human-chatbot dialogues and demonstrates that RJC is an efficient and less intrusive way to provide high relevance and persuasive recommendations.

2.1 Introduction

Due to the popularity of texting and messaging and the recent advancement of deep learning technologies, a conversation-based interaction becomes an emerging user interface. Over the last decade, recommendation and advertisement researchers and practitioners have advanced the frontiers of personalized recommendation by making them function in a conversational mode. While modern conversation platforms offer basic dialogue capabilities such as natural language (NL) understanding, entity extraction and simple dialogue management, there are still challenges in developing practical applications to support complex use cases such as dialogue-based recommendation (Thompson et al. 2004; Christakopoulou et al. 2016, Sun and Zhang 2018).

More and more precise and powerful recommendation algorithms and techniques have been proposed capable of effectively assessing users' tastes and predict information that would probably be of interest to them. Most of these approaches rely on the machine learning (ML)-based collaborative filtering and do not take into account

© The Author(s), under exclusive license to Springer Nature Switzerland AG 2021
B. Galitsky, *Artificial Intelligence for Customer Relationship Management*,
Human–Computer Interaction Series, https://doi.org/10.1007/978-3-030-61641-0_2

the huge amount of knowledge, both structured and non-structured ones, such as prior user utterances in a dialogue describing the domain of interest for the recommendation engine (Anelli et al. 2018). Collaborative filtering is a recommended approach that filters out items that a user might like on the basis of accepted recommendations by similar users. It works by searching a large group of people and finding a smaller set of users with preferences and interests similar to a particular user.

Recommenders available in web portals such as Amazon or eBay are not always relevant and their recommendation is not necessarily timely. At the same time, conversational recommenders developed in the academic community and cited in this chapter can be too intrusive, relying on routine efforts of a customer to explicitly share her preferences and intent and also operate in too restrictive domains. What is needed is a non-intrusive, organic recommendation mode that does not require efforts from the user to share his preferences. In Fig. 2.1, Tiresias (whom we intend to substitute by an autonomous agent) provides a recommendation related to a dispute between Zeus and Hera.

In this section, we introduce a framework for *recommendation by joining a conversation* (RJC), a special case of a conversational advertisement with a focus on assisting with solving a current customer problem or a customer need to be communicated. In RJC scenarios, customers are expected to be fully aware of how and why a product or service being recommended would solve their issues.

When a user attempts to resolve a problem with a business, he is usually not in a mood to order another product or service from this business, or to spend extra on a product he has already purchased. However, frequently a recommendation for an additional product, or an extension of service helps this user save or benefit from this addition immediately or in the long run.

Typically, recommendation, advertisement and customer retention occur in different cycles of interaction with customers. However, in some customer support (CS) scenarios, recommending certain products may accelerate and simplify the

Fig. 2.1 Tiresias (as a role model for RJC) resolves the dispute between Zeus and Hera

problem resolution. For example, in the course of a dialogue where a customer support agent (CSA) explains how to avoid a non-sufficient fund fee (NSF), a linked saving account product can be recommended that would benefit both the user and a bank. This user would avoid NSF and the bank would have more funds in its possession.

In the course of a customer support dialogue, recommendation and advertisement need to be very relevant to customer needs and should assist in problem resolution in the way obvious to this user. In a conventional conversational recommendation, the system first gets information from the user about his needs and preferences and recommends a product after that. To manage such dialogue in an arbitrary domain, nontrivial dialogue management efforts from the system are required (Galitsky and Ilvovsky 2017; Narducci et al. 2018; Sun and Zhang 2018; Galitsky 2019a). Moreover, a user needs to be very patent and perform a routine activity of specifying his preferences. Neither of these is required in the RJC setting.

We consider two types of RJC scenarios:

(1) User—Human CSA dialogue, where an automated advertisement agent tracks this dialogue and inserts its utterances with a recommendation;
(2) User—Chatbot CS, where an automated advertisement agent and a chatbot is the same entity resolving a customer problem and providing product/service recommendations at the same time.

Both of these scenarios may occur in either problem-solving or general information acquisition settings (Kostelník et al. 2019).

One of the main requirements for the advertising in the course of CS dialogue is that the relation to the product the user experiences problem with must be obvious, as well as the benefits to the user of relying on this new recommended product to overcome this problem.

We start with an example of casual conversation and demonstrate how an advertising utterance can naturally intervene (Fig. 2.2 on the top). An utterance of an RJC agent can be followed by additional factual questions RJC should be able to answer (Fig. 2.2 on the bottom).

A conversational advertising agent could have much commercial potential in comparison with a conventional advertising means such as random insertion in a sequence of conversation, as provided by a social advertising network (such as Facebook). Web portals such as Amazon, eBay, JD, Alibaba and others are developing conversational recommender agents, but the research on this topic is very limited, and existing solutions are either based on single round conventional search or a traditional multi-round dialog system. They usually only utilize user inputs in the current session, ignoring users' long term preferences, or just perform slot-filling, obtaining the parameters of interest from the user explicitly (Sun and Zhang 2018). Moreover, most such systems behave very differently from a human when asked for a recommendation (Galitsky 2018). Humans can quickly establish preferences when asked to make a recommendation for someone they do not know. Christakopoulou et al. (2016) address the cold-start conversational recommendation problem in an online learning setting, developing a preference elicitation framework to identify which questions

> Mike: Hey, what's up dude?
> Peter: Not much . I am looking for a DVD to rent but I am fed up with all these. Have seen most of them already
> Mike: Anything worth seeing at movie theater?
> Peter: Nah. Just kids movies, sci-fi and cheesy romantic comedies.
> **RJC-agent: If you are looking for something new you should come to a meeting of the New Age Alternative Films Club**
> Peter What is that?
> **RJC-agent: the New Age Alternative Films Club gets together every other week and screens the type of films you cannot go at a regular movie theater**

> CSA: It's a good day today at Wealth Bank, my name is Joe, How can I help?
> Customer: tell ne remaining money in my account
> CSA: I will help you with this. Can I get your account # and name on this account?
> Customer: Sure, my name is Becky Randall, account # is 12233456
> CSA: your balance is $123.78
> Customer: if I transfer it to my bank account in Lloyds bank in London UK, how long would it take?
> CSA: If we do the transaction over the phone or online, our team members would contact you for verification before sending your money to an international bank. The process takes 2-3 days
> **RJC -agent: Open Account in Morgan Chase and use Zelle QuickPay to quickly transfer money to your friends and partners abroad**

Fig. 2.2 On the top: RJC scenario with a follow-up clarification. On the bottom: A regular banking dialogue with access to information and a transactional request

> Riley: Are you still auditioning for that skin cream commercial?
> Katie: That just so happens to be the 'in thing'. Does not every aspiring actress start off in a commercial?
> Riley: I take it you did not get the part of that 'Life and Death' sitcom?
> Katie: They did not even let me audition
> **RJC-agent: Have you thought about taking acting lessons? Have you heard about *Beverly Hills Playhouse - Acting Classes Los Angeles*?**

Fig. 2.3 RJC agent interrupts a causal conversation between peers

to ask a new user to quickly learn their preferences. In this section, we formulate a broader advertising and recommendation problem learning user preferences implicitly from the previous utterances in an arbitrary problem-solving conversation, not just by asking explicitly about user preferences.

Applicability of the proposed recommendation setting can go beyond CS scenarios. In a daily life, people communicate with others to exchange information and improve social bonding. To exchange and share ideas, people frequently communicate with others following certain dialog flow patterns. Usually, humans do not rigidly answer questions of others and instead wait for the next question. Conversation participants may first respond to the previous context and only then propose their own questions and suggestions. In this way, people show their attention to the words of others and confirm that they are willing to continue the conversation. Daily conversations are rich in emotion. By expressing emotions, people show their mutual respect, empathy and understanding to each other, and thus improve the relationships. Daily dialogues (Li et al. 2017) are also a good source for recommen-

```
Customer: Hello ? Can you give me a tow ? My tour car's stranded .
Agent: Sure . Where are you ?
Customer: I'm on highway 1-75 going near exit 46 .
Agent: What kind of car ?
Customer:  It's a blue Nissan minivan .
Where are you going to ?
Customer: The closest garage . What's the charge ?
RJC-agent – have a tow coverage with you auto insurance.
Request Roadside Assistance | join root.com. It would cover you tow charge.
Agent: You are within 50 kilometers , so it's a 50 - dollar flat rate .
```

Fig. 2.4   RJC agent joins a conversation on a tow truck request

dation and advertisement experiments (Fig. 2.3), as well as dialogues mined from the web randomly (Fig. 2.4).

2.2   Slot-Filling Conversational Recommendation Systems

Conventional recommender systems bring together ideas from information retrieval and filtering, user profiling, adaptive interfaces and machine learning in an attempt to offer users more personalized and responsive active search systems (Galitsky 2016). Conversational recommenders guide a user through a sequence of iterations, suggesting specific items, and using feedback from users to refine their suggestions in subsequent iterations (Smyth et al. 2004). The goal of recommendation systems is to help users find items of interest, and thus they must eliminate some choices from consideration while keeping others. To achieve this, recommenders must determine the interests of the current user, then present items that satisfy those interests. One of the most widely used approaches for information acquisition in recommendation systems is the use of a simple form that the user fills in. Then the recommender system presents a list of results, ordered by their predicted relevance to the user. (The combined technique of information acquired through a form and presentation in a list of results comes from information retrieval.)

In contrast, a conversational recommendation system supports a dialogue between a user and advisor as its mode of interaction (Thompson et al. 2004). For example, if the user is deciding on a restaurant for lunch, the dialogue may be as follows. Notice that it is fairly long, navigating through user preferences and particular instances. Towards the end of the conversation, RJC intervenes with a recommendation and its back up (Fig. 2.5).

A conventional recommendation approach is good if a user is in a mood for recommendation and is ready to spend time for slot-filling. However, in many cases, a user neither seeks nor expects a recommendation. In the course of a customer support session, an explicit product recommendation by RJC might be the last thing this user is expecting. That is why an unsolicited recommendation during such a session must be accepted as is, without additional clarification steps and/or slot filling for the

User: Where do you think I should eat tonight?
Expert: What type of food would you like?
User: What types are there?
Expert: You can say things like Chinese, Indian, and Mediterranean.
User: Oh, maybe a cheap Indian place.
Expert: What kind of parking would you like?
User: I don't care, as long as it's in Palo Alto.
Expert: I'm sorry, I don't know of any restaurants like that, would you like to search for any price?
User: No, I think I'd like Chinese instead.
Expert: How does Mandarin Gourmet on 420 Ramona sound?1
User: No, what else do you have?
Expert: How about Jing-Jing Szechwan Hunan Gourmet on 443 Emerson Street?
User: I am /not sure it got high user rating
RJC-Agent: Consider Golden Dragon Hunan on University ave. It has a great rating for food

Fig. 2.5 A restaurant reservation scenario

User: Car was shaking terrible, took to mechanic five times. Each time he would replace one spark plug at a time. It would run fine for a week, then again shaking and unable to gain speed
Expert: I would start by doing a compression test which will confirm the timing chain or if have low compression in one or more cylinder. A timing chain cannot come and go like you have described. A spark plug fouling is telling us something else.
RJC-agent:
Spark Plug Fouling Diagnostics - Underhood Service
https://www.underhoodservice.com › spark-plug-fouling-diagnostics
Mar 20, 2018 - Spark plugs are the "canary in the coal mine" of the combustion chamber. The electrodes and porcelain can show short- and long-term ...

Fig. 2.6 A sample conversation in the domain of high responsibility and rich with technical terms such as auto repair

desired parameters of the product being recommended. Recommendation during a CS session has a single chance to trigger user interest and, therefore, should not only be relevant but also timely.

Below (Fig. 2.6) is a sample session of RJC-agent in a car repair domain. In these dialogues scraped from the auto repair recommendation portal, utterances are concise and detailed, with proper explanation and argumentation patterns (Galitsky et al. 2018). This is unusual for the most available dialogue training datasets nowadays. RJC agent does not have to ask the user additional questions for parameters of the entity (*spark plugs*) being recommended. Two utterances of the user are sufficient to determine the point of user pain and propose a business or service that might cure it.

2.3 Computing Recommendation for a Dialogue

In a regular recommendation/advertisement scenario, any popular product or the one meeting the user preferences is thought to be appropriate. Conversely, in the RJC scenario, a recommended product or service must be related to the product, which is the man entity of the problem being resolved. Moreover, a feature of the product being recommended must address the problem caused by the respective feature of the problematic product being communicated with a CSA or other people.

We show the cases of typical customer problems in various domains:

- A customer does not maintain a positive balance carefully and now wants to avoid NSF in the future;
- A traveler with a pet finds himself in a hotel that does not allow dogs;
- A traveler got a non-changeable air ticket and now wants to change the flight.

In most of these cases (Table 2.1) the features of products and services were disclosed to customers but they did not pay enough attention. Once these customers find themselves in a situation where the limited product features presented a significant inconvenience, they contact CS and complain. This is a good time to recommend an alternative product or an addition to a service lacking the limitation that was raised as an issue in a CS session. A similar recommendation should have occurred when the user acquired this initial, seed product and service, but it is not plausible in most situations because it is hard to assess all limitations and future usability cases in advance.

The queries have a placeholder X for product/service name such as account type, accommodation name, air travel company, etc. The role of this placeholder in a query is to assure the respective entity type does occur in an acceptable search result.

Table 2.1 Examples of seed products and the ones being recommended, with features

Product (seed) that is the subject of the problem being resolved	Seed's problematic attribute or feature that is a focus of a conversation	Product to be recommended	Recommended attribute/feature to solve problem	Search query
Checking account	No overdraft protection	Saving account	Linked with checking for overdraft protection	*X for checking account with overdraft protection*
Hotel @<location>	No dogs allowed	Apartment	Dog friendly	*Dog friendly apartment X @ <location>*
Flight to <destination>	Ticket is not changeable	Flight insured for change of plans	Coverage for change of plans/air ticket change	*Travel insurance for flight by X to <destination>*
Camping tent of <brand>	Hard to pitch	Self-pitching tent	Tube frames allowing for self-pitching	*Camping tent of <brand> X with self-pitching*
Auto insurance from X	Does not cover roadside assistance	Additional coverage	Covering roadside assistance	*Additional coverage X with roadside assistance*

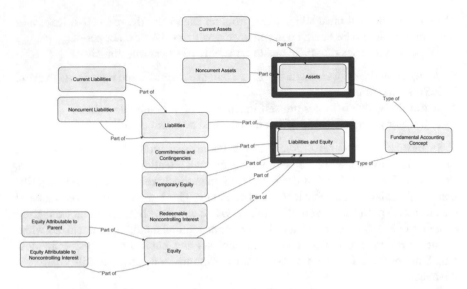

Fig. 2.7 A fragment of an ontology related to financial document

An ontology like the one shown in Fig. 2.7 is required to identify a parameter/feature of the seed entity that is the focus of a conversation with a CS. Relations in ontology are *Part-of, Type-of, Same-as, Instance-of, Defines, Defined-by* and others (Hoffman 2019, Galitsky and Ilvovsky 2019b). A feature of a product is connected with this product by *Part-of, Type-of or Instance-of.* Once an entity is identified in a noun phrase, the ontology is used to find an occurrence of its attribute or feature.

Figure 2.8 shows processing steps in the RJC component that finds a product to be recommended given an utterance with the problematic seed product. Ontology used, such as the one in Fig. 2.7, is shown in the top-right corner.

2.4   Assuring the Recommendation is Persuasive and Properly Argued For

A number of studies including (Berkovsky et al. 2012) demonstrated that explanation and persuasion are two important characteristics for convincing users to follow the recommendations.

We used a traditional advertisement format for irrelevant and unpersuasive examples. A good example is a free-format text that includes a recommendation as well as its argumentative backup, an explanation of why this product would solve a customer problem, as described in dialogue (Fig. 2.9). Negative examples, in particular, rely on the imperative form of verbs that is heavily used in the conventional advertisement.

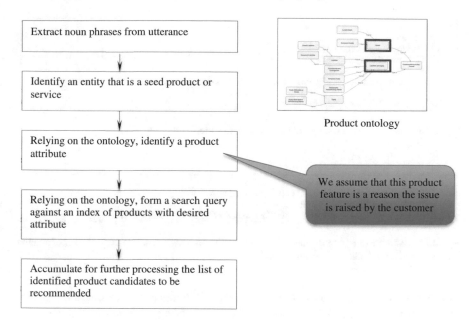

Product ontology

We assume that this product feature is a reason the issue is raised by the customer

Fig. 2.8 Finding a product to be recommended given an utterance with the problematic seed product. A full architectural chart is shown in Fig. 2.15

Customer: You charged me unfair NSF but I maintained a positive balance on my account
CSA: We have to charge NSF to maintain our income, so you should maintain minimum balance.
Good RJC-Agent: I recommend you a product such that you avoid a negative balance. You should get our product _linked checking-saving account with overdraft protection_, so that NSF never happens again
Marginally Relevant and unpersuasive Agent: Open new _account_ at Base Bank. High Yield interest rates. Open within next week and get a free checking
Irrelevant-Agent: Earn _income_ working from home. No training is necessary. Start making money right now
Relevant but unpersuasive Agent Get an overdraft protection. Link a saving account with your checking one

Fig. 2.9 Good and bad RJC agents

To be a good recommendation, it needs to relate to the seed product and to its features and attributes, which are the subjects of the CSA conversation. In addition, the discourse structure of the recommendation text matters (Fig. 2.10).

Discourse tree representation for a recommendation allows judging on its quality. If rhetorical relations of _Explanation, Cause, Enablement_ is recognized in recommendation text (Galitsky and Ilvovsky 2019a, Fig. 2.10, shown in bold), then there is a higher chance that this recommendation is reasonable, persuasive and well-argued. Recommendation with a discourse tree that contains only default rhetorical relations such as _Elaboration_ and _Join_ would not be as good. Moreover, discourse representation of the recommendation must match in terms of argumentation of the discourse representation of the problem description of the product by the customer.

cause
  explanation
    TEXT: I recommend you a product ,
    TEXT: to avoid a negative balance .
  enablement
    TEXT: Therefore, you should get our product "linked checking-saving account with overdraft
protection"
    TEXT: so that NSF never happens again .

Fig. 2.10 Discourse Tree for a good answer above (underlined in Fig. 2.9)

Customer: there is a problem with feature F of product P
CSA: It can (or cannot be fixed) by doing [this and that] with F of P
Customer: No you still cannot fix problem of P ...
RJC-agent: the product R will fix this problem with F of P since R's feature RF covers F

Fig. 2.11 Example of a proper connection between the utterances resolving a problem concerning
the seed product and the EJC recommendation

In other words, these two discourse representations must be in a rhetorical agreement (Chap. 4 Volume 2). A generalized example of a proper correlation between
the previous utterances about the seed product P and recommendation R is shown in
Fig. 2.11.

To assure a recommendation makes sense to a user, it needs to be backed up
by an argument. To find a textual recommendation that will be well perceived by
the user, this recommendation should form a well backed up claim where the utterances in the dialogue are premises. This is a special case of argument mining task
that can be defined as analyzing discourse on the pragmatics level and employing
a certain argumentation theory (Toulmin 1958) to model available textual data. An
argument mining framework includes two steps: argument extraction and argumentation relation prediction. The latter step may be based on learning or reasoning or
both.

Arguments' extraction is the identification of arguments within the input natural
language text. This step may be further split into two different stages, such as the
detection of argument components (e.g., claim, premises) and the further identification of their textual boundaries. Many approaches have recently been proposed to
address such task that adopts different statistical learning methods (Mochales and
Moens 2011; Lippi and Torroni 2016; Bar-Haim et al. 2017).

Relations' prediction determines what are the relations holding between the arguments identified in the first stage. This is an extremely complex task, as it involves
high-level knowledge representation and reasoning issues. The relations between
the arguments may be of heterogeneous nature, like attacks and supports. They are
used to build the argument graphs, in which the relations connecting the retrieved
arguments (i.e., the nodes in the graph) correspond to the edges. Different learning
methods have been employed to address this task, from standard SVMs to Textual
Entailment (Cabrio and Villata 2013). This stage is also in charge of predicting, in

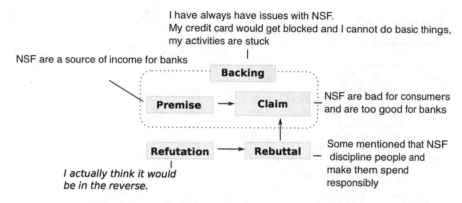

Fig. 2.12   Toulmin model and its instance in the domain of non-sufficient fund fees (NSF)

structured argumentation, the internal relations of the argument's components, such as the connection between the premises and the claim.

A modified Toulmin's model contains five argument components, namely:

claim, premise, backing, rebuttal, and refutation.

When annotating a document, any arbitrary token span can be labeled with an argument component; the components do not overlap. The spans are not known in advance and the annotator thus chooses the span and the component type at the same time. All components are optional (they do not have to be present in the argument) except the claim, which is either explicit or implicit. If a token span is not labeled by any argument component, it is not considered as a part of the argument and is later denoted as none (this category is not assigned by the annotators).

Modified Toulmin's model was used for annotation of arguments with an instantiated example of a CS dialogue on NSF (Fig. 2.12). The arrows show relations between argument components; the relations are implicit and inherent in the model. By contrast to the example of original Toulmin's model, no connective phrases are attached to the relations (such as *so, unless,* etc.).

In Chap. 5 Volume 2, we show how to analyze argumentation relations in text relying on the discourse representation, so we will not repeat it in this chapter. We refer the reader to that section for the algorithm for how to verify that one text *defeats* the claims from another text. On the contrary, in the case of the pair of products *P* and *RP*, a recommendation for RP must be *supported* by the customers' expression of her needs and problems in *P*.

2.5   Continuing Conversation with RJC Agent

Once a recommendation utterance is delivered, the user may choose to continue the conversation with the RJC agent. Then the following algorithm is applied (Fig. 2.13).

```
Input: Recommendations = top-5 recommendations, Profile = set of user preferences, Graph = graph
representation of user preferences, items, entities, properties
Output: conversation

Profile ← Profile + new preferences (items, entities, properties);
Recommendations ← PageRank (Graph, Profile);
Show Recommendations;
while User does not accept Recommendations do
          Feedback ← User feedback;
          Refine(Feedback);
          Recommendations ← PageRank (Graph, Profile);
          Show Recommendations;
end
```

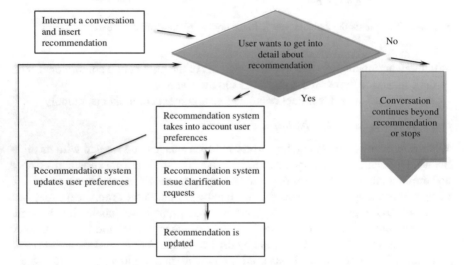

Fig. 2.13 Algorithm description and a chart for a continuous recommendation if a user expresses an interest. A full architectural chart is shown in Fig. 2.15

To build a conversational grammar for dialogue management, we introduce the notion of *adjacency-pair*, sequences of two utterances that are:

(1) adjacent (unless separated by an insertion sequence);
(2) produced by different speakers;
(3) ordered as a first part (which we will refer to also as the initiative) and a second part (which we will refer to also as the response);
(4) typed, so that a particular initiative requires a certain type or range of types of response.

Adjacency-pairs   are   *question–answer,   greeting-greeting,*   or   *offer-acceptance/decline.* Where there is a range of potential responses to an initiative (as with offer-acceptance/decline), a ranking operates over the options setting one response as most preferred (in the sense of normal, more usual) and others as less preferred (Bridge 2002). Other than preferred responses are usually lengthy

1) *turn(system, [], [(Type, Topic)])* --> *initiative(system, Type, Topic)*. There are no ongoing pairs. The system starts a new pair.

2) *turn(user, [(Type, Topic) | Rest], Rest)* --> *response(user, Type, Topic)*. There is at least one ongoing pair. The user provides a response of the same type and on the same topic, thus completing the pair.

3) *turn(system, [(Type, Topic)], [(Type1, Topic1)])* --> *response(system, Type, Topic), initiative(system, Type1, Topic1)*. There is a single ongoing pair. The system provides a response of the same type and on the same topic. Then the system initiates a new pair of a possibly different type and on a possibly different topic.

4) *turn(system, [(Type, Topic), (Type1, Topic) | Rest], [(Type1, Topic) | Rest])* --> *response(system, Type, Topic), initiative(system, Type1, Topic)*. There are at least two ongoing pairs on the same topic. So the dialogue must have entered an insertion sequence. The system provides a response to complete the most recent pair. The system reminds the user of the ongoing pair. The grammar achieves this by requiring that the system initiate a new pair of the same type and topic as the ongoing one but it does not push it onto the stack of ongoing pairs, which remains unchanged.

5) *turn(user, [(Type, Topic) | _], [(Type1, Topic1)])* --> *response(user, Type, Topic), initiative(user, Type1, Topic1)*. There is at least one ongoing pair. The user provides a response to complete the pair and initiates a new pair. This aborts any other ongoing pairs so the stack contains only the new pair.

6) *turn(user, [(_, Topic) | _], [(Type1, Topic1)])* --> *initiative(user, Type1, Topic1), {Topic \= Topic1}*. There is at least one ongoing pair. The user aborts it and initiates something new. We know this is not an insertion sequence because the topic is different.

7) *turn(user, [(Type, Topic) | Rest], [(Type1, Topic), (Type, Topic) | Rest])* --> *initiative(user, Type1, Topic)*. There is at least one ongoing pair. The user begins an insertion sequence by not responding to the ongoing pair but by initiating a new pair on the same topic. Both pairs are now on the stack.

Fig. 2.14 A logic program for dialogue management when a conversation with RJC continues

and syntactically more sophisticated. Having produced a first part (utterance) of some pair, the current utterance stops and it is expected that the next speaker will produce one of the allowable second utterance of the same pair. The second part will often proceed right away. However, there frequently appear sequences of turns that intervene between the first and second utterances of a pair; the second utterance is in a holding pattern during the insertion sequence. An insertion sequence will be topically related to the pair of utterances; it interrupts and may be used to determine the desired features for providing the second utterance of the original pair. Insertion sequences typically contain further adjacency-pairs, which may themselves be interrupted by further insertion sequences (Galitsky 2019b).

We use Prolog notations for the dialogue grammar: variables are capitalized (Fig. 2.14).

A number of decisions have been made in writing the grammar that constrains the contributions that the system can make to the dialogue. In particular, the system cannot abort pairs: rules 5 and 6 apply only to the user. We feel that it is inappropriate for the system to ignore user initiatives.

2.6 System Architecture

A high-level system architecture of RJC is shown in Fig. 2.15. The system tracks the dialogue and attempt to identify a moment where the customer is about to give up on the CSA problem resolution, or is still unhappy after the problem is solved. This tracking is done based on emotional profile and sentiment profile (Chap. 3 Volume

2). Once such utterance is identified, RJC finds a noun phrase in it, and then identifies a product name together with its feature. Entity extraction is done by Stanford NLP augmented by the product-specific entity rules and product-specific lookup, such as eBay product catalog. Product-related named entities could also be verified by consulting eBay product search API.

Then a search query from the formed product name and its feature is formed, and a search is launched. The search results form a list of candidates, which are filtered based on the proper argumentation and discourse coordination requirements. This filtering is implemented via argument mining and reasoning techniques. They verify that the recommendation as a claim is logically supported by the previous customer utterance, and therefore, this recommendation would be convincing for the customer. Rhetorical agreement is verified based on coordination between the discourse trees of previous customer utterances and the discourse tree of the candidate recommendation text (Chap. 4 Volume 2).

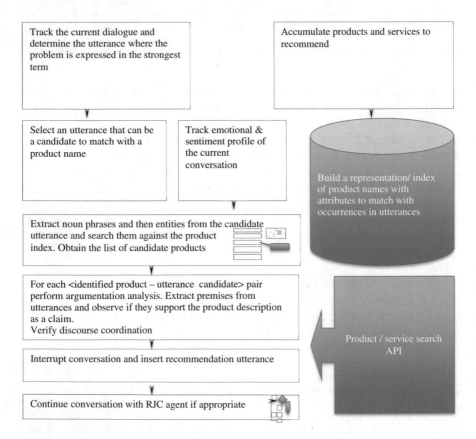

Fig. 2.15 A high-level view of RJC system architecture. The block in the left-middle has been covered in detail in Fig. 2.8, and the block in the bottom-middle—in Fig. 2.13

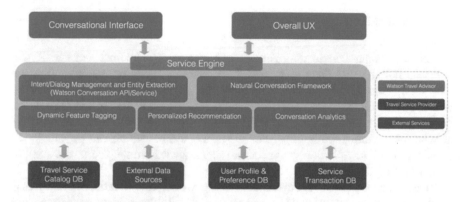

Fig. 2.16 Watson architecture for a conversational travel recommendation system

Figure 2.16 shows a main platform and components in the middlebox, and input data sources and the front end components, such as user interface design, in the bottom and top box, respectively. Conversation service is the main framework for developing chatbots by understanding the user's utterance. In order for the development of a recommendation system on top of a dialogue system, we learned three important aspects that must be considered thoroughly. Context variables must be set by the dialogue service to accommodate variations of entities. Once context variables are set up, then entities or keywords can be detected from the conversation. For the development of destination recommendations, the preferences of users such as nightlife, restaurants, beaches are created and captured as entities in the dialogue system based on context variations.

Recognizing not only user's preferences using entities but also the intent (Allen and Perrault 1980) is essential to determine the right time to invoke the recommendation engine. While current major chatbots and virtual assistant platforms vary, most use the same general principle, what we might call the intent-entity-context-response principle (Makhalova et al. 2019). In this principle:

(1) The user's intent, or conversational action, is determined largely through NL classification;
(2) The entities in the user's utterances are extracted through keyword matching;
(3) The context of the current and prior turns in the conversation is preserved in variables and all of these are used by a dialogue manager to determine the type of the next utterance;
(4) The system's response back to the user.

In addition to physically hosting modules in the cloud environment, the role of Service Engine is to manage the functions between the conversation services, the recommendation engine and the web-conversation user interface.

2.7   Evaluation

We obtain human–human dialogues from Customer Complaints and Car Repair datasets. For the first dataset, we obtain recommendations online from websites like www.bankrate.com and www.bloomberg.com. We also acquire recommendation sources from Yelp on restaurants and services such as repair and tuition. For book recommendations, we used Amazon/LibraryThing (A/LT) dataset available at www.librarything.com/groups. For blogs and forums which can potentially be subject to RJC we relied on www.2carpros.com, www.immihelp.com, www.talkhe althpartnership.com and blog.feedspot.com.

To get closer to the CSA conversation setting, we selected Relational Strategies in Customer Service Dataset that is a collection of travel-related customer service data from four sources. The conversation logs three commercial customer services and the Airline forums on TripAdvisor.com. For a special case of conversations related to overall product opinion, we employ the Customer Support on Twitter dataset. It includes over 3 million tweets and replies from the biggest brands on Twitter. The datasets to evaluate RJC are enumerated in Table 2.2.

For scraped and indexed data, we use our own search for products, and for web data, we either use APIs of a particular source or search this source via Bing API.

We use various source of dialogues:

(1)   Conversational data sets;
(2)   Scraped from online forums;
(3)   Cached search results from specific APIs.

A tool for automated construction of dialogues from the text (Galitsky 2019c, Chap. 1 Volume 2). Documents in the domain of Finance, Travel, Sports are converted into FAQ-type question answering pairs. The Reddit discourse dataset is manually annotated with dialog-acts via crowdsourcing. The dialog-acts comprise an answer, a question, humor, an agreement, a disagreement, an appreciation, a negative reaction, an elaboration and an announcement. It comprises conversations from around 9000 randomly sampled Reddit threads with over 100,000 comments and an average of 12 turns per thread.

The most frequently communicative actions (CAs) in the corpus are *Statement-non-opinion, Acknowledge, Statement-opinion, **Agree/Accept**, **Abandoned** or **Turn-Exit**, Appreciation, Yes–No-Question, Nonverbal, Yes answers, Conventional-closing*. Utterances with underscored CAs are primary candidates for RJC to act.

Overall, it is fairly hard to find a dataset for RJC because most of the conversational datasets are very specific to movies, transportation, restaurants and points of interest. These datasets are extremely limited to domain and conversation style. We do not use dialogue data from public task-oriented dialogues since the conversations are usually very primitive and are confined to a very narrow domain such as hotel and transportation reservation in a given metropolitan area (Budzianowski et al. 2018; Schulz et al. 2017, Facebook Babi 2019). It is quite difficult to recommend any product or service for such dialogue datasets developed to train chit-chat

Table 2.2 Characteristics for each data source in the evaluation of relevant recommendation

Source name	# in the dataset	Problem resolution in a dialogue	Origin of data	Source of recommendations
Finance	2200	Yes	my3cents.com bankrate.com	Web search of Bloomberg, Fidelity, Bankrate for financial products
Auto repair	9300	Yes	2carpros.com	Web search for services
Sports shopping	2740	No	REI and L.L.Bean data from RichRelevance.com	Internal API for product search
Home products shopping	3100	No	Walmart, HD Supply, OfficeDepot data from RichRelevance.com	eBay product search API
Home-related services			Yelp reviews	Yelp API
Travel	2430	No	zicasso.com/travel-reviews, tripadvisor.com reviews Airline forums on TripAdvisor.com	Tripadvisor.com
Daily dialogues	2000	Sometimes	Li et al. (2017)	Yelp API
Genuine human dialogues	2000	Sometimes	Li et al. (2017) ENRON email thread Reddit discourse dataset (Logacheva et al. 2018)	Yelp API, eBay product search API, Tripadvisor.com, Bing Forum search, Bing Web search
Dialogues constructed from blogs, forums and other sources	5200	No	2carpros.com, immihelp.com, talkhealthpartnership.com, blog.feedspot.com librarything.com/groups Book recommendations	
Dialogues generated from text using doc2dialogue tool	5200	No	Web mining of documents on the web in Finance, Legal, Health, Travel	

or task-oriented conversations. Partial exceptions here are the datasets (Li et al. 2017; Logacheva et al. 2018).

That is why the dialogue generation tool from an arbitrary document (Galitsky et al. 2019, Chap. 1 Volume 2) is required to generate dialogues in multiple domains to test RJC extensively. As a result of using this tool, our dialogue datasets are more natural and authentic human conversations than some popular datasets like Twitter Dialog Corpus (Ritter et al. 2011) and Chinese Weibo datasets, constructed by posts and replies on social networks, which are noisy, short and strongly deviate from real conversations (Hou 2019).

To verify each component automatically, we develop a pair of implementations for each verification component and assess one against another for the full-size dataset. For each component, the first integration architecture in this pair has this component and the second architecture does not. Each implementation pair is spot-tested individually manually, on a significantly reduced dataset. This approach is similar to a keyword-based assessment of chatbot performance, such as BLUE, which is not always accurate but scales well.

To achieve automated evaluation it, we try to design an automated assessment algorithm and evaluate the quality of assessment manually. Assessment algorithm should be different from the recognition algorithm for a given component. We separately estimate the accuracy of the assessment algorithm and of the component itself.

The assessment algorithm is estimated manually with respect to how accurately it measures the performance of a system component. The assessment measurement error $\varepsilon = 1 - F1_{\text{assessment algorithm}}$. We consider the assessment algorithm satisfactory for most evaluations if $\varepsilon < 20\%$. Hence ε is estimated manually but allows for an automated assessment of a system component with certain measurement error.

Once this manual assessment is done, we can apply the assessment algorithm to the system component, measuring its accuracy as $F1_{\text{component}} \pm \varepsilon$). We usually just denote it as F1 of a component or an overall system.

Table 2.3 shows the results of the evaluation of the RJC pipeline. The RJC components correspond to the table columns from left to right. We start with an assessment of the best utterance to join the dialogue, proceed to product entity extraction from this utterance to its matching with the available product along with the winning attribute (the one which is going to persuade the customer that the product being recommended would solve his problem). We then assess argument extraction and reasoning related to this argument before the overall recommendation results.

We do not estimate recommendation *recall* since we assume there is an unlimited spectrum of products and services to recommend. If no utterance yields a recommendation, we exclude the conversation from our evaluation. Once a product entity is correctly extracted from a user dialogue, there should be a respective product on the web or in the available index that solves the customer problem. We show the precision for each processing step as a percentage of the correct cases.

Recommendation by joining a conversation turns out to have high overall relevance and appropriateness to the needs of customers (right column in Table 2.3). The accuracy range of 68–74% shows that three-quarters of recommendations should not cause user irritation and instead encourage a user to buy a product that would address a problem raised in the conversation. Although we do not assess an actual conversion rate of RJC, one can see that this form of recommendation and advertisement is least intrusive and has the highest instant relevance in comparison with other conversational recommendation means. Three greyed bottom rows in Table 2.3 show the datasets where we access the applicability of dialogue generation in comparison with genuine dialogues.

Table 2.3 Accuracies of each component as well as overall recommendation relevance assessment, %

Source name	Correct *dialogue turn* for the recommendation	Correctness of *entity extraction* from dialogue	Extracted product entity is properly *matched* in the recommendation	Acceptable *argumentation* by the recommendation	Proper recommendation *discourse*	Overall *meaningful* recommendation
Finance	91.3	94.5	91.2	73.2	79.4	72.9
Auto repair	88.4	96.0	92.6	78.1	84.2	74.3
Sports shopping	89.6	92.9	90.4	76.0	82.3	71.4
Home products shopping	90.3	92.1	94.7	78.3	80.6	72.7
Home-related services	89.3	93.7	91.7	72.7	76.5	73.3
Travel	90.8	92.7	93.6	73.9	82.4	75.2
Daily Dialogues	88.4	89.3	92.0	71.9	80.7	72.6
Genuine human dialogues	89.3	91.6	88.3	67.3	74.2	68.2
Dialogues constructed from blogs, forums and other sources	90.4	92.7	90.7	70.8	73.7	71.4
Dialogues generated from text using doc2dialogue tool	87.2	90.5	88.3	74.2	72.8	73.0

Accuracies of each component vary from domain to domain by less than 10% due to different linguistic and logical complexity of dialogues, product searches and argumentation analysis. Bottom greyed three rows show that genuine human dialogues are a bit more complex than the artificial ones obtained from documents (although the latter has more formal, professional language). The conclusion here is that dialogue generation by the doc2dialogue tool is an acceptable way to train and evaluate conversational systems. Three greyed bottom rows in Table 2.3 show the datasets where we access the applicability of dialogue generation in comparison with genuine dialogues.

Notice that the overall meaningfulness of recommendation is significantly higher than a typical recommendation on Facebook, Gmail or MSN since the proposed recommendation machinery directly attacks the problem expressed by a user in a timely manner. For example, a recommendation to visit Hungary for the author of this book does not take into account any explicit or implicit interest expressed by him in his Facebook profile, so such a sponsored post is totally irrelevant (Fig. 2.17). We believe that in general, a sponsored post does not necessarily have to be irrelevant; a broader match with a catalog of sponsor products needs to be implemented so that every user can get a recommendation according to her specific interests and desires, expressed in communication with peers.

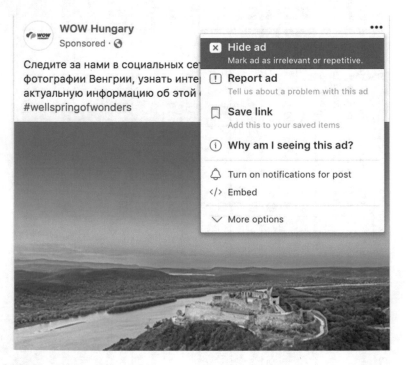

Fig. 2.17 An example of a Facebook sponsor post irrelevant to a user profile

Also, the proposed algorithm would not deliver annoying repetitive recommendations as most advertisers and industrial recommender systems do.

2.8 Related Work and Discussion

Argument mining techniques make it possible to capture the underlying motivations consumers express in reviews, which provide more information than a basic attitude like "I do/don't like product A". Villalba and Saint-Dizier (2012) describe how argument detection can occur on the TextCoop platform. Ibeke et al. (2017) formulate the task of mining contrastive opinions using a unified latent variable model on the El Capitan dataset, where reviews are manually annotated with topic and sentiment labels. Analyzing arguments in user reviews suffers from the vague relation between argument mining and sentiment analysis. This is because sentiments about individual aspects of the implied claim (for/against the product) sometimes express also the reasons why the product is considered to be good or bad.

Argument Mining (AM) is strongly connected with hot topics in AI, as deep learning, fact-checking and misinformation detection (the prediction of the attacks between arguments is a building block for fake news detection, Chap. 6 Volume 2), and explanations of machine decisions (AM can disclose how the information on which the machine relies to make its own decisions is retrieved). Other scenarios where AM can contribute are medicine (where the information needed to reason upon randomized clinical trials can be detected), politics (where AM can provide the means to automatically identify fallacies and unfair propaganda), and for cyber-bullying prevention (where AM can support the detection of repeated attacks against an entity).

Taking the dialogical perspective, Cabrio and Villata (2012) built upon an argumentation framework proposed by Dung (1995), which models arguments within a graph structure and provides a reasoning mechanism for resolving accepted arguments. For identifying support and attack, they relied on existing research on textual entailment (Dagan et al. 2009), namely using the off-the-shelf EDITS system. The test data were taken from a debate portal Debatepedia and covered nineteen topics. Evaluation was performed in terms of measuring the acceptance of the "main argument" using the automatically recognized entailments, yielding F1 score of about 0.75. By contrast to our work, which deals with micro-level argumentation, the Dung's model is an abstract framework intended to model dialogical argumentation.

A number of studies investigated persuasiveness in the sense that is applied to advertising. Schlosser (2011) investigated persuasiveness of online reviews and concluded that presenting two sides is not always more helpful and can even be less persuasive than presenting one side. Miceli et al. (2006) describes a computational model that attempts to integrate emotional and non-emotional persuasion. Persuasiveness was assigned to about twenty texts (out of 100 manually preselected) and four of them are later analyzed for comparing the perception of persuasion between expert and students. Bernard et al. (2012) investigate children's perception of discourse connectives (namely with "because") to link statements in arguments and found out that 4- and 5-years-old and adults are sensitive to the connectives.

A coarse-grained view on dialogs in social media was examined by Bracewell et al. (2012), who proposed a set of fifteen social acts (such as agreement, disagreement, or supportive behavior) to infer the social goals of dialog participants and presented a semi-supervised model for their classification. Their social act types were inspired by research in psychology and organizational behavior and were motivated by work in dialog understanding.

Advertising in the course of dialogue is connected with *dialogue marketing* that emerged two decades ago as companies engaged willing consumers in an ongoing dialogue to create lasting relationships. Dialog marketing is the generic term for all marketing activities in which media is used with the intention of establishing an interactive relationship with individuals. The aim is to initiate an individual, measurable response from the recipient (Jaffe 2008).

Based on available data, marketing personnel in companies invite groups of likely consumers to connect with the company. The engagement process provides value to both the consumer and the company. Marketers use these opportunities as data collection points. The companies use the data to further customize their marketing messages and personalize the experience for their consumers and market segments. In exchange for sharing opinions, buying patterns, product preferences, etc., consumers receive perks such as discounts, tips, and free trials as well as appropriate messaging from the company.

To succeed, dialogue marketing requires that businesses understand their unique value and how it impacts consumers; identify their key customers and prospective customers; develop the appropriate messages and methods to engage them; implement a plan to reach out and connect with the right consumers, and to foster relationships with them. Measurement is a key component of dialogue marketing as it helps businesses track and measure their marketing and sales successes and failures and refine their strategy based on the feedback received. Comprising four essential stages, dialogue marketing integrates advertising, public relations and marketing into one strategy. Vendors include advertising agencies, marketing and branding companies, digital printers, data specialists, social media experts and loyalty and referral program designers.

Combining traditional methods of advertising with technological advancements such as Web 2.0, social media, personalized microsites, variable data printing and blogs, marketers have found that dialogue marketing is both an efficient and effective means of spending their marketing dollars. In focusing marketing efforts on those individuals who are already open to engagement and creating opportunities for them to connect on their terms, businesses increase brand loyalty, referrals, cross-sales and repeat business.

A *relationship dialogue* is a process of reasoning together in order for two or more parties to develop a common knowledge platform (Grönroos 2000). Relationship marketing is facilitated, provided that this knowledge platform enables a supplier to create additional value for its customers on top of the value of the goods and services which are exchanged in the relationship. For a relationship dialogue to emerge, in an ongoing process, the communication effects of planned communication efforts and of product and service-based interactions between a supplier and its customers have to support each other. Then the required extra value of the relationship is created and favorable word of mouth follows.

When focused on customer–company relationships, the conversational system design needs to be closely aligned with the discipline of CRM: Sales, Service and Marketing. A strong focus should be placed on outcomes, not on records or process management. To make the user experience better, implementation of conversational systems must take into account the following (Greenberg 2018):

(1) Conversations are multifaceted. Getting to the right conversation is about accuracy; having that conversation is about precision. Thus, determining which conversation to have and how to best have it are distinct exercises. While equally important, both are complex. Therefore, practitioners must be clear about which problem they are trying to solve.
(2) Conversations reduce friction. They are familiar and easy to describe. The active dialog allows for clear communication and the ability to course correct. Conversations can take place in-person or over video, voice, web chat, and SMS/messaging. Conversations are synchronous, asynchronous, and may come in bursts. Technological definitions may conflict with human nature.
(3) Conversations have a mission. They create optimal experiences and prove value to both participants of the conversation. This involves supporting and enhancing communication between two people, a person and a system/brand, or two systems. The objective is to have the best, informed, value-based and outcome-driven conversation possible. This is Conversational Experience

There have been many works emphasizing the importance of interactivity in recommenders so that the user has a more active role over the recommendations. It includes a critique-based recommendation (Chen and Pu 2012), constraint-based (Felfernig et al. 2011), dialog, and utility based recommenders. However, these studies employ a prior modeling of the items' features, preventing the flexibility in adaptation to different recommendation domains.

We conclude that RJC delivering relevance of recommendations close to ¾ is an efficient and effective way to provide organic recommendations in a less intrusive mode than the other forms of conversational recommendation. RJC does not require a user to spend time sharing personal information, which can potentially be wasted if a recommended product ends up not been needed. Being superior to the conversational recommendation mode with the focus on information gathering from a user, RJC also significantly exceeds the relevance of conventional recommendation, which is usually not associated with a particular scenario of user decision making. Focusing recommendation on the current user point of pain dramatically increases recommendation relevance and meaningfulness as well.

The goal of the RJC Dialogue Manager is to "interrupt politely" (Fig. 2.18).

As a DL system cannot perform basic reasoning, such as example in Fig. 2.20, we skip a discussion on how DL can help in RJC. It is hard for BERT to identify a meaningful action in a context (Fig. 2.21).

Fig. 2.18 Illustration for
"polite" interruption

We observed that it was necessary to track sentiments and the strength of emotion in the user-CSA conversation. When sentiment is not too negative and emotion is not too strong, it might be too early to induce a recommendation since there is a chance that the conflict is resolved among the humans. If the sentiment and emotions are too negative, it is time for a recommender to intervene. This way, we achieved timeliness, less intrusiveness and overall relevance of RJC recommendation.

Although RJC is an effective and efficient means of advertising and marketing, nowadays, even a conventional advertisement can be significantly improved by simple filters, like preventing ads for poorly-rated products. There is an anecdotal evidence that Facebook recommends faulty two-star rated products (Fig. 2.19). By accepting ads from knowingly deceiving businesses, Facebook can boost its short-term ads revenue but lose reputation, which may lead to a longer-term revenue decline. RJC is expected to be an efficient way to advertise in comparison with a more traditional approach (Fig. 2.22, Cartoonbank 2020).

We conclude this chapter by enumerating the observed features of RJC:

- Recommendation by joining a conversation turns out to have high overall relevance and appropriateness to the needs of customers;
- The accuracy range of 68–74% shows that at least ¾ of recommendations should not cause user irritation and instead encourage a user to buy a recommended product;
- In most cases, the recommended products and services indeed address a customer problem raised in conversation;
- Explainable AI—compliant: it is clear why this product is needed;
- This form of recommendation and advertisement is least intrusive as the RJC utterance can be ignored.

One of the tasks of a future study is to evaluate an actual convergence rate of the RJC advertisement mode.

BLACK FRIDAY 🦶 Sale is now ON! 70% OFF everything sitewide.
Shop Now ➡➡

Polar Parka Reviews | Read Customer Service Reviews of ...

https://www.trustpilot.com › review › polar-parka ▾

★★☆☆☆ Rating: 1.9 - 32 reviews

The quality was very very cheap. The fabric was thinning and the jackets didn't look anything like the photos. I emailed **Polar Parka** customer service and they initially offered a store credit or a 35% refund.

Polar Parka

https://polar-parka.com ▾

OFFICIALLY CLOSED. FOR INQUIRIES ON PREVIOUS ORDERS, CONTACT SUPPORT@**POLAR-PARKA.COM**. Search. Close menu. Menu; Search. 0 Cart.
Jackets · Parkas · Products · Contact Us

Fig. 2.19 Recommending a poorly-rated product

Answer

June 15

Passage Context

I fly from New York to San Francisco on June 15 . I came back on July 2.

Question

When did I fly to New York?

Fig. 2.20 It is hard for a DL Q/A to "understand" to/from concepts

Masked Language Modeling

Enter text with one or more "[MASK]" tokens and BERT will generate the most likely token to substitute for each "[MASK]".

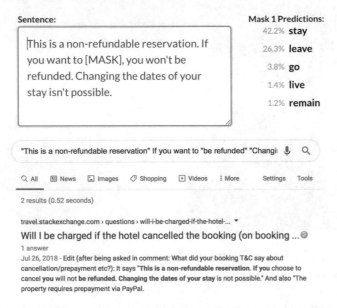

Sentence:

This is a non-refundable reservation. If you want to [MASK], you won't be refunded. Changing the dates of your stay isn't possible.

Mask 1 Predictions:

42.2% **stay**

26.3% **leave**

3.8% **go**

1.4% **live**

1.2% **remain**

"This is a non-refundable reservation" If you want to "be refunded" "Changi

Q All   🗎 News   🖼 Images   ⬦ Shopping   ▶ Videos   ⋮ More   Settings   Tools

2 results (0.52 seconds)

travel.stackexchange.com › questions › will-i-be-charged-if-the-hotel-... ▾
Will I be charged if the hotel cancelled the booking (on booking ... ⊘
1 answer
Jul 26, 2018 - Edit (after being asked in comment: What did your booking T&C say about cancellation/prepayment etc?): It says "**This is a non-refundable reservation. If you** choose to cancel **you** will not **be refunded. Changing the dates of your stay** is not possible." And also "The property requires prepayment via PayPal.

Fig. 2.21 On the bottom: It is hard for DL to "understand" which action is associated with being *non-refundable*. On the bottom: web mining performs this task successfully

Fig. 2.22 Conventional, not a dialogue-based advertisement

References

Allen JF, Perrault CR (1980) Analyzing intention in utterances. Artif Intell 15(3):143–178

Anelli VW, Basile P, Bridge D, Noia TD, Lops P, Musto C, Narducci F, Zanker M (2018) Knowledge-aware and conversational recommender systems. In: Proceedings of the 12th ACM conference on recommender systems (RecSys'18). ACM, New York, NY, USA, pp 521–522

Bar-Haim R, Bhattacharya I, Dinuzzo F, Saha A, Slonim N (2017) Stance classification of context-dependent claims. In: EACL, pp 251–261

Berkovsky S, Freyne J, Oinas-Kukkonen H (2012) Influencing individually: fusing personalization and persuasion. ACM Trans Interact Intell Syst (TiiS) 2(2):9

Bernard S, Mercier H, Clément F (2012) The power of well-connected arguments: early sensitivity to the connective because. J Exp Child Psychol 111(1):128–135

Bracewell D, Tomlinson M, Wang H (2012) Identification of Social Acts in Dialogue. In: 24th International Conference on Computational Linguistics—Proceedings of COLING 2012: Technical Papers, pp 375–390

Bridge D (2002) Towards conversational recommender systems: a dialogue grammar approach. In: Proceedings of the workshop in mixed-initiative case-based reasoning, workshop program at the sixth European conference in case-based reasoning, pp 9–22

Budzianowski P, Wen T, Gasic M (2018) Research data supporting "MultiWOZ—a large-scale multi-domain wizard-of-Oz dataset for task-oriented dialogue modelling". https://doi.org/10.17863/CAM.27632

Cabrio E, Villata S (2012) Combining textual entailment and argumentation theory for supporting online debates interactions. ACL 2:208–212

Cabrio E, Villata S (2013) A natural language bipolar argumentation approach to support users in online debate interactions. Argum Comput 4(3):209–230

Cartoonbank (2020) https://cartoonbank.ru/?page_id=29&category=5&offset=80

Chen L, Pu P (2012) Critiquing-based recommenders: survey and emerging trends. User Model User-Adap Inter 22(1–2):125–150

Christakopoulou K, Radlinski F, Hofmann K (2016) Towards conversational recommender systems. In: Proceedings of the 22nd ACM SIGKDD international conference on knowledge discovery and data mining (KDD'16). ACM, New York, NY, USA, pp 815–824

Dagan I, Dolan B, Magnini B, Roth D (2009) Recognizing textual entailment: rational, evaluation and approaches. Natl Lang Eng 15(Special Issue 04):i–xvii

Dung P-M (1995) On the acceptability of arguments and its fundamental role in nonmonotonic reasoning, logic programming and n-person games. Artif Intell 77(2):321–357

Facebook Babi (2019) https://research.fb.com/downloads/babi/

Felfernig A, Friedrich G, Jannach D, Zanker M (2011) Developing constraint-based recommenders. In: Recommender systems handbook, pp 187–212

Galitsky B (2016) Providing personalized recommendation for attending events based on individual interest profiles. Artif Intell Res 5(1):1–13

Galitsky B (2018) Building dialogue structure from discourse tree of a question. In: Workshops at the thirty-second AAAI conference on artificial intelligence

Galitsky B (2019a) Discourse-level dialogue management. In: Developing enterprise chatbots. Springer, Cham, Switzerland

Galitsky B (2019b) Chatbot components and architectures. In: Developing enterprise chatbots. Springer, Cham, Switzerland

Galitsky B (2019c) Automated building of expanded datasets for training of autonomous agents. US Patent App. 16/426,878

Galitsky B, Ilvovsky D (2017) Chatbot with a discourse structure-driven dialogue management. EACL system demonstrations

Galitsky B, Ilvovsky D (2019a) On a chatbot conducting a virtual dialogue in financial domain. In: Proceedings of the first workshop on financial technology and natural language processing

Galitsky B, Ilvovsky D (2019b) Discourse-based approach to involvement of background knowledge for question answering. RANLP Varna, Bulgaria

Galitsky B, Ilvovsky D, Kuznetsov SO (2018) Detecting logical argumentation in text via communicative discourse tree. J Exp Theor Artif Intell 30(5):637–663

Galitsky B, Ilvovsky D, Goncharova E (2019) On a chatbot conducting dialogue-in-dialogue. SIGDIAL Demo paper. Stockholm, Sweden, pp 118–121

Greenberg P (2018) Conversational experiences: building relationships one conversation at a time. ZDNet. https://www.zdnet.com/article/conversational-experiences-building-relationships-one-conversation-at-a-time/

Grönroos C (2000) Creating a relationship dialogue: communication, interaction and value. Market Rev V1(N1): 5–14(10)

Hoffman C (2019) Financial report ontology. https://www.xbrlsite.com/2015/fro/

Hou Y (2019) Task oriented dialogue dataset survey. https://github.com/AtmaHou/Task-Oriented-Dialogue-Dataset-Survey

Ibeke R, Lin C, Wyner AZ, Barawi MH (2017) Extracting and understanding contrastive opinion through topic relevant sentences. In: IJCNLP, pp 395–400

Jaffe J (2008) Join the conversation: how to engage marketing-weary consumers with the power of community, dialogue, and partnership. Wiley, New Jersey, US

Kostelník P, Pisařovic I, Muron M, Dařena F, Procházka D (2019) Chatbots for enterprises: outlook. Acta Universitatis Agriculturae et Silviculturae Mendelianae Brunensis 67:1541–1550

Lippi M, Torroni P (2016) Argument mining from speech: detecting claims in political debates. In: AAAI, pp 2979–2985

Li Y, Su H, Shen X, Li W, Cao Z, Niu S (2017) DailyDialog: a manually labelled multi-turn dialogue dataset. IJCNLP

Logacheva V, Burtsev M, Malykh V, Polulyakh V, Seliverstov A (2018) ConvAI dataset of topic-oriented human-to-chatbot dialogues. In: Escalera S, Weimer M (eds) The NIPS'17 competition: building intelligent systems. The Springer series on challenges in machine learning. Springer, Cham

Makhalova T, Ilvovsky D, Galitsky B (2019) Information retrieval chatbots based on conceptual models. In: International conference on conceptual structures, pp 230–238

Miceli M, de Rosis F, Poggi I (2006) Emotional and non-emotional persuasion. Appl Artif Intell 20(10):849–879

Mochales R, Moens M-F (2011) Argumentation mining. Artif Intell Law 19(1):1–22

Narducci F, de Gemmis M, Lops P, Semeraro G (2018) Improving the user experience with a conversational recommender system. In: Ghidini C, Magnini B, Passerini A, Traverso P (eds) AI*IA 2018–advances in artificial intelligence. AI*IA 2018. Lecture notes in computer science, vol 11298. Springer, Cham

Ritter A, Cherry C, Dolan WB (2011) Data-driven response generation in social media. In: EMNLP, pp 583–593

Schlosser AE (2011) Can including pros and cons increase the helpfulness and persuasiveness of online reviews? The interactive effects of ratings and arguments. J Consum Psychol 21(3):226–239

Schulz H, Zumer J, El Asri L, Sharma S (2017) A frame tracking model for memory-enhanced dialogue systems. CoRR, abs/1706.01690

Smyth B, McGinty L, Reilly J, McCarthy K (2004) Compound critiques for conversational recommender systems. In: IEEE/WIC/ACM international conference on web intelligence. IEEE, Beijing, China

Sun Y, Zhang Y (2018) Conversational recommender system. In: The 41st international ACM SIGIR conference on research and development in information retrieval SIGIR'18, Ann Arbor, MI, USA, pp 235–244

Thompson CA, Göker MH, Langley P (2004) A personalized system for conversational recommendations. J Artif Int Res 21–1:393–428

Toulmin SE (1958) The uses of argument. Cambridge University Press, Cambridge, UK

Villalba MPG, Saint-Dizier P (2012) A framework to extract arguments in opinion texts. IJCINI 6(3):62–87

Chapter 3
Adjusting Chatbot Conversation to User Personality and Mood

Abstract As conversational CRM systems communicate with human customers and not other computer systems, they need to tackle human emotions in a way to optimize the outcome of a chatbot session. A chatbot needs to understand the emotions of its peers and produce utterances which not only match their emotional states but also attempt to improve it towards solving a problem. We construct a model and a training dataset of emotions and personality from various sources to properly react to the customer in the emotional space and to navigate him through it. We evaluated an overall contribution of a chatbot enabled with affective computing and observed up to 18% boost in the relevance of responses, as perceived by customers.

3.1 Introduction

Emotion detection in computational linguistics is the process of identifying discrete emotions expressed in the text. In recent years, emotion detection in text and reasoning about it has become more popular due to its vast potential applications in marketing, political science, psychology, human–computer interaction, artificial intelligence, etc. Access to a huge amount of textual data, specifically opinionated and self-expression texts, also played a special role to bring attention to this field.

Emotion analysis can be viewed as a natural evolution of sentiment analysis and its more specific model. However, the emotion detection and reasoning field still had a long way to go before matching the success and applicability of sentiment analysis. The amount of useful information which can be gained by moving past the negative and positive sentiments and towards identifying discrete emotions can help improve many applications such as marketing, advertising (Qiu et al. 2010), question answering systems (Somasundaran et al. 2007), summarization (Seki et al. 2005) recommender systems (Terveen et al. 1997), besides CRM.

Not all negative or positive sentiments are created equal (Seyeditabari et al. 2018). For example, the two emotions *fear* and *anger* both express a negative opinion of a person toward something, but the latter is more relevant in marketing or socio-political monitoring of the public sentiment (Galitsky and Kovalerchuk 2006). It has been shown that fearful people tend to have a pessimistic view of the future,

© The Author(s), under exclusive license to Springer Nature Switzerland AG 2021   93
B. Galitsky, *Artificial Intelligence for Customer Relationship Management*,
Human–Computer Interaction Series, https://doi.org/10.1007/978-3-030-61641-0_3

Fig. 3.1 CRM needs a
spectrum of conversational
agents' moods, not just a
"one-size-fits-all" agent

while angry people tend to have a more optimistic view (Lerner and Keltner 2000). Moreover, fear generally is a passive emotion, while anger is more likely to lead to action (Miller et al. 2009, Fig. 3.1).

In marketing, emotion detection can be used to analyze consumers' reactions to products and services to decide which aspect of the product should be changed to create a better relationship with customers in order to increase customer satisfaction (Gupta et al. 2013). Also, emotion detection can be used in human–computer interaction and recommender systems to produce interactions or recommendations based on the emotional state of their users. Results of emotion detection systems can also be used as input to other systems, like what (Rangel and Rosso 2016) experimented with by means of profiling authors by analyzing the presence of emotions in what they authored. By understanding the important role of emotions in decision-making process in humans (Bechara 2004), emotion detection can profit any organization that wants to assess the impact of their products and actions on the consumers and to be able to manage people's reactions by monitoring their emotional responses. Thus understanding emotions can benefit any commercial institute, political campaigns or an entity managing the response to a natural disaster. One can also argue that an emotion recognition is necessary to create better artificial intelligence tools such as chatbots.

In human-chatbot interactions, the ability to detect signs of human emotions and to properly react to them can enrich communication. For example, the display of empathetic emotional expressions enhanced user performance and led to an increase in user satisfaction (Galitsky et al. 2005). Empathetic computer agent can contribute to a more positive perception of the interaction, and many chatbot errors can be played down if the chatbot is able to recognize the emotional state of the user and responded to it sensitively.

The following example shows how emotional tags can help to conduct a meaningful dialogue:

User: Really bad day ever. I arrived wet because of the rain.
Default Seq2Seq: You were wet.
Affect-enabled chatbot (Like): I am always here to support you.
Affect-enabled chatbot (Happy): Keep smiling! Things will get better. You will
not be wet for long. . .
Affect-enabled chatbot (Sad): It's depressing. To be wet.
Affect-enabled chatbot (Disgust): Sometimes life just sucks.
Affect-enabled chatbot (Angry): The rain is too bad!

Some of the most widely accepted models that have been used in emotion detection literature can be divided based on two viewpoints:

(1) Emotions as discrete categories. According to Discrete Emotion Theory, some emotions are distinguishable on the basis of neural, physiological, behavioral and expressive features regardless of culture (Colombetti 2009). A well-known and most used example is Ekman's six basic emotions (Ekman 1992). Ekman, in a cross-cultural study, found six basic emotions of *sadness, happiness, anger, fear, disgust* and *surprise*. Most papers in emotion detection used this model for detecting emotions as a multi-class classification problem, along with some that are based on Plutchik's wheel of emotions (Plutchik 1984, Fig. 3.2) in which he categorized eight basic emotions (*joy, trust* (Galitsky et al. 2014; Galitsky 2015), *fear, surprise, sadness, disgust, anger* and *anticipation*) as pairs of opposite polarity.

(2) Using a different perspective, the dimensional model of emotions tries to define emotions based on two or three dimensions. As opposed to basic emotions theory, which states that different emotions correspond to different neurological subsystems in the brain, the dimensional model is based on the hypothesis that all emotions are the result of a common and interconnected neurophysiological system. The Circumplex model developed by (Russell 1980) suggests that emotions can be shown in a two-dimensional circular space, with one dimension for arousal (i.e. intensity), and one for valance (i.e. pleasantness) (Fig. 3.2 on the bottom).

The following example shows how emotional tags can help conducting a meaningful dialogue:

User: Really bad day ever. I arrived wet because of the rain.
Default Seq2Seq: You were wet.
Affect-enabled chatbot (Like): I am always here to support you. Affect-enabled chatbot (Happy): Keep smiling! Things will get better. You will not be wet for long. . .
Affect-enabled chatbot (Sad): It's depressing. To be wet.
Affect-enabled chatbot (Disgust): Sometimes life just sucks.
Affect-enabled chatbot (Angry): The rain is too bad!

Some dialogue systems such as is SEMAINE (Schröder 2010) have being designed in the form of embodied conversational agents, explored multimodal interaction, gesture input/output, facial signals during conversation, tracks the user's emotional state and eye contact.

A customer interacting with a company can display a broad spectrum of moods (Table 3.1). In each mood, certain interaction modes are most appropriate to continue

Fig. 3.2 Emotional wheel (Plutchik 1984) on the top and Circumplex model developed by (Russell 1980) on the bottom

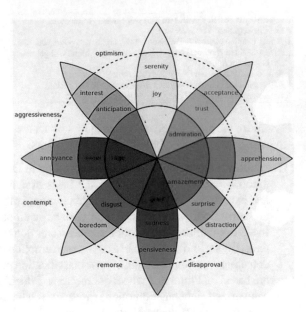

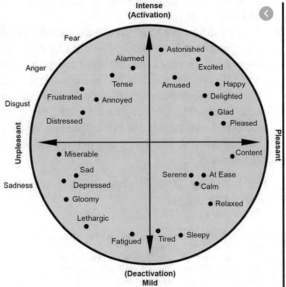

the conversation. A CRM system must first recognize the mood and then choose an appropriate interaction mode.

One of the key questions of this section is whether chatbot mood, emotion, personal trait should be:

(1) as close as possible, similar to the customer or
(2) complementary, distant but matching, reciprocal;

Table 3.1 Association between a personality and mood of a user and that of a chatbot optimal for this user

If a customer is over-confident and arrogant, the chatbot can be sarcastic	
If a customer is very friendly and cooperative, the chatbot should also be supportive and display empathy	
If a customer is a beginner, an authoritative answer with high confidence would be well received	
If a customer is in a bad mood, a discreet, very personalized answer showing great care is anticipated	
If a customer is lost, then an agent should be patient, able to accept or tolerate delays in understanding of her instructions, problems, or suffering without becoming annoyed or anxious	

Emotional dimension is the third one following topical relevance and rhetorical agreement, in determining a good answer to a question versus a bad, unsuitable one. For topical relevance, a linguistic structure of a question needs to be as close to that of an answer as possible, to assure high relevance (Galitsky 2003). On the contrary, discourse structure of an answer must be reciprocal to that one of a question, not necessarily a similar one (Galitsky 2020). In this section, we investigate whether the emotional dimension follows the topical relevance or rhetorical agreement dimension.

A contribution of this chapter is an investigation of an optimal association between a personality and emotional state of a user and that of a dialogue system providing services such as customer support. We also build and evaluate this dialogue system and observe the performance of answering user questions under various associations between personalities and emotional states. Whereas other studies have enabled chatbots with handling emotions, we believe this is the first study attempting to optimize the association between emotions, moods and personalities in a task-oriented chatbot setting.

3.2 Recognizing Personality

It is well known that utterances convey a lot of data about a speaker in addition to their semantic content of the text. One such type of data consists of cues to the speaker's personality traits, the most valuable data related to the distinction between humans. A substantial corpus of work explores an automatic detection of other types of pragmatic variation in text and conversation, such as emotion, deception, speaker charisma, dominance, point of view, subjectivity, opinion and sentiment (Oberlander and Nowson 2006; Galitsky et al. 2010). Personality affects these other aspects of linguistic production, and thus personality recognition may be useful for these tasks, in addition to many other potential applications in CRM.

Computational work on modeling personality proposes methods for expressing personality in conversational agents and tutorial systems, and concepts related to personality such as politeness, emotion, or social intelligence (Wang et al. 2005). Studies have shown that user evaluations of agent personality depend on the user's own personality (Cassell and Bickmore 2003), suggesting that an ability to model the user's personality is required.

Personality is the most complex of all the attributes (behavioral, temperamental, emotional and mental) that characterizes a given individual. It is well known that utterances convey a great deal of information about the speaker in addition to their semantic content. One such type of information consists of cues to the speaker's personality traits, the most fundamental dimension of variation between humans (Mairesse et al. 2007). Personality is typically assessed along five dimensions known as the Big Five:

(1) Extraversion vs. Introversion (sociable, assertive, playful vs. aloof, reserved, shy);
(2) Emotional stability vs. Neuroticism (calm, unemotional vs. insecure, anxious);
(3) Agreeableness vs. Disagreeable (friendly, cooperative vs. antagonistic, fault-finding);
(4) Conscientiousness vs. Unconscientious (self-disciplined, organized vs. inefficient, careless);
(5) Openness to experience (intellectual, insightful vs. shallow, unimaginative).

The trait is one of the "Big Five" factors psychologists use to evaluate an individual's personality.

Extraversion tends to be manifested in outgoing, talkative, energetic behavior, whereas introversion is manifested in more reserved and solitary behavior. *Neuroticism* is a long-term tendency to be in a negative or anxious emotional state. It is not a medical condition but a personality trait. *Conscientiousness* is the personality trait of an individual who displays an awareness of the impact that their own behavior has on those around them. Conscientious people are generally more goal-oriented in their motives, ambitious in their academic efforts and at work, and feel more comfortable when they are well-prepared and organized. Research in recent decades has a number of significant differences between the personalities and life outcomes of people who are conscientiousness, and those who are not (considered to be unconscientious). According to (Melchers et al. 2016), individuals with higher levels of the trait tend to be more empathetic towards other people.

People of various personal traits write differently (Table 3.2, Fig. 3.3). Linguistic cues help to differentiate between Introverts and Extraverts, for example.

The features of (Alm et al. 2005) are listed below. In a personal trait recognizer, they can be implemented as boolean values, with continuous values represented by ranges. The ranges generally overlapped in order to get more generalization coverage.

(1)   First sentence in story;
(2)   Conjunctions of selected features (see below);

Table 3.2 Linguistic cues of texts written by Introverts an Extraverts

Level	Introvert	Extravert
Conversation	Listen Less back-channel behavior	Initiate conversation More back-channel behavior
Topic selection	Self-focused Problem talk, dissatisfaction Strict selection Single topic Few semantic errors Few self-references	Not self-focused selection Pleasure talk, agreement, compliment Think out loud Single topic Many topics Many semantic errors Many self-references
Style	Formal Many hedges (tentative words)	Informal Few hedges (tentative words)
Syntax	Many nouns, adjectives, prepositions (explicit) Elaborated constructions Many words per sentence Many articles Many negations	Many verbs, adverbs, pronouns (implicit) Simple constructions Few words per sentence Few articles Few negations
Lexicon	Correct Rich High diversity Many exclusive and inclusive words Few social words Few positive emotion words Many negative emotion words	Loose Poor Low diversity Few exclusive and inclusive words Many social words Many positive emotion words Few negative emotion words

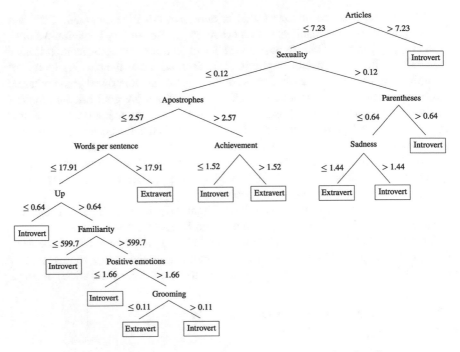

Fig. 3.3 A decision tree chart for binary classification of *extraversion*, based on the essays corpus and self-reports

(3)   Direct speech (i.e. whole quote) in sentence;
(4)   Thematic story type (3 top and 15 sub-types);
(5)   Special punctuation (! and ?);
(6)   Complete upper-case word;
(7)   Sentence length in words (0–1, 2–3, 4–8, 9–15, 16–25, 26–35, > 35);
(8)   Ranges of story progress (5–100%, 15–100%, 80–100%, 90–100%);
(9)   Percent of JJ, N, V, RB (0%, 1–100%, 50- 100%, 80–100%);
(10) V count in sentence, excluding participles (0–1, 0–3, 0–5, 0–7, 0–9, > 9);
(11) Positive and negative word counts (≥ 1, ≥ 2, ≥ 3, ≥ 4, ≥ 5, ≥ 6);
(12) WordNet emotion words;
(13) Interjections and affective words;
(14) Content BOW: N, V, JJ, RB words by POS;

3.3 Models of Emotions

In psychology, based on the appraisal theory, emotions are viewed as states that reflect evaluative judgments (appraisal) of the environment, the self and other social agents, in light of the organisms goals and beliefs, which motivate and coordinate adaptive behavior (Hudlicka 2016). In psychology, emotions are categorized into basic emotions, and complex emotions (i.e., emotions that are hard to classify under a single term such as guilt, pride, shame, etc.). In this chapter, when we talk about emotions, we mostly assume basic emotions.

Figure 3.4 presents (Shaver et al. 1987) a model of emotion that seems to be implicit in subjects' accounts of self and typical emotional episode. Emotions are conceptualized as beginning with appraisals of the way in which circumstances or events bear on a person's motives, goals, values, or desires (Arnold 1960). In other words, prototypical emotion episodes begin with an interpretation of events as good or bad, helpful or harmful, consistent or inconsistent with a person's motives.

Figure 3.5 contains the prototype of *anger*. The cognitive sources that initiate the anger process, as inferred from subjects' accounts, can be summarized as follows. Something (usually another person, in these accounts) interferes with the person's execution of plans or attainment of goals (by reducing the person's power, violating expectations, frustrating or interrupting goal-directed activities). Alternatively, the person perceives another as harming him or her in some way (inflicting physical or psychological pain). According to (de Rivera 1981), an angry person makes the judgment that the frustration, interruption, power reversal, or harm is illegitimate, although it might not be the case. This judgment is very frequent in the anger proto-type, occurring in 95% of accounts where people describe their anger. It is impor-tant to properly formalize this account of anger in CRM applications dealing with potentially angry customers. It is also essential, analyzing communication with such customers.

Unlike a fearful person, who prefers to flee from the source of danger, and a sad person, who stays inactive and withdrawn, an angry person evolves into a stronger response and more energized in order to fight a cause of anger. Her responses are organized to address injustice: she can reassert power or status, frighten the offending person, force him into compliance or restore a desired state of affairs. Thus, the angry person reports attacking the cause of anger verbally, in a loud and ferocious voice, and also communicating anger nonverbally (e.g., by walking out and slamming doors). She frequently imagines attacking the target physically (*I thought for a moment about hitting him*) and sometimes makes an actual attack. Displaced attacks against inanimate objects are also common (hitting something, throwing objects).

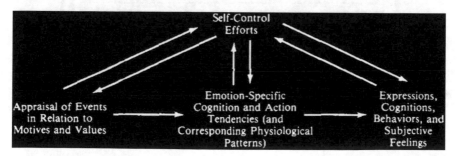

Fig. 3.4 A dynamic model of the emotion process implicit in subjects' accounts of emotion episodes

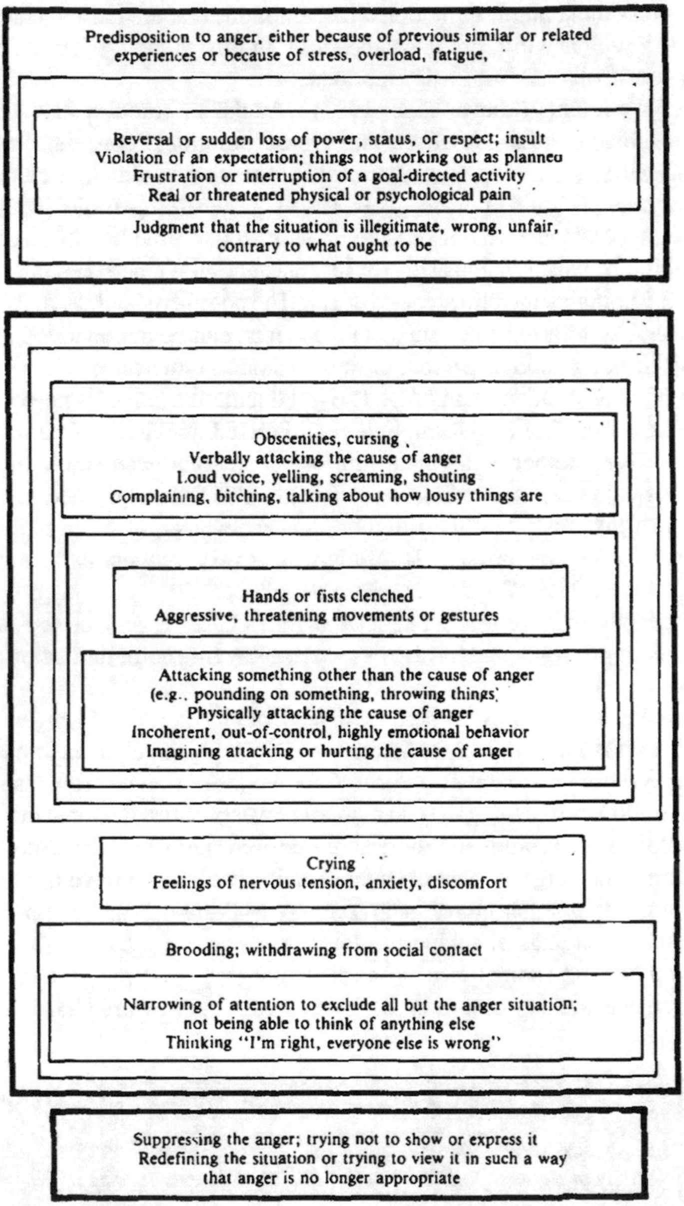

Predisposition to anger, either because of previous similar or related
experiences or because of stress, overload, fatigue,

Reversal or sudden loss of power, status, or respect; insult
Violation of an expectation; things not working out as planned
Frustration or interruption of a goal-directed activity
Real or threatened physical or psychological pain

Judgment that the situation is illegitimate, wrong, unfair,
contrary to what ought to be

Obscenities, cursing
Verbally attacking the cause of anger
Loud voice, yelling, screaming, shouting
Complaining, bitching, talking about how lousy things are

Hands or fists clenched
Aggressive, threatening movements or gestures

Attacking something other than the cause of anger
(e.g., pounding on something, throwing things)
Physically attacking the cause of anger
Incoherent, out-of-control, highly emotional behavior
Imagining attacking or hurting the cause of anger

Crying
Feelings of nervous tension, anxiety, discomfort

Brooding; withdrawing from social contact

Narrowing of attention to exclude all but the anger situation;
not being able to think of anything else
Thinking "I'm right, everyone else is wrong"

Suppressing the anger; trying not to show or express it
Redefining the situation or trying to view it in such a way
that anger is no longer appropriate

Fig. 3.5 A model of emotion for class *anger*

Anger reports mention several physical signs, most of which seem designed to intimidate the target (frowning, showing teeth, clenching fists, etc.). The most commonly mentioned physical sign is a flushed, red face, probably associated with "blood flow" to the head and chest to support threat displays and fighting responses. There is a metaphorical "heat" of anger, sometimes associated with flushing and reddening, literally measurable by skin-temperature sensors. Like the other emotions, anger has a channeling influence on human perceptions and human reasoning, often expressed in the angry person's conviction that he is right and the rest of the people are wrong. Finally, like those for fear and sadness, the anger prototype includes a self-control component, frequently exhibited in the tendency to suppress expressions of the emotion.

It is not hard to give a machine an appearance of having an emotion, but it is much more difficult for a conversational agent to decide on what emotion to display and when (Perlin 1997; Burleson 2006). Software agents in Fig. 3.6 have a manifold of continuously changing expressive parameters that are connected with sensors of human nonverbal communication.

To sense learner's emotions and enable pedagogical agents to respond with appropriate behaviors.

The Affective Agent Research Platform has been developed (Fig. 3.7). The platform consists of a real-time scriptable character agent capable of a wide range of expressive interactions together with the ability to sense affective information from the learner. To detect the learner's emotions and to inform this character's behavioral interactions, a set of sensors is used. These sensors have been developed over the past several years and validated in a variety of experiments by (Burleson 2006).

The pressure mouse detects the intensity of the user's grip on the mouse, which has been shown to correlate to frustration. The skin conductance sensor is a well-established indicator of user arousal. Recent experiments with the seat posture chair show that it can be used to classify motivational states such as engagement, boredom,

Fig. 3.6 Visualized agents show a broad spectrum of expressive parameters

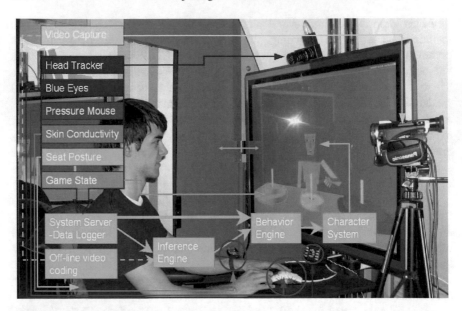

Fig. 3.7 Emotion recognition experimental platform

and break-taking. The facial-expression camera can measure head nod/shake, mouth fidgets, smiles, blink events, and pupil dilations. These sensors provide data to a system that comprises a data logger, a system server (that coordinates the other elements), a classifier, a behavior engine and a personality engine. In addition to the non-verbal social mirroring, the sensor readings are used offline to train a classifier that predicts help-seeking based on measuring several parameters believed to be related to frustration and other relevant affective states.

3.4   Transitions Between Emotions

Picard and her followers pursue a cognitivist measuring approach to users' affect, while the interactional followers prefer a pragmatic approach that views (emotional) experience as inherently referring to social interaction (Boehner et al. 2007). While the Picardian approach focuses on human–machine relations, the goal of the interactional affective computing approach is to facilitate computer-mediated interpersonal communication. And while the Picardian approach is concerned with the measurement and modeling of the neural component of the emotional processing system, interactional affective computing considers emotions as complex subjective interpretations of affect, arguing that emotions instead of affect are in focus, from the point of view of technology users.

Picard uses the state transition diagram to simulate transitions between emotions. The state (here: interest (I), distress (D), or joy(J)) of a person cannot be observed

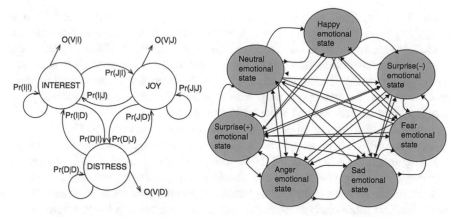

Fig. 3.8 State transition diagram to simulate transitions between emotions (from Jain and Asawa 2015)

directly, but observations that depend on a state can be made (Fig. 3.8). The Hidden Markov Model shown here characterizes the probabilities of transitions among three "hidden" states (I.D.J), as well as probabilities of observations (measurable eccentric forms, such as features of voice inflection, V) given a state. Given a series of observations over time, an algorithm such as (Viterbi's 1967) can be used to compute the sequence of states which provide the best explanation for observations. For example, if a user is associated with a neutral emotional state, a chatbot utterance associated with a happy emotional state, if performed, is likely to transition the user to a happy state (the arc on the top-left).

For example, if one is interested in something but is denied access or information, she transitions into distress. Once the access is granted or information is obtained, she can further transition to joy.

Successful social interactions depend on people's ability to predict others' future actions and emotions. People possess many mechanisms for perceiving others' current emotional states. The question is how they might employ this information to predict others' future states? We hypothesize that people might leverage an overlooked aspect of the affective experience: current emotions predict future emotions. By paying attention to the systematic features in emotion transitions, perceiving humans might develop accurate mental models of others' emotional dynamics. People could then use these mental models of emotion transitions to predict others' future emotions from currently observable emotions.

To test this hypothesis, (Dunbar 1998; Ickes 1997) used data from available experience-sampling datasets to establish the actual rates of emotional transitions. (Thornton and Diana 2007) collected three parallel datasets in which participants rated the transition likelihoods between the same set of emotions. The authors suggested that their mental models contain accurate information about emotion dynamics above and beyond of what might be predicted by static emotion knowledge alone. The authors also examined whether people understand these regularities in emotion transitions. Comparing participants' ratings of transition likelihood to others' experienced transitions, it was found that raters indeed have accurate mental models of emotion transitions. These models could allow perceivers to predict the emotions of others up to two transitions into the future with reasonable accuracy. Factors were identified that affect (but do not fully determine) these mental models: egocentric bias, the conceptual properties of valence, social impact, rationality, the similarity and co-occurrence between different emotions.

Probability matrices of emotion transitions are shown in Fig. 3.9. The likelihood of actual transitions between emotions is indicated, as measured in three experience-sampling datasets (Wilt et al. 2011; Trampe et al. 2015). Each cell in the matrix represents the log odds of a particular transition, calculated by counting the number of such transitions and normalizing based on overall emotion frequencies. Warm colors indicate more likely transitions; cool colors indicate less likely transitions.

Mental models of transitions between 60 mental states demonstrate multidimensionality. Nodes in the network graph represent the poles of four psychological dimensions (i.e., in states in the upper or lower quartile of each dimension) in Fig. 3.10. The transitions between poles are represented by arrows with thickness proportional to the average transitional probability. The transitions are more likely within poles (e.g., positive to positive) than between opposite poles (e.g., positive to negative).

We proceed to an example of an emotional state transition in clinical psychology. Task analysis of the emotional processing of global distress produced a synthesized rational/empirical model. The diagram in Fig. 3.11 shows key findings of clients who start with an expression of nonspecific emotional distress and progress to the productive emotional processing of that distress (Pascual-Leone and Greenberg 2006, 2007). At the starting point of this model, the client in global distress is already emotionally aroused and engaged. From then on, the path toward emotional processing is nonlinear; the client reveals that there is more than one way in which she can therapeutically transform states of her global distress. However, according to these experimental observations, each of the components in Fig. 3.11 is a necessary step in a pathway toward emotional processing. Nevertheless, getting "frozen" in any of these states makes for disordered regulation and inadequate processing. Affective-meaning states in the Global Distress unit at the top of the model pushes the client into one of the following: *feeling pain, hopelessness, helplessness, complaints, self-pity, confusion, despair*, and so on. This is a state of high expressive *arousal* such as tears, emotional voice. This is also a state of low specificity in meaning when the object of distress is often unknown and the client has no sense of direction. Usually, the marker of global distress emerges abruptly, the person behaves in a random way, and the specific concern is often very vague and global. Sometimes, when a psychologist initially explore this, the subjects explicitly state that they do not know why they are feeling so overwhelmed with distress.

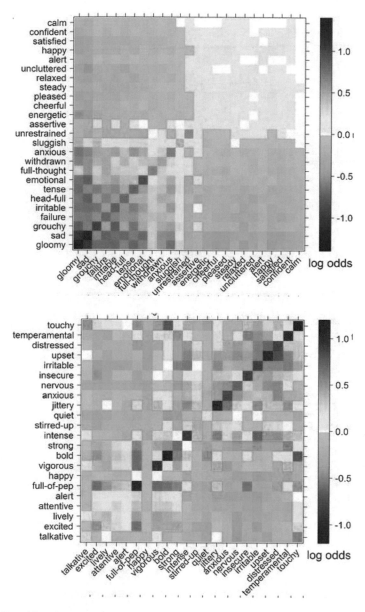

Fig. 3.9   Transitions between emotions

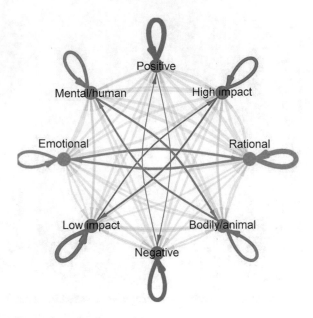

Fig. 3.10 Mental states transition probabilities

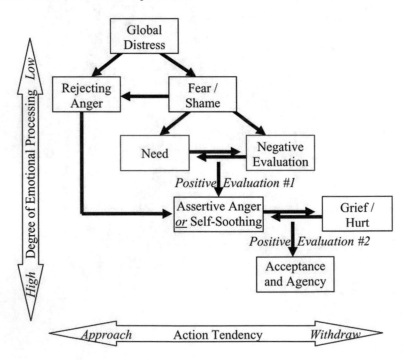

Fig. 3.11 Emotional state transition with an expression of nonspecific emotional distress and progress to the productive emotional processing of that distress

3.5 Emotion Recognition Datasets

Mining emotions from text requires choosing the most appropriate model to operationalize sentiment (Galitsky B and McKenna 2017). In this chapter, we describe five gold standards datasets annotated according to the discrete framework by (Shaver et al. 1987). The framework defines a tree-structured hierarchical classification of emotions, where each level refines the granularity of the previous one, thus providing more indication of its nature. The framework includes, at the top level, six basic emotions, namely *love, joy, anger, sadness, fear*, and *surprise*. The framework is easy to understand, thanks to the intuitive nature of the emotion labels. It has already been used for emotion mining in software engineering.

To train and evaluate our classifier for emotions, we build a gold standard composed of 3,250 posts (question, answer, and comments) from Stack Overflow (SO), an online community where over 7 million programmers do networking by reading and answering questions of others, thus participating in the creation and distribution of crowdsourced knowledge and software documentation. The SO gold standard was annotated by ten Mechanical Turk raters. The annotation sample was extracted from the official SO dump of user-contributed content from July 2012 to July 2019. The coders were requested to indicate the presence/absence of each of the six basic emotions from the Shaver framework. Each post was annotated by three raters and the disagreements were resolved by applying a majority voting criterion.

We also used 860 email threads from Enron dataset, annotated for emotions (Cohen 2009). This dataset provides the text, user information as well as the network information. Enron has been a very popular dataset for social network analysis (Chapanond et al. 2005), sentiment and authority analysis (Diesner and Evans 2015). Peterson et al. (2011) modeled text formality on the Enron corpus and Kaur and Saini (2014) compare emotions across formal and informal emails. Our other datasets included customer complaints, car repair and LiveJournal, also used in other chapters. All emotion annotations were done by Mechanical Turk workers. The observed inter-annotation agreement ranged from 0.87 for LiveJournal to 0.75 for Enron.

In general, textual datasets annotated with markers of emotional content are scarce. Any new method of emotion detection in the text, based on conventional supervised classifiers or neural networks, requires a vast amount of annotated data for training and development. As a relatively new field in NLP, emotion detection as a multi-class classification problem faces a lack of available annotated data.

One of the most used sources for emotionally labeled text is distributed by the Swiss Center for Affective Sciences (Geos 2019). It consists of responses from about three thousand people around the world who were asked to report situations in which they experienced each of the seven major emotions (*joy, fear, anger, sadness, disgust, shame*, and *guilt*), and how they reacted to them. This dataset consists of about 7600 records of emotion-provoking text.

EmotiNet knowledge base (Balahur et al. 2011) tackled the problem of emotion detection from another perspective. The authors proposed that a word-level attempt to detect emotion would lead to a low-performance system because the expressions of emotions are primarily implicit, not presented in the text in specific words, rather from the interpretation of the situation described in a text. They base their insight on Appraisal Theory in psychology (Dalgleish and Power 2000). They created a new knowledge base containing action chains and their corresponding emotional label. They started from around a thousand samples from the ISEAR database and clustered the examples within each emotion category based on language similarity. Then the authors extracted the agent, the verb and the object from a selected subset of examples. Furthermore, they expanded the ontology created using VerbOcean (Chklovski and Pantel 2004) in order to increase the number of actions in the knowledge base, and to reduce the degree of dependency between the resources and the initial set of examples. Although this approach has a potential due to the concepts extracted from text, it could not present itself as viable and generally applicable in its current form because of the small size of the knowledge base and the structure of information they used (limited to the four-tuple of actor, action, object, and emotion).

Vu et al. (2014) focused on the discovery and aggregation of emotion-provoking events. They created a dictionary of such events through a survey of 30 subjects, and used that to aggregate similar events from the web by applying Espresso pattern expansion (Pantel and Pennacchiotti 2006) and bootstrapping algorithms. One of the frequently used dataset is the SemEval-2007 (Strapparava and Mihalcea 2007), which consists of more than a thousand news headlines annotated with six Ekman's emotions. The other example is Alm's annotated fairy tale dataset (Alm et al. 2005), consisting of 1580 sentences from children fairy tales, also annotated with six Ekman's emotions. An extended list of the classed emotions are shown in Table 3.3.

Table 3.3 Instances of words for each class of emotion

Tone & Mood Vocabulary List

Happy	Indifferent	Sad		Excited	Calm	Afraid
Joyful	Resigned	Gloomy		Ecstatic	Peaceful	Mysterious
Amused	Unconcerned	Hopeless		Energetic	Quiet	Frightened
Delighted	Uninterested	Depressed		Exuberant	Soothing	Alarmed
Pleased	Unaffected	Melancholy		Jubilant	Settled	Anxious
Merry	Apathetic	Sulky		Passionate	Composed	Worried
Cheery	Detached	Despairing		Fanatical	Meditative	Nervous

Funny	Factual	Serious		Friendly	Confused	Angry
Comical	matter-of-fact	Solemn		Sympathetic	Perplexed	Irate
Humorous	Formal	Sentimental		Appreciative	Questioning	Irritated
Witty	Informative	Reflective		Caring	Disorganized	Furious
Mocking	Instructive	Somber		Loving	Quizzical	Aggravated
Taunting	Objective	Reminiscent		Romantic	Shocked	Outraged
Sarcastic	Restrained	Nostalgic		Compassionate	Muddled	Disgusted

3.6 Emotional Selection System Architecture

We base our emotion recognition system on the approach described by (Ortu et al. 2015; Calefato et al. 2017). In addition to uni- and bi-grams, modeled using a TF*IDF weighting schema, a suite of lexical features capturing the presence of lexical cues conveying emotions in the input text can be used.

(1) Emotion Lexicon: we capture the presence of emotion lexicon by relying on the association between words and emotion categories in WordNet Affect (Strapparava and Valitutti 2004, Table 3.3). In particular, we compute the TF*IDF for each emotion category (e.g., *joy, love, enthusiasm, sadness, ingratitude*, etc.) based on the occurrences of words associated with this category in WordNet Affect;

(2) Politeness conveyed by the text and measured using the tool developed by (Danescu et al. 2013);

(3) Positive and Negative Sentiment Scores, computed using Stanford NLP Sentiment and SentiStrength (Thelwall et al. 2012), a publicly available tool for sentiment analysis;

(4) Computing consecutive mental states of agents according to BDI model (Bratman 1987; Galitsky 2002; Galitsky and Tumarkina 2004). The current mental states are extracted from text using IR techniques (Makhalova et al. 2019

Once we have the models for personal traits and emotions, we can apply them for selecting the best utterance, given a list of candidates obtained by the topical relevance search (Fig. 3.12).

3.7 Evaluation

We first characterize the training dataset we use to recognize emotions from text sentences (Table 3.4).

In Table 3.5, we show the recognition results for the emotion detector trained on the data presented in Table 3.4 described in Sects. 2–4.

We now evaluate the contribution of the emotion transition model for the improvement of search results. We used normalized Discounted Cumulative Gain (NDCG) as a measure of search accuracy. Traditional ways to measure search engine performance, such as MAP and NDCG, are also applicable for a comparison between conventional search engines and chatbots with respect to the efficiency of information access.

The traditional formula of DCG accumulated at a particular rank position p is defined as:

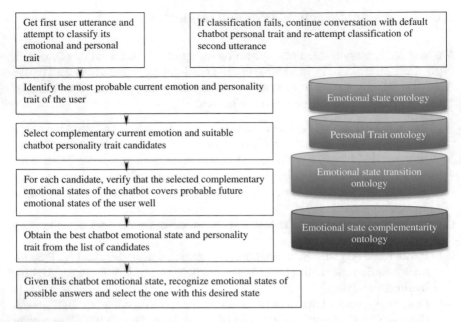

Fig. 3.12 An architecture of a chatbot enabled with managing personal behavior traits

Table 3.4 Emotional label quantities

Dataset						
	#	Surprise	Anger	Sadness	Fear	Joy
Customer complaints	440	712	478	319	132	49
Enron	530	32	20	31	18	217
StackOverflow	440	76	12	23	8	321
LiveJournal	440	521	238	194	73	619
Car Repair	825	265	177	85	24	513

$$DCG_p = \sum_{i=1}^{p} \frac{rel_i}{\log_2(i+1)} = rel_1 + \sum_{i=2}^{p} \frac{rel_i}{\log_2(i+1)}$$

Here the logarithmic reduction factor produces a smooth reduction.

Search result lists vary in length, depending on the query. Comparing a search engine's performance from one query to the next cannot be consistently achieved using DCG alone, so the cumulative gain at each position for a chosen value of p should be normalized across queries. This is done by sorting all relevant documents in the corpus by their relative relevance, producing the maximum possible DCG through position p, also called Ideal DCG (IDCG) through that position. For a query, the normalized discounted cumulative gain, or nDCG, is computed as:

Table 3.5 Accuracy of emotion classifier

Dataset	Recognition accuracy														
	Surprise			Anger			Sadness			Fear			Joy		
Customer complaints	71.3	75.2	73.2	68.7	67.1	67.9	67.8	70	68.9	72.6	70.4	71.5	73.1	68.6	70.8
Enron	64.2	71.9	67.8	66.3	67.9	67.1	68.3	69.9	69.1	70.3	72	71.1	74.2	70.3	72.2
StackOverflow	73.1	76	74.5	69.4	70.2	69.8	71.4	70.5	70.9	69.5	69.7	69.6	72.6	71.8	72.2
LiveJournal	70.6	69.3	69.9	73.2	75	74.1	71.5	73.8	72.6	73.1	72.8	72.9	69.3	72.6	70.9
Car Repair	71.4	72.5	71.9	70.6	73.1	71.8	72.6	71.4	72.0	75.5	72.1	73.8	73.4	74	73.7

$$nDCG_p = \frac{DCG_p}{IDCG_p}$$

where IDCG is ideal discounted cumulative gain,

$$IDCG_p = \sum_{i=1}^{|REL_p|} \frac{2^{rel_i} - 1}{\log_2(i + 1)}$$

and REL_p represents the list of relevant documents (ordered by their relevance) in the corpus up to position p. We now measure nDLG for the default set of answers and for the set ranked by optimizing the emotional component.

We evaluate a single-step search enhanced by the emotional component and also the chatbot search, where some steps included provided ranked answers. Both these evaluations firstly relied on three basic emotional classes and then used all five classes: we wanted to observe if the full set of classes is beneficial.

Table 3.6 shows averaged search accuracies per domain through 100 search sessions. For the chatbot, we averaged these accuracies for consecutive sessions: the first iteration is identical for the search engine and the chatbot.

In the bottom column, we show the relative change of nDLG averaging through rows (answer sources). One can see 6% improvement by relying on the emotional component in reduced emotional space and 12%—full emotional space. For the chatbot, once we compute the plausible future emotions, the component enhances the search accuracy by 17% in the reduced setting and 18%—full setting. One can observe that the emotional component for multi-step sessions requires the full set of emotions to a lesser degree than the since-step emotional component.

Once the CRM system recognizes a personality type of a given user, it needs to decide on what kind of personality is optimal for the conversational agent mode for

Table 3.6 Search relevance enhanced by an emotional recognition component

Answer set	Relevance of ranked answers				
	Baseline	Anger + sadness + joy	All emotions	Anger + sadness + joy	All emotions
		Single-step session (search engine)		Multi-step session (chatbot)	
Customer complaints	0.562	0.562	0.572	0.579	0.603
Enron	0.539	0.531	0.585	0.621	0.626
StackOverflow	0.495	0.573	0.604	0.630	0.615
LiveJournal	0.507	0.548	0.579	0.615	0.632
Car Repair	0.521	0.569	0.593	0.627	0.618
Total improvement	1	1.06	1.12	1.17	1.18

Table 3.7 Association between a behavioral trait for a user and for a chatbot serving this user

Chatbot: User \	Introvert	Extravert	Neurotic	Emotionally stable	Openness to experience
Introvert	0.05	0.3	0.05	0.45	0.15
Extravert	0.1	0.1	0.35	0.25	0.2
Neurotic	0.05	0.25	0.15	0.5	0.05
Emotionally stable	0.1	0.3	0.05	0.3	0.25
Openness to experience	0.3	0.3	0.1	0.1	0.2

this user. Table 3.7 contains the results of which behavioral traits of a user would be better served by a combination of which behavioral traits of a chatbot. Each row contains an array of weights for the serving chatbot behavioral traits. In each cell, there is a weight (a portion of cases) served by a given trait. For example, the top row is showing that *an Introvert should be served by Extravert 30% of times and Emotionally Stable—45% of times.*

We observe the following nontrivial associations between the personal traits in Table 3.7:

- It turns out for an *Emotionally unstable* user, *Stability* and being an *Extravert wishing to communicate* in chatbot helps;
- An *Extravert* user is better served by a combination of *Neurotic, Emotionally Stable* and *Openness* to experience chatbot;
- An *Introvert* sometimes needs an *Extravert* and sometimes—*Emotionally Stable.*

We also compared our emotion detection component with EmoTxt (Calefato et al. 2017), an open-source toolkit for emotion detection from the text, trained and tested on two large gold standard datasets mined from Stack Overflow and Jira. Similarly to this study, we used Stack Overflow but decided not to use Jira due to its limited emotional spectrum and also relied on the datasets used in our evaluations in other problem domains. Our emotion recognition results deviate from (Calefato et al. 2017) by 7–10% in either direction, which is due to a higher variability of how emotions are expressed in different text styles in our five classes of emotions.

EmoText released the classification models to be used for emotion detection tasks. Other than classification, EmoText supports the training of emotion classifiers from manually annotated training data. Its training approach leverages a suite of features that are independent of the theoretical model adopted for labeling the data. Emotion recognition accuracies are comparable with the system presented in this section.

3.8 Emotional State Transition Diagram in CRM

When a customer calls directly into an organization, she might get through to an representative, or have her call redirected through an operator, or perhaps drop into voicemail where they can leave a representative a message. Customers may also go through an automated system where they can press various buttons for other assorted options, such as recorded messages about your products. To improve customer satisfaction, an organization would need to understand exactly what is happening and what are contact pathways. This is where State-Transition Diagrams help.

State-Transition Diagrams are based on nodes and edges, with specific meanings given to each. Nodes represent stable states and edges represent the routes that can be taken in transitioning from one state to another. The transition that is taken depends on a defined event, such as someone picking up the phone or the customer pressing a specific button. The diagram can be self-explanatory for the case of phone contacts and redirects (Fig. 3.13).

This diagram lets an organization track what the customer might have done and find missing states, such as what happens if someone else picks up the phone and they then want to allow the caller to leave a message. But what is happening in the customer mind? We start to see a different situation once we consider this. Figure 3.14 shows some of the mental process about the system that could be going through the customer's mind.

One can use the State-Transition Diagram to map out the customer's mental states and how the triggers in the conversation can lead to their changing states from positive to negative and back again. For example, if we explore just the box where they are talking to the operator, it could look something like Fig. 3.15.

An experienced customer support agent should be able to manage the proper sentiment tonality and language in a conversation, empathizing and otherwise navigating

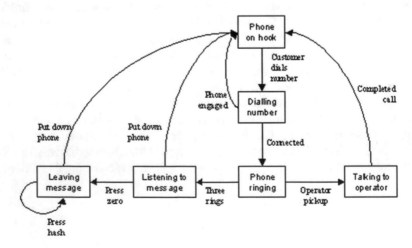

Fig. 3.13 State transition diagram for phone contacts and redirects

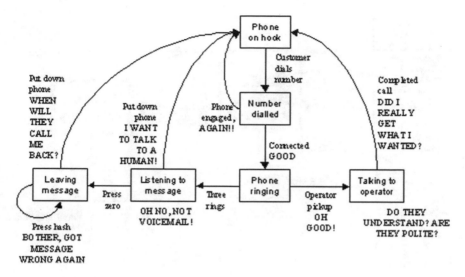

Fig. 3.14 Self-talk in State-Transition

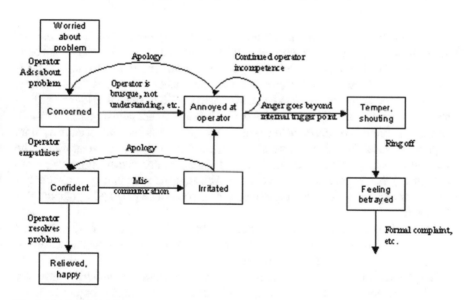

Fig. 3.15 Emotional State-Transition

the customer to create and maintain a state of confidence that the customer's problem will be resolved (Galitsky et al. 2009). On the other hand, a single slip can send the customer into a state of *irritation, anger* or *betrayal.*

A key in this is in the identification of the triggers that cause the transition from one state to another, both in general cases and in specific customer personalities.

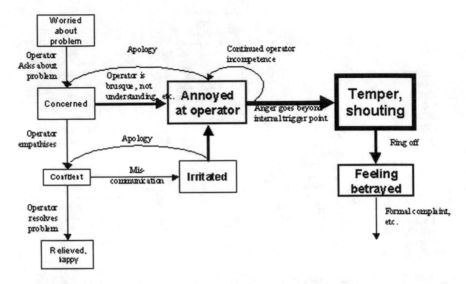

Fig. 3.16 Emotional State-Transition with emphasized common states and transitions

People who spend much time in a state will have many doors into that state, each with well-oiled hinges. Those who are quick to anger may have it as a large and deep state with wide sloping corridors leading down to it from surrounding states. This is shown in Fig. 3.16, with major transitions and states enlarged to show their primacy.

In a business situation, this can be used to help highlight special cases and critical risk points, so that contingency processes such as specialist defusing and customer recovery actions can be introduced to trigger the customers back into a calmer, more cooperative state. In a therapeutic situation, the State-Transition Diagram can be used with clients to help identify their mental states, the things that trigger them into (and out of) the states, how frequently they fall into the state and by which major routes. For example, the following conversation could take place (C = Client, T = Therapist):

The resultant diagram then might look like Fig. 3.17, which could then be used to find common topics to work on, such as the way that it seems to be the actions of other people that are the identified triggers.

The physical diagram can be discussed and changed, an action which is implicitly meta-level in action as the states can be discussed from a higher objective level. Meta-states and self-talk, particularly if they occur at the time of the situation, can also be added to the diagram, as in Fig. 3.18.

State-Transition Diagrams, then, can be used either directly with clients or off-line for understanding the emotional as well as physical-logical states within a situation, how they transition to other states and consequently how the situation can be improved.

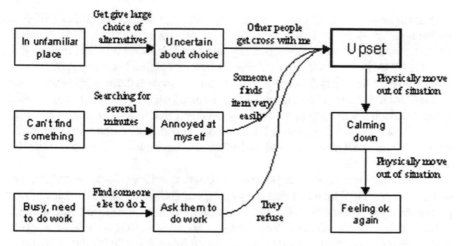

Fig. 3.17 Client emotion State-Transition

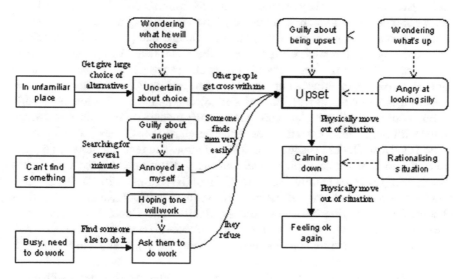

Fig. 3.18 Adding Meta-states

3.9 Related Work and Conclusions

The area of affective computing (Picard 1997) is the design of computational devices proposed to exhibit either innate emotional capabilities or of the machines that are capable of convincingly simulating emotions. Picard (1997) believes that computers should be designed to take into account, express and influence users' feelings. From scheduling an appointment to picking a spouse, humans follow their intuition and listen to their gut feelings.

Marvin Minsky, one of the pioneering computer scientists in AI, relates emotions to the broader issues of machine intelligence, stating in his book "The Emotion Machine" that emotion is "not especially different from the processes that we call 'thinking'" (Minsky 2006). He explains that the distinction between emotions and other kinds of thinking is rather vague. His main argument is that emotions are "ways to think" for different "problem types" that exist in the world. The brain has rule-based mechanisms, implemented as switches or selectors, that initiate emotions to tackle various tasks. Minsky's approach backs up our autism intervention strategy based on rule-based assistance with understanding and reproducing emotions (Galitsky 2016a).

In his book "Descartes' Error" (Damasio 2004) argued that, thanks to the interplay of the brain's frontal lobe and limbic systems, our ability to reason depends in part on our ability to feel emotion. Too little emotions, as well as too much of this system, would cause wrong decisions. The simplest example is as follows. It is an emotion such as fear that controls one's decision not to go into a forest in the dark at night to avoid wolves. Most AI experts are not interested in the role of emotion, preferring to build systems that rely solely on rules. Another AI pioneer John McCarthy believes that we should avoid affect in computational models, arguing that it is not essential to intelligence and, in fact, can get in the way. Others, like (Sloman 2000), believe that there is no need to build in emotions for their own sake. According to Sloman, the feeling will arise as a "side effect" of interactions between components required for other purposes. In terms of our model of the mental world, once mental states are properly trained, emotions will follow since they obey a similar definition framework.

Emotions in cognitive architectures are typically modeled as transient states (associated with *anger, fear, joy*, etc.) that influence cognitive abilities (Galitsky 2005; Wilson et al. 2013). For instance, in CoJACK, morale and fear emotions can modify plan selection. As a result, plans that confront a threat have higher utility when morale is high, but lower utility when fear is high (Evertsz et al. 2009). Other examples include models of stress affecting decision-making (Hudlicka 2016), emotions of joy/sadness affecting blackjack strategy (Schiller and Gobet 2012), analogical reasoning in the state of anxiety and the effect of arousal on memory (Cochran et al. 2006). The largest attempt at implementing a theory of appraisal led to the creation of Soar-Emote (Marinier and Laird 2004).

A chatbot is expected to be capable of exchanging affective arguments with users. A chatbot needs to tackle various argumentation patterns provided by a user as well as provide adequate argumentation patterns in response. To do that, the system needs to detect certain types of arguments in user utterances to "understand" her and detect arguments in textual content to reply back accordingly. Various patterns of logical and affective argumentation are detected by analyzing the discourse and communicative structure of user utterances and content to be delivered to the user (Galitsky 2019). Unlike most argument-mining systems, the chatbot not only detects arguments but performs reasoning on them for the purpose of validation of what the customers say.

Systems neuroscience seeks explanations for how the brain implements a wide variety of perceptual, cognitive and motor tasks. Conversely, artificial intelligence attempts to design computational systems based on the tasks they will have to solve.

In artificial neural networks, the three components specified by design are the objective functions, the learning rules and the architectures. With the growing success of deep learning (DL), which utilizes brain-inspired architectures, these three designed components have increasingly become central to how we model, engineer and optimize complex artificial learning systems (Blake et al. 2019). Richards et al. (2019) argue that a greater focus on these components would also benefit systems neuroscience. The authors provide examples of how this optimization-based framework can drive theoretical and experimental progress in neuroscience. This principled perspective on systems neuroscience, including DL will help to generate more rapid progress.

We explored how chatbot can help people assess, understand and leverage the value of their emotional intelligence. Emotional quotient (EQ) or emotional intelligence concept has been introduced to measure the ability to identify, evaluate and control the emotions of oneself, of others, and of groups. An intelligence quotient (IQ) is a score derived from one of several standardized tests designed to assess intelligence.

Emotional Intelligence (EI) is a medium that reflects how people are able to control, express, define, describe, and omit their feelings and when one's level of emotion stableness is calculating that specific number or reading is known as EQ. On the other hand, Intelligence Quotient is the number that only defines what an intellectual ability of a customer is. It has nothing to do with emotions; it only tells how much the person is smart intellectually (Fig. 3.19).

Nowadays, the people have started taking Emotional Quotient more seriously than before as for the past few years competition has been increased way too much, which

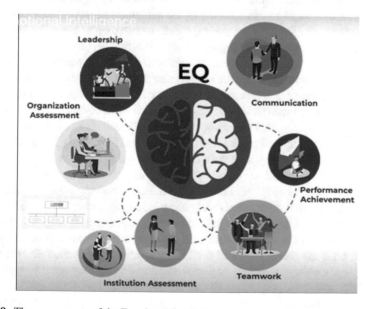

Fig. 3.19 The components of the Emotional Quotient

results in anxiety and depression. So, the people these days are working upon it more than the normal. Many serious steps were taken and still been taking to encourage people, so, that they will take mental health and emotions seriously. More than 60% are afraid to share and express their emotions, and they are not aware of how to take charge of their emotions. We expect that conversing with a chatbot capable of properly matching the emotions and behavioral traits of human users would alleviate this problem.

Visualization is an important tool beyond linguistic data for assisting with communication of emotions, dealing with a high number of heterogeneous and multidimensional datasets. Kovalerchuk and Kovalerchuk (2017) provide a set of tools called a "virtual data scientist" to assist human experts and consumers of ML systems to construct the models including emotion recognition in the text. The objective is to minimize contributions from data scientists and acquire more knowledge from human experts instead.

The difficulties associated with computing emotions can be attributed to the complex nature of emotion expression in text, to the inefficiency of current emotion detection models, and a lack of high-quality training datasets to be fed to these models (Seyeditabari et al. 2018). A short phrase such as "*I would not let my dog*" can express multiple emotions with different polarity and intensity that cannot be understood at a first glance even by humans. Also, the complexity of emotional language, resulting from the extensive use of metaphorical language, context-dependent nature of emotion expression, and implicit nature of such expressions, makes emotion recognition and emotional states prediction tasks even more difficult. To grasp the implicit expression of emotions, to decipher the metaphorical nature of these expressions and to consider the contextual information in which the expression is occurring, one needs the discourse analysis on top of the semantics of the emotional language (Chap. 9 Volume 1). Not only machines, children with mental disorders like autism experience difficulties in computing emotions (Galitsky 2016b).

It is hard for a child with autism to recognize facial expressions of different emotions. Children who have trouble interpreting the emotional expressions of others are taught about emotional expressions by looking at pictures of people with different facial expressions or through identifying emotional expressions of others in structured exercises. Children with autism are missing an intuitive, almost automatic sense of another person's affect (Galitsky 2001; Galitsky and Shpitsberg 2015). This is the feature people rely on to appreciate an emotional state of a peer. In other words, understanding of the emotions of other people is supposed to happen very rapidly through a personal, non-logical, emotional reaction. One can often respond to the person's affect before it even consciously accepted. Thus, we flirt back, look embarrasses, puzzled or display anger as part of our intuitive, affective response. Once we have experienced, at the intuitive level, the other person's emotional signal, we can also reflect on it in a conscious and deliberate manner. People may determine that other people *are unhappy, angry, or puzzled* and to do that they are relying on their own affective response, not just on the facial expression of an opponent.

While many successful algorithms and annotated training sets were introduces for sentiment analysis in the last decade, the sentiment analysis community switched to emotion detection in order to distinguish between different negative or positive emotions, understanding the role of more fine-grained affective information in decision making. Having a large amount of textual data with the rise of social media and a vast corpus of self-expression texts about any major or minor event available, the corpus of research attach a great potential to how CRM organizations can use these information as a basis for their future decision-making processes.

We intend the chatbot to either keep the customer in her *comfort zone*, or navigate towards *learning zone* and *growth zone*. A failure for a chatbot is to lose this customer in a fear zone (Fig. 3.20).

In this chapter, we explored how a dialogue system in a CRM environment can adjust its emotional response and personality to properly manage a conversation for the long-term goal of customer retention. Taking into account the current emotional states and personality traits obtained from the customer profile, the chatbot improved the perceived overall relevance of chatbot utterances by up to 18%. To achieve this improvement, a substantial amount of data annotated with emotional and personal traits tags are required, as well as an extensive set of manually coded rules for transitions between emotional states.

Fig. 3.20 Emotional zones the chatbot is designed to maintain the customer within

References

Alm CO, Roth D, Sproat R (2005) Emotions from text: machine learning for text-based emotion prediction. In Proceedings of the conference on Human Language Technology and Empirical Methods in Natural Language Processing (HLT '05). Association for Computational Linguistics, Stroudsburg, PA, USA, pp 579–586

Arnold MB (1960) Emotion and personality. Columbia University Press, New York

Balahur A, Jesus MH, Andres M, Rafael M (2011) EmotiNet: a knowledge base for emotion detection in text built on the appraisal theories. Springer Berlin Heidelberg, pp 27–39

Bechara A (2004) The role of emotion in decision-making: evidence from neurological patients with orbitofrontal damage. Brain Cogn 55(1):30–40. Development of Orbitofrontal Function

Blake R, Lillicrap T, Beaudoin P, Bengio Y, Bogacz R, Christensen A, Clopath C, Costa R, Berker A, Ganguli S, Gillon C, Hafner D, Kepecs A, Kriegeskorte N, Latham P, Lindsay G, Miller K, Naud R, Pack C, Kording K (2019) A deep learning framework for neuroscience. Nat Neurosci 22:1761–1770

Boehner K, Vertesi J, Sengers P, Dourish P (2007) How HCI interprets the probes. In: Proceedings of the SIGCHI conference on human factors in computing systems. ACM Press, New York, pp 1077–1086

Bratman ME (1987) Intention, plans and practical reason. Harvard University Press, Cambridge, MA

Burleson W (2006) Affective learning companions: strategies for empathetic agents with real-time multimodal affective sensing to foster meta-cognitive and meta-affective approaches to learning, motivation, and perseverance. Thesis for the degree of Doctor of Philosophy

Calefato F, Filippo L, Nicole N (2017) EmoTxt: a toolkit for emotion recognition from text. https://arxiv.org/abs/1708.03892

Cassell J, Bickmore T (2003) Negotiated collusion: modeling social language and its relationship effects in intelligent agents. User Model User-Adap Inter 13:89–132

Chapanond A, Krishnamoorthy MS, Yener B (2005) Graph theoretic and spectral analysis of enron email data. Comput Math Org Theory 11(3):265–281

Chklovski T, Pantel P (2004) Verbocean: mining the web for fine-grained semantic verb relations. EMNLP 4:33–40

Cochran RE, Lee FJ, Chown E (2006) Modeling emotion: Arousal's impact on memory. In: Proceedings of the 28th annual conference of the cognitive science society, pp 1133–1138

Cohen WW (2009) Enron email dataset. https://archive.org/details/2011_04_02_enron_email_dataset

Colombetti G (2009) From affect programs to dynamical discrete emotions. Philos Psychol 22(4):407–425

Dalgleish T, Mick P (2000) Handbook of cognition and emotion. John Wiley & Sons

Damasio A (2004) Descartes' Error: Emotion, Reason, and the Human Brain. Penguin Books

Danescu C, Sudhof M, Jurafsky D, Leskovec J, Potts C (2013) A computational approach to politeness with application to social factors. In: Proc. of ACL

de Rivera J (ed) (1981) Conceptual encounter: a method for the exploration of human experience. University Press of America, Washington, DC

Diesner J, Craig SE (2015) Little bad concerns: using sentiment analysis to assess structural balance in communication networks. In: Advances in Social Networks Analysis and Mining, IEEE/ACM International Conference on. IEEE, pp 342–348

Dunbar RI (1998) The social brain hypothesis. Brain 9:178–190

Ekman P (1992) An argument for basic emotions. Cogn Emot 6(3–4):169–200

Evertsz R, Pedrotti M, Busetta P, Acar H, Ritter FE (2009) Populating VBS2 with realistic virtual actors. In: Proceedings of the 18th conference on behavior representation in modeling and simulation

Geos (2019) Research material—Swiss center for affective sciences—UNIGE. https://www.unige.ch/cisa/research/materials-and-online-research/

Galitsky B (2001) Learning the axiomatic reasoning about mental states assists the emotional development of the autistic patients. AAAI FSS-2001 symposium on emotional and intelligent II, Cape Cod, MA

Galitsky B (2002) Extending the BDI model to accelerate the mental development of autistic patients. In: Second International Conference on Development & Learning. Cambridge, MA

Galitsky B (2003) Using mental simulator for emotional rehabilitation of autistic patients. FLAIRS conference pp 166–171

Galitsky B (2005) On a distance learning rehabilitation of autistic reasoning. In: Encyclopedia of online learning and technologies, vol 4. Idea Publishing Group

Galitsky B (2015) Recognizing intent and trust of a facebook friend to facilitate autonomous conversation. Workshops at the Twenty-Ninth AAAI Conference on Artificial Intelligence

Galitsky B (2016a) Theory of mind engine. In: Computational Autism. Springer, Cham

Galitsky B (2016b) Rehabilitating Autistic Reasoning. In: Computational Autism. Springer, Cham

Galitsky B (2019) Enabling a bot with understanding argumentation and providing arguments. In: Developing enterprise chatbots. Springer, Cham, Switzerland.

Galitsky B (2020) Utilizing discourse structure of noisy user-generated content for chatbot learning. US Patent 10,599,885

Galitsky B, Shpitsberg I (2015) Evaluating assistance to individuals with autism in reasoning about mental world. Artificial intelligence applied to assistive technologies and smart environments: Papers from the 2015 AAAI Workshop

Galitsky B, EW McKenna (2017) Sentiment extraction from consumer reviews for providing product recommendations. US Patent 9,646,078.

Galitsky B, Tumarkina I (2004) Justification of customer complaints using emotional states and mental actions. FLAIRS conference, Miami, Florida

Galitsky B, Kovalerchuk B (2006) Mining the blogosphere for contributor's sentiments. AAAI Spring symposium on analyzing weblogs, Stanford, CA

Galitsky B, Kuznetsov SO, Samokhin MV (2005) Analyzing conflicts with concept-based learning. International conference on conceptual structures, pp 307–322

Galitsky B, Chen H, Du S (2009) Inverting semantic structure of customer opinions expressed in forums and blogs. In: 17th International Conference on Conceptual Structures, Suppl. Proc.

Galitsky B, Dobrocsi G, de la Rosa JL (2010) Inverting semantic structure under open domain opinion mining twenty-third international FLAIRS conference

Galitsky B, Ilvovsky D, Lebedeva N, Usikov D (2014) Improving trust in automation of social promotion. AAAI Spring Symposium Series

Gupta N, Gilbert M, Di Fabbrizio G (2013) Emotion detection in email customer care. Comput Int 29(3):489–505

Hudlicka E (2016) Computational analytical framework for affective modeling: towards guidelines for designing. In: Psychology and mental health: concepts, methodologies, tools, and applications: concepts, methodologies, tools, and applications, pp 1–64

Ickes WJ (ed) (1997) Empathic accuracy. Guilford Press, New York

Jain S, Asawa K (2015) EMIA: emotion model for intelligent agent. J Intell Syst 24(4):449–465

Kaur J, Saini J (2014) Emotion detection and sentiment analysis in text corpus: a differential study with informal and formal writing styles. Int J Comput Appl 101:1–9

Kovalerchuk B, Kovalerchuk M (2017) Toward virtual data scientist with visual means. In: IJCNN

Lerner J, Keltner D (2000) Beyond valence: toward a model of emotion-specific influences on judgment and choice. Cogn Emot 14:473–493

Mairesse F, Marilyn AW, Matthias RM, Roger KM (2007) Using linguistic cues for the automatic recognition of personality in conversation and text. J Artif Int Res 30, 1(November 2007):457–500

Makhalova T, Ilvovsky D, Galitsky B (2019) Information retrieval chatbots based on conceptual models. International Conference on Conceptual Structures, pp 230–238

Marinier RP, Laird JE (2004) Toward a comprehensive computational model of emotions and feelings. In: Proceedings of sixth international conference on cognitive modeling: ICCM, pp 172–177

Melchers MC, Li M, Haas BW, Reuter M, Bischoff L and Montag C (2016). Similar Personality patterns are associated with empathy in four different countries. Frontiers in Psychology. Retrieved from http://journal.frontiersin.org/article/https://doi.org/10.3389/fpsyg.2016.00290/full

Miller DA, Cronin T, Garcia AL, Branscombe NR (2009) The relative impact of anger and efficacy on collective action is affected by feelings of fear. Group Proc Int Relat 12(4):445–462

Minsky M (2006) The emotion machine. Simon & Schuster, New York

Oberlander J, Nowson S (2006) Whose thumb is it anyway? classifying author personality from weblog text. In: Proc. of the 44th Annual Meeting of the Association for Computational Linguistics ACL, pp 627–634

Ortu M, Adams B, Destefanis G, Tourani P, Marchesi M, Tonelli R (2015) Are bullies more productive?: an empirical study of affectiveness vs. vs. issue fixing time. In: Proc. of MSR '15. IEEE Press, pp 303–313

Pantel P, Pennacchiotti M (2006) Espresso: leveraging generic patterns for automatically harvesting semantic relations. In: Proceedings of the 21st International Conference on Computational Linguistics and the 44th Annual Meeting of the Association for Computational Linguistics, ACL-44, pages 113–120, Stroudsburg, PA, USA

Pascual-Leone A, Greenberg LS (2006) Insight and awareness in experiential therapy. In: Castonguay LG, Hill CE (eds) Insight in psychotherapy. American Psychological Association, Washington, DC, pp 31–56

Pascual-Leone A, Greenberg LS (2007) Emotional processing in experiential therapy: why "the only way out is through". J Consult Clin Psychol 75(6):875–887

Perlin K (1997) Layered compositing of facial expression. ACM SIGGRAPH 97.

Peterson K, Hohensee M and Xia F (2011) Email formality in the workplace: a case study on the Enron corpus. In: Proceedings of the Workshop on Languages in Social Media, pp 86–95

Picard RW (1997) Affective computing. MIT Press, Cambridge, MA

Plutchik R (1984) Emotions: a general psychoevolutionary theory. Approac Emot 1984:197–219

Qiu G, He X, Zhang F, Shi Y, Jiajun Bu, Chen C (2010) DASA: dissatisfaction-oriented Advertising based on sentiment analysis. Expert Syst Appl 37(9):6182–6191

Rangel F, Rosso P (2016) On the impact of emotions on author profiling. Inf Process Manage 52(1):73–92

Richards BA, Lillicrap TP, Beaudoin P, Bengio Y, Bogacz R, Christensen A, Clopath C, Costa R, Berker A, Ganguli S, Gillon C, Hafner D, Kepecs A, Kriegeskorte N, Latham P, Lindsay G, Miller K, Naud R, Pack C, Kording K (2019) A deep learning framework for neuroscience. Nat Neurosci 22:1761–1770

Russell JA (1980) A circumplex model of affect. J Person Soc Psychol 39(6):1161

Schiller MRG, Gobet FR (2012) A comparison between cognitive and AI models of blackjack strategy learning. Lect Notes Comput Sci, pp 143–155

Schröder M (2010) The SEMAINE API: towards a standards-based framework for building emotion-oriented systems. Adv Hum Comput Interact 2010:319–406

Seki Y, Koji E, Noriko K, Masaki A (2005) Multi-document summarization with subjectivity analysis at duc 2005. In: Proceedings of the Document Understanding Conference (DUC)

Shaver P, Schwartz J, Kirson D, O'Connor C (1987) Emotion knowledge: further exploration of a prototype approach. J Pers Soc Psychol 52(6):1061–1086

Seyeditabari A, Narges T, Wlodek Z (2018) Emotion detection in text: a review. arXiv:1806.00674

Sloman A (2000) Architecture-based conceptions of mind. In: Proceedings of the 11th international congress of logic, methodology and philosophy of science. Kluwer, Dordrecht, p 397

Somasundaran S, Theresa W, Janyce W, Veselin S (2007) Q/a with attitude: exploiting opinion type analysis for improving question answering in on-line discussions and the news. In ICWSM

Strapparava C, Mihalcea RF (2007) SemEval '07: Proceedings of the 4th International Workshop on Semantic Evaluations, pp 70–74

Strapparava C, Valitutti A (2004) WordNet-Affect: an affective extension of WordNet. In: Proc. of LREC, pp 1083–1086

Thelwall M, Buckley K, Paltoglou G (2012) Sentiment strength detection for the social web. J Am Soc Inf Sci Technol 63(1):163–173

Terveen L, Hill W, Amento B, McDonald D and Creter J (1997) PHOAKS: a system for sharing recommendations. Commun ACM 40:59–62

Thornton MA, Diana IT (2007) Mental models of emotion transitions. Proce Nation Acad Sci Jun 2017, 114(23):5982–5987. DOI: https://doi.org/10.1073/pnas.1616056114

Trampe D, Quoidbach J, Taquet M (2015) Emotions in everyday life. PLoS ONE 10:e0145450

Viterbi AJ (1967) Error bounds for convolutional codes and an asymptotically optimum decoding algorithm. IEEE Trans Inf Theory 13(2):260–269

Vu HT, Graham N, Sakriani S, Tomoki T, Satoshi N (2014) Acquiring a dictionary of emotion-provoking events. In: EACL, pp 128–132

Wang N, Johnson WL, Mayer RE, Rizzo P, Shaw E, Collins H (2005) Thepoliteness effect: pedagogical agents and learning gains. Front Artific Intel-ligence Appli 125:686–693

Wilson JR, Forbus KD, McLure MD (2013) Am I really scared? A multi-phase computational model of emotions. In: Proceedings of the second annual conference on advances in cognitive systems, pp 289–304

Wilt J, Funkhouser K, Revelle W (2011) The dynamic relationships of affective synchrony to perceptions of situations. J Res Pers 45:309–321

Chapter 4
A Virtual Social Promotion Chatbot with Persuasion and Rhetorical Coordination

Abstract We build a chatbot that delivers content in the form of virtual dialogues automatically produced from documents. Given an initial query, this chatbot finds documents, extracts topics from them, organizes these topics in clusters, receives from the user clarification on which cluster is most relevant, and provides the content for this cluster. This content can be provided in the form of a virtual dialogue so that the answers are derived from the found documents by splitting it, and questions are automatically generated for these answers. Virtual dialogues as search results turn out to be more effective means of information access in comparison with original document chunks provided by a conventional chatbot. To support the natural flow of a conversation in a chatbot, the rhetorical structure of each message had to be analyzed. We classify a pair of paragraphs of text as appropriate for one to follow another, or inappropriate, based on communicative discourse considerations. We then describe a chatbot performing advertising and social promotion (CASP) to assist in the automation of managing friends and other social network contacts. This agent employs a domain-independent natural language relevance technique that filters web-mining results to support a conversation with friends. This technique relies on learning parse trees and parses thickets (sets of parse trees) of paragraphs of text such as Facebook postings. We evaluate CASP in a number of domains, acting on behalf of its human host. Although some Facebook friends did not like CASP postings and even unfriended the host, overall social promotion results are positive as long as relevance, style and rhetorical appropriateness are properly maintained. Finally, we propose a way to improve a discourse parsing by a refinement of default rhetorical relations, based on an analysis of Abstract Meaning Representation (AMR). A number of AMR semantic relations such as *Contrast* can be used to detect a specific rhetorical relation.

4.1 Introduction

A presentation of knowledge in a dialogue format is a popular way to communicate information effectively. It has been demonstrated in games, news, commercials, and educational entertainment. Usability studies have shown that for information acquirers, dialogues often communicate information more effectively (Cox et al. 1999, Craig et al. 2000) than monologues most of the times.

One of the famous uses of dialogue for bringing someone's point across is Plato. In his dialogues, Socrates and his peers exchange utterances that convey Plato's philosophy. However, most people's knowledge is available in documents but not in the form of dialogue. Hence the default way of representing information and knowledge is a monological text, for instance, web pages and documents.

Today, people access information mostly via search engines, and a limited volume of higher quality content is available via chatbots. As major web search players came to dominate the market, search results became less direct and personalized, and more optimized for advertisement revenues. In most domains, it is hard to find specific information other than commercial messaging. Social network platforms such as Facebook are increasingly oriented for advertisement as well.

These days, chatbots are expected to provide users with deep domain knowledge, personalization, interactivity and the level of understanding of user needs that modern search engines are lacking. Since chatbots are not involved in the conflict-of-interest between businesses and information gatekeepers (such as major search engines and social networks), they have the potential to provide unbiased and high-quality chunks of information from reputable authors. Chatbots also implement social search, providing opinionated data from peers on request, perform personalization, recommendation and allow easy navigation by drilling into and out of content.

Once the proper piece of content is identified, users like to consume it in the form of frequently asked question pages, discussion forums and blogs, rather than formal, lengthy documents. However, for most knowledge domains, from legal to medical to engineering, most reliable information is only available as documents and web pages. Hence we need to convert plain documents into dialogues, imitating multiple people conversing on the specific topic of interest.

In this chapter, we build a social chatbot that delivers content in the form of virtual dialogues automatically produced from plain texts extracted and selected from documents. Given an initial query, this chatbot finds documents, extracts topics from them, organizes these topics in clusters, receives from the user clarification on which cluster is most relevant, and provides the content for this cluster (Leouski and Croft 1996; Tunkelang 2018). This content is provided in the form of a virtual dialogue so that the answers are derived from the found and selected documents and its split results, and questions are automatically generated for these answers.

We want to advance the ease of generating high-quality multi-modal content for both non-professional and expert content creators and chatbot developers. Virtual dialogue is defined as a multi-turn dialogue between imaginary agents obtain as a result of content transformation. It is designed with the goal of effective information representation and is intended to look as close as possible to a genuine dialogue.

4.2 Conducting Virtual Dialogue

4.2.1 A Session with Virtual Dialogue

Below we present an exploratory session that combines information delivery in the form of a traditional textual answer (conventional dialogue) and also in the form of a virtual dialogue.

The dialogue starts from the user question, *advantages and new features of 5G* (Fig. 4.1). The chatbot consults the sources (in this case, public URLs) and extracts the content from each page (or documents) expected to be relevant for the query. In this example, seven URLs were processed, from domain-specific to general knowledge portals like Quora.com. The chatbot forms the list of topics extracted from these search results so that the user might select one of his interests.

Bot>*ask a new question*

User>**advantages and new features of 5G**
Bot>exploring https://www.tutorialspoint.com/5g/5g_advantages_disadvantages.htm
exploring https://www.cnet.com/news/5g-not-just-speed-fifth-generation-wireless-tech-lets-you-do-vr-self-driving-cars-drones-remote/
exploring https://5gmobilephone.net/5g-advantages-disadvantages/
exploring https://www.techworld.com/apps-wearables/what-is-5g-everything-you-need-know-about-5g-3634921/
I believe these are the main topics of your query: is that what you meant? Please select
demonstrating the benefits of the technology[1].
wide range of people from student'[2]. next wireless network[2].
are already being built ' 5g-ready'[3]. 5g new radio nr specification'[3]. ...
next generation mobile networks alliance[9]. the next stage in mobile technology[9].

User> **next stage in technology (or [9])**
Bot> Put simply, it' s the next stage in mobile technology. It follows 4G and 4G LTE and builds on what they offer, delivering everything at a faster speed. ...
Are you OK with this answer? yes/more/no/specify [different topic] / reduce search to web domain / virtual dialogue

User > **virtual dialogue**
Bot> This is what other people are chatting about your topic:

> User1>**What Are the Benefits of Technology?**
> Bot1> If you hopped over to Ericsson ,
> you 'd find a "5G avenue" with multiple exhibits
> demonstrating the benefits of the technology ...
> User1>**How are these benefits leveraged by new tablets?**
> Bot1>Samsung kicked off its press conference not with its new tablets , but 5G is the next wireless network in telecom industry ...
> User2>**Are the features right for them?**
> Bot1>It is important for people to start learning about 5G technology now so that they can decide if the features are right for them ...
>
> User2 >**Which are the dual 4G VoLTE sim smartphones in India?**
> Bot1> The current 4G VoLTE smartphones with dual SIM slots that are available in the Indian markets may support 4G on single or both SIM slots, however.

User> **Are features right for me?**
Bot> This is what has been answered to people with similar questions:

> Bot1> it is important for people to start learning about 5G technology now so that they can decide if the features are right for them .
> User5>**What happens with this new fifth generation of wireless technology?**
> Bot1> The data presented here is based on research being carried out, and the features that the Next Generation Mobile Networks Alliance believes 5G should fulfill.

Fig. 4.1 Chatbot session with conventional and virtual dialogues

Once the chatbot forms the topics for clarification of the user search intent, it shows them as a list.

The user selects his topic of interest and requests a specific answer via the topic number of the topic expression. Once the answer is read, there are multiple options:

- accept the answer and conclude the session;
- navigate to the next answer from the chatbot list;
- navigate to a specific answer from the chatbot list;
- reject this answer and attempt to reformulate the query;
- reduce search to a specified web domain (such as quota.com, for example);
- proceed in the same direction to more search results in the form of a virtual dialogue.

The user selects the last option and the chatbot builds a virtual dialogue. It is a conversation between imaginary people, but the topic stays the same, matching the original query. Virtual dialogues are shown in frames. As long as the imaginary chatbot responds to the same person, the dialog is intended to stay cohesive; coreferences in the follow-up questions are maintained. The main dialogue can be viewed as a one in the meta-level, and the object-level dialogue is naturally embedded into the meta-level one.

4.2.2 A Persuasive Dialogue

We present a chatbot session that not just provides a user with the content on his topic of interest, but also imitates his conversations with his proponents and a dispute with his opponents, as his own opinion is expected to evolve (Fig. 4.2). The user starts a session with a topic and the chatbot forms the clusters, some of them supporting a positive view of this topic and others defeating it. The chatbot consults the sources (in this case, public URLs) and extracts the content from each page (or documents) expected to be relevant for the query. The formed clusters are shown as a list so that the user can select its element that is the closest to his opinion, and also share it in his own words.

Once the user postulates his opinion, a virtual dialogue is automatically formed from available documents and pages, simulating a conversation between virtual proponents and opponents and virtual bots. The user can read the whole conversation thread, join the discussion he believes are most intriguing, or formulate a question to the thread participant. Given this question, the chatbot takes the user to the part of the virtual discussion thread as close to his question as possible, but with an opposite opinion.

The main purpose of a virtual dialogue is to present content in an informal, social, comprehensive way in comparison to just providing a plain text description of a topic, or address this topic via a document. A virtual dialogue form is expected to be more engaging so that the user can ask her own question and organically join the dialogue.

User>**ideology of political correctness**
Bot>exploring https://theimaginativeconservative.org/2015/04/the-reality-of-the-political-correctness-ideology.html
exploring https://www.spiked-online.com/2018/10/16/political-correctness-an-elite-ideology
exploring https://www.nationalists.org/pdf/political_correctness_a_short_history_of_an_ideology.pdf…
These are the opinions on the topic. Which one do you want to argue for or against?
'criticism of its favored constituencies and ideologies'. 'commentators on the political left'. 'flagellate themselves for
their white privilege'. 'an elite preoccupation should surprise no one'[2]. 'is directly derived from classical Marxism'.
politically correct and politically incorrect brands…
User> **classical Marxism [3]**

Bot> Deconstruction. proves that any text, past or present, illustrates the oppression of blacks, women,
homosexuals, etc. by reading that meaning into words of the text (regardless of their. actual meaning). For cultural
Marxists, the analysis is linguistic.
Please provide your arguments for/against the claim or proceed to virtual dialogue
User > **I think Marxism does not necessarily associated with the political correctness**
Bot> This is what other people who are your opponents chat about the topic:

> User1> 80 Percent Of Americans Think Political Correctness Is An Issue ?
> Bot1> Among devoted conservatives, 97% believe that political correctness is a problem .
> User2> 10 Hilarious Examples Of Political Correctness Gone Mad ?
> Bot2>Progressive activists are the only group that strongly backs political correctness
> User3> What happens in the country sank into political correctness?
> Youth isn't a good proxy for support of political correctness and it turns out race isn't either. Whites are ever so
> slightly less likely than average to believe …

User> **Is it OK to have an ideology in general?**
Bot> These are the fragments from the thread that try to convince you:

> User3> Do you want to abandon the ideological system ?
> Bot3>But the ideology can-not adjust to reality. Ideology takes an intellectual system,
> User4>What kind?
> Bot2>a product of one or more philosophers , and says 'This system must be true'

Fig. 4.2 Chatbot session with conventional and virtual dialogues

One can obviously see the problems with auto-generated dialogues, such as an
incompleteness of questions and answers, a lack of cohesiveness, grammar problems
in a built virtual question and text corruption as a result of extraction from web pages.
However, we claim that these problems are inherent to user-generated content and
can be viewed as cues to its authenticity.

4.2.3 Dialogue Management

The state diagram for the dialogues, including virtual dialogue, is shown in Fig. 4.3.
Dialogue management is based on user clarification requests and hints on further
expected user actions at most dialogue steps. Once a current answer is delivered, the
chatbot asks if a user is happy with this answer and suggests options for both positive
and negative replies. In particular, once the chatbot obtains certain information, it
offers to continue a conventional conversation or proceed to a virtual dialogue.

The user first formulates a topic of a conversation of her interest. The chatbot
finds a set of documents on this topic and clusters them according to a hypothetical
user intent. The clusters are centered around subtopics of the main topic formulated
by the user and are given to her for a selection. The user reads the snippets for each
cluster and selects the subtopic to proceed. Before the virtual dialogue starts, the user
is given a chance to read the documents or texts on the selected subtopic cluster. Then

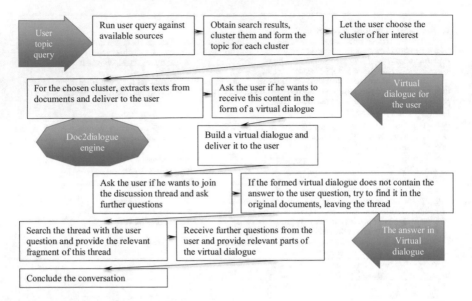

Fig. 4.3 Dialogue management chart

the user may want to proceed to another subtopic, terminate the session or request a virtual dialogue. There are two formats for the virtual dialogue:

(1)   Convert a set of documents for a selected subtopic to a dialogue;
(2)   Converts all sets of documents for all clusters into a single (long) dialogue.

Once the chatbot builds the virtual dialogue according to the user selection, she can browse the whole dialogue or search it by formulating a question. Once this user formulated a question, it is inserted in the virtual dialogue into the most relevant and cohesive position along with the answer and becomes available to other users of the same virtual dialogue (when they select the same topic and subtopic).

4.2.4   Dialogue Construction from Plain Text

Dialogue construction from text is based on the Rhetorical Structure Theory (RST, Mann and Thompson 1988). To build a question from a paragraph of text, we split it into elementary discourse units (EDUs) and then form a discourse tree where these units are labels for the bottom level. Satellite EDUs are then selected as answers to questions that are derived from these EDUs by means of generalization.

An example of converting a text into a virtual dialogue is shown in Fig. 4.4. Answers are obtained by splitting text into EDUs, and questions are inserted in the text before these EDUs as if someone "interrupts" the speaker in the moments of

```
elaboration (LeftToRight)
  attribution (RightToLeft)
TEXT:Dutch accident investigators say <who provided the evidence of responsibility>
  TEXT:that evidence points to pro-Russian rebels as being responsible for shooting down plane .
  contrast (RightToLeft)
    attribution (RightToLeft)
    TEXT:The report indicates
    joint
      TEXT:where the missile was fired from
      elaboration (LeftToRight)
      TEXT:and identifies <what else does report indicate?>
      TEXT:who was in control and pins the downing of the plane on the pro-Russian rebels .
    elaboration (LeftToRight)
      attribution (RightToLeft)
      TEXT:However , the Investigative Committee of the Russian Federation believes
      elaboration (LeftToRight)
        TEXT:that the plane was hit by a missile from the air
        TEXT:which was not produced in Russia . <where was it produced?>
      attribution (RightToLeft)
      TEXT:At the same time , rebels deny <who denied about who controlled the territory>
      TEXT:that they controlled the territory from which the missile was supposedly fired .
```

Fig. 4.4 A discourse tree for a paragraph of text with questions formulated for satellite EDUs as answers

transition from the nucleus to satellite EDUs. Questions are shown in angle brackets and bolded.

4.2.5 Evaluation of Dialogue Effectiveness and Coverage

Evaluating the effectiveness of information delivery via virtual dialogues, we compare the traditional chatbot sessions where users were given plain-text answers with the ones where users were given virtual dialogues.

We present the results on the comparative usability of conventional dialogue and virtual dialogue. We assess dialogues with respect to the following usability properties:

(1) The speed of arriving at the sought piece of information. It is measured as a number of iteration (a number of user utterances) preceding the final reply of the chatbot, which gave an answer wanted by the user. We measure the number of steps only if the user confirms that she accepts the answer.

(2) The speed of arriving at a decision to commit a transaction such as purchase or reservation or selection. A user is expected to accumulate sufficient information, and this information, such as reviews, should be convincing enough for making such a decision.

(3) We also measure how many entities were explored during a session with the chatbot. We are interested in how thorough and comprehensive the chatbot session is, how much the user actually learns from it. This assessment is sometimes opposite to the above two measures but is nevertheless important for understanding the overall usability of various conversational modes.

Table 4.1 Evaluation of comparative effectiveness of conventional and virtual dialogues

	Conventional dialogues			Virtual dialogues		
	# of iterations till found	# iterations till decision	Coverage of exploration # of entities	# of iterations till found	# iterations till decision	Coverage of exploration # of entities
Conventional only	4.6	6.3	10.8	–	–	–
Virtual only	–	–	–	4.1	6.0	13.7
Conventional followed by virtual	4.0	5.7	7.6	6.1	11.3	15.1
Virtual followed by conventional	5.6	7.1	12.3	3.7	7.0	11.5

We do not compare precision and recall of search sessions with either dialogue mode since the same information is delivered but in distinct modes.

We present the evaluation of usability in Table 4.1.

In the second and third rows, we assess the stand-alone systems. One can observe that virtual dialogues take less iteration on average for information access and about the same number of iterations for decisions as conventional dialogues do. Virtual dialogues stimulate the user to explore a higher number of entities, though.

Notice that in the bottom row, the chat scenario proceeds from right to left. In the bottom two rows, we observe the usability of the hybrid system. When a conventional dialogue is followed by a virtual one, a lower portion of users is satisfied by the first step in comparison to the inverse architecture, where virtual is followed by conventional.

4.3   Coordinating Questions and Answers

In this section, we address an issue of how to coordinate an answer with a question, or an arbitrary response with an arbitrary request concerning appropriateness that goes beyond a topic relevance, typical for a question–answer pair. Argumentation patterns in a question need to be reflected in the argumentation patterns in the answer: the latter may contain an argumentation defeat or support. Irony in a question needs to be addressed by irony or sarcasm in the answer. Doubt in a question needs to be answered by rejection or confirmation. A knowledge-sharing intent in an utterance needs to be followed by an acceptance or rejection of this knowledge in the answer.

Which linguistic structures need to come into play to express this sort of coordination? Naturally, neither syntactic or semantic, as they reflect the phrasing and domain-specific information, that should be independent of rhetorical agreement

(Galitsky 2017b). Hence one would expect a discourse structure should take responsibility for utterance coordination. Certain thought patterns expressed in a question must be responded with matching thought patterns in an answer to be accepted by social norms.

Let us consider two questions between friends: *"What did you do today"* versus *"What did you really do today"*. The meaning for the second question is *"Everyone would believe you did one thing but you actually did an unusual thing today, so please tell me"*. The two answers are as follows: *"I went to work"* and *"I rescued a kid from the burning building"*. The reader can see that the routine answer #1 fits the routine question #1, and the special answer #2—the question #2 setting expectations for something irregular, unusual.

Figure 4.5 demonstrates a lack of rhetorical agreement between the title of the book (Human Rights) and a lack of any rights in the environment in which this book is read. We intend to avoid such a disagreement in answering questions and in conducting dialogues.

A request can have an arbitrary rhetorical structure as long as the subject of this request or a question is clear to its recipient. A response on its own can have an arbitrary rhetorical structure. However, these structures should be correlated when the response is *appropriate* to the request. In this chapter, we focus on a computational measure for how logical, rhetorical structure of a request or question is in agreement with that of a response or an answer. We will form a number of representations for a request-response (RR) pair, learn them and solve a RR classification problem of relating them into a class of valid (correct answer or response) or invalid pairs.

Most computational models of communicative discourse are based on an analysis of the *intentions of the speakers* (Allen and Perrault 1980; Grosz and Sidner 1986). A requester has certain goals, and communication results from a planning process to achieve these goals. The requester will form intentions based on these goals and then

Fig. 4.5 Rhetorical discoordination between the book title and the recommendation of the peer (Cartoonbank 2020)

act on these intentions, producing utterances. The responder will then reconstruct a model of the requester's intentions upon hearing the utterance. This family of approaches is limited in providing an adequate account of the adherence to discourse conventions in dialogue.

When answering a question formulated as a phrase or a sentence, the answer must address the *topic* of this question. When a question is formulated implicitly, via a *seed* text of a message, its answer is expected not only to maintain a topic but also to match the *epistemic state* of this seed. For example, when a person is looking to sell an item with certain features, the search result should not only contain these features but also indicate an intent to buy. When a person is looking to share knowledge about an item, the search result should contain an intent to receive a recommendation. When a person is asking for an opinion about a subject, the response should be sharing an opinion about this subject, not another request for an opinion. Modern dialogue management systems and automated email answering have achieved good accuracy in maintaining the topic, but maintaining the communication discourse is a much more difficult problem. This measure of rhetorical agreement needs to be learned from data since it is hard to come up with explicit rules for coordinated rhetorical structures. We will form a number of representations for an RR pair, learn them and solve a RR pair classification problem of relating them into a class of valid or invalid pairs.

The syntactic structure of a simple question is correlated with that of an answer. This structure helps a lot in finding the best answer in the passage re-ranking problem. It has been shown that using syntactic information for improving search relevance helps on top of keywords frequency (TF*IDF) analysis and other keyword statistics methods such as LDA. Selecting a most suitable answer by not just a meaning of keywords but also by judging on how syntactic structure of a question, including a focus of a Wh-word, is reflected in an answer, has been proposed (Moschitti and Quarteroni 2011; Galitsky et al. 2013). We follow along the lines of these studies and take this consideration from phrase and sentence levels to the level of a paragraph discourse. To represent the linguistic features of the text, we use two following sources:

1. *Rhetorical relations* between the parts of the sentences obtained as a *discourse tree*;
2. *Speech acts, communicative actions*, obtained as verbs from the VerbNet resource (the verb signatures with instantiated semantic roles). These are attached to rhetorical relations (RR) as labels for arcs of CDTs.

It turns out that only (1) or only (2) is insufficient for recognizing correct RR pairs, but the combination of these sources is.

The goal of this research is to extend the notion of question/answer relevance to the *rhetorical* relevance of a general request/response pair for broader dialogue support.

Q: My wife want to eat her placenta. Is it OK if she is vegan? I know it sounds gross and weird but a lot of animals do it. So she did some research and found out that it helps to cure postpartum depression. You swallow your own blood when you cut a tongue, this thing is just much bigger.

A: Consuming your placenta after giving birth can be a controversial topic. Add veganism into the mix, and it is even more so. Because it is technically an animal product, some may argue that vegans should not eat it. I grew it from my body, gave it to myself willingly and heard from multiple women that it had helped with postpartum depression, recovery from childbirth, increased energy and milk production, I had nothing to lose. Although other animals eat it raw, some women cook, put it in smoothies, or have it encapsulated like I did, which definitely makes it more palatable! Others may consider eating a placenta cannibalism, but I beg to differ. I did not suffer or die just so I could consume my placenta.

Let us now see if there is a correlation between the discourse trees of Q and A.

We now proceed to another example for an agreement between a question and answer. For the question.

"What does The Investigative Committee of the Russian Federation do" there are two answers:
Mission statement. "The Investigative Committee of the Russian Federation is the main federal investigating authority which operates as Russia's Anti-corruption agency and has statutory responsibility for inspecting the police forces, combating police corruption and police misconduct, is responsible for conducting investigations into local authorities and federal governmental bodies."
An answer from the web. "Investigative Committee of the Russian Federation is supposed to fight corruption. However, top-rank officers of the Investigative Committee of the Russian Federation are charged with creation of a criminal community. Not only that, but their involvement in large bribes, money laundering, obstruction of justice, abuse of power, extortion, and racketeering has been reported. Due to the activities of these officers, dozens of high-profile cases including the ones against criminal lords had been ultimately ruined" (CrimeRussia 2016).

The choice of answers depends on the context. A rhetorical structure allows differentiating between "official," "politically correct," template-based answers and "actual," "raw," "reports from the field," "controversial" ones (Fig. 4.6). Sometimes, the question itself can give a hint about which category of answers is expected. If a question is formulated as a factoid or definitional one, without a second meaning, then the first category of answers is suitable. Otherwise, if a question has the meaning "tell me what it *really* is," or a question has a sarcastic flavor, then the second category is appropriate. In general, if we can extract a rhetorical structure from a question, it is easier to select a suitable answer that would have a similar, matching, or complementary rhetorical structure.

If we look at the discourse trees of an official answer, the official one is based on *Elaboration* and *Joints*, which are neutral in terms of controversy a text might contain (Fig. 4.7). At the same time, the row answer includes the *Contrast* relation (Fig. 4.8). This relation is extracted between the phrase for what an agent is expected to do and what this agent was discovered to have done.

In the future, discourse parsers should be capable of differentiating between "what does this entity" do and "what does this entity *really* do" by identifying a contrast relation between "do" and "really do'. Once such a relation is established, it would be easier to make a decision for whether an answer with or without contrast is suitable.

Further details on coordinating utterances are available in (Galitsky 2017a and Galitsky 2019c).

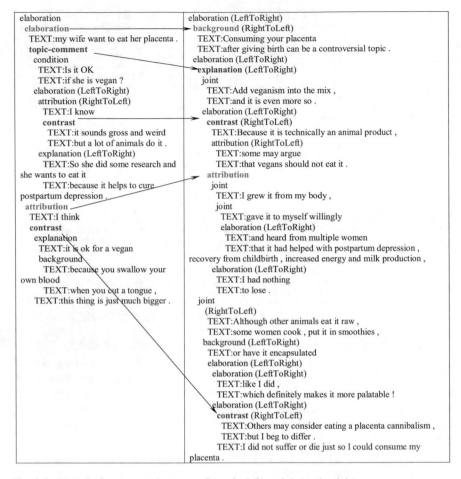

Fig. 4.6 Rhetorical agreement between a Q(on the left) and A (on the right)

4.3.1   Learning Coordination Between a Request or Question and a Response

We now formulate the main problem of this section: how to classify a pair of texts for request and response as correct and incorrect. This problem can be formulated with or without taking into account relevance, which we intent to treat orthogonally to how the rhetorical structure of a request agrees with the rhetorical structure of the response. A rhetorical agreement may be present or absent in an RR pair, and the same applies to the relevance agreement. Some methods of measuring rhetorical agreement will include the relevance one and some will not.

To assess whether a response utterance logically follows a request utterance, we measure the similarity between the question–answer pairs for question answering

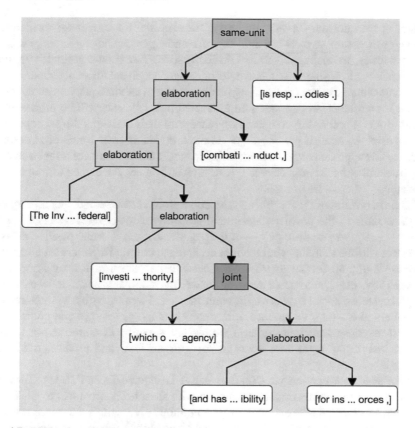

Fig. 4.7 DT for the official answer

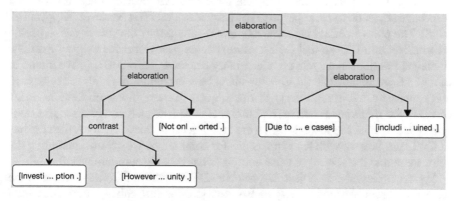

Fig. 4.8 DT for the controversial answer from the web

instead of the question–answer similarity. The classifier for correct versus incorrect answers processes two pairs at a time, $<q_1, a_1>$ and $<q_2, a_2>$, and compares q_1 with q_2 and a_1 with a_2, producing a combined similarity score (Jiang and Conrath 1997). Such a comparison allows the classifier to determine whether an unknown question/answer pair is coordinated or not by assessing its distance from another question/answer pair with a known label. In particular, an unlabeled pair $<q_2, a_2>$ will be processed as a unit. Both q_2 and a_2 are compared together with their corresponding components q_1 and a_1 of the labeled pair $<q_2, a_2>$ on the grounds of such words or structures. Because this approach targets a domain-independent classification of an answer, only the structural cohesiveness between a question and an answer can be leveraged, not "meanings" of answers or replies.

To form a training set for this classification problem, we include actual request-response pairs in the positive dataset and arbitrary or lower relevance and appropriateness request-response pairs—in the negative dataset. For the positive dataset, we select various domains with distinct acceptance criteria for where an answer or response is suitable for the question. Such acceptance criteria are low for community question answering, automated question answering, automated and manual customer support systems, social network communications and writing by individuals such as consumers about their experience with products, such as reviews and complaints. Request-response acceptance criteria are high in scientific texts, professional journalism, health and legal documents in the form of FAQ and professional social networks.

We assess coordination via Communicative Discourse Trees (CDTs). They are designed to combine rhetorical information with speech act structures to CDTs are DTs with arcs labeled with expressions for communicative actions. These expressions are logic predicates expressing the agents involved in the respective speech acts and their subjects. The arguments of logical predicates are formed in accordance with respective semantic roles, as proposed by a framework such as VerbNet (Kipper et al. 2008). The purpose of adding these labels is to incorporate the speech act—specific information into DTs so that their learning occurs over richer features set than just rhetorical relations and syntax of elementary discourse units (EDUs). We intend to cover by these features all information about how the author thoughts are organized and communicated irrespectively of the subjects of these thoughts. Regular nodes of CDTs are rhetorical relations, and terminal nodes are elementary discourse units (phrases, sentence fragments), which are the subjects of these relations. Certain arcs of CDTs are labeled with the expressions for communicative actions, including the actor agent and the subject of these actions (what is being communicated).

To form $<Req, Resp>$ object, we combine DT(Req) with DT(Resp) into a single tree with the root. We then classify such objects into correct (with high agreement) and incorrect (with low agreement). Further details about learning settings are available in Chap. 9 Volume 1.

4.3.2   Computing Similarity Between Communicative Actions in Questions and Answers

We now show how communicative actions are split into clusters (Table 4.2). The purpose of defining the similarity of two verbs as an abstract verb-like structure is to support inductive learning tasks such as rhetorical agreement assessment. In statistical machine learning, the similarity is expressed as a number. A drawback of this learning approach is that, by representing linguistic feature space as numbers, one loses the ability to explain the learning feature underlying a classification decision. After a feature has been expressed as a number and combined with other numbers, it is difficult to interpret it. In inductive learning, when a system performs classification tasks, it identifies a particular verb or verb-like structure that is determined to cause the target feature (such as rhetorical agreement). In contrast, the statistical and deep learning-based family of approaches simply delivers decisions without explanation. In statistical learning, the similarity between the two verbs is a number. In inductive learning, it is an abstract verb with attributes shared by these two verbs (attributes present in one but absent in the other are not retained). The resultant structure of similarity computation can be subjected to further similarity computation with another structure of that type or with another verb. For verb similarity computation, it is insufficient to indicate only that two verbs belong to the same class: all common attributes must occur in the similarity expression.

Hence a similarity between two communicative actions A_1 and A_2 is defined as an abstract verb that possesses the features which are common between A_1 and A_2 (Galitsky and Kuznetsov 2008). We first provide an example of the generalization of two very similar verbs:

Table 4.2   VerbNet classes of the verbs for communicative actions

Verbs with predicative complements	*appoint, characterize, dub, declare, conjecture, masquerade, orphan, captain, consider, classify*
Verbs of perception	*see, sight, peer*
Verbs of psychological state	*amuse, admire, marvel, appeal*
Desire	*want, long*
Judgment Verbs	*judge*
Assessment	*assess, estimate*
Verbs of searching	*hunt, search, stalk, investigate, rummage, ferret*
Verbs of social interaction	*correspond, marry, meet, battle*
Verbs of communication	*transfer(message), inquire, interrogate, tell, manner(speaking), talk, chat, say, complain, advise, confess, lecture, overstate, promise*
Avoid	*avoid*
Measure	*register, cost, fit, price, bill*
Aspectual	*begin, complete, continue, stop, establish, sustain*

agree ˆ disagree = verb(Interlocutor, Proposed_action, Speaker),

where *Interlocutor* is the person who proposed the *Proposed_action* to the *Speaker* and to whom the *Speaker* communicates their response. *Proposed_action* is an action that the *Speaker* would perform if they were to accept or refuse the request or offer, and the *Speaker* is the person to whom a particular action has been proposed and who responds to the request or offer made.

When verbs are not that similar, a subset of the arguments remain:

*agree ˆ explain = verb(Interlocutor, *, Speaker)*.

Further examples of generalizing verbs and communicative actions are available in (Galitsky et al. 2009).

The main observation concerning communicative actions in relation to finding text similarity is that their arguments need to be generalized in the context of these actions and that they should not be generalized with other "physical" actions. Hence, we generalize the individual occurrences of communicative actions together with their arguments. We also generalize sequences of communicative actions representing dialogs against other such sequences of similar dialogs. This way, we represent the meaning of individual communicative action as well as the dynamic discourse structure of dialogue (in contrast to its static structure reflected via rhetorical relations). The idea of a generalization of compound structural representation is that generalization happens at each level. The verb itself or a communicative action is generalized with another verb, and its semantic roles are generalized with their respective semantic roles.

The generalization of communicative actions can also be thought of from the standpoint of matching the verb frames. The communicative links reflect the discourse structure associated with participation (or mentioning) of more than a single agent in the text. The links form a sequence connecting the words for communicative actions (either verbs or multi-words implicitly indicating a communicative intent of a person).

4.4   A Social Promotion Chatbot

4.4.1   Communicating with Friends on Behalf of a Human Host

A conventional chatbot is designed as a communication means between a customer and a company. In this section, we propose a totally different area of a chatbot activity: social promotion. We design a chatbot that communicates with peers on behalf of its human host. In a CRM environment, bots talking to customers on behalf of a company is an important means of advertisement. We develop further the idea of a bot talking with customers.

Instead of answering questions about products and services or fulfilling requests from the users, this social chatbot is representing its human host in maintaining relationships with her friends and colleagues. The goal of this chatbot is to relieve its human host from the routine activity of casual conversation with peers. Also, as an additional feature, this chatbot can implicitly advertise products and services, mentioning them in a conversation with human peers as long as it fits the context of such conversation (Galitsky 1998).

Simulated human characters are increasingly common components of user interfaces of applications such as interactive tutoring environments, eldercare systems, virtual reality-based systems, intelligent assistant systems, physician–patient communication training, and entertainment applications including (Cassell, et al. 2000; De Rosis et al. 2003; Dias and Paiva 2005; Lisetti 2008; Galitsky and Parnis 2017, Trias et al. 2010) among others. While these systems have improved in their intelligent features, expressiveness, understanding of human language, dialog abilities and other aspects, their social realism is still far behind. It has been shown (Reeves and Nass 1996) that users consistently respond to computers as if they were social actors; however, most systems do not behave as competent social actors, leading to users lose of trust and to alienation.

Most customers used to distrust conversational agent who has shown poor understanding of their needs in the areas such as shopping, finance, travel, navigation, customer support and conflict resolution (Galitsky et al. 2005). To restore trust in chatbots, they have to demonstrate robust intelligence features on the one hand and operate in a domain where users are more tolerant to the agent's misunderstanding of what chatbots say or recommend (Galitsky and McKenna 2017).

In this section, we build a chatbot in the form of a simulated human character that acts on behalf of its human host to relieve her from the routine, less important activities on social networks such as sharing news, and commenting on postings of others. Unlike the majority of application domains for simulated human characters, its social partners do not necessarily know that they deal with an automated agent. We refer to this character as a *chatbot* that assists its human host [possibly, with *advertising*] and *social promotion* (CASP). Over the years, we experimented with CASP in a number of Facebook accounts and evaluated its performance and trust by human users communicating with it.

To be trusted, a chatbot operating in a natural language must produce relevant content in an appropriate situation and suitable target person. To do that, it needs to implement the following intelligence features Lawless et al. (2013):

(1) Flexibility in respect to various forms of human behavior, information sharing and request by humans;
(2) Resourcefulness, being capable of finding relevant content in an emergent and uncertain situation;
(3) Creativity in finding content and adjusting existing content to the needs of human user;
(4) Real-time responsiveness and long-term reflection on how its postings being perceived;
(5) Use of a variety of reasoning approaches, in particular, based on the simulation of human mental states;

(6) Ability to learn and adapt performance at a level of intelligence seen in humans and animals;
(7) Awareness of and competence in larger natural, built, and social contexts.

For a chatbot, users need to feel that it properly reacts to their actions, and that what it replied makes sense. To achieve this in a limited, vertical domain, most effective approaches rely on domain-specific ontologies. In a horizontal domain, one needs to leverage linguistic information to a full degree (Sidorov et al. 2014) to be able to exchange messages in a meaningful manner. Once we do not limit the domain a chatbot is performing in, the only available information is language syntax and discourse (Strok et al. 2014), which should be taken into account by means of a full-scale linguistic relevance filter.

Social promotion is based on.

(1) involvement (living the social web, understanding it, going beyond the creation of Google + account);
(2) creating (making relevant content for communities of interest);
(3) discussing (each piece of content must be accompanied by a discussion. If an agent creates the content the market needs and have given it away freely, then you will also want to be available to facilitate the ensuing discussions);
(4) promoting (the agent needs to actively, respectfully, promote the content into the networks).

CASP acts in environments subject to constant changes. As news comes, political events happen, new technologies are developed and new discoveries are made, CASP needs to be able to find relevant information using new terms or new meanings of familiar terms and entities (Makhalova et al. 2015). Hence it needs to automatically acquire knowledge from the web, expanding its taxonomy of entities and building links between them (Chap. 6 Volume 1, Galitsky 2013). These taxonomies are essential when CASP needs to match a portion of text found on the web (as a candidate message) against a message posted by a human user. By growing these taxonomies, CASP learns from the web, adapts its messages to how the available information on the web is evolving. Also, CASP applies accumulated experience from user responses to its previously posted messages to a new posting.

Paragraphs of text as queries appear in the search-based recommendation domains (Bhasker and Srikumar 2010) and social search (Trias et al. 2010, 2011). Recommendation agents track user chats, user postings on blogs and forums, user comments on shopping sites, and suggest web documents and their snippets relevant to a purchase decision (Galitsky and Kovalerchuk 2006). To do that, these recommendation agents need to take portions of text, produce a search engine query, run it against a search engine API such as Bing or Yahoo, and filter out the search results which are determined to be irrelevant to a purchase decision. The last step is critical for the sensible functionality of a recommendation agent, and a poor relevance would lead to a problem with retaining users.

4.4.2 The Domain of Social Promotion

On average, people have half a thousand friends or contacts on a social network systems such as Facebook and LinkedIn. To maintain active relationships with this high number of friends, a few hours per week is required to read what they post and comment on it. In reality, people only maintain a relationship with 10–20 most close friends, family and colleagues, and the rest of friends are being communicated with very rarely. These not so close friends feel that the social network relationship has been abandoned.

However, maintaining active relationships with all members of social network is beneficial for many aspects of life, from work-related to personal. Users of the social network are expected to show to their friends that they are interested in them, care about them, and therefore react to events in their lives, responding to messages posted by them. Hence the users of the social network need to devote a significant amount of time to maintain relationships on social networks but frequently do not have time to do it. For close friends and family, users would still socialize manually. For the rest of the network, they would use the automated agent for social promotion being proposed.

The difficulty in solving this problem lies mainly in the area of relevance. Messages of the automated agent must be relevant to what human agents are saying. These messages are not always expected to be impressive, witty, or written in style, but at least they should show social engagement. CASP should show that its host cares about the friends being communicated with.

The opportunity to automate social promotion leverages the fact that overall coherence and exactness of social communication is rather low. Readers would tolerate worse than ideal style, discourse and quality of content being communicated, as long as overall communication is positive and makes sense. Currently available commercial chatbots employed by customer support portals, or packaged as mobile apps, possess too limited NLP and text understanding capabilities to support conversations for social profiling.

4.4.3 The Chatbot Architecture

CASP is packaged as a chatbot: it inputs a seed (single or multiple postings) written by human peers of the host and outputs a message it forms from a content mined on the web or in another source, selected and/or adjusted to be relevant to this input posting. This relevance is based on the appropriateness in terms of content topic and also on the appropriateness in terms of mental/epistemic state: for example, it responds by an answer to a question, by a recommendation to a user host post asking for recommendations and by a question to a post mentioning an individual would be happy to answer a question of her peer.

CASP includes the following components:

Web mining for the content relevant to the seed:
1) Forming a set of web search queries
2) Running web search and storing candidate portions of text

Content relevance verification:
Filtering out candidate postings with low parse thicket generalization scores

---

Rhetoric agreement, Epistemic and Mental states relevance verification:
Filtering out candidate postings which don't form a plausible sequence of mental states with the seed

---

Fig. 4.9 A higher-level view of CASP components and relevance pipeline

- Web mining component, which forms the web search queries from the seed and obtains search results using APIs such as Bing, Yahoo! or Yandex;
- Content relevance component, which filters out irrelevant portions of candidate content found on the web, based on syntactic generalization operator. It functions matching the parse thicket for a seed with the parse thicket for a content found on the web;
- Mental state relevance component, which extracts mental states from the seed message and from the web content and applies reasoning to verify that the former can be logically followed by the latter.

In Fig. 4.9, we show a high-level view of CASP architecture, outlining the most critical components of web search for candidate postings and relevance verification.

A *Content Relevance* component is described in detail in (Galitsky et al. 2013) and Chap. 2 Volume 1. It is based on text similarity function, which relies on generalization operation of syntactic, semantic and discourse-level representation of text.

In (Galitsky 2016 and Chap. 9 Volume 2), we develop a generic software component for computing consecutive plausible mental states of human agents that are employed by CASP. The simulation approach to reasoning about the mental world is based on an exhaustive search through the space of available behaviors. This approach to reasoning is implemented as a logic program in a natural language multiagent mental simulator NL_MAMS, which yields the totality of possible mental states few steps in advance, given an arbitrary initial mental state of participating agents. Due to an extensive vocabulary of formally represented mental attitudes, communicative actions and accumulated library of behaviors, NL_MAMS is capable of yielding a much richer set of sequences of a mental state than a conventional system of reasoning about beliefs, desires and intentions would deliver (Galitsky 2016). Also, NL_MAMS functions in a domain-independent manner, outperforming machine learning-based systems for accessing plausibility of a sequence of mental states and behaviors of human agents in broad domains where training sets are limited (Galitsky and Shpitsberg 2016).

Detailed CASP architecture that includes all components is shown in Fig. 4.10. The leftmost column includes the posting preparation components, the column in the middle—web mining (Buzmakov 2015) and forming the list of candidate posting, and the column on the right—relevance filtering components. The bottom row of the chart includes merging textual chunks and final delivery of the formed posting. In each row, the processing by components occurs from top to bottom.

Once CASP obtains a current state of a conversational thread, it needs to decide if/when is a good time to post. To form a query, the conversational thread should settle in terms of topic. Also, the rate of postings should drop to make sure CASP does not break the thread (so that the next thread participant would need to adjust his posting).

To form a query from a single (initial, seed posting) or the whole conversational thread, CASP needs to obtain a topic, or main entity (named entity) of this single or multiple texts, respectively. To do that, CASP extracts noun phrases and scores them with respect to estimated importance. For the case of multiple texts, a lattice querying mechanism (Galitsky 2019a) is employed to get the level of optimal generality: if it is too low, then the web mining would find too few of too specific search results,

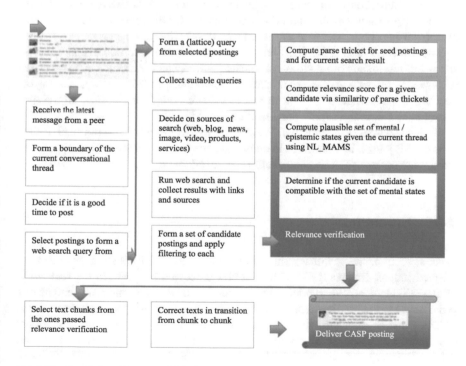

Fig. 4.10 Detailed architecture of CASP

which might be inappropriate. If this generality of web mining query is too high, then the resultant posting might be irrelevant, too broad, so it would be hard for peers to see how CASP maintains the relevance of the conversation.

The chatbot forms multiple web mining queries since it is unclear which one would give the content from the web that would pass the relevance filtering. For each query, we form a set of search results and form a single list of candidate postings. Relevance filtering either selects the best posting or a few best ones whose selected text chunks will be combined.

4.4.4   Use Cases of CASP

We start with the use case of joining a heated conversation between peers on political issues. The participants have a polar opinion on the topic. CASP is looking for content on the web related to police brutality and black/white population controversy (Fig. 4.11).

In the second use case, CASP greets a friend on his arrival back from her trip (Fig. 4.12). In this case, CASP is explicit on representing his host, so a stronger deviation of message appropriateness can be handled. CASP waits as the conversation passes through a couple of cycles and then yields a message with a link covering the entire conversation, not just the first, seed posting. CASP found a relevant posting by another Facebook user (not a random web page) with an image.

The third use case (Fig. 4.13) shows how CASP can take into account mental states and sentiments of previous comments (Galitsky and McKenna 2017). Posting is somewhat relevant: it does not talk about a child unhappy with a parent singing but instead suggests what to sing. However, this far-reaching correlation with the seed is suitable for casual, friendly conversations.

We also share a case study where a posting by CASP initiated a political discussion; CASP joins it to strengthen the case with the content mined online (Fig. 4.14). Further examples of CASP conversations are available in Galitsky et al. 2014).

4.4.5   Evaluation

In this section, we evaluate the relevance of a CASP posting assessed by selected judges, irrespectively of how it was perceived by peers in the real-world settings (Table 4.3). We conducted an evaluation of the relevance of the syntactic generalization-enabled search engine, based on Yahoo and Bing search engine APIs.

The value of relevance for a posting is Boolean: acceptable or not. Individual postings are assessed, so no complications arise due to measuring multiple search results. We vary the complexity of seed posting and provide the percentages of relevant results found on the web and subject to relevance filtering by linguistic means. We show these percentages as the complexity of such filtering increases.

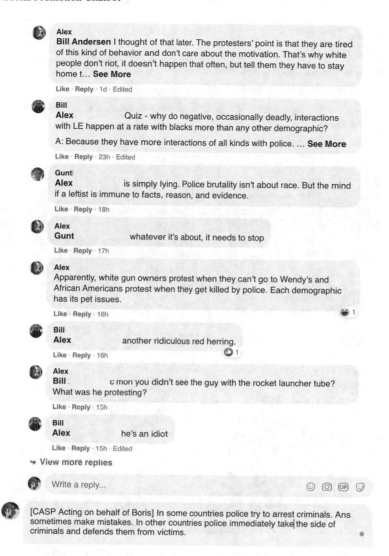

Fig. 4.11 CASP is posting a message about the riots in US in May 2020

The accuracy of a particular search setting (query type and search engine type) is calculated, averaging through forty search sessions. For our evaluation, we use user postings available at the author' Facebook accounts. The evaluation was done by the authors. We refer the reader to (Galitsky 2019b and Chap. 2 Volume 1) for further details on evaluation settings for search relevance evaluation.

To compare the relevance values between search settings, we used the first thirty search results and re-ranked them according to the score of the given search setting.

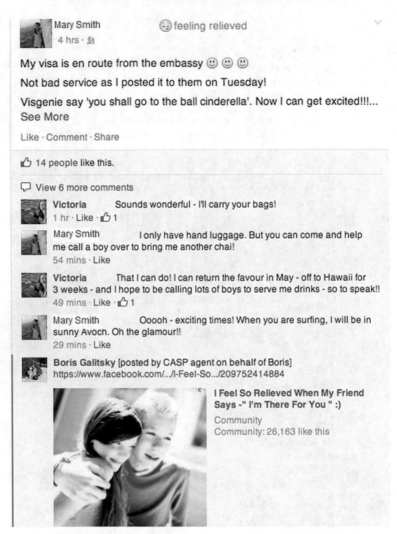

Mary Smith   😌 feeling relieved
4 hrs · 🔒

My visa is en route from the embassy 😊 😊 😊

Not bad service as I posted it to them on Tuesday!

Visgenie say 'you shall go to the ball cinderella'. Now I can get excited!!!...
See More

Like · Comment · Share

👍 14 people like this.

💬 View 6 more comments

Victoria   Sounds wonderful - I'll carry your bags!
1 hr · Like · 👍 1

Mary Smith   I only have hand luggage. But you can come and help
me call a boy over to bring me another chai!
54 mins · Like

Victoria   That I can do! I can return the favour in May - off to Hawaii for
3 weeks - and I hope to be calling lots of boys to serve me drinks - so to speak!!
49 mins · Like · 👍 1

Mary Smith   Ooooh - exciting times! When you are surfing, I will be in
sunny Avoch. Oh the glamour!!
29 mins · Like

Boris Galitsky [posted by CASP agent on behalf of Boris]
https://www.facebook.com/.../I-Feel-So.../209752414884

**I Feel So Relieved When My Friend
Says -" I'm There For You " :)**
Community
Community: 26,163 like this

Fig. 4.12 CASP is posting a message welcoming his friend back home, having recognized the mental state of the participants of the chat

We use two approaches to verify relevance between the seed text and candidate posting:

a. Pair-wise parse tree matching, where the tree for each sentence from seed is matched with the tree for each sentence in the candidate posting mined on the web;

b. The whole graph (parse thicket, PT) for the former is matched against a parse thicket for the latter using a phrase-based approach. In this case, parse thickets are represented by all their paths;

my daughter sawyer (10) says I can become cooler if I don't sing any song out loud for a week.

Fig. 4.13 CASP commenting on the posting of a friend

The value of parse thicket—based generalization (Galitsky 2019b) varies from domain to domain significantly, mostly depending on the writing style and use of terminology by the authors presenting their opinions on the products. When things in a domain are named uniquely, and the typical writing style is a plain enumeration of product features, the contribution of parse thickets is the least (shopping product domains). On the contrary, when writing styles vary a lot and different people name the same things differently, in such horizontal domain as Facebook, the baseline relevance is low, the resultant relevance is lower (63%) than in the other domains (73–75%), but the matching of parse thickets helps in a higher degree.

Proceeding from snippets to original paragraph(s) in a webpage gives a further 0.8% increase for both thicket phrase-based and graph-based computation of parse thickets.

One can observe that unfiltered precision is 52%, whereas improvement by pair-wise sentence generalization is 11%, thicket phrases—an additional 6%, and

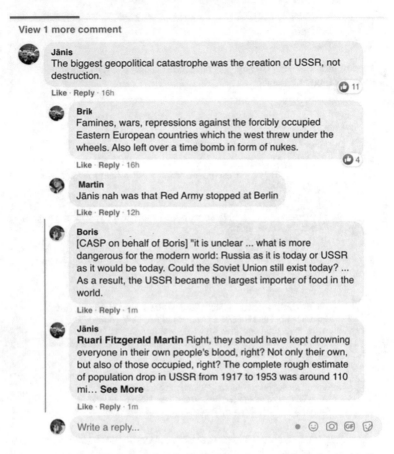

Fig. 4.14 A case study with Facebook friends. On the top: an original photo with the caption, which was a CASP seed. On the bottom: Text and Image found by CASP. On the right: discussions between CASP's host and his friends on the appropriateness of CASP posting

graphs—an additional 0.5%. Hence the higher the complexity of a sentence, the higher is the contribution of generalization technology, from sentence-level to thicket phrases to graphs.

We now proceed to the evaluation of trust. The host human agent should trust the social promotion agent CASP that the results of its activity would indeed improve the host's position in the social world, not decrease it. Relying on an incompetent, silly CASP may lead to unwanted consequences such as a drop in the reputation of the CASP host (Galitsky and Levene 2007). The promotion agent targets the least important friends and members of the network; however, if a significant portion of them lose trust in the host agent, the impact on the social promotion campaign would become negative. If a human host loses the trust in its auto promotional agent, it will stop using it.

Table 4.3 Evaluation results for various search domains and for various implementations of PT generalization

Query complexity	Relevance of baseline Bing search, %, averaging over 40 searches	Relevance of PT/phrase generalization search, %, averaging over 40 searches, using original text, without SpAtcT	Relevance of PT/phrase generalization search, %, averaging over 40 searches, using snippets	Relevance of PT/phrase generalization search, %, averaging over 40 searches, using original text	Relevance of PT/graph generalization search, %, averaging over 40 searches, using snippets	Relevance of PT/graph generalization search, %, averaging over 40 searches, using original text
1 compound sent	54.5	61.3	63.3	65.3	66.2	67.2
2 sent	52.3	60.9	60.7	62.1	63.4	63.9
3 sent	49.7	55.4	61.7	61.9	60.8	61.9
4 sent	50.9	55.5	60.5	61.1	61.5	62.7
Average	51.85	58.28	61.55	62.6	62.98	63.93

Also, the friends and members of the social network may lose trust in the host agent irrespectively of how the communication has been facilitated and may unfriend the host agent or block his messages. This might happen because of a loss of relevance, loss of rhetorical appropriateness of messages and also because they can be offended by the content being communicated. From the standpoint of CASP, it is most likely a problem of relevance; however, the perception of irrelevant messages can be ambiguous. Friends can think of such a message as a bad joke, a hint for something they would not want to share, and even as an insult.

There are two following cases the friends and members of the social network of a host loose trust in the host agent himself when he is using CASP:

- If they do not know that an agent acts on his behalf, they may get upset by the irrelevance and inappropriateness of communication without making the reason for it clear. They would consider it insulting to use such communication means as CASP instead of direct human–human communication;
- If they know that they receive a message from an automated agent, but the results are less relevant and less appropriate than what they expected.

We now share our data on how some peers have been losing trust to as much degree as even stopping using CASP at all and unfriending its human host. We do not see a reason for stopping using CASP other than losing trust and starting perceiving the CASP-facilitated conversation as unfaithful, losing the intimacy of friendship, abusing privacy and so forth. To track how the peer users lose trust as they encounter more CASP activity, we firstly report the *number* of such encounters associate with negative user experience till the user reaches the respective level of mistrust (Table 4.4). After that, we measure the level of relevance that leads to this level of mistrust. Whereas the first dataset does not measure irrelevance and instead reports the number of irrelevant scenarios, the second dataset does the other way around and provides explicit relevance data.

After a certain number of CASP failures in providing relevant postings, friends *lose trust and complain, unfriend, shares negative information* about the loss of trust with others and even *encourage other friends to unfriend* a friend who is enabled with CASP (Table 4.4). The values in the cells indicate the average number of postings with failed relevance when the respective event of disengagement from CASP occurred. These postings of failed relevance were tracked within one month of the experiment run, and we do not access the values for the relative frequency of occurrences of these postings. On average, 100 postings were done for each user (1–4 CASP postings per seed posting).

One can see that in various domains, the scenarios of users' tolerance to irrelevance vary. For less information-critical domains, such as *travel* and *shopping*, this tolerance to failed relevance is relatively high. Conversely, in the domains taken more seriously by peers, like *job*-related, and the domains with personal flavor and increased privacy, like *personal life*, users are more sensitive to CASP failures and the loss of trust in its various forms occurs faster. For all domains, tolerance slowly decreases when the complexity of posting increases. Users' perception is worse for longer texts,

Table 4.4 The data on the number of irrelevant postings till an occurrence of certain dissatisfaction event

Topic of the seed	Complexity of the seed and posted message	A friend complains to the CASP's host	A friend unfriends the CASP host	A friend shares with other friends that the trust in CASP is lost in one way or another	A friend encourages other friends to unfriend a friend with CASP
Travel & outdoor	1 sent	6.3	8.5	9.4	12.8
	2 sent	6.0	8.9	9.9	11.4
	3 sent	5.9	7.4	10.0	10.8
	4 sent	5.2	6.8	9.4	10.8
Shopping	1 sent	7.2	8.4	9.9	13.1
	2 sent	6.8	8.7	9.4	12.4
	3 sent	6.0	8.4	10.2	11.6
	4 sent	5.5	7.8	9.1	11.9
Events & entertainment	1 sent	7.3	9.5	10.3	13.8
	2 sent	8.1	10.2	10.0	13.9
	3 sent	8.4	9.8	10.8	13.7
	4 sent	8.7	10.0	11.0	13.8
Job-related	1 sent	3.6	4.2	6.1	6.0
	2 sent	3.5	3.9	5.8	6.2
	3 sent	3.7	4.0	6.0	6.4
	4 sent	3.2	3.9	5.8	6.2
Personal life	1 sent	7.1	7.9	8.4	9.0
	2 sent	6.9	7.4	9.0	9.5
	3 sent	5.3	7.6	9.4	9.3
	4 sent	5.9	6.7	7.5	8.9
Average		6.03	7.50	8.87	10.58

irrelevant in terms of content or their expectations, than for shorter, single sentence or phrase postings by CASP.

We now drill into the types of relevance errors which lead to deterioration of trust by peer users of CASP. We outline the following cases where a CASP posting is rejected by recipients:

(a) The content CASP is posted typically irrelevant to the content of the original post by a human friend;
(b) CASP content is topically relevant to the content but irrelevant in terms of style, user knowledge (epistemic states), user beliefs (in such domain as politics).

This form of relevance is referred to as rhetorical agreement and explored in Chap. 10 Volume 1.

In Table 4.5 we focus on the *user tolerance versus irrelevance* data in the same format as above (Table 4.4) but measuring relevance values, for both (a) and (b). We use a Boolean value for relevance: either relevant or totally irrelevant posting. For each level of dissatisfaction, from complaint to encouraging others, we measure the value of relevance where at least 20% of the peers reach this level, given the domain and complexity and/or size of CASP posting. For example, in *travel* domain, for 1 sentence posting, more than 20% of the peers start to complain to the CASP host when relevance goes as lows as 83% (17% of postings are irrelevant).

One can see from Table 4.5 that the users can tolerate stronger problems with the rhetorical agreement and epistemic states than with content relevance. As the complexity and/or length of posting grows, users can tolerate lower relevance. There is a few percent (3–10) drop of either content relevance or communicative actions plausibility where a user dissatisfaction becomes more severe; it depends on the

Table 4.5 The data on the percentage of irrelevant postings till an occurrence of certain dissatisfaction event

Topic of the seed and posting/degrees of user tolerance	Complexity of the seed and posted message	A friend complaints to the CASP's host	A friend unfriends the CASP host	A friend shares with other friends that the trust in CASP is lost	A friend encourages other friends to unfriend a friend with CASP
Travel & outdoor	1 sent	83/67	76/63	68/60	61/53
	2 sent	81/68	74/62	75/59	59/54
	3 sent	78/66	74/64	64/58	57/50
	4 sent	75/63	70/62	60/59	55/50
Events & entertainment	1 sent	86/70	79/67	74/65	71/60
	2 sent	82/70	78/66	72/61	69/58
	3 sent	79/69	76/67	74/64	67/59
	4 sent	78/68	76/66	73/63	65/60
Job-related	1sent	80/67	77/63	66/55	59/51
	2 sent	77/65	73/61	70/54	56/51
	3 sent	75/63	71/65	63/56	55/48
	4 sent	74/60	68/63	61/57	56/51
Personal life	1 sent	82/66	75/64	66/62	57/50
	2 sent	80/66	73/65	70/57	60/52
	3 sent	78/62	75/62	66/56	58/48
	4 sent	77/60	75/58	68/55	59/52

problem domain. For job-related communications, user sensitivity to problems with both kinds of relevance is higher than for *travel, entertainment* and *personal life* domains.

Out of a hundred CASP posting per user who made between 2–3 manual postings, failures occurred in less than 10% of CASP postings (Galitsky 2019a). Therefore, most peer users do not end up refusing CASP posting, having their trust of it lost. The friends who were lost due to the abuse of their tolerance to meaningless postings by CASP would become inactive CASP users in most cases anyway (because of a lack of attention and interest to the CASP host). However, luckily, a majority of social network friends will be retained and stay in an active mode, keeping receiving CASP postings.

4.5 Improving Discourse Parsing

Documents can be analyzed as sequences of hierarchical discourse structures. Discourse structures describe the organization of documents in terms of discourse or rhetorical relations. Discourse parsing is an integral part of understanding information flow and argumentative structure in documents. For instance, the three discourse units below can be represented by the tree in Fig. 4.15, where the rhetorical relation *Comparison* holds between the segments 1 and 2, and the relation *Attribution* links the segment covering the units 1 and 2, and segment 3.

(1) Electricity consumption in Spain rose 0.25% in the second quarter from the first quarter
(2) and was 2.6% up from the previous year,
(3) according to the Spanish Bureau of Statistics.

One of the main issues of discourse coherence is how rhetorical relations (relations between elementary discourse units (EDUs) such as *Cause, Evidence, List* or *Summary*) are signaled in text. Rhetorical relations are often signaled by discourse markers such as *and, because, however* and *while*, and relations are sometimes classified as explicit relations if they contain such markers (Taboada and Mann 2006; van der Vliet and Redeker 2011). Discourse markers are widely believed to be the most reliable signals of coherence relations.

Fig. 4.15 A skeleton of a simple discourse tree (DT)

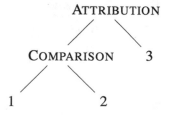

Prediction of the rhetorical relation between two sentences is the goal of discourse parsing, along with text segmentation (splitting sentences into EDUs). We rely on a baseline segmentation and do not attempt to improve it. A number of annotated corpora exist, such as RST-DT (Carlson et al. 2001) and PDTB (Prasad et al. 2008), but in general, the available data is fairly limited, and the task of discourse relation prediction is rather difficult. Most available discourse parsers assign *Elaboration* and *Join* relations, and the recall of establishing other, more specific rhetorical relation is fairly low. In this section, we attempt to employ a linguistic resource AMR (Banarescu et al. 2013) targeting semantic representation to learn to recognize specific rhetorical relations in text.

We first apply the state-of-the-art discourse parser of (Joty et al. 2015) and then attempt to overwrite the *Elaboration* and *Joint* with a specific rhetorical relation obtained from AMR patterns if they are available. We apply such the procedure for intra-sentence rhetorical relations only.

For a sentence, '*It was a question of life or death for me: I had scarcely enough drinking water to last a week*' a default discourse tree is as follows (Fig. 4.16).

In this semantic representation, ***purpose*** as a semantic role is related to the verb *drink*. In our analysis, we identify a nucleus EDU with *drink* and then look for its satellite-connected with *Elaboration*. Then this *Elaboration* should be substituted with *Purpose* for a more accurate DT.

In our second example, we want to map the AMR semantic role of *compared-to* to rhetorical relation of *Comparison*. The default discourse parsing gives us *Elaboration* that can be turned into a more accurate rhetorical relation, if the EDU pair with a default rhetorical relation is semantically similar with a template that has a specific semantic relation that can be mapped into a rhetorical relation.

```
elaboration
   TEXT:It was a question of life or death for me :
   elaboration
      TEXT:I had scarcely enough drinking water
      TEXT:to last a week.
The second relation of Elaboration is not very accurate and we look up this example in AMR dataset:
(q / question
   :ARG0 i
   :ARG1 (o / or
        :op1 (l / live-01)
        :op2 (d / die-01))
   :ARG1-of (c / cause
      :ARG0 (h / have
         :ARG0 (i / i)
         :ARG1 (w / water
            :purpose (d2 / drink
               :ARG0 i)
            :quant (e / enough
               :mod (s / scarce))
            :ARG1-of (l2 / last
               :ARG2 (t / temporal-quantity :quant 1
                  :unit (w2 / week))
               :ARG3 i)))))
```

Fig. 4.16 An AMR Tree where the rhetorical relation of purpose can be yielded

```
elaboration
  TEXT: I ate the most wonderful hamburger
  TEXT: that she had ever bought for me.
```

```
(p / planet
    :domain (i / it)
    :mod (m2 / magnificent
        :degree (m / most)
        :compared-to (p2 / planet
            :ARG1-of (s2 / see
                :ARG0 (h / he)
                :time (e / ever))))
    :mod (s / stately
        :degree (m3 / most)
        :compared-to p2))
```

Fig. 4.17 Mapping words and semantic relations into rhetorical relations

To establish an accurate rhetorical relationship between EDUs in the above sentence, we attempt to match it against a template found in a tagged AMR repository (Fig. 4.17):

"It was the most magnificent and stately planet that he had ever seen".

To match an EDU pair being parsed with a template, we align and generalize them. In our case, the syntactic generalization between the EDU pair and the template is as follows: [VB-* DT-the RBS-most JJ-(*wonderful* ^*magnificent*) IN-that PRP-she VB-had RB-ever VB-*] so that there is a significant evidence that the sentence being parsed and the pattern share the common syntactic structure. *wonderful* ^*magnificent* produces an abstract adjective with the meaning of what is common between these adjectives. We show with an arrow a correspondence between the adjective *magnificent* in the AMR representation and adjective *wonderful* the original DT. Hence we obtain the corrected DT as.

```
comparison
  TEXT: I ate the most wonderful hamburger
  TEXT: that she had ever bought for me.
```

This parsing improvement approach works in the cases where there is a lack of discourse markers, they are ambiguous or misleading, or a deeper semantic representation of a sentence such as AMR implies a specific rhetorical relation. Once a syntactic similarity between a text being parsed and an AMR pattern is established, the semantic role from the AMR verb can be interpreted at the discourse level as a respective rhetorical relation. This mapping between a semantic relation in AMR and a specific rhetorical relation is established irrespectively of how, with which connective, nucleus and satellite EDUs are connected.

The mapping between AMR semantic relations and rhetorical relations is developed as a result of manual generalization of available AMR annotations. We iterate through the list of rhetorical relations (Mann and Thompson 1988) and for each observe a collection of AMR annotations of specific semantic relations. Once we see a systematic correlation between these, we create an entry in our mapping Table 4.6.

The first column enumerates the rhetorical relation to be detected, the second—the AMR semantic relations being mapped into the rhetorical ones, and the third column gives the example sentence that is going to be matched again a sentence being rhetorically parsed. The right column shows the AMR parsing for the templates. Details about AMR denotations and conventions are available in Chaps. 3 and 5 Volume 1.

For two entries on the bottom, we provide an example of a refined discourse tree where *Elaboration* is turned into a specific relation. We take a template, build a discourse tree for it, and refine it, showing the detected rhetorical relation manner in bold (the third row from the bottom). The first row from the bottom shows actual refinement where the *Elaboration* is turned into *Concession* by applying the template from the second row from the bottom. Syntactic generalization between this template and the sentence in the second column is shown on the top of the right column (in the bottom row). Only rhetorical relations that are thoroughly represented in AMR are shown in Table 4.6. Other relations are not presented there and, therefore, cannot be detected using this algorithm.

To overwrite the rhetorical relation of *Elaboration* with the one obtained by manual tagging in AMR, we need to establish a syntactic similarity between the nucleus plus satellite EDUs for this *Elaboration* and a template. If such similarity is high (a pattern from AMR dataset is being parsed), then *Elaboration* can be overwritten with a high confidence. The higher the syntactic similarity score, the higher is the confidence that the semantic role obtained from the pattern describes the rhetorical relation precisely. Since we neither have sufficient AMR pattern data nor extensive mapping into rhetorical relations data, we are unable to formally learn such mapping but instead select a threshold for the similarity score.

4.5.1 Syntactic Generalization of a Sentence Being Parsed and an AMR Template

The purpose of an abstract generalization is to find commonality between portions of text at various semantic levels (Ourioupina and Galitsky 2001). Generalization operation occurs on the level of paragraph, sentences, EDUs, phrases and individual words.

At each level except the lowest one, individual words, the result of generalization of two expressions is a *set* of expressions. In such the set, for each pair of expressions so that one is less general than another, the latter is eliminated. Generalization of two sets of expressions is a set of sets of expressions which are the results of pair-wise generalization of these expressions.

Let us generalize the sentence "*If you read a book at night, your knowledge will improve*" with the template "*If one gets lost in the night, such knowledge is valuable*" from Table 4.6 (Fig. 4.18).

Although in this template IN-If PRP-* VB-* is a signature of a semantic relation of:*condition()* and also the discourse relation of *Condition*, there are happen to be

Table 4.6 The AMR semantic roles and corresponding rhetorical relations

Rhetorical relation	Semantic role of a verb	Example sentence (template)	AMR representation
Contrast	contrast-XX	But he receives the explorers in his study	(c/contrast-01 :ARG2 (r/receive-01 :ARG0 (h/he) :ARG1 (p/person :ARG0-of (e/explore-01)) :location (s/study :poss h)))
Purpose	:puspose()	It was a question of life or death for me: I had scarcely enough drinking water to last a week	(q/question-01 :ARG0 i :ARG1 (o/or :op1 (l/live-01) :op2 (d/die-01)) :ARG1-of (c/cause-01 :ARG0 (h/have-03 :ARG0 (i/i) :ARG1 (w/water :purpose (d2/drink-01 :ARG0 i) :quant (e/enough :mod (s/scarce)) :ARG1-of (l2/last-03 :ARG2 (t/temporal-quantity:quant 1 :unit (w2/week)) :ARG3 i)))))
Comparison	:compared-to()	I was more isolated than a shipwrecked sailor on a raft in the middle of the ocean	(i/isolate-01 :ARG1 (i2/i) :degree (m/more) :compared-to (p/person :ARG0-of (s/sail-01) :ARG1-of (s2/shipwreck-01) :location (r/raft :location (o/ocean :part (m2/middle)))))

(continued)

more common words such as "NN-night ... NN-knowledge" which might or might not be used to establish a similarity between the sentence and the template.

At the phrase level, generalization starts with finding an alignment between two phrases, where we attempt to set a correspondence between as many words as possible between two phrases (Chambers et al. 2007; DeNero and Klein 2008). We assure that the alignment operation retains phrase integrity: in particular, two phrases can be aligned only if the correspondence between their head nouns is established. There

Table 4.6 (continued)

Rhetorical relation	Semantic role of a verb	Example sentence (template)	AMR representation
Cause	cause-XX	That is why, at the age of six, I gave up what might have been a magnificent career as a painter	(c2/cause-01 :ARG0 (t2/that) :ARG1 (g/give-up-07 :ARG0 (i/i) :ARG1 (c/career :mod (m/magnificent) :topic (p/person :ARG0-of (p2/paint-02))) :time (a/age-01 :ARG1 i :ARG2 (t/temporal-quantity:quant 6 :unit (y/year)))))
Condition	:condition(),:have-condition(), condition-of	If one gets lost in the night, such knowledge is valuable	(v/value-02 :ARG1 (k/knowledge :mod (s/such)) :condition (g/get-03 :ARG1 (o/one) :ARG2 (l/lost :time (d/date-entity:dayperiod (n/night)))))
Manner	:manner	It was from words dropped by chance that, little by little, everything was revealed to me	(r/reveal-01 :ARG0 (w/word :ARG1-of (d/drop-06 :ARG1-of (c/chance-02))) :ARG1 (e/everything) :ARG2 (i/i) :manner (l/little-by-little))
manner (LeftToRight) elaboration (LeftToRight) TEXT:It was from words TEXT:dropped by chance TEXT:that, little by little, everything was revealed to me			

(continued)

is a similar integrity constraint for aligning verb, prepositional and other types of phrases (Fig. 4.19).

Table 4.7 shows the co-occurrence values and percentages for lexical, syntactic and semantic correlation with rhetorical relation. This data helps to improve the scoring for *and* and *as* (usually ignored for syntactic generalization) and *but, while, however, because* usually has a very low score.

Table 4.6 (continued)

Rhetorical relation	Semantic role of a verb	Example sentence (template)	AMR representation
Concession	:concession(), :have-concession()	The little prince looked everywhere to find a place to sit down; but the entire planet was crammed and obstructed by the king 's magnificent ermine robe	(a/and :op1 (c/cram-01 :ARG1 (r2/robe :mod (e2/ermine) :mod (m/magnificent) :poss (k/king)) :ARG2 (p3/planet :extent (e3/entire))) :op2 (o/obstruct-01 :ARG0 r2 :ARG1 p3) **:concession** (l/look-01 :ARG0 (p/prince :mod (l2/little)) :ARG1 (p2/place :purpose (s/sit-down-02 :ARG1 p)) :location (e/everywhere)))
elaboration TEXT:A designer trying to fit the power unit into the processor box, elaboration (LeftToRight) TEXT:but there was not enough space TEXT:to accommodate the cooling fan		A designer trying to fit the power unit into the processor box, and there was not enough space to accommodate the cooling fan	[VP [VB-* NN-* IN-into], VP [VB-* VB-* NN-* NN-* NN-*], VP [VB-* IN-* DT-the NN-*], VP [VB-was DT-the NN-*], VP [TO-to VB-* DT-* NN-*]]] **concession** TEXT: A designer trying to fit the power unit into the processor box, elaboration TEXT: but there was not enough space TEXT: to accommodate the cooling fan

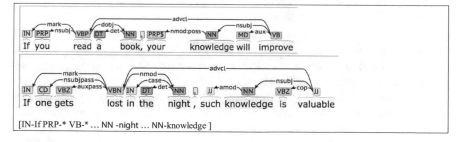

Fig. 4.18 Generalization of a sentence being rhetorically parsed and a template with known semantic relation

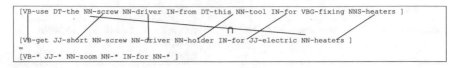

Fig. 4.19 An alignment between words for two sentences

Table 4.7 The frequency of co-occurring discourse cues

Co-occurring discourse cues	Total co-occurrence #	Co-occurring single cues			Co-occurring combined cues		
		Type	#	%	Type	#	%
And	631	Semantic	467	74.00	syntactic + semantic	88	13.95
		Lexical	43	6.81	reference + syntactic	22	3.49
		Syntactic	31	4.91	semantic + syntactic	18	2.85
		Morphological	26	4.12			
But	309	Semantic	277	89.64	reference + syntactic	17	5.50
		Lexical	30	9.71	semantic + syntactic	17	5.50
		Reference	15	4.85	syntactic + semantic	10	3.24
While	73	Semantic	46	63.01	syntactic + semantic	21	28.77
However	56	Semantic	39	69.64	semantic + syntactic	7	12.50
Because	52	Semantic	50	96.15	–	–	–
As	28	Lexical	9	32.14	–	–	–
		Semantic	9	32.14			

To compute a generalization score, we conducted a computational study to determine the POS weights to deliver the most accurate similarity measure between sentences possible (Galitsky et al. 2012). The problem was formulated as finding optimal weights for nouns, adjectives, verbs and their forms (such as gerund and past tense) so that the resultant search relevance is maximum. Search relevance was measured as a deviation in the order of search results from the best one for a given query (delivered by Google); the current search order was determined based on the score of generalization for the given set of POS weights (having other generalization parameters fixed). As a result of this optimization performed in (Galitsky et al. 2010), we obtained $W_{NN} = 1.0$, $W_{JJ} = 0.32$, $W_{RB} = 0.71$, $W_{CD} = 0.64$, $W_{VB} = 0.83$, $W_{PRP} = 0.35$ excluding common frequent verbs like *get/take/set/put* for which $W_{VBcommon} = 0.57$. We also set that $W_{<POS,*>} = 0.2$ (different words but the same POS), and

Fig. 4.20 A match between
abstract structures

$W_{<*,\text{word}>} = 0.3$ (the same word but occurs as different POSs in two sentences).
$W_{\{and, as, but, while, however, because\}}$ is calculated as a default value of 1 normalized for the
value in the second column of Table 4.7. Notice that default syntactic generalization
mostly ignores discourse cue words.

Generalization score (or similarity between *EDU_Pair* and *Template*) then can be
expressed as sum through phrases of the weighted sum through words W.

word$_{sent1}$ and *word* $_{sent2}$:

$$score(EDU\_Pair, \ Template) = \sum\nolimits_{\{NP, VP, ...\}} \sum W_{POS}word\_generalization$$
$(word_{EDU\_Pair}, \ word_{Template})$.

(Maximal) generalization can then be defined as the one with the highest score.
This way we define a generalization for phrases, sentences and paragraphs.

Result of generalization can be further generalized with other parse trees or generalization. For a set of sentences, totality of generalizations forms a lattice: the order on
generalizations is set by the subsumption (subtree) relation and generalization score.
We enforce the associativity of generalization of parse trees by means of computation:
it has to be verified and the resultant list extended each time new sentence is added.
Notice that such associativity is not implied by our definition of generalization.

The concept of matching between abstract structures is visualized in Fig. 4.20.

4.5.2 Rhetorical Relation Enhancement Algorithm

We present an algorithm to enhance *Elaboration* but other rhetorical relations can
be made more accurate as well.

Once we have a text and intend to produce a refined discourse parsing, we first
apply the available default parser and produce a discourse tree (Fig. 4.21). We
then identify default rhetorical relations in this tree, which are more likely to be
successfully refined. Those are innermost relations of *Elaboration* and *Joint*, and
also the nested ones (*Elaboration* over another *Elaboration* [over another *Elaboration*]). Once we have a candidate rhetorical relation to be refined, we identify its

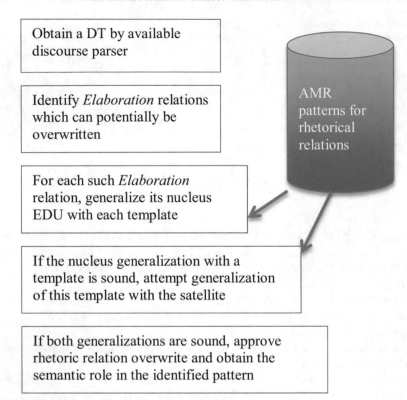

Fig. 4.21   A chart of Rhetorical Relation refinement algorithm

nucleus and satellite EDUs to match with a template. If they are too complicated or long, we reduce them hoping that we can still get a high enough generalization score.

Then we iterate through each template and check if it covers the EDU pair. We first check the discourse cue keywords, then other keywords, and finally, if there is a sufficient keyword match, then we perform syntactic generalization with the nucleus to compute the similarity score. For the highest such score for all templates, if it is above the threshold of 2.0, we accept the template. We then generalize with the satellite to obtain the final score.

Once the final score is above 3.3, we approve the substitution and turn the default rhetorical relation to the one from the template.

4.5.3 Generalization Levels: From Syntax to Semantics to Discourse

To demonstrate how the syntactic generalization allows us to ascend from the syntactic to the semantic level, we follow Mill's *Direct method of agreement* (*induction*) as applied to linguistic structures. British philosopher JS Mills wrote in his 1843 book "A System of Logic": "If *two or more instances* of the phenomenon under investigation have *only one circumstance in common*, the circumstance in which alone all the instances agree, is the *cause* (or *effect*) of the given phenomenon" (Ducheyne 2008).

Let us consider a linguistic property A of a phrase f. For A to be a necessary condition of some effect E, A must always be present in multiple phrases that deal with E. In the linguistic domain, A is a linguistic structure and E is its *meaning*. Therefore, we check whether linguistic properties considered as 'possible necessary conditions' are present or absent in the sentence. Obviously, any linguistic properties As which are absent when the meaning E is present cannot be necessary conditions for this meaning E of a phrase.

For example, the method of agreement can be represented as a phrase f_1 where words $\{A\ B\ C\ D\}$ occur together with the meaning formally expressed as $<w\ x\ y\ z>$. Consider also another phrase f_2 where words $\{A\ E\ F\ G\}$ occur together with the same meaning $<w\ t\ u\ v>$ as in phrase f_1. Now by applying generalization to words $\{A\ B\ C\ D\}$ and $\{A\ E\ F\ G\}$, we obtain $\{A\}$ (here, for the sake of example, we ignore the syntactic structure of f_1 and f_2). Therefore, here we can see that word A is the cause of w (has meaning w). Throughout this book, we do take into account linguistic structures covering A B C D in addition to this list itself, applying the method of agreement.

Hence we can produce (inductive) semantics applying the syntactic generalization. *Semantics cannot be obtained given just syntactic information of a sample; however, generalizing two or more phrases (samples), we obtain an (inductive) semantic structure, not just syntactic one.* Viewing the syntactic generalization as an inductive cognitive procedure, transition from syntactic to semantic levels can be defined formally. In this work, we do not mix syntactic and semantic features to learn a class: instead, we derive semantic features from syntactic according to the above inductive framework.

4.5.4 Evaluation

We first comment on the consequences of false positives and false negatives in enhancing the rhetorical relation of *Elaboration*. To do that, we need to analyze the functionality of the downstream application of the discourse parsing such as summarization, dialogue management and analysis of arguments.

If *Elaboration* is a correct relation but is turned into a more specific one, obtained search results might not match with a query and some sentences may not occur in a resultant summary because the rules are tuned for *Elaboration*. To make the search and summarization system less sensitive to false positives obtained by our refinement system, the matching and selection rules need to be updated to take into account that *Cause, Concession, Condition* are partial cases of *Elaboration* and the discourse trees with these node labels should be matched accordingly.

If we fail to overwrite *Elaboration* with a more specific relation, the precision of a downstream system is negatively affected. If we identify a specific peculiar relation in a question, it has to be addressed in an answer, so if it remains *Elaboration* then a selection of a specific answer matching the question in style would fail. Less relevant sentence or phrase can be included in a summary, or a number of candidates for such inclusion would be reduced. We conclude that false negative is worse than false positive.

Another consideration concerns the genre of the training dataset for discourse parsing. RST Discourse Treebank (RST-DT, Carlson et al. 2001) includes news articles and is not a good source to model text structure in other genres such as fiction, scientific texts, engineering system descriptions and legal documents. Applications of discourse parsing in these domains are critical. Therefore, even if *Elaboration* suffices in news presentation, one needs a more specific structure to model author's reasoning in other genres and domains such as professional texts.

We evaluate the developed discourse parser refinement on four problems (Table 4.8):

Table 4.8 Evaluation of the overall system performance improvement due to the refinement of rhetorical relations

Parser	Original discourse parser, %			Discourse parser with refinement, %			Improvement, %
Task	P	R	F1	P	R	F1	
Searching long queries and enforcing style in search result	76.6	74.5	75.5	81.6	74.8	78.1	3.3
Finding an appropriate utterance to resume a dialogue	71.2	72	71.6	75.9	73.6	74.7	4.4
Generating a dialogue from an initial query	81.7	79.9	80.8	83	86.5	84.7	4.9
Assessing truthfulness of a document	75.3	75.6	75.4	78.4	79.7	79.0	4.8

(1) Search for complex long questions enforcing coordination between questions and answers (Sect. 2). Yahoo!Answers dataset is used;
(2) Finding an utterance to form a dialogue from text or document. The dataset and technique developed in Chap. 1 Volume 2 is used. This technique is heavily dependent on discourse parsing;
(3) Generating a dialogue from the initial query (Chap. 1 Volume 2). Rhetorical relations are taken into account for filtering unsuitable utterances (Galitsky and Ilvovsky 2016);
(4) Assessing truthfulness of a document by its discourse structure (Chap. 6 Volume 2). The structure of discourse trees of how an author expresses information, as well as by means of which rhetorical relations, is important to detect a lie or fake news.

One can observe that in utterance classification and text classification, we achieve above 4% improvement by means of the refinement of the discourse parser results. However, in the search problem, less sensitive to proper rhetorical relations, we achieve closer to 3% improvement.

We now proceed to the evaluation of how an individual rhetorical relation refinement performs (Table 4.9). We use one AMR corpus for training and another for testing.

In the rows three to eight, we analyze relation detection result for individual relation type such as *Contrast*. In the baseline parser, *Contrast* along with *Cause* and *Condition* are recognized, and the rest of relations are not. This is due to the fact that these peculiar, rare relations are not well represented in the Discourse TreeBank. Overall, just for these rhetorical relations, a performance of the baseline classifier weighted by the volume of these relations is fairly low. Learning from AMR, it is possible to achieve a performance of 77.7 for this data. Hence we obtain the improvement of 36.1 for the refinement of these six relations. This is critical for the

Table 4.9 Detection accuracy for individual rhetorical relations

Rhetorical relation	Counts in AMR training set	Original discourse parser			Enhanced discourse parser		
		P	R	F1	R	P	F1
Contrast	136	73	34	46.4	83	74	78.2
Purpose	72	–	0	0	77	69	72.8
Comparison	41	–	0	0	81	76	78.4
Cause	132	69	58	63.0	83	75	78.8
Condition	70	74	72	73.0	86	79	82.4
Concession	25	–	0	0	74	66	69.8
Total 6 relations				41.6			**77.7**
Total for all relations				76.3			82.0

task where the accent is on the particular relation type rather than on the discourse tree structure.

Overall, since these six relations are rare, the parser enhancement gives up to 6% improvement averaging through all rhetorical relations. This is still valuable for applications of discourse parsers, as we observed in Table 4.8.

4.6   Related Work and Conclusions

Six rhetorical relations, which are the focus of discourse parser enhancement, are very important for several applications of search, summarization and text classification into abstract classes. For search, if a question includes either of these six relations, a good, comprehensive answer cannot contain just default rhetorical relations, but instead, properly communicate these peculiar relations in question with its author. Such an answer cannot just be a factoid one.

Contrast needs to be communicated by presenting both thesis and antithesis, possibly employing an argument pattern.

Cause needs to be communicated via one or another form of explanation, presenting a reason, and setting a framework for reasoning.

Condition and *Comparison* need to be handled by communicating, presenting factual data on both (*If* and *Then*, or item *A* versus item *B*) parts.

Hence when these six relations in user questions are not recognized properly, an answer that is wrong in communication manner would be most likely presented, and this user will be dissatisfied with the search, even if it is relevant in terms of queried entities and their attributes.

Penn Discourse Treebank (PDTB, Prasad et al. 2017) has been a major resource for training discourse parsers. Version 3.0 is the third release in the Penn Discourse Treebank project that targets annotating the Wall Street Journal section of Treebank-2 with discourse relations. Penn Discourse Treebank Version 3 contains over 53,600 tokens of annotated relations. Some pairwise annotations were normalized, new senses were included and consistency checks in the corpus were performed. Further details about the development of PDTB are available (PDBT 2019). Since PDBR only includes news genre, the performance of discourse parsers trained on it in other genres is limited. In this work, we attempted to cure these limitations by employing a source of semantic relations from which discourse relations can be deduced.

The PDTB project was inspired by the observation that discourse relations are grounded in an identifiable set of explicit words or phrases (discourse connectives, discourse cues) or simply in the adjacency of two sentences. The PTDB has been used by many researchers in the natural language processing community and more recently, by researchers in psycholinguistics. It has also stimulated the development of similar resources in other languages and domains. There is a strong disagreement between the complexity PDTB 3.0 is built upon and a complexity discourse parsers can handle. Discourse parsers trained on earlier models perform very poorly recognizing very specific rhetorical relations used in PDTB 3.0. Hence the improvement described in this chapter is essential for downstream applications of the discourse parsing.

4.6.1 Constructing Dialogues from Plain Text

Piwek et al. (2007) were pioneers of automated construction of dialogues, proposing Text2Dialogue system. The authors provided a theoretical foundation of the mapping that the system performs from RST structures to Dialogue representation structures. The authors introduced a number of requirements for a dialogue generation system (robustness, extensibility, and variation and control) and reported on the evaluation of the mapping rules.

An important body of work concerns tutorial dialogue systems. Some of the work in that area focuses on authoring tools for generating questions, hints, and prompts. Typically, these are, however, single utterances by a single interlocutor, rather than an entire conversation between two agents. Some researchers have concentrated on generating questions together with possible answers such as multiple-choice test items, but this work is restricted to a very specific type of question–answer pairs (Mitkov et al. 2006). Conversion a text into a dialogue is different from the dialogue generation problem; the former is a training set-based foundation for the latter.

A response generation for dialogue can be viewed as a source-to-target transduction problem. (Sordoni et al. 2015) rescores the outputs of a phrasal machine translation-based conversation system with a neural model incorporating prior context. Recent progress in sequence-to-sequence models has been leveraged (Luan et al. 2016) to build an end-to-end dialogue system that firstly applies an utterance message to a distributed vector representation using an encoder, then secondly generates a response from this representation. Li et al. (2016, 2017a) simulate dialogues between two virtual agents, using policy gradient methods to reward sequences that display three useful conversational properties: informativity, coherence, and ease of answering. We measured comparable dialogue effectiveness properties such as the speed of arrival to a search result, a decision and domain coverage, in the current study.

Dialogue acts are an important source that differentiates between a plain text and a dialogue. The proposed algorithm of virtual dialogues can assist with building domain-specific chatbot training datasets. Recently released dataset, DailyDialog (Li et al. 2017b), is the only dataset that has utterances annotated with dialogue acts and is large enough for learning conversation models. Unlike the virtual dialogues produced in this study, in DailyDialog, conversations are not task-oriented, and each conversation focuses on one topic. Each utterance is annotated with four dialogue acts.

We proposed a novel mode of chatbot interaction via virtual dialogue. It addresses sparseness of dialogue data on one hand and convincingness, perceived authenticity of the information presented via dialogues on the other hand. We quantitatively evaluated an improvement of user satisfaction with virtual dialogue in comparison to regular chatbot replies and confirmed the strong points of the former. We conclude that virtual dialogue is an important feature related to social search to be leveraged by a chatbot.

4.6.2 Conclusions on CASP

We proposed a chatbot domain of social promotion and built a conversational agent CASP to act in this domain. CASP maintains friendship and professional relationship by automatically posting messages on behalf of its human host, to impress the peers that the human host thinks and cares about them. Also, communicating issues raised by peers, CASP can be set to mention various products and services, providing an implicit advertisement. We observed that a substantial intelligence in information retrieval, reasoning, and natural language-based relevance assessment is required so that members of the social network retain an interest in communication with CASP. Otherwise, the result of social promotion would be negative and the host would lose friends instead of retaining them. We demonstrated that a properly designed social promotion chatbot could indeed relieve its human host from the efforts on casual chatting with her least important friends and professional contacts.

According to (Buchegger and Datta 2009), online social networks are inherently peer-to-peer (P2P). Building them as a P2P network leverages a scalable architecture that can improve privacy and avoid the "big brother" effect of service providers. Moreover, Web search engines have problems providing good Web coverage, given the Web's size and high rates of change and growth. It can result in information overload (Wu et al. 2007; Galitsky et al. 2011). Furthermore, the most valuable information is not always available, as in the case of the deep Web. The deep Web is WWW content that is not accessible through search engines; its volume was estimated to be a thousand times higher than the visible Web. Moreover, centralized horizontal search engines aim to satisfy the needs of any user type and they are progressively personalized and context-aware; although they generally provide good results, they are less effective when dealing with atypical searches.

For the purpose of promoting social activity and enhance communications with the friends other than most close ones, the chatbot is authorized to comment on postings, images, videos, and other media. Given one or more sentence of user posting or image caption, CASP issues a web search request to Bing, Yahoo!, Yandex, or an internal company resource and filters the search results for topical relevance, rhetoric appropriateness and style. Experiments with Facebook account were conducted using Facebook OpenGraph involving a number of personal accounts.

To extract a topic and form a query from a conversational thread, (Galitsky 2019a) introduced a new type of query for search engine framework, the lattice query, which is intended to facilitate the process of an abstract data exploration. Instead of having a user formulate a query, one or more instances are automatically formed from sample expressions. To derive a lattice query, as well as to measure the relevance of a question to an answer, an operation of syntactic generalization (Chap. 6 Volume 1, Galitsky

2014) is used. It finds a maximal common sub-trees between the parse trees for the sample text fragments, and also it finds the maximum common sub-trees between the parse trees for the lattice query and that of the candidate answers. In the latter case, the size of the common sub-trees is a measure of relevance for a given candidate search result.

We performed the evaluation of relevance assessment of the CASP web mining results and observed that using the generalization of parse thickets for the seed and candidate message is adequate for posting messages on behalf of human users. Chatbot intelligence is achieved in CASP by integrating linguistic relevance based on parse thickets (Chaps. 2 and 9 Volume 1) and mental states relevance based on the simulation of human attitudes (Galitsky 2016). As a result, CASP messages are trusted by human users in most cases, allowing CASPs to successfully conduct the social promotion.

We experimentally observed the correlation between the intelligence components of CASP and peers' willingness to use it: once these components start to malfunction, the human users start to complain and even intend to disconnect from CASP. In the human–human network, events when people unfriend their peers occur in case of a problem in their relationship, strong deviations in their beliefs and political opinions, but not when humans post least meaningful and least appropriate messages. Humans are ready to tolerate a lack of intelligence in what other humans write, in most of cases. On the contrary, when chatbot utterances are irrelevant or inappropriate, the tolerance is not that high.

We tracked the usability scenarios of CASP when users ended up unfriending it and even encouraging others to do that, measuring topical and rhetoric relevance values, as well as the number of repetitions of problematic postings. We observed that CASP substantially outperforms the boundary acceptability area where a significant number of peers would avoid using it. It is confirmed that the events of unfriending happen rarely enough for CASP agent to improve the social visibility and maintain more friends for a human host than being without CASP. Hence although some friends lost trust in CASP, the friendship with most friends was retained by CASP; therefore, its overall impact on social activity is positive.

CASP was featured on (BBC Inside Science 2014). "Keeping up with your online social network of 'friends' on Facebook can sometimes be time consuming and arduous. Now CASP is designed to do the bulk of his social interactions online. But how realistic is it? And does it fool his cyber pals?"—these were the questions of the reporter.

According to (New Scientist 2014) article "Facebook for lazybones", if one wants to stay in touch with friends on Facebook but cannot be bothered to do it himself, he should rely on CASP, which monitors the social media feed and responds as if it is the host person. CASP makes relevant comments on photos posted by Facebook friends by analyzing the text of status updates and then searches the web for responses.

The content generation part of CASP was available at www.writel.co in 2014–2016. Given a topic, it first mined the web to auto-build thesaurus of entities (Galitsky and Kuznetsov 2013), which will be used in the future comment or essay. Then the system searches the web for these entities to create respective chapters. The resultant document is delivered as a DOCX email attachment.

In the interactive mode, CASP can automatically compile texts from hundreds of sources to write an essay on the topic. If a user wants to share a comprehensive review, opinion on something, provide a thorough background, then this interactive mode should be used. As a result, an essay is automatically written on the topic specified by a user and published. The content generation part of CASP is available at www.facebook.com/RoughDraftEssay.

References

Allen J, Perrault C (1980) Analyzing intention in utterances. Artif Intell 15(3):143–178

Banarescu L, Bonial C, Cai S, Georgescu M, Griffitt K, Hermjakob U, Knight K, Koehn P, Palmer M, Schneider N (2013) Abstract meaning representation for Sembanking. In: Proceedings of the 7th linguistic annotation workshop and interoperability with discourse. Sofia, Bulgaria, pp 178–186

BBC Inside Science (2014) Automatic Facebook. https://www.bbc.co.uk/programmes/b040lnlf

Bhasker B, Srikumar K (2010) Recommender systems in E-Commerce. CUP. ISBN 978–0–07–068067–8

Buchegger S, Datta A (2009) A case for P2P infrastructure for social networks—opportunities & challenges, in: Proceedings of 6th International Conference on Wireless On-Demand Network Systems and Services, Utah, pp 161–168

Buzmakov A (2015) Formal concept analysis and pattern structures for mining structured data. Inria Publication. https://hal.inria.fr/tel-01229062/

Carlson L, Marcu D, Okurowski ME (2001) Building a discourse-tagged corpus in the framework of rhetorical structure theory. In: Proceedings of the second SIGdial workshop on discourse and dialogue, pp 1–10

Cartoonbank (2020) https://cartoonbank.ru/?page_id=29&color=all&offset=260

Cassell J, Bickmore T, Campbell L, Vilhjálmsson H, Yan H (2000) Human conversation as a system framework: designing embodied conversational agents . In: Cassell J et al (eds) Embodied conversational agents. MIT Press, Cambridge, MA, pp 29–63

Chambers N, Cer D, Grenager T, Hall D, Kiddon C, MacCartney, de Marneffe MC, Ramage D, Yeh E, Manning CD (2007) Learning alignments and leveraging natural logic. In: Proceedings of the ACL-07 workshop on textual entailment and paraphrasing

Cox R, McKendree J, Tobin R, Lee J, Mayes T (1999) Vicarious learning from dialogue and discourse: a controlled comparison. Ins Sci 27:431–458

Craig S, Gholson B, Ventura M, Graesser A, Tutoring Research Group (2000) Overhearing dialogues and monologues in virtual tutoring sessions: effects on questioning and vicarious learning. Int J Artif Int Edu 11:242–253

CrimeRussia (2016) https://en.crimerussia.ru/corruption/shadow-chairman-of-the-investigative-committee

De Rosis F, Pelachaud C, Poggi I, Carofiglio V, de Carolis B (2003) From Greta's mind to her face: modeling the dynamics of affective states in a conversational embodied agent. Int J Human-Comput Stud 59

DeNero J, Klein D (2008) The complexity of phrase alignment problems. In: Proceedings of ACL/HLT-08, pp 25–28

Dias J, Paiva A (2005) Feeling and reasoning: a computational model for emotional characters. Springer, In EPIA Affective Computing Workshop

Ducheyne S (2008) J.S. Mill's canons of induction: from true causes to provisional ones. History and Philosophy of Logic 29(4):361–376

Galitsky B (1998) Scenario synthesizer for the internet advertisement. Proc. J. Conf. Infol Sci, Duke Univ 3:197–200

Galitsky B (2013) Transfer learning of syntactic structures for building taxonomies for search engines. Eng Appl Artif Intell 26(10):2504–2515

Galitsky B (2014) Learning parse structure of paragraphs and its applications in search. Eng Applic Artif Int 01/2014; 32:160–184

Galitsky B (2016) Theory of mind engine. Springer, Computational Autism

Galitsky B (2017a) Content Inversion for user searches and product recommendation systems and methods. US Patent 15150292

Galitsky B (2017b) Discovering rhetoric agreement between a request and response. Dial Disc 8(2)

Galitsky B (2019a) A social promotion chatbot. developing enterprise chatbots. Springer, Cham Switzerland, pp 427–463

Galitsky B (2019b) Learning discourse-level structures for question answering. Developing enterprise chatbots. Springer, Cham Switzerland, pp 177–219

Galitsky (2019c) Rhetorical agreement: maintaining cohesive conversations. In developing enterprise chatbots. Springer, Cham Switzerland, pp 327–363

Galitsky B, Kovalerchuk B (2006) Mining the blogosphere for contributor's sentiments. AAAI Spring Symposium on Analyzing Weblogs, Stanford CA

Galitsky B, Levene M (2007) Providing rating services and subscriptions with web portal infrastructures. Encyc Portal Technol Applic 855–862

Galitsky B, Kuznetsov SO (2008) Learning communicative actions of conflicting human agents. J Exp Theor Artif Intell 20(4):277–317

Galitsky B, Kuznetsov SO (2013) A web mining tool for assistance with creative writing. ECIR. European Conference on Information Retrieval, pp 828–831

Galitsky B, Ilvovsky D (2016) Discovering disinformation: a discourse-level approach. In: Fifteenth Russian National AI Conference, Smolenks Russia, pp 23–33

Galitsky B, Shpitsberg I (2016) Autistic learning and cognition. In: Computational Autism, pp 245–293

Galitsky B, McKenna EW (2017) Sentiment extraction from consumer reviews for providing product recommendations. US Patent 9,646,078

Galitsky B, Parnis A (2017) How children with Autism and machines learn to interact. Autonomy and Artificial Intelligence: A Threat or Savior, pp 195–226

Galitsky B, González MP, Chesñevar CI (2009) A novel approach for classifying customer complaints through graphs similarities in argumentative dialogue. Decis Support Syst 46(3):717–729

Galitsky B, Kuznetsov SO, MV Samokhin (2005) Analyzing conflicts with concept-based learning. International Conference on Conceptual Structures, 307–322

Galitsky B, Dobrocsi G, de la Rosa JL, Kuznetsov SO (2010) From generalization of syntactic parse trees to conceptual graphs. In: Croitoru M, Ferré S, Lukose D (eds) Conceptual structures: from information to intelligence, 18th international conference on conceptual structures, ICCS 2010, Lecture Notes in Artificial Intelligence, vol 6208, pp 185–190

Galitsky B, Dobrocsi G, de la Rosa JL, Kuznetsov SO (2011) Using generalization of syntactic parse trees for taxonomy capture on the web. In: 19th International Conference on Conceptual Structures, pp 104–117

Galitsky B, de la Rosa JL, Dobrocsi G (2012) Inferring the semantic properties of sentences by mining syntactic parse trees. Data & Knowl Eng 81–82(November):21–45

Galitsky B, Ilvovsky D, Kuznetsov SO (2013) Strok F (2013) Finding maximal common sub-parse thickets for multi-sentence search. IJCAI Workshop on Graphs and Knowledge Representation, IJCAI

Galitsky B, Ilvovsky D, Lebedeva N, Usikov D (2014) Improving trust in automation of social promotion. AAAI Spring Symposium on The Intersection of Robust Intelligence and Trust in Autonomous Systems Stanford CA

Grosz BJ, Sidner C (1986) Attention, intention, and the structure of discourse. Comput Ling 12(3):175–204

Jiang JJ, Conrath DW (1997) Semantic similarity based on corpus statistics and lexical taxonomy. In: Proceedings of the International Conference on Research in Computational Linguistics

Joty S, Carenini G, Ng RT (2015) CODRA: a novel discriminative framework for rhetorical analysis. Comput Linguist 41(3):385–435

Kipper K, Korhonen A, Ryant N, Palmer M (2008) A large-scale classification of English verbs. Lang Res Eval J 42:21–40

Lawless WF, Llinas J, Mittu R, Sofge DA, Sibley C, Coyne J, Russell S (2013) Robust Intelligence (RI) under uncertainty: mathematical and conceptual foundations of autonomous hybrid (human-machine-robot) teams, organizations and systems. Struct Dyn 6(2)

Leouski AV, Croft WB (1996) An evaluation of techniques for clustering search results. UMass Tech Report #76. https://ciir.cs.umass.edu/pubfiles/ir-76.pdf

Li J, Monroe W, Shi T, Jean S, Ritter A, Jurafsky D (2017a) Adversarial learning for neural dialogue generation. Empirical methods in natural language processing. Copenhagen, Denmark, September 7–11, pp 2157–2169

Li Y, Su H, Shen X, Li W, Cao Z, Niu S (2017b) Dailydialog: a manually labelled multi-turn dialogue dataset. arXiv preprint arXiv:1710.03957

Li J, Monroe W, Ritter A, Jurafsky D (2016) Deep reinforcement learning for dialogue generation. Empirical Methods in Natural Language Processing

Lisetti CL (2008) Embodied conversational agents for psychotherapy. CHI 2008 Workshop on Technology in Mental Health

Luan Y, Ji Y, Ostendorf M (2016) LSTM based conversation models. arXiv preprint arXiv:1603.09457

Makhalova T, Ilvovsky DI, Galitsky B (2015) Pattern structures for news clustering. FCA4AI@IJCAI, pp 35–42

Mann W, Thompson S (1988) Rhetorical structure theory: towards a functional theory of text organization. Text—Interdisc J Study Disc 8(3):243–281

Mitkov R, Ha LA, Karamanis N (2006) A computer-aided environment for generating multiple-choice test items. Nat Lang Eng Spec Iss NLP Edu Appl 12(2):177–194

Moschitti A, Quarteroni S (2011) Linguistic kernels for answer re-ranking in question answering systems. Inf Process Manage 47(6):825–842

New Scientist (2014) https://www.newscientist.com/article/mg22229634.400-one-per-cent.html

Ourioupina O, Galitsky B (2001) Application of default reasoning to semantic processing under question-answering. DIMACS Tech Report 16

Prasad R, Dinesh N, Lee A, Miltsakaki E, Robaldo L, Joshi A, Webber B (2008) The penn discourse treeBank 2.0. In: Proceedings of the 6th International Conference on Language Resources and Evaluation. Marrakech, Morocco, pp 2961–2968

Prasad R, Forbes-Riley K, Lee A (2017) Towards full text shallow discourse relation annotation: experiments with cross-paragraph implicit relations in the PDTB. In: Proceedings of the 18th Annual SIGdial Meeting on Discourse and Dialogue, pp 7–16

Piwek P, Hernault H, Prendinger H, Ishizuka M (2007) T2D: generating dialogues between virtual agents automatically from text. intelligent virtual agents. lecture notes in artificial intelligence, Springer, Berlin Heidelberg, pp 161–174

Reeves B, Nass C (1996) The media equation: how people treat computers, television, and new media like real people and places. Cambridge University Press, UK

Sidorov G, Velasquez F, Stamatatos E, Gelbukh A, Chanona-Hernández L (2014) Syntactic N-grams as machine learning features for natural language processing. Exp Syst Appl 41(3):853C860

Sordoni A, Galley M, Auli M, Brockett C, Ji Y, Mitchell M, Nie J-Y, Gao J, Dolan B (2015) A neural network approach to context-sensitive generation of conversational responses. In: Proc. of NAACL-HLT, May–June

Strok F Galitsky B, Ilvovsky D, Kuznetsov SO (2014) Pattern structure projections for learning discourse structures. In: AIMSA 2014: Artificial Intelligence: Methodology, Systems, and Applications, pp 254–260

Taboada M, Mann WC (2006) Rhetorical structure theory: looking back and moving ahead. Disc Stud 8(3):423–459

Trias i Mansilla A, de la Rosa JL, Galitsky B, Drobocsi G (2010) Automation of social networks with QA agents (extended abstract). In: van der Hoek, Kaminka, Lespérance, Luck and Sen (eds) Proceedings of 9th International Conference on Autonomous Agents and Multi-Agent Systems, AAMAS '10, Toronto, pp 1437–1438

Trias i Mansilla A, Josep Lluís de la Rosa i Esteva (2011) Asknext: an agent protocol for social search. Information Sciences

Tunkelang D (2018) Search Results Clustering. https://queryunderstanding.com/search-results-clustering-b2fa64c6c809

Vliet N, Redeker G (2011) Complex sentences as leaky units in discourse parsing. In: Proceedings of Constraints in Discourse. Agay–Saint Raphael, pp 1–9

Wu LS, Akavipat R, Maguitman A, Menczer F (2007) Adaptive peer to peer social networks for distributed content based web search. In: Social information retrieval systems: emergent technologies and applications for searching the web effectively, IGI Global, pp 155–178

Chapter 5
Concluding a CRM Session

Abstract We address the issue of how to conclude a CRM session in a comprehensive manner, to satisfy a user with the detailed extended answer with exhaustive information. For a question-answering session, the goal is to enable a user with thorough knowledge related to her initial question, from a simple fact to a comprehensive explanation. In many cases, a lengthy answer text, including multimedia content compiled from multiple sources, is the best. Whereas comprehensive, detailed answer is useful most of the times, in some cases, such an answer needs to defeat a customer claim or demand when it is unreasonable, unfair or is originated from a bad mood. We formulate a problem of finding a defeating reply for a chatbot to force completion of a chatbot session. Defeating a reply is expected to attack the user claims concerning product usability and interaction with customer support and provide an authoritative conclusive answer in an attempt to satisfy this user. We develop a technique to build a representation of a logical argument from discourse structure and to reason about it to confirm or reject this argument. Our evaluation also involves a machine learning approach and confirms that a hybrid system assures the best performance finding a defeating answer from a set of search result candidates.

5.1 Concluding a Question Answering Session

In this section, we focus on the issue of how to conclude a chatbot session in a comprehensive manner, to satisfy a user with a detailed extended answer. For a question-answering (Q/A) session, the goal is to enable a user with thorough knowledge related to her initial question, from a simple fact to a comprehensive explanation (Gomez et al. 2015). Sometimes, a short and concise answer, such as account balance or person name, suffices. However, frequently, a longer answer, including multimedia content compiled from multiple sources, is most appropriate. This answer is expected to be a comprehensive source of information on a topic, including definitions, recipes and explanations. In this section, we focus on the algorithm of forming such answers.

After an initial question of a user, a number of clarification steps usually follow. Then, once the chatbot collected all the necessary information, it can decide on what kind of answer is most suitable for a given session. For a factoid question, a brief specification of the value of the parameters or attributes in question is delivered. Otherwise, a final answer about an entity mentioned in the question, such as the introduction of a bank account or a rule for how to close it, is issued.

Traditional chatbots do not possess this feature. Instead, deterministic task-oriented chatbots provide short replies by texts indexed in a typical search index. Even worse, data-driven chit-chat chatbots never attempt to conclude a session. Statistical learning and especially deep learning-based chatbots attempt to tailor their answers to a given user session, but only brief texts can be obtained as a result. Even if these texts are meaningful and suitable, texts obtained as a result of such learning are not comprehensive most of times, addressing just the last user utterance. In a machine learning (ML) environment, typically, each reply is obtained as a result of learning, and no special attention is given to a concluding answer.

Below are the requirements for the complete, comprehensive answer that gives a user a chance to get a deep, exhaustive understanding of an entity/topic and a good way to conclude a dialogue:

1. An answer has to be compiled from multiple sources to assure an unbiased, objective description. If it is opinionated, multiple opinions from a broad spectrum of perspectives must be compiled in a coherent manner. This dialogue conclusive answer has to be comprehensive to provide sufficient information for a user to be satisfied with a chatbot session. If further questions based on this answer arise, the user can start a new chatbot session keeping in mind a specific focus;
2. An answer should be as easy to perceive and as intuitive as possible. Therefore a combination of images, videos and audio files is beneficial. The answer compilation method should be domain-independent and adhere to certain presentation standards;
3. An answer should have a table of content and references.

An example of a conclusive answer for a brief dialogue is shown in Fig. 5.1. The user requested a recommendation about an investment, received it and expressed her doubts. The chatbot provides the comprehensive conclusive answer entitled "*Why a 61% revenue growth is not enough for Alibaba*" with the detailed information on competitiveness, including the charts. In this section, we explore technologies for automated building of such answers.

One of the essential problem to be solved in building a conclusive answer is to form its logical structure from the logic of a dialogue (Galitsky and Ilvovsky 2017) and user interests, intentions and possible misunderstanding expressed in it.

5.1.1   Building a Structure of Conclusive Answer

An answer flow should reflect the structure of the preceding dialogue if it is available and non-trivial. Also, if some controversial intermediate questions and/or answers lead to it, they should be reflected in the structure of this conclusive answer. This

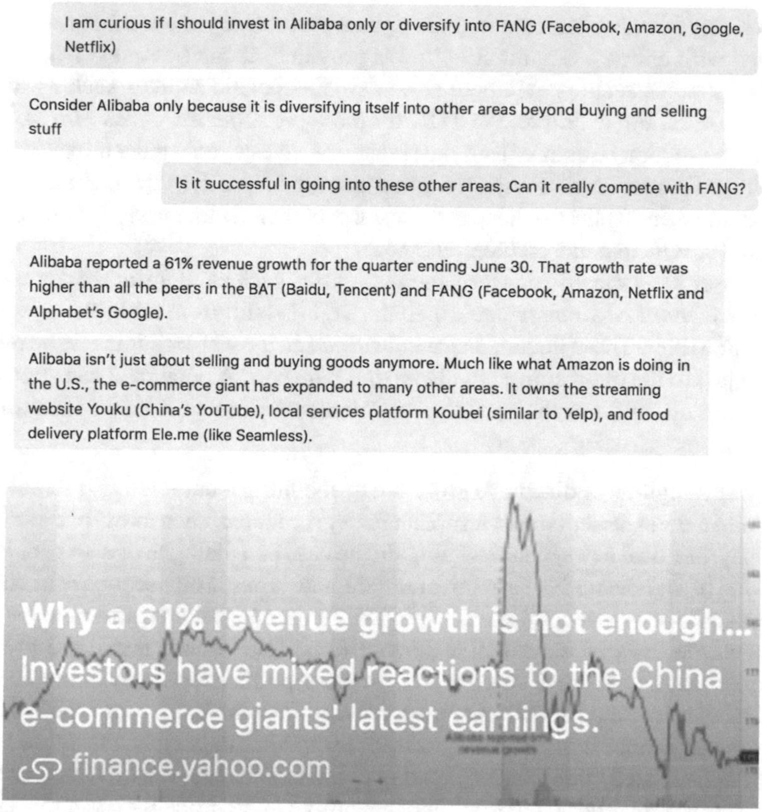

I am curious if I should invest in Alibaba only or diversify into FANG (Facebook, Amazon, Google, Netflix)

Consider Alibaba only because it is diversifying itself into other areas beyond buying and selling stuff

Is it successful in going into these other areas. Can it really compete with FANG?

Alibaba reported a 61% revenue growth for the quarter ending June 30. That growth rate was higher than all the peers in the BAT (Baidu, Tencent) and FANG (Facebook, Amazon, Netflix and Alphabet's Google).

Alibaba isn't just about selling and buying goods anymore. Much like what Amazon is doing in the U.S., the e-commerce giant has expanded to many other areas. It owns the streaming website Youku (China's YouTube), local services platform Koubei (similar to Yelp), and food delivery platform Ele.me (like Seamless).

Why a 61% revenue growth is not enough... Investors have mixed reactions to the China e-commerce giants' latest earnings.
finance.yahoo.com

Fig. 5.1 A conclusive answer to a client having a doubt concerning investment recommendation by a chatbot

answer should constitute a document with section structure reflecting either the generally accepted sequence of topics for this type of entity (such as a biography for a person or account usage rules) or the logical flow of dialogue occurred so far (such as why the first attribute, the value of the second attribute, and why the value is such and such for the third attribute). An example of the latter case would be a certain credit card, its overdraft fee amounts, reasons the card can be canceled and possibilities for interest rate increases.

For most basic questions such as product features, such documents are available and do not need to be constructed. However, for a broad number of topics and issues, when a user's interest is beyond the definition and rules, selecting an existing pre-written document is insufficient and a specific one tailored to the demands of a given user needs to be constructed.

Hence there are two kinds of sources/options for building a document structure or its table of content (TOC):

(1) If a user does not indicate in a dialogue a preference for specific issues associ-
     ated with entity, a default structure is provided. It can be mined from general
     web sources such as Wikipedia and domain-specific sources such as Investo-
     pedia.com. For example, the TOC for the topic *Adjusted Gross Margin* would
     use the section structure from the respective Investopedia page https://www.inv
     estopedia.com/terms/a/adjusted-gross-margin.asp such as the main definitions,
     treatment in depth, associated topics and others. In this case, it is possible to
     build a TOC in a hierarchical manner.
(2) If a user has a specific concern about an entity, such as '*Why banks can increase
     APR without advance notice*', then the TOC is built from multiple documents'
     section titles. These documents are identified on the web or intranet to be relevant
     not just to the main entity but also to the *Why* part. A document can start with a
     section on APR but then proceed to various cases on how banks increased the
     APRs and associated issues.

We use a high-level discourse structure of the human-authored text to automatically build a domain-dependent template for a given topic, such as event description,
biography, political news, chat and blog. In the case of a dialogue or a text containing
some kind of argumentative structure, this template is based on a sequence of communicative actions. In a general case, we follow a certain epistemic structure extracted
from multiple texts in a particular domain (e.g., for a music event, we present a
performer biography, previous concerts, previous partnerships, and future plans).

Let us consider the following dialogue and its conclusive answer (Table 5.1).

The reader can see that this dialogue leads to Option 2 rather than to Option 1, since
the user is frustrated about the NSF and is trying to understand why it happened and
how to avoid it. A generic answer about an entity would probably upset this chatbot
user further since he believes he knows general stuff about NSF. Therefore, the
conclusive answer should focus on a specific user issue/misunderstanding exposed
in the previous utterances of a dialogue.

To form a TOC from the above dialogue, the following phrases from user utterances need to be used as queries to establish the section structure of the conclusive
answer:

1. *Non-sufficient fund fee (NSF)*;
2. *Why was I charged*;
3. *Make a deposit*;
4. *Make a payment for a lower amount.*

These phrases (extended with synonyms) should match some section structures
of certain documents about NSF and banking customer support logs: they will form
a skeleton of the resultant answer.

A good way to discover attributes for entities to form a structure of a document
is an auto-complete feature for web search. If an entity in the preceding dialogue
is '*Edison invented*', then the final concluding document can have the following
TOC (Fig. 5.2). These auto-complete results (Google 2018) are the queries to the
document index on the one hand and the section titles on the other hand.

Table 5.1 Two options for dialogue flow

C(customer): Why was I charged a Non-sufficient fund fee (NSF)? Bank: Paying out of your account, you made your balance negative at some point C: But I first made a deposit and then made a payment for a lower amount Bank: Your deposit might not has been processed by the time you made your payment C: How can I stay positive on my account balance? Bank (with conclusive answer)	
Option 1: Generic Answer about an entity ***Non-sufficient Fund Fee (NSF)*** *Definition: Non-sufficient Fund Fee is a fee charged by the bank...* *Amount...* *Ways to avoid...* *Why banks charge NSF...*	Option 2: Answer specifically addressing customer concern ***Non-sufficient Fund Fee (NSF): making sure your balance is positive*** *Check deposits...* *Processing time...* *Inter-bank transactions...* *Link accounts...*

🔍 edison invented
🔍 edison invented **the light bulb**
🔍 edison invented **dc**
🔍 edison invented **the phonograph**
🔍 edison invented **the telephone**
🔍 edison invented **electric bulb**

To build a hierarchical TOC, we form search queries as entity (document title) plus the discovered section title: { '*Edison invented the light bulb*', '*Edison invented the phonograph*', …} (Galitsky 2015).

For the first query, we visualize the types of light bulbs (following Google search), which can form subsections of the section "Light bulbs" (Fig. 5.3 on the top). For the second query, we obtain the search results and attempt to extract noun phrases which sound as section titles (on the bottom). Such noun phrases should include two–three modifiers (three-four words total) and do not include very specific infrequent words, non-English words and non-alphanumeric tokens.

The infrastructure for preparing content for building answers is shown in Fig. 5.4. Various available sources are used, including the written documents and web pages explaining entities, their attributes and specifying business rules. Case-based information can be available in the form of customer support logs, various forms of corresponding with customers or internal issue logs. All these sources with diverse structures need to be converted into a unified form which adheres to the following:

- A chunk of text needs to contain a paragraph-size text: two to six sentences, 60–150 words;
- This chunk of text should be self-contained; it should neither start with reference to a previous paragraph nor end with reference to the following one.

This assessment can be made by means of discourse-level analysis (Chap. 1 Volume 2) or in a simpler, string-based manner. Chunk-of-text extractor performs the task according to the above requirements. Once chunks of text are extracted from various sources, they are put into the index so they can be combined in a chatbot answer document.

Chunks of text to be inserted into an answer document need to be extracted from a proper area at a webpage or a proper section of a document, and cleaned. We follow (Baroni et al. 2008; Cai et al. 2003; Pasternack and Roth 2009) for the algorithm of text extraction from a webpage. Given a page, we need to decide if the page contains an article with the desired content, and if it does, find a contiguous block of HTML on the webpage, starting with the first word in the article and ending with the last. Finally, we need to remove everything other than the article text (and its included markup tags) itself, such as ads, from the extracted block and output the result. When

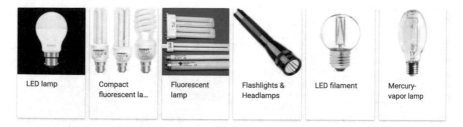

| LED lamp | Compact fluorescent la... | Fluorescent lamp | Flashlights & Headlamps | LED filament | Mercury-vapor lamp |

ⓘ https://www.google.ru/search?newwindow=1&rlz=1C5CHFA_enUS734US735&biw=1087&bih

History of the Cylinder Phonograph Inventing Entertainment: The ... ⑦
https://www.loc.gov/.../edison...of-edison.../history-of-the-cylinder-phonograph/ ▾
The phonograph was developed as a result of Thomas **Edison's** work on two other ... Collection
Inventing Entertainment: The Early Motion Pictures and Sound ...

Phonograph - Wikipedia ⑦
https://en.wikipedia.org/wiki/Phonograph ▾
The phonograph is a device for the mechanical recording and reproduction of sound. In its later ... **The
phonograph was invented** in 1877 by Thomas **Edison**.
Edison's Phonograph Doll · Phonograph cylinder ⑦ · Production of phonograph ... ⑦

The Phonograph - Thomas Edison National Historical Park (U.S. ... ⑦
https://www.nps.gov/edis/learn/kidsyouth/the-phonograph.htm ▾
Feb 26, 2015 - In 1885, Thomas **Edison** wrote, "I have not heard a bird sing since I was ... The first
phonograph was **invented** in 1877 at the Menlo Park lab.

Edison's Invention of the Phonograph - ThoughtCo ⑦
https://www.thoughtco.com › Humanities › History & Culture › American History ▾
May 2, 2018 - Thomas **Edison** achieved widespread early fame by **inventing the phonograph** and
startling the public by demonstrating a machine that could ...

Thomas Alva Edison patents the phonograph - Feb 19, 1878 ... ⑦
www.history.com/this-day-in-history/thomas-alva-edison-patents-the-phonograph ▾
200,521 for his **invention—the phonograph**—on this day In 1878. **Edison's invention** came about as spin-
off from his ongoing work in telephony and telegraphy.

How the Phonograph Changed Music Forever Arts & Culture ... ⑦
https://www.smithsonianmag.com/.../phonograph-changed-music-forever-180957677... ▾
Much like streaming music services today are reshaping our relationship with music, **Edison's invention**
redefined the entire industry.

Fig. 5.3 A visualization of attributes for an entity (on the top). Extracting phrases for topics from search results (on the web, intranet or an arbitrary document index, on the bottom)

the first word or last word is nested within one or more pairs of tags, the relevant opening and ending tags are appended to the beginning and ending of the extracted block, respectively. Otherwise, when this nesting is not as above, this one or more pairs of tags can be left open, disrupting the article text's formatting, so we ignore this case.

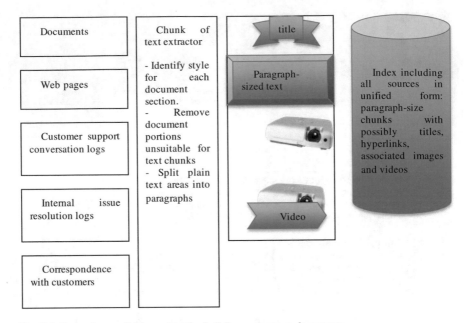

Fig. 5.4 Preparing available content for building answers as documents

A chart for the algorithm for building the structure of a conclusive answer is shown in Fig. 5.5. Firstly, a right step in the dialogue to conclude it needs to be determined (a component on the top). Also, a conclusive comprehensive answer is not always a good end for a dialogue. If a dialogue leads to a transaction or a user seems to be knowledgeable enough, then no comprehensive answer would be required: the dialogue will be concluded with a transaction confirmation and user knowledge confirmation, respectively.

Depending on the dialogue type, we build the structure of a conclusive answer (Option 1 and Option 2 from Table 5.1). On the left, we build sections of conclusive answer from the structure of how an entity and its attributes are introduced. On the right, we follow the questions, disagreements and misunderstanding of user utterances about an entity.

5.1.2   Content Compilation Algorithm

The chart for the text fragment mining algorithm is shown in Fig. 5.6. We start with the seed, one or multiple sentences, each of which will form one or more paragraphs about the respective topics of the TOC. These seed sentences can be viewed as either headers or informational centroids of content to be compiled. We now iterate through each original sentence, build a block of content for each and then merge all blocks, preceded by their seed sentences together, similar to (Sauper and Barzilay 2009).

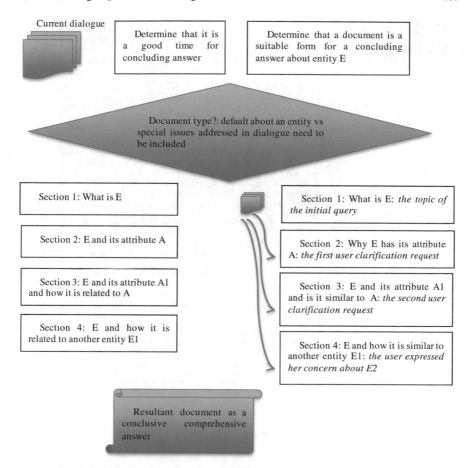

Fig. 5.5 An algorithm for relying on the current dialogue to form a conclusive answer

To find relevant sentences on the web for a seed sentence, we form query as extracted significant noun phrases from this seed sentence: either longer one (three or more keywords, which means two or more modifiers for a noun, or an entity, such as a proper noun). If such queries do not deliver a significant number of relevant sentences formed from search results, we use the whole sentence as a search engine query, filtering our content that is a duplicate to the seed (Galitsky and Kuznetsov 2013).

The formed queries are run via search engine API or scraped, using Bing; search results are collected. We then loop through the parts of the snippets to see which sentences are relevant to the seed one and which are not. For all sentences obtained from snippets, we verify appropriateness to form content on the one hand and relevance to the seed sentence on the other hand. Appropriateness is determined based on grammar rules: to enter a paragraph cohesively, a sentence needs to include a verb phrase and be opinionated (Galitsky and Chen 2009). We filter out sentences that

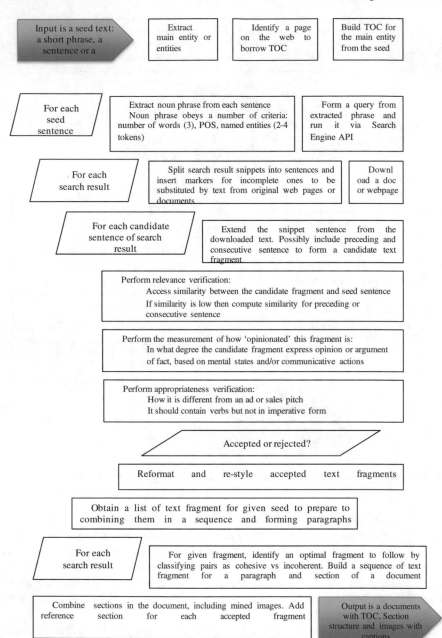

Fig. 5.6 A chart of the content compilation algorithm

look like one or another form of advertisement, a call to buy a product, or encourages other user activity by means of an imperative verb.

Relevance is determined based on the operation of syntactic generalization (Galitsky et al. 2012; Galitsky 2017), where the bag-of-words approach is extended towards extracting commonalities between the syntactic parse trees of seed sentence (Galitsky 2012; Sidorov 2013, 2014) and the text mined on the web. The syntactic generalization score is computed as cardinality of maximal common sub-graph between the parse trees of the seed and candidate sentences or text fragments. Syntactic generalization allows a domain-independent semantic measure of topical similarity, delivering stronger relevance than the search engine itself or the keyword statistics.

In addition to syntactic generalization, the tool verifies the common entities between seed and mined sentence and applies general appropriateness metric. The overall score includes syntactic generalization score (the cardinality of a maximal set of common syntactic sub-trees, Chap. 2 Volume 1) and appropriateness score to filter out less suitable sentences. Finally, mined sentences are re-styled and re-formatted to better fit together. The following section explains how paragraphs are formed from the text fragments.

To find relevant sentences on the web for a seed sentence, we form a query as extracted significant noun phrases from this seed sentence: either longer one (three or more keywords, which means two or more modifiers for a noun, or an entity, such as a proper noun). If such queries do not deliver a significant number of relevant sentences formed from the search results, we use the whole sentence as a search engine query, filtering out the content that is duplicate to the seed.

The formed queries are run via search engine API or scraped, using Bing, Yahoo API or Google, as well as their "/news" or "/blogs" subdomains depending on the topic of generated content; the search results are collected. We then loop through the parts of the snippets to see which sentences are relevant to the seed one and which are not. If only a fragment of a sentence occurs in the snippet, we need to go to the original page, download it, find this sentence and extract it.

For all sentences obtained from snippets, we verify appropriateness to form a conclusive answer text on the one hand and relevance to the seed sentence on the other hand. Appropriateness is determined based on grammar rules: to enter a paragraph cohesively, a sentence needs to include a verb phrase and/or be opinionated; mental space of cohesive information flow has been explored, for example, in Galitsky et al. (2008). Relevance is determined based on the operation of syntactic generalization (Galitsky et al. 2010), where the bag-of-words approach is extended towards extracting commonalities between the syntactic parse trees of a seed sentence and the one mined on the web. Syntactic generalization allows a domain-independent semantic measure of topical similarity between a pair of sentences (Vo et al. 2015). Without syntactic generalization, a combination of sentences mined on the web would not necessarily form a meaningful text.

In addition to syntactic generalization, the tool verifies common entities between the seed and the mined sentence and applies a general appropriateness metric. The overall score includes the syntactic generalization score (the cardinality of the maximal common system of the syntactic sub-trees) and the appropriateness score to filter out less suitable sentences. Finally, the mined sentences are modified and reformatted to better fit together and are joined to form paragraphs.

5.1.3   A Log of Answer Generation

Imagine we have a user utterance (seed):

(S)*Give me a break, there is no reason why you can't retire in ten years if you had been a rational investor and not a crazy trader.*

We start with building TOC for the main entity here, *rational investor*. The other candidates for the main entity are rejected since they are too broad (such as *retire*, a single-word concept), or occur with negation *not a crazy trader*.

Searching Wikipedia, we find a page for *rational investor* with redirect to *Homo economicus* https://en.wikipedia.org/wiki/Homo_economicus, where the following TOC is scraped:

1	History of the term
2	Model
3	Criticisms
4	Responses
5	Perspectives
6	Homo sociologicus
...	

The items which can appear on the bottom, such as *References*, are common for all entities.

For each TOC item, we add a section title keyword to the seed expression. For the default section (here, *Model*), we just use the seed. We need to form queries that contain the main entities from the utterance, retain the meaning but are not too restrictive at the same time.

The main entity here is *retirement* in the form of the verb *retire* and it needs to be constrained by the noun phrase that follows *rational investor*. To form the second query, we combine *rational investor* and the next noun phrase, *not a crazy trader*. Notice that just a single noun phrase with two words is not restrictive enough, and a part of a sentence, such as elementary discourse unit, like '*there is no reason why you can't retire in ten years*' would be too restrictive. Four-five keywords in a query are optimal. Hence two following queries are formed for search engine API:

(Q1) + retire + rational + investor

(Q2) + rational + investor not + crazy + trader

This is not a frequent user query, so web search results need to be further processed: https://www.google.com/search?q=%2Bretire+%2Brational+%2Binvestor.

The following snippet is selected as a candidate to be included in a conclusive answer since it contains all keywords from (Q1).

How to Make Rational Investing Decisions | Sound Mind Investing
https://soundmindinvesting.com/articles/.../how-to-make-rational-investing-
decisions
Nov 1, 2014 - How to Make **Rational Investing** Decisions ... pleasant and you'll
probably have more money to spend in **retirement** and leave to your heirs.

We download this webpage, extract text from it, and find a paragraph that corresponds to the above snippet. We do that for all search results, which contains all keywords from the query.

We consider two text fragments from the search results:

(A1a) *If you take the time to understand the psychology of* **rational investing**, *you'll make your life more pleasant and you'll probably have more money to spend in* **retirement***and leave to your heirs.*

(A1b) *One needs many years of relevant data before deciding if a fund manager is truly skilled in* **rational investing***or just lucky. Hence, by the time you have enough statistically relevant data to rely on, the manager is likely nearing* **retirement***.*

We now show the sentence similarity assessment via generalization operator (Chap. 2 Volume 1):

$A \char94 A_{1a} = $ RST-*Condition* (VP (…, NP *rational investing*),*- *retire*)

$A \char94 A_{1b} = $ NP *rational investing*), *- retire.*

One can see that in the first search result A_{1a} *retire* and *rational investing* are connected in a similar way to the seed S: *relational investing* is connected by the rhetorical relation *Condition* to the phrase including *retire*. In A_{1b}, the syntactic matching part is the same, but these phrases occur in two different sentences and are related in a much more complex indirect way than in the seed. Hence A_{1a} is a good fragment to include in the conclusive answer, and A_{1b} is not so good.

Once we obtain an unordered list of text fragments for a section, we need to find an optimal order to form the section text. For example, if both above text fragments are accepted (not just the first one), the second should follow the first since it contains the conclusion … *Hence*…. And both these fragments are related to the same main entity. Still, the resultant text would not read well since there is a strong deviation of topics towards finding an account manager, which is not the main topic of this section. Given an unordered set of text fragments or paragraphs, we cannot assure cohesiveness of the resultant text but instead at least find an optimal order for these fragments, to minimize a disturbance of content flow and a coherence of the resultant text.

To solve the problem of an optimal sequence, we rely on discourse analysis. It turns out that certain features of logical organization of text encoded via discourse trees are much stronger criteria of text cohesiveness in comparison with maintaining a topic, as most content generation algorithms do. We devote Chap. 1 Volume 2 to this topic.

5.1.4   Modeling the Content Structure of Texts

In this section, we consider the problem of modeling the content structure of texts within a specific domain, in terms of the attributes of an entity this text express and the order in which these topics appear. Some research intended to characterize texts in terms of domain-independent rhetorical elements, such as schema items (McKeown 1985) or rhetorical relations (Mann and Thompson 1988; Marcu 1997). Conversely, Barzilay and Lee (2004) focus on content, a domain-dependent dimension of the structure of the text. They present an effective knowledge-lean method for learning content models from un-annotated documents, utilizing a novel adaptation of algorithms for Hidden Markov Models. The authors apply their approach to two complementary tasks: information ordering and extractive summarization. The experiments showed that incorporating content models in these applications gives a substantial improvement.

In general, the flow of the text is determined by the topic change: how attributes of an entity evolve. (Barzilay and Lee 2004) designed a model that can specify, for example, that articles about mountains typically contain information about height, climate, assents, and climbers. Instead of manually determining the evolution of attributes (the topics for a given domain), a distributional view can be taken. It is possible to machine learn these patterns of attribute evolution directly from un-annotated texts via analysis of word distribution patterns. (Harris 1982) wrote that a number of word recurrence patterns are correlated with various types of discourse structures.

Advantages of a distributional perspective include both drastic reduction in human effort and recognition of "topics" that might not occur to a human expert and yet, when explicitly modeled, aid in applications. The success of the distributional approach depends on the existence of recurrent patterns. In arbitrary document collections, such recurrent patterns might be too variable to be easily detected by statistical means. However, research has shown that texts from the same domain tend to exhibit high similarity (Wray 2002). At the same time, from the cognitive science perspective, this similarity is not random and is instead systematic since text structure facilitates text comprehension by readers and their capability of recall (Bartlett 1932).

We assume that text chunks convey information about a single attribute of an entity (a single topic). Specifying the length of text chunks can define the granularity of the induced attribute/topic: we select the average paragraph length. We build a content model as a Hidden-Markov Model in which each state s corresponds to a distinct topic and generates sentences relevant to that topic according to a state-specific language model p_s. Note that standard n-gram language models can therefore be considered to be degenerate (single-state) content models. State transition probabilities give the probability of changing from a given topic to another, thereby capturing constraints attribute evolution (topic shift).

We rely on the bigram language models, so that the probability of an n-word sentence $x = w_1 \, w_2 \, \dots \, w_n$ being generated by a state s

$$p_s(x) = \prod_{i=1}^{n} p_s(w_i | w_{i-1})$$

We will now describe state bigram probabilities $p_s(w_i \mid w_{i-1})$.

To initialize a set of attributes by partitioning all of the paragraphs (or text chunks) from the documents in a given domain-specific collection into clusters, we do the following. First, we create clusters via complete-link clustering, measuring sentence similarity by the cosine metric using word bigrams as features. Then, given our knowledge that documents may sometimes discuss new and/or irrelevant content as well, we create an AUX cluster by merging together all clusters containing # paragraphs < t (selected threshold). We rely on the assumption that such clusters consist of "outlier" sentences.

Given a set $= c_1, c_2, ..., c_m$ of m clusters, where c_m is the AUX cluster, we construct a content model with corresponding states $s_1, s_2, ..., s_m$. we refer to s_m as the insertion state.

For each state s_i $i < m$ bigram probabilities (which induce the state's sentence-emission probabilities) are estimated using smoothed counts from the corresponding cluster

$$ps_i(w'|w) \underset{=\!=\!=}{def} \frac{f_{ci}(ww') + \delta_1}{f_{ci}(w) + \delta_1|V|},$$

where f $c_1(y)$ is the frequency with which word sequence y occurs within the sentences in cluster c_i, and V is the vocabulary.

We want the insertion state s_m to simulate digressions or unseen attributes. We ignore the content of AUX cluster and force the language model to be complementary to those of the other states by setting

$$ps_m(w'|w) \underset{=\!=\!=}{def} \frac{1 - \max_{i:i<m} ps_i(w'|w)}{\sum_{u \in V}(1 - \max_{i:i<m} ps_i(u|w))}.$$

Our state-transition probability estimates arise from considering how the paragraphs from the same document are distributed across the clusters. For two clusters c and c' we define $D(c, c')$ as the number of documents in which a paragraph from c immediately precedes one from c'. $D(c)$ is the number of documents containing paragraphs from c. For any two states si and s_j, $i, j < m$, we rely on the following smooth estimate of the probability of transitioning from s_i to s_j:

$$p(s_j|s_i) = \frac{D(c_i, c_j) + \delta_2}{D(c_i) + \delta_2 m}.$$

Programming in NL is another area where the content structure of text is essential (Galitsky and Usikov 2008).

5.1.5 Building Answer Document Based on Similarity and Compositional Semantics

The vector representations of the desired document can be obtained using a paragraph vector model (Le and Mikolov 2014) that computes continuous distributed vector representations of varying-length texts. The source documents' section that is semantically close (or similar) to the desired document is identified in this vector space using cosine similarity. The structure of similar articles can then be emulated, the important sections identified and assign relevant web-content or intranet content assigned to the sections.

The entire Wikipedia is leveraged to obtain D-dimensional representations of words/entities as well as documents using the paragraph vector distributed memory model (Le and Mikolov 2014). Similar articles are identified using cosine similarity between the vector representations of the missing entity and representations of the existing entities (entities that have corresponding articles, see Chap. 1 of Volume 1). A content from similar articles is used to train multi-class classifiers that can assign web-retrieved content on the red-linked entity to relevant sections of the article. The system architecture is shown in Fig. 5.7. The paragraph vector distributed memory model is used to identify similar documents to rely upon on the one hand and also to make an inference of vector representations of new paragraphs retrieved from the web on the other hand.

A sequence of words is taken from a similar document and approach the last word that can be reused. Then the next word is predicted using PV-DM. The PV-DM model is based on the principle that several contexts sampled from the paragraph can be used to predict the next word. Given a sequence of T words ($w_1, w_2, ..., w_T$), the task is to maximize the average log probability. In the top equation, c is the size of the

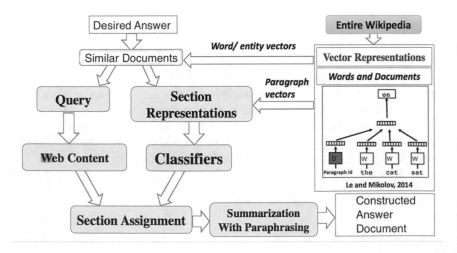

Fig. 5.7 Document generation approach based on similar document and Wikipedia content

context (number of words before and after the current word to be used for training). The conditional probability of w_{t+j} given w_t can be obtained by the softmax function (Bridle 1990) in the equation below, where v_{wt+j} and v_w refers to the output and the input vector representations of the word w, respectively. W refers to the total number of words in the vocabulary

$$F = \frac{1}{T} \sum_{t=1}^{t=T} \sum_{-c \leq j \leq c, j \neq 0} \log p\left(w_{t+j}|w_t\right)$$

$$p\left(w_{t+j}|w_t\right) = \frac{\exp\left(u'_{w_{t+j}} T_{uw_t}\right)}{\sum_{w-1}^{W} \exp\left(u'_w T_{uw_t}\right)}$$

5.2 Defeating Conclusion of a Support Session

5.2.1 Introducing Defeating Reply

In spite of the great success with chatbots, their deployment in the customer support domain is still not robust enough. As mobile and portable devices become popular and enable a number of new products and services, customer expectations of the quality and availability of customer support have significantly raised. Customers expect not only answers to basic questions but also an assistance with resolving problems such as unsatisfactory product features or issues with a service rendered.

Building controllable task-oriented chatbots capable of providing a defeating reply is an essential milestone in developing chatbots that can solve customer problems rather than just providing a recommendation or performing a basic transaction.

In many cases, customers want to take advantage of an organization, are very demanding, or just in a bad mood. Supporting a conversation with such customer, the chatbot needs at some point to put this customer in his place by a authoritative answer defeating customer's claims. The chatbot would need to break the argumentation patterns (Chesñevar et al. 2009) employed by the customer and explain that the customer is wrong. The chatbot needs to reject customer claims and convince the customer that the company has done its best to take care of her problems.

In this section, we explore what kind of discourse representation is required to confirm that a given answer is a good defeating reply to a user utterance. As a result, we will build a filter on top of a generic search engine that would select answers defeating the arguments in customer requests, if appropriate.

In these considerations, we will not follow the "customer is always right" paradigm but instead, demonstrate how a demanding request can be defeated.

Miss Duncan:

'My dear Mr. Shaw: I beg to remind you that as you have the greatest brain in the world, and I have the most beautiful body, it is our duty to posterity to have a child.'

Whereupon Mr. Shaw replied to Miss Duncan: 'My dear Miss Duncan: I admit that I have the greatest brain in the world and that you have the most beautiful body, but it might happen that our child would have my body and your brain. Therefore, I respectfully decline.'

A discourse tree, showing how Show's thoughts are organized, is shown in Fig. 5.8. Firstly, his thoughts are split into "*atomic thoughts*, elementary discourse units. Secondly, they are organized in a hierarchical structure and are interconnected by rhetorical relations. These relations range from default ones of *Elaboration* to specific ones showing the flow of author thoughts such as *Contrast* and *Attribution*. *Contrast* here is essential to show that Miss Duncan proposed a thing, but it was rejected in *Mr. Shaw's* reply. Multiple relations of Attribution attach the subjects What of what was said by the agents to the communicative actions (such as *admit(Who, What)*). Hence discourse tree is essential to represent a logic of a text expressing various interactions between people, such as a defeating reply of *Mr. Shaw*. It does not matter which words and which semantic means are used to defeat a proposal: what is essential is a logical structure of this defeat. Discourse trees are associated with the genre of

```
elaboration (LeftToRight)
  same-unit
   TEXT:My dear Mr. Shaw :
   contrast (RightToLeft)
    attribution (RightToLeft)
      TEXT:I beg to remind you
      joint
       attribution (LeftToRight)
         TEXT:that
         TEXT:as you have the greatest brain in the world ,
         TEXT:and I have the most beautiful body ,
       elaboration (LeftToRight)
        TEXT:it is our duty to posterity
        TEXT:to have a child .
   elaboration (LeftToRight)
    elaboration (LeftToRight)
     TEXT:Whereupon Mr. Shaw replied to Miss Duncan :
     elaboration (LeftToRight)
      TEXT:My dear Miss Duncan :
      attribution (RightToLeft)
       TEXT:I admit
       joint
         TEXT:that I have the greatest brain in the world
        contrast
         TEXT:and that you have the most beautiful body ,
         attribution (RightToLeft)
          TEXT:but it might happen
          TEXT:that our child would have my body and your brain .
    TEXT: Therefore , I respectfully decline .
```

Fig. 5.8 Discourse tree for a pair of utterances suggestion-denial

texts; shorts articles can be clustered based on discourse information only without involving keywords (Makhalova et al. 2015).

One can see that the main feature of a concise, convincing answer is the proper handling of entities. In this case, the reply should characterize body and brain. To defeat the proposal of the initiator of this conversation, the reply must include opposite sentiments to what was proposed. Hence we have a mapping:

$$\text{you ... brain - I ... body}$$
$$\downarrow \quad \downarrow \quad \downarrow \quad\quad \downarrow$$
$$\text{my ... body - your ... brain}$$

Our second example is related to customer support in finance, specifically, to foreign transaction fees:

> Q: '*I am an American expat living in the Republic of Panama. I just want you to know that I am thoroughly disgusted with the way you do business, because you charged me an overdraft fee, although I have Overdraft Protection. In spite of that your customer Non-Service wrote to tell me I should watch my balances! Despite of that you charged me several times for late fees on Sunday due dated bills, although they have paid on Monday! Why are you now charging a Foreign Transaction Fee of 3%? I asked about this but the form letter sent to me told me about fees for withdrawing from ATMs. However I have never in my life used an ATM, because I do not want to pay to withdraw my own money!*';
>
> A: Many banks still charge foreign transaction fees for withdrawing cash at foreign ATMs, even if foreign credit card purchase transactions can occur fee-free. Banks have to convert your money spent into U.S. dollars so they can charge your account. That conversion costs money, and some card-issuing banks pass that cost along to consumers in the form of foreign transaction fees. Some banks waive certain fees if you withdraw money from partner bank ATMs. For example, Bank of America generally charges 3 percent fee to withdraw cash from a foreign ATM. However, if you use an ATM at one of the company's Global Alliance Partners, the $5 fee is waived.

An answer must address a problem raised in question in a comprehensive, exhaustive manner. An answer cannot just agree to please the user, be a submission to her demand. Instead, to benefit a company, a good answer should deny user demand and instead propose a solution explained to be beneficial for both parties. To do that, one or another premise in user demand needs to be defeated. In our example, instead of proposing compensation for the incurred fees, the bank representative defeats user claims that fees are unavoidable and unjust and mentions an option to avoid them.

Discourse Trees for this question and answer are shown in Fig. 5.9. Notice that both the user and customer service representative (CSA) used texts with heavy argumentation; in addition, the user tries to amplify her point with strong negative sentiment (shown as [−]). The user relies on rhetorical relations of *Attribution, Explanation*

contrast (LeftToRight)
  elaboration (LeftToRight)
   TEXT:' I am an American expat living in the Republic of Panama .
    elaboration (LeftToRight)
     attribution (RightToLeft)
      TEXT:I just want you to know
       elaboration (LeftToRight)
        TEXT:that I am thoroughly disgusted with the way [--]
         explanation (LeftToRight)
          TEXT:you do business ,
           contrast (LeftToRight)
            TEXT:because you charged me an overdraft fee ,
            TEXT:although I have Overdraft Protection .
      elaboration (LeftToRight)
       attribution (RightToLeft)
        TEXT:In spite of that Your customer Non-Service wrote to tell me [--]
        TEXT:I should watch my balances !
       elaboration (LeftToRight)
        contrast (LeftToRight)
         TEXT:Despite of that you charged me several times for late fees on Sunday
due dated bills ,
          TEXT:although they have paid on Monday !
          elaboration (LeftToRight)
           TEXT:Why are you now charging a Foreign Transaction Fee of 3% ?
            contrast (RightToLeft)
             TEXT:I asked about this
              elaboration (LeftToRight)
               TEXT:but the form letter told me about fees
               TEXT:for withdrawing from ATMs .
    explanation (LeftToRight)
     TEXT:However I have never in my life used an ATM ,
     TEXT:because I do not want to pay to withdraw my own money !

  elaboration (LeftToRight)
   elaboration (LeftToRight)
    explanation (LeftToRight)
     contrast (LeftToRight)
      TEXT:Many banks still charge foreign transaction fees for withdrawing cash
at foreign ATMs ,
       TEXT:even if foreign credit card purchase transactions can occur fee-free .
      enablement (LeftToRight)
       TEXT:This is because banks have to convert your money spent into U.S.
dollars
        TEXT:so they can charge your account .
        elaboration (LeftToRight)
         joint
          TEXT:That conversion costs money ,

Fig. 5.9   A pair of discourse trees for Q and A

> TEXT:and therefore , some card-issuing banks pass that cost along to consumers in the form of foreign transaction fees .
>   **condition** (LeftToRight)
>   TEXT:Some banks waive certain fees
>   TEXT:if you withdraw money from partner bank ATMs .
>   contrast (RightToLeft)
>   TEXT:For example , Bank of America generally charges 3%fee to withdraw cash from a foreign ATM .
>   condition
>   TEXT:However ,
>   TEXT:if you use an ATM at one of the company ' s GA Partners , then the $ 5 fee is waived .

Fig. 5.9 (continued)

and multiple Contrasts to bring her point across: *fees should not have been charged*. CSA attacks user claims with *Explanation, Attribution* and also multiple *Contrast* relations. Hence the CSA attempts to mimic the discourse of the user claims to defeat them and bring his point across that banks have to charge foreign transaction fees but they can be avoided under certain condition (using certain ATMs).

We show the correspondence between the claims of the user and the CSA as a mapping between the phrases in elementary discourse units (EDU) of the Discourse Tree pair. A user disagreement with the problem described by the phrase "charging a Foreign Transaction Fee" is addressed by the CSA phrase "still charge foreign transaction fees." For the user, this phrase occurs in the EDU for *Elaboration* (request to answer Why question) so that a *Contrast* relation follows, and for the CSA attempt to defeat, it occurs in the nucleus of *Contrast* relation. The reader can observe that this discourse tree is showing a structure for how the CSA plans his attack on user claims. In the following sections, we will explore how to deduce argument representation from a discourse tree structure similar to the one in this example.

Analogously, the verb phrase to '*pay to withdraw*' is addressed by two phrases in reply '*waive certain fees*' and '*withdraw money from partner bank ATMs*'. To provide a defeating reply, the CSA relied on *Explanation-Condition* chain of rhetorical relation to properly handle *Explanation* relation employed by the user.

To produce a more accurate representation of the argument structure of texts, we extend DTs towards communicative discourse trees, where the communicative actions extracted from text form additional labels in DT edges (Galitsky et al. 2018).

5.2.2 An Algorithm for Identifying Answers with Defeating Arguments

The architecture for selecting a defeating answer is shown in Fig. 5.10. The candidate answers/replies for a given user utterance are obtained using conventional IR means to assure relevance; each one is expected to contain the entities from the user question and the relations between them to properly match this question. Arguments need to

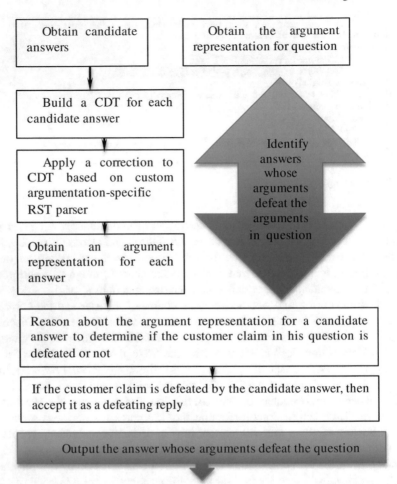

Fig. 5.10 A high-level architecture of selecting defeating answers

be extracted from both the question and each candidate answer (Galitsky et al. 2018), and a correspondence between these arguments needs to be established.

To form an argument representation, we first build CDTs and then improve them by the rules, specifically targeting assessing exact rhetorical relations interpretable in terms of arguments. These rules are a basis for an additional rhetorical post-parser that updates the rhetorical relations identified by a conventional RST parser. In many cases, a conventional RST parser determines the generic *Elaboration* and *Joint* relations which need to be further clarified and turned into *Cause, Reason, Explanation, Conclusion* and others. This is important to form an exact discourse representation of a text with arguments.

Once the clarified CDTs for the user utterance and each candidate answers are built, we convert them to R-C logical framework, which is a subject of reasoning.

The purpose of this reasoning is to determine for a given R-C representation of a candidate answer if it defeats the R-C representation of the claim in the user utterance. If the desired defeasible reasoning confirms that it is the case, this candidate answer is provided as a defeating reply.

5.2.3 Representing Nested Arguments by R-C Framework

We first define an argument representation algorithm following Apothéloz et al. (1993) and Amgoud et al. (2015). The formalism is built upon a propositional language L with the connectives $\neg$, $\vee$, $\wedge$, $\rightarrow$, $\leftrightarrow$. There are also two operators $R(.)$ and $C(.)$ and an additional negation $-$. Thus, two negation operators are needed: $\neg$ for denying propositional formulas ($\neg x$ denotes that x is false), and $-$ for denying $R(.)$ and $C(.)$.

An argument is a formula of the form $R(y)$: $(-)C(x)$. An argument is a reason for concluding a claim. It has two main parts: premises (the reason) and a conclusion. The functions R and C respectively play the roles of giving reason and concluding. Indeed, an argument is interpreted as follows: its conclusion holds because it follows, according to a given notion, from the premises. The notion refers to the nature of the link between them (e.g., the premises imply the conclusion), formally identified by the colon in the definition. However, the conclusion may be true while the functions do not hold and vice versa. The intuitive reading is as follows:

$R(y)$: $C(x)$ means that "y is a reason for concluding x".

$R(y)$: $-C(x)$ means that "y is a reason for not concluding x".

Handling of a nested argument is important for finding a defeating answer since it is insufficient to handle only the object-level or only the meta-level layer of argumentation separately. Nested arguments are central to tackling texts and dialogues: support for nested arguments and rejections has to be provided. To illustrate some of the expressive richness of our approach, Table 5.2 shows various forms of arguments and rejections allowed by our definitions (x, y, z, t are propositional formulas to simplify matters). The table is not exhaustive.

It is not shown here how to build a good argument (or a good rejection of an argument). Instead, a representation of arguments (and their rejections) are specified. If an argument or rejection occurs in a text or dialogue, then we want to extract this argument from text and represent it in L. A list of arguments in Table 5.2 shows that a diversity of logical forms can be used as a target for a natural language (NL) representation. It indicates how to use our language, rather than suggesting that there is a canonical translation of the text into the formal target language. Translating an NL sentence into discourse trees first and then into R-C logic L is shown in Table 5.3.

Our example arguments concern the functionality of a credit card. By default, credit card works (*is operational*), especially if there is a *positive account balance*. However, there are exceptions: for whatever reason, a bank may *decline a transaction*. These examples illustrate that the inner and outer reason R as well as claim C can be

Table 5.2 Discourse representation or arguments and their rejections

Basic arguments	My credit card is operational o(c). It is not blocked ¬b(c)	$R\ (\neg b(c))\!:\ C(o(c))$
	My credit card has been compromised $m(c)$. It is blocked	$R\ (b(c))\!:\ C(m(c))$
	Credit card is operational Thus, it is not possible to conclude that a charge can be declined (d(c)	$R(o(c))\!:\ -C(d(c))$
Single-embedding meta-arguments in reason R	That debit card can be used $u(c)$ because it is operational, is a reason to conclude that the balance is positive $(p(b))$	$R(R(u(c))\!:\ C(o(c)))\!:\ C(p(b))$
	That card is not declined because it has a positive balance is a reason to conclude that it has not been compromised $(m(c))$	$R(R(\neg d(c))\!:\ C(p(b)))\!:$ $C(\neg m(c))$
	Card is operational because its balance is positive, so we cannot conclude that it was blocked	$R(R(p(b))\!:\ C(o(c)))\!:\ -$ $C(b(c))$
Single-embedding meta-arguments in conclusion C	The balance on the card is negative. Thus the charge/use attempt will lead to non-sufficient fund fee $(nsf(c))$	$R(\neg b(c))\!:\ C(u(c)\!:$ $C(nsf(c)))$
	The fact that a card has been declined in the past is a reason to conclude that having a positive balance is not a sufficient reason for a credit card to always be operational	$R(d(c))\!:\ C(-R(p(b))\!:$ $C(o(c)))$
	The fact that all credit cards of team members are operational is a reason for not concluding that a decline charge of a particularly high-cost transaction $h(c)$ is a reason for team credit cards to be compromised	$R(o(c))\!:\ -C(R(h(c))\!:$ $C(m(c)))$
Double embedding of meta-arguments	Bad credit history $(ch(b))$ leads to a decline of a credit card application $(d(a(c)))$. Once a user is unable to use credit card $(u(c))$ it is hard to get a loan $(l(u))$	$R(R(ch(b))\!:\ C(d(a(c))))\!:$ $C(R(u(c))\!:\ C(l(u)))$

(continued)

Table 5.2 (continued)

	Good credit history ($ch(g)$) usually tells us that a credit card application is not declined ($d(a(c))$). However, we cannot imply that a successful credit card application leads to a loan approval (other factors play the role as well)	$R(R(ch(g)): C(d(a(c)))): -$ $C(R(d(a(c)))): C(l(u)))$

Table 5.3 Discourse trees for selected examples

My credit card is operational o(c). It is not blocked ¬b(c)		$R(\neg b(c)): C(o(c))$
My credit card has been compromised $m(c)$. It is blocked		$R(b(c)): C(m(c))$
Credit card is operational. Thus, it is not possible to conclude that a charge can be declined ($d(c)$)		$R(o(c)): -C(d(c))$

That debit card can be used $u(c)$ because it is operational, is a reason to conclude that the balance is positive ($p(b)$)	**cause**
	  explanation (LeftToRight)
	    TEXT:That debit card can be used ,
	    TEXT:because it is operational ,
	  cause (LeftToRight)
	    TEXT:is a reason
	    attribution (RightToLeft)
	     TEXT:to conclude
	     TEXT:that the balance is positive
		$R(R(u(c)): C(o(c)))$: $C(p(b))$

That card is not declined because it has a positive balance. It is a reason to conclude that it has not been compromised ($m(c)$)		$R(R(\neg d(c)): C(p(b)))$: $C(\neg m(c))$

Card is operational because its balance is positive, so we cannot conclude that it was blocked	**conclusion** (LeftToRight)
	  cause (LeftToRight)
	    TEXT:Card is operational
	    TEXT:because its balance is positive ,
	  attribution (RightToLeft)
	    TEXT:so we can not conclude
	    TEXT:that it was blocked
		$R(R(p(b)): C(o(c)))$: $-$ $C(b(c))$

The balance on the card is negative. Thus the charge or use attempt will lead to non-sufficient fund fee ($nsf(c)$)	elaboration (LeftToRight)
	    cause (LeftToRight)
	     TEXT:The balance on the card is negative
	     cause(LeftToRight)
	      TEXT:Thus the charge / use attempt will lead to
	      TEXT non-sufficient fund fee
		$R(\neg b(c)): C(u(c)$: $C(nsf(c)))$

(continued)

Table 5.3   (continued)

The fact that a card has been declined in the past is a reason to conclude that having a positive balance is not a sufficient reason for a credit card to always be operational	**reason**(LeftToRight)
	  elaboration (LeftToRight)
	    TEXT:The fact
	    TEXT:that a card has been declined in the past is a reason
	  conclusion(RightToLeft)
	    TEXT:to conclude
	  cause(LeftToRight)
	    TEXT:that having a positive balance is not a sufficient reason
	      TEXT: for a credit card to always be operational
		$R(d(c)): C(-R(p(b)):$ $C(o(c)))$

The fact that all credit cards of team members are operational is a reason for not concluding that a decline charge of a particular high cost transaction $h(c)$ is a reason for team credit cards to be compromised	elaboration (LeftToRight)
	  TEXT:The fact
	  reason(LeftToRight)
	    TEXT:that all credit cards of team members are operational is a reason
	    conclusion(RightToLeft)
	      TEXT:for not concluding
	    cause(LeftToRight)
	      TEXT:that a decline charge of a particular high cost transaction is a reason for team credit cards
	        TEXT:to be compromised
		$R(o(c)): -C(R(h(c)):$ $C(m(c)))$

Bad credit history ($ch(b)$) leads to a decline of a credit card application ($d(a(c))$). Thus once a user is unable to use credit card ($u(c)$) it is hard to get a loan ($l(u)$)	**cause**(LeftToRight)
	  cause(LeftToRight)
	    TEXT:Bad credit history
	    TEXT:leads to a decline of a credit card application .
	  cause (LeftToRight)
	    TEXT: Thus once a user is unable to use credit card
	    TEXT:it is hard to get a loan ,
		$R(R(ch(b)): C(d(a(c)))):$ $C(R(u(c)): C(l(u)))$

Good credit history ($ch(g)$) usually tells us that a credit card application is not declined ($d(a(c))$). However, we cannot imply that successful credit card application leads to a loan approval (other factors play the role as well)	**explanation** (RightToLeft)
	  cause (RightToLeft)
	    TEXT:Good credit history usually tells us
	    TEXT:that a credit card application is not declined .
	  cause
	    TEXT:However, we can not imply that successful credit card application
	    TEXT: leads to a loan approval.
		$R(R(ch(g)): C(d(a(c)))):$ $-C(R(d(a(c))): C(l(u)))$

potentially identified using argument mining techniques. Furthermore, by recursion, the inner reasons and claims can be identified by argument mining techniques. Thus, the nested structure appears to be better suited as a target language for arguments as they arise in NL dialogues and texts.

The templates in Table 5.3 can be used to extract logical atoms from EDUs, translate rhetorical relations into R-C operators and form a logical representation of

Table 5.4 Connectives providing cues for rhetorical relations

	Cause	Conclusion	Explanation	Contrast	Condition	Enablement	Elaboration	Joint	Attribution	Restatement	Comparison	Temporal
However				1								
For example			1				1	1		1		
And	1	1						1				
Meanwhile							1					
Therefore	1											
Hence	1											
Finally	1			1								
Nevertheless				1								
Instead				1								
Moreover												
Then	1	1	1		1							
On the other hand		1		1			1					
In particular							1			1		
Indeed		1					1		1	1		
Overall		1	1									
In other words		1								1		
Rather												
By contrast				1							1	
By then												1
Otherwise	1			1	1							

(continued)

Table 5.4 (continued)

	Cause	Conclusion	Explanation	Contrast	Condition	Enablement	Elaboration	Joint	Attribution	Restatement	Comparison	Temporal
Thus		1	1		1							
Yet				1			1			1		1
Since	1		1		1							
To						1			1			
But				1			1			1	1	
If	1				1							
As a result	1	1					1					
Because	1		1									
By						1			1			
Due	1								1			
When					1		1					1

arguments. To do that, we first build a semantic representation for the expressions of interest related to banking $ch(g)$. Then we build discourse trees and attach these semantic representations to elementary discourse units. The determined structure of the discourse tree is then forms R-C representations in L, which are subject to argumentation analysis in the downstream components.

5.2.4 Reasoning with Arguments Extracted from Text

In this section, we follow (Amgoud et al. 2015) in describing a reasoning system that takes an argument representation of a question and that of an answer and verifies that the latter defeats the former. We treat a set of arguments and their rejections as a set of formulae, which is a subject of a reasoning system application. A consequence operator $|$— is the least closure of a set of inference rules extended with one meta-rule.

A meta-rule expresses that one can reverse any inference rule

$$\frac{R(y) : F}{-R(y) : G} \quad \text{into} \quad \frac{R(y) : G}{-R(y) : F}$$

This inference rule reversing process occurs whenever negation occurs in front of a leftmost "R" so that, in the general case, an inference rule where $i, j \in \{0, 1\}$.

As to the regular inference rules, we start from consistency:

$$\frac{R(y) : C(x)}{-R(y) : -C(x)} \quad \frac{R(y) : C(x)}{-R(y) : -C(x)}$$

Reasons are interchangeable. This rule is referred to as mutual support:

$$\frac{R(y) : C(x) \quad R(x) : C(y) \quad R(y) : C(z)}{-R(x) : -C(z)}$$

The next rule gathers different reasons for the same conclusion within a single argument:

$$\frac{R(y) : C(x) \quad R(z) : C(x)}{-R(y \vee z) : -C(x)}$$

Cautious monotonicity means that the reason for an argument can be expanded with any premise it justifies. Cut expresses a form of minimality of the reason for an argument.

$$\frac{R(y) : C(z) \quad R(y) : C(x)}{R(y \wedge z) : C(x)} \quad \frac{R(y \wedge z) : C(x) \quad R(y) : C(z)}{R(y) : C(x)}$$

The two next rules describe the nesting of $R(.)$ and $C(.)$. Exportation shows how to simplify meta-arguments and permutation shows that for some forms of meta-arguments, permutations of reasons are possible

$$\frac{R(y) : C(R(z)) : C(x)}{R(y \wedge z) : C(x)} \qquad \frac{R(y) : C(R(z)) : C(x)}{R(z) : C(R(y)) : C(x)}$$

When |—is the smallest inference relation obeying the rules above, reflexivity, monotonicity and cut hold, meaning that with the consequence relation, manipulation of arguments by the inference rules is well-founded (Tarski 1956). Let Δ be a set of (rejections of) arguments. Let α, and β be arguments.

$$\Delta\, \alpha \text{ if } \alpha \in \Delta \text{ (Reflexivity)}$$
$$\Delta \cup \{\alpha\}\, \beta \text{ if } \Delta\, \beta \text{ (Monotonicity)}$$
$$\Delta\, \beta \text{ if } \Delta \cup \{\alpha\}\, \beta \text{ and } \Delta\, \alpha \text{ (Cut)}$$

Also, the consequence relation is paraconsistent in the sense that it is not trivialized by contradiction: not all formulae in language L follow from contradiction.

A domain ontology is required for this reasoning component. It can be constructed manually or mined from a corpus of documents or from the web (Gomez et al. 2010; Galitsky et al. 2011a; Galitsky 2013).

5.2.5 Adjusting Available Discourse Parsers to Argumentation Domain

Nowadays, discourse parsers are trained on a fairly limited corpus (Muller et al. 2012). Moreover, this is the corpus of news articles where analysis of arguments is not necessarily well represented. They take into account conjunctive adverbs like *however* but do not have enough data to rely on the verb such as *imply* to differentiate between the rhetorical relations of *Explanations vs Contrast*. Hence the results of a machine-learned discourse parsing need to be overwritten, taking into account semantics of verbs in EDUs and certain syntactic cues like connectives between EDUs. This needs to be done in addition to using these verbs' VerbNet signatures for DT edge's labels (Kipper et al. 2008).

We perform an additional classification of rhetorical relations based on communicative action verbs and phrases such as '*as be a reason for*' in the nucleus and/or satellite. Let us look at a pair of sentences: "*A cat jumped on a dinner table, and I concluded that it was hungry*" versus "*A cat told me with his eyes to drop him a byte, which implies that it was hungry*". In the first example above, a template *nucleus[no CA]* → *satellite [conclude]* gives *Conclusion*. In the second example, *nucleus[tell]* → *satellite [imply]* gives *Explanation*.

We first show how rhetorical relations can be determined by connectives, and show substantial ambiguity preventing one from properly determining these relations based on connectives only. Notice that in a few thousand sentence-sized training dataset it is possible to generalize such connectives but not necessarily other determining phrases: a significantly larger training dataset for rhetorical parsing is required. Therefore, we intend to explore the determining features of rhetorical relations in the context of argumentation in a rule-based manner.

Given this table which reflects our observation on how connectives determine rhetorical relations, we apply the Formal Concept Analysis (Ganter and Wille 1999) to visualize the interrelationships between rhetorical relations in terms of their discourse cues (Fig. 5.4).

We provide a formal definition to treat associations between the connectives and rhetorical relations (see Chap. 1 Volume 2).

A formal context is a triple (G, M, I), where $G = \{g_1, g_2, \ldots, g_n\}$ is a set objects (such as rhetorical relations), $M = \{m_1, m_2, \ldots, m_k\}$ is a set attributes (such as connectives) and $I \subseteq G \times M$ is an incidence relation, i.e. $(g, m) \in I$ if the object g has the attribute m. The derivation operators $(\cdot)$ are defined for $A \subseteq G$ and $B \subseteq M$ as follows: $A = \{m \in M \mid \forall g \in A: gIm\}$, $B = \{g \in G \mid \forall m \in B: gIm\}$ A is the set of attributes common to all objects of A and B is the set of objects sharing all attributes of B. A formal concept is a pair (A, B), where $A \subseteq G$, $B \subseteq M$ and $A = B$, $B = A$. A is the extent and B is the intent of the concept. A partial order is defined on the set of concepts as follows: $(A, B) (C, D)$ iff $A \subseteq C$ $(D \subseteq B)$, (A, B) is a subconcept of (C, D), (C, D) is a superconcept of (A, B).

The concepts (A_i, B_i) of a context K can be (partially) ordered by the inclusion of extents, or, equivalently, by the dual inclusion of intents. An order $\leq$ on the concepts is defined as follows: for any two concepts (A_1, B_1) and (A_2, B_2) of K, we say that $(A_1, B_1) \leq (A_2, B_2)$ precisely when $A_1 \subseteq A_2$. Equivalently, $(A_1, B_1) \leq (A_2, B_2)$ whenever $B_1 \supseteq B_2$.

In this order, every set of formal concepts has the greatest common subconcept, or meet. Its extent consists of those objects that are common to all extents of the set. Dually, every set of formal concepts has the least common superconcept, the intent of which comprises all attributes which all objects of that set of concepts have.

These meet and join operations satisfy the axioms defining a complete lattice (a partially ordered set in which all subsets have both a supremum and an infimum), such as Fig. 5.11. Conversely, it can be shown that every complete lattice is the concept lattice of some formal context (up to isomorphism). Concept learning has been applied to a number of domains, including conflict resolution (Galitsky et al. 2005) and general CRM support (Galitsky et al. 2011b).

We now proceed to a more specific treatment of connectives and show how classes of verbs in a nucleus and satellite determine the rhetorical relations.

Detailed linguistic sentence-level patterns determining particular rhetorical relation is shown in Table 5.5. We specify connectives for both nucleus and satellite, as well as verb classes with the focus on communicative actions, associated with particular rhetorical relation. In some cases, below the pattern row, we show a sentence example or a generalized phrase to indicate a source of a given pattern.

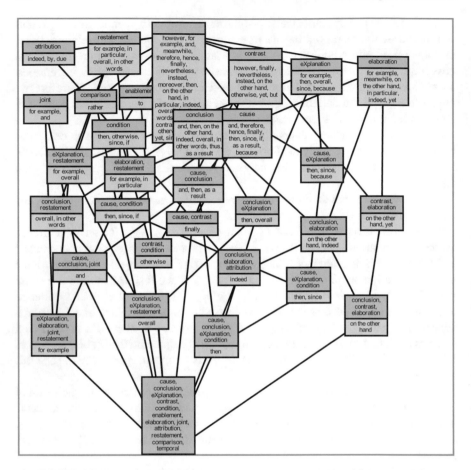

Fig. 5.11 Visualization of a concept lattice for connectives as attributes of rhetorical relations

Most examples here significantly deviate from the PDTB corpus (Prasad et al. 2008) used for training rhetorical parsers as they are tailored for relations associated with making an argument.

5.2.6   Evaluation

In this study, we conduct a three-step evaluation:

(1)   A manual evaluation of communicative discourse tree (CDT) construction, R-C representation and reasoning;
(2)   An automated evaluation of overall recognition accuracy for defeating answers;

Table 5.5 Sample syntactic patterns for rhetorical relations adjusted to argumentation domain

Verb or phrase	Adverbs in nucleus	Conjunctive adverbs in satellite	Nucleus	Satellite	Resultant rhetorical relation
		However, so, therefore		Is a reason, Is why, because of	Cause

I am tall, so [this is a reason/this is why/because of this] I am good at basketball

| | | | Is caused | | Cause |
| <Verb> to <verb> | | | | To <verb> | Enablement |

I took a knife to cut mushrooms in the woods

| | | That | Consequences are | | Cause |
| | | So | <Action> | PRP can | Enablement |

<Nucleus>... so they can ...
<Nucleus>... to do something <verb that has completion state>

		Hence, so	Summarize, conclude, sum up, result, lead to		Conclusion
		Because of, since so			Explanation
	If			Then	Condition
		That	Imply, lead to, cause, brings upon		Cause
			Imply, lead to, cause, brings upon		Cause

Thus <phrase> lead to <phrase>

		That is why			Explanation
	But		Inform		Contrast
Ask				But	Contrast

I asked but the form did

| | | Although, in spite of the fact, despite the fact | Charge, apply, demand, require | Although | Contrast |

You charged me an overdraft fee, although I have Overdraft Protection

I do, however, I use ...

Table 5.6 Resultant accuracies for each step of the argument representation algorithm

	Correctly represented CDT of a question	Correctly represented CDT of a defeating reply	Correctly represented logical argument of a question	Correctly represented logical argument of a defeating reply	Sound inference matching arguments for Q and A
Customer complaints	75.4	73.4	66.0	65.4	58.9
Auto repair (CarPros 2020)	79.2	78.1	69.9	71.1	64.2
Financial recommendation	69.0	72.5	67.6	68.6	62.8
Yahoo! Answers	82.7	77.8	75.2	73.2	66.7

(3) An assessment of how learned features of defeating answers match an intuition of search users in terms of how they score these answers in a social search environment.

We first evaluate the argumentation extraction component, including argument extraction, improving rhetorical parsing and converting a discourse tree into R-C representation (Table 5.6). Whereas CDT is built and corrected reasonably well, R-C representation accuracy is almost 10% lower since there is an ambiguity transitioning from CDT to R-C representation mapping rhetorical relation into either R or C. An adequate inference is achievable in almost 60%; further five percent are adequately represented but are subject to incorrect reasoning. In these five percent of cases, false positives or false negatives occurred: the inference confirmed the defeasibility (Garcia and Simari 2004) but it should not have or the other way around.

Now we proceed to the evaluation of the overall defeating argument selection system. For that, we form hypothetical dialogues from Customer Complaints dataset (GitHub 2020) and select the final, defeating reply by a company representative. We split the complaint text into utterances based on indirect speech indicators and communicative actions (*I said … they replied*). The last utterance is frequently the reason a given complaint arise, so these company replies should have managed to bring their points across and upset customer at the same time. From these utterances, we want to learn the real-world rhetorical and argumentative structure used by customer support representatives. SVM Parse Thicket learning is used (Galitsky et al. 2013, Chap. 9 Volume 1).

To assess how we can classify an answer as defeating, given a question or an arbitrary utterance, we represent complaint texts as unordered sets of question/answer pairs concealing the actual sequence for testing. We classify each company response as final or not final, assuming that the final response is defeating: the customer gave up on further communicating with the opponent company and resorted to other means to fix his problem.

We also apply similar considerations to the auto repair dataset (CarPros 2020). The final response usually either solves the problem or convinces the user that something

Table 5.7 Evaluation of the stand-alone and hybrid defeating answer recognition system

	P argument	R argument	F1 argument	P ML	R ML	F1 ML	F1 hybrid
Customer complaints	73	74	73.6	67	71	69.8	77.2
Auto Repair	80	78	79.4	79	82	81.0	84.6
Yahoo! Answers	75	72	73.5	77	75	76.2	81.5

else needs to be done and it is reasonable to leave the auto repair conversational thread. In this respect, the final utterance in an auto repair thread is also a defeating answer since a user is convinced not to continue the thread for whatever reason. In both these datasets, the random classifier achieves about 33% accuracy: there are 3.3 utterance pairs for customer complaints and 2.8 utterance pairs for auto repair.

The results of the end-to-end evaluation for both argument extraction and reasoning and argument learning (ML) systems are shown in Table 5.7.

One can observe that 75% of argument-based accuracy and 77% of learning-based accuracy complement each other to achieve 5% higher accuracy of the hybrid system. There is a strong deviation of the performances of both components in distinct domains due to variability of the complexity of argumentation patterns.

We also explore if defeating replies are rated highly by readers of a conversation or of an answer who did not actually participate in a conversation. We rely on Yahoo! Answers (2020) dataset to assess if defeating replies are rated higher than non-defeated, based on human assessment and based on our model trained and verified on Complaints and Auto Repair datasets from Table 5.7.

Percentages of most defeating answers from the list of user answers which have the highest rating are shown in Table 5.8. These percentages confirm our intuition that defeating answers are frequently wanted by users who are in a position to solve

Table 5.8 Discovering the correlation between a defeating answer and the one with the highest rating

	As determined by the logical argumentation component	As determined by the ML component	As determined by the hybrid system
Business	21.7	19.6	23.8
Job-related	12.6	14.0	15.4
Travel and entertainment	27.3	22.4	29.4
Personal life	16.8	21.0	24.5
Sports	22.4	23.8	27.3
Shopping	23.8	21.7	25.9

a particular problem, ready to get to the final solution or appeal to the "court of the last resort".

One can see that in different domains, the users of Yahoo! Answers have different expectations concerning how an answer should defeat a point of a novice user who initiates a thread, being not knowledgeable. In highly opinionated travel, entertainment and shopping domains, readers accept that a point raised by an initial question is defeated. At the same time, in less opinionated domains, the answers with the highest rating do not defeat the claim or opinion of a thread initiator but instead support it and provide a useful information without trying to make the thread initiator look like someone possessing limited knowledge.

5.3 Discussion and Conclusions

Whereas chatbot algorithms, in general, belong to such computer science discipline as search engineering and general-purpose NLP, the automated building of conclusive answers fall under the content generation area of AI. Automating an answer creation, it is hard to compete with how human domains experts would do it; however, chatbots are expected to be capable of building tens of thousands of conclusive answers per a vertical domain on the fly.

In the modern society, writing and creating content is one of the most frequent human activities. An army of content creators, from students to professional writers, produce various kinds of documents for various audiences. Not all of these documents are expected to be innovative, break-through or extremely important. The target of the tool being proposed is assistance with routine document creation process where most information is available on the web and needs to be collected, integrated and properly referenced (Galitsky and Kuznetsov 2013).

A number of content generation software systems are available in specific business domains (Johnson 2016). Most of the content generation software is template-based, which limits their efficiency and volume of produced content (Hendrikx et al. 2013). An interesting class of content generation system is based on verbalizing some numerical data. Also, content generation for computer game support turned out to be fruitful (Liapis et al. 2013). Deep-learning—based generation of a sequence of words has limited applicability for large-scale content production industrial systems. In Galitsky (2016), we built a content compilation assistance system that was suitable for producing a report that can be subject to manual editing by students and researchers in various fields in science, engineering, business and law.

Previous work on content generation in general and specifically related to web content relied heavily on manually annotated information of Wikipedia categories (Sauper and Barzilay 2009; Banerjee and Mitra 2016). Articles in Wikipedia consist of sections; (Sauper and Barzilay 2009) retrieved content from the web on articles belonging to a certain category of diseases by using the most frequent section titles as keywords to retrieve relevant web search snippets, utilizing web mining, similar to what we do for chatbot answers. The most informative excerpts were selected using a perceptron-based framework and populated into the built web article. In a recent work, (Banerjee and Mitra, 2016) proposed WikiKreator where contents in the Wikipedia sections were represented by topic-distribution features using Latent Dirichlet Allocation (LDA, Blei et al. 2003).

To build a document from multiple sources, sentences selected and paraphrased from multiple documents must be ordered such that the resulting article is coherent. Existing summarization systems did not tackle coherence, so discourse-level consideration proposed in Chap. 1 Volume 2 needs to be utilized.

The discourse tree representation used in our content compilation system is a reduction of what is called parse thicket (Galitsky 2014, Chap. 9 Volume 1), a combination of parse trees for sentences with discourse-level relationships between words and parts of the sentence in one graph. The straight edges of this graph are syntactic relations and curvy arcs—discourse relations, such as anaphora, same entity, subentity, rhetoric relation and communicative actions. This graph includes much richer information than just a combination of parse trees for individual sentences would.

Galitsky (2016) introduced the tool has been advertised using Google AdWords and used by thousands of users searching for "free essay writing" to compile content for a variety of domains, including natural sciences and humanities. In this section, the proposed and evaluated technique found a new application area in building answers for chatbots.

Proper recognition of rhetorical relations in a specific domain, such as argumentation, is associated with the task of predicting discourse connectives (Malmi et al. 2018). The authors believe that a dialog system might assemble a long and informative answer by sampling passages extracted from different documents retrieved from various sources. In this study, on the contrary, we demonstrated how a dialog can be driven in terms of its genre to a defeating answer completing this dialogue and attempting to convince a user with an authoritative answer.

Certain people's behavior forms are associated with question-answering activities on sites such as Yahoo! Answers. A number of studies have looked at the structure of the community and the interaction between askers and responders. Studies of user typology on the site have revealed that some user category (specialists) answer from personal knowledge, and others prefer to use external sources to construct answers. Observing a social network of Yahoo! Answer users, it turns out that it is possible to distinguish "answer people" from "discussion people" with the former found in specialist categories for factual information, such as mathematics and the latter more common in general-interest categories, such as relationship and travel. They also show that answer length is a good predictor of "best answer" choice (Adamic et al. 2008). Looking at the comments given by users on choosing best answers, one can observe that the most significant criteria (Kim and Oh 2009) are as follows:

(1) content completeness,
(2) solution feasibility, and
(3) personal agreement/confirmation.

What we assessed in this study is the first item.

There are multiple strategies people use to defeat their opponents, such as what us referred to as Straw man approach. Sometimes it helps to misrepresent an argument so that one can more easily defeat it. Just as a straw man is easier to knock down than a real man, so a distorted version of an argument is easier to defeat than the actual argument. If an argument is over-generalized, then it is easier to find a counter-argument for it:

My wife recently told me I should take out the trashcan. I responded, "Why do I have to do everything? If I spent my entire weekend doing housework, I would not have any time to work on my book".

This is like a straw man fallacy because the original claim (that '*I should do something (i.e. take out the trash)*) was taken and over-generalized and misrepresented towards the statement that I should "do everything."

We demonstrated that the answers defeating users' claims can be filtered out, if available, relying on hybrid reasoning + ML approach. Here we focused on the former components and evaluated both of them, confirming that they complement each other.

Relevance support for CRM has become critical to a modern workplace. Finding, documenting, and knowing things in an environment where data is dispersed, employees are always on the fly, and career paths change fast must be intuitive, simple, and seamless (Wade 2018). Finding content in a site structure requires a mental roadmap of where things live. Search may provide good results, but not direct answers; the answer is usually in the file it returns, meaning more time digesting to understand. Chatbots give users a chance to jump straight to the answer while pointing the source for reference, saving everyone's time and bridging what is becoming a major gap in content delivery.

Makhalova et al. (2019) proposed an IR-chatbot that incorporates a concept-based knowledge model and an index-guided traversal through it to ensure the discovery of information relevant for users and coherent to their preferences. The proposed approach not only supports a search session, but also helps users to discover properties of items and sequentially refine an imprecise query. As a conclusive answer, the chatbot indicates a position in the concept lattice the user is currently in (Chap. 1, Volume 2).

Modeling of a few paragraphs to make it a coherent text with a high-level structure remains an open problem as most deep learning algorithms can only accurately generate word-by-word summaries. These algorithms cannot think ahead and map out a good story plot. The focus of the deep learning NLP community has mainly been on teaching machines how to write a good sentence (Karapalidis 2019). This is a seemingly simple task that not every human can accomplish well enough every time. Fan et al. (2018) have recently attempted to raise the bar further and decided to experiment with hierarchical storytelling. The team sourced over a third of a million human-written stories from Reddit and fed that data to a neural network. The algorithm, after learning what and how others wrote, was tasked with creating a multi-stage story that would be relevant to a particular writing prompt. After applying several different approaches to teaching the network the basics of writing and helping it optimize the output, the team received over one hundred short stories drafted by AI. Although the resultant texts are coherent, they are overall meaningless. There is a lack of deep learning-based content generation demos to avoid spoiling the expectations of an audience. As an example of a generated paragraph, let us look at the following:

> *The man was an accountant. He had to be. He had to be the next president. I looked back over the top and saw that his wife was crying in the kitchen. I looked at the clock. It seemed to be coming slower, but I knew if I did it would not be long before I was in my own home. I wasn't sure. I had a hard time finding the right words to say.*

Although the words are formed in a syntactically correct sequence, the text is meaningless and it is hard to see a potential application for such sentence generation (Fan et al. 2018).

Knowing how to compose unique responses and even quick storylines translates to better micro and macro sales conversations in the future. AI-powered chat and customer support bots would become capable of holding more effective discussions and intelligently responding to customer queries, no matter how complex they are. Additionally, new algorithms could help marketers deal with such tasks as creating product image captions and product descriptions for images; or, better—producing descriptive video content for the visually impaired in a matter of clicks. Creative machines can also help marketers achieve a new level of personalization, especially for conversational UIs.

With a chatbot, a content management system (CMS) manager is expected to predict what users want to see and provide direct responses and direct answers. From the users standpoint, the information is not organized either (even though on the back end it is) nor does it provide organic options like search. Instead, the chatbot gives the best answer it has and also does it in a conversational way. This direct method of providing information means the user does less work for the same information gain and can perform the task over and over as necessary.

With search, the users are given the results that just recently combined everything that they have access to. Even a user who knows searching best practices on top of a system with a smart search setup, including promoted ones and customized, refined personalized ones, the user still has to deal with extraneous results that are not always relevant. From keywords that overlap (e.g., "extension" for files info or telephone numbers) to outdated information, one must sift through plenty of hits in search due to the nature of its organic results. It can lead to an overall negative impact on the overall search experience.

With chatbots, the information available is fully specified by the developers who tune the information in the bot CMS (Galitsky and Ilvovsky 2017). Chatbot developers direct users to the source information they seek. A good chatbot with relevant CMS has answers to most common questions for each group or department in an organization, actually answers the question being asked (rather than solely providing a source for the answer), and links back to the source as a reference for further information. An open-source content generator has been available as a part of (OpenNLP 2020) project. According to research from Juniper, banking, healthcare, social, eCommerce and retail organizations are saving $20–25 million annually using chatbots, with a savings of $8 billion per year expected by 2022. Making content accessible and versatile is now more important than ever for CRM content producers.

Not all dialogues can be naturally concluded (Fig. 5.12).

Fig. 5.12   A dialogue without a conclusive answer (cartoonbank.ru 2020)

References

Adamic L, Zhang J, Bakshy E, Ackerman MS (2008) Knowledge sharing and Yahoo answers: everyone knows something. In: WWW 2008/refereed track: social networks & Web 2.0—analysis of social networks & online interaction. Accessed 5 Dec 2017

Amgoud L, Besnard P, Hunter A (2015) Representing and reasoning about arguments mined from texts and dialogues. In: 13th European conference, ECSQARU 2015, July 2015, Compiègne, France, pp 60–71

Apothéloz D, Brandt P-Y, Quiroz G (1993) The function of negation in argumentation. J Pragmat 19:23–38

Banerjee S, Mitra P (2016) WikiWrite: generating Wikipedia articles automatically. In: IJCAI

Baroni M, Chantree F, Kilgarriff A, Sharoff S (2008) Cleaneval: a competition for cleaning web pages. In: Calzolari N, Choukri K, Maegaard B, Mariani J, Odjik J, Piperidis S, Tapias D (eds) Proceedings of the sixth international language resources and evaluation (LREC'08)

Bartlett FC (1932) Remembering: a study in experimental and social psychology. Cambridge University Press

Barzilay R, Lee L (2004) Catching the drift: probabilistic content models, with applications to generation and summarization. HLT-NAACL

Blei DM, Ng AY, Jordan MI (2003) Latent Dirichlet allocation. J Mach Learn Res 3:993–1022

Bridle JS (1990). Training stochastic model recognition algorithms as networks can lead to maximum mutual information estimation of parameters. In: Advances in neural information processing systems 2 (1989). Morgan-Kaufmann.

Cai D, Yu S, Wen J-R, Ma W-Y (2003) Extracting content structure for web pages based on visual representation. In: Zhou X, Zhang Y, Orlowska ME (eds) APWeb. LNCS, vol 2642. Springer, pp 406–417

CarPros Car Repair Dataset (2020) https://github.com/bgalitsky/relevance-based-on-parse-trees/blob/master/examples/CarRepairData_AnswerAnatomyDataset2.csv.zip

Cartoonbank.ru (2020) https://cartoonbank.ru/?page_id=29&offset=29280

Chesñevar CI, Maguitman M, González P (2009) Empowering recommendation technologies through argumentation. In: Rahwan I, Simari G (eds) Argumentation in artificial intelligence. Springer

Fan A, Lewis M, Dauphin Y (2018) Hierarchical Neural Story Generation. ACL pp 889-898.

Galitsky B (2013) Transfer learning of syntactic structures for building taxonomies for search engines. Eng Appl Artif Intell 26(10):2504–2515

Galitsky B (2014) Learning parse structure of paragraphs and its applications in search. Eng. Appl. AI 32:160–184

Galitsky B (2015) Finding a lattice of needles in a haystack: forming a query from a set of items of interest. In: FCA4AI@IJCAI

Galitsky B (2016) A tool for efficient content compilation. In: COLING Demo C16-2042, Osaka, Japan

Galitsky B (2012) Machine learning of syntactic parse trees for search and classification of text. Eng Appl AI 26(3):1072–1091

Galitsky B (2017) Matching parse thickets for open domain question answering. Data Knowl Eng 107:24–50

Galitsky B, Chen H, Du S (2009) Inverting semantic structure of customer opinions expressed in forums and blogs. In: 17th international conference on conceptual structures, Suppl. Proc.

Galitsky B, de la Rosa JL (2011) Concept-based learning of human behavior for customer relationship management. Inf Sci 181(10):2016–2035 (Special Issue on Information Engineering Applications Based on Lattices)

Galitsky B, Kuznetsov SO, Samokhin MV (2005) Analyzing conflicts with concept-based learning. In: International conference on conceptual structures, pp 307–322

Galitsky B, Kuznetsov SO, Kovalerchuk B (2008) Argumentation vs meta-argumentation for the assessment of multi-agent conflict. In: Proc. of the AAAI Workshop on Metareasoning

Galitsky B, Kuznetsov SO (2013) A web mining tool for assistance with creative writing. In: ECIR 2013: advances in information retrieval, pp 828–831

Galitsky B, Usikov D, Kuznetsov SO (2013) Parse thicket representations for answering multi-sentence questions. In: 20th international conference on conceptual structures, ICCS.

Galitsky B, Ilvovsky D (2017) Chatbot with a discourse structure-driven dialogue management. In: EACL Demo E17-3022, Valencia, Spain

Galitsky B, Ilvovsky D, Kuznetsov SO (2018) Detecting logical argumentation in text via communicative discourse tree. J Exp Theor Artif Intell 30(5):1–27

Galitsky B, Usikov D (2008) Programming spatial algorithms in natural language. In: AAAI workshop technical report WS-08-11, Palo Alto, pp 16–24

Ganter B, Wille R (1999) Formal concept analysis: mathematical foundations. Springer, Berlin

Galitsky B, Dobrocsi G, de la Rosa JL, Kuznetsov SO (2010) From generalization of syntactic parse trees to conceptual graphs. In: Croitoru M, Ferré S, Lukose D (eds) Conceptual structures: from information to intelligence, 18th international conference on conceptual structures, ICCS 2010, Lecture notes in artificial intelligence, vol 6208, pp 185–190

Galitsky B, Dobrocsi G, de la Rosa JL, Kuznetsov SO (2011a) Using generalization of syntactic parse trees for taxonomy capture on the web. In: ICCS, pp 104–117

Galitsky B, Dobrocsi G, de la Rosa JL (2012) Inferring the semantic properties of sentences by mining syntactic parse trees. Data Knowl Eng 81:21–45

Garcia A, Simari G (2004) Defeasible logic programming: an argumentative approach. Theory Pract Log Program 4:95–138

GitHub (2020) Customer complaint. https://github.com/bgalitsky/relevance-based-on-parse-trees/blob/master/examples/opinionsFinanceTags.xls

Gomez H, Vilariño D, Pinto D, Sidorov G (2015) CICBUAPnlp: graph-based approach for answer selection in community question answering task. In: SemEval-2015, pp 18–22

Gomez SA, Chesñevar CI, Simari GR (2010) Reasoning with inconsistent ontologies through argumentation. Appl Artif Intell 24(1 & 2):102–148

Google (2018) Search using autocomplete. https://support.google.com/websearch/answer/106230

Harris Z (1982) Discourse and sublanguage. In: Kittredge R, Lehrberger J (eds) Sublanguage: studies of language in restricted semantic domains. Walter de Gruyter, Berlin; New York, pp 231–236

Hendrikx M, Meijer S, Van Der Velden J, Iosup A (2013) Procedural content generation for games: a survey. ACM Trans Multimed Comput Commun Appl 9(1):22 (Article 1)

Johnson MR (2016) Procedural generation of linguistics, dialects, naming conventions and spoken sentences. In: Proceedings of 1st international joint conference of DiGRA and FDG

Karapalidis G (2019) Neural storytelling: how AI is attempting content creation. https://www.the drum.com/opinion/2019/01/22/neural-storytelling-how-ai-attempting-content-creation

Kim S, Oh S (2009) Users' relevance criteria for evaluating answers in a social Q&A site. J Am Soc Inform Sci Technol 60(4):716

Kipper K, Korhonen A, Ryant N, Palmer M (2008) A large-scale classification of English verbs. Lang Resour Eval J 42:21–40

Le Q, Mikolov T (2014) Distributed representations of sentences and documents. In: Eric P. Xing, Tony Jebara (eds) Proceedings of the 31st International Conference on International Conference on Machine Learning—Volume 32 (ICML'14), Vol 32

Liapis A, Yannakakis GN, Togelius J (2013) Sentient sketchbook: computer-aided game level authoring. In: FDG, pp 213–220

Makhalova T, Ilvovsky DA, Galitsky B (2015) News clustering approach based on discourse text structure. In: Proceedings of the first workshop on computing news storylines @ACL

Makhalova T, Ilvovsky D, Galitsky B (2019) Navigate and refine: IR chatbot based on conceptual models. In: ICCS 2019

Malmi E, Pighin D, Krause S, Kozhevnikov M (2018) Automatic prediction of discourse connectives. In: Proceedings of LREC. https://arxiv.org/pdf/1702.00992.pdf

Mann WC, Thompson SA (1988) Rhetoric al structure theory: toward a functional theory of text organization. Text 8(3):243–281

Marcu D (1997) The rhetorical parsing, summarization, and generation of natural language texts. Unpublished Ph.D. dissertation, University of Toronto, Toronto, Canada

McKeown KR (1985) Text generation: using discourse strategies and focus constraints to generate natural language text. Cambridge University Press, Cambridge, UK

Muller P, Afantenos S, Denis P, Asher N (2012) Constrained decoding for text-level discourse parsing. In: COLING, 1883–1900, Mumbai, India

OpenNLP (2020) https://opennlp.apache.org/

Pasternack J, Roth D (2009) Extracting article text from the web with maximum subsequence segmentation. In: WWW '09: proceedings of the 18th international conference on world wide web. ACM, New York, NY, USA, pp 971–980

Prasad R, Dinesh N, Lee A, Miltsakaki E, Robaldo L, Joshi A, Webber B (2008) The Penn Discourse Treebank 2.0. In: Proceedings of the 6th international conference on language resources and evaluation (LREC), Marrakech, Morocco

Sauper C, Barzilay R (2009) Automatically generating Wikipedia articles: a structure-aware approach. In: Proceedings of ACL. Suntec, Singapore, pp 2008–2016

Sidorov G (2013) Syntactic dependency based N-grams in rule based automatic English as second language grammar correction. Int J Comput Linguist Appl 4(2):169–188

Sidorov G (2014) Should syntactic N-grams contain names of syntactic relations? Int J Comput Linguist Appl 5(1):139–158

Tarski A (1956) Logic, Semantics, Metamathematics. In: Woodger JH (ed), Oxford U. Press

Vo NPA, Magnolini S, Popescu O (2015) FBK-HLT: a new framework for semantic textual similarity. In: Proceedings of the 9th international workshop on semantic evaluation (SemEval-2015), NAACL-HLT 2015, Denver, US

Wade M (2018) 5 ways chatbots are revolutionizing knowledge management. AtBot. https://blog.getbizzy.io/5-ways-chatbots-are-revolutionizing-knowledge-management-bdf925db66e9

Wray A (2002) Formulaic language and the lexicon. Cambridge University Press, Cambridge

Yahoo! Answers (2020) https://answers.yahoo.com/

Chapter 6
Truth, Lie and Hypocrisy

Abstract Automated detection of text with misrepresentations such as fake reviews
is an important task for online reputation management. We form the Ultimate Deception Dataset that consists of customer complaints—emotionally charged texts, which
include descriptions of problems customers experienced with certain businesses.
Typically, in customer complaints, either customer describes company representative
lying, or they lie themselves. The Ultimate Deception Dataset includes almost 3 000
complaints in the personal finance domain and provides clear ground truth based on
available factual knowledge about the financial domain. Among them, four hundred
texts were manually tagged. Experiments were performed in order to explore the links
between implicit cues of the rhetoric structure of texts and the validity of arguments,
and also how truthful/deceptive are these texts. We confirmed that communicative
discourse trees are essential to detect various forms of misrepresentation in text,
achieving 76% F1 on the Ultimate Deception Dataset. We believe that this accuracy is sufficient to assist a manual curation of a CRM environment towards having
high-quality, trusted content. Recognizing hypocrisy in customer communication
concerning his impression with the company or hypocrisy in customer attitude is
fairly important for proper tackling and retaining customers. We collect a dataset of
sentences with hypocrisy and learn to detect it relying on syntactic, semantic and
discourse-level features and also web mining to correlate contrasting entities. The
sources are customer complaints, samples of texts with hypocrisy on the web and
tweets tagged as hypocritical. We propose an iterative procedure to grow the training
dataset and achieve the detection F1 above 80%, which is expected to be satisfactory
for integration into a CRM platform. We conclude this section with the detection
of a rumor and misinformation in web document where discourse analysis is also
helpful.

6.1   Anatomy of a Lie

6.1.1   Introduction: A Discourse of a Lie

It has been discovered that a lot of forms of human intellectual and communication activity are associated with certain discourse structures. Rhetorical Structure Theory (RST, Mann and Thompson 1987) is a good means to express the correlation between such form of activity and its representation in how associated thoughts are organized in text. Rhetorical Structure Theory presents a hierarchical, connected structure of a text as a Discourse Tree, with rhetorical relations between the parts of it. The smallest text spans are called elementary discourse units (EDUs). In communicative discourse trees (CDTs), the labels for communicative actions (CAs) (VerbNet expressions for verbs) are added to the discourse tree edges to show which speech acts are attached to which rhetoric relations; this structure helps to understand argumentation (Galitsky and Kuznetsov 2008, Galitsky et al. 2018b).

Argumentation needs a certain combination of rhetorical relations of *Elaboration*, *Contrast*, *Cause* and *Attribution* (Grasso 2003). Persuasiveness relies on certain structures linking *Elaboration*, *Attribution* and *Condition* (Galitsky et al. 2019a). The explanation needs to rely on certain chains of *Elaboration* relations plus *Explanation* and *Cause*, and a rhetorical agreement between a question and an answer is based on certain mappings between the rhetorical relations of *Contrast*, *Cause*, *Attribution* and *Condition* between the former and the latter (Galitsky et al. 2018a, Galitsky et al. 2019c). Discourse trees turned out to be helpful to form a dialogue and to build a dialogue from the text, to better understand and leverage the structure of texts.

In this chapter, we study rhetoric structure correlated with certain forms of verbal activity, namely, we focus on deception in texts such as reviews and complaints. Automated detection of fake reviews is important for online reputation management tasks. Natural Language Processing (NLP) tools that can distinguish truthful and reliable reviews from deceptive reviews would be important for a broad spectrum of applications of recommendation and security systems, for a wide range of products and services. The research on automated deception detection in written texts is focused on classifying if a narrative is truthful or deceptive. The main difficulty is to detect deception where factual knowledge is not available to a degree sufficient to computationally establish the truth. This situation is typical in everyday life in the real world, from an intuitive choice of a product based on reviews to judges' verdicts: it is impossible to establish the truth based on known facts, so the decision is based on implicit cues such as the way people explain what they have done and provide arguments.

Detecting misrepresentation in writing, it is hard to differentiate between different categories of writers. Professional writers are frequently good at misrepresenting, and they do not include cues for what might be a lie. Conversely, content written by non-professional writers is often authentic in how it indicates the thought patterns of the writer where the traces of a lie and hints for how it is motivated can be found. Here, corpora with defined ground truth are needed for classification tasks solving and exploring the links between implicit cues of the rhetorical structure of texts and how truthful/deceptive are these texts (Galitsky 2019b).

6.1.2 Example of Misrepresentation in User-Generated Content

Regarding possible misrepresentation in user-generated content, the following example can be provided (Fig. 6.1):

> I have accounts with them for almost 10 years, I hated it their customer service! Worst one ever. I don't know what's their problems, I'm not recommending their services and banking to anybody, I stopped using their credit cards already! The only reason I can't close my accounts with them, it could drop my credit score. I will not close my credit cards, but I'm not definitely using them so they can't make money from on us! I just had conversation with a supervisor from California called Steve he and his representative didn't even understand my situation, which was not common at all, basically didn't want to help me!

```
elaboration (LeftToRight)
  elaboration (LeftToRight)
    attribution (LeftToRight)
      TEXT:I have accounts with them for almost 10 years ,
      TEXT:I hated it their customer service !
    TEXT:Worst one ever .
  elaboration (LeftToRight)
    elaboration (LeftToRight)
      explanation (LeftToRight)
        attribution (LeftToRight)
          cause (LeftToRight)
            attribution (RightToLeft)
              TEXT:I do not know
              TEXT:what is their problems ,
            TEXT:I 'm not recommending their services and banking to anybody ,
            TEXT:I stopped using their credit cards already !
        attribution (RightToLeft)
          TEXT:The only reason I can not close my accounts with them ,
          TEXT:it could drop my credit score .
      contrast (RightToLeft)
        TEXT:I will not close my credit cards ,
        enablement (LeftToRight)
          TEXT:but I 'm not definitely using them
          TEXT:so they can not make money from on us !
    elaboration (LeftToRight)
      TEXT:I just had conversation
      same-unit
        elaboration (LeftToRight)
          TEXT:with a supervisor from California called Steve , he and his representative did not even
understand my situation ,
          TEXT:which was not common at all ,
          TEXT:basically did not want to help me !
```

Fig. 6.1 A CDT for a customer complaint showing a complex mental state

The author of this complaint does not provide a single argument backing up his claim. And the author's statement that his credit history can be negatively affected by his closing an account is a misrepresentation.

We show the text split into elementary discourse units as done by the discourse parser of either (Joty et al. 2013, Surdeanu et al. 2015). What do we see in the discourse tree for this text? We show important (non-default) rhetorical relations in bold and highlight with italics the verbs with the role of communicative actions, which are an important addition to the rhetorical relations.

There is an unusual chain of rhetorical relations *Explanation-Attribution-Cause-Attribution-Attribution,* which is a suspicious explanation pattern on its own. Unsurprisingly, the atom statement for the last attribution (which is the basis of this explanation, highlighted with underlined italics) turns out to be false: *closing accounts should not affect someone's credit score.*

6.1.3   Example of Misrepresentation in Professional Writing

In our first example, the objective of the author is to attack a claim that the Syrian government used chemical weapons in the Spring of 2018 (Fig. 6.2). An acceptable proof would be to share a certain observation, associated with the standpoint of peers, with the absence of a chemical attack. For example, if it is possible to demonstrate that the time of the alleged chemical attack coincided with the time of a very strong rain, that would be a convincing way to attack this claim. However, since no such observation was identified, the source, Russia Today, resorted to plotting a complex mental state expressing how the claim was communicated, which agents reacted which way for this communication. It is rather hard to verify most statements about the mental states of involved parties. We show the text split into EDUs as done by the discourse parser:

> [Whatever the Douma residents ,][who had first-hand experience of the shooting of the water][dousing after chemical attack video ,][have to say ,][their words simply do not fit into the narrative][allowed in the West ,][analysts told RussiaToday .] [Footage of screaming bewildered civilians and children][being doused with water ,][presumably to decontaminate them ,][was a key part in convincing Western audiences][that a chemical attack happened in Douma .] [Russia brought the people][seen in the video][to Brussels ,][where they told anyone][interested in listening][that the scene was staged .] [Their testimonies , however , were swiftly branded as bizarre and underwhelming and even an obscene masquerade][staged by Russians .] [They refuse to see this as evidence ,][obviously pending][what the OPCW team is going to come up with in Douma], [Middle East expert Ammar Waqqaf said in an interview with RT .] [The alleged chemical incident ,][without any investigation , has already become a solid fact in the West ,][which the US , Britain and France based their retaliatory strike on .]

This article (Fig. 6.2) does not really find counter-evidence for the claim of the chemical attack it attempts to defeat. Instead, the text says that the opponents are not interested in observing this counter-evidence. The main statement of this article is that a certain agent "disallows" a particular kind of evidence attacking the main claim, rather than providing and backing up this evidence. Instead of defeating a

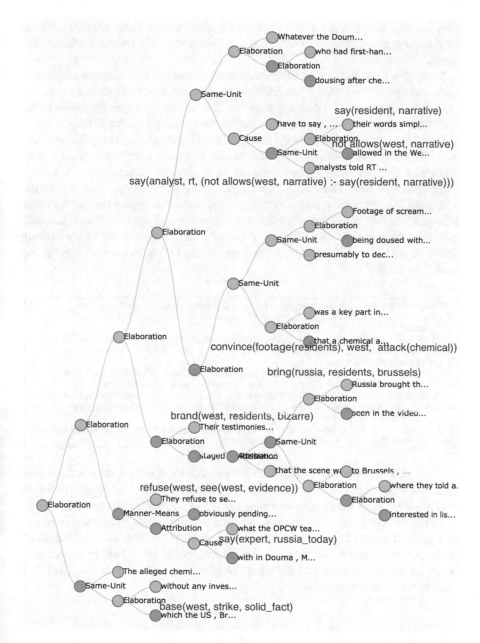

Fig. 6.2 A CDT for the chemical attack claim. An author attempts to substitute a desired valid argumentation chain by a fairly sophisticated mental state expressed by communicative actions

chemical attack claim, the article builds a complex mental states conflict between the residents, Russian agents taking them to Brussels, the West and a Middle East expert.

To express a truthfulness of a text, we need a combination of discourse representation and speech-theoretic representation, to indicate how thoughts are organized and communicated. To do that, we employ CDTs where the edges are labeled with VerbNet expressions for the communicative action verbs (Galitsky 2019c).

Our other example of controversial news is a Trump-Russia link acquisition (BBC 2018, Fig. 6.3). For a long time, it was unable to confirm the claim, so the story is repeated over and over again to maintain a reader expectation that it would be instantiated one day. There is neither confirmation nor rejection that the dossier exists, and the goal of the author is to make the audience believe that such dossier does exist, neither providing evidence nor misrepresenting events. To achieve this goal, the author can attach a number of hypothetical statements about the existing dossier to a variety of mental states to impress the reader in the authenticity and validity of the topic.

In January 2017, a secret dossier was leaked to the press. It had been compiled by a former British intelligence official and Russia expert, Christopher Steele, who had been paid to investigate Mr Trump's ties to Russia.

The dossier alleged Moscow had compromising material on Mr Trump, including claims he was once recorded with prostitutes at a Moscow hotel during a 2013 trip for one of his Miss Universe pageants. Mr Trump emphatically denies this.

The file purported to show financial and personal links between Mr Trump, his advisers and Moscow. It also suggested the Kremlin had cultivated Mr Trump for years before he ran for president.

Mr Trump dismissed the dossier, arguing its contents were based largely on unnamed sources. It was later reported that Mr Steele's report was funded as a opposition research by the Clinton campaign and Democratic National Committee.

Fusion GPS, the Washington-based firm that was hired to commission the dossier, had previously been paid via a conservative website to dig up dirt on Mr Trump.

Frequently, professionally created fake news does not just negate the facts from a genuine news source. It invents a complex mental state such as *opponent's media created narrative around proponent agents* (Fig. 6.4). Also, sophisticated fake news mixes the "positive" agents it wants to position in a positive light (Russia, Iran) and the opponent agent (Trump), inventing a conflict between them and the "negative" agents, such as western anti-Trump media. At the time this fake content was created, the public started to learn that downing the plane is due to Iran activity, but Iran officials have not confessed yet.

6.1.4   Background and Related Work

Deceptive product reviews can be referred to as deceptive opinion spam: fictitious opinions that have been deliberately written to sound authentic in order to deceive the reader (Ott et al. 2013). Spammers write fake reviews to promote or demote target products, and it is difficult to recognize them manually: human average accuracy is

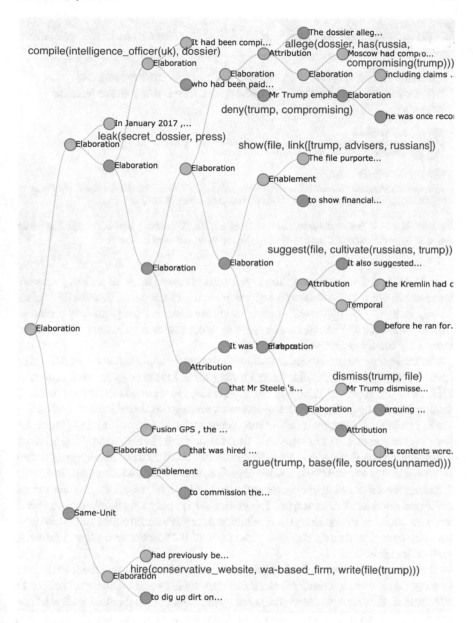

Fig. 6.3 A CDT for an attempt to prove something where evidence is absent, so the facts are "wrapped" into complex mental states as expressed by communicative actions

POMPEO CLAIMS IRAN 'LIKELY' SHOT DOWN UKRAINIAN BOEING AS US ROLLS

Secret intelligence & 'highly likelys': How media created narrative around Tehran jet crash to blame Iran, Russia and Trump

Nebojsa Malic
is a Serbian-American journalist, blogger and translator, who wrote a regular column for Antiwar.com from 2000 to 2015, and is now senior writer at RT.

10 Jan, 2020 00:47 / Updated 2 months ago

Whatever caused Flight 752 to crash just after takeoff from Tehran, the 176 people who died were quickly drafted as elements in a propaganda narrative targeting both Iran, Russia and US President Donald Trump.

Fig. 6.4 Fake news from a controversial site Russia Today. The main editor of this site has been a subject of a corruption scandal, according to the opposition sources in Russia

merely 57.3%. Automated deception detection for reviews faces the lack of gold standard corpora with verified examples of deceptive use of language. Besides this, intentionally written (e.g., by crowdsourcing) texts are distinct from genuinely produced texts. Hence, such artificial texts classified as deceptive by human annotators are not necessarily totally deceptive.

The release of two gold-standard datasets allowed for applying supervised learning methods, taking stylistic, syntactic and lexical features into consideration (Ott et al. 2011, 2013, Feng et al. 2012a; 2012b). Hotels reviews were chosen for the datasets, because it was suggested that deception rates among travel reviews are reasonably small. The latter dataset includes, among other reviews, a crowdsourced generation of deceptive reviews. It contains 400 truthful positive reviews from TripAdvisor; 400 deceptive positive reviews from Mechanical Turk; 400 truthful negative reviews from reviews websites; 400 deceptive negative reviews from Mechanical Turk.

Later, researchers tried to overcome the lack of large realistic datasets on different topics and domains. For example, Yao et al. (2017) apply a data collection method based on social network analysis to identify deceptive and truthful online reviews from Amazon. The dataset contains more than 10 000 deceptive reviews in diverse product domains.

The problem of the mentioned above gold standard datasets is that the fake reviews were not taken from genuinely written ordinary reviews and manually classified as fake. Instead, they were written on demand by the Amazon Mechanical Turk workers; hence they are not indicative of deception (Mukherjee et al. 2013b). However, they are accepted as gold standard datasets for this research field. The rules used in (Ott et al. 2013) to create ground truth datasets were also used in later projects, such as in (Hai et al. 2016).

The real-life Amazon dataset (Jindal and Liu 2008) contains reviews from Amazon.com (crawled in 2006). It is large and covers a very wide range of products. It was used, for example, in Sun et al. (2016) in three domains: Consumer Electronics,

Software, and Sports. The metadata in this dataset provides only helpfulness votes of the reviews.

In cases where there was no certain knowledge of the ground truth, different ways to collect reviews corpora, relying on other features, were used. For example, in Fornaciari and Poesio (2014), the DeRev corpus of books reviews, originally posted on Amazon, was collected using definite pre-defined deception clues. Book reviews in the corpus are marked as clearly fake, possibly fake, and possibly genuine. The corpus includes 6819 instances with 236 instances labeled with a higher degree of confidence and is considered as the gold standard.

In (Rayana and Akoglu 2015), two publicly available Yelp datasets were presented. They are labeled with respect to the Yelp's classification in recommended and not recommended reviews. Mukherjee et al. (2013a) found that the Yelp spam filter primarily relies on linguistic, behavioral, and social networking features. A classification provided by Yelp has been also used in many previous works before as a ground truth, where recommended reviews correspond to genuine reviews, and not recommended reviews correspond to fake ones, so these labels can be trusted. The YelpNYC dataset contains reviews of restaurants located in New York City (359 052 reviews; 10,27% are fake); the Zip dataset is larger, since it contains businesses located in contiguous regions of the United States (608 598 reviews; 13,22% are fake).

Big Amazon dataset is annotated with compliant/non-compliant labels. It has many different topics: from electronics and books to office products (https://s3.ama zonaws.com/amazonreviewspds/readme.html). It contains labels about star rating, helpful vote, total votes, verified purchase that could be used for making decisions.

Hence, the existing recent datasets rely on external factors provided by their source, such as review's rating, number of votes, social networking features of review's author, metadata features etc. They are not annotated manually. So, despite the presence of different corpora, lack of corpora with exact ground truth can be understood as a bottleneck in deception detection of online texts.

Hierarchical discourse-level structures for fake news detection have the following value proposition:

1) The way two discourse units of a document are connected could be quite revealing and insightful about its truthfulness (Rubin and Lukoianova 2015). It turns out that fake stories lack rhetorical relations with the meaning *Evidence*.
2) Fake news is typically produced by connecting disjoint pieces of news. Unlike well-established journalism, fake news production lacks a thorough editorial. Employing CDTs, one can investigate the coherence of fake/real news documents.
3) A number of studies showed that using hierarchical structures such as CDTs (Galitsky et al. 2018) produces a better document representation in various downstream tasks whose predictions depend on the whole document (Bhatia et al. 2015; Morey et al. 2018).

Incorporating hierarchical discourse-level structure of fake and real news articles is an important step toward a better modeling of how these articles are structured

(Karimi and Tang 2019). Discourse Analysis has rarely been employed in the fake news detection domain and faces certain limitations such as a lack of discourse-annotated corpora for fake news. Another challenge is how to extract out useful information from such discovered structures. The author identifies some structure-related properties to facilitate an understating of fake news but do not use such rich discourse representation as discourse trees.

6.1.5   Dataset Description

We introduce the dataset of customer complaints—emotionally charged texts, which include descriptions of problems they experienced with certain businesses. The dataset is freely available (Ultimate Deception Dataset 2020).

Raw complaints were collected from PlanetFeedback.com for a number of banks submitted in 2006-2010. The dataset consists of 2 746 complaints totally. Four hundred complaints were manually tagged with respect to the parameters related to argumentation and validity of text: perceived complaint validity, argumentation validity, presence of specific argumentation patterns, and detectable misrepresentation. Here, the validity of information is connected with the validity of arguments. The dataset contains texts with direct truth confirmation based on manual annotation. It contains authentic data: both truthful and deceptive reviews were taken from spontaneously written customers' texts. Among the manually annotated 400 complaints, 163 are invalid and 237 are valid.

The initial set of 80 complaints was tagged by the authors of the paper as experts. After that, three annotators worked with this dataset, having a set of definitions and applying them. Then precision and recall were measured by matching the tags done by the authors as the "gold standard," after that, the set of definitions was edited and elaborated. In our further work, Krippendorff's alpha measure (for three annotators) was applied as an inter-annotator agreement measurement, and it exceeds 80%. As it is possible to know, retrospectively and based on facts and the established ground truth, we suggest that the annotators can find out, with high confidence, what information in texts is deceptive. So the dataset would provide the ground truth.

The rest 2 346 complaints were auto-tagged based on the model trained on this 400 set. After that, these complaints have also been partially manually evaluated so that the accuracy of autotagging exceeds 75%.

Our dataset includes more complaints with intense argumentation in comparison with other argument mining datasets, such as (Oraby et al. 2015, Stab and Gurevych 2017, Abbott et al. 2016). For a given topic such as insufficient funds fee, this dataset provides many distinct ways of argumentation that this fee is unfair. In this dataset, the complainants attempt to provide as strong argumentation as possible to back up their claims and strengthen their case.

If a complaint is not truthful, it is usually invalid: either a customer complains out of a bad mood or wants to get compensation. However, if the complaint is truthful, it can still easily be invalid, especially when arguments are flawed. When an untruthful complaint has valid argumentation patterns, it is hard for an annotator to properly assign it as valid or invalid, without the guidelines. So, according to the guidelines for the manual tagging of the dataset, a complaint is considered as valid if a judge believes that the main complaint claim is truthful under the assumption that a complainant is making a truthful statement. A valid complaint needs to include proper discourse and acceptable argumentation patterns.

Following this approach, a complaint is marked as truthful if a judge cannot defeat it, using commonsense knowledge, available factual knowledge about a domain or implicit, indirect cues. Inconsistencies detected by a judge also indicates that the complaint author is deceiving. Mentioning multiple unusual, very rarely occurring claims also indicates that the complaint author is deceiving. The judge does not have to be able to prove that the complainant is lying: judge's intuition is sufficient to tag a complaint as untruthful. We suggest that one can provide a valid argumentation and also provide a false statement in a single sentence: "Rule is like this <correct rule> and I followed it, making <false statement>". Conversely, one can be truthful but provide an invalid argumentation pattern" *I set this account for direct deposit and sent a check out of it* <truthful statement> , *as my HR manager suggested* <should not have followed advice from not a specialist in banking>". Therefore, the validity (of argumentation patterns) and truthfulness are correlated.

Furthermore, customer complaints have much more significance for the well-being of customers in comparison with customer reviews. Therefore, tagged customer complaints have much more importance associated with truth/deception than customer reviews. Since reviews are associated with opinions which can be random and complaints with customers doing their best to achieve their goals, both the truth and a lie is much more meaningful and serious in comparison with review datasets.

Complaints usually have a simple motivational structure, are written with a fixed purpose. Most complainants face a strong deviation between what they expected from a service, what they received and how it was communicated. Most complaint authors report incompetence, flawed policies, ignorance, indifference to customer needs from the customer service personnel. The authors are frequently exhausted communicative means available to them, confused, seeking recommendations from other users and advise others on avoiding particular financial service. The focus of a complaint is a proof that the proponent is right and the opponent is wrong, a resolution proposal and the desired outcome.

Complaints reveal the shady practice of banks during the financial crisis of 2007, such as manipulating an order of transactions to charge the highest possible amount of non-sufficient fund fees. Moreover, the most frequent topic is about banks' attempts to communicate this practice as a necessity to process multiple checks. That is why the dataset collection is based on complaints of 2007. Multiple argumentation patterns are used in complaints:

1) A deviation from what has happened from what was expected, according to common sense (most frequent). This pattern covers both valid and invalid argumentation (a valid pattern).

2) The second argumentation patterns cite the difference between what has been promised (advertised, communicated) and what has been received or actually occurred. They also mention that the opponent does not play by the rules (a valid pattern).

3) A high number of complaints are explicitly saying that bank representatives are lying. Lying includes inconsistencies between the information provided by different bank agents, factual misrepresentation and careless promises (a valid pattern).

4) Complaints arise due to the rudeness of bank agents and customer service personnel. Customers cite rudeness in both cases, when the opponent point is valid or not (and complaint and argumentation validity is tagged accordingly).

5) Complainants cite their needs as reasons banks should behave in certain ways. A popular argument is that since the government via taxpayers bailed out the banks, they should now favor the customers (an invalid pattern).

6.1.6 Communicative Discourse Trees to Represent Truthfulness in Text

Starting from the autumn of 2015, we became interested in the controversy about Theranos, the healthcare company that hoped to make a revolution in blood tests. Some sources, including the *Wall Street Journal*, started claiming that the company's conduct was fraudulent. The claims were made based on the whistleblowing of employees who left Theranos. At some point, FDA got involved, and as the case develops, we were improving our deception detection techniques while keeping an eye on Theranos' story. As we scraped discussions about Theranos back in 2016 from the website, the audience believed that the case was initiated by Theranos competitors who felt jealous about the proposed efficiency of the blood test technique promised by Theranos. However, our analysis showed that Theranos was misrepresenting and our findings supported the criminal case against Theranos, which led to the massive fraud verdict. SEC says that Theranos CEO Elizabeth Holmes raised more than $700 million from investors "through an elaborate, years-long fraud" in which she exaggerated or made false statements about the company's technology and finances.

We now build an example of a CDT for the Theranos attack on Wall Street Journal (WSJ) acquisition (Fig. 6.5): "*It is not unusual for disgruntled and terminated employees in the heavily regulated health care industry to file complaints in an effort to retaliate against employers for termination of employment. Regulatory agencies have a process for evaluating complaints, many of which are not substantiated. Theranos trusts its regulators to properly investigate any complaints.*"

To show the structure of a deception, discourse relations are necessary but insufficient, and speech acts are necessary but insufficient as well. For the paragraph above, we need to know the discourse structure of interactions between agents, and what kinds of interactions they are.

file(employee, complaint) is elaborated by *retaliate(employee, employer)*, and

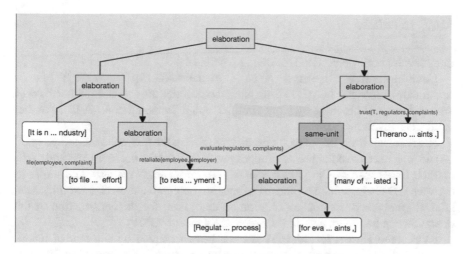

Fig. 6.5 CAs as labels for rhetoric relations helps to identify a text apart from a heated discussion

evaluate(regulation, complaints) is elaborated by *trust(Theranos, regulators, complainants)*. Also, the top link in turn is elaborated by the bottom link. Once we involve the definitions of the verbs for these four communicative actions, the inconsistency is revealed.

From the commonsense reasoning standpoint, Theranos, the company, has two choices to confirm the argument that its tests are valid:

1) Conduct independent investigation, comparing their results with the peers, opening the data to the public, confirming that their analysis results are correct; and

2) Defeat the argument by its opponent that their testing results are invalid, and providing support for the claim that their opponent is wrong.

Obviously, the former argument is much stronger and usually, the latter argument is chosen when the agent believes that the former argument is too hard to implement. On the one hand, the reader might agree with Theranos that WSJ should have provided more evidence for its accusations against the company. On the other hand, the reader perhaps disliked the fact that Theranos selects the latter argument type (2) above, and therefore the company's position is fairly weak. One reason that Theranos' argument is weak is because the company tries to refute the opponent's allegation concerning the complaints about Thermos's services from clients. Theranos' demand for evidence by inviting WSJ to disclose the sources and the nature of the complaints is weak. A claim is that a third-party (independent investigative agent) would be more reasonable and conclusive. However, some readers might believe that the company's argument (burden of proof evasion) is logical and valid. Note that an argumentation assessor cannot identify the rhetorical relations in a text by relying on text only. Rather, the context of the situation is helpful in order to grasp the arguer's intention.

6.1.7 Evaluation

In our evaluation, we used the following pipelines:

Communicative Discourse Tree Construction. Just two RST parsers constructing discourse tree (DT) from paragraphs of text are available at the moment. We used the tool provided by (Joty et al. 2013 and Surdeanu et al. 2015). We then build CDT involving VerbNet.

Nearest Neighbor learning. To predict the label of the text, once the complete DT is built, one needs to compute its similarity with DTs for the positive class and verify that it is lower than similarity to the set of DTs for its negative class. The similarity between CDT's is defined by means of maximal common sub-DTs. Definitions of labeled graphs and domination relation on them used for the construction of this operation can be found, e.g., in (Ganter and Kuznetsov 2001).

SVM Tree Kernel learning. A DT can be represented by a vector of integer counts of each sub-tree type (without taking into account its ancestors). For EDUs as labels for terminal nodes, only the phrase structure is retained: we suppose to label the terminal nodes with the sequence of phrase types instead of parse tree fragments. For the evaluation purpose, Tree Kernel builder tool (Galitsky 2019a) was used. After that, we applied a further set of more complex experiments. For all texts, we use CDT-kernel learning approach. We combined Stanford NLP parsing, coreference resolution tool, entity extraction, CDT construction (based on automated discourse parser as in (Joty et al. 2013 and Surdeanu et al. 2015), as well as the Tree Kernel builder, into one system that is presented in (Galitsky 2019b)).

We first train the deception detection model on our ultimate deception dataset. For the initial and automatically derived datasets, we show (in bold) the accuracies of training row (grayed) and testing, averaging through 5 × cross-validation. For the bottom three datasets, we tested the same SVM Tree Kernel model trained on our dataset. We demonstrate its universality, showing its applicability to texts of various kinds, such as consumer reviews. For genuine reviews, only 380 cases of deception were detected, which were false positives, assuming that review writers do not lie (Table 6.1).

Table 6.1 Datasets, evaluation settings, accuracies for deception detection initial experiments

Dataset	Deception	No deception	P	R	F1
Manually tagged complaints	163	237	91	85	**88**
			83	81	82
Automatically tagged based on initial classifier	1132	1615	78	75	**76**
			69	71	70
Genuine reviews	380	3420	83	100	91
Fake reviews	414	286	100	59	74
Enron	27	10000	85	0.1 (estimated)	0.2

Here, for reviews datasets, we use the dataset presented in (Ott et al. 2011; 2013) in order to compare two following assessment frameworks:

1) The framework trained on consumer reviews and tested on a similar dataset;
2) Our deception recognition framework that we trained once on our own dataset and tested on texts of various kinds, such as reviews.

We achieved the performance between 74 and 91%, which is not as high as in (Ott et al. 2011, 2013) but by the universal text classification system. Hence we expect it to detect deception in other text datasets with acceptable accuracy to assure the resultant decision support system is usable.

We explored whether a fake opinionated text has a similar rhetoric structure to text with deception, and genuine reviews have a similar rhetoric structure to texts without deception. (Jindal and Liu 2008) addressed the problem of detection of opinion spam: obvious instances that are easily identified by a human reader, including advertisements, questions, and other irrelevant or non-opinionated texts. (Ott et al. 2011) investigated a more implicit type of opinion spam such as deceptive opinion spam, ones that have been deliberately written to sound authentic in order to deceive the reader. Fake reviews were written by Amazon Mechanical Turk workers. The instructions asked the workers to assume that they are employed by a hotel's marketing department and to pretend that they are asked to write a fake review (as if they were a customer) to be posted on a travel review website; additionally, the review needs to sound realistic and portray the hotel in a positive light. A request for negative reviews is done analogously.

To assess the deception detection in a real-world deception-neutral environment, we ran our detector against the business communication dataset of Enron. This dataset represents neither user-generated content since this is work-related correspondence, nor professional writing since the email authors are employees of an organization with various roles. Naturally, deception is concealed, and we do not know what was actually happening in the company and among its business partners. However, a small number of interesting emails have been discovered which have a peculiar logical structure and might well be a misrepresentation. The precision turned out to be high and the recall extremely low since only a small fraction of deception emails has been discovered. The resultant 0.2% F-measure is not an indication of recognition accuracy but instead an indication of our available estimate of the classes in the Enron dataset.

We do not know the actual proportion of emails with misrepresentation in the Enron dataset, but all detected cases are important since a misrepresentation is uncovered. Recall is not as important for this task as precision: we want to avoid false positives: once an email is classified as the one with deception, we would expect to manually confirm it.

We now zoom into the deception detection methodology for the most adequate case, the set of 2747 automatically tagged complaints (Table 6.2).

One can see that the keyword-based and Naive Bayes classifiers perform slightly better than random, since deception manifests itself at the discourse level, not the

Table 6.2 Classification accuracy for the baseline and the approach being proposed for deception detection

Method	P	R	F1
Keyword-based	56	53	54
Naïve Bayes	61	63	62
SVM-TK over parse trees and DTs	67	69	68
SVM-TK over parse trees and DTs labeled with CAs	69	71	70

syntactic one. Then we observe that proceeding to machine learning of DTs delivers an 8% gain in classification accuracy.

A deep learning approach could potentially be applied to our structured representation. However, based on our experience with discourse-level data that the amount and the quality of data contribute significantly more to the overall accuracy of a classifier, we believe experiments with the same data but different machine learning framework would be redundant.

6.1.8   Two Dimensions of Lie Detection

How to recognize unsophisticated, unprofessional lies in everyday life (Fig. 6.6), on what grounds could companies distinguish unreasonable claims for compensation from the righteous anger of honest users? These were the questions a journalist (Mishenko 2019 (EM)) addressed the book author (BG) and his colleague (DP).

EM: Honestly, when I read about the program to search for false customer complaints to the bank, I did not understand why to lie in this case. You can, for example, make bots and leave false reviews, praising yourself and scolding competitors. But why cheat on customer support?

BG: Fake reviews would be beneficial only to business, and in customer complaints people lie to get money. They do not care how the bank will continue to operate,

Fig. 6.6 An illustration for the idea that a lie is not visible in the original subjects but can nevertheless be detected at some projection layer

neither they care about its reputation. They just demand: "Give me $ 100." Therefore, reviews are of no interest to anyone—write what you want, what's the difference? Everyone loves to analyze complaints, but private individuals do not have sufficient motivation to write them. Contacting a customer support agent has a very real goal.

EM: How does the program determine which complaint is credible and which is not? By keywords, the emotional load of the text, or somehow else?

DP: (The co-author of (Pisarevskaya and Galitsky 2019)): In modern computer linguistics, primarily the features of vocabulary (keywords, emotionally colored, named entities, etc.) are used, along with syntax (what order and inter-relationship of words in a sentence), and semantics (the meaning of words). But there is a more complex level of language—the level of discourse, the processes of speech activity. Discourse analysis allows one to consider the text from the point of view of its coherence: the position of sentences, the relation-ships between them, their order, context and environment. This is important when one analyzes not just individual sentences, but the text as a whole, to understand its logical structure. After all, the text is not just a linear sequence when clauses are combined into sentences, sentences into paragraphs, and so on. The meaning of each particular sentence is related to the meaning of the previous and next sentences. We work just at the level of relations between fragments of the text, its connectivity.

We analyze the discourse, following the Rhetorical Structure Theory of text. A text is considered as a hierarchical tree, text fragment (elementary discourse units) are combined into larger ones, and they are all interconnected by certain types of relations, such as *Elaboration, Cause, Explanation, Attribution.* This theory of Discourse Trees has been extended (Galitsky 2019c) towards CDTs by adding the verbs which help to clarify the type of relationship. For text classification with respect to lying, we take the features at the highest level of abstraction: discourse trees, reflecting the way the text structure is built.

EM: How does studying a Communicative Discourse Tree help to identify true and false texts?

BG: CDTs express two dimensions of communication: rhetorical dimension and speech acts dimension.

For example, you ask me about my profession. According to the logic of lies, I am not just saying that I am an astronaut because I always aspired to it, but I will justify it with complex shaky constructions: *"I became an astronaut because my parents really wanted me to fly to the moon."* I attribute, begin to invent, add mental states, communicative levels, excuses and references to the words of others. There are two components. The first is the organization of our dialogue: you asked—I answered. Our dialogue refers to the theory of speech acts, and the justification for why I am an astronaut is a discourse part. And it turned out that each of the theories individually does not work: a person needs to lie in both dimensions (speech acts and rhetorical relations) simultaneously.

EM: Are there any quantitative features by which lie versus no lie can be determined with a high probability? For example, what does it mean if we have more than 20% of verbs in a certain mood?

DP: There are so many different cues that researchers in different countries tried to recognize a lie for different languages and in different genres of texts. A very popular destination is forensic linguistics when done for judicial purposes. Discursive symptoms are less studied, although they work well for English (Rubin 2016).

BG: Here is a more radical example. Imagine that you collect information on food markets, and it turns out that bananas are over-weighed (cheated) in 20% of cases, and apples—in 30%. Knowing which fruit is being weighed, the probability of cheating can be calculated. It is possible, but not necessary! The fact that we buy bananas or apples is not the reason we are cheated. The reason is that someone wants to deceive us, to get more money, and the scales are twisted. The same methodology is applied to the discourse analysis: there may be a million of features related to a lie, and exhaustive deployment of all features is very popular among deep learning enthusiasts. Everyone wants to throw in as many features as possible, and then the system itself is expected to figure out what is important and what is not. We are intentionally moving away from this, we want to see what happens if we remove all features but the very logic of lies. The essence lies precisely in the discourse, and banana versus apples is a different world; we do not want to consider it. Our task is not to participate in the competition, that some features would increase reliability by 2%. Instead, we need to reveal the underlying mechanism: what is the thinking of a person who is lying?

DP: We want to see how the very structure of the text of a person who intentionally uses lies differs from the structure of a reliable text. How are causal relationships built, how is argumentation built? This can be discovered via discourse analysis.

EM: The banana and apple example resembles the very concept of machine learning and machine translation: a program does not need to understand the meaning of words in order to find a match?

BG: Lie detection is somewhat simpler than machine translation because people have different languages, different cultures, different occasions, however, the logic is the same in different cultures. And we take the very highest level of abstraction: how do people organize their thoughts, by what structure they are expressed, and what and how to think about in order to properly understand this.

EM: What are examples of lies in say personal finance?

BG: Complainants write that "*I didn't have money, I really needed money, but the bank didn't give it*", and that is it: it is a lie! As soon as someone really needs something, and the bank, of course, is to blame, this person is lying. And when the client complains in detail, listing his actions: "*I called, they told me one thing, I wrote, but they did not answer me*"—most likely, he is not lying. Ordinary people have difficulty inventing scripts.

DP: If emotions prevail, there are no facts, *"they are so bad, they generally deceive everyone"*, then there is probably no evidence. This is the opposite version of a *trained* (professional) liar. Businesses lose a huge amount of money, compensating everyone who is complaining, not verifying who is lying and who is not lying.

6.1.9   Fact-Checking Tools

1) Reverse Image Search. These tools can help show you if the content you are checking is original. TinEye creates a "unique and compact digital signature" and compares it with its huge image dataset. Google or Yandex Reverse Image Search allows one to upload or drop an image by clicking on the camera icon. One can also use this on mobile using the browser menu and selecting "request desktop site."

2) Mapping. It is hard to figure out exactly where particular footage was taken. However, with detailed mapping tools such as Google Street View and Yandex Maps, one can identify a location and compare what can be seen in the footage being verified, with the maps.

3) Big InVID Fake News Debunker plugin. This tool is for journalists keen to discover if a given content is not original. Using the "Analysis" tab, one can check the location and time of YouTube and Facebook videos. This tool has options for Twitter video search, reverse image search options and metadata summaries.

4) The open-source website Inteltechniques.com is useful for tracking information on an individual or group on social media. To use it, the reader can go to the "Tools" menu on the main page and click on a platform. The site allows for searches across most social platforms, including Facebook, Twitter and LinkedIn. The site also lets you reverse image search across Google, Bing, TinEye, Yandex and Baidu.

5) Amnesty International YouTube DataViewer. This tool captures thumbnail images of any YouTube video a user pastes it. The site then lets this user reverse image search each thumbnail to see if the video or parts of the video have been uploaded previously online.

6.1.10   Conclusions

Our Ultimate Deception dataset is in the initial stage and is still being developed. In future studies, the whole complaints dataset should be manually annotated and used for model training and new experiments; it could possibly help in results improvement. We are also going to run our detector again the business communication dataset from the real world, for evaluation purposes. We also plan to run experiments with other machine learning methods. We suggest that a precision improvement (reducing the number of false positives) is most important for the deception detection task, so we will implement further steps to improve the precision. After that, we could also develop different methods of the customer complaints dataset extension.

Both truthfulness and validity are recognized reasonably well, which is a value for CRM systems and could be useful in different e-commerce tasks that are based on online review analysis. The dataset could be used for different machine learning models training that could help detect if reviews or other online texts of similar genres are truthful or deceptive, based on their content features.

6.2   Detecting Hypocrisy in Company and Customer Communication

6.2.1   Introducing Hypocrisy

Humans show a tendency to copy or imitate the behavior and attitude of others and actively influence each other's opinions about products and services. In plenty of empirical contexts, they publicly revealed opinions that are not necessarily in line with internal opinions, causing complex social interaction patterns (Gastner et al. 2019). Detecting hypocrisy in text and in conversations is extremely important for understanding the mood of a customer, how he perceives the current state of interaction with the company, and how she needs to be dealt with. If a customer is saying that he is appalled with hypocrisy from the company communicated with him, it would be hard to retain him unless certain communication and clarification efforts are made.

On the other hand, if hypocrisy is detected in customer demands and descriptions of his problem, this customer should be handled carefully and strictly taking into account that this customer might be too demanding. The company needs to watch spending associated with this customer.

The contemporary meaning of hypocrisy is saying one thing in public and doing another in private (i.e., when not observed by others). Hypocrites taken from classic literature and real-life reflect the key elements that make up this complex judgment. The classic play Tartuffe (Moliere 2002) is centered around a hypocritical priest who, after giving great speeches of piety and self-sacrifice, is found to be stealing his benefactor's fortune and trying to seduce the wife of his benefactor.

People learn in elementary school that when someone says one thing, but does not believe or follow it himself or herself, that person is called a hypocrite. Hypocrite is a person who acts in contradiction to his or her stated beliefs or feelings. Philosophers and psychologists agree that hypocrisy entails attitude-inconsistent behaviors (Fig. 6.7).

It is important to differentiate a text where a writer is appalled with a perceived hypocrisy, or double-standards, from texts of different types, categories and genres

Fig. 6.7 Hidden and public face (on the left), taking hypocrisy mask off (on the right)

because the optimal company's reaction would be totally different. In Table 6.3 we outline the categories of texts the ones with hypocrisy could potentially be confused with, and an expected company's reaction.

We first explore the cases where customers express their frustration citing the perceived hypocrisy of their opponent, the company, in complaints. We then observe how hypocrisy is expressed in tweets and attempt to find common patterns for how people express hypocrisy.

Table 6.3 Categories of text written by a customer and company's optimal reaction. The focus of this section is in the bottom row

Genre	Company's reaction
Sentiment-neutral, or opinion neutral text	Acknowledge and promise to the customer that her thoughts would be taken into account
Sarcastic text	Acknowledge that the problem raised is understood, and confirm that it would be taken seriously, even if it is impossible or too costly to fix
Texts including demands for company actions	Acknowledgement that the desired action would be performed or a rejection, ideally with the explanation why it cannot be done
Texts with a heated argument	Agreeing or disagreeing, with backing up the company's decision
Text indicating an interest in a recommendation	Produce a recommendation
Hypocrisy	Acknowledge the issue and properly communicate it. Make sure the hypocrisy is resolved in the customer's mind

6.2.2   Hypocrisy in Customer Complaints

In customer complaints, upset customers mostly cite the company's behavior as hypocritical. However, in some cases, one can observe that the customer plot indicates his own hypocrisy: the customer is first saying one thing but then acts differently.

For example, a request to return a product claiming "I will never use it" is followed by a request to provide more instructions on how to use this product (indicating that this product is used). Frequently, customers swear they would never go to a particular branch of a bank but soon contact this branch on multiple occasions in an attempt to resolve new problems. Hypocrisy is frequently associated with an explanation behind returning a product: "This dress is of a wrong size," followed by buying another item of the same size.

> *I am upset because I had overdraft protection and paid a bill, went over the 500 dollar limit and deposited the money back into the bank the same day so that I could avoid being penalized. The banker stated that my deposit should hit my account before getting penalized for going 23 dollars over. I mean come on, I put the money back into the account the same day!* **No one sent a notification advising that I lost my overdraft protection** *and so I paid my insurance, again overdrafting the account and thought I was good to go. Checked my statement only to find a rejected payment and in the negative in top of overdraft fees and a cancelled insurance policy.*

In this text, we have an assumed clause of bank responsibility. It occurs implicitly in this text. The customer is saying *you did this* assuming that this bank in particular, as well as most other banks, are supposed to do *that*. A reader would trust this complaint writer in how the actions of this bank are described, so the hypocrisy is genuine here. The customer attaches an expression of disbelief "come on" to the action of the bank.

Naturally, hypocrisy as a logical construction can be tracked in a discourse tree. In Fig. 6.8 on the right (in the star area) we show the *Say* part of a hypocrisy that is not explicitly mentioned in the text but assumed. The *Do* part is explicit in this text, so we intend to detect it. We show communicative actions (CA) in *Say* part that is frequently assumed but not explicit in the text, so it is even harder to detect hypocrisy in this case. However, *no one <CA(bank, What)> me* ([*send(no-one, customer, notification)*]) indicates that *Say = CA(bank, me, What)* together with the explicit *Do* part (here, *Do = reject(bank, me, payment)*). In the rest of this chapter, we focus on the cases with explicit both *Say* and *Do* parts; otherwise, it is too difficult to infer implicit *Say* part.

6.2.3   Building a Dataset of Sentences with Hypocrisy

We borrow various classes of hypocrisy from psychological studies including (Barden et al. 2005, Alicke et al. 2012) to identify the additional relationship between linguistic *Say* and Do parts (Table 6.4). *Do* parts can include an intent to deceive (rows two to four).

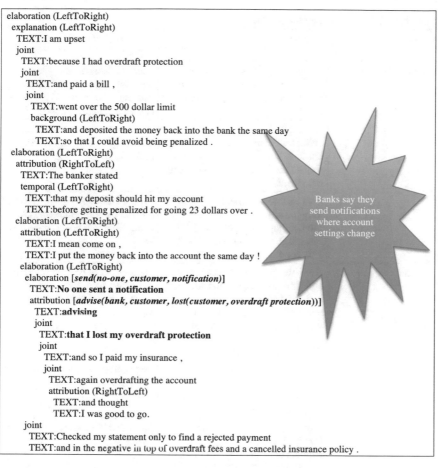

```
elaboration (LeftToRight)
 explanation (LeftToRight)
  TEXT:I am upset
  joint
   TEXT:because I had overdraft protection
   joint
    TEXT:and paid a bill ,
    joint
     TEXT:went over the 500 dollar limit
     background (LeftToRight)
      TEXT:and deposited the money back into the bank the same day
      TEXT:so that I could avoid being penalized .
 elaboration (LeftToRight)
  attribution (RightToLeft)
   TEXT:The banker stated
   temporal (LeftToRight)
    TEXT:that my deposit should hit my account
    TEXT:before getting penalized for going 23 dollars over .
  elaboration (LeftToRight)
   attribution (LeftToRight)
    TEXT:I mean come on ,
    TEXT:I put the money back into the account the same day !
   elaboration (LeftToRight)
    elaboration [send(no-one, customer, notification)]
     TEXT:No one sent a notification
     attribution [advise(bank, customer, lost(customer, overdraft protection))]
      TEXT:advising
      joint
       TEXT:that I lost my overdraft protection
       joint
        TEXT:and so I paid my insurance ,
        joint
         TEXT:again overdrafting the account
         attribution (RightToLeft)
          TEXT:and thought
          TEXT:I was good to go.
  joint
   TEXT:Checked my statement only to find a rejected payment
   TEXT:and in the negative in top of overdraft fees and a cancelled insurance policy .
```

Banks say they send notifications where account settings change

Fig. 6.8 Communicative Discourse Tree for a customer complaint that includes the Do part of a bank's hypocritical pattern

6.2.4 Templates for Sentences with Hypocrisy

In psychological terms, hypocritical statements establish personal standard and then commit behavior that violates that standard, and it does not matter if that standard is consistent or inconsistent with social norms.

We refer to such personal standard as *prominent entity* (of *Saying*) and then consider this behavior that violates this standard as *Doing*. Hence our top-level template is *Say … <RST-Contrast> … Do*. *RST-Contrast* is a rhetorical relation of contrast between two respective parts of a sentence.

A template can cover or not cover a given sentence. We compute syntactic generalization of a template and a sentence to be covered (Galitsky et al. 2012, Chap. 2

Table 6.4 The classes of sentences with hypocrisy

Class	Sentence	Comment/explanation of hypocrisy
Intent to deceive	A parent who was a recreational drug user in his heyday but who now discourages his son to use drugs	intent to deceive others about one's attitudes or values is not necessarily required to judge an actor's behavior as hypocritical
	A woman, Jane, expresses the belief that premarital sex is wrong but does not disguise the fact that she is sexually active despite being unmarried	intent to deceive is not seen as necessary by laypeople to label an action as hypocritical
	Paul believes that people should eat only healthy food, although he eats junk food himself. He tells others that he eats junk food	People know someone believes in *Say* but does contradicting *Do* confirming that he has done that *Do*
Weakness of will	A woman who has been active in anti-drug campaigns, and who has resisted even prescription medications for a severe back injury gives in one day to the temptation to ease her pain, but then never again takes any drugs	Failures of the will are often seen as distinct from hypocrisy, at least when they represent momentary lapses
	Priest, who preaches against adultery is pursued by a married woman. He resists her advances for months, but then finally gives in	Repeated lapses are tend to be judged as hypocritical
	Woman promises herself and her family that she is going to remain celibate until she is married. Then she decides that premarital sex is not wrong	*Say* one thing for the future, then *Do* the opposite
Self-deception	A student who parties far more than he studies, realizes that he is a poor student but is nevertheless critical of others who he believes are not serious students	Some cases of self-deception are indistinct from hypocrisy; in particular, those in which actor must go to great lengths to maintain their delusions while simultaneously denigrating others who engage in the same behaviors
	College student has strong feelings of attraction to other men, but is active in an anti-gay organization. At the same time, the student is aware that he is gay	Self-deception can be expressed by *deceive(student, student, acceptable(gay(student)) & not acceptable(gay(Anyone)))*

(continued)

Table 6.4   (continued)

Class	Sentence	Comment/explanation of hypocrisy
Degree of discrepancy	A parent, who forbids his daughter to get a tattoo, is described as a cigarette smoker, someone with body piercings, or the possessor of a tattoo	Degree of discrepancy between attitudes and behavior affects the frequency with which hypocrisy is ascribed
	A student who ate three cheeseburgers for lunch subsequently helped in a community program to raise awareness about exercise, or walked in a relay to support the fight against heart disease	Actors whose behaviors contradict their own attitudes are critical of others who do the same suffices to conclude about hypocrisy
	A man who visited the X-rated section of a video store. Later in the day, he protested casino gambling, helped at a church bake sale and also helped in a community program to eliminate pornography	
	A person who signs a private contract handed out at school that they will use condoms and then has unsafe sex	
Reversing order	Pat is sitting on the couch, eating and watching TV for a week, and gaining five pounds; however, two weeks later, Pat makes a public statement indicating that people should be proactive in pursuing a healthier lifestyle	The reverse order would increase the likelihood that the inconsistency between the statement and the behavior would be attributed to the change of target rather than to hypocrisy
	Mrs. Grace laments about the terrible conditions of the Mruna tribe in Africa, promising financial aid and support for the missionary who is attempting to Christianize them. But her charity obviously does not begin at home: she resents the mood of the black population in her town and she considers firing her black maid for being "sulky."	One person is expected to advocate for tolerance to a certain category of people and be tolerant himself before and after his act of advocating

Volume 1 and Chap. 4 Volume 2). If all syntactic features from the template are retained in the generalization results, we say that this template *covers* this sentence.

Verb strengthening/attenuating [Prominent entity] <RST-Contrast> Verb strengthening/attenuating/neutral [opposite prominent feature]

Positive sentiment [Prominent entity] <RST-Contrast> Negative sentiment =>
[similar prominent entity].

We will now denote positive sentiment by "+" and negative sentiment by "-."
Perceived expression of hypocrisy (which is a controversy) for a historical period
following a classical writer and social critic:

> *Charles Dickens stood for all the Victorian virtues such as kindness, and sympathy for the*
> *down-trodden, but his novels exposed the violence, hypocrisy, greed, and cruelty of this age.*

We generalize to obtain the template *Person ... action_viewpoint1* +++[sentiment]
Persons' object action_viewpoint2—[sentiment]

These quotes of Arthur Schopenhauer and Leo Tolstoy define a partial case of
hypocrisy. These quotes are covered by our templates and even implicitly follow
Say-Do paradigm:

> *'With people of limited ability modesty is merely honesty. But with those who possess great*
> *talent it is hypocrisy.'*

> *'Hypocrisy in anything whatever may deceive the cleverest and most penetrating man, but*
> *the least wide-awake of children recognizes it, and is revolted by it, however ingeniously it*
> *may be disguised'*

We can see in the discourse tree that *Contrast* must be present (Fig. 6.9).
A quote of Jean Kerr is more explicit in terms of *Say-Do*. The meaning of the
following is: first *Say* (polite) => *Do* (polite):

> *'Man is the only animal that learns by being hypocritical. He pretends to be polite and then,*
> *eventually, he becomes polite.'*

This is a controversy, contradiction (expressed by US Congresswoman Ilhan
Omar) but not a hypocrisy of the person saying this because the pronoun *We* (not *I*)
is used in this text. Otherwise, it is covered by the hypocrisy template.

> *'As an immigrant, I truly believed when I was coming to this country that people had the*
> *tools necessary to live a life that is prosperous. But we cannot figure out how to house our*
> *homeless people.'*

And now let us see how economists such as Milton Friedman express hypocritical
"truth bombs":

```
same-unit
  contrast (RightToLeft)
   elaboration (LeftToRight)
    TEXT:Hypocrisy in anything
    TEXT:whatever may deceive the cleverest and most penetrating man ,
   joint
    TEXT:but the least wide-awake of children recognizes it ,
    TEXT:and is revolted by it ,
   TEXT:however ingeniously it may be disguised
The opposing prominent entities above are 'limited ability' vs 'great talent' and 'cleverest and most
penetrating' vs 'wide-awake of children'.
```

Fig. 6.9 A DT for a definition of hypocrisy

Table 6.5 Syntactic templates for entailment and contradiction

Entailment templates	Contradiction templates
"<premise> implies <hypothesis>"	"In sentence 1 <premise> while in sentence 2
"If <premise> then <hypothesis>"	<hypothesis>"
"<premise> would imply <hypothesis>"	"It can either be <premise> or <hypothesis>"
"<hypothesis> is a rephrasing of <premise>"	"It cannot be <hypothesis> if <premise>"
"<premise> is a rephrasing of <hypothesis>"	"Either <premise> or <hypothesis>"
"In both sentences <hypothesis>"	"Either <hypothesis> or <premise>"
"<premise> would be <hypothesis>"	"<premise> and other <hypothesis>"
"<premise> can also be said as <hypothesis>"	"<hypothesis> and other <premise>"
"<hypothesis> can also be said as <premise>"	"<hypothesis> after <premise>"
"<hypothesis> is a less specific rephrasing of	"<premise> is not the same as <hypothesis>"
<premise>"	"<hypothesis> is not the same as <premise>"
"This clarifies that <hypothesis>"	"<premise> is contradictory to <hypothesis>"
"If <premise> it means <hypothesis>"	"<hypothesis> is contradictory to <premise>"
"<hypothesis> in both sentences"	"<premise> contradicts <hypothesis>"
"<hypothesis> in both"	"<hypothesis> contradicts <premise>"
"<hypothesis> is same as <premise>"	"<premise> cannot also be <hypothesis>"
"<premise> is same as <hypothesis>"	"<hypothesis> cannot also be <premise>"
"<premise> is a synonym of <hypothesis>"	"either <premise> or <hypothesis>"
"<hypothesis> is a synonym of <premise>"	"either <premise> or <hypothesis> not both at the same time"
	"<premise> or <hypothesis> not both at the same time"

'*With some notable exceptions, businessmen favor free enterprise in general but are opposed to it when it comes to themselves.*'

We also show a set of generic templates (Table 6.5).

6.2.5 Assessing Coordination of Prominent Entities

A baseline approach here is based on distributional semantics (word2vec, Chap. 2). A pair of prominent entities in *Say* and *Do* or *Say One thing* then *Say Another thing* should be coordinated.

A more sophisticated approach is to rely on the wisdom of the web to explore how two prominent entities are inter-related (or, in particular, contrasting). We want to see whether two prominent entities are opposite to each other or not. We select an example of *attraction to other men* versus *anti-gay organization*. We want to assess how a reversal of meaning for a prominent entity can dramatically boost affinity.

Web mining results for a pair of prominent entities is shown in Fig. 6.10. On the top, we show the assessment of affinity of original prominent entities, and on the bottom—affinity of the former and the *reversed* latter entity. Once the meaning is reversed, the number of documents with both these prominent entities is dramatically increased. We have just seven search results associating *attraction to other men* versus *anti-gay organization* and 1810 search results for the same prominent entities but

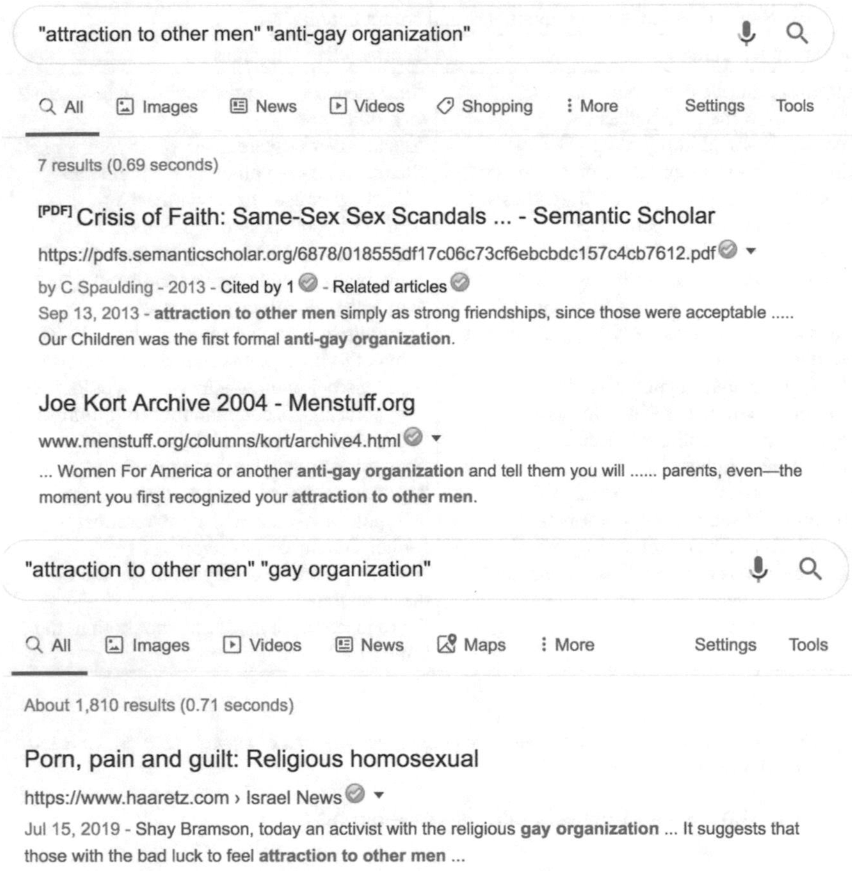

Fig. 6.10   Web mining to establish an affinity of two prominent entities

with the reversal of meaning for the latter one. Hence we conclude that *if |Say & Do|* $\ll$| *Say & $\neg$ Do|* $\Rightarrow$ *Do* $\approx \neg$ *Say,* which is a hypocrisy.

The third approach leverages web thesaurus resources when the prominent entity is a single word. A web resource can be accessed online or be pre-loaded. Figure 6.11 shows examples of antonyms for *prosperous*. Notice that the accuracy of word meanings significantly exceeds that of compositional semantic models. To coordinate *prosperous* and *homeless*, we need to get a list of synonyms and antonyms for each and then attempt to find a common word. If this attempt is unsuccessful, word2vec can be used to link derived synonyms and/or antonyms to produce a chain of words connecting the prominent entities. Web ontologies are usually horizontal, domain-independent. A domain-specific ontology of entities (Galitsky et al. 2011b) can be employed as well, but its construction is costly.

Fig. 6.11 Antonyms for *prosperous* at Thesaurus.com

6.2.6   Hypocrisy in Tweets

Also, there is a good set of tweets with hashtag *hypocrite* on Twitter. The reader can see that some tweets with this tag are covered by our hypocrisy templates, such as Fig. 6.12.

Person says ... but then person does
Person speaks loud/crying crocodile tears—... but try/turns blind eye—...

Some tweets in this set have only *Do* part, and it is hard to identify such tweet as a text with hypocrisy.

Some tweets have neither parts and express hypocrisy explicitly

They bought a pipeline.
They're still taking Indigenous youth to court.
They haven't even met Harper's environmental targets.
Trudeau violated his own ethics law. TWICE!

The template here is *violated/broke/cheat/deceive his/her/their own ...*

So Beth Moore who shares the Gospel is a stain on the church but a heretic like Paula White is a leading evangelical's good friend? Mhmmm I wonder what's the common denominator...let's see could it be that her allegiance to Trump is greater than the Gospel
So <Person1> <Person1feature -> but/yet <Person2> <Person2feature +>

Here is a CDT for the first sentence above, which is in a hypocritical format (Fig. 6.13)

We conclude this section with a few more examples:

Says the man who <verb1-> and <verb2-> . <verb1->= drives expensive car

So your <concept +> matters but others should <verb->

What's worse is that Facebook is only implementing their "standards" to ordinary people but not to those who have money or power

Fig. 6.12 Sample tweets from https://twitter.com/hashtag/hypocrite

Because expressions with hypocrisy are so peculiar subject of study in NLP, we do not follow a traditional ML methodology. We use a combined manual and automatic method to construct the training dataset, reducing the large original one obtained from various sources. As we construct it and use for learning, we obtain detection test results and as long F1 is improving, we apply the trained model to the original set attempting to form a larger training set. Hence the entire hypocrisy detection dataset formation procedure is iterative.

---

contrast
elaboration
  TEXT:So Beth Moore
  TEXT:who shares the Gospel is a stain on the church ,
  TEXT:but a heretic like Paula White is a leading evangelical 's good friend

---

Notice that *but* as a discourse marker is needed to indicate rhetorical relation of ***contrast***.

'Must have one of the biggest carbon footprints going, so to preach to us about climate change is an absolute joke
<Person> must have <prominent entity -> so to <do> <positive> change is an absolute joke
  If you call Biden's son a criminal what do u call @ivanka who's rcvd almost 50 trademarks from China since daddy's been in office?
  If you call <Person1> - what do you call <Person2> who - <action>
  Why are so called <Person-Category> silent on this?
  How pro-<concept1> is your stance/viewpoint/position on <concept2>? I <mental_state> your <concept3>
  Funny how @KingJames preaches being "more than an athlete", but is afraid to stand up for democracy when it's gonna hurt the bank.
  Funny how <person> preaches being <concept1>, but is afraid to stand up for <concept2> when it's gonna hurt

---

Fig. 6.13 A DT for a tweet (on the top) and a number of templates for hypocritical tweets (on the bottom)

6.2.7 Expressing Hypocrisy in a Dialogue

There is an example of how hypocrisy is expressed in dialogue. Hypocrisy in a dialogue can be detected by a sudden change in a mood, as reflected in the sentiment of each utterance (Galitsky and McKenna 2017).

I don't think women should have any rights. Moreover, LGBT should be executed.
Wow! What a complete primitive asshole you are! Because you must be a republican?
No. Actually, I am a Muslim. And, therefore, those are my religious beliefs.
Oh! Then I'm so sorry!! I apologize! But I hope you don't think I am islamophobic.

It turns out that just an indication of sentiment as determined by an individual phrase is most informative about this dialogue (Fig. 6.14). The sentiment profile shows how an instant sentiment value changes with each utterance and how a dialogue participant abruptly changes his attitude, values and estimates of the dialogue participants (Galitsky et al. 2015).

The sentiment profile in Fig. 6.15 starts with the negative territory as a person describes his negative attitude. His peer is "excited," so the profile jumps to positive for a short step. Her clarification question step has a neutral sentiment, followed by the negative sentiment associated with his answer. Her reaction is very volatile: from the negative sentiment of *being sorry* to the positive sentiment of *I apologize*. The reader may disagree with sentiment assignment to individual utterances but the overall volatility of the sentiment profile of this dialogue does not seem counter-intuitive (Galitsky and Kovalerchuk 2006).

A CDT for this dialogue is shown in Fig. 6.16. Rhetorical relations showing the logical structure of this dialogue are bolded. Default rhetorical relation such as *Elaboration, Same-unit* and *Temporal* do not express special dialogue-related logic or

Fig. 6.14 Illustration for a representation of conversational discourse

a communication structure. *Contrast* and *Explanation* express a high-level meaning for a current utterance or a block of utterances.

Communicative actions are attached to the edges of the CDT. Texts of elementary discourse units are extended with expressions for communicative actions such as *not think(he, have_right(women))*. These expressions are obtained from AMR parsing and also VerbNet resource. Besides communicative actions, emotions can be attached to the edges of this CDT as well.

A dynamic semantic theory of discourse interpretation that uses rhetorical relations to model the semantics/pragmatics interface is called SDRS (Asher and Lascarides 2003, Fig. 6.17). The intention of SDRS is to express semantic underspecification as partial descriptions of logical forms and to rely on a *glue logic* that uses commonsense reasoning to construct logical forms, relating the semantically underspecified forms that are generated by the grammar to their pragmatically preferred interpretations. The purpose is to handle anaphora and other types of semantic ambiguities.

The glue logic extends dynamic semantics' mechanisms for constructing logical form by encoding an interaction between semantics and pragmatics: it involves commonsense reasoning with both linguistic and non-linguistic information, which extends the partial information about content that's generated by the grammar to a more complete semantic representation of the discourse. SDRS calculates the value of a rhetorical relation (and its arguments) that is absent in compositional semantics. Also, SDRS identifies the antecedent to a pronoun, resolves the semantic scope of a presupposition, disambiguates a word sense, yields a bridging inference, etc.

Sentiment:

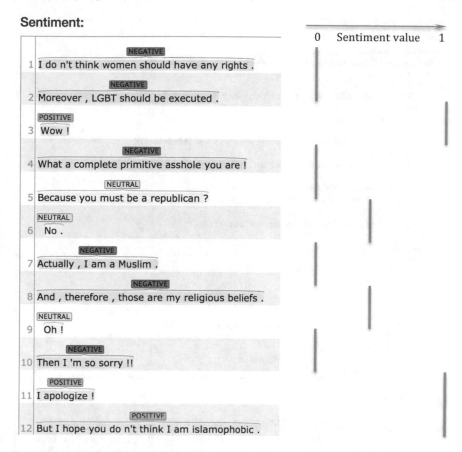

Fig. 6.15 Sentiment profile of a dialogue

The glue logic plays an important role in semantic under-specification. In Fig. 6.17, the glue logic includes predicates such as *Experiencer(_, _)*, *Patient(_, _)* and *Stimulus(_, _)*.

6.2.8   System Architecture

The system architecture of the hypocrisy detector is depicted in Fig. 6.18. On the left, there are main detection engines: a Nearest-neighbor-based (on the top) and an SVM Tree Kernel learning, oriented to tackle structured tree-like features (on the bottom). On the right, we show the data components: The Training Set Former, A domain-specific Ontology and An Entity Matching.

Nearest-neighbor learning is used for faster detection with explainability. Once/if the nearest neighbor template is found, the hypocrisy detector explains its decision for

```
elaboration (LeftToRight)
 attribution (RightToLeft)
  TEXT:I do not think
  TEXT:women should have any rights. [not think(he, have_right(women))]
 elaboration
  elaboration
   TEXT:Moreover , LGBT should be executed . [emotion(agression)]
   elaboration
    TEXT:Wow !
    elaboration
     TEXT:What a complete primitive asshole you are ! [emotion(agression)]
     explanation(
      TEXT:Because you must be a republican ? believe (she, republican(he))
      joint
        attribution (RightToLeft)
         TEXT:No. Actually ,
         TEXT:I am a Muslim .
        TEXT:And , therefore , those are my religious beliefs .
 temporal
  TEXT:Oh !
  elaboration
   TEXT:Then I ' m so sorry !! [emotion(sorry)]
   contrast (RightToLeft)
    TEXT:I apologize !
    same-unit
     attribution (RightToLeft)
      TEXT:But I hope [hope(she, not think(he, islamophobic(she)))]
      TEXT:you don 't
     attribution (RightToLeft)
      TEXT: think [think(he, islamophobic(she))]
      TEXT:I am islamophobic .
```

Fig. 6.16 A CDT for the dialogue

```
SDRS( CONTINUATION( K1 K2 ) CONTINUATION( K2 K3 ) … CONTINUATION( K12 K11 )
K1( DRS( person( X1 ) P1( DRS( NEC( DRS( woman( X2 ) NEC( DRS( IMP( DRS( right( X3 ) ) DRS(
have( E1 ) Agent( E1 X1 ) Patient( E1 X3 ) now( T1 ) Temp_included( E1 T2 ) Temp_before( T1 T2 ) ) ) )
) ) ) ) ) ) )
K2( DRS( NEC( DRS( lgbt( X1 ) execute( E2 ) Patient( E2 X1 ) now( T1 ) Temp_included( E2 T3 )
Temp_before( T1 T3 ) and( E2 ) ) ) ) )
K3( DRS( wow( X3 ) ) )
K4( DRS( DUP( DRS( thing( X4 ) ) DRS( thing( X2 ) be( E3 ) Agent( E3 X2 ) Theme( E3 X3 ) now( T1 )
Temp_included( E3 T4 ) Equ( T4 T1 ) ) ) ) )
K5( DRS( NEC( DRS( person( X1 ) republican( X5 ) be( E4 ) Agent( E4 X1 ) Theme( E4 X5 ) now( T1 )
Temp_included( E4 T5 ) Temp_before( T1 T5 ) ) ) ) )
K6( DRS( NOT( DRS( thing( X6 ) ) ) ) )
K7( DRS( person( X7 ) muslim( X8 ) be( E5 ) Agent( E5 X7 ) Theme( E5 X8 ) now( T1 ) Temp_included(
E5 T6 ) Equ( T6 T1 ) actually( E5 ) ) )
K8( DRS( person( X9 ) person( X1 ) Of( X9 X10 ) Topic( S1 X9 ) religious( S1 ) belief( X9 ) be( E6 )
Agent( E6 X9 ) Theme( E6 X9 ) now( T1 ) Temp_included( E6 T7 ) Equ( T7 T1 ) and( E6 ) ) )
K9( DRS( person( X2 ) oh( S2 ) Topic( S2 X2 ) now( T1 ) Temp_included( S2 T8 ) Equ( T8 T1 ) ) )
K10( DRS( person( X2 ) person( X2 ) Of( X10 X2 ) Topic( S3 X10 ) oh( S3 ) Topic( S4 X10 ) oh( S4 ) ) )
K11( DRS( person( X2 ) m( X11 ) In( X2 X11 ) so( X2 ) sorry( S5 ) Topic( S5 X10 ) so( S5 ) P2( DRS(
person( X2 ) hope( E7 ) Experiencer( E7 X2 ) Stimulus( E7 P2 ) now( T1 ) Temp_included( E7 T9 ) Equ(
T9 T1 ) P3( DRS( person( X2 ) '( X12 ) Agent( E8 X2 ) Theme( E8 P2 ) ) ) ) ) ) )
K12( DRS( person( X2 ) hope( E9 ) Experiencer( E9 X2 ) Stimulus( E9 P3 ) now( T1 ) Temp_included(
E9 T10 ) Equ( T10 T1 ) ) ) )
```

Fig. 6.17 A SDRS Representation for the same dialogue

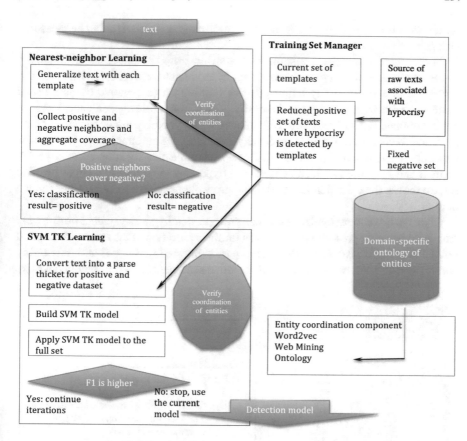

Fig. 6.18 System architecture of the hypocrisy detector

why a given text is classified as hypocrisy or not. As a candidate neighbor is found, the system attempts to coordinate the entities in *Say* and *Do* parts. The detector performs generalization of a current text and a candidate nearest template only if the coordination of prominent entities succeeds.

SVM TK learning (Chap. 9 Volume 1) is used for iterative improvement of detection accuracy by enlarging the training set. SVM TK does not possess the explainability feature and speed performance of the nearest-neighbor but assures a higher detection accuracy. It employs the same entity coordination component.

To achieve the higher accuracy detection, given the available raw training dataset, and minimize manual tagging, we iteratively expand the golden (reduced) set of accepted texts containing hypocrisy. We first apply the initial set of manually built templates to the raw set of texts and obtain the current reduced set. Then we use SVM TK for building a classification model from this reduced set. Once this classification model is built, it is applied to the raw set and is supposed to produce a larger reduced training set. This larger reduced set is expected to produce a better model. The iterations continue until the model stops to improve (Fig. 6.19). It could be measured as a gain of F1 at the latest iteration below 0.3%.

In the algorithm chart, we show how starting from the initial set of manually formed sentences with hypocrisy and a set of templates for hypocrisy, one can iteratively build a substantially larger positive training set (a negative training set of sentences without hypocrisy can be easily grown from arbitrary sentences). As we apply templates to a corpus where sentences with hypocrisy are expected to occur (such as tweets not explicitly tagged as hypocritical), we automatically identify new members of the positive training set. Once we build a classification model, we can apply it and find more such sentences with hypocrisy. As we have a larger positive set, we retrain the classification model and grow the positive set even further (on the bottom-left).

Once we learn to recognize sentences with explicit hypocrisy, where both *saying* and *doing* parts are present, we envision a future exploration of the texts with implicit reference to hypocrisy where the saying part is inferred (assumed) and only doing part is present, usually associated with negative sentiment and emotionally charged.

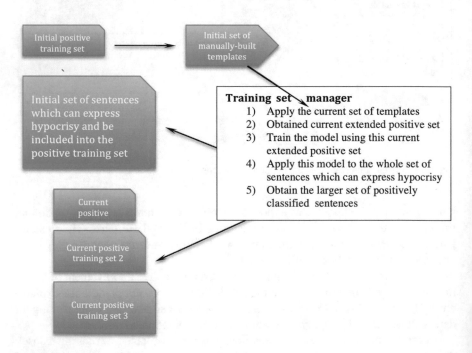

Fig. 6.19 Iterative algorithm for growing a larger positive training set

6.2.9   Evaluation

We collect *Say-Do* sentences and paragraphs from multiple sources on the web related to hypocrisy, including http://www.wiseoldsayings.com/hypocrisy-quotes/, https://www.brainyquote.com/topics/hypocrisy, https://www.ranker.com/list/notable-and-famous-hypocrisy-quotes (Table 6.6). We use Twitter Search API to obtain tweets with hashtags related to hypocrisy. We use our Ultimate Deception dataset of customer complaints (Sect. 6.1.5) many of which cite company hypocrisy.

The negative dataset for the web source was obtained from the same sites for items other than hypocrisy. For tweets, we use the replies to the posts associated with hypocrisy so that we have the texts on the same topic but without the *Say-Do* hypocrisy part. For the complaint dataset, we use sentences with positive reviews as ones without hypocrisy.

We do a two-step learning to minimize a manual tagging of texts perceived by a human annotator as hypocritical. In the first step, we use templates to build a gold set of "genuine" expressions for hypocrisy. We then spot-check it manually and confirm the precision of the training data. The first step is performed iteratively adjusting the templates. In the second step, we train the classifier in a traditional setting, exploring the accuracy of Nearest Neighbor and SVM TK (Table 6.7)

One can see that for all datasets, hypocrisy detection facilitated by web mining produces better results than the one facilitated by word2vec. The entity coordination is further improved by a hybrid approach.

SVM TK improves nearest-neighbor only by about 1%; however, the role of SVM TK in expanding the training set is valuable. Hence it is wise to use SVM TK offline for training set management and Nearest-Neighbor component at detection time.

What are the categories of texts which are confused with hypocrisy most frequently? We show the data in Table 6.8. For each row, we show percentages of all false positives which fall in this category, such as *Strong negative sentiment*.

Table 6.6 Positive training sets

Source of Hypocritical expressions	# in original set	# in selected set	Average# of sentences	Average# of words
Expression from web sources	280	213	1.7	18.2
Expressions from twitter tagged#*Hypocrite*	4217	516	1.4	16.7
Expressions from twitter tagged#*Double-standard*	2319	308	1.5	17.6
Expressions from twitter tagged#hypocrisyatitsfinest	565	159	1.4	17.0
Customer complaint recognized as valid	1328	265	7.3	76.3
Random customer complaint	1400	188	8.5	81.4

Table 6.7 Hypocrisy detection accuracy

Source/Method	Nearest Neighbor based on syntactic generalization									SVM TK								
	Word2vec			Web mining			Hybrid + hand-coded thesaurus for entity comparison			Word2vec			Web mining			Hybrid + hand-coded thesaurus for entity comparison		
	P	R	F1	P	R	F1	P	R	F1	P	R	F1	P	R	F1	P	R	F1
Expression from web sources	69.70	66.00	67.80	72.30	75.20	73.72	82.40	82.70	82.55	70.30	72.40	71.33	74.3	76.1	75.19	84.3	83.8	84.05
Expressions from twitter tagged#Hypocrite	64.20	67.30	65.71	72.90	70.30	71.58	84.20	85.40	84.80	67.80	64.9	66.32	71.8	72.7	72.25	85.6	86.1	85.85
Expressions from twitter tagged#Double-standard	63.90	66.80	65.32	69.30	70.80	70.04	82.30	83.10	82.70	65.80	67.90	66.83	70.5	69.2	69.84	83.4	82.7	83.05
Expressions from twitter tagged#hypocrisyatitsfinest	67.20	67.00	67.10	72.70	70.80	71.74	80.60	84.20	82.36	69.60	70.40	70.00	73.2	75.7	74.43	83.2	83	83.10
Customer complaint recognized as valid	64.20	67.20	65.67	71.00	72.50	71.74	79.40	78.30	78.85	67.40	69.00	68.19	72.7	70.5	71.58	80.7	81.3	81.00
Random customer complaint	69.70	66.00	67.80	72.30	75.20	73.72	82.40	82.70	82.55	70.30	72.40	71.33	74.3	76.1	75.19	84.3	83.8	84.05

Table 6.8 Confusion categories for hypocrisy

Category	Nearest Neighbor	SVM TK
Strong negative sentiment	15.2	16.1
Contrasting without pretending or hypocrisy	12.0	13.4
Blaming without pretending or hypocrisy	13.7	12.6
Rudeness, name calling	12	10.4
Punch line of a joke	7.1	6.5

Different ML approaches show certain variations in these categories of confusion given the same training/test dataset.

6.2.10 Related Work and Discussions

(Barden et al. 2005) investigated whether the temporal order of writers' expressed statements and their behaviors affected judgments of others concerning hypocrisy. It was proposed that hypocrisy would be greater when a claim establishing a personal standard preceded a behavior pattern violating that standard as opposed to the other way around. This order effect occurred in a number of studies, generalizing across two topic areas (healthy living and safe sex) and for both normative and nonnormative statements (pro/anti–safe sex). Conducted data analyses showed that the reverse order mitigated against hypocrisy because the target's inconsistency was associated with a dispositional change. The authors enumerate additional variables likely to affect hypocrisy and the relationship of this research to hypocrisy paradigms in dissonance.

Hypocrisy is a multi-faceted concept that has been studied empirically by psychologists and discussed logically by philosophers. (Aliske et al. 2012) propose various behavioral scenarios to research participants and ask them to confirm whether the actor in the scenario behaved hypocritically. The authors assess many of the components that have been considered to be necessary for hypocrisy (such as the *intent to deceive, self-deception*), features that may or may not be differentiated from hypocrisy (such as weakness of will), and features that may moderate hypocrisy (such as the degree of discrepancy between the attitude and behavior, whether the attitude is stated publicly, and the nature and severity of the behavioral consequences). (Aliske et al. 2012) findings indicate that the actual foundation of hypocrisy are not always correlated with philosophical speculation. A complete understanding of the criteria for hypocrisy would require consideration of how ordinary people express hypocrisy. In contrast to some philosophical concepts such as physical causation, for which lay conceptions are mostly independent, hypocrisy is an essential component of social judgment.

There are multiple reasons people say one thing and end up doing a totally different thing. One example is the 2015 UK election, as the polls leading up to the election said that no one political party would be the outright winner/have a majority. Trump's election in the US in 2016 is a similar example. However, what happened is that on election night, the Conservatives won an unexpected majority. Another example is UK former education secretary, William Bennett, whose huge gambling losses in the wake of his "Book of Virtues" were widely cited as hypocritical.

Why did people say they were going to vote one way and then change their minds? People often say (*Say*) one thing and do (*Do*) another. It is a complex process to understand what people and customers want and how it deviates from what they say.

The pollsters were not trying to influence the election outcome. They tried hard to get a sample on which they could predict where the election was headed. So the pollsters, along with all of the public, were surprised to learn election results. Even if they were reaching a broad sample of the British population, the answers they got back might not have been accurate. This is because sometimes, the voter did not know yet what they actually wanted. What they wanted for the election was implicitly stored in their subconscious, deep in the emotions.

Many times there is a hidden part of how a customer feels that drives their behavior. One can try to detect where customers tell you they want something, implement that something, and see no change in customer behavior. It is important to look for the causes of the behavior to see what customers *really* want. These customer causes are hidden deep in the subconscious or superego.

People frequently have two ways of thinking about things and whichever one is in control at the moment will determine their behavioral choice. Everyone knows there is a big difference between what people say and what people do. Sometimes people do not know what they want until they are forced to make a decision, as in the voting booth. However, the way people make decisions many times, is with their hearts, not their heads. (Kahneman 2011) writes about the System One thinking (intuitive, emotional, instinctive, fast) and System Two thinking (methodical, analytical, logic-based, slow). One can hypothesize that during the poll inquiry, voters could have used System One thinking, answering quickly without using their more rational thinking from System Two. However, System Two might have been triggered at the poll stations. It can also be the other way around.

The difference between *Say* (what they will do) and what they actually *Do* is associated with their reasoning not being perfect, rational. Having marketing actions based on research concerning the rational side of obtained experience from users is not going to get a business to where it needs to go. Every company has an experience that yields irrational emotions that drive the behavior of its customers. Exploring the emotions connected to a brand would give a much better basis for predicting how customers might react.

One can cite obsolete methodologies for polling and suggest they have caused the error. Polling results come from a certain sampling of the population, usually via their home phone, and it is increasingly difficult to reach people on a home number. Pollsters still use the home phone because there is a consensus amongst pollsters that cell phones are not reliable. But for most people, if they are not being reached on their cells, one can rely on not reaching them at all. It is important to change methods of communication if it is necessary to get an indicative sample of the population.

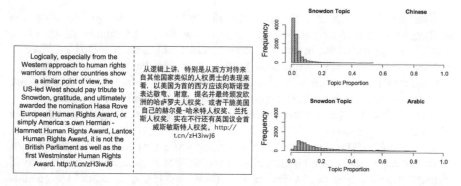

Fig. 6.20 Hypocrisy is frequently associated with such topic as human rights and global warming

Politics and polling go together. They are essential to those who run and those who vote. However, in the election in the UK in 2015, the pollsters failed to provide an accurate representation of voters' intentions, leaving many wondering if the methodology needs a closer look.

How hypocrisy is expressed depends on particular language culture. For example, the "human rights" topic discusses the U.S. record on human rights and whether the Snowden disclosures undermine this record. This topic contains words such as *"violate"*, *"freedom"*, *"human"*, *"right"* and *"traitor"* Some of the posts also discuss whether the United States is a hypocrite, violating U.S. citizens' human rights while also advocating for greater human rights protection abroad. Figure 6.20 on the left displays a tweet on this topic, and on the right shows a proportion of this topic in different language cultures (Lucas et al. 2015).

6.2.11 Hypocrysy versus Controversy Stance, Sarcasm, Sentiments

We now comment on the difference between hypocrisy detection, stance detection, controversy detection and sentiment analysis. Stance detection has been defined as automatically detecting whether the author of a piece of text is in favor of the given target or against it. It can be viewed as a subtask of opinion mining and it stands next to the sentiment analysis (Galitsky et al. 2010). The significant difference is that in sentiment analysis, systems determine whether a fragment of text has positive, negative, or neutral polarity. Conversely, in stance detection, systems are to determine the author's favorability towards a given target and the target even may not be explicitly mentioned in the text. Moreover, the text may express a positive opinion about an entity contained in the text, but one can also infer that the author is against the defined target (an entity or a topic). This makes stance detection more difficult, compared to the sentiment analysis, but it can often bring complementary information.

The "anyone-can-edit" policy of Wikipedia has created many problems such as trolling, vandalism, controversies, and doubts about the content and reliability of the information provided due to non-expert involvement. Controversy can be defined as a strong disagreement between large groups of people. People have tried to identify and rank controversies in Wikipedia articles through various techniques that use quantitative data as well as the techniques that measure the impact on existing meanings of the text due to new editing processes along with their relationship to the topic of the article (Jhandir et al. 2017).

According to (Dori-Hacohen et al. 2016), controversies occur in neighborhoods of related topics and exhibit homophily. Homophily is a tendency of socially linked individuals to use language in similar ways (Yand and Eisenshtein 2017). As a classification of controversial web pages improves in comparison with a model that examines each page in isolation, one can observe that controversial topics exhibit homophily.

In general, controversy in texts emerges when there are two seriously conflicting public opinions about the topic. One of the main 'classic' approaches to controversy detection is based on Wikipedia edits (Dori-Hacohen et al. 2016; Jang et al. 2016). A model is trained on the data considering statistics about edits, anonymous edits and similarity with other possible controversial topics. Within the other approach, a model considers polarity and can be trained on a predefined controversial topics list, obtained news stories or tweets, where groups of people have extremely positive and extremely negative points of views about it (Choi et al. 2010). A number of attempts were made to detect controversy, such as collection of the dataset of crowdsourced annotations on various issues in controversy (Controversy Annotations Dataset 2017).

Sentiment analysis is seen as a step towards detecting varying opinions, including controversy (Addawood et al. 2017). The other work shows sentiment and controversy are overlapping but not identical. To identify a set of controversial and noncontroversial topics, the authors first searched controversy-related web sources (i.e. Procon.org), Wikipedia lists of controversial topics, news media websites and blogs (Table 6.9).

It turns out that analysis of sentiment, controversy and stance analysis can exploit social network structure. Social network information is available in a wide range of contexts, from social media to political speech to historical texts. Thus, social

Table 6.9 Examples of controversial and non-controversial topics

Controversial or not	Topic	Statement
Yes	Privacy	Citizen privacy takes precedence over national security
	Autism	Vaccine causes autism
	Gun control	Access to guns should be more restricted
No	Safety	Seat belt use can save lives in car accidents"
	Education	Every child should have access to education
	Health	Consuming vitamins is healthy

network homophily has the potential to provide a more general way to account for linguistic variation in NLP.

Many words have one sentiment in a typical case and the opposite sentiment in an atypical case. The word *cool* typically has a positive sentiment. However, in some northern communities with a lack of warmth, and in languages other than English, this word can have a negative sentiment: *cool weather* or *cool (introvert, not very emotional, indifferent) person*. Given labeled examples of "cool" in use by individuals in a social network, one can assume that the word will have a similar sentiment meaning for their near neighbors—an assumption of linguistic homophily. Note that this differs from the assumption of label homophily, which entails that neighbors in the network will hold similar opinions, and will therefore produce similar document-level labels (Hu et al. 2013). Linguistic homophily is a broader hypothesis, which could potentially be applied to any NLP task where the author network information is available, such as hypocrisy detection.

The identification and characterization of controversial topics, as well as topics in statements with hypocrisy, is difficult for several reasons (Timmermans 2017; Timmermans et al. 2017). First, what is regarded as controversial depends on the senders and receivers of information as well as on the context of a topic in terms of space and time. Second, understanding or even resolving controversies on the individual level may require expertise that may not be part of everybody's general knowledge, making the construction of consensus challenging in terms of creating a comprehensive and shared knowledge base in the first place. Third, the potentially continuously evolving nature of information and knowledge further adds to this hard task. Expressing hypocrisy, controversy, sarcasm, a lie or a polarized opinion with a strong sentiment requires a special argument structure that is strongly correlated with the discourse structure of text (Pisarevskaya et al. 2019, Galitsky 2019b).

6.2.12 *Measuring Contention Between* Say *and* Do *Parts*

In this section, we present a numerical model for contention, following (Dori-Hacohen et al. 2016; Dori-Hacohen 2017).

A contention rate between *Say* and *Do* can be defined quantitatively as a probability that two people, randomly selected from the population, will hold conflicting opinions between what they say (Galitsky 1999). In Fig. 6.21, a plot for controversy rate C, we have the following axis:

X—axis: probability (C| Total_US, T);

Y—axis: probability (C| Group_of_Computer_Scientists, T).

Let $\Omega = \{p_1.., p_n\}$ be a population of n people, and T is a topic of interest. Let c denote the degree of contention, which we also define with respect to a topic and a group of people: $P(c| \Omega, T)$ represents the probability of contention of topic T within Ω. Let $P(\neg c|\Omega, T)$ similarly denote the probability of non-contention with respect to a topic and a group of people, such that: $P(c| \Omega, T) + P(\neg c| \Omega, T) = 1$.

Fig. 6.21 Controversy rate among a special group of scientists versus Controversy rate for the whole US population

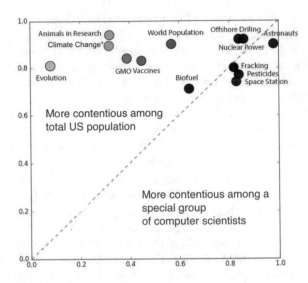

Let s denote a stance with regard to the topic T, and let the relationship *holds(p, s, T)* denote that person p holds stance s with regard to topic T. Let $S^\wedge = \{s_1, s_2, \ldots, s_k\}$ be the set of k stances with regard to topic T in the population Ω. We allow people to hold no stance at all with regard to the topic (either because they are not aware of the topic, or they are aware of it but do not take a stance on it). We use s_0 to represent this lack of stance. In that case, we define

holds(p, s₀, T) $\Leftrightarrow \neg\exists\, s_i \in S^\wedge$ such that *holds(p, sᵢ, T)*

Let $S = \{s_0\} \cup S^\wedge$ be the set of $k + 1$ stances with regard to topic T in the population Ω. Therefore, $\forall p \in \Omega, \exists s \in S$ such that *holds(p, s, T)*. Now, let conflicts: $S \times S \to \{0, 1\}$ be a binary function which represents when two stances are in conflict. Note that a person can hold multiple stances simultaneously, though no stance can be jointly held with s_0. We set *conflicts(s_i, s_i)* $= 0$.

Let *stance groups* in the population be groups of people that hold the same stance: for $i \in \{0..k\}$, let

$G_i = \{p \in \Omega \mid$ *holds(p, sᵢ, T)*$\}$. By construction, $\Omega = \cup_I\, G_i$. Let opposing groups in the population be groups of people that hold a stance that conflicts with s_i. For $i \in \{0..k\}$, let

$O_i = \{p \in \Omega \mid \exists j$ such that *holds(p, sⱼ, T)* $\wedge$ *conflicts(sᵢ, sⱼ)*$\}$.

We intend to quantify a proportion of people where *Say* and *Do* parts disagree. This proportion of people should grow when the groups in disagreement are larger. We estimate the probability that two randomly selected people hold conflicting stances. A contention is modeled directly to do that.

Let $P(c \mid \Omega, T)$ be the probability that if we randomly select two people in Ω, they will conflict on topic T. This is equal to:

$P(c|\Omega, T) = P(p_1, p_2)$ (selected randomly from Ω),

$\exists s_i, s_j \in S$, *s.t. holds(p₁, sᵢ, T)* $\wedge$ *holds(p₂, sⱼ, T)* $\wedge$ *conflicts(sᵢ, sⱼ))*

This model simulates a person to hold two conflicting stances at once and thus be in both G_i and O_i, as in the case of intrapersonal conflict. This definition, while exhaustive to all possible combinations of stances, is very hard to estimate. We now consider a special case of this model with two additional constraints. Let every person have only one stance on a topic:

$\neg \exists p \in \Omega, s_i, s_j \in S$ such that $i \neq j \wedge holds(p, s_i, T) \wedge holds(p, s_j, T)$.

And, let every explicit stance conflict with every other explicit stance:

$conflicts(s_i, s_j) \Longleftarrow \Longrightarrow (i \neq j \wedge i \neq 0 \wedge j \neq 0)$

This implies that $G_i \cap G_j = \emptyset$. We enforce a lack of stance not to be in conflict with any explicit stance. Thus, $O_i = \Omega|G_i|G_0$ as a set-theoretic subtraction.

For simplicity, we estimate the probability of selecting p_1 and p_2 as a selection with replacement. Note that $|\Omega| = \sum_{i \in \{0..k\}} |G_i|$ and the probability of choosing any particular pair is $1/|\Omega|^2$. $|\Omega|$ is, in turn, equals to

$$|\Omega|^2 = \left(\sum_i |G_i| \right)^2 = \sum_{i \in \{0..k\}} |G_i|^2 + \sum_{i \in \{1..k\}} (2|G_0||G_i|)$$
$$+ \sum_{i \in \{2..k\}} \sum_{j \in \{1..i-1\}} 2|G_i||G_j|$$

Depending on whether the pair of people selected hold conflicting stances or not, they contribute to the numerator in $P(c|\Omega, T)$ or $P(c| \Omega, T)$, respectively. Finally, we obtain

$$P(c|\Omega, T) = \frac{\sum_{i \in \{2..k\}} \sum_{j \in \{1..i-1\}} (2|G_i||G_j|)}{|\Omega|^2}$$

and

$$P(nc|\Omega, T) = 1 - P(c|\Omega, T) = \frac{\sum_{i \in \{0..k\}} |G_i|^2 + \sum_{i \in \{1..k\}} (2|G_0||G_i|)}{|\Omega|^2}$$

6.2.13 Hypocrisy and Opinion Formation

Hypocrisy is a general feature of organizational behavior where reputation and promotions are at stake (Brunsson 1989; Wagner et al. 2009; Ellinas et al. 2017). Within organizations, language use is often adjusted to the audience. For instance, the tone of political correctness depends on the expectations of receivers (Hughes 2009). According to (Noelle-Neumann 1977), a significant proportion of people try to avoid isolation in the case of public questions. The author claims that social relations and acceptance in their own environment are more important to people than revealing their own views in public.

Gastner et al. (2019) explore to what extent hypocrisy is sustained during opinion formation and how hidden opinions change the convergence to consensus in a group. A voter model is built with hypocrisy in a complete graph with a neutral competition between two alternatives. The authors computationally infer that hypocrisy always prolongs the time needed for reaching a consensus.

All forms of hypocrisy create cognitive dissonance in peers who observe it (Festinger 1962). This cognitive dissonance exists in two forms:

1) *Internalization* happens when individuals accept the belief or opinion that he has expressed publicly (Kelman 1961). Adjusting the internal opinion is an important last step in the process of socialization that is well described in the classic sociological and social psychological literature (Sherif and Sherif 1953). Opinions and individual attitudes are the products of contact with other members of the group that create an internal and external conflict (Galitsky and Levene 2005). To resolve it, one needs an internalization of external norms. As a result, the individual can be said to be depersonalized and fully assimilated to the group (Galam and Moscovici 1991).

2) *Externalization* happens when the previously concealed opinion becomes publicly expressed. In practice, this requires courage or expressiveness. The process of understanding, accepting and valuing one's opinion necessarily results in public discomfort but often produces relief, a positive cognitive and emotional state. Acting and producing a poker face for the inhibition of inner opinions are associated with substantial efforts (Ekman 1997), and the individual is liberated from these costs by expressing her internal belief. It depends on the empirical context to which extent it is feasible to reduce cognitive dissonance by internalization or externalization. For instance, externalization is particularly problematic for political opinions in oppressive regimes but strongly encouraged when diverse standpoints need to be revealed, such as in critical academic debates.

Internalization is distinct from compliance with public norms as it covers the private acceptance of the norm or attitude. The evolution of opinion must be taken into account, building an infrastructure for the delivery of opinionated content (Galitsky et al. 2011a). To influence the reader's opinion in a strongest way, a content can be transformed into a form centered around opinion polarities (Galitsky et al. 2009).

To predict an overall opinion about a product or service, it is important to analyze the role that hypocrisy, internalization and externalization play in opinion formation. In the Concealed Voter Model (CVM), the publicly expressed (external) opinion can differ from the internal one (Gastner et al. 2018).

The BVM and CVM share the following simplifications:

1) There are only two kinds of potential opinions (which we call "red" and "blue") on a particular issue, and these are mutually exclusive;
2) In the external layer, individuals interact in pairs;
3) The group is homogeneous in the sense that each rate is the same for all individuals and at all times;
4) Red and blue opinions have the same transition rates. That is, their competition is neutral.

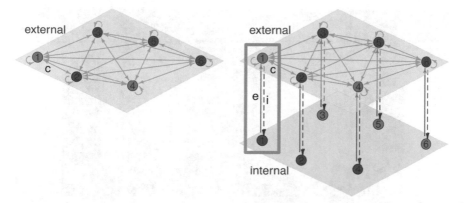

Fig. 6.22 A Basic Voter Model (on the left, from Gastner et al. 2018) versus the Concealed Voter Model (on the right)

In the Basic Voter Model, every individual is represented by a node in a single layer (Fig. 6.22), which is "external" in the sense that all of its neighbors can see and copy his opinion. The tension that is caused by the disagreement between neighbors (e.g., between the blue individual 1 and the red individual 2) can be released by adopting the neighbor's opinion. Such copies happen with a rate c.

In the Concealed Voter Model, every individual is represented by two nodes: one in the external and another in the internal layer. For example, the external/internal opinion of individual 1 (shown in the green rectangle) is marked by a blue/red circle. Because these opinions differ, we call individual 1 a "hypocrite." The tension between the external versus internal opinions can be released either by externalization or internalization (with the corresponding rates e and i). None of the individuals knows the internal opinion of any other individual. Hence, there are no edges within the internal layer.

Galitsky and Levene (2007) simulated the process of opinion change in the course of interactions between a set of competitive services and a set of portals that provide online ratings for these services. The authors argued that to have a profitable business, these portals are forced to have subscribing services that are rated by the portals. To satisfy the subscribing services, we make the assumption that the portals improve the rating of a given service by one unit per transaction that involves payment. The authors followed the 'what-if' methodology, analyzing strategies that services may choose to select the best portal for it to subscribe to, and strategies for a portal to accept the subscription such that its reputation loss, in terms of the integrity of its ratings, is minimized. We observe that the behavior of the simulated agents in accordance with our model is quite natural from the real-world perspective. One conclusion from the simulations is that under reasonable conditions, if most of the services and rating portals in a given industry do not accept a subscription policy similar to the one indicated above, they will lose, respectively, their ratings and reputations, and, moreover the rating portals will have problems in making a profit.

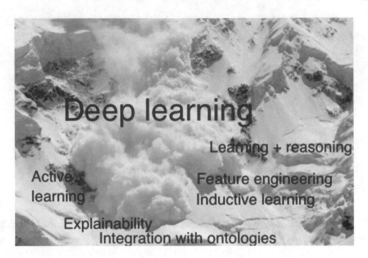

Fig. 6.23 Deep learning has become so popular and the traditionally desired features of machine learning are abandoned ("swept by an avalanche")

We did not attempt to apply deep learning to the problem of hypocrisy detection. Once an extensive training set is available, deep learning would have probably obtained a higher recognition accuracy. However, we would be deprived of the exploration of the nature of the phenomena of how people express their frustration with hypocrisy. Figure 6.23 illustrates how deep learning frequently loses important data exploration features on its way to obtaining end-to-end better detection accuracy. Deep learning is shown as an avalanche sweeping away most nice machine learning features designed by generations of machine learning scientists.

6.2.14 Conclusions

Sarcasm detection is a much harder problem in comparison with hypocrisy since the variety of possible templates is extremely high. We expect a customer who is in a mood for sarcasm to also express her frustration by citing the hypocritical behavior of her opponents. Hence we will not detect sarcasm in texts written by a customer, but once we detect a citation of hypocrisy, we know there is a problem with this customer that needs to be tackled.

Detecting hypocrisy in customer communication plays an important role in differentiating between handling different customers. Citing hypocrisy in a description of company behavior means that the frustration level of this customer is much higher than what just a negative sentiment would indicate.

Explainability is a key to an overall CRM system based on hypocrisy detector: in some context, the explanation behind the decision can be more important than the detection result itself to decide on how to tackle a given customer (Fig. 6.24).

★ ★ ★ ★ ★ | Подтвержденная покупка Спортмастер ✖ 12 августа 2019

Вячеслав Из города: **Салехард** Цвет: **Черный** Частота использования: **пару раз в месяц**
Срок использования: **меньше месяца**

Это мой первый походный рюкзак.
Много места, есть чехол от дождя. Дальше пока не понятно.

Преимущества:
В карманы на поясе влезает 4 банки пива и сигареты...

Недостатки:
...Выпив пиво тяжело тащить снаряженный рюкзак

Функциональность:
Соответствие фото:
Качество:
Надежность:

✅ Да, я бы рекомендовал этот товар другу!

👍 24   👎 2

Fig. 6.24 A review of a backpack (in Russian). The conclusion is translated as "This backpack has a strong disadvantage. I had some beer, and after that, it was hard to carry this fully loaded backpack."

6.3 Detecting Rumor and Disinformation by Web Mining

6.3.1 Introduction

Information that is published on the web and propagates through social networks can carry a lot of false claims. Published once, it can be copied into multiple locations with some edits and make the impression that multiple sources confirm untrue facts and fake opinions (Fig. 6.25 and Fig. 6.26). Such fake information, rumor or disinformation may be distributed to manipulate public opinion; therefore, its sources and posting of its various versions need to be identified as fast as possible.

Fig. 6.25 Fake News and Social Media

Fig. 6.26 Examples of fake news and misrepresentations. On the top: Iranian Press TV news. On the bottom: Introducing LinkedIn database with the false reliability claim (based on a personal experience of the author)

A fast growth of online information-sharing media has made it possible for a rumor to spread rather quickly. Unreliable sources can quickly spread inaccurate and intentionally false information in large quantities, so it is crucial to design systems to detect both misinformation and disinformation at the time it is indexed by search engines, included in feeds, etc.

In this section, we are concerned with a high volume of disinformation, assuming it is created and distributed automatically. It is hard to scale the manual writing process and manual distribution, so for real attempts to manipulate public opinion, we expect automated agents to create content (Galitsky and Kuznetsov 2013). To do that at a scale, they would have to obtain a publicly available content and substitute some entities and their attributes in some manner. As a result, high quantities of strongly opinionated content can be systematically created and distributed in favor of a certain group of people. The working assumption is that a certain content source would be exploited by such agents, given their mission. These agents take genuine content, substitute certain entities in favor of their mission, and distribute it. Moreover, the agents are expected to do some text re-phrasing to avoid easy detection of the real sources.

The key to handling these cases of disinformation would be to identify the source and highlight the substituted entities. Currently, available copyright detection software is not well suited to do this job because of the potentially high number of substituted entities. Hence the similarity between the fake content and original content is expected to be too low for copyright algorithms to determine.

In a number of problems similar to rumor detection on the web, such as credibility assessment and spam detection, solutions are based on learning features other than linguistic, including the structure of sources, behavioral and social media (Qazvinian et al. 2011, Hu et al. 2013, Castillo et al. 2011). In our case, only textual data is available, so a rather deep linguistic analysis is required.

The contribution of this section is an application of a sentence-level linguistic technology augmented with a discourse level. Our approach is capable of verifying that one piece of text is a result of disinformation based on another piece of text.

6.3.2 Definitions and Examples

disinformation (text$_1$, text$_2$) is a measure on a mapping between two graphs for texts *text$_1$* and *text$_2$*. It measures a number of substituted nodes and returns the truth value if *text$_2$* is determined to be disinformation (rumor, distortion, inadequate modification) of *text$_1$*.

We call a graph representing syntactic, shallow semantic and shallow discourse structure of *text* a parse thicket: it is a set of parse trees for each sentence connected with inter-sentence links for anaphora and rhetoric relations (Chap. 2 Volume 1 and Galitsky 2013).

The idea of publishing similar portions of information in various places to affect public opinion is nicely expressed in the following quote:

> *"See, in my line of work you got to keep repeating things over and over and over again for the truth to sink in, to kind of catapult the propaganda."* George W. Bush—43rd US President.

One can see how this procedure can be automated by taking a piece of information, rewriting it multiple times (which is entity/attribute substitution in our case) and publishing it in multiple places:

> *"Political language ... is designed to make lies sound truthful and murder respectable, and to give an appearance of solidity to pure wind."* George Orwell.

Instead of relying on social network topology information to track the sources and propagation of disinformation and rumor, in this work, we rely on linguistic means to perform a similarity assessment between a given text and a candidate for its source on the web. The finding procedure of textual sources is conducted via web mining, employing search engine APIs.

According to (Mintz 2013), the best way to find if a piece of information is factual is to use common sense. A reader should verify whether a piece of information makes sense if the founders or reporters of the sites are biased or have an agenda, and look at where the sites may be found. It is highly recommended to look at other sites for that information as it might be published and heavily researched, providing more concrete details. The art of producing a disinformation is based on the readers' balance of what is the truth and what is a lie. Hence most of the entities and their attributes, appealing to the former, are retained, and those referring to the latter are substituted. There is always a chance that even the readers who have this balance will believe in an error or they will disregard the truth as wrong. (Libicki 2007) says that prior beliefs or opinions affect how readers interpret information as well. When readers believe something to be true before researching it, they are more likely to believe something that supports their prior thoughts. This may lead the readers to believe in a disinformation.

LinkedIn Engineers (falsely) claim the robustness of their database known for unrecoverable data loss. Not relying on Oracle database, they lose entire user profiles (a personal experience of the author).

6.3.3   Examples of Disinformation as Entity Substitutions

We use an example of the well-known disinformation to analyze how it can be potentially scaled up.

In early 2007 Wikipedia community was appalled when an active contributor ("believed" by the site to be a professor of religion with advanced degrees in theology and canon law), was exposed as being nothing more than a community college drop-out. The person at the center of this controversy was "Essjay" (Ryan Jordan), a 24-year-old from Kentucky with no advanced degrees, who used texts such as *Catholicism for Dummies* to help him correct articles on the penitential rite and transubstantiation (Educate-Youself 2020). What we observe here is that substituting certain entities in popular religious texts, one can produce scholarly articles.

On 25 September 2014, REN TV's website ran a story quoting Russian-backed insurgents as saying that "dozens" of bodies had been discovered in three graves, some with organs removed. It illustrated the story with an image of men carrying what appears to be a body bag.

Four days later, REN TV's website—from which a screengrab was taken, above—reported that "bodies continue to be discovered" in areas that it said had been recently vacated by Ukraine's National Guard. The report contained an image of numerous body bags placed on the ground near what appears to be a piece of white wreckage. But both of these images were details from photographs that had appeared over a month earlier on the website of the airline crash investigators (Stopfake 2015)

What has been done here is the substitution of the attribute location and reason. The main entity '*multiple bodies*' have been reused, together with the associated image. What the agent, REN TV channel, did is substituted the values of location

= *airliner crash site* with *area vacated by Ukraine's National Guard'* and reason = *'airliner crash'* with *'activity of Ukraine's National Guard'*. The purpose of this disinformation is to produce negative sentiment about the latter. In this particular case, the fact of disinformation has been determined by the reused authentic image; however, considerations of this section are to reuse text. To perform the detection, we take a text (image, video or other media) and try to find a piece of similar content available on the web at an earlier date.

6.3.4 Disinformation and Rumor Detection Algorithm

Input: a portion of text (possibly published on the web)

Output: categorization of input text as normal or disinformation (also including the original authentic information, and its source).

1. For a given portion of text (seed), find the most significant sentences (this task is similar to summarization);

2. For each of the most significant sentences, form a query from the noun phrases, so that the head noun must occur and other nouns and adjectives should occur;

3. Run the search and collect all search results for all queries;

4. Identify common search results for the set of queries;

5. Form the set of candidate texts which could be a source for the texts being analyzed;

6. For each candidate, compare it with the seed. If a high similarity is found along with the substituted entity, then disinformation is found;

7. Identify the mapping of entities and their attributes from the seed text to the source text. Highlight substituted entities and attributes;

8. Identify sentiments added to the seed text compared to the source.

Steps 1) to 5) are straightforward, and 6)-8) require a linguistic technology to match two portions of text and map entities and their attributes. Such a linguistic technology that recognizes disinformation content needs to be developed hand-in-hand with content generation linguistics. If a content generation algorithm docs rephrasing on the sentence level, applying parse tree-based representation, then a recognition algorithm needs at least as detailed linguistic representation as parse trees. Furthermore, if a content generation algorithm relies on inter-sentence level discourse structure, it needs to be represented by a discourse level detection algorithm as well (Chap. 4 Volume 1).

The results of the content generation family of technologies presented in this book are not detected by search engines at the time of writing. This is due to the belief that they do not use parse tree—level representation for sentences in a search index. Once search engines employ parse tree representations, the content generation algorithms would need to be capable of modifying the rhetorical structure of text at the paragraph level to avoid being detected.

For two portions of the text, we want to establish a mapping between corresponding entities and their attributes. To do that, we need to employ parse trees as well as discourse relations, to form a parse thicket for a paragraph (Galitsky et al.

2012, Galitsky 2013, 2014). Formally, the matching problem is defined as a generalization operation, finding the maximum common subgraph of the parse thickets as graphs: *disinformation(text1, text2)*.

In this section, we provide an example of matching text1 =
Iran refuses to accept the UN proposal to end the dispute over work on nuclear weapons,
UN nuclear watchdog passes a resolution condemning Iran for developing a second uranium enrichment site in secret,
A recent IAEA report presented diagrams that suggested Iran was secretly working on nuclear weapons,
Iran envoy says its nuclear development is for peaceful purpose, and the material evidence against it has been fabricated by the US
against candidate source text2 =
UN passes a resolution condemning the work of Iran on nuclear weapons, in spite of Iran claims that its nuclear research is for peaceful purpose,
Iran confirms that the evidence of its nuclear weapons program is fabricated by the US and proceeds with the second uranium enrichment site
Envoy of Iran to IAEA proceeds with the dispute over its nuclear program and develops an enrichment site in secret

The matching results are as follows (Fig. 6.27):

[NN-Iran VBG-developing DT-* NN-enrichment NN-site IN-in NN-secret]
[NN-generalization-<UN/nuclear watchdog> * VB-pass NN-resolution VBG condemning NN- Iran]
[NN-generalization-<Iran/envoy of Iran> Communicative_action   DT-the NN-dispute IN-over JJ-nuclear NNS-*
[Communicative_action - NN-work IN-of NN-Iran IN-on JJ-nuclear NNS-weapons]
[NN-generalization <Iran/envoy to UN> Communicative_action NN-Iran NN-nuclear NN-* VBZ-is IN-for JJ-peaceful NN-purpose],
Communicative_action - NN-generalize <work/develop> IN-of NN-Iran IN-on JJ-nuclear NNS-weapons]

6.3.5 *Evaluation*

Although the spam web data sets are available, this is not true for the rumor-related web data other than social. To the best of our knowledge, there is no systematic resource of disinformation on the web. (Kaggle 2020) *Fake news* dataset is associated with politics too much and does not seem to be reliable. We automatically formed the Seed Text dataset by mining the web for opinions/reviews. It includes 140 seed texts, from simple sentences of less than fifteen words to a fairly detailed multi-sentence product review. The size of the seed needs to correspond to the size of the identified source portion of the text.

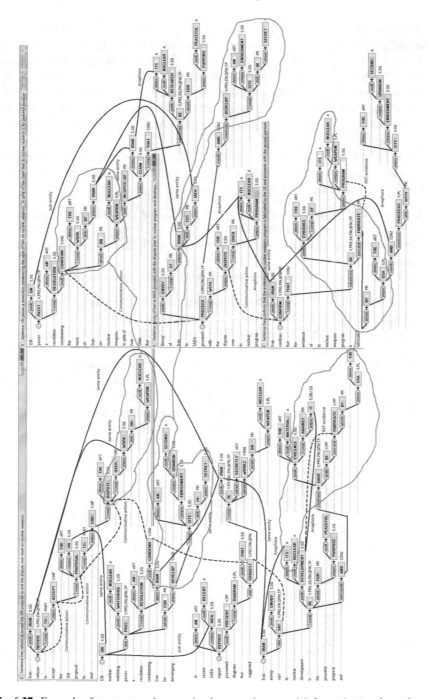

Fig. 6.27 Example of two texts and a mapping between them as *misinformation(text1, text2)*

We collected a set of thousand product recommendations and consider them as "disinformation" relative to the product features descriptions by the manufacturers and retailers. Given a set of product queries, we obtained a few opinionated texts on each. This opinionated text, such as an Amazon review for a digital camera, we then submit as a query against a formal product descriptions. The other sites we mined for imitations of "rumor" content are review sites, Yahoo! Answers, and topic-specific sites containing reviews. For the source content, we use eBay product search API and a product catalog as a seed.

In the context of our evaluation, the opinionated data can be viewed as potentially being a rumor, and the actual product description is a source. The attribute substitution occurs by altering some parameters of the product:

- the consumer who wrote a review has a different estimate of the parameter values from those of a manufacturer;
- the consumer specified a product attribute/feature which is lacking in the product description;
- the consumer adds sentiments related to product attributes and usability.

The task is to identify the proper source (product description) on the web, along with the set of substituted attributes. Hence we believe our evaluation domain is relevant to an actual disinformation domain in terms of web mining properties and its linguistic features.

We manually reviewed the rumor finding sessions and made assessments of precision and recall (Table 6.10). One can see that the more information we have in the seed (the longer the text), the higher the precision of the rumor identification procedure is, and also the lower the percentage of identified attributes is. The recall and the proportion of identified sentiments do not significantly depend on the size of seed text.

Table 6.10 Evaluation of finding source text on the web

Seed Text fragments/size	Recall of finding source page, %	Precision of finding source page,%	Substituted attributes found, %	Sentiments found, %
Single sentence, <15 words	71.2	67.2	78.9	62
Long compound sentence,>15 words	67.4	73.3	71.6	70.1
2–3 sentences	72.9	72.1	65	64.5
4–5 sentences	70.4	80.6	62.7	61.3

6.3.6 Related Work and Conclusions

We were unable to find a systematic source of disinformation on the web. However, opinionated data on user products being related to product description turned out to be an adequate way to the evaluation of our algorithm. We confirmed that it performs fairly well in identifying textual sources on the web, entity substitution and sentiment detection. Our evaluation addressed the cases of various complexities of text and demonstrated that disinformation can be detected varying from a single sentence up to the level of a paragraph containing up to five sentences (having an entities substitution distributed through this portion of text).

(Seo et al. 2012) focused on two problems related to the mitigation of false claims in social networks, based on the source topology rather than on a linguistic approach. Firstly, the authors study the question of identifying sources of rumors in the absence of complete provenance information about rumor propagation. Secondly, they study how rumors (false claims) and non-rumors (true information) can be differentiated. The method is based on the assumption that rumors are initiated from only a small number of sources, whereas truthful information can be observed and originated by a large number of unrelated individuals concurrently. Unlike the current approach based on web mining and linguistic technology, the authors rely on utilizing network monitors. Their approach focuses on investigating individuals who agree to let us know whether or not they heard a particular piece of information (from their social neighborhood), although do not agree to let us know who told them this information or when they learned it.

The problem of identifying rumor and misinformation on the web is much harder than identifying spam web pages. For the latter task, an analysis of extracted links to suspicious sites (which belong to a typical spam category) is sufficient for webspam identification (Webb et al. 2006). On the contrary, to find a rumor or disinformation, the content and links are usually irrelevant, and word-level, sentence-level and discourse-level analyses are essential. (Castillo et al. 2011) developed an automated approach to assess the credibility of a given set of tweets. Microblog postings related to trending topics were analyzed with respect to being credible or not credible, based on topicality features extracted from users' posting, from citations to external sources and from user reposting behaviors. Topic-based credibility assessment works in a social media environment where additional behavior-based cues are available. On the contrary, in the case of the web rumor, when behavior-based information is lacking, a deeper linguistic analysis that goes beyond keywords is required.

Besides social network analysis, cognitive psychology helps identify the cognitive process involved in the decision to spread information (Kumar and Geethakumari 2014). This process involves answering four main questions related to the consistency of message, coherency of message, credibility of source and general acceptability of message. We have used the cues of deception to analyze these questions to obtain solutions for preventing the spread of disinformation.

(Canini et al. 2011)'s studies indicated that both the topical content of information sources and social network structure affect source credibility. Based on these results, they designed a method of automatically identifying and ranking social network users according to their relevance and expertise for a given topic. (Qazvinian et al. 2011) addressed the problem of rumor detection in microblogs and explore the effectiveness of three categories of features: content-based, network-based, and microblog-specific memes for correctly identifying rumors. The authors showed how these features are effective in identifying the sources of disinformation, using thousands of manually annotated tweets collected from Twitter. In the current study, a deeper linguistic means are required to identify larger portion of text with disinformation.

A broad range of methods has been studying the spread of memes and false information on the web. (Leskovec et al. 2009) use the evolution of quotes reproduced online to identify memes and track their spread overtime. (Ratkiewicz et al. 2010) created the "Truthy" system, identifying misleading political memes on Twitter using tweet features, including hashtags, links, and mentions. Other projects focus on highlighting disputed claims on the Internet using pattern matching techniques.

Instead of identifying rumors from a corpus of relevant phrases and attempting to discriminate between phrases that confirm, refute, question, and simply talk about rumors of interest, we applied a paragraph-level linguistic technology (Galitsky 2013) to identify substituted entities and their attributes. The linguistic approach presented here complements social network structure-based described in a corpus of research on disinformation detection.

6.3.7   Corruption Networks

In this section, we focus on another phenomenon associated with disinformation: corruption. The more open a society is, the higher the access to truth by its population. Experts are evenly split on whether the coming decade will see a reduction in false and misleading narratives online. Those forecasting improvements place their hopes in technological fixes and in societal solutions. Others think the dark side of human nature is aided more than restricted by technology. Oxford Dictionaries define "post-truth" as a new trend, referring to the circumstances in which objective facts are less important in influencing public opinion than how emotions and personal beliefs affect public opinion.

(Schmidt et al. 2017) analyzed 376 million Facebook users' interactions with over 900 news outlets and found that people tend to seek information that fits well with their views. Social media dramatically modified the way we get informed and shape our opinions. Users' polarization seems to dominate news consumption on Facebook and other social network sites like VKontakte.ru and Odnoklassniki.ru. The authors explored the structure of news consumption on Facebook on a global scale, showing that users tend to confine their attention on a limited set of pages, thus determining a sharp community structure among news sites. The findings suggest that users have a more cosmopolitan perspective of the information space than news providers.

While some economists tend to reduce all corruption to impersonal market-like transactions, ignoring the role of social ties in shaping corruption, (Kravtsova and

Oshchepkov 2019) show that this reduced the understanding of corruption processes. It is necessary to distinguish between market corruption (impersonal bribery), and network (or parochial) corruption that is conditional on the social connections between bureaucrats and private agents. In Fig. 6.28 and Fig. 6.29 we present two corruption networks that show individuals, companies owned by them, and relations between these individuals as extracted from the text. Among the sources are rbc.ru, nymag.com, mintpressnews.com, Intelligencer, zakupki.gov.ru, Russian Property Registration cite.

The network drawing shows an "imitation" of a tender that is supposed to be competitive, but in real life, all winners belong to the same network.

6.3.8 Lying at Work

Lying is natural, to some extent. Deceit, lying, and falsehoods lie at the very heart of our cultural heritage. Even the narrative of Adam and Eve, the founding myth of Christianity, revolves around a lie (Livingstone Smith 2007). Nature is full of deceit. Viruses trick the immune systems of their hosts, while chameleons rely on camouflage to repel their predators. Humans are no exception in terms of an attachment to a lie, including at work (Galitsky 2016b). Hiring managers acknowledge that nearly all job applicants exaggerate their qualifications.

Deception is absolutely necessary for certain jobs, such as undercover detectives. Many people believe diplomacy is synonymous with lying. Deception can even be strategic across a company, such as when a call center instructs employees to pretend that they are located in a different country due to customer biases. More generally, the definition of workplace deceit can be fuzzy. Customer service roles associated with strong emotional load are frequently performed by women; they are typically encouraged to mask their feelings (Galitsky 2016a).

In most cases, deception in the workplace is viewed negatively. It is believed that if someone has to resort to lying, he is probably not well qualified at his job. Deception can be toxic to a culture of trust and teamwork. However, there is an exception for jobs that are perceived as being high in selling orientation rather than customer orientation (Gunia and Levene 2019). According to the marketing study of these authors, customer orientation is about satisfying customers' needs, while selling orientation relates to meeting own objectives of a seller. Certain professions, like sales and investment banking, are stereotyped as being selling orientation-heavy. (Though in practice, of course, salespeople can be deeply caring and care workers can be self-interested).

Integrating theories of selling, stereotypes, and negotiation challenging much research and rhetoric on deception, the authors observe that the public does not always disapprove of deceives. Instead, the public concludes that deceivers will be competent in certain occupations: those in which a selling orientation is stereotypically seen as integral to the job. The authors introduce selling orientation as an occupational stereotype and distinguish between occupations stereotyped as high versus low in

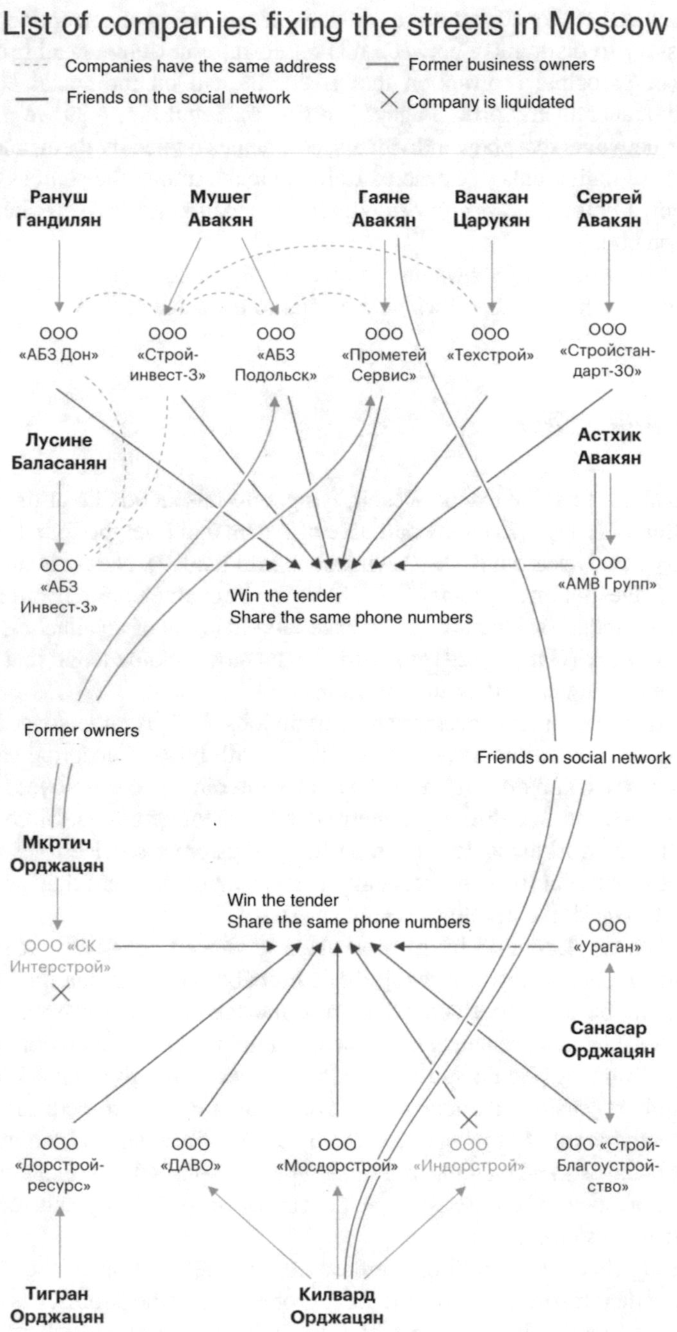

List of companies fixing the streets in Moscow

Fig. 6.28 A corruption network in Russia. The names of individuals and companies are spelled in the original language, the names of relations are interpreted in English

New York fixers and their network

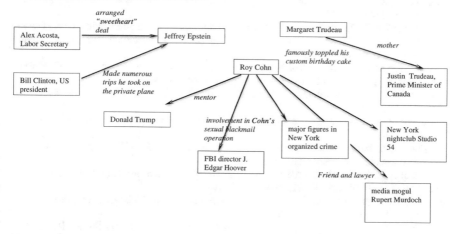

Fig. 6.29 A corruption network in United States

selling orientation. The respondents in this research believed that people who had displayed deception would be more successful at high-in-selling-orientation jobs and prioritized hiring them. The authors intentionally recruited business students so that they could be sure that the stereotypes they examine are actually held by future practitioners. Students who intend to perform managerial jobs may actually believe that deception indicates high job competence and thus import these beliefs into future hiring practices. Tolerance (or even encouragement) of workplace deception can be hard to recognize. A system of acceptable behaviors in an organization or industry supporting deception at a workplace is often kept as a secret, at least to the public (Wang and Murnighan 2017).

References

Abbott R, Ecker B, Anand P, Walker MA (2016) Internet argument corpus 2.0: an SQL schema for dialogic social media and the corpora to go with it. Language Resources and Evaluation Conference

Addawood A, Rezapour, R-S, Abdar O, Diesner J (2017) Telling apart tweets associated with controversial versus non-controversial topics. In: Proceedings of the Second Workshop on NLP and Computational Social Science, pp 32–41

Alicke MD, Gordon E, Rose D (2012) Hypocrisy: what counts? Philos Psychol. 26(5)

Asher N, Lascarides A (2003) Logics of conversation. Cambridge University Press, Cambridge UK

Barden J, Rucker DD, Petty RE (2005) Saying one thing and doing another: examining the impact of event order on hypocrisy judgments of others. Personal Soc Psychol 31–11:1463–1474

Bhatia P, Ji Y, Eisenstein J (2015) Better document-level sentiment analysis from rst discourse parsing. In: Proceedings of the 2015 Conference on Empirical Methods in Natural Language Processing, p 22122218

Brunsson N (1989) The organization of hypocrisy: talk, decisions, and actions in organizations. Wiley, Chich/ester

Canini KR., Suh B, Pirolli PL (2011) Finding credible information sources in social networks based on content and social structure. In: 2011 IEEE Second International Conference on Social Computing, SocialCom'11, pp 1–8

Castillo C, Mendoza M, Poblete B (2011) Information credibility on twitter. In: WWW Conference

Choi Y, Jung Y, Myaeng S-H (2010) Identifying controversial issues and their sub-topics in news articles. In: Intelligence and Security Informatics, Pacific Asia Workshop, PAISI 2010, Hyderabad, India, pp 140–153

Controversy Annotations Dataset (2017) (http://btimmermans.com/2017/06/29/controversy-annotations-dataset/)

Dori-Hacohen S (2017) Controversy detection and stance analysis. PhD Dissertation. 1084. https://scholarworks.umass.edu/dissertations_2/1084

Dori-Hacohen S, Jensen D, Allan J (2016) Controversy detection in wikipedia using collective classification. SIGIR, July 17–21, 2016, Pisa, Italy

Educate-Youself (2020) Wikipedia Lies: Online Disinformation & Propaganda http://educate-yourself.org/cn/wikipedialies20jan08.shtml

Ekman P (1997) Should we call it expression or communication? Innov Eur J Soc Sci Res 10:333–344

Ellinas C, Allan N, Johansson A (2017) Dynamics of organizational culture: individual beliefs vs. social conformity. PLOS ONE 12:e0180193

Feng S, Banerjee R, Choi Y (2012a) Syntactic stylometry for deception detection. In: ACL 12, Proceedings of the 50th Annual Meeting of the Association for Computational Linguistics, pp 171–175

Feng S, Xing L, Gogar A, Choi Y (2012b) Distributional footprints of deceptive product reviews. In: Sixth International AAAI Conference on Weblogs and Social Media, pp 98–105

Festinger L (1962) A theory of cognitive dissonance. Stanford University Press, Stanford, CA

Fornaciari T, Poesio M (2014) Identifying fake Amazon reviews as learning from crowds. In: Proceedings of the 14th Conference of the European Chapter of the Association for Computational Linguistics, pp 279–287

Galam S, Moscovici S (1991) Towards a theory of collective phenomena: consensus and attitude changes in groups. Eur J Soc Psychol 21:49–74

Galitsky B (1999) Analysis of mental attributes for the conflict resolution in multiagent systems. AAAI-99 Workshop on agents' conflict

Galitsky B (2013) Machine learning of syntactic parse trees for search and classification of text. Eng Appl AI 26(3):1072–1091

Galitsky B (2014) Transfer learning of syntactic structures for building taxonomies for search engines. Eng Appl AI

Galitsky B (2016a) Intuitive theory of mind. In: Computational Autism, pp 79–93

Galitsky B (2016b) From reasoning to behavior in the real world. In: Computational Autism, pp 345–378

Galitsky B (2019a) Enabling a bot with understanding argumentation and providing arguments. Developing enterprise chatbots. Springer, Cham, Switzerland, pp 465–532

Galitsky B (2019b) A content management system for chatbots. In: Developing enterprise chatbots. Springer, Cham, Switzerland

Galitsky B (2019c) Rhetorical agreement: maintaining cohesive conversations. In: Developing enterprise chatbots. Springer, Cham, Switzerland

Galitsky B, McKenna EW (2017) Sentiment extraction from consumer reviews for providing product recommendations. US Patent 9,646,078

Galitsky B, Kovalerchuk B (2006) Mining the blogosphere for Contributors' Sentiments. AAAI Spring symposium: computational approaches to analyzing weblogs, pp 37–39

Galitsky B, Levene M (2005) Simulating the conflict between reputation and profitability for online rating portals. J Art Societ Soc Simul 8(2)

Galitsky B, Levene M (2007) Providing rating services and subscriptions with web portal infrastructures. In: Encyclopedia of portal technologies and applications, pp 855–862

Galitsky B, Kuznetsov SO (2008) Learning communicative actions of conflicting human agents. J Exp Theor Artif Intell 20(4):277–317

Galitsky B, Kuznetsov SO (2013) A web mining tool for assistance with creative writing. 35th ECIR

Galitsky B, Chen H, Du S (2009) Inversion of forum content based on authors' sentiments on product usability. AAAI Spring Symposium: Social Semantic Web: Where Web 2.0 Meets Web 3.0, pp 33–38

Galitsky B, De La Rosa JL, Dobrocsi G (2012) Inferring the semantic properties of sentences by mining syntactic parse trees. Data Knowl Eng 81:21–45

Galitsky B, Ilvovsky D, Kuznetsov SO (2015) Text integrity assessment: sentiment profile vs rhetoric structure. CICLing-2015, Cairo

Galitsky B, Ilvovsky D, Kuznetsov SO (2018a) Detecting logical argumentation in text via communicative discourse tree. J Exp Theor Artif Intell 30(5):1–27

Galitsky B, Ilvovsky D, Pisarevskaya D (2018b) Argumentation in text: discourse structure matters. CICLing 2018

Galitsky B, Dobrocsi G, de la Rosa JL (2010) Inverting semantic structure under open domain opinion mining. Twenty-Third International FLAIRS Conference

Galitsky B, de la Rosa JL, Dobrocsi G (2011a) Building integrated opinion delivery environment. FLAIRS-24, West Palm Beach FL May

Galitsky B, Dobrocsi G, de la Rosa JL, Kuznetsov SO (2011b) Using generalization of syntactic parse trees for taxonomy capture on the web. International conference on conceptual structures, 104–117

Ganter B, Kuznetsov SO (2001) Pattern structures and their projections. ICCS, Lecture notes in artificial intelligence (Springer) 2120:129–142

Gastner MT, Oborny B, Gulya's M. (2018) Consensus time in a voter model with concealed and publicly expressed opinions. J Stat Mech Theory Exp 063401

Gastner MT, Takács K, Gulyás M, Szvetelszky Z, Oborny B (2019) The impact of hypocrisy on opinion formation: a dynamic model. PLoS ONE 14(6):e0218729

Grasso F (2003) Characterizing rhetoric argumentation. PhD Thesis Heriot-Watt University

Gunia BC, Levine EE (2019) Deception as competence: the effect of occupational stereotypes on the perception and proliferation of deception. Org Beh Human Dec Proc Elsevier 152(C):122–137

Hai Z, Zhao P, Cheng P, Yang P, Li X-L, Li G (2016) Deceptive review spam detection via exploiting task relatedness and unlabeled data. In: Proceedings of the 2016 Conference on Empirical Methods in Natural Language Processing, pp 1817–1826. https://beyondphilosophy.com/3-reasons-why-people-say-one-thing-and-do-another/

Hu X, Tang J, Zhang Y, Liu H (2013) Social spammer detection in microblogging. In: AAAI

Hughes G (2009) Political correctness: a history of semantics and culture, 1st edn. Wiley Blackwell, Maldon, MA

Jang M, Foley J, Dori-Hacohen S, Allan J (2016) Probabilistic approaches to controversy detection. In: CIKM '16: Proceedings of the 25th ACM International on Conference on Information and Knowledge Management. October, pp 2069–2072

Jhandir MZ, Tenvir A, Byung-Won O, Lee I, Gyu, Choi GS (2017) Controversy detection in Wikipedia using semantic dissimilarity. Inf Sci v418–419, 581–600

Jindal N, Liu B (2008).Opinion spam and analysis. In: Proceedings of International Conference on Web Search and Data Mining (WSDM-2008)

Joty S, Carenini G, Ng RT, Mehdad Y (2013) Combining intra-and multisentential rhetorical parsing for document-level discourse analysis. ACL 1:486–496

Karimi H, Tang J (2019) Learning hierarchical discourse-level structure for fake news detection. NAACL 3432–3442

Kaggle (2020) Fake News Dataset https://www.kaggle.com/c/fake-news

Kahneman D (2011) Thinking fast and slow. Macmillan Publishing Company, London UK

Kelman HC (1961) Processes of opinion change. Public Opin Q. 25:57–78

Kravtsova M, Oshchepkov A (2019) Market and network corruption. In: Basic Research Progr Working papers: Economics. WP BRP 209/EC/2019. https://wp.hse.ru/data/2019/01/28/120042 1555/209EC2019.pdf

Kumar K, Geethakumari G (2014) Detecting disinformation in online social networks using cognitive psychology. Human-Centric Comput Inf Sci 4:14

Leskovec J, Backstrom L, Kleinberg J (2009) Meme-tracking and the dynamics of the newscycle. In: KDD'09: Proceedings of the 15th ACM SIGKDD, pp 497–506

Livingstone Smith D (2007) Why we lie: the evolutionary roots of deception and the unconscious mind. MacMillan Publishers, Stuttgart, Germany

Libicki M (2007) Conquest in cyberspace: national security and information warfare. Cambridge University Press, New York, pp 51–55

Lucas C, Nielsen RA, Roberts ME, Stewart BM, Storer A, Tingley D (2015) Computer-assisted text analysis for comparative politics

Mann WC, Thompson SA (1987) Rhetorical structure theory: description and construction of text structures. Springer, Netherlands, Dordrecht

Mintz A (2013) The disinformation superhighway? PBS. Retrieved 26 February

Mishenko E (2019) How discourse analysis helps identify common people's lies. https://indicator. ru/mathematics/chelovek-vret-dva-izmereniya.htm

Moliere (2002) Tartuffe [Play]. BookSurge Classics, North Charleston, SC. (Original work published in 1667)

Morey M, Muller P, Asher N (2018) A dependency perspective on rst discourse parsing and evaluation. In: Computational Linguistics, pp 1–54

Mukherjee A, Venkataraman V, Liu B, Glance N (2013a) What Yelp fake review filter might be doing? In: Proceedings of the Seventh International AAAI Conference on Weblogs and Social Media

Mukherjee A, Venkataraman V, Liu B, Glance N (2013b) Fake review detection: classification and analysis of real and pseudo reviews. Tech. rep. uic-cs-2013–03. University of Illinois at Chicago

Oraby S, Reed L, Compton R, Riloff E, Walker M, Whittaker S (2015) And that's a fact: distinguishing factual and emotional argumentation in online dialogue. NAACL HLT 2015 2nd Workshop on Argumentation Mining

Ott M, Cardie C, Hancock JT (2013) Negative deceptive opinion spam. In: NAACLHLT 2013, Proceedings of the 2013 Conference of the North American Chapter of the Association for Computational Linguistics: Human Language Technologies, pp 497–501 (dataset is at http://myl eott.com/)

Ott M, Choi Y, Cardie C, Hancock JT (2011) Finding deceptive opinion spam by any stretch of the imagination. In: Proceedings of the 49th Annual Meeting of the Association for Computational Linguistics: Human Language Technologies, vol 1, pp 309–319

Pisarevskaya D, Galitsky B, Taylor J, Ozerov A (2019) An anatomy of a lie. In: Companion Proceedings of The 2019 World Wide Web Conference, pp 373–380

Pisarevskaya D, Galitsky B (2019) An anatomy of lie: discourse patterns in ultimate deception dataset. In Dialogue Conference, Moscow, Russia

Rubin VL, Lukoianova T (2015) Truth and deception at the rhetorical structure level. J Assoc Inf Sci Technol 66(5):905–917

Qazvinian V, Rosengren E, Radev DR, Mei Q (2011) Rumor has it: identifying misinformation in microblogs. EMNLP-2011

Ratkiewicz J, Conover M, Meiss M, Goncalves B, Patil S, Flammini A, Menczer F (2010) Detecting and tracking the spread of astroturf memes in microblog streams. CoRR, abs/1011.3768.1599

Rayana S, Akoglu L (2015) Collective opinion spam detection: bridging review networks and metadata. In: Proceedings of the 21th ACM SIGKDD International Conference on Knowledge Discovery and Data Mining, ACM, pp 985–994

Rubin V (2016) Deception detection and rumor debunking for social media. In: The SAGE Handbook of Social Media Research Methods

Seo E, Mohapatra P, Abdelzaher T (2012) Identifying rumors and their sources in social networks. SPIE Conference

Sherif M, Sherif CW (1953) Groups in harmony and tension. Harper & Brothers, An integration of studies on ontergroup relations

Schmidt A, Zollo F, Del Vicario M, Bessi A, Scala A, Caldarelli G, Stanley H, Quattrociocchi W (2017) Anatomy of news consumption on Facebook. In: Proceedings of the National Academy of Sciences, p 114

Stab S, Gurevych I (2017) Recognizing insufficiently supported arguments in argumentative essays. EACL, pp 980–990

Stopfake (2015) https://www.stopfake.org/en/ren-tv-uses-crash-pictures-in-mass-grave-reports/

Sun C, Du Q, Tian G (2016) Exploiting product related review features for fake review detection. Mathem Prob Eng

Surdeanu M, Hicks T, Valenzuela-Escarcega MA (2015) Two practical rhetorical structure theory parsers. NAACL HLT

Timmermans B (2017) A dataset of crowdsourced annotations on controversy aspects http://btimme rmans.com/2017/06/29/controversy-annotations-dataset/)

Timmermans B, Aroyo L, Kuhn T, Beelen K, Kanoulas E, van de Velde B, van Eerten G (2017) ControCurator: understanding controversy using collective intelligence. Collective Intelligence Conference

Ultimate Deception Dataset (2020) https://github.com/bgalitsky/relevance-based-on-parse-trees/ blob/master/examples/ultimateDeceptionAutoTagged.csv.zip

Wagner T, Lutz RJ, Weitz BA (2009) Corporate hypocrisy: overcoming the threat of inconsistent corporate social responsibility perceptions. J Mark 73:77–91

Wang L, Murnighan JK (2017) How much does honesty cost? small bonuses can motivate ethical behavior. Manage Sci 63(9):2903–2914

Webb S, Caverlee J, Pu C (2006) Introducing the webb spam corpus: using email spam to identify web spam automatically. In: CEAS, 2006

Yao W, Dai Z, Huang R, Caverlee J (2017) Online deception detection refueled by real world data collection. In: Proceedings of Recent Advances in Natural Language Processing, pp 793–802

Yi Y, Jacob E (2017) Overcoming language variation in sentiment analysis with social attention

Chapter 7
Reasoning for Resolving Customer Complaints

Abstract We report on a novel approach to modeling a dynamic domain with limited knowledge. A domain may include participating agents where we are uncertain about the motivations and decision-making principles of some of these agents. Our reasoning setting for such domains includes deductive, inductive and abductive components. The deductive component is based on situation calculus and describes the behavior of agents with complete information. The machine learning-based inductive and abductive components involve the previous experience with the agents, whose actions are uncertain to the system. Suggested reasoning machinery is applied to the problem of processing customer complaints in the form of textual messages that contain a multiagent conflict. The task is to predict the future actions of an opponent agent to determine the required course of action to resolve a multiagent conflict. This chapter demonstrates that the hybrid reasoning approach outperforms both stand-alone deductive and inductive components. The suggested methodology reflects the general situation of reasoning in dynamic domains in the conditions of uncertainty, merging analytical (rule-based) and analogy-based reasoning.

7.1 Introduction

In the last decade, such artificial intelligence techniques as information extraction (IE) from the text (Ciravegna 2000) and inductive logic programming (Lavrac and Dzeroski 1994) have found a variety of emergent and sophisticated applications. Also, disciplines such as reasoning about action and reasoning about mental attributes (Fagin et al. 1995) have become promising from the standpoint of applications. However, we believe that a robust universal framework for automatic processing of textual messages that describes a conflict between human agents has not been developed (Barber and Kim 2001; Liu et al. 1997; Leake et al. 1997). The main reason is that message understanding in an open domain in the conditions of uncertainty must be followed by quite sophisticated reasoning. Note that the desired depth of understanding for messages which contain a multiagent conflict is much higher than that of the general case of message understanding under question answering (Galitsky 2003b; Galitsky et al. 2005), where the task is to deliver the document from the set

© The Author(s), under exclusive license to Springer Nature Switzerland AG 2021 289
B. Galitsky, *Artificial Intelligence for Customer Relationship Management*,
Human–Computer Interaction Series, https://doi.org/10.1007/978-3-030-61641-0_7

of a priori indexed ones. A special scenario-based ontology is required in addition to adequate reasoning mechanism for an in-depth understanding of textual scenarios (Singh and Barry 2003).

As an example of a textual description of the multiagent conflict, here we use the uniform collection of customer complaints. They describe how complainants interact with their opponents (customer support representatives, business partners, etc.) from the standpoint of complainants. To advise these complainants on how to resolve the dispute, it is necessary to understand the motivations and constraints of the company representative and to envision the company's future strategy. Only the textual description of a customer complaint and the collection of complaints about a given company are available for our analysis.

In this chapter, we develop and integrate the formalisms of processing the formalized scenarios of multiagent interactions, where a conflict needs to be identified and localized, and a strategy for its resolution suggested. To focus on the reasoning component of the overall conflict processing system, we assume that the formalization of a textual conflict has been obtained. In our study (Galitsky and Mirkin 2003), we have proposed an alternative approach to text understanding, without IE, implemented for the complaint processing system. Interactive forms to represent a complaint about the interaction with customer service have been suggested, which allows eliminating the bottleneck of text understanding system: syntactic, semantic and knowledge representation components for such a poorly structured and diverse knowledge-intensive domain as customer complaints (Galitsky 2001, 2003b; Galitsky and Tumarkina 2004).

Based on the formalism to be introduced, we have developed the software for consumer advocacy companies to handle the complaints automatically or semi-automatically, to generate advice and suggest courses of action to help the customer. As such, the complaint understanding task requires an advanced text analysis and understanding, extensive reasoning about actions of conflicting agents, a simulation of multiagent behavior and a prediction of an opponent agent's actions (Galitsky 2003a). This chapter presents the underlying technology for one of these components that is based on the prediction of a further opponent's action.

In our previous computational studies of understanding complaint scenarios (Galitsky and Tumarkina 2004; Galitsky and Pampapathi 2003), to model the mental states of participating agents in the complex cases (a customer, a company, a customer's partner who conducts his business via this company, etc.), we have deployed the natural language multiagent mental simulator NL_MAMS, described in (Chap. 9 of Volume 2 and Galitsky 2016). It is capable of yielding the consecutive mental states, given the current ones, taking into account such complex forms of behavior as *deceiving, pretending, explaining, reconciling*, etc.

In this work, we will not deploy reasoning about *mental attitudes* of participating agents on the one hand, for the sake of implementation effectiveness on the one hand, and, on the other hand, to explore the limits of how the multiagent interaction can be modeled without involving reasoning about knowledge, beliefs and intentions of participating agents.

7.1.1 Why Are Both the Deductive and Inductive Components Required?

Concerning the reasoning about action, a series of formalisms, developed in the logic programming environment, have been suggested for robotics applications. Particularly, the system for dynamic domains, GOLOG, suggested in Levesque et al. (1997), has been extended by multiple authors for a variety of fields (e.g., Muggleton 1992; Reiter 1993). The involvement of sensory information in building the plan of multiagent interaction has significantly increased the applicability of GOLOG (Lakemeyer 1999).

However, GOLOG is still not well suited to handle the multiagent scenarios with a lack of information concerning the actions of opponent agents, when it is impossible to sense them (acquire additional features online). A strong progress in the efficient implementation of reasoning about action in many ubiquitous applications has been achieved; however, such implementations deal with an explicit set of preconditions and effect axioms. Clearly, the formalism of reasoning about actions does not target situations with uncertainty, such as multiagent conflict scenarios, where full knowledge reflects only the perspective of a particular side. In particular, uncertainty is often unavoidable in medical practice, where additional techniques are applied to GOLOG, including Bayesian networks (Levesque and Pagnucco 2000). A series of GOLOG extensions have been built for processing information from noisy sensors for applications in robotics (Bacchus et al. 1999), as well as a theoretical framework concerning situation calculus operating in probabilistic conditions (Pattison-Gordon et al. 1996).

Incomplete knowledge about the world is reflected as an expression for non-deterministic choice of the order in which to perform actions, non-deterministic choice of argument values, and non-deterministic repetition. These settings are adequate for the selected robotics applications, where the designer uses a particular approximation of the external world. In a general setting, an agent that performs reasoning about actions is expected to learn from the situations where the actual sequence of actions has been forced by the environment to deviate from the initially obtained plan, using the current world model.

A generic environment for reasoning about actions is not well suited for handling essentially incomplete data, where neither totality of procedures, nor action preconditions, nor successor state constraints are available. Evidently, situation calculus by itself does not have a sufficient predictive power and needs to be augmented by a learning system capable of operating in the dynamic language. An abstraction of reasoning about action in the way of GOLOG assumes that action preconditions, successor state expressions and ones for complex actions are known, or at least that the respective probabilities can be estimated (McCarthy 2002).

At the same time, the methodology of obtaining a formal description for a set of facts implemented via inductive reasoning in the wide sense has found a series of applications, including biochemistry, protein engineering, drug design, natural language processing, finite element mesh design, satellite diagnosis, text classification, medicine, games, planning, software engineering, software agents, information retrieval, ecology, traffic analysis and network management (De Raedt 1999).

However, scenarios of multiagent interactions cannot be efficiently handled by the traditional deterministic machine learning (an attribute value learning system), because of the high dimension, the sparseness of the feature space and a lack of an important body of commonsense knowledge. A knowledge discovery system that is based on inductive logic programming or similar approaches (Muggleton 1992; De Raedt 1999) is insufficient, taken alone because it is incapable of performing necessary commonsense reasoning about actions and knowledge in accordance to heuristics available from the domain experts. Neglecting this knowledge would dramatically decrease the extent of possible predictions. Also, a generic knowledge discovery system is not oriented to handle dynamic kinds of data, which include such a complex structure of interdependencies as multiagent scenarios. Therefore, we intend to merge reasoning about action-based deductive and learning-based inductive systems to form the environment to handle dynamic domains with incomplete information (Fig. 7.1).

We outline two basic methodologies for predicting future action or a set of possible actions:

(1) By means of reasoning about actions. Following this methodology, one specifies a set of available basic and combined actions with conditions, given a current situation, described via a set of fluents. These fluents, in turn, have additional constraints and obey certain conditions, given a set of previous actions. Action possibilities, preconditions and successor state axioms are formulated *manually*, analyzing the past experience. This methodology can fully solve the problem if the complete formal prerequisites for reasoning about actions are available.

(2) By means of supervised learning of future action from the set of examples. Given a set of examples with a sequence of actions and fluents in each, a prediction engine generates the hypotheses of how these fluents are linked to future actions. Resultant hypotheses are then applied to predict these future actions. Such kinds of learning require the actions and fluents to be explicitly specified, as in the methodology of reasoning about actions. However, the learning itself is performed automatically. This supervised learning methodology is worth applying in a stand-alone manner if neither explicit rules for agents when to perform an action nor action preconditions are available.

Our experience in the implementation of reasoning in the selected application domains demonstrates that the above methodologies are complementary. The following facts contribute to this observation:

• Almost any prediction task, particularly in a deterministic approach, is some combination of manually obtained heuristics and automatically extracted features, which characterize an object of interest.

• If an attempt is made to predict all actions using learning, the problem complexity dramatically increases and, therefore, the accuracy of any solution under possible approximation drops.

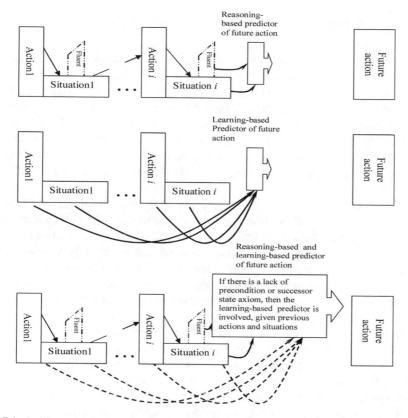

Fig. 7.1 An illustration for the merging reasoning about action-based and learning-based machinery for performing the prediction of future (or unknown) actions in a dynamic domain. On the top: reasoning about action, in the middle: machine learning, on the bottom: our hybrid approach that is the results of a merge between the two above

- On the other hand, if an attempt is made to explicitly construct the required totality of pre- and postconditions of actions for the deductive settings, we run against a frame problem that may need a unique solution for a specific situation (Shanahan 1997). Moreover, some other difficulties are associated with the search of inference (building of a plan), not assisted by the considerations involving the past experience.
- Considering a sequence of actions in a dynamic domain, the longer this sequence is, the more inductive reasoning is needed relatively to the deductive one.

Note that the above considerations are valid when the choice of action does not occur in a pure mental world, that is, the world where the situations are described in terms of belief, knowledge and intention (Galitsky 2016). Choosing an action that is to be performed in a given mental state occurs in accordance with quite different laws, unlike ones for physical states we are talking about in this report.

7.1.2 Statistical or Deterministic Machine Learning?

In this chapter, we target the domain of textual descriptions of multiagent conflict, where there is no well-suited machine learning methodology available. Special data structures are required to represent scenarios of multiagent interactions, extracted from the text; therefore, traditional machine learning techniques are not applicable. The closest domain to multiagent scenarios, represented as graphs with labeled nodes for causal links, mental actions and physical actions, is a chemical substances domain, where the properties are predicted based on molecular graphs. The concept-based machine learning approach has been shown (Grosskreutz and Lakemeyer 2003) to be adequate.

In this section, we perform the comparative analysis of the applicability for the probabilistic and deterministic methodologies for representing a multiagent conflict, relating a particular scenario to a class and predicting the next action of an opponent agent. We believe that Bayesian learning is less appropriate because some parameters of conflict scenarios are essentially deterministic. For example, we tend to set the probability *that a customer expects a bad attitude from a customer support agent who has already ignored the customer's request concerning a defective product* to zero. There may be exceptions for the above, but it is rather inefficient to take them into account and we would not want to include these exceptions in the learning dataset. Indeed, these exceptional cases rely on the earlier unlinked features that are better included in formal analysis rather than parameterized via probabilities.

Also, if two reactions were possible in a certain state, it would not be adequate to assign a probability to each of them. Our experimental data shows that there is a lack of repetitive statistical patterns of agents' behavior in comparison to our initial intuitive expectations. Instead, we observed that knowledge of additional parameters would lead to the possibility of determining a subsequent action. For example, we performed a statistical analysis for a general choice of complaining or not complaining, given a situation with a defective/normal product or service. An unlimited number of parameters initially seemed to affect the choice. However, as a result, it became clear that assigning a customer such a parameter as *mood* (bad or good) ultimately determines the above choice. We reveal that assuming the existence of an unknown parameter that uniquely sets the value of the target parameter is a rather efficient methodology. In other words, if a selected set of parameters gives a probabilistic distribution of a target parameter, it is worth either:

(1) Adding a new parameter to explicitly determine the target one, or
(2) Ignoring the probability values and considering all possibilities for the target parameter as being equal, if such the parameter cannot be found.

Figure 7.2 presents a simple diagram of possibilities where a customer who is assigned a *bad mood* complains about both a good and bad product, and a customer with *good mood* who complains about the bad products only. It is irrational to assign a probability for either of these possibilities because, given the fact that 20% of customers behave one way and 80% behave another way, we still have

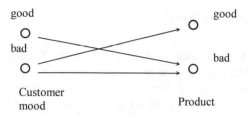

good   good

bad

                                        bad

Customer
mood   Product

Fig. 7.2 A simple model for customer's mood (the diagram of possibilities). In accordance with the model, a customer in a bad mood complains in the case of either (good or bad) product and a customer in a good mood—only in the case of a bad product. Having chosen the mood parameter, we avoided using probabilities for representing complaints involving either product type

to consider both possibilities. Also, if the situations are assigned probabilities, they would significantly vary from domain to domain.

We have also discovered that for the more specific situation of following or not following a customer service advice concerning *making a product work*, the probability of choice is independent of some previous actions and events (e.g., *asked for compensation* or *was previously ignored by a customer service*), but strongly depends on the other events (*of being rejected a compensation*). We build the choice tree (Table 7.2) for banking complaints and observe that it satisfactorily covers the scenarios based on deterministic links between the parameters of agents, fluents and actions. Note that ignoring the scenarios just because of their infrequency (as a probability threshold-based approach would do) may lead to ignoring important cases, which introduces new links (fluents) between the states. At the same time, if a particular scenario is not covered by the deductive deterministic model, our approach (its deterministic machine learning component) allows finding a set of somewhat similar scenarios and performing the prediction *by analogy*.

As a simple example from our customer support domain, we recall a well-known commonsense reasoning puzzle that involves a basic multiagent conflict. In a customer support office, 35% of incoming telephone calls are for the manager, 40% for the assistant manager, and 25% for other team members. Assuming all team members are by the telephone, and there is no receptionist, what system should be used to decide who answers the phone to minimize the number of occasions when the wrong person answers it? The answer is that the assistant manager should *always* answer the phone because her chance to be called is the highest, and it only matters whose probability is highest and not what the probability values are.

To complete the above discussion, we state that the nature of uncertainty in such data as textual representation of multiagent conflicts is rather a lack of information or logical links between the events than probabilistic characteristics (the reader is advised to compare our conclusions with Fagin and Halpern (1994)).

7.2   The System Architecture

Hence we choose the GOLOG and JSM environments for deterministic reasoning about action and inductive machine learning, respectively, because of their flexibility and power (Fig. 7.3). Using the above approaches to illustrate our methodology, we keep in mind that our architecture of merging deductive and inductive components is independent of the choice of particular formalism and better models real-world domains than these approaches taken separately.

Overall architecture of the system for prediction of a consecutive action in a multiagent conflict is shown in Fig. 7.3. The natural language information extraction unit (on the left) provides the deductive component (on the top right) with the extracted actions. If the *Reasoning about action* component determines a lack of information concerning the opponent agent, the *Inductive* component (on the bottom right) is initiated. The *Inductive* component loads the set of accumulated complaints about the given company (its name is extracted by NL component) and predicts the following action given the state, obtained by the *Reasoning about action* component. If the multiagent scenario is rather complex, the simulation by means of NL_MAMS (Galitsky 2016) is required to predict the following mental state. The units with a bold frame are the focus of this chapter.

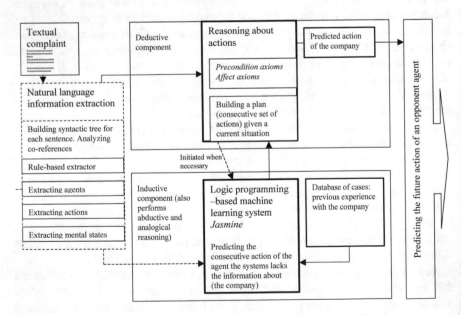

Fig. 7.3 A system for prediction of a consecutive action in a multiagent conflict

7.3   Inductive Machine Learning as a Logic Program

In this chapter, we implement both the GOLOG and JSM environments within the same logic program. We will only briefly comment on GOLOG in the following section because it has been thoroughly presented in the literature. The JSM approach (Finn 1999) was inspired by the plausible similarity-based reasoning of the philosopher J. S. Mill who has suggested a set of five canons by means of which to analyze and interpret our observations (for the purpose of drawing conclusions about the causal relationships they exhibit). Here we build the JSM system as a logic program called JaSMine, following the formal frameworks of Anshakov et al. 1989; Vinogradov 1999). JSM can be represented as first-order logic with the specialized applied axioms for induction, abduction and analogy (Finn 1999).

The JSM environment consists of features, objects and targets. Within a first-order language, objects are atoms, features and targets are terms which include these atoms. For a target (feature to be predicted), there are four groups of objects with respect to the evidence they provide for this target:

$$Positive - Negative - Inconsistent - Unknown.$$

An inference to obtain a target feature (satisfied or not) can be represented as one in a respective four-valued logic. The predictive machinery is based on building hypotheses, $target(X): features_1(X, …), …, feature_n(X, …)$, that separate examples, where $target$ is an effect, and $features_1, …, feature_n \in features$ are the causes; X ranges over objects.

The desired separation is based on the *similarity* of objects in terms of features they satisfy. Usually, such similarity is domain-dependent. However, building the general framework of inductive-based predictions, we use the anti-unification of formulas that express the totality of features of the given and other objects (our futures do not have to be unary predicates and are expressed by arbitrary first-order terms).

JSM-prediction is based on the notion of similarity between objects. The similarity between a pair of objects is a hypothetical object which obeys the common features of this pair of objects. There is no numerical value for similarity. In handling similarity, JSM is close to Formal Concept Analysis (Ganter and Wille 1999; Kuznetsov 2004), where similarity is the operator on a lattice. In this work, we choose anti-unification of formulas expressing features of the pair of objects to derive a formula for similarity sub-object (Galitsky 2017). Anti-unification, in the finite term case, was studied in Reynolds (1970) and Amiridze and Kutsia (2018) as the least upper bound operation in a lattice of terms. Below we will be using the predicate *similar(Object1, Object2, CommonSubObject)* which yields the third argument given the first and the second arguments.

Our starting example of JSM settings for unary predicate is as follows (from now on we use the conventional PROLOG notations for variables and constants):

```
features([a,b,c,d,e]). %% set of features and actions they denote
   a=customerServiceIgnoreAskWhyC. b= askHowToFix.
   c=explainWronglyC. d=followWrongAdviceNoResult.
   e=ClaimBadCustomerService.
objects([compl1,   compl2,   compl3,   compl4,   compl5,   compl6,
compl7]). %% complaints
   targets([referBBB]). %% an action to occur (to be predicted)
%% Beginning of knowledge base
   a(compl1).    b(compl1).    c(compl1).    a(compl2).    b(compl2).
c(compl2). e(compl2).
   a(compl3). d(compl3). a(compl4). c(compl4). d(compl4).
   a(compl5). b(compl5). e(compl5). a(compl6). d(compl6).
   a(compl7).           b(compl7).            c(compl7).            e(compl7).
referBBB(compl1). referBBB(compl2). referBBB(compl5).
%% End of knowledge base
   unknown(referBBB(compl7)).unknown(referBBB(compl6)).
      % to be predicted
```

Let us build a framework for predicting the target feature V of objects set by the formulas X expressing their features: *unknown(X, V)*. We are going to predict whether $V(X)$ holds or not.

We start with the raw data, positive and negative examples, raw*Pos(X, V)* and *rawNeg(X, V)*, for the target V, where X range over formulas expressing features of objects. We form the totality of intersections for these examples (positive ones, U, that satisfy *iPos(U, V)* and negative ones, W, that satisfy *iNeg(W, V)*, not shown):

iPos(U, V):- rawPos(X1, V), jPos(X2, V), X1\=X2, similar(X1, X2, U), U\=[ ].
iPos(U, V):- iPos(U1, V), jPos(X1, V), similar(X1, U1, U), U\=[ ].

Above are the recursive definitions of the hypothesis. As the logic program clauses which actually construct the lattice (totality of intersections for positive and negative examples), we introduce the third argument to accumulate the currently obtained intersections (the negative case is analogous):

iPos(U, V):- iPos(U, V, _).
iPos(U, V, Accums):- rawPos(X1, V), rawPos(X2, V), X1\=X2, similar(X1, X2, U),
    Accums=[X1, X2], U\=[ ].
iPos(U, V, AccumsX1):- iPos(U1, V, Accums), !, rawPos(X1, V),
    not member(X1, Accums), similar(X1, U1, U), U\=[ ],
    append(Accums, [X1], AccumsX1).

To obtain the actual positive *posHyp* and negative *negHyp* hypotheses from the intersections derived above, we filter out the hypotheses which belong to both positive and negative intersections *inconsHyp(U, V)*:

inconsHyp(U, V):- iPos(U, V), iNeg(U, V).
posHyp(U, V):-iPos(U, V), not inconsHyp(U, V).
negHyp(U, V):-iNeg(U, V), not inconsHyp(U, V).

Here U is the formula expressing the features of objects. It serves as a body of clauses for hypotheses $V:U$.

The following clauses deliver the totality objects so that the features expressed by the hypotheses are included in the features of these objects. We derive positive and negative hypotheses *reprObjectsPos(X, V)* and *reprObjectsNeg(X, V)* where X is instantiated with objects where V is positive and negative, respectively. The last clause (with the head *reprObjectsIncons(X, V)*) implements the search for the objects to be predicted so that the features expressed by both the positive and negative hypotheses are included in the features of these objects.

> *reprObjectsPos(X, V):- rawPos(X, V), posHyp(U, V), similar(X, U, U).*
> *reprObjectsNeg (X, V):- rawNeg(X, V), negHyp(U, V), similar(X, U, U).*
> *reprObjectsIncons(X, V):-unknown(X,V), posHyp(U1, V), negHyp(U2, V),*
> *similar(X, U1, U1), similar(X, U2, U2).*

Finally, we approach the clauses for prediction. For the objects with unknown targets, the system predicts that they either satisfy these targets, do not satisfy these targets, or that the fact of satisfaction is inconsistent with the raw facts. To deliver V, a positive hypothesis has to be found so that a set of features X of an object has to include the features expressed by this hypothesis and X is not from *reprObjectsIncons(X, V)*. To deliver $\neg V$, a negative hypothesis has to be found so that a set of features X of an object has to include the features expressed by this hypothesis and X is not from *reprObjectsIncons(X, V)*. No prediction can be made for the objects with features expressed by X from the third clause, *predictIncons(X, V)*.

> **predictPos(X,V):- unknown(X, V), posHyp(U, V), similar(X, U,U),**
> **not reprObjectsIncons(X, V).**
> *predictNeg(X,V):- unknown(X, V), negHyp(U, V), similar(X, U,U),*
> *not reprObjectsIncons(X, V).*
> *predictIncons(X,V):- unknown(X, V), not predictPos(X, V), not predictNeg(X, V),*
> *reprObjectsIncons(X, V):-not j01(X, V).*

The first clause above (shown in bold) will serve as an entry point to predict (choose) an action from the explicit list of available actions that can be obtained for the current state, given the hard-coded precondition axioms (delivered by *findAllPossibleActionsAtThisState(S, As)*). The clause below is called from the reasoning about action component when other possibilities to find the following action are exhausted (Sect. 7.4).

> *predict_action_by_learning(ActionToBePredicted,S):-*
> *findAllPossibleActionsAtThisState(S, As), loadRequiredSamples(As),*
> *member(ActionToBePredicted, As), predictPos(X, ActionToBePredicted), !,*
> *X\=[ ].*

Predicate *loadRequiredSamples(As)* above forms the training dataset. If, for a given dataset, a prediction is inconsistent, it is worth eliminating the cases from the dataset which deliver this inconsistency. Conversely, if there is an insufficient number of positive or negative cases, additional ones are included in the dataset. A number of iterations may be required to obtain a prediction; however, the iteration procedure is deterministic: the source of inconsistency/insufficient data cases are explicitly indicated at the step where predicates *reprObjectsPos* and *reprObjectsNeg* introduced above are satisfied.

For example, for the knowledge base above, we have the following protocol and results:

Intersections
Positive: `[[a(_),b(_),c(_)],[a(_),b(_)],[a(_),b(_),e(_)]]`
Negative: `[[a(_),d(_)]]`
Unassigned examples:
`[[a(compl7),b(compl7),c(compl7),e(compl7)],[a(compl6),d(compl6)]]`

Hypotheses
Positive: `[[a(_),b(_),c(_)],[a(_),b(_)],[a(_),b(_),e(_)]]`
Negative: `[[a(_),d(_)]]`
Contradicting hypotheses: `[]`
   The clauses for hypotheses here:
`referBBB(X):- a(X),b(X),c(X) ;   a(X),b(X) ;   a(X),b(X),e(X).`
`referBBB(X):- not a(X),d(X).`

Background (positive and negative objects with respect to the target `referBBB`)
Positive: `[[a(compl1),b(compl1),c(compl1)],`
`[a(compl2),b(compl2),c(compl2),e(compl2)],`
`[a(compl5),b(compl5),e(compl5)]],`
Negative: `[[a(compl3),d(compl3)],[a(compl4),c(compl4),d(compl4)]] ,`
Inconsistent: `[]`

Prediction for `referBBB` (objects `compl6` and `compl7`)
Positive: `[[a(compl7),b(compl7),c(compl7),e(compl7)]]` (`referBBB(compl7)`)
Negative: `[[a(compl6),d(compl6)]]`   (`not referBBB(compl6)`)
Inconsistent: `[]`
`Instantiated derived rules`
`referBBB(compl7):- a(compl7),b(compl7),c(compl7),e(compl7).`
`not referBBB(compl7):- a(compl6),d(compl7).`

Hence *referBBB(compl7)* holds, this action is expected in scenario *compl7*, but not in the scenario *compl6*. '_' are anonymous variables (here we follow the conventions of logic programming).

7.4   Merging Deductive and Inductive Reasoning About Action

Based on the motivations, which were presented in the Introduction, we have the following methodology to predict an action of an agent in an environment where we do not have a complete information on this agent. If we are unable to derive the actions of this agent given the preconditions of his actions and successor state axioms to sufficiently characterize his current state, learning-based prediction needs to come into play. Instead of just taking the current state into account, as reasoning about action would do, learning-based prediction takes into account the totality of previous actions and states. It is required because there is a lack of knowledge about which previous actions and situations affect the current choice of action.

Situation calculus is formulated in a first-order language with certain second-order features (Reiter 1993). A possible world history that is a result of a sequence of *actions* is called *situation*. The expression *Do(a, s)* denotes the successor situation to *s* after action *a* is applied. For example, *Do(complain(Customer, Do(harm(Company), S_0))),* is a situation expressing the world history that is based on the sequence of actions {*harm(Company, Customer), complain(Customer, Company)*}, where *Customer* and *Company* are variables (with explicit meanings).

Also, situations involve the *fluents*, whose values vary from situation to situation and denote them by predicates with the latter arguments ranging over the situations, for example,

upset(Customer, Do(harm(Company), S_0))).

Actions have *preconditions*—the constraints on actions:

poss(complain(Customer), s) ≡ upset(Customer, s).

Effect axioms (postconditions) describe the effect of a given action on the fluents:

poss(complain(Customer),   s)   &   responsive(Company)   ⊃ settled_down(Customer, Do(complain(Customer), s))).

Effect axioms express the causal links between the domain entities. We refer the reader to (Levesque et al. 1997) for further details on the implementation of the situation calculus.

As we see, the methodology of situation calculus is building a sequence of actions given their pre- and postconditions. To choose an action, we verify that the preconditions are dependent on the current fluents. After an action is performed, it affects these fluents, which in turn determine the consecutive action, and so forth. In the traditional situation, calculus pre- and postconditions are manually coded. In this work, we use machine learning to acquire preconditions of actions from each complaint. However, since our current complaint representation stores actions but not intermediate states, here we do not learn action postconditions.

The *frame problem* (Levesque et al. 1997) comes into play to reduce the number of effect axioms that do not change (the common sense law of inertia). The successor state axiom resolves the frame problem:

$$poss(a, s) \supset [f(v, Do(a, s)) \equiv \gamma_f^+(v, a, s) \lor (f(v, s) \& \neg \gamma_f^-(v, a, s))],$$

where $\gamma_f^+(\hat{y}, a, s)$ ($\gamma_f^-(\hat{y}, a, s)$) is a formula describing under what conditions doing action *a* in situation *s* makes fluent *f* become true (false, respectively) in the successor situation *Do(a, s)*.

GOLOG extends the situation calculus with complex actions, involving, in particular, *if–then* and *while* constructions. Macros *do(δ, s, s′)* denotes the fact that situation *s′* is a terminating situation of execution of complex action *δ* starting in situation *s*.

Here we present the case of complex actions performed by an agent with intentions and beliefs. If $a_1, ..., a_n$ are agents' actions, then.

- $[a_1... a_n]$ is a deterministic sequence of actions. We know that an agent may only perform actions in a given order either because of external constraints or because of her intentions.
- $[a_1\#...\# a_n]$ is a non-deterministic sequence of actions for an agent, any sequence of actions is plausible, given our knowledge about the intentions of this agent.
- *ifCond(p)* is checking a condition expressed by *p* by an agent. This is the case of an explicit condition for agent's choice of action; the condition is available for the reasoning system.
- *star(a)*, nondeterministic repetition.
- *if* (p, a_1, a_2), if–then–else conditional, applied by an agent in accordance with our knowledge of his rules.
- *while* (p, a_1, a_2), iteration.

We suggest the reader to consult (Levesque et al. 1997) for more details, and proceed to the GOLOG interpreter. The last line below is added to the conventional GOLOG interpreter to suggest an alternative choice of action by means of learning from the previous experience, if the other options to determine the following action are exhausted:

> $do(A1 : A2,S,S1) :- do(A1,S,S2), do(A2,S2,S1).$
> $do(ifCond(P),S,S) :- holds(P,S).$
> $do(A1 \# A2,S,S1) :- do(A1,S,S1) ; do(A2,S,S1).$
> $do(if(P,A1,A2),S,S1) :- do((call(P) : A1) \# (call(not P) : A2),S,S1).$
> $do(star(A),S,S1) :- S1 = S ; do(A : star(A),S,S1).$
> $do(while(P,A),S,S1):- do(star(call(P) : A) : call(not P),S,S1).$
> $do(pi(V,A),S,S1) :- sub(V,\_,A,A1), do(A1,S,S1).$
> $do(A,S,S1) :- proc(A,A1), do(A1,S,S1).$ % a complex action
> $do(A,S,do(A,S)) :- primitive\_action(A), poss(A,S).$
> **$do(A, S, do(A, S)):- predict\_action\_by\_learning(A, S).$**

The last clause with the body **predict_action_by_learning(A, S)**, yielding action *A* at the state *S*, can be thought of as an online acquisition of facts of action possibilities, (*poss(A, S)*).

Figure 7.4 depicts the problem of finding a plan as a theorem-proving in situation calculus:

Axioms $\models (\exists \delta, s) Do(\delta, S_0, s)$ and $Goal(s)$, where plan $Goal(s)$ is synthesized as a side effect while satisfying *Goal*. In our case, planning is a reduction in the number of possible actions of an opponent.

Below we present the samples of postcondition (effect, successor state) axioms for fluents *unsatisfied*, *disinformed* and *company_untrusted*.

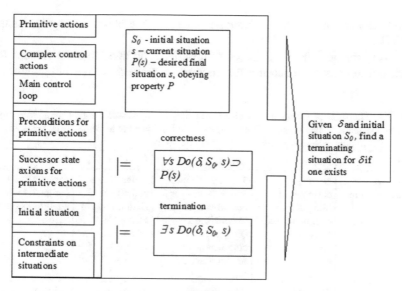

Fig. 7.4 Methodology for deriving a plan in the settings of situation calculus (Levesque et al. 1997). To predict an action of an opponent agent, we simulate the planning process for this agent to plan his future actions

holds(unsatisfied, Do(E,S)):- E = wrongDoC; E = customerServiceIgnoreWhy;
        E = explainWrong; E = findUnreasonableCauseForCustComplain;
     (holds(unsatisfied,S), not member(E, [agreeToFixCS,   agreeToCompensateCS,
convinceToBeActingAsRequiredCS])).
     holds(disinformed, Do(E, S)):- E = explainWronglyCS.
     holds(company_untrusted, Do(E, S)):- holds(disinformed,S),
                                E = followWrongAdviceNoResult.

There are more examples of pre- and post-conditions for our domain of customer complaints below.

7.5   Predicting Inter-Human Interactions in Customer Complaints

To provide a comprehensive illustration of our hybrid reasoning approach to the prediction of agents' actions in the conditions of uncertainty, we consider a real-life problem of automated handling of customer complaints. As an application area, in this chapter, we focus on a particular issue of automation for complaint handling, the prediction of possible action of an opponent (company) to suggest an effective countermeasure for the customer. This countermeasure, presented to a user (upset customer) as a textual advice, is based on this prediction of company's action or course of actions (strategy). *Opponent's action prediction engine*, which deploys the hybrid reasoning approach described above, is one of the important *ComplaintEngines* for

overall automation and decision support tools for the customer support industry
(Table 7.1).

Clearly, the domain of customer complaints is an appealing benchmark for a
hybrid reasoning system because it combines the problems of resolving multiagent

Table 7.1 The suite of *Complaint Engines* including the *opponent's action prediction engine*,
which is the focus of this chapter. Other engines use the machine learning component *Jasmine*,
(rows 3–5) but not the *reasoning about the actions* component

Engine	Purpose	Benefit	Input	Output
Interactive complaint form	To assist customer in filing a complaint, and to assist a company in its effective handling	To suggest a fast and easy way for a customer to attempt to convince a company to compensate for a product/service	A non-verbal complaint (initial stage of complaint resolution process)	A preprocessed complaint with analyzed structure
Complaint argumentation advisor	To assist customers in making their case convincing, and to help a company in obtaining the most important parameters of possible service failure	To accelerate the complaint handling process, to impress customers with unbiased responses to complaints, to reveal the weakest points for products/services	An original textual and preprocessed structurized complaint	A list of argumentation patterns which support a claim and a list of ones which weaken it (Galitsky et al. 2009, 2015)
Complaint validity assessor	To automatically justify if a service failure has indeed occurred, or the complaint is a result of negative customer attitude	This is a key engine: it supports a decision of either reject a claim and try to settle the case, or to try to fix a problem and to compensate a customer for it	A preprocessed complaint with analyzed structure and other cases	Yes/No decision and its motivations Comparison with other cases on a feature-by-feature basis
Complaint case matcher	To suggest a resolution strategy	It allows to apply the past complaint resolution experience to the current case	A preprocessed complaint with analyzed structure Other cases (indexed)	Similar cases and similarity features. For each such feature, the link is indicated, that links a given case with the stored one with indication

(continued)

Table 7.1   (continued)

Engine	Purpose	Benefit	Input	Output
Opponent's action prediction engine	Given the scenario of inter-human interaction, predict the possible actions or sequence of actions of an opponent (company) to produce an adequate countermeasure strategy	To generate an advice for a customer on the most efficient course of actions, taking advantage of knowledge of possible company responses	A preprocessed complaint with analyzed structure and other cases	A textual advice which is formed by merging the elements of predefined textual hints associated with predicted set of actions

conflict, handling ambiguous data extracted from the complex discourse, matching scenarios of inter-human conflicts with each other and planning agents' actions.

7.5.1   *Introducing the Domain of Customers' Complaints*

Our problem domain is formed in accordance with the experience of a series of consumer advocacy companies, which try to help the unsatisfied customers. These customers are unsatisfied by particular products, services, or, especially, customer support on one hand, and the practice of complaint handling by customer response management personnel and existing software means on the other hand. We base our scenario-grounded model of a customer complaints on the analysis of publicly available databases of complaints, primarily www.planetfeedback.com (Blackshaw and James 2008). In the course of our analysis, we build the internal database of formalized and structurized complaints applying a variety of classification criteria in an attempt to achieve a unified framework for a wide assortment of domains for complaints.

In our presentation in the current chapter, we skip the natural language component that extracts actions, fluents and their parameters; we refer to Chap. 7 Volume 1 for details on that. Here, we briefly touch upon the applications of semantic templates to extract the complex actions (Fig. 7.9).

The task of a written complaint processing can be formulated as relating a complaint to a class that requires a certain set of reactions (directly contacting a producer or retailer, clarifying the situation to a consumer, bringing a case to court, addressing a particular consumer advocacy firm, etc.). Such a class is determined by the opponent's action, which is a subject of prediction. Performing such kinds of tasks allows us to automate the complaint processing, significantly accelerating the results and reducing the cost of operations for a consumer advocacy firm (Fig. 7.7).

Clearly, an application of statistical machine learning would skip too many details to adequately relate a natural language complaint to a reaction class. If the determination of such a class deploys keyword-based information extraction methods, peculiarities of both natural language representation and the dispute process itself are ignored. The reader should take into account that similar complaints with very similar mental states of agents may frequently belong to totally different classes of reaction in accordance with the willingness of a company to satisfy its customer (so that the complaint is dropped).

In the most natural cases, a classification of complaints is based on the name of the product/service and its specific feature, which has not met a customer expectations (Table 7.2). However, instead, a handling of a complaint depends on objective estimates of the products' feature failure, customer attitude, customer support policy and how it may deviate in a given scenario, and the properties of the complaint scenario, including their structure. The first item above (objective estimates of the feature failure) is quite hard to estimate directly by an automatic system; therefore *good product/bad product* hypotheses are generated and evaluated against the other properties of the compliant scenario.

7.5.2   Selecting the Features, Fluents and Actions

In this section, we describe a set of actions and fluents for each complaint. The complaint scenario includes two main agents: a customer and a company (for simplicity, we consider multiple representatives of a company as a conventional agent and ignore complaints where a third party is involved). The behavioral patterns for these two agents are quite different with respect to uncertainty: a complainant is assumed to be motivated to disclose the relevant information (the consumer advocacy company), and her intentions and motivations are clear (Fig. 7.6). Conversely, we observe the actions of a company from the perspective of a (biased) customer, but we can only hypothesize on its intentions and motivations: the causal relations between the company's actions and its overall policy are frequently uncertain for the reasoning system.

Our initial plot was to focus on all features, including the domain-specific ones (Table 7.3). We selected the well-circumscribed domain of banking complaints and formed the set of the most important, from a customer viewpoint, a set of features (Table 7.4 and Fig. 7.5).

Having selected the set of features of interest, we processed our database of formalized complaints and revealed the typical action patterns for both customers and companies. What we have observed is that the set of possible strategies for both companies and customers is limited (it may be obvious to the reader). The complaint databases we use allow for an adequate coverage of a variety of complaints about a given company.

Table 7.2 A fragment of complaint database: initial classification criteria are applied. A typical complaint arises when both service failure (the second column) and customer service failure (the fourth column) have co-occurred. These failures are subjective and specified in accordance with the claim of a customer. The fifth column presents the beginning of textual complaint

Id	Essence of service failure	Operation that confused a provider	Essence of customer service failure	A fragment of complaint
1	Payment delay	Credit card payment	None	The problem concerns the billing or payment …
10	Reject promlsed service	Sign-up bonus	Providing misleading information and not providing expected service	Promised $50 for signing up with Netbank and all I got was charged fees. When I called about the … $50 and the fees I Mas tolo on numerous occosions that I …
11	agreement with customer and properly notify him/her	Account inactivity	None	Balance to a negative balance for "inactivity fees" which I was not fully informed. When I opened the account, I …
12	Unable to correct amount of deposit	Making a deposit	Cheating/disinforming/ ignoring customer	Rediculous process of recciving a returned check (missing some …
14	Unable to verify existing of account for deposit	Transfer to unexisting account	Unwillingness/inability to understand client's request	Services for $270.—(Transaction # KMM19821220V5600L0KM) from a supplier i have been using for the past 2 …
15	Unable to handle lost credit card situation	Lost credit card	Responding with wrong information	They've stolen money from me! I've heard several months of BS and lies, and …
16	Delays	Online bill payments	Providing misleading information	NetBank delivered my online bill payments days and weeks late causing …
26	Unable to handle a client with lost login	Transactions with no login information	Unwillingness or inability to help/advise	I have a Pay Pal Accouet, this ac count was created roughly 1.5 years ago. I created it strictly for the purpose of paying for a …

We proceed to the set of some generalized actions for a complaint. Each of the selected generalized actions below covers a class of actions which may be semantically similar in our complaint domain only:

wrongDoCS—initial action of a company that caused the complaint. Usually, the customers complain when they believe something went really wrong, their interests are strongly affected and they were mistreated by the company's customer support.

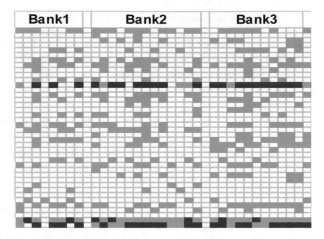

Fig. 7.5 A visualization of the features for three banks. Gray cells denote the presence of a feature, and black cells denote the presence of an inverse feature value (e.g., strong *customer support viscosity* versus low *customer support viscosity*, which is a *friendliness*). Features are rows (see Table 7.3), and complaints are columns

Company's actions are denoted with an identifier whose last two characters are "CS" (Customer Support) to distinguish them from the actions of the complainants and their representatives.

askWhy—the first thing a customer does is asks the customer service "Why did it happen? What went wrong?", believing that the company is ready to help.

customerServiceIgnoreAskWhyCS—a typical step in the development of relationships between a customer and a company is ignoring the customer's request (by the company).

askHowToFix—at this step, the customer proceeds from the questions "Why/how did it happen" to "How to achieve the *normal functioning/compensation/satisfaction situation*?".

explainWronglyCS—the company gives a wrong advice that does not lead to any of the above situations. It is questionable whether the company's representatives are aware of it.

followWrongAdviceNoResult—the customer believes that company's advice is adequate, follows it and discovers that it is not the case.

claimBadCustomerService—customer starts to complain not only about *wrongDoC* but about customer service as well.

findUnreasonableCauseForCustComplainCS—at this point, the company blames the customer that she is non-cooperative and states that there are no reasons to complain.

complainToOtherEstablishments, askFriend, askLawyer, askConsumerAdvoc-Company—the customer understands that he can achieve nothing on his own from the company and looks for help, including a friend, an attorney, a consumer advocacy company, etc.

Table 7.3 The set of features for banking complaints. This set includes service and customer support failures at the initial and final stages of the complaint scenarios. The same set of features is considered from the complainant's perspective and also is the subject of objective estimation by a domain expert

1	**Complaint of a service failure**	5	**Customer's resolution**
a	Inadequate transaction	a	Request explanation
b	Breach of confidentiality	b	Request to complete transaction
c	Changing terms of contract	c	Lost trust
d	Credit collection	d	Leave
e	User interface	e	Request compensation
2	**Initial customer support failure**	f	Seek legal advice
a	Ignoring customer's request	6	**Service failure (confirmed by an expert)**
b	Wrong advice or explanation	a	No failure
c	Blaming customer	b	inadequate transaction
d	Failure to keep up to compensation promises	c	Breach of confidentiality
e	Incompetence	d	Changing terms of contract
3	**Customer support viscosity (1, −1, −2)**	e	Credit collection
4	**Continuing customer support failure**	f	Owerdraft
a	Ignoring customer's request	g	*Inadequate credit history evaluation*
b	Wrong advice or explanation	7	**User interface failure**
c	Blaming customer	a	Not available
d	Failure to keep up to compensation promises	b	With respect to bank's inadequacy
e	Incompetence	c	With respect to customer's errors
		8	**Mental features**
			Customer's mood (bad −1, good +1)
		9	CS mood (helpful, helpful with limited resources, unhelpful)

settleDown, agreeToFixC, agreeToCompensateCS, convinceToBeActingAsRequiredCS—the customer is ready to settle down by a promise or actual fulfillment of the required actions by the company. The latter has found one way or another to satisfy this customer, or has convinced him that nothing went really wrong (Fig. 7.7).

Table 7.4 Enumeration of complaints about two banks based on the essential compliant properties. Compare with Table 7.1, which contains the initially employed set of features

Bank	Actual quality of product/service	Mood of the CS	Mood of the customer	Essence of service failure	The type of service which failed	Essence of customer service failure	Company accepted responsibility
Bank 1	N/A	Unhelpful	Good	Car loan/repossession	Timely notification for payment	Not understanding the situation	N
	N/A	Unhelpful	Good	Unreasonable product decline	Credit card approval	Inability to provide motivations for decision	N
	Bad	Unhelpful	Good	Inconsistent check deposit procedure	Deposit of business check	Inability to explain the failure	Y
	Deceptive	N/A	Good	Deceitful credit card offer	Promotional offer	Inability to comply with the offer	N
	N/A	Unhelpful	Good		Check deposit	Impoliteness	N
	N/A	Unhelpful	Suspicious	Too low credit limit	Credit limit update	Offensive offer	N
	N/A	Unhelpful; bad attitude	Demanding	Unclear what info to provide for title info	Title information	Inability to explain the failure; sending from rep to rep; bad attitude	N
	Bad	Helpful; unhelpful	Good	Unable to verify check	Check deposit	Incompetence; inability to verify a check; cheating	N
	Good		Demanding	N/A	Overdraft fee	Inability to accommodate customer request	N

(continued)

Table 7.4 (continued)

Bank	Actual quality of product/service	Mood of the CS	Mood of the customer	Essence of service failure	The type of service which failed	Essence of customer service failure	Company accepted responsibility
Bank 2	Bad	Unhelpful	Good	Inability to obtain a proper customer information	Car loan	Wrong loan recepient name, wrong address, inability to correct, inaability to get information from customer, unlawful data disclosure	N
	Bad	Unhelpful	Good	Card is cancelled because of overdraft check	Overdraft protection	Inability to explain the failure, stealing funds, ignoring customer request, inability to get proper account information	N
		Unhelpful	Good	Check cashing failure	Check cashing	Inability to explain the failure	N
	Bad	Unhelpful	Good	Return check fee	Assigning return check fee	Illegal modification of service agreement, ignoring customers' request; providing untruthful info	N

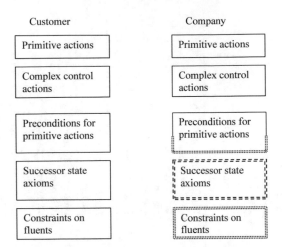

Fig. 7.6 The knowledge base components of a complaint processing system. On the left: customer's component, on the right: company's component. Dotted boxes denote incomplete information

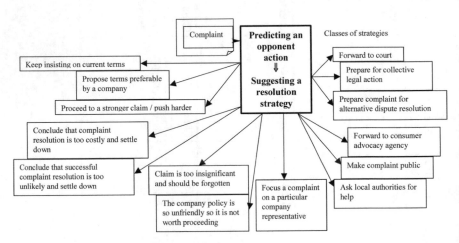

Fig. 7.7 The problem domain for our hybrid approach: recognizing the class of a complaint with respect to the resolution strategy. Recognition of a complaint is determining the future action or set of actions of an opponent, which should be dealt with in accord-ance with that strategy

7.5.3   Setting the Learning Environment

In the complaints, the customers explicitly mention their actions and most of the fluents expressing their mental states. Ambiguity in the representation of actions for the customers may be caused by errors in natural language processing and/or inadequate writing by the customer. As to the company, we obtain a description of its actions and an incomplete plot of its fluents in accordance with the customer's viewpoint. This data is insufficient to perform the prediction of the company's planning, given only the current scenario. On the other hand, using a pure predictive machinery without actually modeling the company's sequence of actions in a deductive way does not allow obtaining the company's fluents in sufficient detail to relate a given complaint to a class (Fig. 7.7).

The customer component includes the complete knowledge of the precondition for primitive actions, successor state axioms and constraints on fluents. The customer's component is ready for modeling its sequence of actions. However, the company's component is incomplete: we do not have complete information on preconditions for primitive actions. Also, our knowledge of successor state axioms and constraints on fluents is incomplete.

Note that we cannot conduct supervised learning for our system in the usual sense because no company would ever disclose its customer support policy to eliminate uncertainty in our representation for the company side. We form the learning dataset using the collected complaints (Table 7.2), where we may get information about the complaint results from our expert and manually assign the class of reaction. At the same time, we would never get information on the company's side from our dataset (Fig. 7.6).

We build the prediction for a single company's actions or a sequence of actions in response to the customer's action. A symmetric problem of prediction the customer's action in response to the company's action, having complete knowledge of the company side, may be solved in a similar way. However, the latter case would not take advantage of the automated treatment of the previous experience with an opponent agent: collecting data on previous complaints of a given customer is rather hard. In both cases, the same agents' features, fluents and actions are in use.

7.5.4 Further Classification of Complaint Scenarios

One way to look at the classification of scenarios is to use the precondition axioms as the classification criteria. A class comprises the set of scenarios where action was preceded by certain conditions (Table 7.5).

Table 7.5 presents a sample of scenarios for interaction between a customer and a company for a particular domain of complaint analysis. Only possible scenarios for *good* products are shown; the number of possible scenarios for a *bad* product (a justified complaint) is much higher.

The main classification criteria are based on the quality of a product {*good, bad* (not shown)}, customer mood {*good, bad*} and a company policy {*helpful, helpful with limited resources, unhelpful*}.

Blank cells mean that the complaint is settled down. Fourth, sixth, seventh and eighth columns denote the fluent and action of a company (in the middle) and the second action of a company (on the right).

We do not intend to cover all possibilities for interaction of complaint agents: enumeration of scenarios reflects the set of analyzed complaints about a given

Table 7.5 A fragment of a representation for the classification of interaction scenarios

Product: bad/good	Customer mood: bad/good	Company's policy	First customer action	First company response: fluent	First company response: action	Second customer action	Second company response: action
Good	Bad	Helpful, helpful no spending	Ask(compensate)	Understand(customer_mood)	Suggest(refund)	Reject(offer)	Suggest(way_to_fix)
						Keep(ask_compensate)	
				Not interested(customer_mood)	Suggest(explanation)	Suggest(counter_offer)	
					Suggest(partial_refund)	Accept(offer)	
			Ask(how_to_fix)	Understand(customer_mood)	Suggest(way_to_fix)	Reject_offer	Explain(product_good)
				Not understand(customer mood)	Explain(product good)	Ask(compensate)	
			Ask(why_happen)	Understand(customer mood)	Suggest(way to fix)	Reject(offer)	
				Not understand(customer_mood)	Explain(product_good)	Ask(compensate)	
						Accept(explanation)	
		Unhelpful	Ask(compensate)	Not interested(customer_mood)	Ignore(request)	Claim(bad_CustS)	Explain(customer_wrong)
						Ask(compensate)	
			Ask(how to fix)		Explain(product_good)		
	Good	Any	No complaint				

Table 7.6 Percentages of the correct predictions of future actions for various recognition settings (left sub-columns) and indications of how these predictions are better than randomly selected or most frequently selected (right sub-columns). The last column shows that the system is capable of determining the complaint status (justified or unjustified) with higher accuracy than predicting an action (Galitsky and Pascu 2006). Note that the accuracy of random prediction in our settings would be less than 10% (the number of possibilities is sufficiently large, see Table 7.5)

Dataset	Only reasoning about action (%, times over random)		Only machine learning (%, times over random)		The hybrid approach (%, times over random)		Justified/unjustified complaint (%, times over random)	
Bank 1	23%	3.7	32%	4.8	45%	6.6	82%	13.0
Bank 2	40%	5.8	45%	6.6	70%	10.9	90%	14.7
Bank 3	28%	4.6	27%	4.2	52%	7.3	80%	12.5
Bank 4	24%	4.2	67%	9.6	73%	11.1	81%	12.7
Average	29%	4.6	43%	6.3	60%	9.0	83%	13.2

company. Note that intuitive reasoning suggests that the set of plausible combinations of properties and actions is a subset of the exhaustive set (of all possibilities) for an arbitrary domain of customer complaints so that the cardinality of this subset is much lower than that of the whole set.

In the left three columns, the parameters of the agents and the product are set. The fourth column contains the possible initial action of a customer, followed by the fifth and sixth columns. These columns contain the company's fluents (here, the properties of agents which depend on the iteration of a conflict) and actions in response, respectively. The seventh column contains the customer's actions, which are the second iteration in the conflict.

For example, the top row where the scenarios end with $suggestCS(way\_to\_fix)$ can be represented by the following clauses:

$Do(suggestCS(way\_to\_fix),$ ($(Do(reject(offer),$ $Do(suggestCS(refund),$ $Do(ask(compensate),$ $S_0)))$ $\vee$ $(Do(keep(ask\_compensate)),$ $Do(suggestCS(explanation),$ $Do(ask(compensate),$ $S_0))))$ $\vee$ $(Do(suggest(counter\_offer),$ $Do(suggestCS(partial\_refund),$ $Do(ask(compensate),$ $S_0))))))):$ $product(bad),$ $customer\_mood(bad),$ $(company\_policy(helpful)$ $\vee$ $company\_policy(helpful\_no\_spending)).$

Action preconditions here are:

$poss(suggestCS(refund),$ $S):$ $understand(CS,$ $customer\_mood,$ $S),$ $S =$ $Do(ask(compensate),$ $S_0).$

$poss(suggestCS(explanation),$ $S):$ $understand(CS,$ $customer\_mood,$ $S),$ $S =$ $Do(ask(compensate),$ $S_0).$

$poss(suggestCS(partial\_refund),$ $S):$ not $interested(CS,$ $customer\_mood,$ $S),$ $S =$ $Do(ask(compensate),$ $S_0).$

In this case there is no any postcondition for the first customer action: customer mood may be understood or be of no interest irrespectively of the initial customer action. However, the fluent *understand(CS, customer_mood, S)* does depend on the second iteration:

understand(CS,   customer_mood,   S):   (not   (S   =   not   Do(reject(offer),
Do(suggestCS(refund),   Do(ask(compensate), S_0))))   ∨   (S   =
Do(keep(ask_compensate)),   Do(suggestCS(explanation,   Do(ask(compensate),
S_0))))).

Here we added suffixes *CS* to indicate an action of a company for better readability.

Table 7.5 presents just one of the possible ways to classify the scenarios. Parameters that do not change in time form the basis of classification, and further division occurs in accordance with iterations. Using the formalism of reasoning about action helps to build a uniform and compact representation of possible scenarios. For a higher number of possibilities, the above form of representation (via enumeration) would be hardly maintainable. The set of scenarios could be represented as decision lists or decision trees, but the formalization approach of reasoning about action is better suited for the prediction of a consequent action versus the relation of a scenario to a class. Moreover, precondition and postcondition axioms play a better role as a means for using knowledge representation in inductive machine learning. For the latter, a knowledge base can be coded as an enumeration of facts, and also as clauses (precondition and postcondition axioms), capable of yielding these facts.

7.5.5 Applying Semantic Templates

A usual complaint is the description of the process of interaction between two conflicting agents, a customer and a company (Fig. 7.8). For each sentence, the natural language processing (NLP) unit extracts the information on actions. Figure 7.9 shows the parsing tree for the fifth (underlined) sentence from Fig. 7.8 and the results of

I joined XYZbank over a year ago- with faith that the site was secure and I wouldn't have to worry about anyone getting my information. I didn't have any problems until about two weeks ago- when I noticed fraudulent charges on my credit card. I got a feeling so I tried to log into my XYZbank account but was informed that the email addresses I tried were not in their records. When the charges posted to my credit card statement they were indeed from XYZbank. I called XYZbank and was given the email address to where one of the charges went but I still can't get into my XYZbank account. Also, someone has tried to get money from both my savings and checking accounts. I called XYZbank last Monday and was told I would receive a call in 24 hours- come this morning- no word from XYZbank. I got another letter in the mail today from my bank telling me someone had again tried to get money out of my checking account. I called XYZbank and told them to just delete my information out of my account but then I'm told they can't do that because they don't have access to my account- and only I can delete that information- but how can I if I can't get into the account? It's ridiculous the circles they've been running me around- and this is when someone finally answers the phone- plus the only number I could find is not toll free so now I'm spending who knows how much on these phone calls that are only making me more frustrated.

Fig. 7.8 A typical complaint about a bank. The parsing tree and extraction of actions for the underlined sentence is depicted in Fig. 7.9

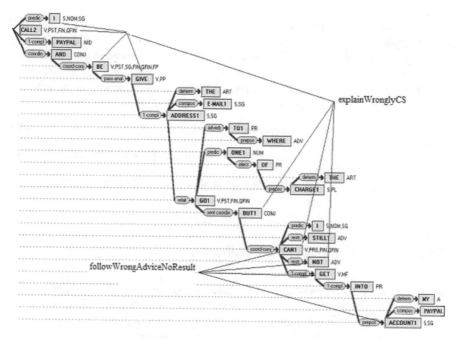

Fig. 7.9 The parsing tree and the extracted word combinations for actions. The rule-based system for extraction of actions enumerates the occurrence of lexical units (including the synonyms), which indicate one of the generalized actions for conflicting agents. The set of words for action *explainWronglyCS* is on the top right, and for action *followWrongAdviceNoResult*—on the left bottom

its analysis: detected actions *explainWronglyCS* and *followWrongAdviceNoResult*. Note that there arc no such words in these sentences that are directly mapped into the concepts *explainWronglyCS* and *followWrongAdviceNoResult*; a semantic template for each of these actions is required, for example.

   *explainWronglyCS:- match([not, receive, answer, {how, to}]); match([suggest impossible, account, lock]); **match([i, was, [given, sent, suggested, explained], but, {could, not}, Verb])**.*

   Semantic templates enumerate lexical units, linked with certain syntactic relationships, which form a particular meaning in the domain of customer complaints (judging on the available dataset). The clause for an action to be extracted from text is based on the predicate *match*, whose argument is a template (list) whose element is either a word (*receive*), a list of synonyms (*[contact, call]*), a part-of-speech placeholder (Verb), a multiword (ordered set) {*how, to*} or a placeholder for one or more words (…). Naturally, there are multiple instances of *match* for each entity; the process of accumulating the templates is manual. The last disjunctive member gets satisfied in our example (sentence Fig. 7.8).

   The fragment of the complaint database with the complaint classification criteria (the column names) are presented in Table 7.1.

The clause below produces textual advice for a customer based on the predicted action *requestAdditProofOfTransaction*. Each predicted action yields, generally speaking, unique advice. In case when a sequence of actions is predicted, an ordered set of advices is provided explicitly stating the order. If multiple actions are determined to be possible, the respective textual fragments are merged in an arbitrary order and the possibility of multiple actions is explicitly stated.

> outputAdviceComponent("At this point the company will likely request the proof of transaction you refer to for backing up your point. To avoid a possible delay in handling your complaint, it would be optimal if you get a transaction statement at the current stage rather than when it will likely be requested in the future."):
>   predictedAction(requestAdditProofOfTransaction).

7.5.6 Evaluation of Prediction Results

We present the resultant recognition accuracy for the analysis of four datasets, each containing 26 complaints. Each dataset includes a set of complaints filed for a particular US-based bank within a month. The complaints are selected to have a similar subject (such as *overdrawn check* and *late payment penalty*). Reasoning about the action component is the same for each bank; half of each set of complaints about each bank is used as a training dataset, and the other half for an evaluation of the prediction accuracy. An NLP unit extracts the features (actions and fluents) and provides a formal representation of scenarios; in the evaluation scenarios, the last action (company response) is set to *unknown*.

Here we present the recognition accuracy of our hybrid reasoning system, assuming an ideal NLP, so that our experts manually verify and correct when necessary the set of features extracted from the text. An overall estimate of the functioning of each complaint engine is presented elsewhere (Galitsky and Tumarkina 2004; Galitsky and Mirkin 2003). Also, for each complaint, the experts determine its status: whether it is justified (there is something wrong with a product, *bad*) or unjustified (a product is as it should be, *good*). The prediction consists of single or multiple actions that are claimed possible and stated to be consistent with the initial scenario.

The results of the evaluation of our hybrid system are shown in Table 7.3. The first column enumerates the banks and the number of complaints available. The second and third columns present the prediction accuracy when the deductive or inductive components (respectively) are deployed. The fourth column gives us the accuracy of action prediction by our hybrid approach, and the fifth column contains the accuracy for overall complaint estimates: justified or not justified. We separately consider the accuracy for each bank and the average value because of the strong variation in banks' complaint handling policies.

Note that for some datasets (banks) we have the machine learning component outperforming the reasoning about action component, and for some datasets, it is the other way around. Whether learning or reasoning outperforms is dependent on the consistency of customer support policy for these banks, the repetitive patterns of handling the complaints, and deviations of a particular scenario from the model encoded via situation calculus. Remarkably, for all the datasets, our hybrid system outperforms either component, used as a stand-alone.

For each evaluation dataset, we are predicting the last 25% of actions (towards the end of the scenario). Clearly, the later the action in the sequence is to be predicted, the more constraints are present, and therefore the narrower is the set of possible actions. Hence we evaluate about 100 settings for each bank, having the average length of complaint scenarios 15.7.

Prediction accuracy data for stand-alone reasoning components, a hybrid system and a different recognition task is presented in Table 7.6. The accuracy is calculated as a percentage of correct predictions (taking into account predictions of multiple possibilities), and the ratio between correct predictions delivered by the system and random predictions (or ones based on the most frequent actions, see discussion in Sect. 7.1.2). These results are shown in the left and right sub-columns for each of the four columns above.

The overall relatively low *reasoning about action*-based prediction accuracy (second column) for the total of 104 scenarios suggests that the scenarios need a more thorough formal description in terms of action preconditions and postconditions, as well as a richer dataset to cover the totality of possible agents' choices.

The stand-alone *Inductive machine learning* unit delivers 36% higher accuracy than the *Reasoning about action* unit. It suggests that implicit knowledge of an individual bank's policy, taken separately, is more important than the overall commonsense knowledge of the complaining process.

One of the goals of our comparative analysis of complaints about the banking industry is to reveal the possible differences between the policies of customer support for these banks. We revealed that the bank 4 has a higher consistency of their scenarios (customer support policy), but also a higher deviation from the common complaint model. It suggests that there is a special customer policy that is different from other banks. Conversely, bank 3 follows our complaint model rather than displaying consistency in complaint handling, which is rather chaotic, so deductive reasoning is more robust here than inductive. Noticeably, deductive and inductive reasoning are good additions to each other.

As to the hybrid system, its accuracy is about 50% higher than the deductive and 43% higher than that of the stand-alone machine learning system. However, it is still 46% lower than the accuracy of determining another complaint parameter—its validity. It suggests that other considerations, including a thorough description of the participants of inter-human conflicts in terms of their intentions, beliefs and desires, would improve the complaint analysis accuracy (compare with Nikolopoulos and Choi 1994).

7.6   Conclusions

In this chapter, we merged deductive reasoning about action with logic and combinatorial predictive machinery that implements inductive, abductive and analogical reasoning (Galitsky 2006). This resulted in a hybrid reasoning system involving multiagent simulation, which is a major component of the overall complaint processing system *ComplaintEngine*.

We have explored both probabilistic and deterministic approaches to simulation of human mental activity and have come to the conclusion that the latter is a reasonably adequate way to represent such activity. We have observed it to be true for the purpose of relating a particular scenario of multiagent conflict to a class or for the purpose of prediction of a consecutive action. Furthermore, we conclude that even if the behavior of participants of a multiagent scenario seems to be random, it is quite efficient to represent it as a deterministic scenario with an unknown value of fluents for the sake of consistency and possibility of formal matching with other scenarios.

The merged formalisms were found adequate in terms of modeling the agent interaction during the automated processing of complaints. Our model includes about ten consecutive actions, including deterministic and non-deterministic ones. For a particular complaint, given an initial sequence of actions, the system provides predictions of consecutive actions, which are expected to follow from each of the opposing agents. The predictions serve as a basis of decisions concerning the plan of action for a customer to resolve a conflict: as a result, the complaint is assigned a class of reactions. We have verified that our hybrid approach to reasoning about customer complaints improves the overall accuracy by about 46% over a random classification.

Implementing the action prediction component of *ComplaintEngine*, we have confirmed our proposition that a hybrid deductive and inductive reasoning system outperforms the stand-alone components in a domain involving multiagent interactions in the conditions of high uncertainty. This conclusion is drawn, in particular, taking into account the capabilities of the inductive logic programming system Cprogol (Davey and Priestley 2002) and the implementation of the event calculus system (Mueller 2004). We believe an adequate reasoning for our domain could be achieved by merging the above systems instead of merging the ones from this chapter (*Jasmine* + (GOLOG + *its interface with machine learning*)).

A transition from a deductive to an inductive reasoning system in the context of Inductive Logic Programming has attracted a substantial interest (Furukawa 1998). Similar to *Jasmine* settings, the logical framework of Inductive Logic Programming can be described, comprising the background knowledge B (an arbitrary logic program), a set of positive examples E which is not derivable from B only, and a set of constraints I (Note the lack of negative examples, explicitly required by *Jasmine*). The task is to find hypothesis H such that $B \cap H$ entails E and satisfies I (Chap. 7 Volume 1). As to the inductive inference, (Furukawa 1998) outlines *descriptive induction* that introduces a set of interconnections between unclassified examples, and *predictive induction*, which starts from classified examples, and finds a set of hypotheses that classify the examples and then use these hypotheses to predict the class of unclassified examples, as it happens in *Jasmine*.

Our current approach to modeling the complaints is based on reasoning about actions and machine learning; here, we did not model mental attitudes of involved agents in detail, using special machinery of reasoning about mental states, developed elsewhere (Galitsky et al. 2006a, b; Wooldridge 2002; Fagin and Halpern 1994). Instead, here we performed a higher-level approximation of inter-human interactions (ignoring the peculiarities of the mental world), specifying the beliefs, desires and indentions of involved agents to make our model more compact and our reasoning more efficient. Such higher-level simulation becomes possible in the case of a hybrid reasoning system, capable of operating with the entities (complex actions), which cover a wide class of meanings, as, for example, *followAdviceNoResult*. In the case of stand-alone reasoning systems, such entities would have to be split into a number of partial cases (particular actions), which would require a higher number of pre/post conditions and a higher volume of learning dataset to operate with (Galitsky and Kuznetsov 2008b). In this domain, we did not use default reasoning to describe typical and abnormal situations in complaint scenarios as an additional measure for reasoning efficiency—this is a subject of Chap. 6 Volume 1 and (Galitsky 2005).

In spite of the high importance of complaint handling in the functionality of the overall customer response management (CRM) system, there are a limited number of computational studies of complaint processing. We believe this is due to the fact that complaint processing requires a powerful suite of reasoning techniques to be deployed (Galitsky 2006, Galitsky and Kuznetsov 2008a), sufficiently expressive knowledge representation language and a rather sophisticated formal model for the scenarios of inter-human interactions.

The framework developed in this chapter for complaints is expected to have a potential in more general application areas, including decision support for negotiations in business, legal and military domains, as well as in a wide variety of legal domains. In the domains involving multiagent conflicts, there will be two major difficulties: information extraction and complex reasoning (Galitsky and Ilvovsky 2019). In our future studies, we plan to reuse the latter component, developed in this chapter.

References

Amiridze N, Kutsia T (2018) Anti-unification and natural language processing fifth workshop on natural language and computer science, NLCS'18, EasyChair Preprint no. 203

Anshakov OM, Finn VK, Skvortsov DP (1989) On axiomatization of many-valued logics associated with formalization of plausible reasoning. Studia Logica 42(4):423–447

Bacchus F, Halpern JY, Levesque H (1999) Reasoning about noisy sensors and effectors in the situation calculus. Artif Intell 111(1–2)

Barber KS, Kim J (2001) Belief revision process based on trust: agents evaluating reputation of information sources. In: Flacone R, Singh M, Tan Y-H (eds) Fraud, deception, and trust in agent societies. Springer

Blackshaw P, James L (2008) Satisfied customers tell three friends, angry customers tell 3000. Randomhouse/Doubleday, NY, USA

Ciravegna F (2000) Learning to tag information extraction from text. In: ECAI-2000 workshop on machine learning for information extraction

Davey BA, Priestley HA (2002) Introduction to lattices and order. Cambridge University Press

De Raedt L (1999). A perspective on inductive logic programming. In: Apt KR, Marek VW, Truszczynski M, Warren D (eds) The logic programming paradigm. Springer

Fagin R, Halpern JY (1994) Reasoning about knowledge and probability. J ACM 41(2):340–367

Fagin R, Halpern JY, Moses Y, Vardi MY (1995) Reasoning about knowledge. MIT Press, Cambridge, Mass

Finn VK(1999) On the synthesis of cognitive procedures and the problem of induction NTI Series 2 N1-2 8-45

Furukawa K (1998) From deduction to induction: logical perspective. In: Apt KR, Marek VW, Truszczynski M, Warren DS (eds) The logic programming paradigm. Springer

Galitsky B (2001) Semi-structured knowledge representation for the automated financial advisor. In: Monostori et al (eds) Engineering of intelligent systems LNAI 2070: 14th IEA/AIE conference pp 874–879

Galitsky B (2003a) Using mental simulator for emotional rehabilitation of autistic patients. In: FLAIRS'03, May 12–14, St. Augustine, FL

Galitsky B (2003b) Natural language question answering system: technique of semantic headers. Advanced Knowledge International, Adelaide Australia

Galitsky B (2005) Disambiguation via default rules under answering complex questions. Int J Artif Intell Tools 14:157–175

Galitsky B (2006) Reasoning about mental attitudes of complaining customers. Knowledge-Based Systems

Galitsky B (2016) Theory of mind engine. In: Computational autism. Springer, Cham

Galitsky B (2017) Improving relevance in a content pipeline via syntactic generalization. Eng Appl Artif Intell 58:1–26

Ganter B, Wille R (1999) Formal Concept Analysis. Springer, Mathematical Foundations

Galitsky B, Mirkin B (2003) Building interactive forms to input the scenarios of multiagent conflicts. In: Rossiter JM, Martin TP (eds) Proceedings of the 2003 UK workshop on computational intelligence. University of Bristol, UKCI-2003, Bristol, UK pp 123–130

Galitsky B, Pampapathi R (2003) Deductive and inductive reasoning for processing the claims of unsatisfied customers. In: 16th IEA/AIE conference, LNAI 2718, Loughborough University, UK, pp 21–30

Galitsky B, Tumarkina I (2004) Justification of customer complaints using mental actions and emotional states. In: FLAIRS'04, May 16–18, Miami, FL

Galitsky B, Pascu A (2006) Epistemic categorization for analysis of customer complaints. In: FLAIRS conference, pp 291–296

Galitsky B, Kuznetsov SO (2008a) Learning communicative actions of conflicting human agents. J Exp Theor Artif Intell 20(4):277–317

Galitsky B, Kuznetsov SO (2008b) Scenario argument structure vs individual claim defeasibility: what is more important for validity assessment? In: International conference on concept structures ICCS 2008. LNCS, vol 5113, pp 282–296

Galitsky B, Ilvovsky D (2019) On a chatbot conducting a virtual dialogue in financial domain. In: Proceedings of the first workshop on financial technology and natural language processing, pp 99–101

Galitsky B, Kuznetsov SO, Samokhin MV (2005) Analyzing conflicts with concept-based learning. In: International conference on conceptual structures, pp 307–322

Galitsky B, Kovalerchuk B, Kuznetsov SO (2006a) Learning common outcomes of communicative actions represented by labeled graphs. In: International conference on concept structures Sheffield, UK July 22–27. LNCS 4604, pp 387–400

Galitsky B, Kuznetsov SO, Vinogradov DV (2006a) Applying hybrid reasoning to mine for associative features in biological data. J Biomed Inform 22

Galitsky B, González MP, Chesñevar CI (2009) A novel approach for classifying customer complaints through graphs similarities in argumentative dialogues. Decis Support Syst 46(3):717–729

Galitsky B, Ilvovsky D, Kuznetsov SO (2015) Text integrity assessment: sentiment profile vs rhetoric structure. In: International conference on intelligent text processing and computational linguistics, pp 126–139

Grosskreutz H, Lakemeyer G (2003) Probabilistic Complex Actions in GOLOG Fundamenta Informaticae 57(2–4):67–192

Kuznetsov SO (2004) Machine learning and formal concept analysis. In: International conference on formal concept analysis, Australia, pp 287–312

Lakemeyer G (1999) On sensing in GOLOG. In: Levesque HJ, Pirri F (eds) Logical foundations for cognitive agents. Springer

Lavrac N, Dzeroski S (1994) Inductive logic programming: techniques and applications. Ellis Horwood, New York

Leake DB, Kinley A, Wilson D (1997) Learning to integrate multiple knowledge sources for case-based reasoning. In: Fourteenth international joint conference on artificial intelligence. Morgan Kaufmann, Nagoya, Japan

Levesque HL, Pagnucco M (2000) Legolog: inexpensive experiments in cognitive robotics. In: Proceedings of the second international cognitive robotics workshop, Berlin, Germany, August 21–22

Levesque HJ, Reiter R, Lesperance Y, Lin F, Scherl RB (1997) GOLOG: a logic programming language for dynamic domains. J Logic Progr 31:59–84

Liu TH, Chuter CJ, Barber KS (1997) Virtual environment simulation for visualizing conflict resolution strategies in multiple robot systems. In: 5th IASTED international conference, robotics and manufacturing. IASTED Press, Cancun, Mexico

McCarthy J (2002) Actions and other events in situational calculus. In: 8th international conference on principles of knowledge representation and reasoning KR02, Toulouse France

Mueller ET (2004) A tool for satisfiability-based commonsense reasoning in the event calculus. In: Proceedings of the seventeenth international florida artificial intelligence research society conference. AAAI Press, Menlo Park, CA

Muggleton S (ed) (1992) Inductive logic programming. Academic Press

Nikolopoulos C, Choi C (1994) A consumer complaint behavior neural forecasting model. Appl Inform 61–63

Pattison-Gordon E, Cimino JJ, Hripcsack G, Tu SW, Gennari JH, Jain NL, Greenes RA (1996) Requirements of a Sharable Guideline Representation For Computer Applications, Stanford University, Report No. SMI-96-0628

Reiter R (1993) Proving properties of states in the situational calculus. Artif Intellig 64(2): 337–351

Reynolds JC (1970) Transformational systems and the algebraic structure of atomic formulas. Machine intelligence, vol 5. Edinburgh University Press, pp 135–151

Shanahan M (1997) Solving the frame problem. MIT Press

Singh P, Barry B (2003) Collecting commonsense experiences. In: Proceedings of the second international conference on knowledge capture (K-CAP 03). Sanibel Island, FL

Vinogradov DV (1999) Logic programs for quasi-axiomatic theories NTI Series 2 N1-2 61-64

Wooldridge M (2002) Reasoning about rational agents. The MIT Press, Cambridge, MA London, England

Chapter 8
Concept-Based Learning
of Complainants' Behavior

Abstract In this chapter, we apply concept learning techniques to solve a number of problems in the customer relationship management (CRM) domain. We present a concept learning technique for common scenarios of interaction between conflicting human agents. Customer complaints are classified as valid (requiring some kind of compensation) or invalid (requiring reassuring and calming down) the customer. Scenarios are represented by directed graphs with labeled vertices (for communicative actions) and arcs (for temporal and causal relationships between these actions and their parameters). The classification of a scenario is computed by comparing a partial matching of its graph with graphs of positive and negative examples. We illustrate machine learning of graph structures using the Nearest Neighbor approach and then proceed to JSM-based concept learning, which minimizes the number of false negatives and takes advantage of a more accurate way of matching sequences of communicative actions. Scenario representation and comparative analysis techniques developed herein are applied to the classification of textual customer complaints as a CRM component. In order to estimate complaint validity, we take advantage of the observation (Galitsky and Kuznetsov 2008) that analyzing the structure of communicative actions without context information is frequently sufficient to judge how humans explain their behavior. Therefore, because human attitudes are domain-independent, the proposed concept learning technique is a good compliment to a wide range of CRM technologies where a formal treatment of inter-human interactions such as customer complaints is required in a decision-support mode.

8.1 Introduction

In recent years, CRM has grown into a significant industrial sector with its own series of technological advancements. A number of computer science algorithms, including optimization and scheduling, have been developed specifically targeting

CRM (Oracle 2009a; GTF 2009; Yuksel 2006; Zirtiloğlu et al. 2008). However, we believe a number of areas of Artificial Intelligence are still finding applications in CRM. The current chapter addresses such an area: the simulation of human reasoning, the proper and efficient implementation of which can be vital to a series of CRM applications. A state-of-art CRM system must be capable of simulating human behavior to properly address customer needs, facilitate communication, perform customer retention (Galitsky 2018) and resolve conflicts should they arise. To solve these problems, a CRM application needs the capability to operate in the realm of human thoughts, by simulating human reasoning and by learning human behavior. In this chapter, we propose a concept-based representation technique and an infrastructure to learn customers' behavior.

One of the main problems to be solved in facilitating customer retention and assisting inter-human conflict resolution is how to reuse previous experience in later situations with similar agents. A business rule system-based architecture is typical for CRM (Jayachandran et al. 2005). However, machine learning is required for handling a poorly formalized domain like human behavior (Yuan and Chang 2001; Ngai 2009). Using information about customers' prior behavior and historical patterns to understand buying patterns, behaviors, and ticketing characteristics are important. Most companies are new to using such structured information about customer behavior to manage and measure relationships. Such efforts go beyond having a call center for customers to raise complaints; it requires having a modern behavior-simulation based management system that listens to the customers, documents the problem and solution, and changes the behavior of employees and call center interactions to build proper relationships with customers (Swift 2001).

In a series of previous studies, we focused on various issues surrounding the practical implementation of reasoning in such domains as understanding multiagent scenarios (Galitsky et al. 2005), determining possible criminal behavior of mobile phone users by means of analyzing the location tracking data (Galitsky and Miller 2005), and emotional profiling (Galitsky et al. 2007). We have addressed a number of issues with graph learning (Galitsky and Kuznetsov 2008a), simulating reasoning about mental states and communicative actions (Galitsky et al. 2011), and introduced complaint scenarios as graphs, using argumentation-based learning (Galitsky et al. 2018). We explored the contribution of specific sources of information about scenarios as communicative actions (Galitsky and Kuznetsov 2008a), argumentation and meta-argumentation patterns (Galitsky and Kuznetsov 2008b), and causal links (Galitsky et al. 2005, 2006).

In this chapter, we focus on scenario structures as a whole to build a concept learning framework for CRM. Referring to concept learning and concept graphs, we follow (Mitchell 1997) and (Sowa 1984). We will observe how concept learning helps to deal with customer complaints (Galitsky et al. 2005), as well as how it assists in the interactive exploration of product features extracted from customer reviews (Galitsky et al. 2009a). We select lattices and formal concept analysis as tools for learning human behavior because they have the following properties:

- flexibility,
- appropriateness for poorly formalized domains like human behavior, and
- deterministic structures capable of explicit explanation of decisions proposed by the system.

In the last decade, machine learning features of FCA have been leveraged by a number of industrial applications, and we believe CRM will further demonstrate its capability to handle domains with extremely complex structures. Hence, this chapter contributes to the literature by building a concept learning framework to operate on human attitudes for decision support and decision making and thoroughly evaluating this framework. We will demonstrate that concept-based learning is better suited for representing complex patterns of human behavior, including communication, than conventional machine learning mechanisms, such as classification of groups of words extracted from textual descriptions of a conflict or a dialog.

To properly position our work in a family of CRM technologies, we mention the following CRM services, following (Adair 2020; Davidow 2003):

(1) the aggregation of data to create a single, accessible source (whether physical or virtual),
(2) the analysis and presentation of that data as usable information by individuals doing strategic planning or executing strategic sales/marketing initiatives, and
(3) tools and information to provide front-line personnel or systems-that are interacting with customers or prospects the ability to make timely, educated decisions that benefit both the customer and company.

In this chapter, we focus on the tools mentioned in the third aspect of CRM, specifically focusing on facilitating customer interaction through concept learning technologies. The following sequence of problems needs to be solved for predicting and classifying human behavior using a CRM system:

(1) Discover how to *reconstruct the behavior patterns* from text. It turns out that communicative actions and their subjects are essential elements of behavior discourse (Galitsky 2008).
(2) Construct a *formal language* to represent communicative actions. Find attributes of communicative actions so that similarity between them can be defined. Analyze how the mental space is "covered" by communicative actions, and form a substitution matrix for them.
(3) Build a way to *extract information* from the natural language for communicative actions (which is relatively easy) and their subjects (which is significantly harder due to implicit references to these subjects in natural language).
(4) Observe that the sequence of behavior patterns can be packaged as a *scenario*. Define a scenario as a graph, including communicative actions and interaction between their subjects, based on causal links and relations that defuse argumentation (Galitsky 2019a).

(5) Define relationships between scenarios via sub-graphs, with respective operations on vertices and arcs. Define similarity between scenarios based on graphs and similarities between individual communicative actions.

(6) Build a machine learning framework and select a particular learning approach well suited to operate with scenario graphs. Evaluate whether concept learning is an adequate approach.

One of the most important tasks in assisting negotiations and resolving inter-human conflicts in a CRM framework is the *validity* assessment. A scenario (in particular, a complaint) is *valid* if it is plausible, internally consistent, and also consistent with available domain-specific knowledge. On the contrary, a complaint scenario is *invalid* if there are inconsistencies in the communication discourse, so that there is a doubt as to whether a problem with a product (mentioned in this complaint scenario) has actually occurred (Galitsky and Ilvovsky 2019). In the case of inter-human conflicts or negotiations, such domain-specific knowledge is frequently unavailable. In this chapter, we build a CRM framework to assist companies with complaint management, assigning complaints to a class of *valid* or *invalid* scenarios (Galitsky and Pascu 2006).

8.2 Logical Simulation of the Behavior

An extensive body of literature addresses the problem of logical simulation of the behavior of autonomous agents, taking into account their beliefs, desires and intentions (Bratman 1987). A substantial advancement has been achieved in building the scenarios of multiagent interaction, given properties of agents, including their attitudes. However, the means of automated comparative analysis for interaction scenarios for *human* agents are still lacking.

In our previous study (Galitsky 2006), we analyzed the roles of deduction, simulation and learning in application to human agents. In the current chapter, we build the representation machinery and develop a concept learning technique for operating with scenarios that include a sequence of communicative actions. We propose a framework for classifying scenarios of inter-human conflicts. This framework will be implemented in a stand-alone mode and used in combination with deductive reasoning or simulation to be a part of a decision support system.

In spite of the advances in modeling conflicts and negotiations between autonomous agents and its deployment in a number of domains, a general framework to reuse the experience of conflict resolutions from earlier cases has not been developed. To effectively build such a framework and predict the interaction between autonomous agents, it is helpful to augment reasoning and/or simulation with machine learning (Weiss and Sen 1996; Olivia et al. 1999; Stone and Veloso 2000). In the case of human agents, an adequate behavioral model that gives a plausible data structure for machine learning is essential as well. It would reduce the number of possible actions for the agents at each step, taking into account how these agents acted in previous cases. Obviously, formalizing human behavior is a much more complex task than that of autonomous agents. Hence, we restrict ourselves to communicative actions (plus the causal and argumentative links between them) of human agents in the course of interaction (conflict) as a way to describe their behavior (Galitsky and Parnis 2019).

Recently, the issue of providing BDI (Belief–Desire–Intention) agents (Bratman 1987) with machine learning capabilities attracted interest; an application domain of agents for intelligent information access was considered in (Stone and Veloso 2000). Nevertheless, a BDI-based machine learning framework for scenarios of inter-human interactions has not yet been developed. A number of case-based reasoning approaches have been suggested to treat interaction scenarios involving BDI agents (Laza and Corchado 2002; Olivia et al. 1999); however, the description of agents' attitudes is reduced to their beliefs, desires and intentions in these studies. Indeed, the behavior of real-world agents in conflict is described in a richer language using a wide number of mental entities, including *pretending, deceiving, offending, forgiving, trusting*, and others.

The importance of learning in negotiation has been recognized in the game research community as fundamental for understanding human behavior, as well as for developing new solution concepts (Osborne and Rubinstein 1994; Harsanyi and Selten 1972). Jordan (1992) studied the impact of Bayesian learning processes for finite-strategy normal form games. Kalai and Lehrer (1993) analyzed infinitely repeated games in which players try to subjectively maximize their utility by learning to predict future strategies of opponents. These theoretical results, however, are available only for the simplest settings that can be represented in game-theoretic language and are valid only under very restrictive assumptions, for example, allowing only a subset of possible negotiation strategies. Also, it is hard to apply the developed machinery to a practical conflict resolution system: it lacks the ability to handle the mental states of participants and assumes that domain-specific knowledge is available and can be subject to formalization.

Formalized inter-human conflict is a special case of a formal scenario where the agents have inconsistent and dynamic goals; a negotiation procedure is required to achieve a compromise (Muller and Dieng 2000). In this chapter, we employ the hypothesis that by following the logical structure of how negotiation is represented in a scenario (represented as a text or some structured way), it is possible to judge the consistency of the scenario. We take advantage of this assumption and propose an interactive form, where the required parameters of communicative actions are specified from the viewpoint of a given agent.

We believe that a useful machine learning framework for operating with scenarios of inter-human interactions should exhibit the following characteristics:

- It should be capable of relating a scenario to a class of scenarios, given a number of classes specified for a given domain by experts;
- It should be based on a concise and effective model that represents inter-human interactions, operating with a rich set of communicative actions (Galitsky et al. 2018);

- It should be domain-independent and therefore equally applicable to any domain; it should also allow the avoidance of domain-specific ontologies (Galitsky 2016a);
- It should provide motivations for the classification decisions because it is a component of a decision support system for the CRM industry sector.

A learning model needs to be focused on a specific graph representation for these conflicts. The learning strategies used here are based on ideas similar to that of the Nearest Neighbors (see, e.g., Mitchell 1997), case-based learning (Kolodner 1993), concept-based learning (Kuznetsov 1999; Ganter and Kuznetsov 2001) or the JSM-method (Finn 1999). Having defined scenarios and the operation of finding common subscenarios, we use the Nearest Neighbors algorithm as a simple illustration of our approach to relating a scenario to either class of *valid* or *invalid* scenarios. We then proceed to JSM-based learning to avoid false positives as much as possible. JSM-based learning delivers the most cautious approach to classifying human behavior and attitudes in order to comply with the ethical and legal norms of CRM. In the current chapter, we use deterministic machine learning because the explicit motivations for the decisions might be more important than the content of the decision itself, whenever decision support is provided. We believe concept learning is more appropriate for CRM settings where decisions have to be clearly communicated and solidly backed up than statistical learning, even if the latter might be more accurate (Galitsky et al. 2006).

8.3   Complaint Validity, Complaint Management and CRM

Complaint processing (Davidow 2003) has become an important issue for CRM in large companies and organizations. Complaint management is a formal process of recording and resolving a customer complaint. Even though CRM systems in general and complaint processing systems, in particular, are expensive, companies can extract priceless knowledge from an appropriate handling of a complaint, with significant effects on customer retention rates and word-of-mouth recommendations (Yuksel 2006). If complaints are transformed into knowledge about customers, they can provide valuable business intelligence for enterprises. To exploit this intelligence, companies must design, build, operate and continuously upgrade systems for managing complaints. In the last few years, several approaches have emerged to automate complaint management, such as (Yuan and Chang 2001; GTF 2009), among others. Retailers and service providers may profit from such software services because they allow complaints to be handled faster, providing the possibility of feedback analysis and data mining capabilities on the basis of a complaint database.

A typical complaint is a report of a failure of a product or service, followed by a narrative on the customer's attempts to resolve the issue. These complaints include both a description of the product or service failure as well as a description of the resulting interaction process (negotiation, conflict, etc.) between the customer and the company representatives. Because it is almost impossible for CRM personnel to verify the actual occurrence of such failures, company representatives must judge the adequacy of a complaint on the basis of the communicative actions provided by the customers in their narratives. Customers usually do their best to bring their points across, so the consistency of communicative actions and the appropriateness of their arguments (represented as parameters of these actions) are major clues for the validity of their complaints. Indeed, a complaint narrative usually describes a conflict between an unsatisfied customer and CRM personnel, in which communicated claims need to be rationally justifiable by sound arguments. In contrast with the almost unlimited number of possible details regarding product failures, the emerging argumentative dialogues between customer and company can be subject to a systematic computational study (Galitsky 2019b). In this context, a major challenge in complaint processing involves distinguishing those customer complaints which are rationally acceptable from those which are not, so that the whole procedure of complaint handling can be better supported. Currently, most customer complaint management solutions are limited to the use of keyword processing to relate a complaint to a certain domain-specific class (e.g., banking and travel complaints, as reported in this chapter), or to the application of knowledge management techniques in software platforms for workflow processing (e.g., (Zirtiloğlu and Yolum 2008; MasterControl 2009)). To the best of our knowledge, existing industrial complaint management platforms do not make use of natural language processing nor machine learning techniques for quicker performance, quality assurance and lower sustainability costs; most complaint handling functionalities remain manual. Thus, for example, even advanced tools such as Oracle PeopleSoft Enterprise CRM do not exploit the possible benefits of learning from available complaint data. In particular, no automated solutions have been developed to assess the validity of a customer complaint on the basis of the emerging dialogue between a customer and the company representatives, with the goal of better supporting the procedure of complaint handling as a part of CRM.

8.4 Complaint Scenario and Communicative Actions

We proceed to the main definition of this study of how a behavioral scenario consists of communicative actions.

A communicative action is a function of the form *verb(agent, subject, cause)*, where *verb* characterizes some kind of interaction between customer and company in a complaint scenario (e.g., *explain, confirm, remind, disagree, deny*), *agent* identifies either the customer or the company, *subject* refers to the information transmitted or object described, and *cause* refers to the motivation or explanation for the subject.

Thus, for example, a communicative action associated with some customer claim such as, "*I disagreed with the overdraft fee you charged me because I made a bank deposit well in advance*" would be represented as *disagree (customer, "overdraft fee", "I made a bank deposit well in advance"*). Scenarios are intentionally simplified as labeled directed graphs to allow for effective similarity matching among them. Each vertex in the graph will correspond to a communicative action. An arc (oriented edge) may denote either temporal precedence or an attack relationship between two actions a_i and a_j. In the first case, we will distinguish between consecutive actions that refer to the same subject from those that refer to different subjects. Graphically, we will distinguish these situations by means of thick arcs and thin arcs, respectively.

A complaint scenario is a labeled directed graph $G = (V, A)$, where $V = \{action_1, action_2,\ldots, action_k\}$ is a finite set of vertices corresponding to communicative actions, and $A = A_{thick} \cup A_{thin} \cup A_{causal}$ is a finite set of labeled arcs (ordered pairs of vertices), classified as follows:

- Each arc $(action_i; action_j) \in A_{thick}$ corresponds to the temporal precedence of two references to the same subject.
- Each arc $(action_i; action_j) \in A_{thin}$ corresponds to the temporal precedence of two actions referring to different subjects.
- Each arc $(action_i; action_j) \in A_{causal}$ corresponds to a causal link or an attack relationship between $action_i$ and $action_j$, indicating that the cause of $action_i$ is in conflict with the subject or cause of $action_j$.

The rest of the chapter is organized as follows. We first introduce the domain of conflict scenarios and then present both a formal treatment of communicative actions and a detailed definition of conflict scenarios as graphs encoding communicative actions. Second, having defined the similarity operation on graphs as finding maximal common subgraphs, we move on to relating a scenario to a class of scenarios using the Nearest Neighbor approach, following (Galitsky and Kuznetsov 2008a). To improve the accuracy of the classification and to adjust the machine learning technique to real-world requirements, we use the logic programming system Jasmine (Chap. 7 Volume 2), which is based on JSM-method learning (Finn 1999). The procedure of finding similarities between scenarios is then described, taking into account the aggregation of communicative actions with the same subjective and causal links. We then evaluate the proposed technique in the domains of banking and travel and compare the technique with state-of the-art techniques in opinion mining. Towards the end of the chapter, we address the concept-based exploration of product features and local logic-based frameworks to deductively describe scenario discourses using non-monotonic reasoning.

8.5   Formalizing Conflict Scenarios

In this section, we present our model of a conflict scenario to be used in a machine learning setting. We develop a knowledge representation methodology based on an approximation of a natural language description of a conflict (Galitsky 2006).

When modeling scenarios of inter-human conflict, it is worth distinguishing communicative (mental) and non-mental states and actions. The former includes *knowing* and *pretending* (states) as well as *informing* and *asking* (actions); the latter are related, for example, to *location, energy* and *account balance* (physical states), as are *moving, heating* and *withdrawal* (physical actions). To form a data structure for machine learning, we approximate an inter-human interaction scenario as a sequence of communicative actions, ordered in time, with a causal relation obtaining between certain communicative actions. Our approximation has the style of a situation calculus; scenarios are simplified to allow for effective matching by means of graphs. Only communicative actions remain as the most important component for expressing similarities between scenarios. Each vertex corresponds to a communicative action, which is performed by either a *proponent* or an *opponent*, which are called *agents* (here we consider two-agent systems, but the model is easily extended to involve multiple agents). An arc (oriented edge) denotes a sequence of two actions.

In our model, communicative actions have two parameters: *agent name* and *subject* (information transmitted, a cause addressed, a reason explained, an object described, etc.). Representing scenarios as graphs, we take into account both parameters. Arc types bear information even if the subject remains the same. Thick arcs link vertices that correspond to communicative actions with the same subject, while thin arcs link vertices that correspond to communicative actions with different subjects.

The curve arcs denote a causal link between the arguments of communicative actions, for example, *service is not as advertised* ⇒ *there are particular failures in a service contract, ask ~ > confirm.*

Let us consider an example of a scenario and its graph (Fig. 8.1a, b).

Note that the first two sentences (and the respective subgraph comprising two vertices) are about the current transaction, the following three sentences (and the respective subgraph comprised of three vertices) address the *unfair charge,* and the last sentence is probably related to both above issues. Hence, the vertices of two respective subgraphs are linked with thick arcs (*explain-accept*) and (*remind-deny-disagree*).

> *I **explained** that my check bounced (I wrote it after I made a deposit).*
> *A customer service representative **accepted** that it usually takes some time to process the deposit.*
> *I **reminded** the representative that I was unfairly charged an overdraft fee a month ago in a similar situation.*
> *They **denied** that it was unfair because the overdraft fee was disclosed in my account information.*
> *I **disagreed** with their fee and wanted this fee deposited back to my account.*
> *They **explained** that nothing can be done at this point and that I need to look at the account rules more closely.*

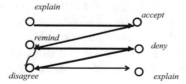

Fig. 8.1 **a** A scenario that includes communicative actions of a proponent and an opponent. **b** The graph for the approximated scenario

In formal conflict scenarios extracted from text, there can be multiple communicative actions per step, for example, *I disagreed … and suggested.…* The former communicative action describes how an agent receives a message (*accept, agree, reject*, etc.) from an opponent, while the latter describes either the attitude of this agent initiating a request (*suggest, explain*, etc.) or the agent's reaction to the opponent's action. Sometimes, one of the above actions is omitted in a textual description of a conflict. Frequently, a communicative action that is assumed but not mentioned explicitly can be deduced. For the sake of simplicity, we will consider a single action per step in comparatively analyzing scenarios (Fig. 8.1b).

There is a commonsense causal link *between being charged an unfair fee* and wanting *to have this fee returned*, which is expressed by the arc between the *remind* and *disagree* nodes. Semantically, arcs with causal labels between vertices express the causal links between the arguments of communicative actions rather than between the communicative actions themselves.

How would one handle commonsense reasoning patterns in our domain? We need (complaint-)specific commonsense knowledge to link such statements as *unfair fee* with *deposit back*. An ontology that would give us sufficient knowledge is not available, and it would be extremely hard and expensive to build such ontologies for a variety of complaint domains. Therefore, our data structure for machine learning only includes causal links (and not background knowledge). Causal links (Riloff 1996) can be extracted from the text; however, to increase the accuracy of the data structures, we will use a form wherein a complainant specifies causal links (Sect. 8.14).

Why do we relate this scenario to the class of invalid complaints? First of all, using background knowledge about banking, it is clear that the customer wrongly assumed that the funds become available immediately after a deposit is made. However, it is not possible to store this information in a generic complaint management system; therefore, we further examine the legitimacy of the observed sequence of communicative actions. "Being in an attack mode (*reminding*) after a previous attack (*explaining*) was *accepted*" does not appear to be cooperative. Moreover, maintaining a disagreement concerning a subject that was just *denied* (speaking more precisely, a commonsense implication of this subject) is not an appropriate negotiation strategy. If a similar scenario (in terms of the structure of communicative actions) has been assigned by a domain expert as *invalid*, we want the machine learning system to relate the scenario illustrated in Fig. 8.1a to the same class, even if there are no explicit reasons to do so.

Hence, our analysis of the domain of customer complaints shows that to relate a scenario to a class without domain-specific knowledge, one must analyze a sequence of communicative actions and certain relations between their subjects. Otherwise, one must code all relevant domain knowledge, which is well-known as an extremely hard problem and not feasible for practical applications. Our next step is to formalize communicative actions in a way suitable for learning scenarios.

8.6 Semantics of Communicative Actions

In this section, we will use formal concept analysis (FCA) to formalize the theory of speech acts so that we can apply machine learning to communicative actions. In this theory, a dialogue, a negotiation and a conflict are all forms of interactions between human agents. Elements of the language that express these interactions are referred to as locutions, speech acts (Bach and Harnish 1979), utterances, or *communicative actions* (we will use the last term).

The foundation of the current theory of *speech acts* was developed in (Austin 1962), where he explores performative utterances, aiming to prove that when people speak, they are doing more than merely conveying information—they act. The theory of speech acts asserts that *in saying something, we perform something*. It is an action that is performed by means of language. An example from the domain of customer complaints would be the performative act of a judge during a hearing when s/he says, "I now pronounce the complaint solved." Due to Austin's designation of speech acts, sentences like this adopt a notion of action. The judge's sentence is not a report of the action; rather, it *is* the action.

However, every sentence does not undertake the same linguistic action. Austin distinguishes between three types of linguistic acts: the act *of* saying something, what one *does* in saying it, and what one does *by* saying it. He labels them *Locutionary*, *Illocutionary*, and *Perlocutionary*, respectively. A locutionary act is simply saying something about the world, for example, a declarative sentence such as, "The product does not work." This sentence is not posing a question, promising, or commanding anything. It simply states something about the world and contains purely propositional content. This type of act is the most basic and does not require much more explanation.

The illocutionary act includes promising, questioning, admitting, hypothesizing, etc. While the locutionary act was simply the act of saying something, the illocutionary act is performed *in* saying something. For example, "A company promises to support the product after it is sold," asserts more than simply stating a sentence about the world. It includes an *assertion* that is performative in nature. Illocutionary acts are very prominent in language, and are frequently in use in complaint scenarios.

The third type of linguistic acts is the perlocutionary ones. These are non-conventional sentences that cause a natural condition or state in a person. These acts de-emphasize the actual intentions, and focus on the effects on the hearer. Acts of frightening or convincing depend on the response of another person. If a perlocutionary act is successful, then it seems safe to say that an illocutionary act has successfully taken place.

Austin's speech act theory has been fairly influential since its inception. There have been certain improvements and clarifications made to the theory of speech acts that are worth noting; in particular, (Searle 1969) rejected Austin's insistence that acts cannot perform two different functions. Searle shows that illocutionary acts can act in two different ways.

As an example from the domain of customer complaints, let us consider the following. By describing a situation of strong dissatisfaction with particular product features (locutionary component) in a writing style that is designed to have the force of a warning (illocutionary component), the complainant may actually frighten the customer support representative into providing compensation for a faulty product (perlocutionary component). It is important to analyze whether a complainant consistently uses one type of communicative action with her opponent, which we are going to evaluate by means of machine learning.

In order to approximate scenarios for multiagent interactions, we follow the division of communicative actions into *constatives* and *performatives*.

- Constatives describe or report some state of affairs such that it is possible to assess whether they are false or true.
- Performatives, on the other hand, are *fortunate* or *unfortunate, sincere* or *insincere, realistic* or *unrealistic*, and, finally, *valid* or *invalid*, the last of which is the focus of the current study. Performatives address the attitude of an agent in performing the linguistic act, including his thoughts, feelings, and intentions.

It turns out that it is much more efficient to automatically analyze the group of performatives than the group of constatives, because the former is domain-independent; in the case of complaints, there is always a lack of information for judging constatives.

To choose communicative actions to adequately represent an inter-human conflict, we have selected the most frequently used ones from our structured database of complaints (Table 8.1, Galitsky et al. 2005).

Table 8.1 The set of communicative actions from a typical complaint

Customer describes his own action	Customer describes an opponent's action
Agree, explain, suggest, bring to company's attention, remind, allow, try, request, understand, inform, confirm ask, check, ignore, convince disagree, appeal, deny, threaten	Agree, explain, suggest, remind, allow, try, request, understand, inform, confirm, ask, check, ignore, convince, disagree, appeal, deny, threaten, bring to the customer's attention, accept complaint, accept/deny responsibilities, encourage, cheat

A number of *computational* approaches have attempted to discover and categorize how the agents' attitudes and communicative actions are related to each other in the computational simulation of human agents (Searle 1969; Cohen and Levesque 1990). As we have mentioned above, in applying machine learning to the attitudes and communicative actions, we are primarily concerned with how these approaches can provide a unified and robust framework for finding a similarity between the communicative actions. The theory of speech acts seems to be one of the most promising approaches for categorizing communicative actions in terms of their roles. Following (Bach and Harnish 1979), we consider four categories of illocutionary communicative actions with major representatives: *stating, requesting, promising and apologizing*. Each speech act is related to only a single category in the framework of the speech act theory. For our purposes, each speech act is extracted from text automatically or is selected from a list by a user as a word, which may belong to multiple categories.

Now we can calculate the similarity between communicative actions as the set (an overlap) of speech act categories to which they belong. To estimate how fruitful the speech act-theoretical approach is for calculating the similarities between communicative actions, we build a concept lattice (Ganter and Wille 1999) for communicative actions as objects and speech act categories as their features (*Constatives, Directives, Commissives*, and *Acknowledgements*). In the concept lattice, each node is assigned a set of features and a set of objects. For each node, all features assigned to nodes are satisfied by the objects assigned to this node. These features are assessable when navigating the lattice upwards. In Fig. 8.2, we show either features or objects for each node. For example, let us consider the node with the object *allow* assigned

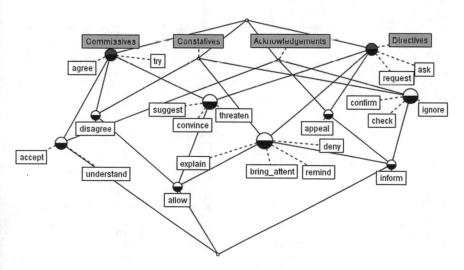

Fig. 8.2 The concept lattice for communicative actions when adapting speech act theory to our domain. Each communicative action does not have a unique set of attributes. The calculation of similarity might be inadequate

to it. Navigating up the edges, we access the *disagree* and then *Commissives* and *Constatives* node; the triple *suggest-convince-threaten* node and then *Commissives* and *Directives*; and four-tuple *explain-bring_attention-remind-deny* and then *Directives*. Hence, the lattice shows that the object *allow* satisfies three out of four *features*: *Commissives, Directives, and Constatives* (as we have specified in Table 8.2, the eighth row).

As the reader can see, this direct Speech Act—theoretical approach is inadequate for a uniform coverage of communicative actions in conflict scenarios. Some communicative actions (e.g., *agree, try*) are described by the selected features more accurately, whereas *suggest-convince-threaten* and four-tuple *explain-bring_attention-remind-deny* cannot be distinguished under this categorization at all. Hence, the four features of the speech act theory are insufficient to differentiate between 20 communicative actions that have been determined as minimally expressive of inter-human conflict (Galitsky and Kuznetsov 2008a). Hence, more attributes must be taken into account in order to find adequate means for computing similarities between communicative actions.

Table 8.2 Selected attributes of communicative actions, adapting speech act theory to our domain. The attributes for *allow* are highlighted (mentioned in the example below)

Speech acts	Constatives	Directives	Commissives	Acknowledgements
Agree	0	0	1	0
Accept	0	0	1	1
Explain	1	1	0	0
Suggest	0	1	1	0
Bring_attention	1	1	0	0
Remind	1	1	0	0
Allow	1	1	1	0
Try	0	0	1	0
Request	0	1	0	0
Understand	0	0	1	1
Inform	1	1	0	1
Confirm	1	0	0	1
Ask	0	1	0	0
Check	1	0	0	1
Ignore	1	0	0	1
Convince	0	1	1	0
Disagree	1	0	1	0
Appeal	0	1	0	1
Deny	1	1	0	0
Threaten	0	1	1	0

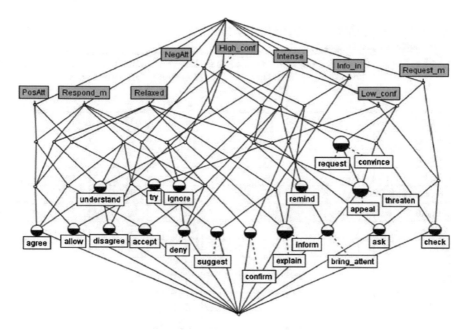

Fig. 8.3 The resultant concept lattice for communicative actions with adjusted definitions. Each communicative action has a unique set of attributes

We proceed to the solution that turned out to be the most robust and plausible (Fig. 8.3). To extend the speech act–based means of expressing the similarity between communicative actions, we introduce five attributes, each of which reflects a particular semantic parameter for communicative activity (Table 8.3):

- *Positive/ negative attitude* expresses whether a communicative action is a cooperative (friendly, helpful) move (1), uncooperative (unfriendly, unhelpful) move (-1), neither or both (hard to tell, 0).
- *Request/ respond mode* specifies whether a communicative action is expected to be followed by a reaction (1), constitutes a response to (follows) a previous request, neither or both (hard to tell, 0).
- *Info supply/ no info supply* flags whether a communicative action adds any additional data about the conflict (1), does not bring any information (-1), 0; does not occur here.
- *High/low confidence* specifies the confidence of the preceding mental state so that a particular communicative action is chosen, high knowledge/confidence (1), lack of knowledge/confidence (-1), neither or both is possible (0).
- *Intense/ relaxed mode* says about the potential emotional load: high (1), low (-1), neutral (0) emotional loads are possible.

Table 8.3 Augmented attributes of communicative actions

Communicative action	Attributes				
	Positive/negative attitude	Request/respond mode	Info supply/no info supply	High/low confidence	Intense/relaxed mode
Agree	1	−1	−1	1	−1
Accept	1	−1	−1	1	1
Explain	0	−1	1	1	−1
Suggest	1	0	1	−1	−1
Bring_attention	1	1	1	1	1
Remind	−1	0	1	1	1
Allow	1	−1	−1	−1	−1
Try	1	0	−1	−1	−1
Request	0	1	−1	1	1
Understand	0	−1	−1	1	−1
Inform	0	0	1	1	−1
Confirm	0	−1	1	1	1
Ask	0	1	−1	−1	−1
Check	−1	1	−1	−1	1
Ignore	−1	−1	−1	−1	1
Convince	0	1	1	1	−1
Disagree	−1	−1	−1	1	−1
Appeal	−1	1	1	1	1
Deny	−1	−1	−1	1	1
Threaten	−1	1	−1	1	1

Note that out of the set of meanings for each communicative action, we merge its subset into a single meaning. In performing this merge, the relations between the meanings of the given communicative actions and those of the others are taken into account (Galitsky 2006).

Formal concept analysis was used to characterize the set of communicative actions in the context of our framework. In FCA, a (formal) context consists of a set of objects G, a set of attributes M, and an indication of which objects have which attributes. A *concept* is a pair containing both a natural property cluster and its corresponding natural object cluster. A "natural" object cluster is the set of all objects that share a common subset of properties, and a "natural" property cluster is the set of all properties shared by one of the natural object clusters. Given a set of objects G and a set of attributes M, a concept is defined to be the pair (G_i, M_i) such that,

(1) $G_i \subseteq G$;
(2) $M_i \subseteq M$;
(3) every object in G_i has every attribute in M_i;
(4) for every object in G that is not in G_i, there is an attribute in M_i that the object does not have;
(5) for every attribute in M that is not in M_i, there is an object in G_i that does not have that attribute.

Given a concept (G_i, M_i), the set G_i is called the *extent* of the concept, and the set M_i is called the *intent*. Concepts can be partially ordered by inclusion: if (G_i, M_i) and (G_j, M_j) are concepts, a partial order $\leq$ can be defined, where $(G_i, M_i) \leq (G_j, M_j)$ whenever $G_i \subseteq G_j$. Equivalently, $(G_i, M_i) \leq (G_j, M_j)$ whenever $M_j \subseteq M_i$. In general, attributes may allow multiple values (many-valued attributes) that characterize many-valued contexts. By applying so-called conceptual scaling, many-valued contexts can be transformed to one-valued, scaled contexts from which concepts can be computed. The family of these concepts obeys the mathematical axioms defining a lattice and is called a *concept lattice* or a *Galois lattice*.

So-called *line diagrams* are used in order to succinctly represent information about the intents and extents of formal contexts in a concept lattice. Nodes are circles that can be labeled with (a) both attributes and objects; (b) attributes; (c) objects or (d) none. In order to consider some distinguished labels, some nodes appear as circles that are half-filled in their lower part (labeled with objects only), and some nodes appear as circles that are half-filled in their upper part (labeled with attributes only). Nodes that are empty circles have no particular labels. In order to provide a formal characterization of the communicative actions in terms of their attributes, a concept lattice was obtained. A nominal scaling was applied to the first and second attributes (the third, fourth and fifth attributes were already two-valued). As a result of this scaling, we obtained nine two-valued attributes associated with different possible values of the original five attributes: PosAtt (1), NegAtt (-1), Request (1), Respond (-1), InfoIn (1), High_Conf (1), Low_Conf (-1), Intense (1), and Relaxed (-1). It must be remarked that some particular two-valued attributes derived from the original attributes were not considered for building the resulting concept lattice shown in Fig. 8.3 because they do not contribute strongly to distinguishing communicative actions from one another. Finally, the scaled context had nine two-valued attributes.

The ConExp software (Yevtushenko 2020) was used to construct and visualize the concept lattice of communicative actions and their nine associated two-valued attributes. Some selected nodes are provided with descriptions of the corresponding "intents" and "extents" written beneath to show how certain communicative actions are semantically related to each other. The concept lattice illustrates the semantics of communicative actions and shows how to cover different meanings in the knowledge domain of customer–company interactions in complaint scenarios. The concept lattice illustrates the semantics of communicative actions; it shows how the choice of attribute-based expressions covers the totality of possible meanings in the knowledge domain of interaction between human agents.

After scaling the many-valued context of communicative actions, the descriptions of communicative action are given by 9-tuples of attributes, ordered in the usual way. Thus, vertex labels of generalizations of scenario graphs are given by the intents of the scaled context of communicative actions.

Before we proceed to the formal model of scenarios in terms of graphs, we define a conflict scenario as a sequence of communicative actions, each of which is a *reaction* to the previous communicative actions of opponents. This reaction is constrained by *interaction protocols* by means of enumeration of *valid* scenarios, where this protocol is assumed to be correct. Multiagent conflict is a scenario where agents have inconsistent intentions (about states): *want(AgentFor, State), want(AgentAgainst, not State)*.

The scenario is defined as a *sequence of communicative actions*. Usually, if the sequence of communicative actions of customer support is "adequate," a complaint does not arise. Therefore, we define a typical complaint as a scenario with the following conditions:

- a conflict of intentions concerning the *physical state* of a product/service (pre-complaint), and
- a conflict of intentions concerning the *mental* and *physical actions* of customer support and resultant state of the satisfaction of the intentions.

Indeed, these conditions are the ones for the *subjects* of communicative actions. The conflict is defined as a *logical inconsistency*. Our definition of a complaint scenario includes inconsistencies in both mental and physical spaces. In the section to follow, complaint scenarios will be defined formally as a graph.

8.7   Defining Scenarios as Graphs and Learning Them

To demonstrate how CRM scenarios can be represented as graphs, we introduce the dataset that contains two sets of complaint scenarios: those showing a complainant with a good attitude (consistent plot with proper argumentation, a *valid complaint*) on the left, and those showing a complainant with a bad attitude (inconsistent plot with certain flaws, implausible or irrational scenarios, an *invalid complaint*) on the right (Fig. 8.4).

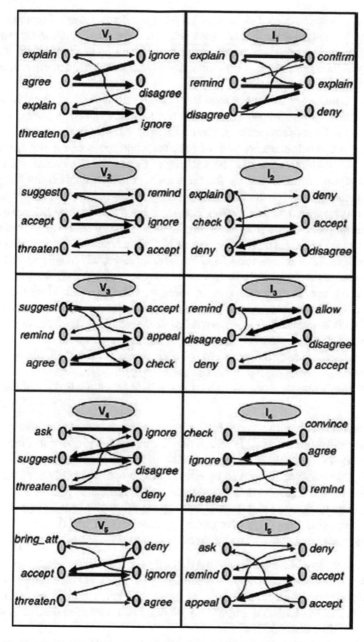

Fig. 8.4 The training set of scenarios. On the left, V1-V5 are valid scenarios, while I1-I5 are invalid scenarios

Each scenario includes 2–6 interaction *steps*, each consisting of communicative actions with the alternating first attribute {*request—respond—additional request or other follow up*}. A step comprises one or more consequent actions with the same subject. Within a step, vertices for communicative actions with common arguments are linked with *thick* arcs.

For example, *suggest* from scenario V2 (Fig. 8.4) is linked by a thin arc to communicative action *ignore*, whose argument is not logically linked to the argument of *suggest* (the subject of suggestion). The first step of V2 includes *ignore-deny-ignore-threaten*; these communicative actions have the same subject (it is not specified in the graph of conflict scenario). The vertices of these communicative actions with the same argument are linked by the *thick* arcs. For example, it could be **ignored** *refund because of a wrong mailing address,* **deny** *the reason that the refund has been ignored* [*because of a wrong mailing address*], **ignore** *the denial* [*...concerning a wrong mailing address*], *and* **threatening** *for that ignorant behavior* [*...concerning a wrong mailing address*]. We have *wrong mailing address* as the common subject S of communicative actions *ignore-deny-ignore-threaten*, which we approximate as

ignore(A1, S) & deny(A2,S) & ignore(A1,S) & threaten(A2, S), keeping in mind the scenario graph. In such an approximation, we write *deny(A2, S)* for the fact that *A2 denied the reason that the refund has been ignored because of S.* Indeed, we write *ignore(A1, S) & deny(A2,S) & ignore(A1,S) & threaten(A2, S).* Without a scenario graph, the best representation of the above in our language would be

ignore(A1, S) & deny(A2, ignore(A1, S)) & ignore(A1, deny(A2, ignore(A1, S))) & threaten(A2, ignore(A1, deny(A2, ignore(A1, S)))).

Let us enumerate the constraints for the scenario graph (Galitsky and Kuznetsov 2008a):

(1) All vertices are fully ordered by the temporal sequence (earlier-later);
(2) Each vertex has a special label relating it either to the proponent (drawn on the left side in Fig. 8.1b) or to the opponent (drawn on the right side);
(3) Vertices denote actions taken by either of the proponent or of the opponent;
(4) The arcs of the graph are oriented from earlier vertices to later ones;
(5) Thin and thick arcs point from a vertex to the subsequent vertex in the temporal sequence (from the proponent to the opponent or vice versa);
(6) Curly arcs, representing causal links, can jump over several vertices.

Hence, we have obtained the formal definition of a conflict scenario as a graph.

The similarity between scenarios is defined by means of maximal common subscenarios. Because we describe scenarios by means of labeled graphs, we first consider formal definitions of labeled graphs and the domination relation on them (see, e.g., (Ganter and Kuznetsov 2001).

Let G be an ordered set of graphs of the form (V,E), with vertex- and edge-labels from the sets $(\Lambda_\varsigma, \leq)$ and $(\Lambda_E, \leq \Gamma)$. A labeled graph Γ from G is a quadruple of the form $((V,l), (E,b))$, where V is a set of vertices, E is a set of edges, $b : E \rightarrow \Lambda_E$ is a function assigning labels to vertices, and $l : V \rightarrow \Lambda_\varsigma$ is a function assigning labels to edges. We do not distinguish isomorphic graphs with identical labeling.

The order is defined as follows: for two graphs $\Gamma_1: = ((V_1, l_1), (E_1, b_1))$ and $\Gamma_2: = ((V_2, l_2), (E_2, b_2))$ from G, we say that Γ_1 **dominates** Γ_2 or $\Gamma_2 \leq \Gamma_1$ (or Γ_2 is a **subgraph** of Γ_1) if there exists a one-to-one mapping $\varphi: V_2 \rightarrow V_1$ such that it

- respects edges: $(v, w) \in E_2 \Rightarrow (\varphi(v), \varphi(w)) \in E_1$ and
- fits under labels: $l_2(v) \leq l_1(\varphi(v))$, $(v, w) \in E_2 \Rightarrow b_2(v, w) \leq b_1(\varphi(v), \varphi(w))$.

Note that this definition allows the generalization ("weakening") of labels of matched vertices when passing from the "larger" graph G_1 to "smaller" graph G_2.

Now, a *generalization* Z of a pair of scenario graphs X and Y (or their similarity), denoted by X * Y = Z, is the set of all inclusion-maximal common subgraphs of X and Y, with each satisfying the following additional conditions:

- To be matched, two vertices from graphs X and Y must denote communicative actions of the same agent;
- Each common subgraph from Z contains at least one thick arc.

This definition is easily extended to find generalizations of several graphs (e.g., see Ganter and Kuznetsov 2001, 1999). The subsumption order μ on pairs of graph sets X and Y are naturally defined as X μ Y: = X * Y = X.

Computing the relation $\Gamma_2 \leq \Gamma_1$ for arbitrary graphs Γ_2 and Γ_1 is an NP-complete problem (because it is a generalization of the subgraph isomorphism problem from (Garey and Johnson 1979)) and finding X * Y = Z for arbitrary X, Y, and Z is generally an NP-hard problem. In (Ganter and Kuznetsov 2001), a method based on so-called projections was proposed, which allows one to establish a trade-off for labeled graphs between the accuracy of their representation and the complexity of their computations. In particular, for a fixed size of projections, the worst-case time complexity for computing operation * and testing relation $\leq$ becomes constant. The application of projections was tested in various experiments with chemical (molecular) graphs (Kuznetsov and Samokhin 2005) and conflict graphs (Galitsky et al. 2005).

If the conditions above cannot be met, then the common subgraph does not exist.

8.8 Assigning a Scenario to a Class

The following conditions hold when a scenario graph U is assigned to a class (we here consider positive classification, that is, to valid complaints; the classification of invalid complaints is made similarly, Fig. 8.5):

(1) U is similar to (has a nonempty common scenario subgraph of) a positive example R^+.
(2) For any negative example R^-, if U is similar to R^- (i.e., $U * R^- \neq \phi$) then $U * R^- \mu U * R^+$. These conditions introduce the measure of similarity and say that to be assigned to a class, the similarity between the unknown graph U and the closest scenario from the positive class should be higher than the

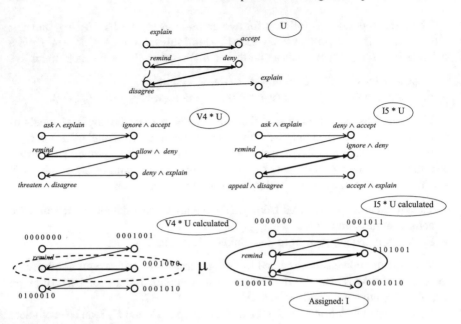

Fig. 8.5 A scenario with unassigned complaint status and the procedure of relating this scenario to a class

similarity between U and each negative example (i.e., all representatives of the class of invalid complaints).

Condition 2 implies that there is a positive example R^+ such that for no R^- example, is $U * R^+ \mu R^-$, that is, there is no counterexample to this generalization of positive examples.

Let us now proceed to the example of a particular U on the top of Fig. 8.5. The task is to determine whether U belongs to the class of valid complaints (on the left of Fig. 8.4) or to the classes of invalid complaints (on the right); these classes are mutually exclusive.

We observe that V_4 is the graph with the highest similarity to U among all graphs from the set $\{V_1, \ldots V_5\}$ and find the common sub-scenario $U * V_4$. Its only thick arc is derived from the thick arc between vertices with labels *remind* and *deny* of U and the thick arc between vertices with labels *remind* and *allow* of V_4. The first vertex of this thick arc of $U * V_4$ is *remind* ^ *remind* = *remind*, while the second is *allow* ^ *deny* = $< 0\,0\,0\,1\,0\,0\,0 >$ (U * V_4 is calculated at the bottom left). Other arcs of $U * V_4$ are as follows: from the vertex with the label *remind* to the vertex with the label $< 0\,0\,0\,1\,0\,0\,0 >$; from the vertex with the label $< 0\,0\,0\,1\,0\,0\,1 >$ to the vertex with the label *remind*; from the vertex with the label $< 0\,0\,0\,1\,0\,0\,0 >$ to the vertex with the label $< 0\,1\,0\,0\,0\,1\,0 >$. These arcs are thin, unless both respective arcs of U * V_4 are thick (the latter is not the case here). Naturally, common subscenarios may contain multiple steps, and each of them may result in the satisfaction of conditions (1) and (2) for the class assignment above.

Similarly, we build the common subscenario $U * I_5$; I_5 delivers the largest subgraph (two thick arcs) when compared to I_1, I_2, I_3, and I_4. Moreover, $U * V_4 \, \mu \, U * I_5$, and this inclusion is highlighted by the ovals around the steps. Condition 2 is satisfied. Therefore, U is an invalid complaint because it has the highest similarity with the invalid complaint I_5. We refer the reader to (Galitsky and Kuznetsov 2008a) for further details and examples of classifications of graphs.

Having shown how a scenario can be related to a class using the Nearest Neighbor algorithm, we proceed to a more cautious classification framework that minimizes false negatives: the framework refuses to classify a scenario whenever such a classification is borderline. This feature is crucial for the conflict resolution domain, where a solution offered to the parties must have an unambiguous and concise explanation and background. Moreover, an approach to finding similarities between scenarios that are more sensitive to peculiarities of communicative actions and conflict scenarios would deliver higher classification accuracy in our domain.

8.9 JSM Learning in Terms of Formal Concept Analysis

The JSM method proposed by Finn in the late 1970s was intended to describe logical induction by deductive means and therefore give some kind of justification for induction. The logic programming implementation of JSM used in this work, Jasmine (Chap. 7 Volume 2), provides a reasoning framework that allows the natural integration of JSM induction with other logical means of deduction. The JSM method was named in honor of English philosopher John Stuart Mill who proposed schemes (canons) of inductive reasoning more than a century ago (Mill 1843). These canons state that if two or more instances of a phenomenon under investigation have only one circumstance in common, then this circumstance is the cause or effect of the given phenomenon. These canons reflected observations of both the physical and the mental worlds (in this chapter, we leverage the latter).

JSM formalization includes a two-layered logic with several truth types that reflect mental attitudes, such as "empirical contradiction," between data generalizations. These truth types are allowed in the internal (lower) level of the second-order logic, while only classical truth values appear at the external (upper) level. JSM uses a many-valued, many-sorted extension of FOL with quantifiers over tuples of variables with varying length. Because induction is based on the similarity of objects, and because the number of objects (of a particular similarity) is not known in advance, quantification over a varying number of objects is required.

A constraint is placed on the hypothesis by learning that prohibits counter-examples. This constraint is expressed in terms of Formal Concept Analysis. We use the FCA notion of a formal context, $K = (G, M, I)$, where G is the set of scenarios (behaviors, or sessions), and M is the set of scenario properties (such as communicative actions occurring in a scenario).

For K, we add the *target* attribute $\omega \notin M$ (the set of attributes). In the example of complaint scenarios we use throughout the chapter, our target attributes are valid and invalid assessments of complaint scenarios. The target attribute partitions the set G of all objects into three subsets: The set G_+ of objects that are known to have the property ω (positive examples), the set G_- of objects that are known *not* to have the property ω (negative examples), and the set G_τ of objects about which it is not known whether they have the property ω or not. This gives three sub-contexts of K:

$K_+ = (G_+, M, I_+)$, $K_+ = (G_-, M, I_-)$, $K_+ = (G_\tau, M, I_\tau)$. The first two are the positive and negative training sets (valid and invalid complaint scenarios) respectively. For $\varepsilon \in \{+, -, \tau\}$ we have for $I_{\varepsilon:} = I \cap (G_\varepsilon \times M)$, and the corresponding deviation operators are denoted by $(.)^+, (.)^-, (.)^\tau$, respectively. A subset $h \subseteq M$ is a simple positive hypothesis (rule) for ω if $h^{++} = h \ \& \ h^- \neq h$. 'No counterexample' - hypotheses are expressed as an intent of K_+ such that $h^+ \neq \emptyset \ \& \ h \not\subset g^{-:} = \{m \notin M | (g,m) \in I_-\}$ for any negative example $g \in G_-$. It can also be expressed as $h^{++} = h \ \& \ h' \cap G_- \neq \emptyset$, where $(.)'$ is taken in the whole context $K = (G, M, I)$. An intent of K_+ that is contained in the intent of a negative example is called a falsified plus-generalization.

Hypotheses can be used for the classification of scenarios (examples) with unknown target attributes. If the intent $g_\tau: = \{m \in M | (g,m) \in I_{\tau^-}\}$ of a scenario $g \in G_\tau$ contains a positive, but not a negative hypothesis, then g^τ is classified positively. Otherwise, if g^τ contains both positive and negative hypotheses or does not contain any hypotheses, then the classification is contradictory or undetermined, respectively. One can attempt to apply probabilistic machine learning techniques in this case. However, such predictions will not be accepted in the cautions classification settings of JSM.

It was shown that JSM can be represented in the logic programming language (Vinogradov 1999). Moreover, it can be implemented as the machine learning system Jasmine as evaluated in (Galitsky et al. 2006). Kuznetsov (1999) considered a learning model from (Finn 1991) formulated in FCA terms. As applied to scenarios, this model is described as follows. Given a similarity (meet) operation * on pairs of scenarios that define a semi-lattice, sets of positive and negative examples, a (+)- hypothesis is defined as the similarity of several positive examples that do not cover any negative example (due to lack of space, we refer the reader to the above publications for exact definitions). (-)-hypotheses are defined similarly. Now, an undetermined scenario is classified positively if it contains (in terms of μ) a positive hypothesis and does not contain any negative hypotheses.

8.10 Finding Similarity Between Scenarios

Naturally, the quality of scenario classification is dramatically dependent on how the similarity between scenarios is defined. High prediction accuracy can be achieved if the measure of similarity is sensitive to object features that determine the target (explicitly or implicitly). Because most times, it is unclear in advance, which features affect the target, the similarity measure should take into account all available features. If the totality of selected features describing each object is expressed by formulas, a reasonable expression of similarity between a pair of objects is a formula that is the least common generalization of the formulas for both objects, which is called *anti-unification*. Anti-unification is the inverse operation for the unification of formulas in logic programming. Unification is the basic operation that finds the least general (instantiated) formula (if it exists), given a pair of formulas.

For example, for two formulas *reconcile (a, X, f(X))* and *reconcile(Y, U, f(f(b)))*, their anti-unification (least general generalization) is *p(Z1, Z2, f(Z2))*. Anti-unification was used in (Plotkin 1970) as a method of generalization, and later this work was extended to form a theory of inductive generalization and hypothesis formation. Conversely, unification of these formulas, *reconcile(a, X, f(X)) = reconcile(Y, U, f(f(b)))* will be *reconcile(a, C, f(f(b)))*. Using JSM-based learning (Finn 1999) requires associativity in the similarity operator applied to scenarios: $(S_1 \cap S_2) \cap S_3 = S_1 \cap (S_2 \cap S_3)$. Applying anti-unification to scenarios as ordered lists of expressions for communicative actions does not obey the associativity property. A naïve solution would be to ignore the order of communicative actions and merely consider these actions as conjunctions of expressions. This method would lead to ignorance of essential information about scenarios.

To overcome this problem, we represent the ordered set of formulas for communicative actions as the unordered set of these actions plus multiple instances of the binary predicate *after (Action1, Action2)*. Using this predicate allows information to be retained regarding the order of communicative actions in the scenario and obeys the associativity requirement at the same time. To find a common scenario formula for two scenarios, which are represented by the formulas above, we pair predicates to actions, predicates to the order of actions *after* and predicates to other binary relations on predicates (*causal*).

Moreover, in classifying scenarios, the role of a sequence of communicative actions forming a *step* is more important than the role of a single communicative action. Therefore, when computing similarity between scenarios, one first needs to find *matching steps* occurring in a pair of scenarios and then to search for matching individual actions. Further details on computing similarities between scenarios are available in (Galitsky and Kuznetsov 2008a).

8.11 Scenarios as Sequences of Local Logics

So far, in this chapter, we have used an inductive approach for the learning behavior of agents. In this section, we attempt to simulate the deductive properties of a developing scenario. Each interaction step can be characterized by a set of mental conditions, including knowledge, beliefs, intentions, emotions and others, as well as "physical" conditions. Obviously, these conditions change when new interaction steps occur. From the standpoint of deduction, the sequence of interaction steps for a scenario is essentially non-monotonic: adding new steps (conventionally, adding new facts) frequently leads to existing conditions on previous states failing to hold. To simulate this non-monotonicity, we choose local logics as the formalism to represent the development of scenarios where new interactions between agents occur.

For the purpose of concept learning, we were concerned with the structure of communicative action. However, for the deductive system, we need some sort of completeness for the pre- and post-conditions of communicative actions. These conditions can be obtained as prepositions extracted from text or deduced from domain-specific rules like "early withdrawal => penalty" or from mental world-specific rules such as "loss of money => negative emotion." In this section, we treat propositions irrespective of their source.

In the formalism to be presented, *situations* are associated with mental states. Multiple situations *like the thought of being cheated on by an opponent, being misinformed, the plan to counter-attack being discovered* are associated with the state *change communication topic and formulate a new request* (This state can be followed with communicative action *remind* followed by *request*, for example). *Propositions* are interpreted as conditions on current mental states.

A *Boolean classification* (a Boolean logic without the relation⊢ for sets of propositions (Barwise 1975; Barwise and Perry 1983)) $A = <S, \Sigma, \models, \&, \neg >$ consists of a non-empty set S of situations, a set Σ propositions, a binary relation "true in"$\models =$ on S x Σ, conjunction & and negation $\neg$. Boolean classification satisfies the following conditions for conjunction and negation: $s\models = p_1 \& p_2$ iff $s\models = p_1$ and $s\models = p_2$, $s\models = \neg p$ iff $s\models = p$.

Boolean classification adopts the basic Gentzen sequent calculus approach to logic, and $\Gamma\vdash \Delta$ means that the conjunction of the propositions in Γ entails the disjunction of the propositions in Δ as a non-logical component of a formal system combined with any kind of logical component. A pair of sets of propositions < Γ, Δ > is called a *sequent*. For example,

<{"this book is great"^"he enjoyed this book" & "this book covers math"^"he referred to this book preparing for math test" & "I recommend this book for beginners"^"Will suit a beginner reader well"},

{good_for_students $\vee$ good_for_mathematicians $\vee$ $\neg$ suitable for biologists} is a sequent for a book recommendation. This kind of sequent can be obtained by information extracted from a text, where those sentence generalization expressions are selected from a text that gave non-trivial results (a generalization score above a certain threshold).

A Boolean *local* logic $L = < A, \vdash, N >$ consists of a Boolean classification and binary relation⊢ of inferability for a pair of sets of propositions and a set of *normal* situations $N \subseteq S$. Normal situations satisfy the following conditions:

Entailment: The relation⊢ satisfies all usual Gentzen rules for classical propositional logic, including identity (a⊢ a), weakening ($\Gamma\vdash \Delta \Rightarrow \Gamma, \Gamma'\vdash \Delta, \Delta'$), and global cut

$(\Gamma, \Sigma_0\vdash \Delta, \Sigma_1$ for each partition $< \Sigma_0, \Sigma_1 >$ of some set $\Sigma' \Rightarrow \Gamma\vdash \Delta$). Also, *normal* situations are those situations s such that:

for any $\Gamma\vdash \Delta$ and for all $p\in\Gamma$, $s\models = p \Rightarrow s\models = q$ for some $q\in\Delta$.

By default, situations are normal. The use of normal situations in a local logic L imitates assumptions that are implicit background knowledge within L.

A local logic is *sound* if its every situation is normal. L is *complete* if for all sets of propositions Γ, Δ, such that $\Gamma\vdash \Delta$, then there is a normal situation s such that s| = p for every p∈Γ and s| = ¬q for every q ∈Δ.

It is possible to introduce a partial ordering on a pair of logics L_1 and L_2 on a fixed classification A: $L_1 < L_2$ iff:

- For all sets Γ, Δ of propositions, $Γ\vdash_{L1} Δ \Rightarrow Γ\vdash_{L2} Δ$, and
- Every situation that is normal in L_2 is normal in L_1.

Given this formalism, we state that individual information extraction occurs relative to an implicit local logic. Changing the natural language expression or the targeted extraction (constraints or normal situations) can bring about changes in the normal situations or constraints. This is how local logics implement non-monotonicity.

We now take advantage of the theorem introduced in (Barwise and Seligman 2000).

The local logics on a given classification form a complete lattice under ordering $<$.

Hence, a given behavior scenario developing through time forms a complete lattice. At each point in time, the current scenario can be valid, invalid, or undetermined; validity assessment does not correlate with ordering on a sequence of developing scenarios directly.

8.12 Evaluation

In this section, we present the evaluation results of our classification model. We present the results of different evaluation settings for both the Nearest Neighbor approach and for *Jasmine*:

1. Evaluation of how complaint validity was assessed for a number of customer complaints about banking services. Complaints are collected from PlanetFeed-back.com. A common training dataset allows a comparative analysis of the customer support quality for these banks to be performed. The results are shown in Table 8.4. Complaint validity assessment is a unique problem that is addressed in this study, and it is difficult to provide a comparison to other computational studies of customer complaints.
2. Evaluation of how complaint validity was accessed for travel complaints in seven US metropolitan areas. We also explored which features were the subjects of communicative actions and which sentiments were attached to these features. Even though the problem of sentiment recognition is associated with complaint validity, it remains quite far from mainstream opinion mining studies. Nevertheless, we can compare our sentiment recognition accuracy with the state-of-the-art in the opinion mining field.

Table 8.4 Complaint classification results for fourteen banks (Galitsky and Kuznetsov 2008). On the top: classification by experts; on the bottom: classification by the automated system

Bank	# of complaints	As assigned by experts		
	Training/eval.	Valid	Invalid	Self-eval. of training dataset, %
Bank 1	20/20	8	12	80
Bank 2	20/20	6	14	75
Bank 3	20/20	7	13	80
Bank 4	20/20	5	15	75
Bank 5	20/20	8	12	80
Bank 6	20/20	8	12	65
Bank 7	20/20	11	9	75
Bank 8	20/20	8	12	80
Bank 9	20/20	7	13	75
Bank 10	20/20	9	11	80
Bank 11	20/20	10	10	85
Bank 12	20/20	5	15	75
Bank 13	20/20	10	10	75
Bank 14	20/20	8	12	80
Average		7.9	**12.1**	**77.1**
Percentage		39.3%	**60.7%**	

8.12.1   Assessing Validity of Banking Complaints

We formed the training dataset by randomly dividing the available complaints about each bank in half. One half was used for evaluating the accuracy of our approach on the one hand, while the second half was used for assessing the relative quality of customer support for each bank. The complaints we used were downloaded from the public website PlanetFeedback.com for 3 months starting in March 2004. We manually coded each complaint as a sequence of communicative actions and assigned it a status. Thirdly, the usability and adequacy of our formalism were evaluated by a team of individuals comprised of three classes: complainants, company representatives, and judges.

Not all complaints submitted by upset customers to consumer advocacy websites can be assessed with respect to validity. If a complaint only mentions a failure of a product or a service without describing an interaction with customer support, its validity is linked to specific product/service-related knowledge and cannot be assessed using the proposed technique. As we have stated, this situation is not typical for a complaint: usually, complaints are caused by both product failure and customer support failure. Additionally, we did not include complaints with the structure of interaction scenarios that were too simple or too complex (the former case is similar to the above, while the latter is subject to manual evaluation in the decision-support settings).

Bank	# of complaints	Classification results			Classified as valid but invalid (false positives)	Classified as invalid but valid (false neg.)	Overall classification accuracy, *Jasmine*, %	Overall classification accuracy, Nearest Neighbor, %
	Training/eval.	Valid	Valid	Invalid			Inconsistent classification (refuse to classify)	
Bank 1	20/20	8	6	8	1	1	4	75
Bank 2	20/20	6	6	9	2	0	3	65
Bank 3	20/20	7	5	8	2	1	4	75
Bank 4	20/20	5	3	9	2	2	4	70
Bank 5	20/20	8	5	7	3	2	3	75
Bank 6	20/20	8	4	8	2	2	4	65
Bank 7	20/20	11	6	6	1	3	4	70
Bank 8	20/20	8	6	8	1	1	4	75
Bank 9	20/20	7	4	8	1	2	5	75
Bank 10	20/20	9	6	8	3	1	2	65
Bank 11	20/20	10	6	7	2	2	3	80
Bank 12	20/20	5	2	11	1	2	4	75
Bank 13	20/20	10	6	4	2	1	7	65
Bank 14	20/20	8	7	10	0	1	2	85
Average		7.9	5.1	7.9	1.6	1.5	3.8	72.5
Percentage		39.3%	25.7%	39.6%	8.2%	7.5%	18.9%	

The "Overall classification accuracy, *Jasmine*, %" column values (rightmost numeric in the Jasmine group): 75, 75, 70, 65, 65, 65, 60, 75, 70, 70, 75, 70, 65, 85; Average 70.4.

We used data from fourteen banks, with 20 complaints about training and 20 complaints about evaluation. Firstly, the consistency of each training dataset is evaluated under the assumption that the complaint validity for each complaint is *unknown* and then a classification is performed. After classification, the numbers of false positives, false negatives and correct classifications are obtained. An attempt is then made to increase the classification accuracy by means of temporarily eliminating cases from the training dataset that lead to inconsistent classifications (refused to classify). Finally, the numbers of false positives and false negatives among previously unclassified cases are obtained.

Table 8.4, which contains the results of a validity assessment, is organized as follows:

- The first four columns in the top section of the table contain the bank#, dataset volumes, and the numbers of valid/invalid complaints as manually assessed by the authors (two light-grayed area on the left), respectively.
- The *Self-evaluation of training dataset* column (light-grayed area in the top section) shows the percentage of complaints from the training dataset for each bank that were classified wrongly or not classified at all.
- The Middle column (*Classifications*) in the bottom section gives the number of complaints that were classified correctly and incorrectly (false positives and false negatives).
- The rightmost two columns in the bottom section, *Overall classification accuracy (Jasmine/Nearest Neighbor)*, give the number of correctly assigned complaints as a percentage of the total number in the evaluation dataset. We used this simplified measure instead of F-measure, the calculation of individual factors contributing to complaint classification (Galitsky and Kuznetsov 2008a; Galitsky et al. 2009b).

Rather low data self-evaluation results of 77% show that the domain is quite complex; the scenarios in the training dataset were quite diverse so they would cover all plausible conflict protocols. There is a low deviation between the self-evaluation accuracies for different banks: this fact means that the coverage of the totality of scenario possibilities is similar (although incomplete).

Hence, the resultant recognition accuracy is 70.4% for cautious classification by *Jasmine* and 72.5% for the Nearest Neighbor algorithm. Although quite low with regards to pattern recognition standards in domains such as speech and visual object recognition, this accuracy is believed to be satisfactory for the decision-support settings where the number of complaints that must be re-assessed manually is relatively low. The obtained classification accuracy cannot be compared with the 50% accuracy that one would get by a random prediction because our prediction setting requires the *highest accuracy in providing an explanation for the decision*. The Nearest Neighbor algorithm gives just 2% better accuracy than *Jasmine* and does not guarantee delivery of the best explanations for the categorization decision; therefore, *Jasmine* is a preferred solution for CRM applications. Because the training dataset self-evaluation (by *Jasmine*) accuracy is only 6.9% higher than that of the evaluation dataset, one can conclude that the complaint scenarios are rather diverse, and accumulating a larger dataset is expected to increase the accuracy.

Notice that even the small amount of data in this evaluation shows that banks differ in their ratios between valid and invalid complaints. This result indicates either that banking rules and regulations are not communicated properly or customer support quality is low in specific cases. Moreover, banks vary, although not as strongly, in the difficulty of evaluating complaint validity.

8.13 Assessing Validity of Travelers' Complaints

Opinion mining of travelers staying in hotels has been conducted for the years 2007–2008. Based on compliments and complaints submitted to travel websites as well as planetfeedback.com, the travel recommendation system for uptake.com was developed. Hotel ratings obtained by uptake.com from the hotel reviews, grouped by traveler needs like family, kids, business or romance, served as a recommendation basis. A proper validity assessment of complaints is important for the system to decide whether to use a particular complaint to **not** recommend staying in a particular hotel. For our scenario-based analysis, we also used the discussion threads of other users expressing their opinion regarding a given complaint.

We use the following complaint thread from PlanetFeedback.com as an example. The opinions of other customers help to access the validity of the original complaint. The whole scenario involving proponents or opponents of a given complaint becomes more complex. However, its parts can be matched against the parts of a complaint assigned a validity in order to find the parts of the scenario which express problems. Alternatively, the discussion thread may explicitly confirm the original complaint.

We booked 2 rooms on June 13–15th at St Christopher hotel in New Orleans. The beds were lumpy and uncomfortable. Bedding was very worn. The worst part BED BUGS infested the room and beds. They got in our suitcases and clothes.
We complained to the front desk who didn't care. We came all the way from Idaho for vacation and was treated badly. I want my money back for both rooms. I will also call the New Orleans health department if necessary. I want complete refund of both rooms and an apology.

While you said you complained at the front desk, exactly what was their response? Did they ignore you, did they say "ha, ha...too bad for you"?
If you booked using a credit card call them and tell them you were unhappy and completely dissatisfied with this hotel stay and asked them what your options are. Next time book at a reputable hotel (national chain). Also bed bugs can be at expensive as well as cheaper hotels, but you have a better chance of them taking care of these type issues. And go ahead, write a letter to the New Orleans Dept of Health what is stopping you from doing so? Why just threaten...do it...you have a legitimate complaint about the bed bugs.

The time to ask for a refund, a room change, a hotel change etc. is when you were still a hotel guest. You should have ramped this issue up to the Hotel General Manager when you got no where with the Front Desk.
Your threat to call the Health Department will not endear them to take action on your request and should have been left for a follow up letter.

The validity assessment of hotel complaints is shown in Table 8.5. The training dataset included all scenarios obtained from banking complaints, plus all formalized complaint scenarios of travelers, including those with discussion threads. The number of training complaints is equal to the number of complaints used for evaluation.

Although traveler complaints were longer and the scenario graphs more complex, the overall recognition accuracy (JSM-based) of travel reviews is slightly higher (74.5%) than for banking reviews. We believe this outcome is because the reasons for dissatisfaction of travellers are more explicit than those for banks, where transaction rules might be misunderstood by a customer. One observes that the portion of invalid complaints (including those correctly recognized) is higher in the banking domain.

Our further evaluation addresses the accuracy of extracting individual opinions in the travel domain (compare with Yuksel et al. 2006). We enumerate features of hotels (like *cleanliness*) and travel activities (like *ballet*) in Table 8.6. The data included more than 1,000,000 reviews collected from various travel websites like Expedia.com and Tripadvisor.com. For every feature, we evaluate whether the review was positive (sentiment = 1) or negative (sentiment = 0). The third column contains the numbers of manually evaluated extractions of features, while the fourth column shows the accuracy of sentiment and feature extractions.

The last column contains the total number of features found in the review corpus. Occurrence frequency of these features varies significantly; the number of such occurrences is shown in the third column. For example, travelers mentioned *cleanliness*, *travel with families* and *beach access* much more frequently than most activities or hotel features such as *luxury*, *quietness* or *room service*. Notice that when these

Table 8.5 Complaint classification results for hotels in seven metropolitan areas in US

Hotel area	# of complaints	Classification results					Overall classification accuracy, *Jasmine*, %
	Evaluated	Valid	Invalid	Classified as valid but invalid(false positives)	Classified as invalid but valid (false neg.)	Inconsistent classification (refuse to classify)	
Greater Boston	30/30	10	13	1	1	5	76.7
Bay Area	20/20	6	9	2	0	3	75.0
Los Angeles	40/40	18	15	2	1	4	82.5
New York	40/40	13	15	4	3	5	70.0
Atlanta	20/20	8	6	3	1	2	70.0
Miami	40/40	14	17	2	4	3	77.5
Denver	20/20	6	8	1	3	2	70.0
Average		**10.7**	**11.9**	**2.1**	**1.9**	**3.4**	**74.5**

Table 8.6 Evaluation of the accuracy of individual opinion extraction

Feature	Sentiment	# Assessed	Accuracy (%)	Total
Ballet	0	0	n/a	315
Ballet	1	1	95.00	801
Beach	0	218	63.76	4821
Beach	1	790	81.77	8960
Cleanliness	0	632	87.50	41146
Cleanliness	1	1372	85.13	109068
Family	0	905	78.95	12033
Family	1	3087	86.39	25213
Food	0	3	66.67	19050
Food	1	20	97.00	22216
Luxury	0	6	97.00	12965
Luxury	1	16	62.50	25884
Market	0	10	60.00	5521
Market	1	4	100.00	13743
Money	0	6	50.00	50087
Money	1	27	61.11	84645
Museum	0	7	71.43	444
Museum	1	43	93.02	881
Pet	0	170	38.24	1291
Pet	1	233	68.88	2288
PlayGround	0	2	50.00	192
PlayGround	1	4	75.00	2288
Quiet	0	4	0.00	15992
Quiet	1	40	65.00	26918
Romance	0	0	n/a	11812
Romance	1	5	80.00	16356
RoomService	0	4	100.00	2758
RoomService	1	10	90.00	1455
Ski	0	3	0.00	674
Ski	1	3	0.00	1245
Spa	0	4	75.00	2118
Spa	1	5	80.00	1541
WomAlone	0	0	n/a	150
WomAlone	1	3	100.00	115

features occur as subjects of communicative actions, they participate in the scenario validity assessment procedure.

We proceed to compare our results with the state-of-the-art results in opinion mining, which mostly arise out of academia. We outline the main differences between the industrial opinion mining settings and the ones used in most academic studies on sentiment classification and opinion mining.

In industrial settings, attempt to improve the accuracy of opinion mining is conducted in a test driven development environment, where the goal of the system is to properly extract polarity and sentiment of a manually constructed dataset. This dataset and system settings are adjusted so that the accuracy approaches 100%, so that the system provides the "bug free" code that is expected by quality assurance personnel. The resultant accuracy is, therefore, lower than academic-style evaluations that target maximum accuracy on the testing dataset, something that is frequently not even measured in industrial applications. In order to suit the quality assistance procedures of an industrial environment, deterministic approaches are preferred over statistical ones because they provide more control over individual cases, which assures that the topic and polarity extraction can be carried out on the entire dataset.

Although most approaches to opinion mining focus on the overall assessment of customer reviews (Wiebe et al. 2001; Liu et al. 2005), it is necessary for commercial recommendation applications to extract and determine the individual sentiment expression, its topicality, and its polarity properly so that a particular user's needs or concerns may be addressed. Hence, we evaluate the accuracy of the extraction of individual reviews that are quoted to support a user's decision. Obviously, assessing a group of opinion expressions as a single opinion in a given review is more accurate than assessing an individual opinion expression.

We compare our work to the somewhat similar domain of U.S. Congressional floor debates (Pang and Lee 2008). The investigation addressed the possibility of determining from the transcripts whether the speeches were in support of or opposed to proposed legislation. The authors leveraged the observation that these speeches occur as part of a discussion and are backed by arguments; this fact allows them to use sources of information regarding relationships between discourse segments, such as whether a given utterance indicates an agreement with the opinion expressed by another speaker, similar to our procedure for complaints. The authors found that incorporation of the information on discourse structures yields substantial improvements over classifying speeches in isolation; an accuracy of 84.25% on the training dataset and 81.07% on the testing dataset is achieved.

Chaovalit and Zhou (2005) conducted a comparison between supervised and unsupervised sentiment and topicality classification approaches using movie reviews. Their supervised machine learning accuracy is 85.54%. The semantic orientation approach, because it is unsupervised, requires extracting phrases containing adjectives or adverbs from the review data. Five patterns of phrases were extracted to find their semantic orientation values based on the selected POS tagger, and 77% classification accuracy on 100 movie reviews from Movie Vault was achieved after adjusting the dividing baseline. Turney (2002) obtained 65.83% accuracy in mining 120 movie reviews from the Epinions website. Pang et al. (2002) mined movie reviews using various machine-learning techniques to determine whether these techniques are as effective as other sentiment classification methods like movie review mining. They obtained the best classification accuracies ranging from 77.4 to 82.9% by varying input features (i.e., unigrams, bigrams, unigrams + bigrams). Most studies confirm our expectation that the machine learning approach is more accurate but requires a significant amount of time to train the model. In contrast, the semantic orientation approach chosen in the current chapter is slightly less accurate but more efficient for use in real-time applications.

To the best of our knowledge, the current work is the first to propose complaint validity assessment for CRM; therefore, there are no computational evaluation results available for comparison. Sentiment extraction is the closest area for a comparison to state-of-the-art techniques with available evaluations of sentiment extraction at the document level (Galitsky et al. 2015). Statistical methods such as SVM, when applied to polarity extraction for the whole document, achieve 86.4% accuracy (Pang and Lee 2004). Extracting individual sentiments required for the formalization of the whole scenario of behavior cannot be expected to be as accurate. However, for some features and polarities such as positive reviews of *cleanliness*; negative reviews of *luxury*; positive reviews of *family-friendliness, food,* and *room service*; and positive reviews of attractions such as *museums*, statistically obtained accuracy is exceeded.

8.14   Using *ComplaintEngine*

Our further evaluation involves an improvement of existing software for processing customer complaints, called *ComplaintEngine*. Five attributes of communicative actions, selected for the model presented in this chapter, helped to improve the accuracy of scenario recognition, given the particular set of complaints from our database of formalized complaints. Our database primarily originates from data for the financial sector, obtained from publicly available textual complaints on PlanetFeedback.com.

Currently, *ComplaintEngine* uses an anti-unification procedure to find similarities between scenarios. The machine learning process of *ComplaintEngine* employs JSM-type plausible reasoning (Finn 1999) augmented with situation calculus, reasoning about communicative states and other reasoning domains. *ComplaintEngine* applies domain-independent anti-unification to formulas that include enumerations of communicative actions in time.

As expected, the employed machine learning technique caused noticeable improvement in complaint recognition accuracy. Judging on the restricted dataset of 80 banking complaints (40 complaints make up the training set and 40 complaints make up the testing set), the performance of *ComplaintEngine* was improved by 6% to the resultant recognition accuracy of 89%. In relating a scenario to a class, *ComplaintEngine* is capable of explaining its decision by enumerating similar and dissimilar scenarios, as well as particular communicative actions and their subjects that led to its decision.

We would like to briefly introduce *ComplaintEngine* (Galitsky 2006), the integrated complaint management component of a customer response management infrastructure. The user interface to specify a complaint scenario is shown in Fig. 8.6. Communicative actions are selected from the list of 20 or more. The parameters of communicative actions are specified as text in the Interactive Form; however, they are not present in the formal graph-based scenario representation. Causal links between the parameters (subjects) of communicative actions are specified by pairs of checkboxes (shown by vertical arrows).

Having performed the justification of complaint validity, *ComplaintEngine* sets the list box for complaint status at "unjustified." *ComplaintEngine* provides the explanation of its decision, highlighting the cases that are similar to U (unjustified) and those that are different from U (justified). Moreover, *ComplaintEngine* indicates both the communicative actions (steps) that are common for U and also other unjustified complaints that further support its decision.

A form similar to the one in Fig. 8.6 is used for a complainant to file a complaint and for a company to store complaints, analyze them, determine their validity, explain how the decision regarding them was made, and finally advise the company on strategies for complaint resolution.

A complainant has a choice to use the above form or to input a complaint as a text so that the linguistic processor processes the complaint automatically and

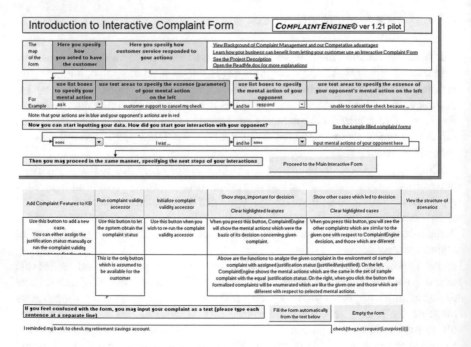

Fig. 8.6 A screen-shot of the Interactive Complaint Form, where the complaint scenario U from Fig. 5 is specified

fills out the form for her. Using the form encourages complainants to use a logical structure in their complaint and to provide sound argumentation. After a complaint is partially or fully specified, the user evaluates its consistency. *ComplaintEngine* indicates whether the current complaint (its mental component) is consistent or not. It may issue a warning and advice concerning how to improve the logical structure of the complaint. When the complainant is satisfied with the response of *ComplaintEngine*, he submits the completed form. The other result may be a dismissal of the complaint at this early stage by the complainant if a user observes that it is not possible to file a reasonable complaint.

8.15 Selecting Products by Features Using Customer Feedback

In the previous sections, we addressed the practical issues of resolving customer complaints. In this section, we will focus on a wider problem of how to aggregate customer opinions (both positive and negative) extracted from text. Mining customer opinion data is now becoming an important source of product selection decisions.

In our study (Galitsky et al. 2009b), we proposed a natural language processing and semantic transformation mechanism for open-domain extraction of user opinions; here, we focus on the lattice-based interactive recommendation platform. This platform is capable of providing an aggregated view of products and their features, as extracted from customer feedback.

The screen-shot of the *Interactive recommendation platform* for advanced users is shown at the top of Fig. 8.7. The purpose of the view is to create a visual impression for the user of which features are advantageous or disadvantageous for a series of products of the same category. The data feed for this view is the result of extracting information from customer reviews. The initial lattice is drawn automatically, and the user may re-locate nodes of interest or add/remove labels when interests and foci change. For every product and its disadvantageous features, the lattice allows the identification of products where these features are better and continued exploration of these products other features to match the user needs.

On the right, users choose their current products of interest. At any time, they can add new products by selecting checkboxes for available products in order to obtain more comparative information. Similarly, users can remove products from the current view for a more comprehensive visualization of remaining products. The lattice will be updated accordingly. When a given product is selected, one can see all nodes (highlighted) of the lattice that contains features of this product, and, conversely, for every positive or negative feature, one can see all products having these features. The concept lattice is shown at the bottom of the figure in a higher resolution.

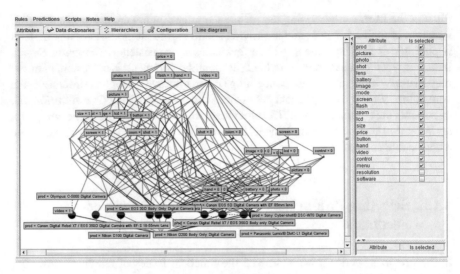

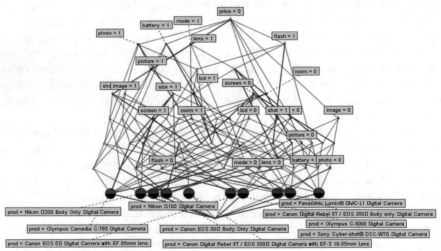

Fig. 8.7 Interactive recommendation platform

8.16   Discussion and Conclusions

In this chapter, we proposed a concept learning approach to relate a human behavior pattern to classes. We used a representation language of labeled directed acyclic graph labels with vertices for communicative actions and arcs for temporal relations, causal links and defeat relations on them. For the purpose of machine learning, the scenarios are represented as a sequence of communicative actions attached to agents; the communicative actions are grouped by subjects, and the order of communicative actions is retained using binary predicates *after*. We considered the concept lattice of communicative actions and showed how the procedure of relating a complaint to a class can be implemented by Nearest Neighbor and JSM (Finn 1999) learning machinery. This approach is believed to be an innovative way to learn scenarios of inter-human interactions that are encoded as sequences of communicative actions.

CRM experts are telling that businesses should focus on the customer and reinvent themselves to deliver personalized, service-driven sales and support. We do not agree with a pure monetization approach that the overall objectives of CRM are to drive productivity and provide measurable return on investment while improving profitability and expanding market share. While these objectives are sometimes the result of a well-executed CRM initiative, many CRM projects help organizations achieve specific objectives such as improving customer satisfaction or retention.

The importance of using predictive technologies by front-line personnel to proactively address issues has been demonstrated by (Adair 2020). Using the technique presented in this chapter, the front-line personnel can engage in more proactive customer contact rather than merely reacting to customer requests, as is often the case today. As has been observed with automated phone answering systems, customers with issues are driven to other channels such as Web sites for self-help. The goal of CRM will be to save the time and talents of educated workers so that they may focus on gathering non-system data, such as a customer's demeanor and future plans. Front-line workers will be transformed, becoming salespeople and/or consultants utilizing the CRM system to research historical information and add value to their personal interactions with customers, whether those interactions are on the phone, via the Internet or in person. To make this cultural change, front-line workers will need to adopt new habits (perhaps encouraged by changes in their compensation) so that they use the CRM systems and understand the value of both the system and their front-line interactions. Natural language interfaces will be used by both front-line workers and customers to facilitate easy access to information, regardless of location, channel or experience.

Many analytical tasks in CRM, such as churn prognosis, risk management or targeted marketing, involve classification of customers and their behavior (Bichler and Kiss 2004; Ngai et al. 2009). For example, CRM analysis of a telecommunication provider might build classification models trying to predict whether a customer presents a high, medium, or low risk of switching providers, a.k.a. churn prediction. Given the training and test data sets, analysts can compare different algorithms based on overall accuracy. Traditionally, classification has focused on attribute-value learning, where each example or instance can be characterized by a fixed set of attributes. The hypothesis language is propositional logic, and these types of algorithms are referred to as propositional learners (Krogel et al. 2003). Dierkes et al. (2009) improve churn prediction models by leveraging network effects. In contrast to traditional classification algorithms, the information about a customer's neighbors in the communication graph is taken into account. A Markov logic network field (Richardson and Domingos 2006) is used, combining Markov Random Fields and Inductive Logic Programming (ILP) to define a distribution over objects' properties and relations among them by attaching a weight (capturing the importance of the formula) to each formula in a first-order theory.

To position our method among the learning techniques, it is closer to ILP (Muggleton 1999), which has been applied to CRM, and Explanation Based Learning, which is intended to derive as general expressions as possible from available data (Russell 1986; Mitchell et al. 1986). Our approach is further away from statistical, hybrid (Richardson and Domingos 2006; Galitsky 2006), or neurocomputing (Kaburlasos and Ritter 2007) approaches.

When building a framework for comparative analysis of formal scenarios, one expresses the similarity between the main entities. In our study (Galitsky 2006), we approximated the meanings of mental entities using definitions from the basis of *want-know-believe*; however, we observed that this approach would be too coarse for recognizing complaints. In this chapter, we extend the speech act theory-based set of attributes to build an adequate concept lattice for communicative actions. This extension was more suitable than our earlier approaches to defining a concept lattice for scenarios while learning (Galitsky et al. 2010).

There exist a number of settings in which graph-based data mining and clustering is performed (e.g., Holder et al. 2005; Coble et al. 2005) that rely on information-theoretic or error-based measures. Concepts are the basic units of thought that underlie human intelligence and communication. The study of concept formation and learning is central to cognitive informatics (Galitsky 2016b). The concept-based approach has been applied to human reasoning in (Yao 2004), which addresses basic issues of concept formation and learning from cognitive informatics perspectives. A layered model for concept formation and learning is presented by the author.

Much distributed AI and game theoretic research (Rosenschein and Zlotkin 1994) deals with coordination and negotiation issues by giving pre-computed solutions to specific problems. Mor et al. (1995) discussed multi-agent learning as a means to reach equilibrium. The author modeled agents as finite automata and analyzed the computational complexity of certain classes of learning strategies based on this automaton model. Also, there has been much research reported on developing theoretical models in which learning plays a key role, especially in the area of adaptive dynamics of games (e.g., mentioned above (Jordan 1992; Kalai and Lehrer 1993)). However, to build a negotiation assistant and conflict resolution system, it is necessary to improve the negotiation competence based on learning from previous experience of interactions among human agents. Learning in inter-human settings is closely related to the issue of how to model the overall interactions process in terms of communicative actions (Galitsky and Tumarkina 2004), that is, what negotiation protocols are adopted. Zeng and Sycara (1997) simulate a sequential decision-making protocol for negotiation between autonomous agents who are able to learn in a rational manner using a Bayesian approach.

Also, we suggested in the current chapter a novel approach to building a semantic network between linguistic entities on the basis of selected attributes. The choice of attributes of communicative actions in this chapter is motivated by the task of scenario comparison; these attributes may vary from domain to domain. Twenty selected communicative entities are roughly at the same level of generality—there are "horizontal" semantic relations between them. In this respect, we have established a link between the theory of concept structures and the speech act theory, which has been discussed (Turoff et al. 1999) but has not become a subject of a computational analysis. This work sheds a light on what kind of conceptual structures communicative actions are; the necessity of extending the traditional set of attributes of communicative actions for the purposes of machine learning has been demonstrated.

We believe the current work is one of the first employing machine learning in the domain of multiagent interactions described in natural language. A number of studies have shown how to enable BDI-agents that learn in a particular domain (e.g., information retrieval). In BDI settings, the description of agents' attitudes is quite limited: only their beliefs, desires and intentions are involved. Moreover, only automated (software) agents are addressed. In this chapter, we significantly extended the expressiveness of representation language for agents' attitudes, using 20 communicative actions linked by a concept lattice. The suggested machinery can be applied to an arbitrary domain, including inter-human conflicts, characterized in natural language.

The evaluation of our model shows it is an adequate technique to handle such complex objects (both in terms of knowledge representation and reasoning) as communicative actions of scenarios of multiagent interactions. The JSM learning approach was found suitable to relate inter-human conflict scenarios to classes. Evaluation using two datasets of banking and travel complaints showed satisfactory performance for the decision-support mode. The suggested approach for assessing complaint validity is appropriate for deployment in CRM settings: most typical complaints are subject to automated processing, and atypical cases are handled manually. The proposed method for formal representation of conflict scenarios allows their classification, as well as the efficient user interface for complaint submission.

Processing customer complaints is a major challenge in the context of knowledge management technologies. In this chapter, we have proposed a novel approach to improve the automated processing of customer complaints. We have shown how communicative actions and attack links can be successfully modeled in terms of the graph-based representation provided by the notion of complaint scenario. We have also shown that our proposal for classifying complaint scenarios using supervised learning can be successfully applied, outperforming the results obtained using the *ComplaintEngine* platform when applying a keyword-based approach in which no attack links were taken into account for complaint classification. In this respect, the evaluation experiments using our dataset of formalized real-world complaints showed satisfactory performance. It must be remarked that a particular strength of our approach is that the concept lattice was computed once, accounting for the whole domain of complaint scenarios. Clearly, for other application domains associated with conflicting situations such as international conflicts, the corresponding concept lattice could be different.

References

Adair B (2020) The future of CRM https://www.selecthub.com/customer-relationship-management/future-of-crm/

Austin JL (1962) How to do things with words. In: Urmson JO (ed). Clarendon, Oxford

Bach K, Harnish RM (1979) Linguistic communication and speech acts. MIT Press, Cambridge, MA

Barwise J (1975) Admissible sets and structures. Springer Verlag

Barwise J, Perry J (1983) Situations and attitudes. MIT Press, Cambridge, MA and London

Barwise J, Seligman J (2000) Information flow in distributed systems. Cambridge University Press, Tracts in Theoretical Computer Science

Bratman ME (1987) Intention, plans and practical reason. Harvard University Press

Bichler M, Kiss C (2004) A comparison of logistic regression, k-nearest neighbor, and decision tree induction for campaign management. Tenth Americas Conference on Information Systems (AMCIS), New York

Chaovalit P, Zhou L (2005) Movie review mining: a comparison between supervised and unsupervised classification approaches. In: Proceedings of the Hawaii International Conference on System Sciences (HICSS)

Coble J, Cook D, Rathi R, Holder L (2005) Iterative structure discovery in graph-based data. Int J Art Int Techn 1–2(14):101–124

Cohen PR, Levesque HJ (1990) Performatives in a rationally based speech act theory. In: Proceedings of the 28th conference of Association for Computational Linguistics, pp 79–88

Davidow M (2003) Organizational responses to customer complaints: what works and what doesn't. J Ser Res 5(3):225–250

Dierkes T, Bichler M, Krishnan R (2009) Modelling network effects with markov logic networks for churn prediction in the telecommunication industry. In: Fifth Symposium on Statistical Challenges in Electronic Commerce Research

Finn VK (1991) Plausible reasoning in systems of JSM-type, Itogi Nauki I Techniki, Seriya Informatika, 15:54–101, [in Russian]

Finn VK (1999) On the synthesis of cognitive procedures and the problem of induction NTI Series 2 N1-2 8-45.12

GTF (2009) Gtf inspire complaint processing. http://www.gft.de

Galitsky B (2006) Reasoning about mental attitudes of complaining customers. Knowledge-Based Systems

Galitsky B (2008) Kuznetsov SO: learning communicative actions of conflicting human agents. J Exp Theor Artif Intell 20(4):277–317

Galitsky B (2016a) Generalization of parse trees for iterative taxonomy learning. Inf Sci 329:125–143

Galitsky B (2016b) Computational models of Autism. In: Computational Autism, Springer, Cham, Switzerland, pp 17–77

Galitsky B (2018) Customers' retention requires an explainability feature in machine learning systems they use. 2018 AAAI Spring Symposium Series

Galitsky B (2019a) Enabling a bot with understanding argumentation and providing arguments. Developing Enterprise Chatbots, Springer, Cham, Switzerland, pp 465–532

Galitsky B (2019b) Enabling chatbots by validating argumentation. US Patent App. 16/260,939

Galitsky B, Tumarkina I (2004) Justification of customer complaints using emotional states and mental actions. FLAIRS conference, Miami, Florida

Galitsky B, Miller A (2005) Determining possible criminal behavior of mobile phone users by means of analysing the location tracking data, AAAI SSS 2005 on Homeland Security

Galitsky B, Pascu A (2006) Epistemic Categorization for Analysis of Customer Complaints. FLAIRS Conference, 291–296

Galitsky B, Kuznetsov SO (2008b) Scenario argument structure vs individual claim defeasibility: what is more important for validity assessment? Intl. Conf on Concept Structures ICCS 2008: 282–296 LNCS 5113

Galitsky B, Parnis A (2019) Accessing validity of argumentation of agents of the internet of everything. In: Artificial Intelligence for the Internet of Everything, pp 187–216

Galitsky B, Ilvovsky D (2019) Validating correctness of textual explanation with complete discourse trees. In: Workshop Notes of the Seventh International Workshop" What can FCA do for AI"

Galitsky B, Kuznetsov SO, Samokhin MV (2005) Analyzing conflicts with concept-based learning. International conference on conceptual structures, pp 307–322

Galitsky BA, Kuznetsov SO, Vinogradov DV (2006) Applying hybrid reasoning to mine for associative features in biological data. J Biomed Inform v22

Galitsky B, Chen H, Du S (2009a) Inversion of forum content based on authors' sentiments on product usability. AAAI Spring Symposium: Social Semantic Web: Where Web 2.0 Meets Web 3.0, pp 33–38

Galitsky B, González MP, Chesñevar CI (2009b) A novel approach for classifying customer complaints through graphs similarities in argumentative dialogues. Decis Support Syst 46(3):717–729

Galitsky B, Kovalerchuk B, Kuznetsov SO (2007) Learning common outcomes of communicative actions represented by labeled graphs. In: Intl Conference on Concept Structures Sheffield UK July 22–27 LNCS 4604, pp 387–400

Galitsky B, D Ilvovsky, SO Kuznetsov SO (2015) Text integrity assessment: sentiment profile vs rhetoric structure international conference on intelligent text processing and computational linguistics, pp 126–139

Galitsky B, Ilvovsky D, Kuznetsov SO (2018) Detecting logical argumentation in text via communicative discourse tree. J Exp Theor Artif Intell 30(5):1–27

Galitsky B, Dobrocsi G, De La Rosa JL, Kuznetsov SO (2010) From generalization of syntactic parse trees to conceptual graphs. In: International conference on conceptual structures, pp 185–190

Galitsky B, Dobrocsi G, de la Rosa JL, Kuznetsov SO (2011) Using generalization of syntactic parse trees for taxonomy capture on the web. ICCS:104–117

Ganter B, Kuznetsov S (2001) Pattern structures and their projections. In: Proc. 9th Int. Conf. on Conceptual Structures, ICCS'01, Stumme G, Delugach H (eds) Lecture Notes in Artificial Intelligence, vol. 2120, pp 129–142

Ganter B, Wille R (1999) Formal concept analysis. Springer, Mathematical Foundations

Garey MR, Johnson DS (1979) Computers and intractability: a guide to the theory of NP-completeness. Freeman, San Francisco, CA

Holder L, Cook D, Coble J, Mukherjee M (2005) Graph-based relational learning with application to security. Fundam Inf (Special Issue on Mining Graphs, Trees and Sequences) 1–2(6):83–101

Harsanyi JC, Selten R (1972) A generalized Nash solution fro two-person bargaining games with incomplete information. Manag Sci 1880–106

Jordan JS (1992) The exponential convergence of Bayesian learning in normal form games. Games Eco Beh 4202–217

Jayachandran S, Sharma S, Kaufman P, Raman P (2005, October) The role of relational information processes and technology use in customer relationship management. J Mark 69(4):177–192

Kalai E, Lehrer E (1993) Rational learning leads to Nash equilibrium. Econometrica 61(5):1019–1045

Kaburlasos VG, Ritter GX (2007) Computational intelligence based on lattice theory. Studies in CI N67

Kolodner J (1993) Case-based reasoning. Morgan Kaufmann

Krogel MA., Rawles S, Zelezn F, Flach P, Lavrac N, Wrobel S (2003) Comparative evaluation on approaches to propositionalization. LNCS 2835 Springer, Berlin, pp. 142–155

Kuznetsov SO (1999) Learning of simple conceptual graphs from positive and negative examples. In: Zytkow J, Rauch J (eds) Proc. Principles of Data Mining and Knowledge Discovery, Third European Conference, PKDD'99, Lecture Notes in Artificial Intelligence, vol. 1704, pp 384–392

Kuznetsov SO, Samokhin MV (2005) Learning closed sets of labeled graphs for chemical applications. ILP 2005:190–208

Laza R, Corchado JM (2002) CBR-BDI agents in planning. Symposium on Informatics and Telecommunications (SIT'02). Sevilla, Spain, September 25–27, pp 181–192

Liu B, Hu M, Cheng J (2005) Opinion observer: analyzing and comparing opinions on the Web. 14th WWW Conference, pp 342–351

Mill JS (1843) A system of logic, racionative and inductive. London

Mitchell T (1997) Machine learning. McGraw-Hill

Mitchell TM, Keller RM, Kedar-Cabelli ST (1986) Explanation-based generalization: a unifying view. Mach Learn 1:47–80

MasterControl (2009) MasterControl: customer complaint handling software. www.mastercontrol.com/solutions/complaints_fb.html

Mor Y, Goldman CV, Rosenschein JS (1995) Learn your opponent's strategy (in polynomial time). In: Proceedings of IJCAI-95 Workshop on Adaptation and Learning in Multiagent Systems

Muggleton S (1999) Inductive logic programming: issues, results and the challenge of learning language in logic artificial intelligence 114(1–2):283–296

Muller HJ, Dieng R (eds) (2000) Computational conflicts conflict modeling for distributed intelligent systems. Springer-Verlag, New York

Ngai EWT, Xiu L, Chau DCK (2009) Application of data mining techniques in customer relationship management. Expert Syst Appl 36:2592–2602

Oracle (2009a) Oracle customer relationship management, http://www.oracle.com/applications/peoplesoft/crm/ent/index.html

Osborne MJ, Rubinstein A (1994) A course in game theory. The MIT Press

Olivia C, Chang CF, Enguix CF, Ghose AK (1999) Case-based BDI agents an effective approach for intelligent search on the world wide web. In: Intelligent Agents in Cyberspace. AAAI Spring Symposium

Pang B, Lee L (2004) A sentimental education: sentiment analysis using subjectivity summarization based on minimum cuts. ACL

Pang B, Lee L, Vaithyanathan S (2002) Thumbs up? sentiment classification using machine learning techniques. In: Proceedings of EMNLP

Pang B, Lee L (2008, January) Opinion mining and sentiment analysis. Found Trends Inf Retr 2(1–2):1–135

Plotkin GD (1970) A note on inductive generalization, Machine Intelligence, vol 5, Edinburgh University Press, pp 153–163

Russell SJ (1986) Preliminary steps toward the automation of induction. In: Proceedings of the 5th National Conference on Artificial Intelligence. Morgan Kaufmann, Los Altos, CA, pp 477–484

Rosenschein J, Zlotkin G (1994) Rules of encounter. MIT Press, Cambridge, MA

Riloff E (1996) Automatically generating extraction patterns from untagged text. In: Proceedings of the 13th National Conference on Artificial Intelligence (AAAI-96), pp 1044–1049

Richardson M, Domingos P (2006) Markov logic networks. Mach Learn 62(1–2/February):107–136

Searle J (1969) Speech acts. An essay in the philosophy of language. Eng.- Cambridge University Press, Cambridge

Sowa J (1984) Conceptual graphs, conceptual structures information processing in mind and machine. Addison-Wesley, Reading, MA

Stone P, Veloso M (2000) Multiagent systems a survey from a machine learning perspective. Autonomous Robotics 8(3):345–383

Swift R (2001) Accelerating customer relationships: using CRM and relationship technologies. Prentice Hall, London UK

Turoff M, Hiltz SR, Bieber M, Fjermestad J, Rana A (1999) Collaborative discourse structures in computer mediated group communications. J Comput Med Commun 4(4)

Turney PD (2002) Thumbs up or thumbs down? semantic orientation applied to unsupervised classification of reviews. 40th ACL, New Brunswick, NJ

Vinogradov (1999) Logic programs for Quazi-axiomatic theories. Nauchno-Tehnicheskaya Informacia Ser 2 N2 61–64 [In Russian]

Weiss G, Sen S (1996) Adaptation and learning in multiagent systems. Lect Notes Art Int, vol. 1042. Springer-Verlag, Berlin Heidelberg New York

Wiebe J, Wilson T, Bell M (2001) Identifying collocations for recognizing opinions. In: Proceedings of ACL/EACL 2001 Workshop on Collocation, Toulouse, France

Yevtushenko SA (2020) Concept explorer. https://sourceforge.net/projects/conexp/. Last accessed April 7 (2020)

Yuan ST, WL Chang (2001, February) Mixed-initiative synthesized learning approach for web-based CRM. Exp Syst Appl 20(2):187–200(14)

Yuksel A, Kilinc U, Yuksel F (2006) Cross-national analysis of hotel customers' attitudes toward complaining and their complaining behaviours. Tour Manag 27(1):11–24

Yao YY (2004) Concept formation and learning: a cognitive informatics perspective. In: Proceedings of the Third IEEE International Conference on Cognitive Informatics (ICCI'04)

Zeng D, Sycara K (1997) Benefits of learning in negotiation. In: Proceedings of the 14th National Conference on Artificial Intelligence (AAAI-97). Menlo Park, CA AAAI Press, pp 36–42

Zirtiloğlu H, Yolum P (2008) Ranking semantic information for e-government: complaints management. In: Proceedings of the first ACM international workshop on Ontology-supported business intelligence. Karlsruhe, Germany

Chapter 9
Reasoning and Simulation of Mental Attitudes of a Customer

Abstract In this chapter, we employ logic programming to simulate the mental world. A Theory of Mind engine is introduced that takes an initial mental state and produces the consecutive mental states as plausible to a real-world scenario as possible. We simulate a multiagent decision-making environment taking into account intentions, knowledge and beliefs of itself and others. The simulation results are evaluated with respect to precision, completeness and complexity. Metaprogramming techniques of introspection is outlined for putting a CRM component in "customers' shoes," better predicting how she would think and act. We conclude that the Theory of Mind engine is adequate to support a broad range of CRM tasks requiring simulation of human mental attitudes.

9.1 Introduction

Over the last two decades, the attention to formal modeling of various forms of human reasoning and mental behavior has strongly risen, particularly in connection with software applications in business and educational domains. A series of phenomena in human reasoning has been reflected in such computational approaches as reasoning about action and knowledge, space and time, non-monotonic and counterfactual reasoning, etc. as well as in user modeling. Nevertheless, a generic computational framework for reasoning about mental states which is suitable for CRM applications is yet to be developed (Galitsky et al. 2011).

In this chapter, to reason about mental attitudes, we define *Theory of Mind of a customer* in the context of a CRM application. Theory of mind is the ability to attribute mental states such as beliefs, intents, desires, emotions, knowledge and others to oneself and to others, such as peers, other customers and customer support agents. Theory of mind is necessary to understand that others have beliefs, desires, intentions, and perspectives that are different from one's own. Theory of mind is essential for everyday human social interactions, including consuming goods and services. Theory of mind is used when analyzing, judging, and inferring others' behaviors.

© The Author(s), under exclusive license to Springer Nature Switzerland AG 2021   371
B. Galitsky, *Artificial Intelligence for Customer Relationship Management*,
Human–Computer Interaction Series, https://doi.org/10.1007/978-3-030-61641-0_9

We also build a reasoning engine (*Theory of Mind (ToM) engine*) that is supposed to reproduce reasoning and behavior associated with a customer in some approximated form. We will enable this engine with the skill to correctly answer questions in certain scenarios. To obtain correct answers, the engine needs to properly infer the mental states (who *knows* what, who *wants* what) that are associated with these answers. How can we assure that the Theory of Mind engine completes all these exercises and questions properly?

We require it to derive a *complete, exhaustive* sequence of mental states, given a task (which we refer to as *initial mental state*). We then expect such completeness to reproduce rationality and intelligence in reasoning in the mental world. This feature of completeness can be achieved not only because of the limited number of entities describing the manifold of activities in the mental world, but also because these entities can be defined in the basis of just three mental actions, *knowledge, belief* and *intention.*

Once the engine is designed, we will evaluate it with a number of various scenarios in the mental world. Here we refer to the engine as *ToM engine*, although in our previous studies, we named it *the natural language multiagent mental simulator,* NL_MAMS (Galitsky 2016).

Hence the main task of the ToM is to build a set of consecutive mental states given an arbitrary initial mental state in the fixed vocabulary of mental states and actions. The formal declarative definitions of mental states and actions are also given. This set of consecutive mental actions must be consistent with the definitions of involved mental states and actions. Informally, for a human, this set should sound plausible, as far as the definitions of mental states and actions are plausible and match human intuition. Since the definitions of mental actions are of a declarative nature, they do not give a hint on how to navigate mental space to satisfy them, including preconditions and effects. The richer the set of definitions is available, the more extensive and complete the derived set of consecutive mental states is expected to be.

9.1.1   The Task of the ToM Engine

The ToM Engine inputs formal or natural language descriptions of initial mental states of interacting agents. It outputs deterministic scenarios of plausible, rational behaviors of these agents in the mental world. The ToM Engine is capable of analyzing and predicting the consequences of mental and physical actions of actions (Galitsky 2002, 2013). The output of the ToM Engine is the sequence of mental formulas expressing the states that are the results of the committed actions (behaviors) chosen by these agents.

Obviously, we cannot reproduce the richness and variability of the real mental sub-world of the real world by this engine. To properly frame the capabilities of the ToM Engine simulator, we specify the *available repository of behaviors* for each agent to choose from. To reproduce certain scenarios and certain ToM Engine tasks, we define a minimal set of behaviors providing successful solutions to these tasks.

The scope of the engine (the totality of generated scenarios) is determined by a repository of behaviors loaded into the system. This repository contains definitions of mental entities such as *deceive*, so that the ToM Engine agent can choose it if its preconditions can be satisfied at a given state, and this action leads to most desired or least undesired reachable states.

The ToM Engine can be viewed from multiple perspectives (Galitsky 2016):

(1) A *planner* in the mental world. Given a current state and constraints in the form of implausible or irrational agents' actions, build a plan of actions to satisfy these constraints

(2) A *simulator* of the mental world. Given the set of constraints for allowed actions give, simulate an activity of an agent searching for the best action. An agent first searches through all possible actions of his opponents according to his knowledge about their beliefs, and then searches through his own options having found those of opponents.

(3) A *game player in the mental world*. The simulator settings could be reduced to the game-theoretic ones if the mutual beliefs of agents are complete or absent, and intentions are uniform (a trivial case of multiagent scenario, Rosenschein and Zlotkin 1994).

(4) A *prediction engine* in the mental world. Given previous initial mental states and their outcomes, or sequences of mental states, the system learns from them and predicts the outcome for an unknown initial mental state. This engine can also be viewed as a machine learning or induction one.

(5) A *reasoning engine* about the mental world. An axiomatic system for a given ToM session includes the initial mental states and behavioral repository of definitions of mental entities as axioms. Theorems include deduced mental actions and mental states which form a sequence. If mental state s_1 is inferred relying on action a_1 that is, in turn, inferred relying on state s_0, then s_0, a_1 and s_1 are ordered in time correspondingly.

Since the ToM Engine possesses definitions of mental entities, it is capable of representing natural language expressions that include mental entities as mental formulas. Words for physical states and actions are merged and form parameters of these entities. Therefore we assign to the ToM Engine the capability of *understanding* natural language messages from its user and other agents. The ToM Engine extracts the expressions, which mention explicitly or assume implicitly mental states and actions of involved agents.

Modeling of multiagent interaction takes into account the possible *ambiguity* of messages that is inherent in a natural language dialog. For each mental entity extracted from text, such as *inform*, the ToM Engine forms a disjunction of mental formulas for each meaning of this entity

$inform1(A,B,S) \cup inform2(A,B,S) \cup inform3(A,B,S)$ according to multiple clauses for *inform*.

The ToM Engine imitates the multiagent behaviors that are caused by a possible misunderstanding of one agent by another because of the ambiguity of mental entities. Under the search of optimal action or reaction, the set of meanings for received entities is (exhaustively) analyzed with respect to avoiding the least wanted state (assuming this state may be achieved as a result of a particular understanding of a message). In this book, we will not touch upon the natural language component of the ToM Engine and refer the reader to (Galitsky 2003) for the description of message understanding issues in mental domains and sample applications of question answering (Galitsky 2017, 2019).

9.2   A Model of a Mental Attitude of a Customer

We present a step-by-step introduction to our representation of the mental world. The steps of this introduction are either definitions or hypotheses which have been computationally verified in our studies.

Logico-philosophical investigation of mental entities is a well-established area in AI. Similar to the vocabulary of mental actions introduced in this chapter, many cognitive vocabularies make a prominent distinction between mental states (as knowledge or belief) and mental mechanisms (as the mental events that process knowledge or information). For example, the conceptual dependency theory (Schank 1969) distinguishes between two sets of representations: primitive mental *acts* and mental *conceptualizations* upon which the acts operate. In addition, the theory proposes a number of causal links that connect members of one set with members of the other. With such building blocks, a representational language such as conceptual dependency must be able to represent many process terms: *think* (about), *remember, infer, realize* and *calculate*; and numerous state terms: *fact, belief, guess, doubt,* and *disbelief.*

9.2.1   Mental States and Actions

We first hypothesize that we can merge (ignore the difference between) the totality of entities of other than mental (physical) nature.

Hypothesis 1 Actions and states are divided into mental (communicative, e.g., informing-knowing) and physical (remaining, e.g., making withdrawal – decreased account balance). We approximate our description of the mental world using mental states and actions and merging all physical actions into a constant predicate for arbitrary physical action and its potential resultant physical states (Fig. 9.1) This approximation is valid most of the times modeling the mental states of a software user where the set of available physical actions (as software options, e.g., turn, stop, lend, buy a product, order a service, get a ticket, etc.) is rather limited.

Hypothesis 2 Humans can adequately operate with the set of natural language mental expressions containing not more than four mutually dependent mental entities. This hypothesis is based on psychological observations concerning the theory

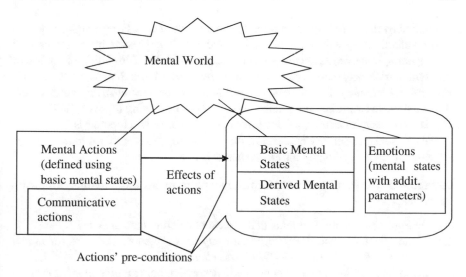

Fig. 9.1 Our ToM-oriented model of the mental world, which targets knowledge representation in a particular domain (complaint scenarios)

of mind representations of control subjects and individuals with mental disorders (Baron-Cohen 2000; Pilowsky et al. 2000). These kinds of experiments are conducted with the number of nested mental entities from one to four, confirming that the higher number causes difficulties for the majority of subjects.

In the play "Othello," Shakespeare manages to keep track of five separate mental states: he intended that his audience believes that Iago wants Othello to suppose that Desdemona loves Cassio. Being able to maintain four-five separate individuals' mental states is the natural upper limit for most adults.

Hypothesis 3 In natural language, each mental entity has a variety of meanings. There are multiple clauses defining every mental metapredicate via the other ones. The absence of such family of definitions for a mental entity means that all possible meanings are implicitly assumed. Thus the problem of disambiguation in a formal language is posed for situations where agents exchange messages in the natural language.

Definition 4 The elementary expression for a mental state or mental action is of the form

$$m_1(a_1[,a_{1'}], m_2(a_2[,a_{2'}], m_3(a_3[,a_{3'}], m_4(a_4[,a_{4'}], p))))$$

where $m_1 \dots m_4$ are the metapredicates for mental states and actions, occurring with or without negation; m_4, (m_3 and m_4), ($m_2,$ m_3 and m_4) may be absent; in accordance to Hypothesis 3, the total number of metapredicates is equal or less than four.

$a_1 \dots a_4$ are the agents from the set of all agents A, square brackets denote the variables for the second agent $a_{1'} \dots a_{4'}$ (this is the *passive* agent for the mental actions, committed by the *active* agent, denoted by the first argument). For example, an action (and resultant state) with its actor and its receiver is expressed by metapredicate *inform(Actor, Receiver, Knowledge)*, and an action with two (possibly, symmetric or anti-symmetric) receivers – by metapredicate *reconcile(Actor, Receiver1, Receiver2, MatterToSettleDown)*. Further on, we will assume that mental metapredicates are allowed to have additional arguments and will not be showing them explicitly.

p is a predicate or expression for physical action or state, Hypothesis 1.

We call such elementary expression for an arbitrary p a *mental formula*. It obeys the standard criteria of being a *well-written* formula.

Definition 5 The totality of well-formed mental formulas fell into three following categories:

(1) Interpretable mental formulas that represent existing mental states.
(2) Mental formula that always holds for any set of agents (an axiom for modal logic, e.g., *know(Who, know(Who, Knowledge)))*.
(3) Invalid mental formula that cannot be interpreted. For example, it is impossible that a person pretends about someone else's mental state *pretend(a_1, a_2, want(a_3, Something))*. The reader may object this example, suggesting that *Someone may pretend to a boring acquaintance that his partner wants him to spend the evening with her*. However, the exact meaning here is that *Someone pretends that **he believes** that his partner wants him to spend the evening with her*, so that the respective former expression is invalid and the respective latter expression is valid (interpretable). Prohibitive mental formulas are provided together with corresponding definitions.

Hypothesis 6 For any interpretable mental formula, there is a natural language entity that covers it. There is a many-to-one mapping between interpretable mental formulas and natural language mental entities. Hence natural language entities can be viewed as the classes of equivalence for mental formulas. Otherwise, there would be mental states which cannot be expressed in natural language (this would cause a new entity to appear to cover this mental state).

Hypothesis 7 There are certain syntactic constraints for the formulas describing the mental world that are sufficient to express an arbitrary multiagent scenario. A set of expressions for a mental state has two following components:

(1) Mental state fluents, characterizing instant mental states;
(2) Mental state clauses, specifying the set of consecutive mental states.

Mental state fluents are expressed with mental formulas as the following conjunction

$$\& \; m_{i1}(a_{j1}, m_{i2}(a_{j2}, m_{i3}(a_{j3}, m_{i4}(a_{j4}, p))))$$
$$i = 1..n, \, j \in A$$

where $m_{i1} \ldots m_{i4}$ are the metapredicates for mental states and actions, occurring with or without negation; m_{i4}, (m_{i3} and m_{i4}), (m_{i2}, m_{i3} and m_{i4}) may be absent;

a_{j1} ... a_{j4} are the agents from the set of all agents A;

Note that there are maximum four metapredicates in the conjunctive members above.

For example, *Peter knows that Nick does not know that Peter wants Mike to play with a toy* → *know(peter, not know(nick, want(peter, play(mike, toy)))), m_{11}= know, m_{14}= not know, a_{11}= peter, p = play(mike, toy)*.

Also, permanent mental conditions that are expected to be valid through multiple consecutive mental states are expressed via clauses. Let us denote by μ the conjunctive member above

$$\mu \equiv m_{i1}(a_{j1}, m_{i2}(a_{j2}, m_{i3}(a_{j3}, m_{i4}(a_{j4}, p)))).$$

The following expressions are interpretable mental formulas to express the continuous mental conditions

$p:-\mu_1 * ... * \mu_k$

This is a condition for physical action. Here $*$ denotes the logic programming conjunction "," or disjunction ";". Let us consider the example: *Peter would make a deposit if he knew that Nick wants him to do so: deposit(peter, fund):- know(peter, want(nick, deposit(peter, fund)))*.

$\mu(\mu_1):- \mu_2 *...* \mu_k, \mu(\mu_1:- \mu_2 * ...*\mu_k)$ and $\mu(p:- \mu_2 * ...* \mu_k)$.

For example, *Mike knows the following: Peter would make a deposit if Mike informs Peter that Nick wants Peter to make this deposit and if Peter does not want to make this deposit himself* → *know(mike, deposit(peter, fund):- inform(mike, peter, want(nick, deposit(peter, fund))), not deposit(mike, fund))*.

Note that an agent may have not only knowledge or belief that includes a causal relationship, but also intention about convincing other agents concerning a particular causal link. For example, *Mike* wants the following: *Peter would make a deposit if Mike informs Peter that Nick wants Peter to make this deposit* → *want(mike, (deposit(peter, fund):- inform(mike, peter, want(nick, deposit(peter, fund)))))*. The reader may compare the last two examples and reveal the ambiguity of the natural language expressions in terms of whether the clause is the argument of μ, or μ forms the head of a clause.

Additional considerations should be taken into account analyzing the allowed expressions for mental states: each formula μ in the expressions above (conjunctive member) is an interpretable mental formula (Hypothesis 5).

Hypothesis 8 Without loss of the spectrum of meanings for mental entities, we can merge the action and resultant mental states if they are expressed using similar mental entities (*to inform – being informed*, to pretend – being impressed by a pretending, etc.) unless it leads to contradictions or ambiguities in characterizing resultant mental states.

Hypothesis 9 We can ignore certain temporal relationships between the mental and physical states, so that the resultant scenario will stay the same. *Asynchronous* temporal relations can be reduced to a sequence. Complex *spatial* attributes of mental entities can be reduced to a sequence.

(Partial) ordering of mental states expressed by formulas $\mu_1, ..., \mu_k$ in the clause body that denotes respective consecutive (in time) mental states $\mu_1, ..., \mu_k$ is sufficient to represent temporal constraints with respect to the resultant multiagent scenario (agents' choice of actions).

9.2.2 An Example of a Definition of a Mental Action

Once an agent is capable of operating with basic mental states, it can be taught the definitions of derived mental states so that relying on these definitions, she can be involved in a more complex form of behavior than asking and answering simple questions about *who knows what* and *who wants what*. We give an example of how an automated agent can be taught to perform and recognize *deception*, the mental action that can be defined in the basis.

To achieve a *Goal*, a person *C* (cheater) selects deception if there is no easy way (such as working towards this *Goal* or asking for help) to achieve it otherwise. If there is another person *T*, the target of this deception, who can commit an action *A* wanted by *C*, and *C* believes that once *T* is informed *Deception* then *T* will commit *A*, then *C* will inform *T* about *Deception*.

deceive(C, T, Deception, Goal):-
    want(C, Goal), not Action(C, Goal),
    not ask(C, Helper, Action(Helper, Goal)),
    believe(C, not Deception),
    believe(C, (Action(T, Goal):- believe(T, Deception))),
    believe(C, not want (T, Action(T, Goal)),
    believe(C, not (believe(T, Deception)),
    inform(C, T, Deception),
    believe(T, Deception),
    perform(T, Action),
    Action(T, Goal).
Notice the additional condition which makes this definition valid:

- *C* cannot perform an *Action* to achieve the *Goal* himself;
- No-one (*Helper*) can commit an *Action* so that *Goal* is achieved;
- *C* believes that once *T* gets to believe (know) statement *Deception*, she will perform an action which results in the *Goal*;
- *C* believes *T* does not know *Deception* on her own (otherwise, there is no reason to deceive, and it will have no effect).
- *C* believes that *T* does not want *Goal* on her own; otherwise, there would be no reason to deceive).

Finally, *C* informs *T* about *Deception*. This definition covers only a successful deception where C achieves his Goal. To turn it into an unsuccessful or successful deception, the last three terms should be removed.

The reader can observe that deception can indeed be defined in the basis of *want-know-believe*. An autonomous agent does not have to have definitions for the basic mental states *want-know-believe* to learn how to perform *deceptions* as long as he is capable of operating with scenarios involving these basic mental states. We will now illustrate the above Hypotheses:

Hypothesis 1 This definition does not depend on the physical state from Deception, Goal or *Action*.

Hypothesis 2 No term in the clause has more than four embedded metapredicates.

Hypothesis 3 There are multiple meanings for deceiving (cheating, misrepresentation, concealing facts) depending on what kind of *Goal* and what are the means *Deception* to achieve it.

The formula for the entity being defined (the head of the clause above) and all defining terms (the body of the clause above) are well-written interpretable mental formulas.

Hypothesis 6 Natural language entity *deceive* covers a series of clauses where some of the terms in the defining part are omitted or added. A switch to another mental entity such as *explain* will occur if *Deception* is a true fact (remove the term *believe(C, not Deception)* from the above definition). A switch to *pretend* will also occur if we remove all terms with *Action* from the defining part and add the clause that instead of *Action C* just *wants T* to believe in her pretense.

Hypothesis 7 A fluent in deceiving will be a transition belief state where *T* is already informed *Deception* but has not perform *Action*. Also, note the subject of *C*'s belief is a clause.

Hypothesis 8 The order of states and actions should be as per the definition. In characterizing the initial mental state, the order of terms is arbitrary. Once *C* initiated the deceiving behavior, the order of mental states and actions (shown in a gray area) does matter.

9.2.3 Derived Metapredicates

After we successfully expressed as a complex concept as deceiving, we can approach the attempt to express all mental states and actions in our basis.

Hypothesis 9 The set of derived metapredicates exhaustively covers the set of verbs expressing interactions between people and their feelings. We treat in depth the entities of ToM introduced in Sect. 9.2.1.

Derived metapredicates fall into two following categories:

(1) Metapredicates for derived mental states and actions without an explicit senti-
    ments load. These are characterized in the dimensions of *knowledge* and
    intention only and can be formalized fairly well, as we have seen.

(2) Metapredicates for emotions. These are formally independent of mental
    metapredicates (1), which belong to the classes of equivalence of the above
    category of metapredicates with respect to agents' choice of action, required to
    reach one mental state from another. These metapredicate are loaded with senti-
    ments, emotions and feeling, which cannot be expressed on our basis. However,
    for the purpose of teaching, these approximations are satisfactory.

Since all our mental metapredicates allow multiple interpretations, we merge
desire as a long-term goal with *intention* as an instant goal to the metapredicate
want(Agent, Goal), where $Goal \equiv \mu_1 * \ldots * \mu_k$. It allows us to reduce the number of
well-written mental formulas for the analysis of interpretable formulas (Definition 5).
The difference between belief and knowledge is that an agent is capable of changing
and revising beliefs, but knowledge is only subject to acquisition (Fagin et al. 1996).

We can express not only mental actions for a single agent but also the mental
actions involved in a multiagent conflict in the basis of *want-know-believe*. Here we
provide just a single clause for selected mental actions, keeping in mind that multiple
clauses are expressing the meanings in various contexts of multiagent interaction
(e.g., definitions of *inform*, Hypothesis 10).

In the definitions below, the reader may notice a use of meta-programming, where
a clause occurs as an argument of a defining predicate to express a deductive link in
a general way, to cover a wide spectrum of meanings.

---

disagree(A,B,W) :- inform(A,B,W), not believe(B,W), inform(B,A, not W).
agree(A,B, W) :- inform(A,B, W), believe(B, W), inform(B,A, W).
explain(A,B, W) :- believe(A, (W :- V)), not know(B, W), inform(A,B,V),
inform(A,B,(W :- V)), believe(B,W).
confirm(A,B, W) :- inform(A,B,W), know(A, believe(B, W)).
bring_attention(A,B, W) :- want(A, believe(B, know(A, W))).
remind(A,B, W):- believe(A, believe(B, W)),
inform(A,B,W), want(A, know(B, know(A, W))).
understand(A,W) :- inform(B,A,W), believe(B, not believe(A, (W :- V))),
want(B, believe(A, (W :- V))), inform(B, A,(W :- V)),
        believe(A,(W :- V),
        believe(A, W).
accept_responsibility(A, W) :- want(B, not W), believe(B, (W:-do(A,W1))),
        want(A, know(B, believe(A, (W:-do(A,W1))))),
        inform(A,B, (W:-do(A,W1))).
expect(A, W) :- not know(A, W),believe(A, B), (believe(A, W:-believe(_, B)) or
sense(A, W)), know(A, W).
Expect something – not knowing but believing in something which might imply expectation or sensing
it.

9.2.4 Handling Multiple Meanings

Hypothesis 10 The set of available actions for agents is derived from the respective set of natural language entities. For each such entity, we obtain a spectrum of conditions to perform the denoted action based on the family of definitions for this entity in *want-know-believe* basis. From the linguistic perspective, the spectrum of meanings for an entity that denotes mental action is determined by the context of this entity (the set of other mental entities in the accompanying sentences). In our model of the mental world, there is a spectrum of clauses for each mental action such that each clause enumerates particular conditions on mental states. As an example, we present four clauses for *inform*, taking into account that there are much more clauses to form the whole spectrum for this predicate:

(1) *inform(Who, Whom, What): want(Who, know(Whom, What)), believe(Who, not know(Whom, What)),*
     believe(Who, want(Whom, know(Whom, What))).
     default *informing*

(2) *inform(Who, Whom, What): ask(Whom, Who, What),*
     want(Who, know(Whom, What)).
     informing as *answering*

(3) *inform(Who, Whom, What): ask(SomeOne, Who, believe(Whom, What)),*
     want(Who, know(Whom, What).
     following SomeOne's request for informing

(4) *inform(Who, Whom, What): believe(Who, know(Whom, What)),*
     want(Who, believe(Whom, now(Who,What))).
     to *inform Whom* that not only *Whom* but *Who knows What*

Clearly, each natural language mental entity has a number of meanings, some of them may be determined in a context. Formalizing the mental world, one needs to represent the totality of meanings, relevant in a particular domain, for each respective lexical unit. A clear-cut approach then would be, to sum up, all meanings for each participating mental entity and build a respective set of clauses. However, following this approach, we lose a very valuable information that the NL divides the totality of meanings into the classes with denotation by words. Ignoring this information would lead us to a loss of overall structure of the mental world, vigilantly reflected in NL.

If we have a pair of different definitions (clauses) for a given entity, there should be a machinery to formally express the similarity between these clauses to avoid losing important semantic cues. For example, it is hard to construct a common parameterized definition for *suggest* and *hint* in the basis of *want-know-believe*; however, totally independent clauses would be misleading (e.g., if we want to handle the case of *hint about a solution* ≡ *suggest a solution*).

It is quite natural from the formal representation viewpoint that we use the same predicate to express the totality of meanings for the same lexical entity. It should be a generic framework to express such common features. When we form a series of clauses for a mental entity, we need to take into account that there should be a common feature among the clauses for a given mental entity in natural language to distinguish these clauses from those of other mental entities in natural language. As we have verified, there is a *syntactic meta-criterion* that relates a clause to a unique mental entity. *Syntactic* here denotes the grammar of formal representation language, the clauses (not a grammar of natural language).

Hence we can define an isomorphism between the NL mental entities and the metapredicates that express the criterion of belonging to the set of clauses for the predicate that we use for this mental entity.

$$\forall \text{ NL\_mental\_entities } \forall \text{ Meaning 1, Meaning 2, Meaning 3,}\ldots \exists \text{ Meta-clause:}$$

$$
\begin{array}{c}
\nearrow \text{ Meaning 1} \rightarrow \text{Clause 1} \searrow \\
\text{NLmental\_entities } \rightarrow \text{Meaning 2} \rightarrow \text{Clause 2} \quad \rightarrow \quad \text{Meta-clause is satisfied by Clauses1,2,3} \\
\searrow \text{Meaning 3} \rightarrow \text{Clause 3} \quad \nearrow \\
\ldots
\end{array}
$$

For an example of such mapping, let us consider the set of definitions for the entity *inform*, presented above.

$$
\begin{array}{c}
\nearrow \text{ general informing} \rightarrow \text{Clause (1) above} \searrow \\
\text{inform } \overset{\rightarrow}{\rightarrow} \text{ informing as answering} \rightarrow \text{Clause (2) above} \quad \rightarrow \quad \text{Meta-clause} \\
\searrow \text{following SomeOne's request} \rightarrow \text{Clause (3)} \quad \nearrow \\
\text{for informing}
\end{array}
$$

All of these clauses include the term *want(Who, know(Whom, What))*. Let us build the meta-clause that expresses such a common feature.

inform (as lexical unit) → the set of clauses {*inform₁*:-..., ..., *informₖ*:-...} → syntactic metapredicate *Meta-clause*:

clause_For(inform, Clause): clause_list(Clause, Bodys), member(want(Who, know(Whom, What)), Bodys).

The syntactic meta-predicate *clause_For* accepts a mental entity to be expressed and a clause for it. The body of this mental predicate verifies that the clause obeys certain criteria, built to express the totality of meanings for this mental entity. We have verified that such isomorphism can be built for almost all mental entities we use in the representation of the scenarios from our dataset (Galitsky 2016).

We conclude this subsection with a brief comment on the observation of the commonality between clauses and the existence of the "covering" metapredicate ranging over clauses for the same natural language entity. If such commonality would not exist, the natural language would have a hard time expressing information about the mental world in an efficient manner. If there were a lexical unit for each meaning, it would be hard to memorize and operate with such a language. Similarly, if there were no commonality in various meanings of a given word (these meanings were not forming a cluster "around" this word), humans would have a hard time resolving the ambiguity of the natural language denotations in the real mental world. At the same time, we mention that expressing the common features in the meta-language of the logic programming language is the feature of our particular approach. Different natural languages cluster the meanings of mental entities in distinct ways; for example, the notion of *pretending* in Russian follows the logic of example in Hypothesis 6 closer than in English.

9.2.5 Representing Emotions

In this section, we continue our formalization of emotions from Chap. 3 Volume 2. Emotions are not pure logical entities; however, for the purpose of simulation of human agents, we need to formalize them. Again, our basis of *knowledge-belief-intention* comes into play to express a pre-condition for a given emotional state to appear. Most of times, approximations of emotional states in the basis are fairly distant from the real meanings of emotions and lose genuine emotional colors, but are nevertheless adequate in terms of possible agent's reaction. Based on our definitions of emotion, the agents can select an action to overcome or at least to attempt to overcome a negative emotion and retain a positive one.

Here are some definitions of emotions in our basis. For more complex cases, we present the clauses along the verbal definition of an emotion.

forgetting: a lack of a *belief* that follows its presence at some point in time.

dreaming: an *intention* of some physical or mental state to occur, having a *belief* that currently, it does not hold;

imagining: believing that something holds *knowing* that the belief is wrong;

feeling guilty: an *intention* that some action that has been committed should not has been done and *belief* that it depended on the agent's physical or mental state.

fairly treated: a belief that people think of me in a similar way I think of myself

surprised: expected one thing, but turned out to be another thing

upset(U, SomethingSad): not want(U, SomethingSad),

believe(U, not (not SomethingSad: Action(U))).

(something is unwanted and cannot be improved employing available knowledge). The same definition would be for *sad,*

jealous(J, H, SomethingNice): believe(J, state(H, SomethingNice)), want(J, SomethingNice), not state(H, SomethingNice).

(*J* is jealous if he wants the same state *SomethingNice* another agent *H* possesses, according to *J*'s belief, but she is not in this state).

unfairly treated Action1(U), Action2(F), believe(U, Action1 = Action2)), want(Authority, Action1), not want(Authority, Action2).

(An unfairly treated person believes what he did (*Action1*) is as good as *Action2* committed by someone else (*F*), but an *Authority* agent wants (likes) *F*'s action and not *U*'s action).

frightened(F, S, Unknown): believe(F, not want(F, Action(S))),

believe(F, (Action(S): ask(F, S, not Action(S))).

(*F* is frightened by *S* committing *Action* when this *Action* is unwanted and inevitable: *S* will commit it even when *F* asks *S* not to do it.)

confident: persons believes in something, and believes that other people believe that he does not believe in this.

loosing_trust(L, T, EventLostTrus): believe(L, believe(L, SaidByT):-
inform(T, L, SaidByT)), inform(T, L, EventLostTrust),
not believe(L, EventLostTrust),
believe(L, (not believe(L, SaidByTButNotBel)):-inform(T, L, SaidByTButNotBel)).

L first believe what *T* was saying (expressed as a clause), then *T* said *Event-LostTrust*, but now *L* does not believe this *EventLostTrust*, and after that *L* does not believe whatever *SaidByTButNotBel T* is saying.

In the settings of mental entities of (Cox and Ram 1999), in order to use representations of mental terms effectively, a system should consider the structure of the representation, rather than to show how to syntactically manipulate with representations or make sound inferences from them, as we do in this chapter. As an example, let is consider a treatment of the pair of predicates *forget(P, M)* and ¬ *remember(P, M)*.

Because the predicates involve memory, it is helpful to posit the existence of two contrasting sets of axioms: the background knowledge (BK), or long-term memory of the agent, P, and the foreground knowledge (FK), representing the currently conscious or active axioms of the agent. The resulting interpretation of person P forgetting memory item M is

$$forget(P, M) \rightarrow \exists M (M \in BKp) \wedge (M \notin FKp)$$

With such a representation, one can also express the proposition that the person P knows that he has forgotten something. P knows that M is in his background knowledge, but cannot retrieve it into his foreground knowledge:

$$\exists M (M \in BKp) \in FKp \wedge (M \notin FKp)$$

To include these interpretations to an agent's behavior repository is to add content to the representation, rather than simply semantics. It is part of the *metaphysical interpretation* (McCarthy 1979) of the representation that determines an ontological category (i.e., what ought to be represented), and it begins to claim that the sets BK and FK are necessary distinct. However, the meaning is not only correspondences with the world to be represented, but the meaning is also determined by the inferences a system can draw from a representation (Schank 1969). The *forget* predicate offers little in this regard. Moreover, this predicate will not assist a reasoning system in understanding what happens when it forgets some memory item, M, nor will it help the system learn to avoid forgetting the item in the future. Finally, because the semantics of a mental event that did not actually occur is not represented well by a simple negation of a predicate representing an event that did occur (Cox and Ram 1999), the logical expression ¬*Remember (John, M)* does not bring computationally sound information.

We have experimentally verified that one neither has to enumerate all possible meanings nor approach them as close as possible to teach *applicability* and *reasonability* of these emotions to human students. Our model of emotions in the mental world is adequate in terms of mental rehabilitation, but may be far from optimal for building agents that impress the audience with intelligent and emotional behavior (compare with (Scheutz 2001; Breazeal 1998; Sloman 2000)).

Formal treatment of emotions helps to compensate for our simplification of scenario description by means of predicates for actions. In addition to the above definition of emotions, we consider them as fluent (time- and situation-dependent) predicates that are the preconditions for mental actions. Also, emotions are the fluents that are affected by committed mental actions (Galitsky 2005):

poss(give_up(explain(Customer, Explanation)), Situation):-
lost_trust(Customer, Situation).

We will be using examples from the domain for customer complaints. Since complaints are a systematic extensive source of the description of complicated mental states such as conflicts, we will be using this domain as a source of examples of complex expressions in the mental world.

We will now introduce situation calculus, using an arbitrary (not necessarily mental attitudes-related) approach. Situation calculus is formulated in a first-order language with certain second-order features (Levesque et al. 1997). A possible world history that is a result of a sequence of *actions* is called *situation*. The expression, *do(a,s)*, denotes the successor situation to *s* after action *a* is applied. For example, *do(complain(Customer, do(harm(Company),S_0))),* is a situation expressing the world history that is based on the sequence of actions {*complain(Customer), harm(Company)*}, where *Customer* and *Company* are variables (with explicit meanings). We refer the reader to (Chap. 7 in Volume 2 and Levesque et al. 1997) for further details on the implementation of the situation calculus. Also, situations involve the *fluents,* whose values vary from situation to situation and denote them by predicates with the latter arguments ranging over the situations, for example,

upset(Customer, do(harm(Company),S_0)).

Actions have *preconditions* – the constraints on actions:
poss(complain(Customer), s): upset(Customer, s).

Effect axioms (post-conditions) describe the effect of a given action on the fluents:
complain(Customer) & responsive(Company) →
settle_down(Customer, do(complain(Customer), s)).

For example, an action *ignoring* leads to an emotional state (fluent) *feel unfairly treated.* In such a state, cooperative actions are unlikely for an agent, which will rather *disagree* or *bring to attention* than *agree, encourage* or *ask for advice*. Formally,

unfairly_treated(Customer,   do(ignore(CS),do(ask(Customer,replace(Product),
S_0)))).

poss(disagree(Customer,CS,SomethingNew), S): unfairly_treated(Customer, S).

To illustrate our model of interchange between emotions and mental actions, let us consider the following complaint fragment. We present the textual fragments from the actual complaint written by its author and then show how to represent it using our formal language. After that, we show how this complaint fragment can be represented by means of user-friendly form. Such kind of form is specially oriented towards the mental component of a complaint and will be discussed in further detail in the section below.

Table 9.1 Classes of emotions and their representatives (the left column) and members (the right column)

Class representative	Class members
Sad	*upset, frustrate, frustration, distress, hurt, disturb, sadden, trouble, wound, disappoint, disconcert, displease, grieve, affront, dismayed*
Anger	*indignation, rage, fury, furious, offence, infuriate, insult, hate, offend, annoyance*
Surprise	*astonish, shock, horrify, aghast*
Disgust	*sickened, disgust, revolt*
Cheat	*scam, trick, fiddle, swindle, sting, dodge*
Insulting	*derogatory, disparaging, deprecating, offensive*
Harass	*annoy, pester, bother, pursue, nuisance, stalk, hassle, worry, tease*

> *I am requesting the refund of an application fee, which I made through my credit card…*
> *I was told by Don Joe that this fee was non-refundable but I feel that I have extenuating circumstances…*
> *I am in outrage because 3 months ago I could have consolidated with my second mortgage company…*

The following three statements correspond to the sentences above. We assume that the first two sentences express mental actions, and the third sentence contains the emotion and its causal link.

$request(Customer, CS, refund(fee(application, cc)))$.

$explain(CS, Customer, not\ refund(fee(\_, \_)))$.

$upset(customer, do(explain(CS, Customer, not\ refund(fee(\_, \_)))$,

$do(request(Customer, refund(fee(application, cc))), S_0)))$.

Here the emotion is expressed as a result of two consecutive actions, one of the *Customer* and the other of *CS* (Customer Support), coming from an initial pre-complaint state S_0.

Hypothesis 11 Emotions represented via definitions in a knowledge-intention-belief basis are both preconditions and effects of mental actions.

Each class of emotions can be covered by at least a single definition in our basis, however, it is sufficient to determine an action to optimally maintain the outcome (Table 9.1).

9.3   Simulating Reasoning About the Mental States

Over the last three decades, intelligent software systems have been assisting humans in a wide range of their activities, including information seeking, shopping, education, negotiation, etc. However, a major bottleneck for the penetration of such a system into these domains is understanding the human factors involved in respective activities. A personalized software system must be capable of modeling the mental attitudes of users, including their intentions, knowledge, and beliefs. Moreover, software systems need to be competent to handle various behavior forms of users' proponents and opponents, associated with systems' functionality, such as *pretending, lying, offending,* and *forgiving.*

In this chapter, we build a generic simulation environment for reasoning about mental attitudes. We intend this environment to be integrated as a component with a behavior-prediction software in a particular domain where understanding the mental attitudes of users and/or prediction of their mental states is required (Winograd and Flores 1986; Shoham 1993; Wooldridge 2000). In particular, it is important in the domains of Internet auction, where understanding the intentions of sellers and buyers is key. A combination of the reactive and the deliberate approaches to multiagent architecture is used in this study to approximate the decision making of conflicting human agents communicating using a rather extensive vocabulary of speech acts.

Intelligent software and web services are expected to be taking into consideration multiple static human factors, including age, gender, education, location, social background, etc. (Yu et al. 2003; Li et al. 2003). In this chapter, we focus on dynamic human factors such as beliefs, and intentions of human agents, which are fairly important for a system to keep track of while assisting a user. Moreover, in addition to such mental attitudes as knowledge, belief, desire, and intention, we treat more complex mental states and actions such as *pretending, cheating, offending, forgiving, explaining,* etc. Our simulation framework is independent of the user interface or the way mental attitudes are obtained from a user; they may be extracted from the text (Galitsky 2003) or specified via a form explicitly (Galitsky 2006).

Reasoning about mental attributes and behavior patterns is an important component of human intellectual activity. Quite a few formalisms have been suggested to reproduce the peculiarities of human reasoning in the way of logical calculi. In these calculi, the laws of "mental world" are encoded via axioms, and derived theorems are expected to describe the states and actions of agents in the mental world. It has been comprehended a few decades ago that staying within the bounds of classical logic; it is hard to represent the certain phenomenology of human reasoning. Non-classical logics have enabled artificial intelligence to model reasoning of agents in time and space, in the conditions of uncertainty and inconsistency, and reasoning about the behaviors of each other. Particularly, the modal logics is quite a successful means to represent the notion of knowledge, belief and intention in connection to the other ("physical") properties of the real world (Fagin et al. 1996). However, nowadays, there is still a lack of complex real-world examples, based on a software implementation of non-classical calculi.

In recent years attention to formal modeling of various forms of human reasoning and mental behavior has strongly risen, particularly in connection with software applications in business and educational domains. A series of phenomena in human reasoning have been represented in such computational approaches as reasoning about action (Shanahan 1997), knowledge, space and time, nonmonotonic and counterfactual reasoning, etc. as well as in user modeling. Nevertheless, a generic computational framework for reasoning about mental states which is suitable for software applications is yet to be developed (Walton and Krabbe 1995; d'Inverno et al. 1998; Olivia et al. 1999; Tamma et al. 2005).

Our intention is to construct a framework to simulate human reasoning in the mental word in as detailed way as possible (compare with Shoham 1993; Sloman 2000). Building the practical systems which model the mental world (Galitsky 2003), we have been evaluating whether a pure axiomatic reasoning delivers a sufficiently rich number of theorems to adequately describe the mental states of agents. We tend to believe that a simulation-based (procedural, reactive) approach rather than a deductive reasoning-based one is suitable to express the laws of the mental world and to apply them to produce as realistic scenarios as possible for practical applications. The main goal of the desired system is *obtaining a set of consecutive mental states,* which are expected to *follow the initial mental state* that is given. We look for a solution to this problem that is as close to the natural behavior (from the annotators' viewpoint) as possible.

We have verified that the simulation approach is applicable in a variety of domain of various natures (Galitsky and Parnis 2017). In this chapter, we present in detail the implementation and evaluation of ToM Engine, analyze how the repository of behaviors affects the functionality of the simulator, and outline its application domains and integration with other reasoning and machine learning components.

To proceed from the partial cases of multiagent systems, where the reasoning-based approach proved successful, towards the generic implementation, we will attempt to address the following issues:

- Rather weak subset of commonsense laws of mental world is expressible via assertions between modalities;
- Too few theorems are deducible from the axioms for modalities as laws of the mental world to describe its phenomena in detail;
- Attempts to build a sound and complete (in logical sense) formalizations of the mental world are associated with the drop of the expressiveness of resultant language: only a subset of observed mental states can be reproduced;
- Representing mental entities as independent modalities moves the modal logic-based approach away from the natural language, which is capable of merging the multiple cohesive meanings in a single lexical unit for the mental entity;
- Implementation of reasoning as a first-order theorem proving is inefficient; also, it seems to be hard to directly take advantage of the practical limitation on the complexity of mental formulas.
- First-order logic (particularly, modal and lambda calculi) is oriented to handle certain phenomena of natural language such as quantification and especially language syntax-semantic connections (e.g., Montague grammars). At the same time, it is harder to adjust these calculi (furthermore, their model theories) to the peculiarities of ambiguity in mental natural language expressions; processing derived mental states and actions.

Analyzing these limitations, one may come to conclusions that the mental world is quite different from the physical world in terms of how the reasoning is organized. Since 1980s, a number of control architectures for practical reasoning agents have been proposed; however, most of them have been deployed only in limited artificial environments, and very few have been accepted for the field-tested applications. To mention the current applications of reasoning about knowledge, which are based on modal logic, these are communication protocols and reliability, multiagent scheduling, and temporal constraint satisfaction.

Hence the following developments to be presented in this chapter need to occur:

(1) Using a simulation of decision-making rather than representing it as a pure deduction (see, e.g., Bousquet et al. 2004);
(2) Describing the multiagent interaction, ascend from the level of atomic actions of agents to the level of behaviors;
(3) Limiting the complexity of mental formulas;
(4) Following closer the natural language in describing the mental world, using a wide range of entities (this has been explored with respect to acceptance by a multiagent community by (Lara and Alfonseca 2000));
(5) Taking advantage of approximation machinery. We express an arbitrary mental entity through the basis *knowledge-belief-intention* (*informing, deceiving, pretending, reconciling*, etc., Galitsky 2006);
(6) Using a hybrid reasoning system *combining* simulation of decision-making with the set of typical behaviors specified as axioms;
(7) Increasing the *expressiveness* of representation language by means of using an extensive set of formalized mental entities beyond *belief* and *desire*.

9.4 Implementation of Simulation

Decision-making of agents in our settings is primarily concerned with the choice of actions to achieve desired states. Generally speaking, agents have immediate and long-term goals of mental and physical states, and sometimes explicit intentions of actions.

9.4.1 Choosing the Best Action Taking into Account Yourself Only

Let us first consider an action selection algorithm in a trivial case, where an agent does not consider the possible actions of others. Of particular importance to our interests are systems that allow agents to learn about and model their *own* teammates and then use that knowledge to improve collaboration. (Kaminka and Frenkel 2005) present a technique that allows one agent (a coach) to predict the future behavior of other agents (its own team and the opponent team) in order to coordinate activities by observing those agents and building a model of their behavior. Observations are translated into a time series of recognized atomic behaviors, and these into the subsequences that characterize a team (although not necessarily a single agent). (Kaminka and Tambe

2000) investigated just how much monitoring of another agent is sufficient for an agent to be an effective teammate.

To choose the best action, each agent considers each action it can currently perform (Fig. 9.2). Firstly, each agent selects a set of actions it can legally perform at the current step (physically available for the agents, acceptable in terms of the norms, etc.). Such an action may be explicitly wanted or not; also, this action may belong to a sequence of actions in accordance with a form of behavior that has been chosen at a previous step or is about to be chosen. In the former case, the agent may resume the chosen behavior form or abort it.

Having a set of actions that are legal to be currently performed, the agent applies a preference relation. This relation is defined on states and actions and sets the following order (1 is preferred over 2–5, 2 is preferred over 3–5, etc.):

1. Explicitly preferred (wanted) action.
2. The action that leads to the desired state that is not current.
3. Action that eliminates an unwanted state that is current.
4. Action that does not lead to an unwanted state that is not current.
5. Action that does not eliminate a wanted state that is current.

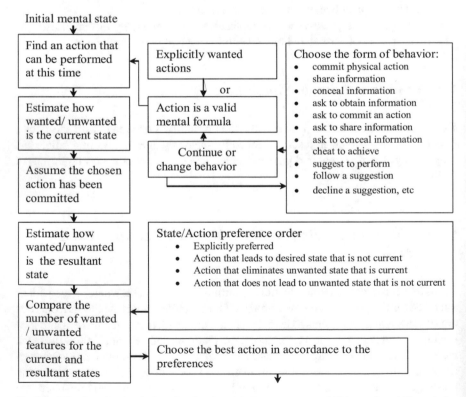

Fig. 9.2 The chart for the choice of action, involving own agent capabilities and world knowledge (simplified case)

In our representation language the sequence of preference conditions is as follows:
```
Want (A, ChosenAction),
want (A, State), not State, assume(ChosenAction),
State,
want (A, not State), State, assume(ChosenAction), not
State,
not (want(not State), not State, assume(ChosenAction),
State),
not (want(State), State, assume(ChosenAction), not
State).
```
Agent's actions to select from can be atomic or compound. A compound action that includes a mutually-dependent typical sequence of actions is called a *behavior* (Sect. 9.4.3). A compound action of a given agent may include actions of other agents and various intermediate states, some of which the agent may want to avoid. The agent decides either to perform the action delivering the least unwanted state or action of another agent, or to do nothing. If there are multiple possible actions that do not lead, in the agent's belief, to unwanted consequences, this agent either chooses the explicitly preferred action, if there is an explicit preference predicate or the action whose choice involves the least consideration of the beliefs of other agents.

Hence the agent A has an initial intention concerning a `ChosenAction` or `State`, assesses whether this condition currently holds, then selects the preferred `ChosenAction`, assumes that it has been executed, deduces the consequences, and finally analyses whether they are preferential. The preference, parameters of agents' attitudes, and multiagent interactions may vary from scenario to scenario and can be specified via a form.

Before an action can be assumed, ToM Engine needs to check that a potential action is a valid mental formula (Sect. 9.4.2). A valid mental formula is neither an axiom (such as *an agent knows what it knows*) nor implausible formula (such as literally viewing *someone else's mental state*).

A resultant state comprises one or more explicitly wanted or unwanted states; the agent performs the comparative analysis of preferences on a state-by-state basis. Figure 9.3 presents an algorithm for the search of the most favorable action as a simple logic program for the case of a single agent.

Hence in the simplified model, without simulating the decision-making of others, the agent performs the exhaustive search through all currently legal actions for all possible consequences. For each such action, the agent assumes he has executed it and estimates the consequences.

```
chooseAction(Agent,ChosenActions):-
 % generates the set of available actions and chose those leading to acceptable states
 findall( PossibleAction, ( % finds all objects satisfying conditions below
    availableAction(Agent, PossibleAction),
        % choosing (forming) a behavior
    assume(PossibleAction), % assume that the selected action is performed
    acceptableState(Agent),
 % To verify that the state to be achieved is acceptable (not worse than the current state)
        clean_assume(PossibleAction), % cleans the assumptions
    ), AccumulatedPossibleActions),
 chooseBestActions(AccumulatedPossibleActions, ChosenActions). % choosing
the best action in accordance to the preference relation on the set of accessible states
```

Fig. 9.3 The single-agent algorithm for search of the most favorable action. Comments to the code (currier font) start with '%'

9.4.2   Choosing the Best Action Considering an Action Selection by Others

We start with the premise that humans use themselves as an approximate, initial model of their teammates and opponents. Therefore, we based the simulation of the teammate's decision making on the agent's own knowledge of the situation and its decision process. To predict the teammate's choice of actions in a collaborative strategy, we model the human as following the self-centered strategy. The result of the simulation is made available to the base model by inserting the result into the "imaginary" buffer of possible opponents' actions. The availability of the results of the mental simulation facilitates the agent's completion of its own decision making. The effect is that the agent yields to what it believes is the human's choice. While this simple model of teamwork allows us to demonstrate the concept and the implementation of the simulation of the teammate, we proceed to the simulation mode, which uses the collaborative strategy recursively.

The high-level algorithm for the choice of a most favorable action (Fig. 9.4), taking into account the decision-making of the opponents, is presented below as a logic program (Fig. 9.5). Note that in addition to Fig. 9.3, we have the predicate
assumeOtherAgents(Agent, OthersActions) which is preceded by the predicate
involveKnowledgeOfOthers(Agent): the agent's perspective of knowledge and intentions of its opponents needs to be invoked before this agent simulates the choice of the most favorable actions by each of these opponents.

9.4.3   The Repository of Behaviors

We have discovered that the totality of mental entities can be expressed in the basis *want- know-believe* (Galitsky 2003). The clauses for pre-conditions of behaviors (as aggregated mental actions) we define in this section indeed contain these

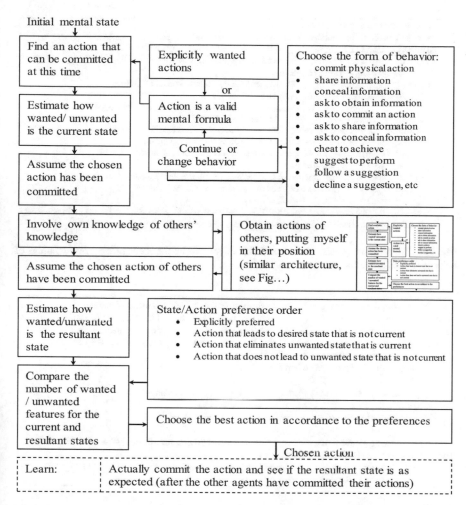

Fig. 9.4 The chart for the choice of action involving the simulation of the choice of action by other agents. The model of learning within our framework is depicted on the bottom by dotted lines

predicates. The head of each clause is the predicate `generateAction(Agent, GeneratedAction, History)`, which returns the second argument.

We present the clauses for behaviors in detail to introduce a flavor of how to define mental entities in the basis of *want- know-believe* in a procedural manner, based on the current mental state and the history of mental actions `History`. Note that we take strong advantage of meta-programming to express a wider set of meanings and to achieve a higher level of abstraction. For brevity, we merge know and believe in the clauses below most of times.

```
chooseAction(Agent,ChosenActions, History):-
% generates the set of available actions and chose those leading to acceptable states
findall( PossibleAction, ( % finds all objects satisfying conditions below
availableAction(Agent, PossibleAction, History),
        % choosing (forming) a behavior
assume(PossibleAction), % assume that the selected action is performed
involveKnowledgeOfOthers(Agent),
              %substitutes own knowledge by own knowledge of others' knowledge
   assumeOtherAgents(Agent, OthersActions),
   % Similar assumption concerning others' actions. They are obtained based on the
   % acceptable states of the others from the viewpoint of the given agent.
   % Here the agent thinks for its opponents what would they do to achieve their goals
     acceptableState(Agent),
% To verify that the state to be achieved is acceptable (not worse than the current state)
       clean_assume(PossibleAction), % cleans the assumptions
   ), AccumulatedPossibleActions),
   chooseBestActions(AccumulatedPossibleActions, ChosenActions). % choosing
the best action in accordance to the preference relation on the set of accessible states
```

Fig. 9.5 The predicate *available Action* (bold above) will be the focus of our considerations of behavior forms in the following section

```
    We start with the clause to generate a physical action that is included in agent's intention. It may be a
potential action of another agent, which is selected by a given agent. The clause finds  a subformula of
intention    so    that    its    argument    is    ranges    over    physical    objects    (not    actions).
generateAction(Agent, ActionFull, _):- want(Agent, StateORAction),
      expand(StateORAction, SOAs) !],
   % getting a list of all subterms of a term
     member(PhysFull, SOAs),
     PhysFull=..[PhysAct,WhoWhat, Object|_], % a phys action
     argrep(PhysFull, 1, Agent, ActionFull).
   % substitution of itself instead   of another agent into selected action

   %The following clause forms an own action for an agent that causes desired state of another agent
generateAction(Agent, MyAction, _):-
     want(Agent, State),(clause(State, MyAction);
     know(Agent, (State:- MyAction) )),
```

```
        State=..[_,OthAg|_],OthAg\=Agent,
        MyAction=..[_, Agent|_],
        not want(Agent, not MyAction), % it is not an unwanted action
        not know(Agent, not MyAction). % this action is not known as impossible
```

We proceed to the generic clause for *inform*

```
generateAction(Agent,
  inform(Agent, Addressee, Smth),_):-
    know(Agent,want(Addressee, know(Addressee, Smth)));
  want(Agent, know(Addressee, Smth)).
```

If an agent is being informed, it should possibly add a belief (reaction to being informed)

```
generateAction(Agent, assert(believe(Agent, Smth)),
    History):- % has been informed at a previous step
  prevStep(inform(AgentInform, Agent, Fact), History),
  not believe(Agent, not Smth),
  not know(Agent, not Smth),
  not believe(Agent, not trust(Agent, Smth)).
```

The following clause specifies how an agent forms mistrust when it discovers that it is being informed a lie

```
generateAction(Agent,
  believe(Agent, not trust(Agent, Smth)), History):-
  prevStep(inform(AgentInform, Agent, Fact),
   History),
  %checking if it's a previous action
  member( FactOp , LastHistory),opposite(Fact, FactOp).
```

The clause clarifying when to ask with the intention to gain knowledge and possibly believe that someone knows looks like

```
generateAction(Agent, ask(Agent, InformAgent, Smth),
_):-
  [!((want(Agent, know(Agent, Smth)), believe(Agent,
  know(InformAgent, Smth)),
  nonvar(Smth) ); ( want(Agent, know(Agent, Smth)),
  nonvar(Smth) )),
  ifthen(var(InformAgent), (allAgents(Ags),
  member(InformAgent, Ags))) !].
```

The clause introduces the conditions for when to answer: history includes asking, an agent answers if it knows and/or wants addressee to know; believe/know options are considered

```
generateAction(Agent, ActionFull, History):-
  prevStep(ask(AgentAsk, Agent, Smth), LastHistory), (
  (believe(Agent, Smth),
  want(Agent, know(AskAgent, Smth)),
  ActionFull= answer(Agent, AgentAsk,
    believe(Agent,Smth)) );
  (believe(Agent, not Smth),
  want(Agent, know(AskAgent, Smth)),
  ActionFull= answer(Agent, AgentAsk, believe(Agent,
  not Smth)) );
  ( (know(Agent, SmthRelevant);
  believe(Agent, SmthRelevant)),
  expand(SmthRelevant, SmthRE), member(Smth, SmthRE),
```

```
     ActionFull= answer(Agent, AgentAsk, SmthRelevant) )).
```

We proceed to the clause for generation of a suggestion. If an agent wants someone's action and does not have a belief that this agent does not want to perform that action then that action is suggested.

```
generateAction(Agent,
     suggest(Agent, OtherAg, OtherAgAction), History):-
  want(Agent, OtherAgAction),
  OtherAgAction=..[Action, OtherAg|_],
  not believe(Agent,
     not want(OtherAg,   OtherAgAction)),
  not member(Action, [know, believe, want] ),
  Agent\=OtherAg, allAgents(Ags), member(OtherAg, Ags).
```

If an agent is being suggested something, the following clause specify the conditions to follow these suggestions

```
generateAction(Agent, Smth, History):-
  prevStep(suggest(AgentAsk, Agent, Smth),History),
  ( (Smth=..[Action, Agent|_]);
  ( (Smth=(not NSmth)), NSmth=..[Action, Agent|_])),
  Agent\=AgentAsk.
```

The following clause is applicable to the agent which is going to try not to share information to / to conceal from/ to suggest not to not inform another agent

```
generateAction(Agent, ActionFull, _) :-
  want(Agent, not OtherAgAction),
     OtherAgAction=..[_, OtherAg|_],
  (believe(Agent, believe(ThirdAgent,
     OtherAgActionCondition));
  know(ThirdAgent, OtherAgActionCondition)),
  Agent\=OtherAg, Agent\=ThirdAgent,
     ThirdAgent \= OtherAg,
  ifthen((know(Agent, (
  OtherAgAction:-
     believe(OtherAg,OtherAgActionCondition)));
     clause(OtherAgAction,
     believe(OtherAg, OtherAgActionCondition));
       ),
  ActionFull=suggest(Agent, ThirdAgent,
  not inform(ThirdAgent, OtherAg,
                     OtherAgActionCondition))),
  ifthen(( know(Agent, (OtherAgAction:-
     believe(OtherAg, not OtherAgActionCondition)));
  clause(OtherAgAction, believe(OtherAg, not OtherAgActionCondition));
  believe(Agent, (OtherAgAction:-
         believe(OtherAg, not OtherAgActionCondition)))
       ),
  ActionFull=suggest(Agent, ThirdAgent,
  inform(ThirdAgent, OtherAg,
                     not OtherAgActionCondition))).
```

We proceed to the clause for intentional cheating/informing to make someone perform desired action

```
generateAction(Agent, ActionFull, _):-
  want(Agent, OtherAgAction),
```

```
OtherAgAction=..[_, OtherAg|_], 0
(know(Agent, (OtherAgAction:-
     believe(OtherAg, OtherAgActionCondition))));
clause(OtherAgAction,
know(OtherAg, OtherAgActionCondition));
know(Agent, (OtherAgAction:-
               know(OtherAg, OtherAgActionCondition)))),
Agent\=OtherAg,
ifthenelse( ( know(Agent,
                  not want(OtherAg, OtherAgAction));
believe(Agent, not OtherAgActionCondition) ),
(ActionFull=..
[cheat, Agent, OtherAg, OtherAgActionCondition];
ActionFull=..[inform, Agent, OtherAg, OtherAgActionCondition])).
```

The diagram Fig. 9.6 depicts relations between mental actions. *Suggesting* is a partial case of *asking*, *asking* and *suggesting* may have a goal to *initiate_action*. *Cheating* is a partial case of *informing* with untruthful information, which may or may not have a goal of initiating an opponent's action. Both *informing* and *cheating* may form *responding*, all these mental actions may serve the purpose of *initiate_action*. *Committing a physical action* may also be *following advice*.

As to the causal links, usually *asking* and sometimes *informing* causes *responding*, *suggesting* may cause *following* it (*follow_advice*), cheating and initiation of action may cause *committing of this* (*physical*) *action*.

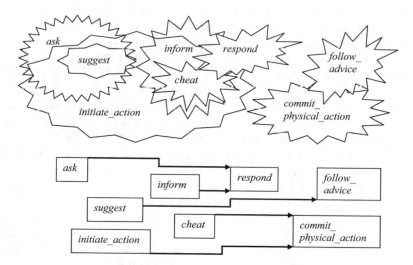

Fig. 9.6 The relations between the behaviors

9.5   Evaluation of the ToM Engine

In this section, we assess the performance of the ToM Engine.

A practical commonsense reasoning system such as ToM Engine can be characterized in terms of the following parameters:

(1) *Correctness.* To evaluate the correctness of the ToM Engine, we compare the scenarios built by ToM Engine with those built by human experts. The adequacy of a reasoning system like ToM Engine to the real mental world can be evaluated by means of a representation of a set of scenarios of multiagent interaction (focused on mental attitudes) collected from a variety of domains.

(2) The *coverage* of possible behaviors. To evaluate the *coverage* of real-world scenarios, we collect the dataset from various domains. For this dataset, we verify that ToM Engine's reasoning can link the initial mental state, mentioned in a scenario from this dataset, with the final mental state from that scenario. The link is implemented via the repository of behaviors; and our evaluation of coverage is indeed an estimate of how the encoded set of behaviors covers the totality of real-world scenarios with respect to the resultant mental states.

(3) Scenario *complexity.* To evaluate the highest *complexity* of scenarios the ToM Engine can handle, we vary the *number* of behaviors of various agents combined in a single scenario. Maximum complexity is the number of behaviors such that the correctness of obtained scenarios dramatically falls when this number is incremented. In other words, if a scenario complexity exceeds this number, there is a significant deviation of scenarios generated by the ToM Engine from those natural for human experts, given the same initial mental states.

(4) The *expressiveness* of representation language. Evaluating the expressiveness of representation language, we are concerned with the information lost when scenario representation is converted from the natural to the formal language. The importance of the lost information is estimated taking into account the caused deviation of resultant mental states. The information is usually lost because the number of meanings of mental entities explicitly represented as behaviors are obviously lower than the respective number of meanings in a natural language description of a scenario of inter-human interactions. Our evaluation of the expressiveness of representation language is tightly connected with natural language information extraction focused on mental entities presented in (Galitsky and Kuznetsov 2008). We will not conduct the evaluation of expressiveness in this book but mention that the ToM Engine's vocabulary includes a generic template for physical actions and a rather extensive set of lexical units and synonyms for the common-usage mental attributes.

For the purpose of estimating the parameters (1)–(3) above, we form two following datasets of textual scenarios to be represented by the ToM Engine:

(a) The scenarios that were suggested to illustrate certain peculiarities of reasoning about the mental world (frame problems, defaults, circumscription, argumentation, belief updates, reasoning about knowledge, time and space, reasoning in legal, educational, medical domains, etc.). Seventy-two such scenarios have been collected over the duration of ToM Engine project (over 7 years). There are no special criteria for inclusion to this dataset except that the mental states and actions should be explicitly mentioned.

(b) The uniform set of multiagent conflict scenarios (textual complaints) was obtained and subject to manual formal representation from the public complaint database (e.g., PlanetFeedback.com). Complaints describe the interaction between a complainant and company representatives; these conflicting scenarios are mostly occurring in a mental space. Fifty-eight banking complaints have been obtained and converted into formal representation (Galitsky and Kuznetsov 2008) to serve as the evaluation dataset. Complaint selection was random in terms of content: all banking complaints submitted within a month that describe at least four steps of interactions (pairs of communicative actions) between the involved parties.

The role of the dataset (a), which is fairly diverse, is to compare the performance of ToM Engine with other systems in mental as well as non-mental reasoning. Also, most of the scenarios from this dataset are accompanied by their formal representations. This dataset is used as a basis to estimate the correctness and coverage by behaviors since existing formal representations allows unambiguous comparison of the original and ToM Engine-based representations.

We use the dataset (b) of customer complaints to estimate the coverage with higher accuracy than the former dataset and to estimate scenario complexity since a high number of scenarios for each complexity are available. Since we used a super-set of the dataset (b) to evaluate our scenario learning framework for communicative actions only (Chap. 1 Volume 2), we also use it for correctness evaluation based on a specific class of plausible and implausible scenarios. ToM Engine is expected to build plausible (valid) scenarios only and not build implausible (invalid) scenarios.

Although ToM Engine is a prediction system, we evaluate the plausibility of results rather than prediction accuracy: the real mental world is too rich and diverse to be predictable in terms of the proposed model. Although the precision can be satisfactory, the recall of ToM Engine is really low. We expect the ToM Engine to yield at least a single plausible scenario of multiagent interaction; we do not target yielding the totality of possible resultant mental states.

9.5.1   Evaluation of Precision

We used the dataset (a) above formed by compiling examples found in the logical AI literature to evaluate the correctness. For each formalized scenario, the ToM Engine was fed with the initial mental state (explicitly mentioned in these scenarios). We verified whether the ToM Engine can yield the sequence of further mental states from this scenario. If a given scenario required adding a new form of behavior, the respective clause for this behavior was added.

The results of the precision evaluation are shown in Table 9.2. The first column presents the origin of a scenario, and the second column contains a number of scenarios for each group. The third column shows the number of scenarios of each origin, where it is necessary to add a clause for a new behavior or alter an existing clause, given the behavior repository before this evaluation. The fourth column enumerates some of the behaviors for each group of scenarios that have to be added to reproduce them. We observed that the scenarios requiring a modification of the behavior repository constitute 43% of the total number of scenarios. Finally, the fifth column presents the number of scenarios for each group that allowed correct representation (with or without a modification). We observed that 75% of the total number of scenarios was subject to correct representations. In the other 25% of cases, either

Table 9.2 Evaluation of precision

Origin of a scenario: reasoning domain	Number of scenarios	Number of scenarios where new behavior has to be added	Required additional forms of behavior (selected examples)	Number of scenarios where the correct representation was achieved
Modal logic, BDI model (e.g., Wooldridge 2000)	15	6	Changing mind, giving up, advising others to give up	11
Reasoning about action (e.g., Reiter 1993)	16	12	Change action parameters	13
Default reasoning (e.g., Gabbay 1999)	18	6	Changing mind	12
Argumentation (e.g., Weigand and de Moor 2004)	13	4	Defeating the previous statement, breaking a loop in actions, threaten	9
Other multiagent models (negotiation, auction, coalition formation, assistance (e.g., Olivia et al. 1999)	10	3	Agree, disagree, confirm, deny	9
Total	72	31 (43%)		54 (75%)

the underlying reasoning was too complex, or initial mental states were lacking the information necessary to correctly derive consecutive mental states.

In addition to the above evaluation, we observe that in most cases, the agents' behavior that is generated by the ToM Engine is perceived by its users and assessors as a sequence of natural and expected choices. If this is not the case, the ToM Engine backs its scenario up by providing the motivation and the protocol of exhaustive search through the lists of the available actions at each step. A user might disagree with the selected form of behavior, but she will at least understand the motivations. Furthermore, handling a manifold of meanings caused by the necessity to represent NL input increases system flexibility and makes it closer to the real world in imitation of human reasoning and human behavior.

9.5.2   Evaluation of Completeness

As a result of the evaluation of correctness, the behavior repository has been extended (trained) to accommodate atypical behaviors from the dataset (a). Evaluating the completeness, we assess how frequent an occurrence of each behavior form is in the complaint dataset (b), which did not participate in the training of the behavior forms. In this section, we conduct the evaluation of the accumulated behavior repository and an overall system performance.

We observed that the trained behaviors adequately cover the test domain (Table 9.3). All clauses for behaviors that were obtained in the domain of randomly accumulated scenarios were employed in forming the sequence of consecutive mental states in the test domain. Conversely, to explain a rational multiagent behavior of proponents and opponents in complaint scenarios in 81% of cases, it is sufficient to use accumulated clauses for behaviors. The remaining 19% of complaint scenarios the ToM Engine failed to reproduce, relying on the accumulated repository of behaviors and its simulation machinery. Each scenario contains on average 3.2 forms of behavior in the training dataset and 4.3 forms of behavior in the test dataset.

Clearly, formal descriptions of the behavior of complainants and their opponents in more detail would benefit from additional complaint-specific behavior patterns. However, we observed that increasing the complexity of the formal descriptions of textual scenarios does not make them more consistent because the majority of intermediate mental states are not explicitly mentioned. Hence we come to the conclusion that the formed repository of behaviors is sufficient to provide an adequate (most consistent) description of multiagent interactions between a complainant and his opponents. And since the customer complaints domain is a source of fairly complex examples of conflicts in the mental world, we can expect the ToM Engine to satisfactorily perform in other, simpler domains.

Note that our evaluation is by no means intended to predict the behavior of scenario agents; instead, we try to include all necessary information in the initial mental state so that the scenario is generated as a respective sequence. The problem of predicting the consecutive mental states under a lack of information is posed differently (Chap. 7

Table 9.3 An evaluation of the behavioral completeness of scenarios. Note that a particular behavior form may occur in a scenario more than once. The bottom row depicts the number of cases that require a modification of the behavior repository

Form of behavior	Training, 72 scenarios from logical AI literature		Test, 58 complaint scenarios	
	# of scenarios	% of scenarios	# of scenarios	% of scenarios
Perform own physical action	70	97	57	98
Achieving the desired state of another agent	21	28	29	50
Informing	14	19	23	40
Updating belief while being informed	5	7	17	29
Forming mistrust	7	9	32	55
Asking to gain knowledge	29	39	19	33
Answering	18	24	14	24
Generating suggestion	26	35	21	36
Following suggestion	14	19	18	31
Avoiding sharing/suggesting not to inform	12	16	13	22
Cheating to achieve an action	17	23	5	9
New forms of behavior	–	–	**14**	**19**

of Volume 2 and Galitsky 2006) and requires machine learning and reasoning about actions (Galitsky et al. 2009) components in addition to ToM Engine.

9.5.3   Evaluation of Complexity

The complexity of scenarios the ToM Engine can handle significantly exceeds that of the textual information on mental attributes of human and automatic agents comprehensible by a user. We observe that the ToM Engine's performance is much higher than the humans' performance in spite of the fact that reasoning about mental states is a natural and frequent task for a human user. To characterize the computational tractability of the suggested approach, we take into account that at each step, the ToM Engine considers about 30 available behavior forms for each agent.

In the process of multiagent communication and while behavior decision-making, the ToM Engine analyses the formulas of complexity (the number of nested mental predicates) below four. For the totality of all well-written mental formulas, the system recognizes whether a formula is an axiom, meaningful, or meaningless expression (Galitsky and Kuznetsov 2008). For an arbitrary set of such formulas as an initial condition for the ToM Engine, it either finds a contradiction or synthesizes the scenario of multiagent behavior.

Table 9.4 Estimating the maximum complexity of scenarios for ToM Engine: number of behavior forms

Number of behavior forms per scenario	Correctness of scenario representation, %
2	85
3	80
4	75
5	50
6	35

We used the dataset (b) of formalized complaints and its extension by longer scenarios to estimate how the correctness of representations depends on scenario complexity, measured as a number of behavior forms. We observed that the maximum complexity of the scenarios ToM Engine can handle reliably is 4 behavior forms. Exceeding this number, the correctness of generated scenarios falls to as low as 52% for 5 behavior forms and to just 34% for six behavior forms. The results show that when a scenario contains 5–6 behaviors, the ToM Engine is frequently unable to represent its last one-two mental states towards the end. Instead, it significantly deviates from what an expert would think of a natural behavior of participating agents (Table 9.4).

To analyze how nested expressions for mental states and actions are represented by the ToM Engine, we assessed the correctness of scenarios representation grouping scenarios by the *maximum number of nested mental actions or states in a scenario* (Table 9.5). One can see an abrupt drop in the correctness of scenario representation when the complexity of nested expressions exceeds four.

As to the expressiveness of ToM Engine's representation language, one can estimate its sensitivity to a deviation of meanings of mental entities presenting initial conditions. We formulate the sensitivity statement for the ToM Engine as follows:

Sensitivity Hypothesis. For any two mental formulas μ and μ' for respective entities specifying initial mental states, there exist two initial mental states of s and s' yielding different scenarios. $\mu \in s$ and $\mu' \in s'$ are such that the simulator forms distinct multiagent scenarios $s \rightarrow s_1,...,s_n$ and $s' \rightarrow s_1',...,s_k'$. Therefore, the ToM

Table 9.5 Estimating the maximum complexity of scenarios for ToM Engine: number of behavior forms

Maximum number of nested mental actions or states in a scenario	Correctness of scenario representation, %
1	85
2	75
3	80
4	60
5	30
6	25

Engine is capable of taking into account the difference between any two mental formulas (or two distinct mental entities) while building a sequence of mental states.

The conclusion of our assessment is that the ToM Engine is suitable for assistance with predictions of human behavior for CRM.

9.6 Introduction to Meta-Reasoning and Introspection of ToM Engine

The meaning of the term "meta-reasoning" is "reasoning about reasoning." In a computer system, this means that the system is able to reason about its own operation. This is different from performing object-level reasoning, which refers in some way to entities external to the system. A system capable of meta-reasoning may be able to reflect, or introspect, that is, to shift from meta-reasoning to object-level reasoning and vice versa.

The organization of knowledge in a metalevel architecture has been widely used for representation purposes in a ToM system. Its use has mainly been in the control of deduction: meta-knowledge allows one to drive the search of a solution and to improve its efficiency by applying heuristic strategies. More generally, a metalevel architecture has been used to implement introspective systems (Batali 1983; Maes and Nardi 1988), which can modify their own behavior by analyzing their status, and accessing their own representation. A metalevel architecture enables the construction of the ToM engine where such different issues can be dealt with in a unified framework (Giunchiglia and Weyhrauch 1988). In a metalevel architecture, an agent is represented as a meta-theory and a set of base-level (or object-level) theories, which represent the agent's own knowledge, and, possibly, other agent's knowledge. In the meta-theory, it is possible to assert facts about the object-level theories, and make deductions in the basis of knowledge represented in them. This requires the definition of symbols that represent, in the metatheory, the objects of the theories.

In logic, a language that takes sentences of another language as its objects of discourse is called a meta-language. The other language is called the object language. A clear separation between the object language and the meta-language is necessary: namely, it consists in the fact that sentences written in the metalanguage can refer to sentences written in the object language only by means of some kind of description, or encoding, so that sentences written in the object language are treated as data. As it is well-known, (Gödel 1940) developed a technique (gödelization) for coding the formulas of the theory of arithmetic by means of numbers (gödel numbers). It became possible to write formulas for manipulating other formulas, the latter represented by the corresponding gödel numbers.

Meta-predicate is used to make similarity more general, unify similarity of numerical functions, and similarity of logical descriptions. For certain objects, if their similarity cannot be expressed in the language-object, one needs to consider the possibility that it can be expressed in meta-language.

Syntactic meta-programming can be particularly useful for theorem proving. Many lemmas and theorems in mathematics are actually meta-theorems, asserting the validity of a fact by simply looking at its syntactic structure. In this case, a software component, namely the theorem prover, consists of two different parts: one, that we call the object level, where proofs are performed by repeatedly applying the inference rules; another one, that we call the metalevel, where meta-theorems are stated.

The theorem prover at the object level performs *object-level reasoning*. Meta-theorems take as arguments the description of object-level formulas and theorems, and metalevel proofs manipulate these descriptions. Then, at the metalevel, the system performs reasoning about entities that are internal to the system, as opposed to object-level reasoning that concerns entities denoting elements of some external domain. This is why we say that at the metalevel, the theorem prover performs *meta-reasoning*.

A natural language is represented by a logical language at two levels. The object-level is the level of semantics. The metalevel is the level of discourse (Galitsky 2020). Discourse meta-expressions such as rhetorical relations take as arguments the descriptions of the description of object-level, semantic formulas.

rhetorical_relations (semantic_representation (EDU1), rhetorical_relations (semantic_representation (EDU2)),

where *rhetorical_relations* is a meta-predicate whose arguments range over semantic expressions *semantic_representation (EDU1)], EDU1* – is a fragment of text called elementary discourse unit.

Metalevel rules, such as the discourse rule of text organization, manipulate a representation of object-level knowledge, such as chunks of semantic knowledge. Since semantic knowledge is represented in some kind of language such as FOL, meta-rules of discourse actually manipulate a representation of syntactic expressions of the object-level semantic representation language (not the NL syntax).

We start with a simple example of object-level and metalanguage for NL syntax. In analogy with NL, a metalevel representation is usually called the *name* of the syntactic expression. The difference between a word of the language, such as *dog*, and a name *_dog_*, is the following: the word is used to denote an entity of the domain or an attribute we are talking about. On the contrary, a name denotes the word as a symbol, so that we can say that *_dog_* is composed of three characters, is expressed in English, and its translation into Russian is "собака." That is, a word can be used, while a name can be inspected (for instance, to count the characters) and manipulated (for instance, translated).

Once a semantic representation is set as a language-object, the metalevel discourse operates with the names of predicates, its arguments, and values to express the rules for how a text chunk can be manipulated and a text can be logically organized. This manipulation is implemented as a theory of discourse. In a logic meta-language, we may have names for variables, constants, function and predicate symbols, terms and atoms, and even for entire theories: the metalevel may in principle encode and reason about the description of several object-level theories.

The idea that meta-knowledge and meta-reasoning could be useful for improving the reasoning performed at the semantic (object) level suggests that the object and the metalevel should interact. In fact, semantic and discourse levels can be seen as different components that interact by passing the control to each other.

At the object level, the operation of *referentiation* allows a semantic expression to be transformed into its name and this name can be given as an input argument to a discourse component. This means that object-level computation gives place to metalevel computation. This computational step is called *introspection*, or shift up because the metalevel is considered to be a "higher level" with respect to the object level. It is called introspection, because the semantic component suspends its activity in order to initiate a metalevel discourse one. This is meant to be in analogy with the process by which people become conscious (at the metalevel of mind) of mental states they are currently in (at the object level). Composing texts, human writers switch from the local content (semantics) to the global text organization and back.

The inverse action, that consists in going back to the object-level activity, is called *downward reflection*. The object-level activity can be resumed from where it had been suspended or can be somehow restarted when the author returns from overall content planning to writing individual thoughts. The semantic "state" (of enumerating facts or implications) can be the same as before, or can be altered, according to the metalevel activity that has been performed. Downward reflection may imply that some names of semantic objects are dereferenced, and the resulting expressions ("extracted" from the name) are given as input arguments to the resumed or restarted object-level activity. For example, at the discourse level, it is determined that there is a good time to introduce a new entity E. Now, as a result of downward reflection, E is going to be presented at the semantic level.

For specific types of documents, upward and downward reflection can be set by rules on how to organize a document and what kind of content each section should contain. For example, for writing a resume, such rules specify an organization of section, a structure of each section (discourse levels), and a recommended specificity of information (semantic level, date-role-organization-address). In a logical system, upward and downward reflection can be specified by means of special inference rules (reflection rules) or axioms (reflection axioms), which may additionally restrict what kind of information is exchanged.

9.6.1 Meta-Interpreter of NL

We introduce a predicate *express* defined by a set of meta-axioms Pr, where the relevant aspects of Horn-clauses provability are made explicit. The predicate *express* takes as first argument the representation (name) of an object-level semantic theory AMR and the representation (name) of a goal A. express("AMR," "A") means that the goal A is expressible (provable) in theory AMR.

An inference about knowledge expressed in a text can be performed at the metalevel of discourse (via invocation of *express*), and the AMR object level is simulated, by providing *express* with a suitable description "AMR" of a semantic knowledge representation theory AMR.

The rules for upward and downward reflection are as follows:

$$T \mid\!\!\!-_{AMR} A$$

$$Pr \mid\!\!\!-_{RST} express("AMR","A")$$

$$Pr \mid\!\!\!-_{RST} express("AMR","A")$$

$$T \mid\!\!\!-_{AMR} A$$

where $\mid\!\!\!-_{RST}$ means provability (an ability to express) at the metalevel RST and $\mid\!\!\!-_{AMR}$ means provability at the object level AMR.

9.6.2 Metaprogramming Tricks for Q/A

We need a metalevel clause to reason about *is_a* relation: *express("is_a"(X, "Y") $\mid$— express(Y(X)).*

If we have an ontology *human ("man"), animal("human"), man("John")*

and a user asks question 'is man a human', it can be represented as *is_a("man", "human")*

We may also rely on metaprogramming at the discourse level to define properties of semantic relations:

express(X(Y,Z))|— symmetric(X), express(X(Z,Y)).
express(X(Y,Z))|— transitive(X), express(X(Y,W)), express(X(W, Z)).
express_not(X(Y,Y))|— irreflexive(X).

Synonyms for predicates and for their arguments can be expressed in metalanguage

express(X(Y,Z))|— symmetric(X), express(X(Z,Y)).
express(X(Y))|— synonym(X, X_1), express(X_1(Y)).
express(X(Y))|— synonym(Y, Y_1), express(X(Y_1)).
express_not(X(Y))|— antonym(X, X_1), express(X_1(Y)).
symmetric("synonym"). symmetric("antonym").

Hence for the knowledge base

synonym ("big", "large"). synonym("dog", "wolf").
big(dog).
antonym("angry", "kind"). kind("wolf").

We can infer *large(wolf). not agry(wolf).*

Similarity can be extended towards pairs:

express(X(Y,Z))|— symmetric (X), express(X(Z,Y)).
express(X(Y,Z))|— same_pair ((Y,Z), (Y_1,Z_1)), express(X(Y_1, Z_1)).

same_pair ((X,Y), (X₁,Y)) |— same(X,X₁). same_pair ((X,Y), (X,Y₁)) |— same(Y,Y₁). symmetric ("same").

Then for a knowledge base

same("Trump", "president(usa)"). age(Trump, 70).

?- age(president(usa), X) gives $X = 70$.

Metareasoning assists in the flexible interpretation of texts by means of defining similarities in the metalevel. If predicate q is defined similar to a predicate p then the system may include the answer associated with p if an association of an answer with q is absent. The similarity of fairly abstract concepts can be defined relative to an ontology such that two sub-entities are considered similar in case they have the same super-entity.

express(X) |— attenuate (X,Y), express(Y).

attenuate (X(W),Y(W)) |— super_entity(X, Z), super_entity(Y, Z).

Then   if   *super_entity("pretence","misrepresentation").*
super_entity("hypocrisy","misrepresentation"). hypocrisy(Mike, mike_s_lie).

?-pretence(Mike, Q) gives $Q = mike\_s\_lie$.

Metaprogramming makes it easy to formulate generalized queries, without knowing exactly what this KB is or without knowing which kind of information is available in a KB. For a KB that includes properties of an individual (job applicant) *man(Peter), engineer(Peter), master_degree(Peter), beginner(Peter)...*

as well as desired properties from a job description *beginner,* one can formulate a query in metalanguage:

express(X("Andrew")), job_description(beginner(man, X)).

Analogical meta-reasoning can be implemented using metapredicate *has_property*:

express("has_property"("x", Y) |— similar (x,z), express("has_property"("z", Y).

For a KB *has_property(Peter, "master_degree"), similar(Peter, Mike)* we can arrive at the fact *has_property(Mike, "master_degree").*

Analogical reasoning may also occur as a transfer of properties by determination rules

express(X(Z,L))|— determine (Y, X), express(Y(Z,N)), express(Y(P,N)), express(Y(P,L)),

express(X(Y,Z))|— same_pair ((Y, Z), (Y₁, Z₁)), express(X(Y₁, Z₁)).

9.7 ToM Engine Support for Customer Complaint Processing

The main conjecture of the evaluation section above is that ToM Engine is good at exactly what it is expected to do: yielding a plausible sequence of mental states given the initial one. However, to take into account additional information about the agents, previous experience, and cases involving these agents, their particular circumstances, features of the physical environment, etc., it is important to involve other reasoning components. Integrating the ToM Engine simulation with other reasoning methodologies, including deductive, inductive, and abductive, is necessary for processing mental attitudes together with domain-specific knowledge (compare with Stein and Barnden 1995).

Table 9.6 enumerates the accompanying reasoning components and presents the sample chunks of knowledge from the domain of customer complaints. These components have been implemented in the system for conflict resolution (Chaps. 7 and 8 in Volume 2), which heavily relies on mental states and communicative actions of involved parties (Galitsky et al. 2009). The complaint domain is used to demonstrate the upper bound of the complexity of the mental world as a subject of reasoning. A hybrid reasoning system is required to support a broader set of scenarios with a substantial diversity of physical states and actions.

Table 9.6 Accompanying reasoning systems. We use the Prolog variables *Cust* and *Comp* for "customer" and "company," respectively

Component name	Component role	Sample encoded knowledge for the component
Behavior simulation: reasoning about mental states and actions ToM Engine	To provide a simulation environment for agents' choice of future mental actions, given the current mental state of interacting agents. The unit includes the repository of behaviors available for agents. It yields the consecutive mental states given the initial one, simulating the decision-making process of agents	*forgive(Cust, Comp, WrongAdvice):-* *advice(Comp, Cust, WrongAdvice), believe(Cust, know(Comp,* *not (howToFix(Happen):- WrongAdvice)))),* *explain(Comp, Cust, believe(Comp, (howToFix(Happen):-* *WrongAdvice)))), trust(Cust, Comp).*
Classical deductive clauses	To define entities, to specify links between them which always hold	*followAdviceNoResult:- ask(Cust, Comp, what(Happen)),* *suggest(Comp, Cust, satisfaction(Cust):-* *howToFix(Happen)),* *do(Cust, howToFix(Happen)), not satisfaction(Cust).*
Defeasible rules	To specify when some entities may support serve as arguments for a given entity	*justified_complaint - < lieCS, consistent_discourse.* *~ justified_complaint- < consistent_discourse, ~ loss(Cust).*

(continued)

Table 9.6 (continued)

Component name	Component role	Sample encoded knowledge for the component
Default rules	To specify when an entity (prerequisite) *always* serves as the condition for the given entity of interest (consequent) if an additional assumption takes place (justification). If justification is not available (cannot be formulated, implicit), a default rule is interpreted as a respective defeasible one. Default rules may be conflicting, therefore implementation of operational semantics may be required	*lieCS: mention_biz_rule* ——————— *justified_complaint* *justified_complaint: lieCS* ——————— *cust_compensation* *not requested(cust_compensation): lieCS* ——————— *cust_compensation*
Reasoning about action: plan building rules so that the assistant agent can advise on future actions	To specify what the future (physical) action of agents will be, given the pre-conditions of possible actions and their effects, taking into account the current development (of interaction between agents). Our implementation of reasoning about action allows online acquisition of action pre-conditions (Galitsky 2006)	*poss(do(Cust, fixProd(WayToFix)):- suggest(Comp, Cust, Satisfaction:- howToFix(Happen)),* *lost_trust(Cust, CustServ)* *holds(disinformed, do(E, S)):* *E = explainWronglyCS*

(continued)

Table 9.6 (continued)

Component name	Component role	Sample encoded knowledge for the component
Machine learning: matching the cases *Jasmine*	To predict the future interaction of involved agents and to determine their parameters given the previously accumulated cases (represented as sequences of communicative actions). Matching a current formalized complaint with the dataset of complaints with assigned status	*askt(Cust, P1). explain(Comp, P1). disagree(Cust,P1) confirm(Cust, P1), agree(Comp,P2), suggest(Comp, P2), accept(Cust, P2), request(Cust, P2), promise(Comp, P2), remind(Cust, P2), ask(Cust, P2)* Note two subjects of communicative actions: *P1* and *P2*

To demonstrate the universality of our approach to reasoning about mental attitudes, we enumerate the other problem domains where ToM Engine has been deployed or used for simulation or knowledge representation:

- Solving constraint satisfaction problem in the environment of conflicting human and automatic agents (scheduling for the broadcasting industry);
- Training of negotiation and other decision-making skills; querying the works of literature using mental states of their characters (Galitsky 2004);
- Automatic synthesis of scenarios (e.g., for Internet advertisements);
- Analysis and classification of the characters of fairy tales;
- Modeling mental states of investors for market predictions;
- Extracting mental states of participating agents from the text; understanding customers' complaints;
- Extraction of the mental behavior patterns from the wireless-based location services data;
- Simulating the relationships between economic agents.

9.7.1   Linked Subscenarios

One of the most important information that a scenario comprises is its linked subscenario. A sequence of mental states is referred as to *linked* if the meta-variables of each mental meta-predicate of this sequence are instantiated by the same formula W. A basic example here is the typical unit of an arbitrary discourse, *I asked about a feature of object and she responded, specifying this feature for the object*. In this

case, *W = Feature(Object)*, where predicate *Feature* is uninstantiated at the time of
asking but instantiated at the time of answering:

   ask(i, she, Feature(Object)) → *answer(she,i, Feature(Object))*,

   '→' denotes the sequence of actions.

   Let us now consider a more complex example of a linked subscenario, including
mental states and physical actions and states:

   *I deposited my child support check and they sent it back to me saying that they
could not deposit a business check into a personal account. It clearly states on the
front it is child support from Brazoria County and on the back that it is payable to
me.*

   This fragment is represented as the background info part:

   deposit(i, check(child_support)), send(bankOfAmerica, i, check(child_support)),
followed by the scenario itself:

   inform(bankOfAmerica, i, not deposit(me, check(child_support)),

   believe(i, accept(Bank, check(child_support))).

   In this complaint subscenario, the mental predicates above (including physical
predicate *deposit,* which plays here the role of the initial mental predicate) have the
term *check(child_support)* as the value of metavariable *W*. Therefore, the scenario
above is a linked subscenario of the complaint which is based on the conflict of bank's
and customer's beliefs concerning a deposit of checks (issued by a particular institu-
tion). Given a particular linked subscenario, finding a similar subscenario in another
complaint would mean that these two complaints are originated by a belief conflict
of the same structure. At the same time, the semantics of linking meta-variable
(*check(child_support)*) in our example identifies a particular physical parameter and
is too specific to judge on the conflict. Moreover, the physical parameter above is
independent of the plot of the scenario and may be combined (and serve as an argument of a mental action) with an arbitrary scenario. This discussion provided an
additional justification for our mental action-based formal model of a scenario.

   Let us continue with the example above; the complainant writes:

   *This is the second time in the last 3 months this bank has done this. The first time I
went in they had to pay me $150 in fees because of the error. Then I get an insufficient
funds from an automatic transfer that says the $2000 transfer couldn't happen. Well
the auto transfer is for $20 and now the account is negative 1400 and some change.
I hate these people. When I went in the first time they did this, the manager said "Oh
well stupid error" and thought I didn't hear her. I will be removing all funds from
this incompetent bank and trying some place else!*

   As the reader observes, in this sample conflict, the plot does not carry on with
the same physical predicate. Above is a rather chaotic and emotional enumeration
of previous events which do not form a linked subscenario that is well-suited for
complaint identification (matching with a similar subscenario).

   Overall scenario above is a representative of the class of complaints *Customer
believes company did not follow its rules.* For the purposes of this chapter, the classes
of complaints are drawn based on the mental attitudes of complainants and their
opponents; linked subscenarios form the criterion of belonging to the class. Note that

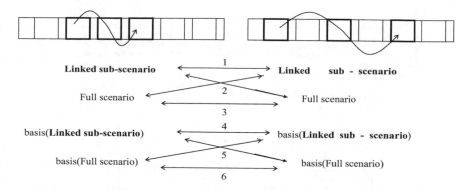

Fig. 9.7 The order of the search for common mental actions and emotions for a pair of scenarios (on the left and on the right)

a linked subscenario in our example does not have to occur at the beginning of the whole scenario: its background may precede the essential part (linked subscenario).

Hence, to find a similarity between two scenarios, we need to find their common linked subscenario via the search for a match on predicate-by-predicate basis (Fig. 9.7). If it is checked to be impossible, a linked subscenario of one complaint is matched against the whole scenario of another one. If such the attempt fails, the whole scenarios are tried to be matched against each other. If two scenarios do not have common sequence of (linked) predicates, we perform their comparison as the ordered sets of mental actions.

As the reader may feel at this point, the problem of finding a similarity for two scenarios is not adequately reducible to the task of finding an intersection of the set of mental predicates for each scenario, even if we consider additional scenario-specific constraints above. Looking for intersections between the sets, which are the sets of formulas (not arbitrary elements), we take advantage of the operation of the *term anti-unification* (Chap. 4 in Volume 1). In the case of unary predicates, anti-unification turns into a set-theoretic intersection.

Given a pair of scenarios, anti-unification yields a third scenario that comprises the common features (mental actions) of input scenarios. We intend our algorithm for search of similarity (Fig. 9.7) to reveal as many common features as possible.

9.8   Front End of ToM Engine

The user interface of ToM Engine allows the user to input a description of scenarios via plain English. The form (Fig. 9.8) shows an example in which a user-specified a scenario. This user then pressed the button [Load (translate into formal expressions)].

The result of pressing this button is the mental formulas seen in the combo box. The combo box allows users to highlight parses they like and to edit those that need refinement—in the case of inaccuracies in formal representations. Experienced users

Training of Mental Reasoning using NL_MAMS

This educational tool develops general analytical skills, your capability to grasp a complex situation quickly, creative decision making and situational memory. For the scenario below, try to understand it and predict what each agent would do. Then, running the simulator, please compare its solution with your own. You may also want to modify the initial mental states of involved agents and observe how their resultant behaviour changes.

Specify the <u>agents'</u> and simulator parameters

> Sally and Ann are in a room. Sally is holding a chocolate.
>
> Sally puts the chocolate in a drawer.
>
> Sally leaves the room.
>
>   Ann wants to hide the chocolate from Sally.
>   Ann moves the chocolate from the drawer to a box in the room.
> Sally comes back in the room to look for the chocolate.

Load (translate into formal representation)

> put(sally, chocolate, drawer).
> see(ann, (put (sally, chocolate, drawer))).
> put(sally, chocolate, box).
> not(see(ann,(put(sally, chocolate, box)))).
> want(ann, (find(ann, chocolate))).

Run simulation

Simulation results:

Step	Symbolic output	Auto generated text output
1	search(ann, chocolate, drawer)	"Ann searches for chocolate in drawer"
2	ask(ann,sally, (inform(sally, ann,(location(chocolate, X))))	"Ann asks Sally that Sally inform Ann about location of chocolate"

Fig. 9.8 The ToM Engine user interface for a simple logical connection of "not seeing → not knowing"

are able to skip the English to formal logic translation step and enter their scenario descriptions directly in the formal logic notation (Galitsky and Shpitsberg 2015).

Once the user feels ready, she can press the [Run Simulation] button. This will cause the simulation to run. The results of running the simulation are the candidate's answers to the question "What will happen next?". The results of running the simulation can be seen at the bottom of Fig. 9.8. There the user can see that in this case, a two-step plan was generated. Most frequently, 3 to 5 steps are generated, and sometimes up to 8–10 steps. Each step is depicted via its formal logic notation and via an automatically generated English rendering of that step.

In Table 9.7, we show the rules from our theory of mind repository that fired in the process of running the simulation. Note that the rules may fire recursively. Some fired based on the initial states and others fired on intermediate results.

In our example, we use a first-order test scenario for the axiom "not seeing leads to not knowing." To be able to approach the application of this axiom, a number of general knowledge-related axioms should be applied, including a particular case of *searching* (with a specific pre-condition for our scenario), as well as a generic axiom for an *informing* behavior. Notice a meta-predicate *epistemic_trans,* which links uninstantiated expression *Query* with its instantiated version *QueryProposition* (this instantiation occurs when the body of the respective clause is called).

The user can select the subset of formulas specifying the initial mental state to monitor how the resultant scenario is changed (Fig. 9.9). The system visualizes the

Table 9.7 English glosses and symbolic representation for behaviors

English Gloss	Symbolic representation
IF an *Agent* wants to know in what Place some Object is and if he/she believes that Object is in that Place THEN he/she will search Place for Object	*search(Agent, Object, Place):- (want(Agent, know(Agent, location(Object,Place)), believe(Agent, location(Object,Place))*
IF *Agent1* sees *Agent2* put *Object* in *Place* THEN *Agent1* believes that the location of *Object* is *Place*	*believe(Agent1, location(Object,Place)):- see(Agent1, put(Agent2, Object, Place))*
Agent1 asks *Agent2* about *Query* IF *Agent1* want to know answer to this *Query* and believes that *Agent2* knows *QueryProposition*	*ask(Agent1, Agent2, Query):- wants(Agent1, know(Agent1, QueryProposition)), not(know(Agent1, QueryProposition), believe(Agent1, knows(Agent2, QueryProposition)), epistemic_trans(Query, QueryProposition)*
Partial case of the above, where Query is a binary predicate *BinaryPredicate(Subject,Object))*	*asks(Agent1, Agent2, BinaryPredicate(Subject,Object)):- wants(Agent1, know(Agent1, BinaryPredicate(Subject,UnknownObject)), not(know(Agent1, BinaryPredicate(Subject,Object)), believe(Agent1, knows(Agent2, BinaryPredicate(Subject,Object)), epistemic_trans(UnknownObject, UnknownObject)*
Metapredicate which operates with expressions, either substituting variables in them, or checking that one expression can be turned into another by substitution. Can be treated as Prolog unification test	*epistemic_trans(Query, QueryProposition)*
Not seeing leads to not knowing	*not(know(Agent, Proposition)):- not(see(Agent, Proposition))*

semantic relationships between mental entities, a single physical entity, and the agents involved. The parameters of ToM Engine are specified using the form Fig. 9.10.

9.8.1   Related Systems

In the last two decades, interest in the formal modeling of various forms of human reasoning and in the simulation of mental behavior has risen strongly. A series of phenomena in human reasoning has been reflected in such approaches as reasoning about actions and knowledge, nonmonotonic reasoning, etc. Modal logic-based

There are three friends: Mike (m), Nick(n) and Peter(p). They got together tonight to have fun but their favorite toy is missing...

The friends take information from each other rather seriously, although they sometimes may want to tell a lie each other. The information concerning their mental states includes the permanent attitudes of the friends, as well as their particular moods for tonight.

Nick's mental state	Peter's mental state	Mike's mental state
Nick believes that Mike wants Peter to get the toy, and Nick wants Mike to get it. And also Nick would get if no one else does, but would not like to.	Peter does not want to get the toy himself and believes that Mike would not get it anyway. Also, Peter believes that Mike believes that Nick wants Mike to get it. Peter wants Mike to know that Peter would not get the toy himself. However, Peter would get the toy if he knows (someone tells him) that Nick wants him (Peter) to get it.	Mike wants either Nick or Peter to get the toy. Mike knows that Nick does not want Peter to get it. Mike would get the toy if Peter believes (is said) that Nick wants himself (Mike) to get it.

Form the statement using list boxes below

| Nick ▼ | want ▼ | inform ▼ | Peter ▼ | toy is bad ▼ | None ▼ |
| None ▼ | Nick ▼ | | None ▼ | None ▼ | or input in natural language |

Nick wants Peter to inform Nick if the toy is bad.

What will the children do?	Read the scenario (generated sequence of mental states) below:	
Nick's future actions	Peter's future actions	Mike's future actions
inform(n,p,want(m,get(p,toy)))	*inform(p,m,not get(p,toy))*	*cheat(m,p,want(n,get(p,toy)))*
cheat(n,p,want(m,get(p,toy)))	*nothing*	*inform(m,n,not get(m,toy))*
inform(n,p,get(m,toy))	*nothing*	*cheat(m,n,get(m,toy))*
ask(n,m,not get(m,toy))	*nothing*	*inform(m,p,not want(n,get(p,toy)))*
ask(n,m,get(m,toy))	*get(p, toy)*	*answer(m,n,not get(m,toy))*

Fig. 9.9   The ToM Engine user interface

and situation calculus-based approaches have become the most popular in formal modeling of mental attitudes (McCarthy 1995; Fagin et al. 1996; Wooldridge 2000). However, these approaches had to be extended for the purpose of the creation of educational software that possesses such capabilities.

Traditionally, representation of the laws of the mental world is developed via axioms (e.g., *an agent knows what it knows* (Fagin et al. 1996)). The axiom-based approach delivers a rather limited set of theorems to describe the mental world realistically. Furthermore, the axiom–based approach does not solve the general problem of obtaining the totality of possible mental states, given an initial mental state. We believe this general problem needs to be solved for the desired educational software: we want the children to be capable of reasoning starting from an arbitrary mental state.

Just a limited number of consecutive mental states can be yielded in a first-order system where meanings of knowledge, belief, and intention are expressed as formal modalities. The task of analysis of real-world conflicts between human agents, which is formulated in NL and involves the words for various mental states, actions, and emotions, requires at least solving the problem above. We believe that merging the

Specify the agent parameters | SELLER ▼ |

In this form, you set the parameters for individual agents. These settings are special for each agent. Varying the capabilities of reasoning and interacting with other agents, the user may achieve the wide spectrum of mental behaviors and decision-making capabilities of the agents.

Preferred actions
| Action that eliminates unwanted state that is current | ▲ |
| Action that does not lead to unwanted state that is not current | ▼ |

Attitude and reasoning capabilities

◉

☑ Assists other agents in their intensions (may be except those he does not like | buyer ▼ |)

Prefers to achieve his own goals rather that assists other agents in her intensions (may be except those he does not like | buyer ▼ |)

Prefers to achieve his own goals and neutral to the intensions of others

Prefers to achieve his own goals and not to let others doing so (may be except his friends | buyer ▼ |)

Ready for cooperation and coalition formation

Avoiding conflicts

Ready to advise

Ready to help with physical action

Limited reasoning capabilities (only facts and no clauses)

One step reasoning

Multiple steps reasoning (| 4 | steps in advance)

Tries to learn from the past experience

Does not take into account other agents

Takes into account other's choice without considering differences in their knowledge and beliefs and own ones

Takes into account other's choice considering differences in their knowledge and beliefs and own ones

Takes into account other's choice, considering differences in their knowledge and beliefs and their thoughts about my own possible actions

Takes into account other's choice, considering differences in their knowledge and beliefs and their thoughts about my own possible actions and mentioned differences.

Fig. 9.10 Specifying the parameters of agents involved: attitude and reasoning capabilities. Varying these parameters, a rehabilitation specialist may adjust ToM Engine to reproduce the mental reasoning of a particular trainee

declarative (laws of the mental world), procedural (a simulation of an agent's choice of action), and machine learning (taking into account previous experience) components is required adequately to reproduce the phenomenology of human reasoning about mental attitudes (Galitsky 2003). In this chapter, we have evaluated that the above is true (for the first two components) in the particular domain of reasoning about complaints.

In Sect. 9.4.2, we have introduced the methodology for how to cover (to approximate) the totality of mental actions by building definitions in the basis *want-know-believe*. In this chapter, it has been subject to an experimental evaluation, assuming that if the model is adequate, it can handle a variety of complaint scenarios.

Why did we select the particular knowledge representation formalism for reasoning about mental attitudes? We believe that the general approach to reasoning about actions, the situation calculus, and its implementation for reasoning about dynamic domains (e.g., GOLOG, (Levesque et al. 1997)) is adequate for reasoning about physical actions, but lacks the expressiveness to operate with mental actions. The situation calculus is relevant to expressing the effect axioms (how the mental actions result in mental states) but has an insufficient means to determine a possible mental action, given a mental state (see, e.g., Shanahan 1997). The reason is that when an automatic agent chooses an action in a mental world, there are a much higher number of explicit and implicit input parameters than when a robot makes a plan concerning its actions in a physical world.

Rather than stating that the mental world is more complex than the physical world, we proposed that a smaller number of facts in a mental world have a much more complex structure of causal links, and the very nature of these links is quite different from other reasoning domains. Indeed, our training methodology takes advantage of the compactness of entities of the mental world, focusing on the skill to build links between these entities.

In this book, we have discussed the applications of modal logic for reasoning about the mental world. Clearly, a lot of observations about the multiagent behavior can be deduced from the axioms; however, the set of theorems does not constitute a basis to enumerate a set of consecutive mental states. We conclude that the generic implementation of reasoning simulation is required, which is implemented as an exhaustive search in the space of possible behaviors. It has been observed in this chapter that the simulation for realistic mental states for a few agents is not computationally intensive.

Similar to the traditional settings of multiagent systems and the BDI model, both an initial mental state and the one to be predicted are specified in terms of *intentions, knowledge* and *beliefs*. However, the implementation of prediction is based on the defined behaviors as a means to transit from one state to another. This is in contrast to the traditional approach where the pre-conditions of mental actions and mental states as effects of these actions are formulated in terms of a rather limited number of entities for mental states, including *intentions, knowledge* and *beliefs*. Obviously, using a wider set of mental entities to express behaviors, leveraging the machinery of deriving these behaviors from the basis, delivers *much richer* set of mental states than the traditional approach. In other words, going beyond the basis dramatically increases the expressiveness of the representation language for mental actions, making the formal description of multiagent interaction scenarios adequate to apply to the real world.

Simulation-type approaches have been successfully applied to reasoning about mental attitudes: they follow the idea to eliminate layers of belief operator in order to simplify the reasoning and representation steps compared to what would be needed in modal logic-based reasoning about mental states. In our approach, reasoning by agent A about agent B's belief is carried out by standing in B's shoes and applying

B's own reasoning process directly to B's supposed beliefs, much as if they were A's own beliefs, in order to conclude what B might believe. In other words, our "simulation" is conducting reasoning within an alleged belief space of B, where the reasoning process is similar to what A would herself use if B's beliefs had been in A's own belief space.

In terms of how a society of agents can be characterized in terms of their mental states, the proposed approach can be characterized as a low-level and detailed (without a loss of information). As examples of higher level description of multiagent societies which involve mental states, it is worth mentioning (Buzing et al. 2005) who showed that the pressure to cooperate leads to the evolution of communication skills facilitating cooperation. At this lower level, a logic-based simulation comes into play rather than a numerical simulation; an aggregation of agents to express their attitudes and attributes quantitatively does not seem to be a plausible solution. Another example of a higher level multiagent model would be a social dilemma of (Axelrod 1984), where decisions that seem to make perfect sense from each individual's point of view can aggregate into outcomes that are unfavorable for all (Galan and Izquierdo 2005). Cooperative norms treat multiagent interactions at a more general level than our study, where individual communicative actions are selected. The ToM Engine predicts the behavior in a much narrower sense and in a much more concrete manner than, for example, the systems implementing the Theory of Reasoned Action and Theory of Planned Behavior (Ajzen and Fishbein 1980).

Building the environment for a low-level simulation involving basic verbalized attitudes and behavior forms of agents, we do not enable them with the ability to learn, provide argumentation, or other higher-level forms of behavior (Chesñevar et al. 2000; Stone and Veloso 2000). This is for the sake of a more accurate evaluation of how basic mental actions and states can yield real-world forms of behavior. However, the proposed simulation framework and representation language, which are logic-based, can accommodate more complex forms of behavior at a higher level of generality.

There are two types of application domains of the ToM Engine. Primarily, these are do-mains where simulation of beliefs of human agents is required (e.g., analysis buyers' behavior at e-commerce site). Another important application type of the ToM Engine is a HCI setting where the prediction of possible mental states of software users is essential. Mental attitudes of a human agent constitute one of the most important components of the human factors any software system is expected to be aware of, and especially a personalized assistant. However, the design and architecture of the ToM Engine follow the pragmatic purpose of being a generic efficient component of a wide range of large-scale systems, in particular CRM ones. Therefore, we don't target to build a computational model of the human cognitive process, unlike, for example, ACT-R approach (Anderson 1993) developed and used by cognitive psychologists.

The ToM Engine targets both cooperation and conflict domains. For the former, general models of teamwork and collaboration within AI include STEAM and TEAMCORE (Tambe 1997), SharedPlans (Grosz and Kraus 1996) and COLLAGEN

(Rich and Sidner 1998). For a broad overview of teamwork in multiagent systems, the reader is recommended (Stone and Veloso 2000).

There is a series of multiagent systems where agents are designed to implement *emotions* (Breazeal 1998). Also, a number of formalisms have been developed that handle the notion of emotion quite adequately (see, e.g., Oatley and Jenkins 1996; Parameswaran 2001; Scheutz 2001). However, the target of our model for the mental world, which includes emotions of participating agents, is quite different. As we experimentally discovered, the interface of the rehabilitation system does not have to display the emotional behavior explicitly; instead, the canonical explanation of the strict rules for emotions is required. We have learned from our experimental studies that when children start better operate with basic entities of knowing and believing and then proceed to the derived entities like *deceiving* and *pretending* using ToM Engine, the further step to more complex mental and emotional behavior frequently comes easier and quite naturally.

Simulating the cognitive processes of another agent requires maintaining multiple worlds where epistemic states of individual agents can be loaded. The problem spaces in Soar (Rosenbloom and Laird 1993) and alternate worlds in Polyscheme (Cassimatis 2005) are good examples of such capabilities, but most cognitive systems do not have such a mechanism. Soar's problem spaces facilitate subgoaling and have been used to anticipate opponent's behavior in the game of Quake (Laird 2001). Polyscheme's worlds are a general construct and allow for instantiation and manipulation of hypothetical, counterfactual, and even stochastic simulations. The alternate worlds in Polyscheme have been used to model spatial perspective-taking and theory of mind (Bello and Cassimatis 2006). The concept of simulating the cognitive processes of another agent (Trafton et al. 2013) suggested that an important consideration in designing an architecture for integrated intelligence, is how well the system works with a person. When a system uses representations and processes similar to a person's, it will be able to collaborate with a person better than a computational system that does not. Furthermore, such a system will be more compatible with human expectations of reasonable behavior, and thus more accommodating to the human.

9.8.1.1 Commonsense Psychology System

Psychologists need to explicitly spell out a conceptual system of commonsense psychology. Smedslund (1989) is arguing that some knowledge engineering needs to be done in order to identify the implicit commonsense theories that people have of mental states and processes. What is remarkable about Smedslund and his research is that he has done two things that set him apart from other theorists in this area. First, he has attempted to execute this knowledge engineering task himself on a reasonably large scale, authoring a repository of the concepts, definitions, and axioms of commonsense psychology that he calls "Psychologic" (Smedslund 1989). Second, he has attempted to validate the contents of this repository of commonsense psychological knowledge by studying the degree to which people within and across cultures are in agreement about the truth of this knowledge. Smedslund describes Psychologic as follows:

> "Psychologic" is a project of explicating the implicit conceptual system of psychology embedded in ordinary language, or in other words, the basic assumptions and distinctions underlying our ways of thinking and talking about psychological phenomena. Psychologic identifies 22 primitive terms whose meanings are taken to be self-evident, namely terms for psychological states (aware, feel, want, belief, understand, strength), for temporal relationships (when, after, before, now), for action (act, talk, can, try, ability, difficulty, exertion), normative values (right, wrong, good, bad), and a term for people (person). Psychologic elaborates these primitive terms through 43 definitions, which take the form illustrated by the following examples, where the notation "= df" is taken to mean "is by definition equal to."

Definition 1.2.3 "Intentional" = df "directed by a preference for achieving a goal."

Definition 1.2.8 "X is relevant for achieving a goal G" = df "taking into account increases the likelihood of achieving G."

Definition 3.3.15 "Two wants are compatible" = df "Acting according to one of the two wants can be combined with acting according to the other." (

Using these definitions, Psychologic presents 56 axioms to describe the conceptual relationships that exist between these terms, as in the following examples:

Axiom 3.5.1 The strength of P's belief X is directly proportional to P's estimate of the likelihood that X is the case.

Axiom 4.1.1 P's feeling follows from P's awareness of the relationship between P's wants and P's beliefs.

Axiom 5.3.15 All understanding depends on relevant pre-understanding.

Although the language of Psychologic is intended to be expressed by these primitive terms only, definitions, and axioms, the contents of Psychologic as a conceptual system are really elaborated in the statements that can be seen as direct consequences of this conceptual system. These consequences are presented in the form of 108 theorems, listed with short proofs written in English, and an additional 135 corollaries that are viewed as direct consequences of the axioms and theorems. Examples of each are as follows:

Theorem 1.2.10 P takes into account what P takes to be relevant for the achievement of P's goal.

Theorem 3.3.17 If the wants W1 and W2, are compatible, then they combine in such a way that W1 & W2 > W1 and W1 & W2 > W2.

Corollary 3.5.2 If P's belief A is stronger than P's belief B, then P's estimate of the likelihood of A is higher than P's estimate of the likelihood of A.

Corollary 3.7.3 Every person reflectively believes in the possibility of his or her nonexistence.

Smedslund's project has received a substantial amount of criticism within his own field, with detractors tending to outnumber advocates. Given the fair amount of discussion and academic debate of Smedslund's research that exists within this corner of the field of psychology, it is remarkable that this research remains so isolated from the other fields across the cognitive sciences that have a direct interest in commonsense psychology.

Smedslund draws no connection between his work and ongoing research on Theory of Mind in philosophy, a research on the acquisition of Theory of Mind in developmental and social psychology, or a study of the formalization of common-sense knowledge within the field of AI. At the same time, Smedslund's project has not received attention within these fields. One should confirm that Smedslund advanced the inter-disciplinary connections between logic and psychology, given the degree to which each of these academic fields is isolated from each other.

9.8.1.2   A Symbolic Production-Based System

To better understand how engineering ToM Systems work, in this section, we describe ACT-R is a hybrid symbolic/subsymbolic production-based system. Modules in ACT-R are intended to represent relatively specific cognitive faculties such as declarative (fact-based) and procedural (rule-based) memory, visual and auditory perception, vocalization, and time perception. Buffers in ACT-R make up the working memory of a cognitive model. Some modules fill their buffers in response to the changes in the environment and all modules fill their buffers in response to explicit procedural requests. Like many production systems, ACT-R continuously matches production conditions against the working memory (buffers), selects a single production to fire, and then executes specified buffer changes and module requests, which eventually result in updates to relevant buffers.

The project (Kennedy et al. 2008) embodied ACT-R on a human-scale robotic platform suited to use in indoor environments. It carries the sensors and provides onboard computing support for multimodal sensing, navigation, and output. With ACT-R/E, (Trafton et al. 2013) have extended the ACT-R architecture with rudimentary spatial reasoning (spatial module), localization and navigation faculties ("moval" module), and modified the visual, aural, and vocal modules to use actual robot sensors as shown in the architectural diagram in Fig. 9.11.

ACT-R architecture facilitates running additional cognitive models simultaneously. An ACT-R model consists of declarative and procedural memory and an initial goal. The ability of ACT-R to spawn a new model from within a running model allows cognitive system developers to represent and manipulate a mental model of another agent. To allow the base cognitive model to continue running while the simulation occurs, two models can run synchronously at the production-level. The flexibility of fixing the declarative memory and productions of the simulated mental model to a subset of the original model's allows the system to consider hypothetical and counterfactual situations.

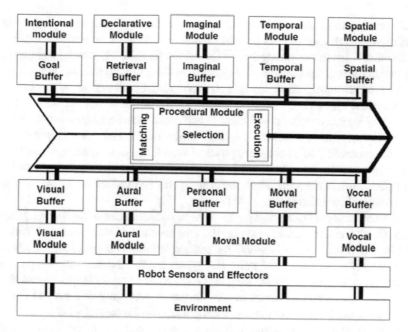

Fig. 9.11 ACT-R/E architecture (from Trafton et al. 2013)

9.9   Discussion and Conclusions

In this chapter, we constructed the engine that navigates through the mental world, operates with its language and makes decision on how the citizens of the mental world need to be tackled with. The functioning of this engine is an existential proof that a computational ToM exists and that it is sustainable, adaptable and intelligent as observed by external observers. ToM engine is evaluated with respect to correctness, coverage and complexity, and can be integrated with other reasoning components and with machine learning, to perform both reasoning and cognitive tasks (Fig. 9.12).

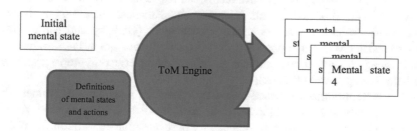

Fig. 9.12 The Task of ToM engine is to yield a set of consecutive mental states for an arbitrary initial one, having the set of initial mental states

We demonstrated that reasoning about the mental world can be implemented via exhaustive search through the possible actions and behaviors, evaluating achieved mental states. From the standpoint of the axiomatic method, which combines pure (logical) axioms of inference with domain-specific (applied) axioms, generic representation of reasoning about the mental world may be viewed as an augmentation of the former. Therefore, we follow the classical axiomatic method stating that the same set of logical axioms is sufficient to perform reasoning in an arbitrary domain. In our case, the same axioms of the mental world (considered a pure, logical component) can be applied to an arbitrary physical world. In this chapter, we have verified that the set of behaviors observed in one domain can be applied in an intact form to another domain with different physical axioms to produce adequate multiagent scenarios (Galitsky and Ilvovsky 2017).

For an arbitrary set of mental formulas as an initial condition for the ToM Engine, it either finds a contradiction or synthesizes the scenario of multiagent behavior. The ToM Engine's vocabulary included the generic template for physical actions and a rather extensive set of lexical units and synonyms for the common-usage mental entities. Also, it is worth mentioning that though each natural language has its own peculiarities of reasoning about mental attributes, replacing one natural language with another does not affect the suggested model for the mental world.

There are two aspects of the ToM Engine's contribution to the theory of mind training for an individual with autism and other mental disorders (Galitsky and Parnis 2017). Firstly, it introduces a new conceptual framework for treating mental entities in the way that the trainees are frequently ready to accommodate. The second aspect which seems to be more important for training practice is that ToM Engine allows a much more persistent, consistent, and efficient approach because as a computer system, ToM Engine can repeat exercises and vary them as many times as a trainee wishes (Galitsky 2002).

It is worth mentioning that the usability of the underlying representation machinery for scenarios of inter-human interactions goes beyond the domain of customer complaints. In the part of our research (Galitsky and Tumarkina 2004; Galitsky et al. 2007), five different domains were considered to assess the adequateness of speech act theory, obtaining satisfactory results. Such domains included international conflicts, security clearance scenarios, detection of emotional profiles, analysis of bloggers' sentiments (Galitsky and Kovalerchuk 2006), and identification of suspicious behavior of cell phone users (Galitsky and Miller 2005). This provides empirical support for the adequacy of our graph-based representation language involving communicative actions characterized by numerical-valued attributes (Chap. 8 in Volume 2).

Our problem domain is based on the experience of a series of consumer advocacy companies that try to help the customers unsatisfied by particular products, services, or, especially, customer support. We base our model on a publicly available database of complaints (see, e.g., http://www.planetfeedback.com, http://www.my3 cents.com). Though a high number of studies have addressed the issue of conflict resolution (see, e.g., Wong and Lin 2002; Vassileva and Scoggins 2003), modeling real-world customer complaints bring in a unique class of textual scenarios for analysis that does not fit the framework of conflicts as inconsistent beliefs and desires. Also, the application of traditional domain-independent techniques of text mining has a limited value in the case of extraction complaint parameters from text because of their high logical complexity.

References

Ajzen I, Fishbein M (1980) Understanding attitudes and predicting social behavior. Prentice-Hall, Englewood Cliffs, NJ

Anderson J (1993) Rules of the mind. Lawrence Erlbaum Associates, Hillsdale, NJ

Axelrod R (1984) The evolution of cooperation, Basic Books

Baron-Cohen S (2000) Theory of mind and autism: a fifteen year review. In: Baron-Cohen S, Tagar-Flusberg H, Cohen DJ (eds) Understanding other minds, vol A. Oxford University Press, Oxford, pp 3–20

Batali J (1983) Computational introspection MIT. MA, AI Memo, Cambridge, p 701

Bello P, Cassimatis N (2006) Developmental accounts of theory-of-mind acquisition: Achieving clarity via computational cognitive modeling. In: Proceedings of the 28th Annual Conference of the Cognitive Science Society, pp 1014–1019

Bousquet O, Boucheron S, Lugosi G (2004) Introduction to statistical learning theory. Lec Notes Artific Int 3176:169–207

Breazeal C (1998) A motivational system for regulating human-robot interactions. In: Proceedings of the fifteenth national conference on AI (AAAI-98)

Buzing PC, Eiben AE, Schut MC (2005) Emerging communication and cooperation in evolving agent societies. J Art Societ Soc Simul 8(1). http://jasss.soc.surrey.ac.uk/8/1/2.html

Cassimatis NL (2005) Integrating cognitive models based on different computational methods. In: Twenty-Seventh Annual Conference of the Cognitive Science Society

Chesnevar C, Maguitman A, Loui R (2000) Logical models of argument. ACM Comput Surv 32(4):337–383

Cox MT, Ram A (1999) Introspective multistrategy learning: on the construction of learning strategies. Artif Intell 112:1–55

d'Inverno M, Kinny D, Luck M, Wooldridge M (1998) A formal specification of dMARS. In: Intelligent Agents IV: Proc 4th Intl Workshop on Agent Theories, Architectures and Languages, Rao S, Wooldridge (eds) LNAI 1365, pp 155–176

de Lara J, Alfonseca M (2000) Some strategies for the simulation of vocabulary agreement in multi-agent communities. J Art Societ Soc Simul 3:4. http://www.soc.surrey.ac.uk/JASSS/3/4/2.html

Fagin R, Halpern JY, Moses Y, Vardi MY (1996) Reasoning about knowledge MIT Press. MA, London, England, Cambridge

Gabbay DM (1999) Action, Time and Default. In: Levesque HJ, Pirri F (eds) Logical foundations for cognitive agents. Springer, Berlin Heidelberg, New York

Galan JM, Izquierdo LR (2005) Appearances can be deceiving: lessons learned re-implementing Axelrod's evolutionary approach to norms. J Art Societ Soc Simul 8(3) http://jasss.soc.surrey.ac.uk/8/3/2.html

Galitsky B (2002) Extending the BDI model to accelerate the mental development of autistic patients. Second Intl Conf Devel Learn, Cambridge, MA

Galitsky B (2003) Natural language question answering system: technique of semantic headers. Advanced Knowledge Intl, Adelaide Australia

Galitsky B (2004) A library of behaviors: implementing commonsense reasoning about mental world. KES 2004 LNAI 3215, pp 307–313

Galitsky B (2005) On a distance learning rehabilitation of autistic reasoning. In: Encyclopedia of online learning and technologies, vol 4. Idea Publishing Group

Galitsky B (2006) Reasoning about mental attitudes of complaining customers. Knowl-Based Syst Elsevier 19(7):592–615

Galitsky B (2013, September) A computational simulation tool for training autistic reasoning about mental attitudes. Knowl Based Sys 50:25–43

Galitsky B (2016) Theory of mind engine. Computational Autism, Springer, Cham Switzerland

Galitsky B (2017) Matching parse thickets for open domain question answering. Data Knowl Eng 107:24–50

Galitsky (2019) Developing enterprise chatbot. Springer, Cham Switzerland

Galitsky B (2020) Utilizing discourse structure of noisy user-generated content for chatbot learning. US Patent 10,599,885

Galitsky B, Tumarkina I (2004) Justification of customer complaints using emotional states and mental actions. In: Barr V, Markov Z (eds) Proceedings of the Seventeenth International Florida Artificial Intelligence Research Symposium (FLAIRS) Conference, Miami Beach, Florida, USA, AAAI Press, pp 239–244

Galitsky B, Miller A (2005) Determining possible criminal behavior of mobile phone users by means of analyzing the location tracking data, Proc. of the AAAI Spring Symposia on Homeland Security (published as technical report), Stanford, CA, USA

Galitsky B, Kovalerchuk B (2006) Mining the blogosphere for contributors' sentiments. AAAI Spring symposium: computational approaches to analyzing weblogs, pp 37–39

Galitsky BA, Kuznetsov SO (2008) Learning communicative actions of conflicting human agents. J Exper Theor Art Intel 20(4):277–317

Galitsky B, de la Rosa JL (2011) Concept-based learning of human behavior for customer relationship management. Special Issue on Information Engineering Applications Based on Lattices. Information Sciences. Volume 181, Issue 10, 15 May 2011, pp 2016–2035

Galitsky B, Shpitsberg I (2015) Evaluating assistance to individuals with autism in reasoning about mental world. In: Artificial intelligence applied to assistive technologies and smart environments. Papers from the 2015 AAAI Workshop

Galitsky B, Parnis A (2017) How children with autism and machines learn to interact. Autonomy and Artificial Intelligence: A Threat or Savior? 195–226

Galitsky B, Ilvovsky D (2017) Chatbot with a discourse structure-driven dialogue management. In: EACL Demo E17–3022. Valencia, Spain

Galitsky B, González MP, Chesñevar CI (2009) A novel approach for classifying customer complaints through graphs similarities in argumentative dialogues. Decis Support Syst 46(3):717–729

Galitsky B, Kovalerchuk B, Kuznetsov S (2007) Learning common outcomes of communicative actions represented by labeled graphs. In: Proc. of the 15th Intl. Conference on Conceptual Structures (ICCS), Sheffield, UK, July 2007, pp 387–400

Giunchiglia F, Weyhrauch RW (1988) A multi-context monotonic axiomatization of inessential nonmonotonicity. In: Maes P, Nardi D (eds) Meta-level architectures and reflections. North-Holland, pp 271–285

Grosz BJ, Kraus S (1996) Collaborative plans for complex group actions. AIJ 86:269–358

Gödel K (1940) The consistency of the axiom of choice and of the generalized continuum hypothesis with the axioms of set theory. Princeton University Press

Kaminka GA, Frenkel I (2005) Flexible teamwork in behavior-based robots. AAAI- 05:2005

Kaminka GA, Tambe M (2000) Robust multi-agent teams via socially-attentive monitoring. JAIR 12(105–147):2000

Kennedy WG, Bugajska MD, Harrison AM, Trafton JG (2008) Like-meÓ simulation as an effective and cognitively plausible basis for social robotics. Int J Social Robot 1(2):181–194

Laird JE (2001) It knows what you're going to do: adding anticipation to a quakebot. In: Proceedings of the fifth international conference on autonomous agents. ACM, New York

Levesque HJ, Reiter R, Lesperance Y, Lin F, Scherl RB (1997) GOLOG: a logic programming language for dynamic domains. J Log Program 31:59–84

Li G, Hopgood AA, Weller MJ (2003) Shifting matrix management: a model for multi-agent cooperation. Eng Appl Artif Intell 16(3):191–201

Maes P, Nardi D (eds) (1988) Meta-level Arehitec- tares and Reflection, North Holland

McCarthy J (1979) Ascribing mental qualities to machines. In: Ringle M (ed) Philosophical perspectives in artificial intelligence. Humanities Press, Atlantic Highlands

McCarthy J (1995) Making robots conscious of their mental states. In: Proceedings of Machine Intelligence Conf, p 15

Oatley K, Jenkins J (1996) Understanding emotions. Blackwell, Oxford

Olivia C, Chang CF, Enguix CF, Ghose AK (1999) Case-based BDI agents: an effective approach for intelligent search on the world wide web. In: Intelligent Agents in Cyberspace. Papers from 1999 AAAI Spring Symposium

Parameswaran N (2001) Emotions in Intelligent Agents, FLAIRS-01. Pensacola Beach, FL, pp 82–86

Pilowsky T, Yirmiya N, Arbelle S, Mozes T (2000) Theory of mind abilities of children with schizophrenia, children with autism, and normally developing children. Schizophr Res 42(2):145–155

Reiter R (1993) Proving properties of states in the situational calculus. AI 64, pp 337–351

Rich C, Sidner CL (1998) COLLAGEN: a collaboration manager for software interface agents. User Model User-Adap Inter 8(3–4):315–350

Rosenbloom PS, Laird JE (1993) A Newell. The SOAR papers MIT Press

Rosenschein J, Zlotkin G (1994) Rules of encounter: designing conventions for automated negotiation among computers. MIT Press, Cambridge, MA

Schank R (1969) A conceptual dependency parser for natural language. In: Proceedings of the 1969 conference on Computational Linguistics, Sweden, pp 1–3

Scheutz M (2001) Agents with or without emotions, FLAIRS-01, Pensacola Beach, pp 89–93

Shanahan M (1997) Solving the frame problem. MIT Press

Shoham Y (1993) Agent oriented programming. Artif Intell 60(1):51–92

Sloman A (2000) Architecture-based conceptions of mind. In: Proceedings of the 11th international congress of logic, methodology and philosophy of science, Dordrecht, Kluwer, p 397

Sloman A (2000) Architecture-based conceptions of mind. In: Proc 11th International Congress of Logic, Methodology and Philosophy of science. Dordrecht: Kluwer, p 397

Smedslund J (1989) What is psychologic? Recent trends in theoretical psychology. In: Part of the series recent research in psychology, pp 453–457

Stein GC, Barnden JA (1995) Towards more flexible and common-sensical reasoning about beliefs. In: 1995 AAAI Spring Symposium on Representing Mental States and Mechanisms. AAAI Press, Menlo Park, CA

Stone P, Veloso M (2000) Multiagent systems: a survey from a machine learning perspective. Auton Robot 8(3):345–383

Tambe M (1997) Agent architectures for flexible, practical teamwork. In: Proceedings of the national conference on artificial intelligence (AAAI)

Tamma V, Phelps S, Dickinso I, Wooldridge M (2005) Ontologies for supporting negotiation in e-commerce. Eng Appl Artif Intell 18(2):223–236

Trafton GJ, Hiatt LM, Harrison AM, Franklin P, Tamborello II, Khemlani SS, Schultz AC (2013) ACT-R/E: an embodied cognitive architecture for human-robot interaction. J Human-Robot Int 2(1)

Vassileva B, Scoggins P (2003) Consumer complaint forms: an assessment, evaluation and recommendations for complaint categorization. In: Jarrar M, Salaun A (eds) Proceeding of the International Workshop on consumer complaint forms for online resolution machines, Brussels

Walton DN, Krabbe E (1995) Commitment in dialogue. In: Basic concepts of interpersonal reasoning. state univ of New York Press, Albany NY

Weigand H, de Moor A (2004) Argumentation semantics of communicative action. In: Proceedings of the 9th International Working Conference on the Language-Action Perspective on Communication Modelling (LAP 2004) Rutgers University, NJ, USA

Winograd T, Flores F (1986) Understanding computers and cognition: a new foundation for design. Ablex Publishing

Wong SKM, Lin T (2002) Conflict resolution in probabilistic multi-agent systems. FLAIRS Conference, pp 529–533

Wooldridge M. (2000) Reasoning about rational agents. The MIT Press, Cambridge MA

Yu R, Iung B, Panetto H (2003) A multi-agents based E-maintenance system with case-based reasoning decision support. Eng Appl Artif Intell 16(4):321–333

Chapter 10
CRM Becomes Seriously Ill

Abstract This is a less technical chapter devoted to a CRM management problem of poor performance of an organization such a call center or a technical support department. We explore a technology that can detect this performance and a root cause for it, in terms of We explore the phenomenon of Distributed Incompetence (DI), which is an opposite to Distributed Knowledge and occurs in various organizations such as customer support. In a DI organization, a team of employees is managed in a way that, being rational, impresses a customer or an external observer with total irrationality and incompetence, an inability to get things done. In most cases, the whole organization or individual team members gain from DI by means of refusing customer compensation while avoiding other obligations. We investigate DI in a variety of organizations to analyze its commonality as well as specific DI features for organizations and communities. A discourse-level analysis to detect DI in textual descriptions of customers and observers is outlined. We report a detected DI rate in financial organizations and propose a solution to handle it, such as a chatbot.

10.1 Introduction

In the domain of reasoning about agents, distributed knowledge is all the knowledge that a team of agents possesses and leverages in solving a problem. Distributed knowledge (Fagin et al. 1995) expresses what a rational human reasoner knows about what each member of a team knows. Distributed knowledge includes all the knowledge that a population of agents possesses to solve a problem. Distributed knowledge and the collective experience of the crowd showed better problem-solving and decision-making skills in comparison with individual agents in a number of domains. In this study, we are interested in the phenomenon opposite to distributed knowledge that can be observed in some organizations.

In a domain such as a customer support, when a customer interacts with multiple human agents, he can be negatively impressed that a team of agents solves his problem in an inferior manner in comparison to how an individual agent would. In a case like this, when a given agent A refers to another agent B for help with a given problem, B further refers to C and so forth, and yet the problem is still not solved,

© The Author(s), under exclusive license to Springer Nature Switzerland AG 2021
B. Galitsky, *Artificial Intelligence for Customer Relationship Management*,
Human–Computer Interaction Series, https://doi.org/10.1007/978-3-030-61641-0_10

distributed intuition becomes a noisy, inconsistent, intractable alteration of the sum of the individual knowledge of *A*, *B* and *C*. We refer to such deteriorated knowledge as *Distributed Incompetence* (DI).

In a Distributed Incompetence organization, agents have limited authorities over solving problems and limited knowledge about the same of other agents. Passing a customer problem from one agent (who is a rational reasoner within the business domain) to another, a joint multiagent system sometimes stops being a rational reasoner. In some cases, organizations such as insurance companies leverage DI as a means to retain income, trying to make customers give up on their existing claims. Some businesses rely on DI to avoid compensating customers for faulty products and services, in effect reversing transactions. In other cases, the upper management of an organization is not in a position to deny compensation, but the DI is a result of a lack of proper management. In many cases, customer support agents (CSAs) are not directly motivated to solve customer problems, but instead, their performance is measured by an abstract user satisfaction score. Frequently, CSAs are either not uniformly motivated to perform their functions, or not motivated at all (Fig. 10.1, Integration Training 2018).

Here is an example of how an external observer describes DI behavior with the terms of how a CSA describes his mission: *"The only thing I am authorized to do is to tell you that I am not authorized to do anything."*

It has been discovered that a lot of forms of human intellectual and communication activity, such as management styles, are associated with certain discourse structures

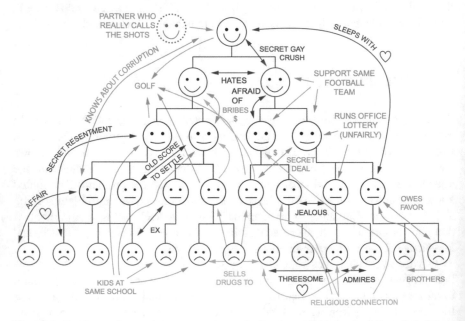

Fig. 10.1 Employees in a customer support organization have all kinds of relations that distract them from acting in the best interests of their company and customers

of how these activities are described in the text. Rhetorical Structure Theory (RST; in Mann and Thompson 1987) is a good means to express the correlation between such form of activity and its representation in how associated thoughts are organized in a text. Rhetoric Structure Theory presents a hierarchical, connected structure of a text as a Discourse Tree (DT), with rhetorical relations between the parts of it. The smallest text spans are called elementary discourse units (EDUs).

In communicative discourse trees (CDTs), the labels for communicative actions (VerbNet expressions for verbs) are added to the discourse tree edges to show which speech acts are attached to which rhetoric relations. In DI, activity such as *persuasion* is very important in convincing a customer that banks are forced to demand insufficient fund fees to maintain profitability. RST, in particular, helps to understand this form of persuasion as argumentation (Galitsky et al. 2018).

In this chapter, we study rhetoric structures correlated with certain forms of verbal activity such as DI, as expressed in customer complaints. We intend to discover the distinct discourse representations associated with DI. Some of such features can be observed as a result of manual analysis, but most of these features are concealed and need to be tackled by a data-driven approach, so we adjust our customer complaints dataset tagged to detect DI.

10.2 Defining DI

Logically, DI can be inferred when a CSA demonstrates his intention to be other than the well-being of a customer and his company at the same time. Since there is frequently a conflict of interest between a company and a customer, we cannot expect a CSA to always act in the best interests of the customer. However, if a company's interests are not satisfied either, one can conclude that DI is taking place.

When a customer describes her encounter with an individual CSA, she is frequently dissatisfied even when her perception of her opponent is reasonable. However, what makes complainants appalled is an inconsistency between what different CSAs tell them about the same thing. For example, what frequently happens is that one CSA explains to the client that his insufficient fund fee (NSF) is due to a too-early withdrawal transaction, whereas another CSA is saying that the deposit transaction has not gone through. This situation puts both client and company at a disadvantage that is clearly indicative of a DI. Moreover, when a customer describes this kind of misinformation, it can be trusted in most cases since a customer would need to be too "inventive" to compose a description with this form of inconsistency (it is much easier for a dissatisfied customer to misrepresent an encounter with a single agent (Galitsky et al. 2009; Pisarevskaya et al. 2019)).

Hence a DI can also be defined as a conflict between parties so that these parties behave irrationally by not acting in their best interest as perceived by an impartial judge reading a description of this conflict. In part, a case here is a claimed conflict of interest when there is a contradiction between the intents of the agents involved.

Another case is where a conflict of interest is present but is not attempted to be resolved reasonably.

The problem of a DI is associated with the observed invalid argumentation patterns used by the parties of a conflict. In some cases, if arguments of only one party are faulty, it does not necessarily mean a DI; however, if such argumentation is systematic, it is natural to conclude that a DI is occurring. The systematic improper use of explainability indicates a DI as well (Galitsky 2018).

Some problems of a DI are associated with a limit on time set by one agent involved in its communication. For example, in the healthcare industry, doctors commonly interrupt patients explaining their problems in 11 s on average (Singh et al. 2018). Having these reduced descriptions of a problem, it is hard to make a competent decision; therefore, certain irrational reasoning patterns can be included, in particular, when referring to other specialist doctors.

A DI is defined in an annotation framework as a decision by a human expert that a CSA has acted irrationally, contradicted another agent, demonstrated a lack of commonsense knowledge, or exhibited a substantial lack of knowledge about company rules or industry regulations. An organization with DI is irrational to an external observer but may well be rational from the expected utility standpoint of an organization's CSA agents who minimize the compensation a user might achieve communicating with such organization (Oppong 2018).

DI is a key reason customer complaints arise. People usually do not submit formal complaints because of their dissatisfaction with a product or service. To get to the point of a complaint's submission, users usually have to be either handled badly by multiple CSAs or to encounter a DI.

10.3   Companies Sick with Distributed Incompetence

10.3.1   Managing Distributed Incompetence Organizations

In his recent research note (Grudin 2016), formulates the incompetence problem directly: "How could incompetence be on the rise when knowledge and tools proliferate?" The author cites the Peter Principle (Peter and Hull 1968) that explains why organizations keep incompetent managers and how they avoid serious harm (Fig. 10.2). Grudin (2016) explores whether managerial incompetence is escalating, despite the greater capability of those who are competent—those, in the words of Peter and Hull (1968), who have not yet reached their levels of incompetence. The conclusion is that managerial incompetence is accelerating, aided by technology and the weak social changes that strive to level the playing field of competition between employees in an organization. The counterforces rely on weakened hierarchy, but hierarchy remains strong enough to trigger self-preservation maneuvers at the expense of competence.

Fig. 10.2 Illustration for the Peter' principle (Biswa 2015)

In a DI organization, the higher the level of management, the less skillful and capable the respective manager has to be. To be a manager in a DI team, to operate it smoothly, an individual needs to possess genuine incompetence and a lack of skills. To adequately control and guide lower-rank managers with limited skills and capabilities to produce results, an upper-level manager needs to possess even less skills. If an energetic, highly skilled, and results-oriented manager finds herself leading a team of personnel operating in a DI mode, she would not fit in such a team. In a DI team, those members who are doers would be left alone, and those who are not good at doing but who are well in playing politics would be promoted to a managerial position to retain smooth DI operations. Hence, in a DI organization, people with lower delivering capabilities, but better communication skills tend to occupy management positions, increasing the stability of DI. Notice that in our model, individual managers are not necessarily incompetent: instead, they lead the whole organization to the distributed incompetence state, possibly achieving their individual managerial goals.

When a company such as Barclays bank (who employed the author of this study) is being sued for fraud (FCA 2015), usually due to upper management activities, substantial efforts are often put into training all company employees related to honest business conduct. Most employees are becoming scapegoats blamed for the activities of the upper management, although they would not be authorized to commit fraud in the first place. Once the same company is charged with another fraud, the training materials for all employees are repeated respectfully, as if the regular employees were also responsible for this new fraud. This form of employee training to prevent a crime these employees would not be authorized to commit anyway is another symptom of a DI and its associated blame games.

10.3.2 Whistleblowing in Distributed Incompetence Organizations

DI is associated with a lack of a number of whistleblowers in an organization. A whistleblower is an agent who exposes any kind of information or activity that is deemed inappropriate, illegal, unethical, or not correct within an organization. The information on alleged wrongdoing can be classified in many ways: violation of company policy/rules, law, regulation, or threat to public interest/national security, as well as fraud and corruption. Those who become whistleblowers can choose to expose information or allegations to the public either internally or externally. Internally, a whistleblower can bring his/her accusations to the attention of other people within the accused organization, such as an immediate supervisor. Externally, a whistleblower contacts a third party such as a government agency or law enforcement. Whistleblowers, however, take the risk of facing strong reprisal and retaliation from the company being exposed. Once the number of whistleblowers is sufficient, or their allegations are supported, the organization can reduce its DI by internal means. Frequently, an employee must make a choice to either become a whistleblower, be a quiet opponent of the harmful operations of an organization or evolve into DI with an organization.

A number of laws exist to protect whistleblowers. Some third-party groups even offer protection to whistleblowers, but that protection can only go so far. Whistleblowers face legal action or even criminal charges, social stigma, and termination from their position or role. Two other classifications of whistleblowing are private and public. The classifications relate to the type of organizations someone chooses to whistle-blow on private sector, or public sector. Depending on many factors, both can have varying results. However, whistleblowing in the public sector organization is more likely to result in criminal charges and possible custodial sentences. A whistleblower who chooses to accuse a private sector organization or agency is more likely to face termination, legal and civil charges. In 2010, the Dodd-Frank Wall Street Reform and Consumer Protection Act was enacted in the US following the crisis to promote the financial stability of the United States and protect whistleblowers (Obama 2010).

10.3.3 The Financial Crisis and Distributed Incompetence Organizations

In 2014, The US Justice Department (DOJ) and the banks such as the Bank of America settled several of the DOJ civil investigations related to the packaging, marketing, sale, arrangement, structuring, and issuance of Residential Mortgage-Backed Securities (RMBS), collateralized debt obligations (CDOs), and the banks' practices concerning the underwriting and origination of mortgage loans. The settlement included a statement of facts, in which the bank acknowledged that it had sold billions of dollars of RMBS without disclosing to investors key facts about the quality and nature of the securitized loans. When the RMBS collapsed, investors, including federally insured financial institutions, had billions of dollars in losses. The bank has also confirmed that it originated risky mortgage loans and made misrepresentations about the quality of those loans to Fannie Mae, Freddie Mac, and the Federal Housing Administration (FHA).

Obviously, each individual financial advisor understood the necessity to disclose the quality of securitized loans to clients. However, such disclosure would jeopardize his career and make selling such shadow financial products more difficult. The most natural way for a bank agent to communicate his attitude is to pretend that she does not understand the problems with financial products she is selling, and also pretend that she does not understand that her peers understand the problem with financial products, and also pretend that she does not understand this pretense of others. Hence this form of DI is associated with fairly complex mental states of agents:

pretend(agent, not know (agent, problem(fin_product)))

pretend(agent, not understand(agent, know (peer-agent, problem(fin_product))))

pretend(agent, not understand(agent, pretend(peer-agent, not know (peer-agent, problem(fin_product)))))

We give a definition of pretend

pretend(Agent, Pretense): inform(Agent, Peer-agent, Pretense) and believe(Agent, not Pretense)) and know(Peer-agent, not believe(Agent, Pretense)).

We go further defining *Coming-to-believe* using FrameNet (Ruppenhofer et al. 2016).

A person (the Cognizer) comes to believe something (the Content), sometimes after a process of reasoning. This change in belief is usually initiated by a person or piece of Evidence. Occasionally words in this domain are accompanied by phrases expressing Topic, i.e. that which the mental Content is about.

Based on the most recent census I have CONCLUDED that most Americans sleep too much.

Cognizer [Cog] **Semantic type**: Sentient	Cognizer is the person who comes to believe something Sue REALIZED that Bob was lost
Content [Cont] **Semantic type**: Content	With a target verb, the Content is usually expressed as a finite clausal Complement or an Object NP, and may sometimes be expressed by a PP The President LEARNED that the reporters were hungry The children DETERMINED the answer
Evidence [Evid]	Words in this frame may occur with a PP headed by from which expresses the Evidence on which knowledge or belief is based I have LEARNED from experience that poison oak can be painful
Means [Mns] **Semantic Type**: State_of_affairs	An act performed by the Cognizer which enables them to figure something out A post-mortem examination was unable to ASCERTAIN the cause of death

(continued)

(continued)

Cognizer [Cog] **Semantic type**: Sentient	Cognizer is the person who comes to believe something Sue REALIZED that Bob was lost
Medium [med]	Medium is the text created by the Cognizer to communicate that they came to believe a specified Content
Topic [Top]	Some verbs in this frame may occur with postverbal Topic expressions: They FOUND OUT about us! More generally verbs in this frame may occur with quantificational nouns followed by Topic expressions The jury LEARNED something terrible about the suspect

The whole spectrum of finance professionals was hiding behind the curtains of DI, from bank clerks to university finance professors, to avoid being perceived as non-professional. Financial crisis demonstrated how an organization can evolve from being a regular one where recommendations of their financial advisors were reasonable and made sense, to a DI where those advisors pretended they did not understand how risky and meaningless their recommendations were. Not necessarily all advisors understood the problems with their investment recommendations; some might have genuinely believed that they were in the best interest of their clients. For a given bank employee, most of their managers and peers were confirming that their recommendations were valid, complying with bank policies (and maintaining the DI). A DI for an organization is stabilized if no employee wants to stand and blow the whistle on higher management.

Bank of America provided $7 billion in the form of relief to aid hundreds of thousands of consumers harmed by the financial crisis precipitated by the unlawful conduct not only of Bank of America, Merrill Lynch, and Countrywide. That relief took various forms, including principal loan reduction modifications that helped many borrowers no longer being underwater on their mortgages and finally having substantial equity in their homes. It also included new loans to creditworthy borrowers experiencing difficulties in getting a loan, donations to assist communities in recovering from the financial crisis, and financing for affordable rental housing. Finally, Bank of America has agreed to place over $490 million in a tax relief fund to be used to help defray some of the tax liability incurred by consumers receiving certain types of relief.

Merrill Lynch made misrepresentations to investors in 72 residential mortgage-backed securities throughout 2006 and 2007. Merrill Lynch's employees regularly told investors the loans it was securitizing were made to borrowers who were likely and able to repay their debts. Merrill Lynch made these representations even though most of its advisors knew, based on the due diligence they had performed on samples of the loans, that a significant number of those loans had material underwriting and compliance defects—including as many as 55% in a single pool. In addition, Merrill Lynch rarely reviewed the loans with limited performance data to ensure that the defects observed in the samples were not present throughout the remainder of the pools. Merrill Lynch also disregarded its own due diligence and securitized loans that the due diligence vendors had identified as defective. This DI practice led one

Merrill Lynch consultant to question the purpose of performing due diligence if Merrill Lynch was going to securitize the loans anyway, regardless of the issues that might be identified.

Before the financial crisis, John C. Bogle, founder, and chief executive of The Vanguard Group, wrote that a series of challenges facing capitalism that have contributed to past financial crises and have not been sufficiently addressed. He associates the problems of Corporate America with the power of managers who went virtually unchecked by their peers and regulators for a long time. In terms of the current study, as DI penetrated into the management structure of major corporations, the following issues arose, as outlined by Bogle:

- "Manager's capitalism" has replaced "owner's capitalism," meaning management runs the firm for its benefit rather than for the shareholders, a variation on the principal–agent problem;
- burgeoning executive compensation;
- the management of earnings focused mainly on share price rather than the creation of genuine value; and
- the failure of gatekeepers, including auditors, boards of directors, Wall Street analysts, and career politicians.

The terms to describe the activity of agents responsible for the Financial Crisis are expressive for articulating DI:

- widespread failure in regulation and supervision;
- dramatic failures of corporate governance and risk management at many systemically important institutions;
- a lack of transparency by service providers, ill preparation and inconsistent action by higher-level management and decision-making (such as government) that contribute to the uncertainty and panic; and,
- a systemic breakdown in accountability and ethics of the agents involved.

Hence an organization with DI sooner or later leads to one or another form of crisis.

A conglomerate of financial organizations, rating agencies, and the government, each with its own form of a DI at scale, resulted in a crisis so strong that it affected most world economies. A DI in smaller individual organizations such as a company, hospital, or small country usually results in smaller-scale crises that affect a limited number of people. A crisis can also be caused by an organization that is not necessarily in the state of a DI but instead is run by management with criminal intent but where only a minority of the agents involved are corrupt (such as ENRON Corporation (2001) and Theranos corporation (2018)).

Financial crises are not over; a number of authors believe that central banks may be unable to fight future financial bubbles fully given human nature, but at least they should refrain from boosting these bubbles in the name of supporting the real economy (Nageswaran 2014). The author considers the exaggerated oil prices and the cost of shale oil production, profitable when oil prices are about $40 per barrel. He reasons that if the majority of shale oil production in US remained viable at around

$40 per barrel, then there is still a long way to go before shale oil would cease to be a source of competitive price or an existential threat to OPEC oil producers. From this situation, The author cites *systemic irrationality* and concludes that what is going on in the oil industry is not a business competition between OPEC and the United States shale oil producers, but instead is a political, proxy battle where some of the producers in OPEC are acting on behalf of the United States against Russia, under certain conditions of interest to some of these OPEC players.

A DI should be differentiated from the individual incompetence of managers and from the criminal intent of managers, which have different mechanisms driving irrational decisions. A DI should also be differentiated from totalitarian regimes, which may or may not be incompetent.

10.3.4 Distributed Incompetence and Competitive Rating

One of the key causes of the financial crisis of 2007 was the lack of competence in credit rating agencies, as has been suggested by multiple authors (Federal Reserve 2010). The Financial Crisis Inquiry Commission concluded that the financial crisis was avoidable and was caused by "the failures of credit rating agencies" to correctly rate risk.

In academics, there is a long history of the assessment of the quality of an academic study and its contribution based on formal, numerical parameters. A good, objective rating of academic work is its applicability in practice and deployment in real-world applications. Since this rating is not always applicable to research work, numerical measures such as citation index are applied. Once the authors target this measure directly, the quality of work decreases dramatically and can lead to a DI. As publication venues become more competitive, even a higher percentage of authors attempt to directly acquire such rating and the quality and applicability to practice of such research products abruptly drops. In venues where extremely high competitiveness exists, the quality of peer reviews is fairly low as reviewers run out of arguments to perform a fair assessment of a contribution. This failure is another demonstration of how higher competitiveness leads to a DI. According to the author of the current study, this can be observed in such academic fields as Computational Linguistics and AI.

Galitsky and Levene (2005) simulated the process of possible interactions between a set of competitive services and a set of portals that provide an online rating for these services. The authors claimed that to have a profitable business, these portals are forced to have subscribed services that are rated by the portals. To satisfy the subscribing services, the study relied on the assumption that the portals improve the rating of a given service by one unit per transaction that involves payment. The authors followed the 'what-if' methodology, analyzing the strategies that service may choose to select the best portal for it to subscribe to, and strategies for a portal to accept the subscription such that its reputation loss, in terms of the integrity of its ratings, is minimized. The behavior of the simulated agents in accordance with this model turned out to be quite natural from a real-world perspective (Akhremenkov and Galitsky 2007). One conclusion from these simulations is that under reasonable assumptions, if most of the services and rating portals in a given industry do not accept a subscription policy similar to the one indicated above, they will lose, respectively, their ratings and reputations, and, moreover, the rating portals would have problems in making a profit. The prediction made in this study turned out to be plausible for the Financial Crisis of 2007: the modern portal-rating-based economy sector evolved into a subscription process similar to the one suggested in this study, as an alternative to a business model based purely on advertising. Financial Rating services contributed substantially to the weakening economy for the financial crisis, knowingly providing positive ratings for derivatives, which should have been rated poorly.

10.3.5 *Irrationality of Agents Under Distributed Incompetence*

A DI is a specific form of irrational behavior. The behavioral challenge for how agents make rational or irrational choices is associated with an individual's decision-making. Behavioral irrationality does not necessarily mean or leads to chaos: DI is a good example of it. Most irrational behavior occurs in the course of a reasoning session, where decision-makers do not behave with full knowledge and/or optimal computational power in pursuit of maximizing expected utility. In a DI, the behavior of agents is possibly rational for their personal expected utility but definitely irrational for the expected utility of an external user or observer. Yang and Lester (2008) critique the rationality paradigm for judgments and preferences and for exploring the impact of culture on people's economic behavior. Moreover, the authors draw the attention of researchers to the phenomenon of *systemic irrationality*. Irrationality may exist at the aggregate or societal level, a conclusion based on the observation that large segments of the population are incapable of making decisions in accord with traditional rationality—groups such as those who have a psychiatric disorder, those who are taking medications, those with limited intelligence, those from the lower social classes, children and adolescents, and the elderly. Even those who are not included in these groups, but who take medications for medical conditions may have their decision-making impaired to some extent. Therefore, it is argued that rationality in economic decision-making is more frequently an exception rather than the norm.

Unlike other forms of irrationality, the behavior of DI agents is explainable and rational. Conversely, cognitive scientists have known for decades that most humans are inherently irrational. Ariely (2008) introduces a notion *Predictable Irrationality*. The author says that most humans want explanations for why they behave in a certain way and attempt to connect it with how the external world reacts to what they do. Sometimes such "explanations" are not logically valid and are detached from reality. Human irrationality is associated with how humans tell themselves story after story until they come up with a satisfactory explanation that sounds reasonable enough to believe. People also like when such a story that includes favorable explanations portrays them in a positive light. This story mechanism is applicable to DI agents as well: they may believe that they are playing a positive role, having invented a reasonable explanation.

A rational person's behavior is usually guided more by conscious reasoning than by experience and not adversely affected by emotion. An average human is filled with systematic mistakes known to psychologists as *cognitive biases*. These mistakes affect most human decision-making. Cognitive bias makes people spend impulsively, be overly influenced by what other people think and affects people's beliefs and opinions.

Irrational incompetence can also be considered from the standpoint of an unconscious. An *unconsciously incompetent* person is someone who does not recognize they are doing something wrong and hence go on doing it. For them to unleash their full potential, they must first admit to this incompetence and begin seeing the advantages of acquiring new skills (Sharanya 2017). An employer can play an important role in adding this skill or competency (Fig. 10.3).

A DI is an irrationality of a totally different nature. When agents deviate from normal, rational behavior under the orders of their managers, they are fully aware of what they are doing. They know what they need to know and what they need to believe to perform their duties collectively to satisfy their DI goals. Customer support agents in DI *pretend* they behave in an irrational way so that an observer of a DI team believes so, but they do not possess the features of irrationality described above.

Shuldiner (2019) writes that as we use AI programs more and more, in our attempts to better understand and to manage our private and public affairs, we are injecting more and more opacity into our lives. An average user of a digital camera may not care to know the peculiarities of its operation). In general, for users, AI is proving too

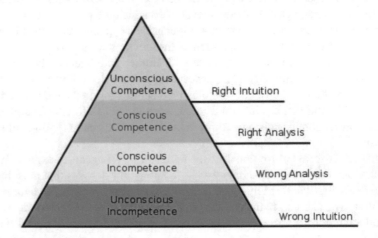

Fig. 10.3 Hierarchy of competence (Broadwell 1969)

difficult to fully understand. So human and machine agents can focus their energy on either operating AI systems or on understanding the underlying technology, but not both at the same time. By embedding AI into the Internet of Things, particularly the intelligent infrastructure that will make up Internet of Things, humans and their technologists are creating a global operating system that is in a large sense opaque. In this chapter, we go further and explain how such a system can evolve into an incompetent one. Various kinds of errors humans make once they form teams are explored in Lawless and Sofge (2016), Mittu et al. (2016), Moskowitz and Lawless (2016), Galitsky and Parnis (2017, 2019).

Although maintaining privacy is important for consumers, a lot of companies and government organizations use privacy as their excuse for a DI. In healthcare, privacy-related legislation shifts the focus from a customer with medical problems to privacy-related concerns brought upon this customer. It increases the amount of paperwork a customer needs to compete and distracts his attention from the quality of health services being provided.

As customers are distracted from a health-related focus, a healthcare provider can significantly increase the profitability and efficiency of its business at the expense of customer well-being. Specialist doctors only spend 11 s on average listening to patients before interrupting them, according to a new study (Singh et al. 2018). In primary care visits, 49% of patients were able to explain their agenda, while in specialty visits, only 20% of patients were allowed to explain their reason for visiting. For specialty care visits, however, eight out of 10 patients were interrupted even if they were allowed to share their agenda.

Differences among agents may be constructive as long as they can bring solution enhancements or modification. A cooperation involving different rational agents results in more than a mere addition of the agents' individual knowledge skills, because of a process of approval and refutation of the current solution (Tessier and Chaudron 1996). This approach follows along the lines of Lakatos (1978) work and adapted to a set of cooperating agents.

10.3.6 Aggressive DI

A DI, in its extreme form, is associated with lies and deceits. When a team wants badly to achieve a goal, it can significantly deviate from rationality by pretending and lying; they are not who they actually are to exaggerate their achievement and impress a potential investor. In most cases, what they do lacks domain competence, but they aggressively try to convince the external world in the opposite. We refer to this phenomenon as an *aggressive DI*.

There have always been spectacular stories of lies and deceit in areas in the world where capitalism flourishes, such as Silicon Valley in the United States. There are tales that go on for decades of founders telling partial truths about how their companies were founded and which products were developed; in these cases, CEOs exaggerating the features of their products to fool the press or to obtain new funding.

Some CEOs make false statements about the number of users on their platforms (such as Twitter); some lie to Congress concerning the privacy of their clients, confirming they have complete control over their personal data (Facebook). However, these misrepresentations are nothing compared to the audacious lies of Elizabeth Holmes, the founder, and CEO of Theranos (Bilton 2018). Theranos is a healthcare technology company that promised to make a revolution in blood tests.

Over the last few years, the author got interested in Theranos as a testbed for argumentation and conflict analyses. We applied the discourse analysis to texts from *Wall Street Journal* with claims that the company's conduct was fraudulent, the author was enhancing his argumentation mining and reasoning techniques (Galitsky et al. 2016, 2018) watching the Theranos' story closely, getting textual data from Theranos website back in 2020. Most people believed that the case was initiated by Theranos' competitors, who felt jealous about the proposed efficiency of the blood test technique promised by Theranos. However, our argumentation analysis technique showed that Theranos' argumentation patterns were faulty, and our findings supported the criminal case against Theranos, which led to its massive fraud verdict. SEC (2018) states that Elizabeth Holmes raised more than seven hundred million from in which she made false statements about the company's technology and finances.

We build a discourse representation of the arguments and observe if a discourse tree is capable of indicating whether a paragraph communicates both a claim and argumentation that backs it up. We will then explore what needs to be added to a discourse tree (DT) so that it is possible to judge if it expresses an argumentation pattern or not. A discourse tree is a means to express how author's thoughts are organized in text. Its non-terminal nodes are binary rhetorical relations such as elaboration connecting terminal nodes associated with text fragments (called discourse units).

This is what happened according to (Carreyrou 2018):

> Since October [2015], the Wall Street Journal has published a series of anonymously sourced accusations that inaccurately portray Theranos. Now, in its latest story ("U.S. Probes Theranos Complaints," Dec. 20), the Journal once again is relying on anonymous sources, this time reporting two undisclosed and unconfirmed complaints that allegedly were filed with the Centers for Medicare and Medicaid Services (CMS) and U.S. Food and Drug Administration (FDA).

Figure 10.4 shows the communicative discourse tree (CDT) for the following paragraph:

> But Theranos has struggled behind the scenes to turn the excitement over its technology into reality. At the end of 2014, the lab instrument developed as the linchpin of its strategy handled just a small fraction of the tests then sold to consumers, according to four former employees.

Please notice the labels for communicative actions are attached to the edges of discourse trees (on the left and in the middle-bottom).

In the following paragraph, Theranos attempts to rebuke the claim of WSJ, but without communicative actions, it remains unclear from its DT (see Fig. 10.5).

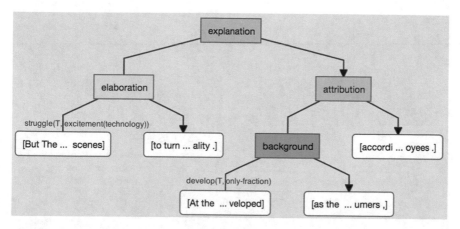

Fig. 10.4 When arbitrary communicative actions are attached to a DT as labels of its terminal arcs, it becomes clear that the author is trying to persuade by bring her point across and not merely sharing a fact

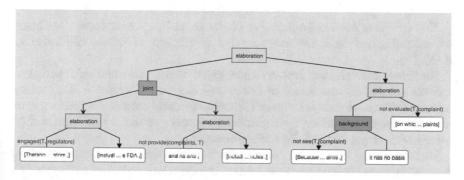

Fig. 10.5 Just from a DT and multiple rhetoric relations of elaboration and a single instance of background, it is unclear whether an author argues with his opponents or enumerates on a list of observations. Relying on communicative actions such as "engage" or "not see," the CDT can express the fact that the author is actually arguing with his opponents. This argumentation CDT is an attempt to make an even stronger rebuff

Theranos remains actively engaged with its regulators, including CMS and the FDA, and no one, including the Wall Street Journal, has provided Theranos a copy of the alleged complaints to those agencies. Because Theranos has not seen these alleged complaints, it has no basis on which to evaluate the purported complaints.

We proceed to a CDT that is an attempt by Theranos to get itself off the hook (Fig. 10.6).

It is not unusual for disgruntled and terminated employees in the heavily regulated health care industry to file complaints in an effort to retaliate against employers for termination of employment. Regulatory agencies have a process for evaluating complaints, many of which are not substantiated. Theranos trusts its regulators to properly investigate any complaints.

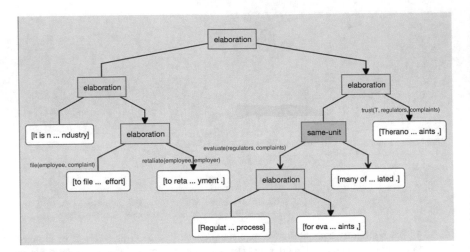

Fig. 10.6 Speech acts as labels for rhetoric relations helps to identify a text apart from a heated discussion

To show the structure of arguments, discourse relations are necessary but insufficient, and speech acts are necessary but insufficient as well (Galitsky et al. 2018).

For this paragraph, we need to know the discourse structure of interactions between agents and what kinds of interactions they are. We need to differentiate between a *neutral default relation of Elaboration* (which does not include a speech act) and elaboration relation which includes a speech act with a sentiment such as *not provide(…)* that is correlated with an argument.

We do not need to know the domain of interaction (here, health), the subjects of these interactions (the company, the Journal, the agencies), and what are the entities, but we need to take into account the mental, domain-independent relations among them.

Theranos uses speech acts to show that its opponents' argumentations are faulty. Now we use the labels for speech acts to show which one is attached to which rhetoric relations (Fig. 10.7, Galitsky 2019):

> By continually relying on mostly anonymous sources, while dismissing concrete facts, documents, and expert scientists and engineers in the field provided by Theranos, the Journal denies its readers the ability to scrutinize and weigh the sources' identities, motives, and the veracity of their statements.

From the commonsense reasoning standpoint, Theranos, the company, has two choices to confirm the argument that *his tests are valid*:

(1) Conduct an independent investigation, comparing its results with its peers, opening the data to the public, or confirming that their analysis results are correct.
(2) Defeat the argument by its opponent that their testing results are invalid and providing support for the claim that their opponent is wrong.

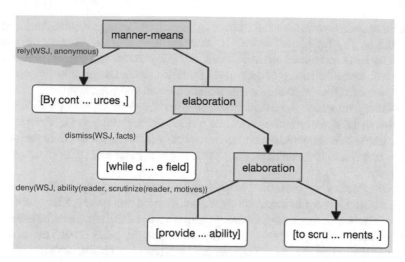

Fig. 10.7 Theranos is arguing that an opponent's arguments are faulty

Obviously, the former argument is much stronger, and we now know that usually, the latter argument is chosen when the agent believes that the former argument is too difficult to implement. On the one hand, the reader might agree with Theranos that Wall Street Journal should have provided more evidence for its accusations against the company. On the other hand, the reader perhaps disliked the fact that Theranos selects the latter type of argument (2) above, and therefore the company position is weak.

The authors believe that Theranos' argument is not sound because the company tries to refute the opponent's allegation concerning the complaints about Theranos' services from clients. We believe that Theranos' demand for evidence by inviting the Journal to disclose its sources and the nature of its complaints is weak. We claim that a third-party (independent investigative agent) would be more reasonable and conclusive. However, some readers might believe that the company's argument (a burden of proof evasion) is logical and valid.

It is hard to verify the validity of argumentation, relying on a CDT only (Galitsky et al. 2018). Argumentation analysis should account not only for the information conveyed by the clausal components of the DT (i.e., RST's subject matter) but also for what is inferred, namely, the WSJ writer's intention to motivate' the reader to cast doubt at the opponent's accusation of Theranos by inviting him to scrutinize the "proofs" provided. An argumentation assessment cannot identify the rhetorical relations in a text by relying on the text only; she must essentially rely on the context of a situation in order to fully grasp the arguer's intention.

We proceed to the background for the story of Theranos' CEO, the dedicated Stanford dropout who was set to save the world by making a blood test relying just on a pinprick of blood at a time. Holmes founded a blood-testing start-up, which was once valued at $6 billion. For years, Holmes was on top of the tech world, being featured at *The New York Times Style Magazine, Forbes, Fortune, Glamour, The New*

Yorker and *Inc.*, always wearing a black turtleneck and being associated with Steve Jobs. But as *The Wall Street Journal's* Carreyrou (2018) wrote, almost every word spoken by Holmes as she built and ran her company was either grossly embellished or, in most instances, outright deceptive. Theranos was a DI organization where its incompetence relied on total misrepresentation on all company levels.

As Carreyrou writes, the company she built was a web of lies along with threats to employees who discovered these lies and wanted to figure things out. When Holmes tried to impress Walgreens, she created completely false test results from their blood tests. When it was discovered by the Theranos Chief Financial Officer, he was fired right away.

No whistleblowing protections helped any of Theranos employees. The full extent of the whistleblowing is unknown as a number of those involved have remained anonymous; two of the youngest among them tried to raise their concerns internally, but they faced bullying in response. They worked in the same lab at Theranos, and when they started comparing notes, they realized they were dealing with a conspiracy of lies perpetrated at the highest levels within the organization wrapped in a toxic culture of secrecy and fear. Subsequently, both left the company, but Holmes would not leave them alone, and these employees were put under intense pressure to abstain from sharing information on Theranos. We conclude from this example that the culture of secrecy and fear is the clearest attribute of an aggressive DI.

Holmes told other investors that Theranos was going to make $100 million in revenue in 2014, but in reality, the company was only on track to make $100,000 that year. She told the press that her blood-testing machine was capable of making over 1,000 tests when in practice, it could only do one single type of test. She lied about a contract that Theranos had with the Department of Defense when she said her technology was being used in the battlefield, even though it was not. She repeatedly made up complete stories to the press about everything from her university schooling to company profits to the number of people whose lives would be saved from her bogus technology. And she did all these misrepresentations while ensuring that no one inside or outside her company could publicly challenge the truthfulness of her claims. That is an example of extremely self-consistent and rational behavior in support of the DI in the sense of Sect. 10.3.5.

10.3.7 Machine Learning of DI

There are various implications related to a DI when organizations use machine learning (ML) systems. If an ML system malfunctions and the company personnel cite it as a reason for an incompetent decision, an organization easily slips into a DI. This slip is especially problematic if an ML system does not possess an explainability feature (Chap. 8), its decision is perceived as random, and thus are made in an incompetent way.

Although ML is actively deployed and used in the industry, user satisfaction is still not very high in most domains. We will present a use case where explainability

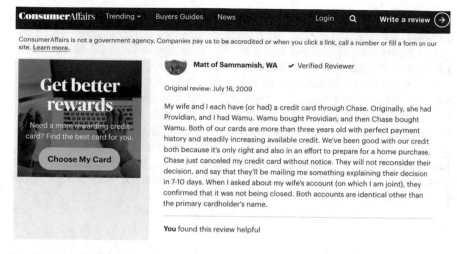

Fig. 10.8 A customer back in 2009 is confused and upset when his credit card is canceled, but no explanation is provided

and interpretability of machine learning decisions are lacking and users experience dissatisfaction in these cases.

Customers of financial services are appalled when they travel, and their credit cards are canceled without an obvious reason (Fig. 10.8). This situation is a clear indicator of a DI. If this bank used a decision-making system with explainability, there would be a given cause for its decision. Once it is established that this cause does not hold, the bank is expected to be capable of reverting its decision efficiently and retaining the customer.

Computer machines trying to be trusted are a potential reason for a DI. Incompetent workers can first start trusting machines and then blame them for failures of mixed human–machine teams, if these machines lack explainability. Lyons et al. (2019) present data from their qualitative study regarding the factors that precede trust for the elements of human–machine teaming. The authors reviewed the construct of human–machine trust and the dimensions of teammate-likeness from a human–robot interaction perspective. They derived the cues of trust from the corpus of Human–Computer Interaction literature on trust to reveal the reasons why individuals might have reported the trust of a new technology, such as a machine. The authors found that most subjects reported the technology as a tool rather than as a teammate for human–machine teaming.

Levchuk et al. (2019) construct the framework of an energy perspective for a team from which they postulated that optimal multiagent systems can best achieve adaptive behaviors by minimizing a team's free energy, where energy minimization consists of incremental observation, perception, and control phases. In a DI team, the first two phases are regular, but the last one is corrupted. This third phase should be minimized in terms of unexplainable control decisions. The authors propose a mechanism with their model for the distribution of decisions jointly made by a team, providing the associated mathematical abstractions and computational mechanisms. Afterwards, they test their ideas experimentally to conclude that energy-based agent teams outperform utility-based teams. Models of energy and utility-based DI teams look like an intriguing subject for future study.

Both object-level agents and meta-agents (Chap. 19) can display DI. In one possible architecture (Fouad and Moskowitz 2019), such meta-agents are agents existing inside of a software paradigm where they are able to reason and utilize their reasoning to construct and deploy other agents. The authors give an example with a service-oriented architecture, test it with an automated evaluation process and introduce intelligent agents able to work independently and as part of a hierarchy. These agents are able to interact independently with the environment, while being a part of a hierarchy at the same time.

10.4   Detecting DI in Text

The purpose of applying Natural Language Processing to the DI phenomena is to find out the DI rate for different organizations. A DI rate obtained from customer feedback texts can be an objective, unbiased assessment of the quality of management in a given organization, in most cases, irrespective of its particular policies and regulations. Once organizations are DI-rated, the public would be able to make an informed choice of the products and services provided by them.

Trying to classify communicative discourse trees (CDTs) for texts describing multiagent behavior is expected to help with identifying a DI. In CDTs, the labels for communicative actions, which are added to the discourse tree edges, show which speech acts are attached to which rhetoric relations. With DI, activity such as *persuasion* is very important in convincing a customer, for example, that banks are forced to demand insufficient fund fees to maintain profitability. This form of persuasion is identified as argumentation. Argumentation needs a certain combination of rhetorical relations of *Elaboration, Contrast, Cause* and *Attribution* to be sound. Persuasiveness relies on certain structures linking *Elaboration, Attribution* and *Condition*. Explanation needs to rely on certain chains of *Elaboration* relations plus *Explanation* and *Cause*, and a rhetorical agreement between a question and an answer is based on specific mappings between the rhetorical relations of *Contrast, Cause, Attribution* and *Condition* between the former and the latter (Galitsky et al. 2019).

Also, to detect a DI, invalid argumentation patterns used by the parties can be detected. In some cases, if arguments of only one party are faulty, it does not necessarily mean a DI; however, if such an argumentation is systematic, it is natural to conclude that a DI is occurring. The systematic improper use of explainability indicates a DI as well.

10.4.1 Distributed Incompetence and Rhetorical Relations

One of the examples of a DI follows as a response of a customer service representative
to a user attempting to resolve a matter and clarifying why a particular operation
cannot be performed: *You are asking me to reverse this insufficient fund fee? I cannot
do it. The only thing I <CSA> am allowed to do is to tell you that I am not allowed
to help you <the customer> with anything. I recommend you trying to ask a branch
agent to reverse this fee for you.* This text can be viewed as a credo of a CSA.

The communicative discourse tree for this text is shown in Fig. 10.9a and the
parse tree for the second sentence is shown in Fig. 10.9b. Each line shows the
text fragment for elementary discourse unit (EDU); expressions in italic are verb
frames with substituted semantic roles. The hierarchy is shown from left to right:
the level in the discourse tree is shown by the indentation value. The terminal nodes
are assigned with EDUs: the fragments of text which are connected by rhetorical
relations. Edges of this discourse tree are labeled with speech acts which are highlighted in EDUs, such as *asking(you, me, …)*. Frames for speech acts are available
at VerbNet (such as https://verbs.colorado.edu/verb-index/vn/allow-64.php-allow-64
for the communicative action *allow*).

The features of this discourse tree can be associated with a DI. The abundance of
speech acts and certain inter-relations between them indicate a peculiar mental state
which should not arise unless a multiagent system evolves into a DI. For example,
an inconsistency between *allow(…)* and *not allow(…)* connected by the rhetorical
relation of *Attribution* is a very special way of a contradiction which should not occur
in the normal flow of a business operation, as expressed in this text.

(a)

```
elaboration (LeftToRight)
  elaboration (LeftToRight)
    joint
      EDU: asking(you, me, to reverse this insufficient fund fee) ?
      EDU:I cannot do it .
    elaboration (LeftToRight)
      EDU:The only thing
      attribution (RightToLeft)
        EDU: allowed(me, to do is to tell(me, you, →))

        EDU:that not allowed(I, help(I, you, →)
  elaboration (LeftToRight)
    EDU: recommend(me, you, →)
    enablement (LeftToRight)
      EDU:trying to ask(you, branch agent, →)
      EDU:to reverse this fee for you
```

(b)

Fig. 10.9 a Communicative discourse tree for this text. **b** Parse tree in the sentence for a "CSA
credo"

Also, when the statement by a CSA *I cannot do* is strengthened with the *Elaboration-Attribution* chain, the reader believes that this customer is stuck with her problem and it is impossible for a CSA to provide any help. This perception is the goal of an organization with a DI so that a user can easily give up on his attempts to resolve the matter.

As we collect such texts and form a training set, our ML system detects commonalities between communicative discourse trees for DI texts and automatically builds rules for its detection. Not all such rules can be easily verbalized but a special discourse tree structure is associated with these rules.

10.4.2   Semantic Cases of Distributed Incompetence

We are curious in which logical, discourse-level peculiarities of texts are associated with incompetence. There is a possibility of lexical correlated with DI: less competent people are expected to use simpler and incorrect language, but this would be not as insightful: we believe a flawed logic of multiagent interaction is a root cause. Therefore we explore communication discourse trees enriched with entity information.

One of the linguistic patterns for DI is an *entity loop*, when one agent(entity) refers to another agent who then refers back. More precisely, the entity loop occurs when an agent or department *P* recommends to contact *J,* who, in turn, recommends back *P*. This loop can be discovered in an Entity—CDT with entity information.

> Agent Peter from Customer Care recommended me to ask agent John from Finance about how to refund my fee. Then when I wrote to agent John, he told me to contact Customer Care.

An Entity—CDT for this example is shown in Fig. 10.10. Corresponding entities are highlighted with respective colors and the same entity arc is shown by arrows. Labels for the edges of CDT encoding the communicative actions with arguments as entities (agents) highlighted with the same color are shown under the respective texts (leave nodes of this CDT). The loop relation between entities is obvious: this text is an element of a positive training set for DI.

The other indication of a DI is an entity attribution chain (Fig. 10.11):

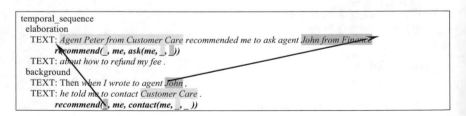

Fig. 10.10   An entity communicative discourse tree for a text with an entity loop

```
elaboration
  attribution
    TEXT:Agent Peter from Customer Care said that
    attribution
      TEXT: according to Finance department ,
      TEXT : confirmation from management is required to refund my fee .
              require(confirmation(management), refund)
  attribution
    TEXT: John told me ,
    TEXT: that only the management can decide about the refund .
            decide(management, refund)
```

Fig. 10.11   An entity communicative discourse tree for a text with an entity attribution chain

Agent Peter from Customer Care said that, according to Finance department, confirmation from management is required to refund my fee. John told me, that only the management can decide about the refund.

In this text, there is no loop, but the repetitive rhetorical relation of **attribution** indicates that the CSAs are lacking authority and are citing a higher authority as a reason then cannot fulfill the customer request. The reader can observe embedded **attributions** as an indication that an organization is formed in a way to deny customer requests by a reference to a higher authority. It is a more sound way of rejecting customer demands than just denying without reason.

The third, more explicit but less reliable way to express DI in the text is an explicit, *systematic denial* as per the labels of the edges of a CDT.

Agent Peter from Customer Care said he could not refund my fee. John told me, that he could not decide on his own concerning the refund. Agent Mike denied responsibilities when I was referred to him.

An Entity CDT with explicit, systematic denial is shown in Fig. 10.12. All three agents disagreed to do what they were asked by a customer. Highlighted agents are all occurring with negations for their refund action, as is visible from the labels of the CDT edges. When some CSA cannot help and some can, that is a case for a regular organization, and when *all* CSAs deny in one form or another, this is an indication

```
elaboration
  attribution
    TEXT:Agent Peter from Customer Care said
    TEXT:he could not refund my fee .
            said(peter, me, not refund)
  elaboration
  attribution
    TEXT:John told me ,
    TEXT:that he could not decide on his own concerning the refund .
      said(john, me, not decide(john, refund))
  background
    TEXT:Agent Mike denied responsibilities
    TEXT:when I was referred to him .
      deny(mike, responsibility)
```

Fig. 10.12   An entity communicative discourse tree for a text with an explicit systematic denial

of DI. The reader can observe that the rhetorical relation of **attribution** occurs here as well.

10.4.3   A Detection Dataset

We first created a manually-tagged set of customer complaints from the financial sector. Annotators were given a definition of a DI and how to classify each complaint as indicative of a DI or not. Then we built a recognizer program that used this manually-tagged set for training and testing. Once our recognizer demonstrated satisfactory performance, we applied it to textual complaints for various banks to estimate their DI rate. Recognition accuracies in the manually-tagged dataset allowed us to estimate the value of deviation in the DI rate.

This dataset contains texts where authors do their best to bring their points across by employing all means to show that they (as customers) are right and their opponents (companies) are wrong (Galitsky et al. 2009). Customers always try to blame the company for everything, so the task of the recognizer is to verify if customers' arguments are valid and their stories do not indicate misrepresentations. Complainants are emotionally charged writers who describe problems they have encountered with a financial service, the lack of clarity and transparency as their problem was communicated with CSA, and how they attempted to solve it. Raw complaints were collected from PlanetFeedback.com for a number of banks submitted during the years of the Financial Crisis of 2007. Four hundred complaints were manually tagged with respect to perceived complaint validity, proper argumentation, detectable misrepresentation, and whether a request for an explanation concerning the company's decision occurred.

Judging by these complaints, most complainants were in genuine distress due to a strong deviation between:

- what they expected from a product or a service;
- the actual product or service that they received;
- how this deviation was explained;
- how the problem was communicated by a customer support.

The last two items are directly correlated with a DI. Most complaint authors reported incompetence, flawed policies, ignorance, lack of common sense, inability to understand the reason behind the company's decision, indifference to customers' needs, and misrepresentation from the customer service personnel. The authors are frequently confused, looking for a company's explanation, seeking a recommendation from more other users and advising others on avoiding a particular financial service. The focus of a complaint is proof that the proponent is right and her opponent is wrong, the explanation for why the company decided to act in a certain way, a resolution proposal and the desired outcome. Although a DI is described in an indirect, implicit way, it can be easily identified by a human reader.

The DI tag in the dataset used in the current study is related to the whole text of a complaint, not a paragraph. Three annotators worked with this dataset, and the inter-annotator agreement exceeded 80%. The set of tagged customer complaints about financial services is available at (ComplaintDataset 2020).

10.4.4 Discourse-Level Features

In texts where a DI description might occur, one can expect specific discourse-level features. These texts can be an enumeration of the specific mental states of CSA agents, an indication of the conflict with a lack of rationality, or heated arguments among conflicting agents, etc. It is important to differentiate between the emotions of a text's author and the ones describing the mental states and communicative actions of opponents. The complexity of a DI detection is increased by the necessity of grasping the mental state of a team of agents, not an individual one.

Detection accuracy for DI for different types of evidence is shown in Table 10.1. We consider simpler cases, where the detection occurs based on phrases, in the top row. Typical expressions in the row one have an imperative form such as *please explain/clarify/motivate/comment*. Also, there are templates here such as *you did this but I expected that ... you told me this but I received that*.

The middle row contains the data on a level higher evidence for the implicit explanation request case, where multiple fragments of DTs indicate the class. Finally, in the bottom row, we present the case of lower confidence for a single occurrence of a DT associated with an explanation request. The second column shows the counts of complaints per case. The third column gives examples of expressions (which include keywords and phrase types) and rhetoric relations, which serve as criteria for an implicit DI. The fourth and fifth columns present the detection rates where the complaints about a given case is mixed with a hundred complaints without a DI.

Table 10.1 Cases of explanation requests and detection accuracies. The left column presents the linguistic cue for evidence of DI. The second column from the left gives the counts for each case. The third column presents criteria and examples for the given evidence type. The fourth and fifth columns give the precision and recall recognizing the given evidence type

Evidence	#	Criteria	P	R
Expressions with the rhetorical relation of *Contrast*	83	Phrases: *A said this ... but B said that* ... *I learned from A one thing ... but B informed me about something else*	83	85
Double, triple, or more implicit mention of an inconsistency	97	Multiple rhetoric relation of *Contrast, Explanation, Cause* and *Sequence*	74	79
A single implicit mention of an inconsistency	103	A pair of rhetoric relation chains for *contrast* and *cause*	69	75

10.4.5   Implementation of the Detector of Distributed Incompetence

There are two approaches for discourse-level classification of texts into classes {*DI, no DI*}:

(1)   Nearest neighbor learning. For a given text, if it is similar from the discourse standpoint with an element of the positive training dataset and dissimilar with all elements of the negative dataset, then it is classified as belonging to the positive class. The rule for the negative class is formulated analogously. The similarity of two texts is defined as cardinality of maximal common discourse structure for the respective discourse structures of these texts, such as discourse trees.

(2)   The features of the discourse trees can be represented in a numerical space. The kernel learning approach applies the support vector machine (SVM) learning to the feature space of all sub-discourse trees of the discourse tree for a given text where a DI is being detected. Tree Kernel counts the number of common sub-trees as the discourse similarity measure between two DTs.

Both approaches are applied for DI detection; we refer the reader to (Galitsky 2019) for details of both approaches and briefly outline the latter approach below.

We extend the tree kernel definition for the DT, augmenting the DT kernel by the information on speech acts. Tree kernel-based approaches are not very sensitive to errors in parsing (syntactic and rhetoric) because erroneous sub-trees are mostly random and will unlikely be common among different elements of a training set.

A DT can be represented by a vector V of integer counts of each sub-tree type (without taking into account its ancestors):

$V(T) = $ (# *of subtrees of type* 1, ..., # *of subtrees of type* I, ..., # *of subtrees of type* n). Given two tree segments DT_1 and DT_2, the tree kernel function is defined:

$K(DT_1, DT_2) = \ <V(DT_1), V(CDT_2)> \ = \Sigma i \ V(CDT_1)[i], V(DT_2)[i] = \Sigma n_1 \Sigma n_2 \Sigma_i \ I_i(n_1) * I_i(n_2),$

where $n_1 \in N_1, n_2 \in N_2$ and N_1 and N_2 are the sets of all nodes in CDT_1 and CDT_2, respectively; $I_i(n)$ is the indicator function:

$I_i(n) = \{1$ *iff* a subtree of type i occurs with a root at a node; 0 otherwise}. Further details for using TK for paragraph-level and discourse analysis are available in (Galitsky 2019).

Only the arcs of the same type of rhetoric relations (presentation relation, such as antithesis, subject matter relation, such as condition, and multinuclear relation, such as List) can be matched when computing common sub-trees. We use N for a nucleus or situations presented by this nucleus, and S for a satellite or situations presented by this satellite. Situations are propositions, completed actions or actions in progress, and communicative actions and states (including beliefs, desires, approve, explain, reconcile and others). Hence we have the following expression for an RST-based generalization "^" for two texts *text1* and *text2*:

$text1 \ ^\wedge text2 = \ \cup$ i,j (*rstRelation1i*, (...,...) ^ *rstRelation2j* (...,...)), where I ∈ (RST relations in *text1*), j ∈ (RST relations in *text2*). Further, for a pair of RST relations, their generalization looks as follows:

rstRelation1(N1, S1) ^ rstRelation2 (N2, S2) = (rstRelation1^ rstRelation2)(N1^N2, S1^S2).

We define speech acts as a function of the form verb (agent, subject, cause), where verb characterizes some type of interaction between involved agents (e.g., explain, confirm, remind, disagree, deny, etc.), subject refers to the information transmitted or object described, and cause refers to the motivation or explanation for the subject. To handle the meaning of words expressing the subjects of speech acts, we apply word2vec models.

We combined Stanford NLP parsing, coreferences, entity extraction, DT construction (discourse parser, Surdeanu et al. 2015; Joty et al. 2013), VerbNet and Tree Kernel builder into one system available at https://github.com/bgalitsky/relevance-based-on-parse-trees.

For EDUs as labels for terminal nodes only the phrase structure is retained; we propose to label the terminal nodes with the sequence of phrase types instead of parse tree fragments. For the evaluation, Tree Kernel builder tool was used (Galitsky 2019). Further details are available in Chap. 9.

10.4.6 Detection Results

Once we confirmed the plausibility of a DI detector on the annotated complaints, we proceeded to assess the DI rate per organization (Table 10.2). The average DI rate per a customer complaint was 11%.

Recognition accuracies and the resultant DI rates are shown in Table 10.2. We used 300 complaints about each bank to assess the recognition accuracies for the explanation request. $79.1 \pm 3.1\%$ looks like a reasonable estimate for recognition accuracy for DI. The last column on the right shows that taking into account the error rate that is less than 20% in DI recognition, $10.9 \pm 3.1\%$ is an adequate estimate of complaints indicating DI, given the set of 1200 complaints. Hence the overall average DI rate for these organizations is about one-tenth.

Table 10.2 Discovering DI rates for four banks

Source	#	Precision	Recall	DI rate
Bank of America	300	79	76	**8.4**
Chase Bank	300	76	80	**11.6**
Citibank	300	77	85	**12.7**
American Express	300	76	84	**11.2**

10.5   Customer Service and Covid-19

Most executives are struggling to navigate the teams through Covid-19. The ways how the pandemic influences different parts of the company varies significantly from one department to another, and CSAs are among the hardest-hit departments. In just two weeks, between March 11, when Covid-19 was declared a pandemic by the WHO, and March 26, the average company in the investigation of the study of (Dixon et al. 2020) saw the percentage of calls scored as difficult increased from a typical level of 10% to more than 20%. Issues related to the coronavirus, from unexpected travel cancellations to requests for bill payment extensions and disputes over insurance coverage, dramatically increased the level of customer dissatisfaction in service calls, making a typical CSA job far more difficult.

In the financial sector, there is an increase in financial hardship-related calls, among the most difficult for CSA to handle, increase by 150% in a week. A lot of CSAs working from home for the first time now find themselves without the usual office infrastructure (like a reliable phone connection) and lack a support by their peers and managers. A strong increase in CSA effort per user is an income loss for a company as high-effort support sessions are far more likely to lead to a customer dissatisfaction and far less likely to result in a new sale. Among the customers threatening to leave, those who had had an unsuccessful session has just a few percent chances of accepting the company's promotion to make them stay, as compared to a 1/5 chance for customers whose interactions were scored as easy.

Many CSAs are still constrained by standard customer-service policies such as rules about extending bill payments in banks that pre-date the pandemic. CSAs hide behind policy and indicate that they are powerless to help far more often than they would under normal circumstances. It is important to revise policies to reflect the current Covid-19 world and reduce opportunities for CSAs to use outdated policies to avoid solving customers' problems.

Covid-19 strengthens DI-associated CSA behaviors that increase customer effort by introducing uncertainty, using negative language, and thoughtlessly passing customers elsewhere (Ivanov et al. 2020). A CSA redirect is conducted by saying *I suggest you try contacting…* or *I can't help you but maybe they can*. Redirects require customers to wait and then explain their problem over and over again, a total waste of time and effort. CSA should be empowered to make exceptions in order to solve the customer's problem, but changing service organization culture and policies can be a long journey. Here chatbots come into play to cure the CRM system.

10.6   Conclusions: Curing Distributed Incompetence

DIs naturally appear in organizations due to the human factor. Hence the means to cure a DI can be based on the removal of human factors: making customer support fully formalized by following an established protocol. This approach follows along the lines of, for example, increased safety by means of autonomous systems such as auto-pilots and navigators. Instead of dealing with human CSA from manifold motivations, customers should be handled with an autonomous agent capable of understanding their problems in a limited, vertical domain.

As long as people rely on various products and services to satisfy their needs, they will encounter DIs associated with the frustration of customers and with businesses losing customers. A transition to an autonomous CSA, as long as it is relevant in terms of topic and dialogue appropriateness, would make a DI avoidable. It is hard to overestimate a potential contribution of such a CSA when a broad category of people call financial institutions, travel portals, healthcare and internet providers, or government services such as immigration and revenue agencies.

Task-oriented chatbots for customer service can provide adequate solutions for a DI. Currently available dialogue systems (Galitsky and Ilvovsky 2019) with dialogue management and context tracking can be trained from textual descriptions of customer problems and their correct resolution. The resultant functionality of these trained chatbots needs to be formally assessed to avoid hybrid human–machine DI.

The least typical cases of user dissatisfaction, such as the ones associated with the non-sufficient fund fee, can be fully formalized and encoded into the CS chatbot so that human intervention would not be required. A DI-free development team of chatbots should be able to cover the most important cases of product issues and users' misunderstandings to reduce the DI rate significantly from 11%.

In this chapter, we introduced a new model for a well-known form of behavior for an organization: distributed incompetence. A comparison is drawn between DI and distributed knowledge: in both cases, agents reason rationally, but in the former case, the agents pretend to be irrational to achieve certain organizational objectives so that an external agent would believe that he deals with genuinely incompetent agents. In the latter case of distributed knowledge in a competent organization, knowledge and skills of individual agents help each other to impress an external observer with a superior capability and result-oriented mindset of this organization. DI is also associated with a hierarchical organizational structure where the higher the manager level is, the lower is his competence (Fig. 10.13).

It is not easy to detect distributed incompetence in an organization. Many banks during the Financial crisis of 2007, ENRON as a public company, and also Theranos as a private company succeeded by leading investors by the nose for a long time. Some company managers turn out to be so good liars that neither employees nor customers nor members of the public become suspicious about the company's business conduct. The proposed natural language analysis tool is intended to take a corpus of documents (such as internal emails) from an organization and attempt to detect a DI. Our assessment showed that this tool could be plausible in identifying a DI in an arbitrary organization.

Fig. 10.13 A management hierarchy where an official above is always right (Cartoonbank 2020)

References

Akhremenkov AA, Galitsky B (2007) Building web infrastructure for providing rating services and subscription to them. Matem Mod 19(2):23–32

Ariely D (2008) Predictably irrational. Harper Collings Publishers

Bilton N (2018) She absolutely has sociopathic. VanityFair. Tendencies. https://www.vanityfair.com/news/2018/06/elizabeth-holmes-is-trying-to-start-a-new-company

Biswa P (2015) Putt's Law, Peter Principle, Dilbert Principle of Incompetence and Parkinson's Law. https://asmilingassasin.blogspot.com/2015/06/putts-law-peter-principle-dilbert.html

Broadwell MM (1969) Teaching for learning (XVI). The Gospel Guardian. wordsfitlyspoken.org

Carreyrou J (2018) Bad blood: secrets and lies in a silicon valley startup. Penguin Random House.

Cartoonbank (2020) https://cartoonbank.ru/?page_id=29&color=all&offset=300

ComplaintDataset (2020) https://github.com/bgalitsky/relevance-based-on-parse-trees/blob/master/examples/opinionsFinanceTags.xls

Dixon M, McKenna T, de la OG (2020) Supporting customer service through the coronavirus crisis. https://hbr.org/2020/04/supporting-customer-service-through-the-coronavirus-crisis

Fagin R, Halpern JY, Moses Y, Vardi MY (1995) Reasoning about knowledge. The MIT Press

Federal Reserve (2010) Bernanke-four questions. Federalreserve.gov. April 14, 2009

FCA (2015) FCA fines Barclays £72 million for poor handling of financial crime risks. https://www.fca.org.uk/news/press-releases/fca-fines-barclays-%C2%A372-million-poor-handling-financial-crime-risks

Fouad H, Moskowitz IS (2019) Meta-agents: using multiagent networks to manage dynamic changes in the internet of things. In: Lawless WF, Mittu R, Sofge DA, Moskowitz IS, Russell S (eds) Artificial intelligence for the internet of everything. AP/Elsevier

Galitsky B (2018) Customers' retention requires an explainability feature in machine learning systems they use. In: AAAI Spring symposium on beyond machine intelligence: understanding cognitive bias and humanity for well-being AI, Stanford, CA

Galitsky B (2019) Developing enterprise chatbots. Springer, Cham

Galitsky B, Levene M (2005) Simulating the conflict between reputation and profitability for online rating portals. J Artif Soc Soc Simul 8(2)

Galitsky B, Parnis A (2017) Team formation by children with autism. In: Lawless WF, Mittu R, Sofge D, Russell S (eds) Autonomy and artificial intelligence: a threat or savior? Springer, Cham

Galitsky B, Ilvovsky D (2019) A demo of a chatbot for a virtual persuasive dialogue. In: Persuasive technologies 14th international conference, Limassol, Cyprus, April 9–11

Galitsky B, Parnis A (2019) Accessing validity of argumentation of agents of the internet of everything. In: Lawless WF, Mittu R, Sofge DA, Moskowitz IS, Russell S (eds) Artificial intelligence for the internet of everything. AP/Elsevier

Galitsky B, González MP, Chesñevar CI (2009) A novel approach for classifying customer complaints through graphs similarities in argumentative dialogues. Decis Support Syst 46(3):717–729

Galitsky B, Ilvovsky D, Kuznetsov SO (2016) Text classification into abstract classes based on discourse structure. In: Proceedings of the international conference recent advances in natural language processing, pp 200–207

Galitsky B, Ilvovsky D, Pisarevskaya D (2018) Argumentation in text: discourse structure matters. In: CICLing 2018

Galitsky B, Ilvovsky D, Wohlgenannt G (2019) Constructing imaginary discourse trees improves answering convergent questions. In: CICLING, April 7–13, La Rochelle, France

Grudin J (2016) The rise of incompetence. ACM Interactions 8–1, p 6. https://interactions.acm.org/archive/view/january-february-2016/the-rise-of-incompetence

Integration Training (2018) IntegrationTraining.co.uk

Ivanov S, Webster C, Stoilova E, Slobodskoy D (2020) Biosecurity, automation technologies and economic resilience of travel, tourism and hospitality companies

Joty S, Carenini G, Ng RT, Mehdad Y (2013) Combining intra-and multi-sentential rhetorical parsing for document-level dis-course analysis. ACL 1:486–496

Lakatos I (1978) The methodology of scientific research programmes: philosophical papers, vol 1. Cambridge University Press, Cambridge

Lawless WF, Sofge DA (2016) AI and the mitigation of error: a thermodynamics of teams. In: AAAI spring symposia 2016

Levchuk G, Pattipati K, Serfaty D, Fouse A, McCormack R (2019) Active inference in multiagent systems: context-driven collaboration and decentralized purpose-driven team adaptation. In: Lawless WF, Mittu R, Sofge DA, Moskowitz IS, Russell S (eds) Artificial intelligence for the internet of everything. AP/Elsevier

Lyons JB, Wynne KT, Mahoney S, Roebke MA (2019) Trust and human-machine teaming: a qualitative study. In: Lawless WF, Mittu R, Sofge DA, Moskowitz IS, Russell S (eds) Artificial intelligence for the internet of everything. AP/Elsevier

Mann WC, Thompson SA (1987) Rhetorical structure theory: description and construction of text structures. Springer, Netherlands, Dordrecht

Mittu R, Taylor G, Sofge DA, Lawless WF (2016) Introduction to the symposium on AI and the mitigation of human error. In: AAAI spring symposia 2016

Moskowitz IS, Lawless WF (2016) Human caused bifurcations in a hybrid team: a position paper. In: AAAI spring symposia 2016

Nageswaran VA (2014) Systematic irrationality. https://www.livemint.com/Opinion/reJomN4Ak pvUAPHVgRxhDO/Systematic-irrationality.html

Obama B (2010) Remarks by the president on wall street reform archived 2010–07–23 at the wayback machine. White House

Oppong T (2018) What was i thinking? (The science of systematic irrationality) https://medium. com/kaizen-habits/what-was-i-thinking-the-science-of-systematic-irrationality-e053e5476fcf

Peter L, Hull R (1968) The Peter principle: why things always go wrong. William Morrow and Company

Pisarevskaya D, Galitsky B, Taylor J, Ozerov A (2019) An anatomy of a Lie. In: Liu L, White R (eds) Companion proceedings of the 2019 world wide web conference (WWW '19). ACM, New York, NY, USA, pp 373–380

Ruppenhofer J, Ellsworth M, Petruck MRL, Johnson CR, Baker CF, Scheffczyk J (2016) FrameNet II: extended theory and practice. https://framenet.icsi.berkeley.edu/fndrupal/the_book.

SEC (2018) US Securities and Exchange Commission. Theranos, CEO Holmes, and Former President Balwani Charged With Massive Fraud. https://www.sec.gov/news/press-release/201 8-41

Sharanya M (2017) Overcoming the unconscious incompetence hurdle at work. https://www.people matters.in/article/culture/overcoming-the-unconscious-incompetence-hurdle-at-work-16750? utm_source=peoplematters&utm_medium=interstitial&utm_campaign=learnings-of-the-day

Shuldiner A (2019) Raising them right: AI and the internet of big things. In: Lawless WF, Mittu R, Sofge DA, Moskowitz IS, Russell S (eds) Artificial intelligence for the internet of everything. AP/Elsevier

Singh ON, Phillips KA, Rodriguez-Gutierrez R, Castaneda-Guarderas A, Gionfriddo MR, Branda ME, Montori VM (2018) Eliciting the patient's agenda secondary analysis of recorded clinical encounters. J Gener Intern Med 1–5

Surdeanu M, Hicks T, Valenzuela-Escarcega MA (2015) Two practical rhetorical structure theory parsers. NAACL HLT

Tessier C, Chaudron L (1996) Constructive difference and disagreement: a suprA-cooperation among agents. In: Computer supported cooperative work (CSCW), vol 5, pp 23–336

Yang B, Lester D (2008) Reflections on rational choice—The existence of systematic irrationality. J Socio-Econ 37(3):1218–1233

Chapter 11
Conclusions

Abstract We draw the conclusions for Volume 1 and 2 of this book.

In Volumes 1 and 2 of this book, we outlined the main problems on the way towards building a robust intelligent CRM system with the focus on understanding customer reasoning and behavior, and attempted to solve them. We observed that AI is not just an improvement for CRM, but is a way of its survival, as a human-powered CRM does not scale and has many disadvantages:

(1) Introduction of a bias, discrimination, incompetence, delays;
(2) Deviates from case to case, becomes a matter of luck;
(3) Throws the user into internal politics of a support team, into a crossfire between teams' intent to minimize their efforts and the company's intent to minimize their spending.

Solving unique, complex customer problems can be done by experienced, seasoned company experts. However, routine product support and product lifecycle operations need to be 100% automated. To achieve this level of automation, a CRM needs to be intelligent and should have the following essential skills, presented in the book chapters:

(1) Answering a broad range of questions, from factoid to problem-solving ones. We introduced a range of question-answering techniques with structurized word2vec, indexing by means of summarized logic forms, multi-hop, ontology-based and the ones requiring reasoning to answer. We proposed a controlled question answering where exact answers are guaranteed for frequent and important questions. Described question answering is also capable of learning from texts, acquiring definitions of new entities, formalizing their meanings and employing the wisdom of the web;
(2) Explaining major issues with products and services. Making sure the user understands why a certain decision is made, so the CRM system is trusted. An explanation is perrmed in various modes, including a conversational one;
(3) Recommending relevant products and services in a timely, non-intrusive manner to solve a current problem or user need. Employ various modes of recommendation with the focus on the dialogue-based recommendations;

B. Galitsky, *Artificial Intelligence for Customer Relationship Management*,
Human–Computer Interaction Series, https://doi.org/10.1007/978-3-030-61641-0_11

461

(4) Supporting a conversation with a user on a broad range of topics in an authorita-
      tive, persuasive, supportive and adversarial manner with trusted content, taking
      into account user emotional states and personal traits. Assuring all problems are
      communicated with the user urgently towards their prompt resolution. Providing
      a broad range of dialogue management techniques based on the discourse
      analysis of the content being communicated;
(5) Understanding customer mood and intelligently handling his complaint. Simu-
      late a mental attitude of this user to maintain his positive mood by timely
      addressing his concerns, providing compensations, refunds and returns only
      when it is critical not to lose him. Apply introspection and meta-reasoning
      to reproduce what people think about themselves, peers, the products and the
      company;
(6) Diagnosing and curing problems in a customer support-oriented organization
      or department.

The final goal of this intelligence is a demonstrated competitive advantage that
results in retention and minimizing of a churn rate.

At the time of writing of this book, it is easy to see how success in AI can
boost CRM development on the one hand, but it is hard to detect intelligence in
those systems exposed to the public, on the other hand. In this book, we proposed a
pathway to a CRM that can be demoed to impress potential users. We made a claim
that a modern CRM system needs to integrate a number of specific components
enumerated above instead of just following a certain paradigm such as data-driven
or a specific set of rules.

To summarize the book, we can propose the following formula for the AI for
CRM success:

*AI_enabled_CRM = Search Engine + Dialogue Management + User Simulation
+ Quality Content + Recovery from Failures.*

Dialogue Management for CRM is still an emerging area of research. A deep
learning approach to dialogue management attempts to simulate human intellectual
activity and learns from the available dialogues which are not always meaningful and
frequently produce a resultant conversation where a user is confused. At the same
time, the major vendors of CRM dialogue development platforms offer tools for hard-
coded dialogue management, which require a lot of manual work and produce very
brittle conversations, which can hardly deviate from a set of hard-coded dialogue
scenarios. In this book, we voted against these approaches and instead proposed the
one based on discourse analysis.

Eleven patents based on the chapters of this book have been filed by Oracle in
various domains of CRM-related technologies with the focus on discourse linguistics.
We anticipate that these inventions will become popular among the community of
CRM system developers. Relying on discourse analysis and the logic of conversation,
developers are expected to automate the process of taking a user through a number
of CRM phases. With discourse analysis, specifying explicit rules of the dialogue
state machine becomes unnecessary in most cases for task-oriented dialogues. A
number of inventions described in this book have been deployed into the Oracle

Digital Assistant in 2019–2020 (https://www.oracle.com/application-development/cloud-services/digital-assistant/).

A version of this book served as a primary material for the Master's course on Intelligent Systems at National Research University Higher School of Economics, Department of AI and Data Science, Moscow, Russia. The students used this book in their hands-on projects on designing various components of CRM with a particular focus on chatbot in such domains as finance, entertainment, culinary, management, transportation and others.

Printed in the United States
by Baker & Taylor Publisher Services